Symbol	Chapter Introduced	Meaning
$P(z)$	19	price level in market z
PPI	1	producer price index
PPP	16	purchasing-power parity
r	7	real interest rate
r^e	7	expected real interest rate
$\tilde{r}$	13	after-tax real interest rate
$\hat{r}$	14	real discount rate for people with poor collateral
R	3	nominal interest rate
R^d	17	nominal interest rate on deposits
s	11	gross saving rate
S	15	nominal amount of national saving
$(\cdot)^s$	5	quantity supplied
$t\ (T)$	12	individual's (aggregate) nominal taxes
$(\cdot)_t$	2	price or quantity in period t
T	4	interval between withdrawals of money
u	10	unemployment rate
$u(\cdot)$	2	utility function
U	10	number of persons unemployed
$v\ (V)$	8	individual's (aggregate) nominal transfers
w	6	nominal wage rate
$\overline{w}$	10	reservation wage rate
w^u	10	income received while unemployed
x	3	real present value of consumption
$y\ (Y)$	2	individual's (aggregate) real output
z	19	index of markets
α	12	substitution of public services for private consumption
β	12	marginal product of public services
γ	4	nominal transactions cost
δ	9	depreciation rate
Δ	2	change of some price or quantity
ϵ	16	exchange rate
λ	20	rate of price adjustment
μ	8	growth rate of money
ν	20	marginal propensity to consume (or to spend)
π	7	inflation rate
π^e	7	expected inflation rate
$\hat{\pi}$	19	choice of inflation under discretionary policy
π^*	20	rate of change of market-clearing price level
σ	10	job-separation rate
τ	13	marginal tax rate
ϕ	10	job-finding rate
$\Phi(\cdot)$	4	aggregate function for real demand for money
$\psi(\cdot)$	19	function for policymaker's choice of inflation

signifies that it corresponds to a market-clearing condition.

MACROECONOMICS

THE MIT PRESS   CAMBRIDGE, MASSACHUSETTS   LONDON, ENGLAND

FIFTH EDITION

MACROECONOMICS

Robert J. Barro

Fourth printing, 2001
© 1997 Massachusetts Institute
of Technology

This book was set in Melior and
MetaPlus by Windfall Software
using ZzTEX and was printed and
bound in the United States of
America.

Images copyright © 1997
PhotoDisc, Inc.

Library of Congress Cataloging-in-
Publication Data

Barro, Robert J.
    Macroeconomics / Robert J.
Barro.—5th ed.
        p.   cm
    Includes bibliographical
references and index.
    ISBN 978-0-262-02436-5
    1. Macroeconomics.   I. Title.
HB172.5.B36   1997
339—dc21   97-26136
                            CIP

Contents

PREFACE

M acroeconomics has been in an unsettled state since the early 1970s. The Keynesian model, which was almost universally accepted as the basic paradigm until the late 1960s, is regarded by most economists as scientifically not quite respectable. Periodically, some group of economists tries to patch up the Keynesian framework—the most recent effort was by the new Keynesians in the 1980s—but the results have never really been successful.

The initial loss in popularity of the Keynesian model was caused by embarrassments over economic events, especially the failure of the model to deal satisfactorily with inflation and supply shocks. The reduced enthusiasm also reflected the theoretical and empirical progress of an alternative "market-clearing approach," which began in the 1970s and was more closely related to the microeconomics that economists use successfully to study the behavior of individual households and businesses. There is a reasonable consensus among economists that this market-clearing approach is the correct one for longer-term studies, such as analyses of a country's long-run rate of economic growth. In short-term contexts—that is, for studies of business fluctuations—some important problems remain. Nevertheless, this alternative approach provides a more satisfactory macroeconomics than the one we had before. By more satisfactory, I mean that the approach avoids internal inconsistencies and also provides a better understanding of the real world.

Although the Keynesian model has been subject to skepticism by economists for at least 25 years, it has nevertheless continued to be the main organizing model in most textbooks. As a result, it has continued to dominate the way the subject has been taught to the majority of students. Many textbooks now present aspects of market-clearing models, but these models are usually not taken seriously in the study of real-world events or policy proposals. This gap between textbook material and the knowledge gained since the early 1970s motivated me to write the first edition of this book in 1984.

My purpose in the book is to present the market-clearing approach as a general method for analyzing real-world macroeconomic problems. The stress on this approach means that the book is not a balanced treatment of alternative macroeconomic models. There is no book—and probably could be none of substance—that is balanced in this respect. Although I deal in a serious manner with the Keynesian model—and show carefully how it relates to the market-clearing approach—I do not use the Keynesian framework for most of the analyses of economic events or policies. In any case, whatever one's ultimate judgment about the value of the Keynesian model, there is a good reason not to start the study of macroeconomics with it. The Keynesian model is an advanced topic that makes specific assumptions about the ways that private markets malfunction. The nature of the malfunctions and the special features of the model cannot be fully understood and appreciated until the market-clearing analysis has been worked out.

I think that the favorable reception of this book in previous editions reflects the widespread eagerness for a macroeconomic framework that outperforms the Keynesian model. Although the Keynesian model can be appealing as a teaching device, it leaves students with a poor understanding of how the economy works and how governmental policies can help or hinder it. In addition, I have found that many instructors have become convinced, after some initial skepticism, that the more satisfactory market-clearing approach really is accessible to undergraduates.

As with previous versions, this fifth edition discusses the material in as simple a fashion as I have found possible so that the book can be used for undergraduate courses in intermediate macroeconomics. Many years of experience have demonstrated that the book works well for these courses. However, the feedback from users has helped me to simplify the exposition in many places. Therefore, I am confident that students will find this fifth edition even more accessible than the earlier ones.

I am grateful to Betsey Stevenson for her tireless assistance with data, empirical examples, and improvements of my prose. I also appreciate Elin Lee's efforts in learning Scientific Word and preparing the manuscript for the publishers. Finally, I am grateful to my son Josh for his skill in the construction of some of the figures.

MACROECONOMICS

THE APPROACH TO MACROECONOMICS

In macroeconomics we study the overall or aggregate performance of an economy. We consider, for example, the total output of goods and services as measured by the **gross domestic product (GDP)**. We look also at the aggregates of employment and unemployment, and at the breakdown of GDP into consumer expenditures, private investment (purchases of new capital goods by the private sector), government consumption and investment, and net exports.

These terms refer to the quantities of goods or work effort. We shall also be interested in the prices that relate to these quantities, for example, the dollar prices of the goods and services that the U.S. economy produces. When we look at the price of the typical or average item, we refer to the **general price level**. However, we are also interested in the prices of particular items in the economy, such as the **wage rate** (which is the price of labor services), the **interest rate** (which determines the cost of borrowing and the return to lending), and the **exchange**

rates (which are the prices of a country's currency in terms of foreign currencies).

We shall want to know how the economy determines the various quantities and prices and how government policies affect these variables. Specifically, we shall consider monetary policy, which involves the determination of the quantity of **money** and the design of monetary institutions, and fiscal policy, which pertains to the government's expenditures, taxes, and budget deficits.

The performance of the overall economy is a substantial concern for everyone because it influences job prospects, incomes, and prices. Thus, it is important for us—and even more important for our government policymakers—to understand how the macroeconomy works. Unfortunately, as is obvious from reading the newspapers, the theory of macroeconomics is not a settled scientific field. There is much controversy among economists about what is a useful basic approach, as well as about the detailed analyses of particular economic events and policy proposals. There has, however, been a great deal of progress in recent years in designing a more satisfactory macroeconomic theory. The main objective of this book is to convey that progress to students in an accessible form.

THE BEHAVIOR OF OUTPUT, UNEMPLOYMENT, AND THE PRICE LEVEL IN THE UNITED STATES

[1] *The figure uses a proportionate (logarithmic) scale, so that each unit on the vertical axis corresponds to an equal percentage change in real GDP. On this scale, the slope of the curve at any point equals the growth rate of real GDP. Because of data availability, the numbers refer to real gross national product (real GNP) up to 1958 and to GDP thereafter.*

To get an overview of the subject matter, consider the historical record on some of the major macroeconomic variables for the United States. Figure 1.1 shows the total output of goods and services in the United States from 1869 to 1996. (The starting date is determined by the available data.) The measure of aggregate output is the gross domestic product, expressed in terms of values for a base year, which happens to be 1992. This measure, which we discuss in a later section on national-income accounting, is called **real GDP**.[1]

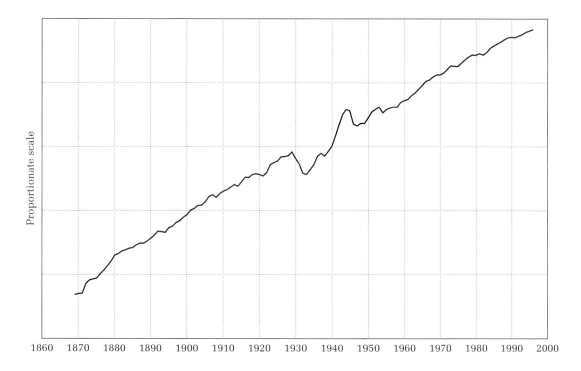

FIGURE 1.1

THE BEHAVIOR OF OUTPUT IN THE UNITED STATES, 1869–1996

The figure shows real gross domestic product on a proportionate scale. Values prior to 1959 are for gross national product.

Sources for Figures 1.1–1.5 are as follows:

For real GDP (or GNP) and the GDP (or GNP) deflator: Recent values are from the U.S. Department of Commerce, *Survey of Current Business*, March 1997, and DRI data bank. Figures from 1929 to 1958 are from U.S. Department of Commerce (1986). For 1869–1928, the values are from Christina Romer (1987, 1988).

For the unemployment rate: The figures are the number unemployed divided by the labor force (inclusive of military personnel up to 1990 and consisting only of the civilian labor force thereafter). Data since 1930 are from DRI data bank and from *Economic Report of the President*, 1988, Table B–32; 1983, Table B–29; 1970, Table C–22. The data for 1933–43 are adjusted to classify federal emergency workers as employed, as discussed in Michael Darby (1976). Values for 1890–1929 are based on Christina Romer (1986, Table 9).

The general upward trend of real GDP in Figure 1.1 reflects the long-term growth or economic development of the U.S. economy. The average growth rate of real GDP from 1869 to 1996 was 3.3% per year. Consequently, over 127 years, the total output increased 64-fold. If we divide through by population to determine real per capita GDP, we find that the average growth rate was 1.8% per year—the 3.3% average growth rate of real GDP less the 1.5% average growth rate of population. Hence, over 127 years, output per person increased by a factor of 10.

Figure 1.2 shows the growth rate of real GDP for each year. Notice in this figure the recurring ups and downs of output. These movements are called aggregate business fluctuations or the business cycle.[2] When real GDP falls toward a low point or trough, the economy is in a **recession** or an economic contraction. Conversely, when real GDP expands toward a high point or peak, the economy is in a **boom** or an economic expansion. The dates indicated in Figure 1.2 show the major U.S. recessions since 1869. Note especially the **Great Depression** of 1930 to 1933, during which output fell 30% below the peak value reached in 1929. The other major economic contractions before World War II occurred in 1893–94, 1907–08, 1914, 1920–21, and 1937–38. For the post–World War II period, the most significant recessions were those for 1958, 1974–75, 1980–82, and 1990–91.

On the up side, notice first the high rates of growth in output during World Wars I and II and the Korean War. Other periods of economic boom—in the sense of unusually high growth rates of real GDP—were 1982–88, 1975–78, 1961–73 (except for the brief recession in 1970), the recovery from the Great Depression from 1933 to 1940 (aside from the recession of 1937–38), much of the 1920s, the period from 1896 to 1906, and the years from 1875 to 1880.

Figure 1.3, which reports the unemployment rate for each year, provides another way to look at recessions and booms. The unemployment rate is the fraction of the labor force that has no job. (We discuss the precise meaning of this variable in Chapter 10.) Over the period 1890 to 1996, for which data are available, the median unemployment rate was

[2] *The term* business cycle *is somewhat misleading because it suggests a more regular pattern of ups and downs in economic activity than actually appears in the data. But the term is too entrenched in the economics literature to avoid entirely.*

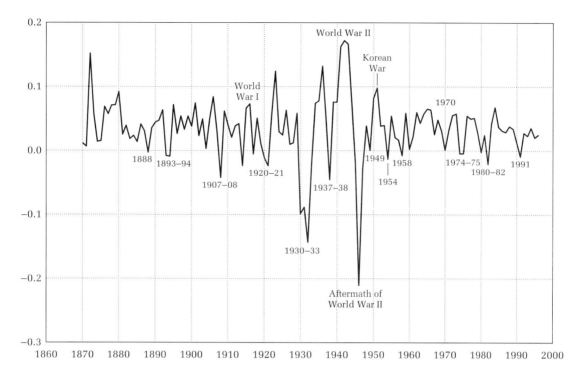

FIGURE 1.2

GROWTH RATES OF OUTPUT IN THE UNITED STATES, 1870–1996

The figure shows the annual growth rate of real gross domestic product (real gross national product prior to 1960).

5.4%. (The mean was 6.4%.) During recessions, the unemployment rate rises above the median. The extreme is the Great Depression, in which unemployment reached 22% of the labor force in 1932. Also noteworthy are the average rates of 18% for 1931–35, 12% for 1938–39, 11% for 1894–98, and 8% for 1921–22, 1975–76, and 1980–86.

Figures 1.2 and 1.3 show the turbulence of the economy during the two world wars and the 1930s. But suppose that we abstract from these episodes and compare the post–World War II performance with that from before World War I. Then the major message from the data is the similarity between the post–World War II and pre–World War I

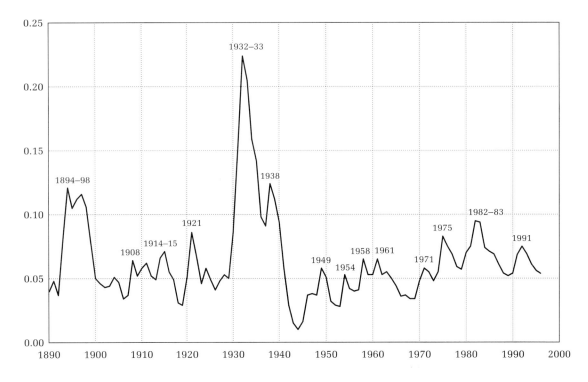

FIGURE 1.3

U.S. UNEMPLOYMENT RATE, 1890–1996

experiences. The average growth rate of real GDP was 3.1% per year from 1947 to 1996, compared with 3.8% from 1870 to 1914. The median unemployment rates were 5.5% from 1947 to 1996 and 5.2% from 1890 to 1914 (the means were 5.6% and 6.4%, respectively). The extent of fluctuations—in terms of the severity of recessions and booms—was only moderately larger in the earlier period than in the later one.[3] Therefore, although the economy has changed greatly over a century—including a larger role for government, a diminished share of agriculture in the GDP, and dramatic alterations in the monetary system—the data suggest no major change in the intensity of business fluctuations.

Figure 1.4 shows an index of the general level of prices in the United States from 1869 to 1996. (We discuss the details of the particular measure—the deflator for the gross domestic product—toward the end

[3] *For a detailed comparison of real GDP and unemployment rates over the different periods, see Christina Romer (1986, 1987, 1988).*

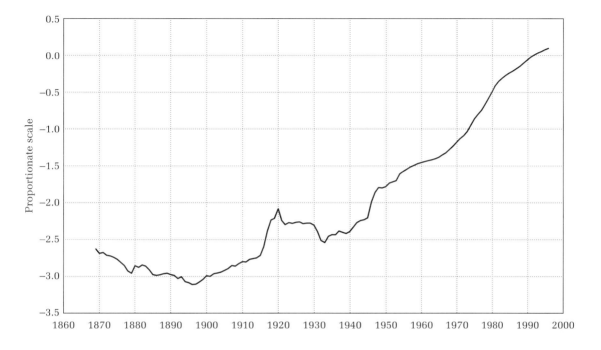

FIGURE 1.4

U.S. PRICE LEVEL, 1869–1996

The figure shows the GDP deflator (GNP deflator prior to 1959) on a proportionate scale.

of this chapter.) One striking observation is the persistent rise in prices since World War II, contrasted with the movements up and down before the war. There are long periods in the earlier history—1869–92 and 1920–33—during which prices fell persistently.

Figure 1.5 looks at the year-to-year growth rate of the general price level, that is, the **inflation rate**. Almost all of the inflation rates since World War II were positive, whereas those from earlier periods were sometimes positive and sometimes negative. Note also that the inflation rate fell sharply from a peak of nearly 10% in 1980–81 to 3.2% for 1983–96.

In subsequent chapters we shall relate the behavior of the general price level to monetary developments, especially to changes in the quantity of money. This monetary behavior depends, in turn, on the nature of

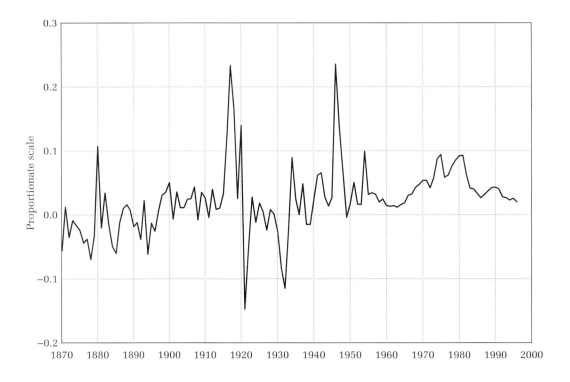

FIGURE 1.5

U.S. INFLATION RATE, 1870–1996

The figure shows the annual rate of change of the GDP deflator (GNP deflator through 1959).

monetary institutions, such as whether the United States was on the **gold standard** (as it was from 1879 until World War I and, to some extent, from World War I until 1933), on the presence of the Federal Reserve System (which began in 1914), and on the characteristics of the banking sector.

SOME KEY FACTS ABOUT U.S. BUSINESS FLUCTUATIONS

We now examine some detailed characteristics of U.S. business fluctuations, using quarterly data for the recent period 1959–96. We start in 1959 because a major revision of the national accounts has, thus far, been

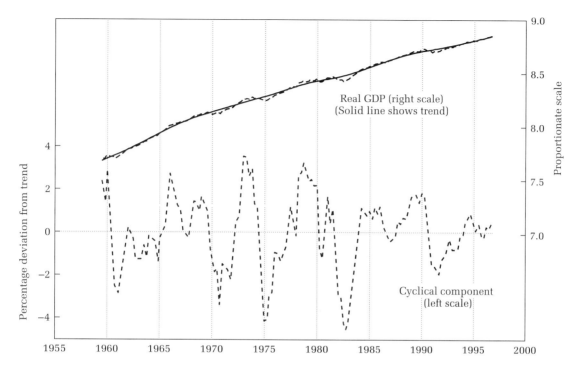

FIGURE 1.6

THE BREAKDOWN OF REAL GDP INTO TREND AND CYCLICAL COMPONENTS

The dashed line is chain-weighted real GDP, the solid line is the trend (see footnote 4), and the dotted line is the cyclical component, which equals the difference between real GDP and its trend.

extended back only to that year. The facts on business fluctuations are interesting in themselves but will also help to focus the theoretical discussion in later chapters. We shall want to see how well the economic model that we develop fits these facts.

The dashed line in the upper part of Figure 1.6 shows the path of real GDP on a proportionate scale, essentially a magnified picture of the right end of the graph in Figure 1.1. A good way to assess business fluctuations is to look at the departure of real GDP from a trend line that captures the longer run evolution of output. The solid line in the upper part of the figure represents such a trend.[4] The gap between real GDP and the trend line, which we refer to as *detrended GDP* or the *cyclical component of*

[4] *Finn Kydland and Edward Prescott (1990) describe a simple way to fit a trend line like that shown in Figure 1.6. Basically, they find a curve that explains as much as possible of the movements in the underlying variable (real GDP in this case) without wiggling around too much.*

GDP, is shown by the dotted line at the bottom of the figure. The average of detrended GDP is zero by construction, and the value at any date—read off the left scale—shows the percentage deviation from the trend. In the fourth quarter of 1991, for example, real GDP was 2.0% below trend, whereas in the fourth quarter of 1996 it was 0.5% above trend.

We can use the bottom part of Figure 1.6 to pinpoint the main recessions: the proportionate shortfalls of real GDP at the troughs were 2.8% in 1961.1, 3.4% in 1970.4, 4.2% in 1975.1, 4.5% in 1982.4, and 2.0% in 1991.4.[5] The recession for 1990–91 was the first significant downturn in the United States since late 1982.

A useful measure of the volatility of real GDP is the standard deviation of the cyclical component,[6] which is 1.7%. (This number and other figures presented in this section are collected in Table 1.1.) The cyclical fluctuations are, in other words, large enough so that quarterly real GDP is often 1.7% or more above or below its trend line.

THE COMPONENTS OF GDP

We can get more information about business fluctuations by comparing detrended real GDP with the detrended data for its various components. We look here only at the domestic parts of spending and defer until Chapter 15 a discussion of the foreign sector.

Figure 1.7 deals with consumer expenditure on nondurables and services, a form of spending that accounted on average for 58.9% of real GDP from 1959 to 1996. The solid line in the figure reproduces the cyclical part of real GDP from the bottom of Figure 1.6, whereas the dotted line shows the cyclical part of real consumer spending on nondurables and services. One observation is that consumer spending typically moves in the same direction as GDP: the correlation between the cyclical components is 0.83.[7] If this correlation is positive—that is, if a variable usually moves cyclically in the same direction as real GDP—then economists say that the variable is **procyclical**. A variable that moves in the opposite direction is **countercyclical**, and one that has little

[5] *Using an earlier concept of real GDP, two other post–World War II recessions were in 1954.2 (real GDP 2.0% below trend) and 1958.2 (3.7% below trend).*

[6] *The standard deviation is the square root of the variance. The variance is the average squared value of the cyclical component.*

[7] *The correlation, which must lie between −1 and 1, shows how closely two variables move together. If the correlation equals 1, then the two move precisely together in the same direction, whereas if it equals −1, then the two again move precisely together, but in opposite directions. If the correlation equals 0, then an increase in one variable is equally likely to go along with an increase or decrease in the other variable. Formally, for the two variables A and B, the correlation equals $Cov(A,B)/(\sigma_A \sigma_B)$, where σ_A and σ_B are the standard deviations of the cyclical components of each variable (see footnote 6), and Cov is the covariance between the two cyclical components. The covariance is the average value of the product of the two cyclical components.*

TABLE 1.1

SOME KEY FACTS ABOUT U.S. BUSINESS FLUCTUATIONS, 1959–96

	Average Share of Real GDP	Standard Deviation	Correlation with Real GDP
Components of real GDP:			
Real GDP	1.000	.017	1.00
Consumption, nondurables and services	.589	.008	.83
Nondurables	.236	.012	.79
Services	.353	.007	.77
Broad private investment	.203	.065	.93
Consumer durables	.066	.049	.82
Gross private investment	.140	.077	.90
Fixed nonresidential	.089	.049	.81
Fixed residential	.046	.109	.65
Inventory change	.005	.0053[a]	.60
Government consumption and investment	.226	.017	.02
Federal	.106	.027	.04
State and local	.119	.012	.35
Net exports	−.014	.008[a]	−.32
Exports	.064	.044	.28
Imports	.078	.051	.75
Labor variables:			
Employment	—	.010	.81
Worker-hours	—	.015	.88
Output per employee	—	.011	.84
Output per worker-hour	—	.008	.41
Unemployment rate	—	.0075[b]	−.90
Price level:			
GDP deflator	—	.009	−.65

The data are quarterly from 1959 to 1996. All variables are in proportional (logarithmic) units except where noted otherwise.

[a] These variables are measured as fractions of trend real GDP. (The variables cannot be expressed in proportional units because they are sometimes negative.)

[b] The unemployment rate has not been transformed into proportional units. The sample mean is .061.

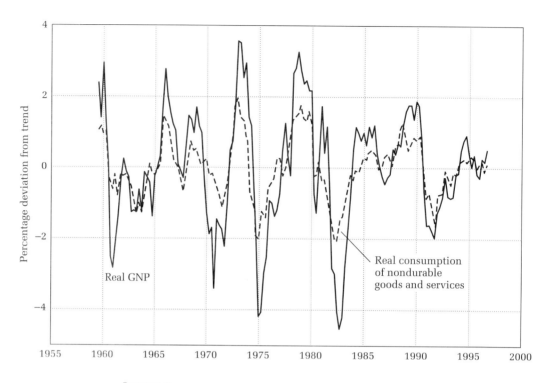

FIGURE 1.7

THE CYCLICAL COMPONENTS OF REAL GDP AND REAL CONSUMER EXPENDITURE ON NONDURABLES AND SERVICES

The solid line is the cyclical part of real GDP, and the dashed line is the cyclical part of real consumer spending on nondurables and services.

relation to real GNP is **acyclical**. Consumer spending on nondurables and services is therefore a procyclical variable.

Figure 1.7 and Table 1.1 also show that the cyclical component of consumer expenditure on nondurables and services is less volatile than that of real GDP: the standard deviation for consumer spending is 0.008, about one-half that for GDP. Because spending on nondurables and services is relatively stable, this component contributes much less to business fluctuations than would be expected from the average size of this component (58.9% of GDP).

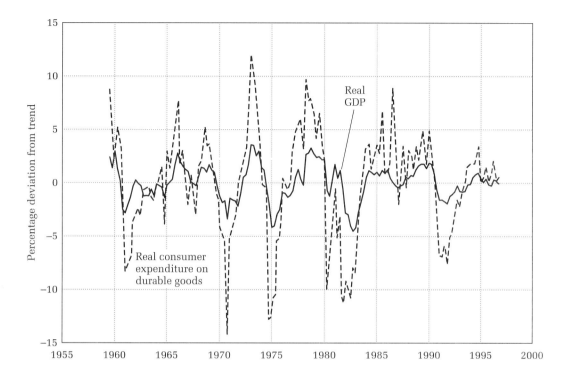

FIGURE 1.8

THE CYCLICAL COMPONENTS OF REAL GDP AND REAL PURCHASES OF CONSUMER DURABLES

The solid line is the cyclical part of real GDP, and the dashed line is the cyclical part of real purchases of consumer durables.

Figures 1.8 and 1.9 show the behavior, respectively, of purchases of consumer durables (another part of consumer spending) and the standard measure of gross private investment—spending on structures, equipment, and inventories by businesses and purchases of residential housing by households. Durables purchases and gross private investment are procyclical: the correlations of the cyclical components with detrended real GDP are 0.82 and 0.90, respectively. The contrast with consumer spending on nondurables and services is that the two new variables are each substantially more volatile than real GDP. (Note that the scales in Figures 1.8 and 1.9 are much wider than that in Figure 1.7.)

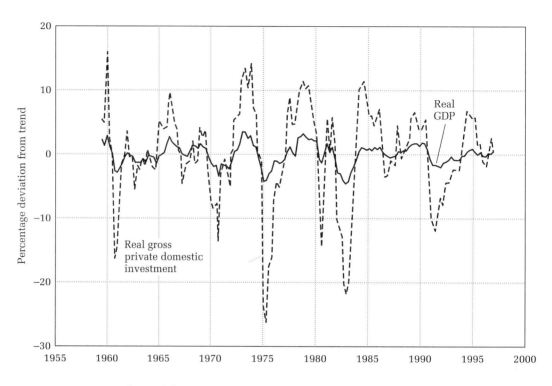

FIGURE 1.9

THE CYCLICAL COMPONENTS OF REAL GDP AND REAL GROSS PRIVATE DOMESTIC INVESTMENT

The solid line is the cyclical part of real GDP, and the dashed line is the cyclical part of real gross private domestic investment.

The standard deviation for consumer durables is 0.049 and that for gross investment is 0.077, compared with 0.017 for GDP (see Table 1.1). Thus, these components contribute far more to business fluctuations than would be expected from their average shares of real GDP (6.6% for consumer durables and 13.7% for gross private investment). Table 1.1 also provides information for the breakdown of gross private investment into its various parts, nonresidential and residential investment and accumulation of inventories.

Because consumer durables are the equipment used by households, it is not surprising that the purchases of these durables behave simi-

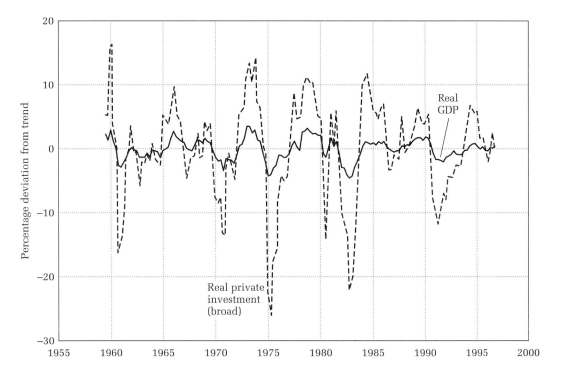

FIGURE 1.10

THE CYCLICAL COMPONENTS OF REAL GDP AND REAL PRIVATE INVESTMENT, BROADLY DEFINED

The solid line is the cyclical part of real GDP, and the dashed line is the cyclical part of real gross private
domestic investment plus real purchases of consumer durables.

larly to the spending on equipment by businesses, a component of gross
private investment. It is therefore useful to add purchases of consumer
durables to gross private investment to get a broader measure of private investment. Figure 1.10 shows that broad private investment is
markedly procyclical: the correlation with detrended real GDP is 0.93.
The cyclical component of broad private investment has a standard deviation of 0.065, almost four times that of GDP. Thus, although broad
private investment averages only 20.3% of GDP, the volatility of this
component and the high correlation with detrended GDP mean that
it accounts for the bulk of overall business fluctuations. It will there-

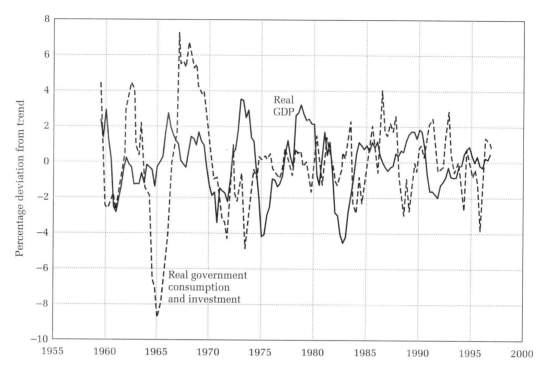

FIGURE 1.11

THE CYCLICAL COMPONENTS OF REAL GDP AND REAL GOVERNMENT CONSUMPTION AND INVESTMENT

The solid line is the cyclical part of real GDP, and the dashed line is the cyclical part of real government expenditures for consumption and investment.

[8] *Earlier versions of the U.S. national accounts referred to this component as government purchases of goods and services. These purchases were partly for consumption and partly for investment (on public capital goods). The new concept of government consumption also includes some implicit rental income on the outstanding stock of public capital.*

fore be important later on (especially in Chapter 9) to see whether our economic model can explain the key role of investment in business fluctuations.

Government consumption expenditure and gross investment averaged 22.6% of GDP from 1959 to 1996.[8] Figure 1.11 shows that this component is about as volatile as GDP, with a standard deviation of 0.017. This component is, however, negligibly related to detrended GDP: the correlation is only 0.02. Thus, although the government component of GDP is large and moderately variable, the lack of correlation with GDP indicates that this component is acyclical and has little to do with the typical pattern of business fluctuations.

LABOR INPUT AND PRODUCTIVITY

The cyclical fluctuations in real GDP have underlying them substantial movements of labor input. We consider here two measures of labor input—total employment (the number of persons with jobs) and total worker-hours (the number employed multiplied by the average weekly hours worked per employee). Figures 1.12 and 1.13 show that both labor

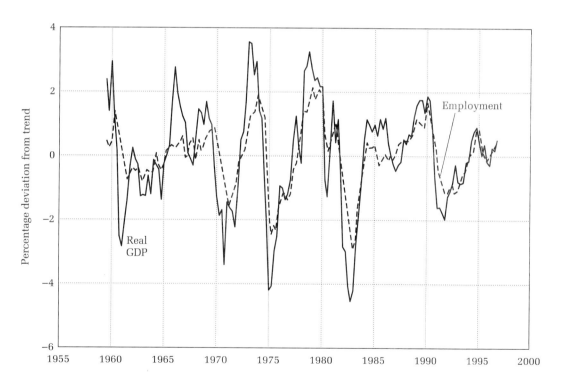

FIGURE 1.12

THE CYCLICAL COMPONENTS OF REAL GDP AND EMPLOYMENT

The solid line is the cyclical part of real GDP, and the dashed line is the cyclical part of total civilian employment.

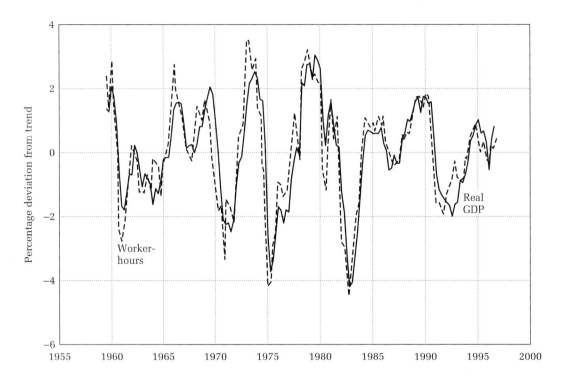

FIGURE 1.13

THE CYCLICAL COMPONENTS OF REAL GDP AND TOTAL WORKER-HOURS

The solid line is the cyclical part of real GDP, and the dashed line is the cyclical part of total worker-hours (employee hours in nonagricultural establishments).

variables are procyclical: the correlations of the cyclical components with detrended GDP are 0.81 and 0.88, respectively. The volatility of employment (standard deviation = 0.010) is substantially less than that of GDP, whereas the volatility of worker-hours (standard deviation = 0.015) is slightly smaller than that of GDP.

Output (real GDP) and labor input both rise in booms and fall in recessions. The cyclical behavior of *labor productivity*—the output generated per unit of labor—depends on the relative movements of output

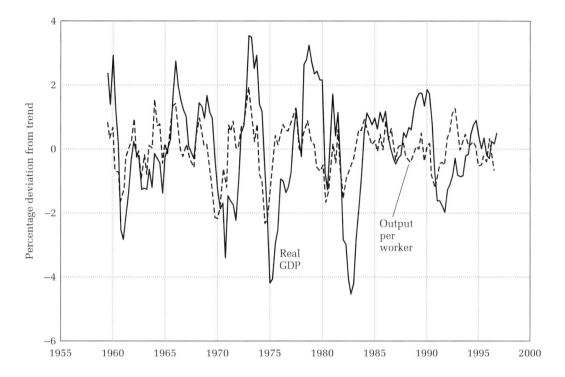

FIGURE 1.14

THE CYCLICAL COMPONENTS OF REAL GDP AND OUTPUT PER WORKER

The solid line is the cyclical part of real GDP, and the dashed line is the cyclical part of output per worker (real GDP divided by total civilian employment).

and labor. We consider here two measures of productivity—output per worker (real GDP divided by the number employed) and output per worker-hour (real GDP divided by total worker-hours). The two measures of productivity are both procyclical: the correlations with detrended GDP are 0.84 for output per worker and 0.41 for output per worker-hour (see Figures 1.14 and 1.15). These results mean that output expands proportionately more than labor in a boom and falls proportionately more than labor in a recession. The second measure of labor productivity

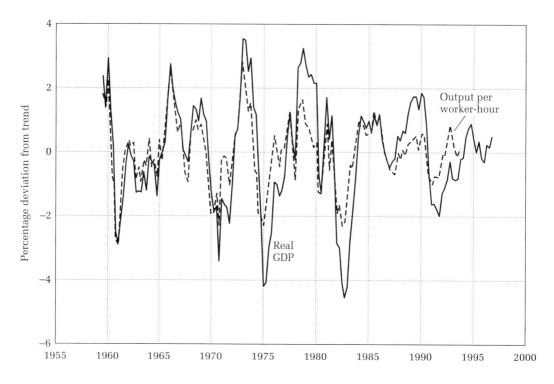

FIGURE 1.15

THE CYCLICAL COMPONENTS OF REAL GDP AND OUTPUT PER WORKER-HOUR

The solid line is the cyclical part of real GDP, and the dashed line is the cyclical part of output per worker-hour
(real GDP divided by total worker-hours).

(based on total worker-hours) is less procyclical than the first (based on employment) because the hours worked per worker tend to rise in booms and fall in recessions.

Because employment is procyclical, it is not surprising that the unemployment rate is countercyclical. The correlation of the detrended unemployment rate with detrended GDP is −0.90 (see Figure 1.16).

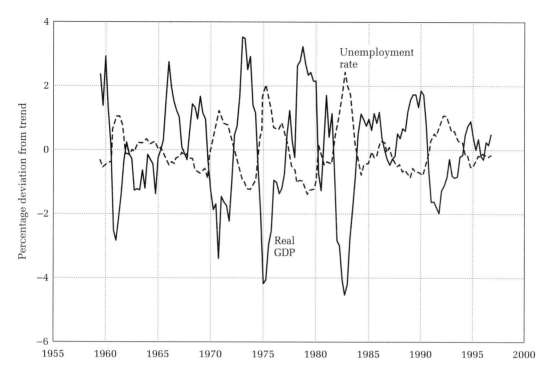

FIGURE 1.16

THE CYCLICAL COMPONENTS OF REAL GDP AND THE UNEMPLOYMENT RATE

The solid line is the cyclical part of real GDP, and the dashed line is the cyclical part of the civilian unemployment rate.

THE PRICE LEVEL

We shall find it useful later to see how the general level of prices relates to business fluctuations. We use the measure of the price level shown in Figure 1.4, the deflator for the GDP. Figure 1.17 shows that the overall price level was countercyclical from 1959 to 1996: the correlation of the detrended price level with detrended GDP is −0.65. The volatility of the price level (standard deviation = 0.009) is about one-half that of GDP.

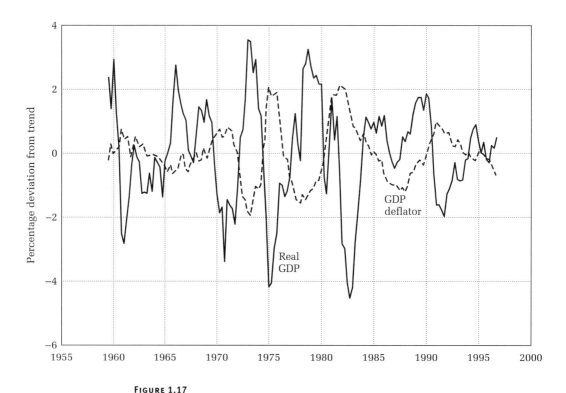

FIGURE 1.17

THE CYCLICAL COMPONENTS OF REAL GDP AND THE GDP DEFLATOR

The solid line is the cyclical part of real GDP, and the dashed line is the cyclical part of the GDP deflator.

THE APPROACH TO MACROECONOMICS

This section describes the basic theoretical approach that this book uses to design a useful macroeconomic model. In setting up this model, we shall spend a good deal of time on economic theory. In this context we worry about whether the theory seems sensible, whether it is internally consistent, and so on. However, the main test of the model will be its ability to explain the behavior of macroeconomic variables in the real world. We therefore devote considerable space to comparisons of the theory with the real world, that is, with empirical evidence.

MICROECONOMIC FOUNDATIONS OF MACROECONOMICS

We begin by developing the basic price theory—or **microeconomic foundations**—that underlies the macroeconomic analysis of the aggregate variables in an economy. Much of this microeconomics will be familiar to students from previous courses in economics. In that sense, the macroeconomic approach in this book is a continuation of the economic reasoning used to explain the behavior of individual households and businesses. Here we apply this same economic science to understand the workings of the overall economy, that is, to study real GDP, employment and unemployment, the general price level and inflation, the wage rate, the interest rate, the exchange rate, and so on. Many basic textbooks in economics unfortunately do not follow this general approach when dealing with macroeconomics. Students could, in fact, easily reach the conclusion that macroeconomics and microeconomics were two entirely distinct fields. A central theme of this book is that a more satisfactory macroeconomics emerges when it is linked to the underlying microeconomics. The term *more satisfactory* means, first, that the macroeconomic theory avoids internal inconsistencies, and second, that it provides a better understanding of the real world.

In Chapter 2 we examine the choice problems of an isolated individual, similar to the Robinson Crusoe of Daniel Defoe's novel. We assume that Crusoe's choices are guided by enlightened self-interest; that is, we exploit the central economic postulate of optimizing behavior. In the initial framework, the only choice variable is the level of work effort, which then determines the quantities of production and consumption. By studying Crusoe's behavior, we can understand in a simple way the trade-off between leisure and consumption that applies analogously in complicated market economies. Also, by looking at an isolated individual, we bring out the role of a resource or **budget constraint** in its simplest form. When goods cannot be stored over time, Crusoe's budget constraint dictates that his consumption equals his production. As we shall see, extensions of this simple constraint are central to correct macroeconomic analyses in economies that include many consumers and producers, as well as a government.

We can use the model of Robinson Crusoe to predict his responses to changes in production opportunities, for example, to harvest failures or to discoveries of new goods or methods of production. Many of these results carry over to the predictions for aggregate output and employment in more realistic settings. In particular, when we consider the economy's responses to changes in production opportunities—such as the oil crises of 1973–74 and 1979—we usually get the right answer by thinking of the parallel situation for Robinson Crusoe.

Chapter 3 develops the microeconomic foundations needed to go from an analysis of Robinson Crusoe to a study of many people who interact on various marketplaces. Once again we exploit the postulate of optimizing behavior, subject to budget constraints, to assess the responses of individuals to different circumstances.

To simplify matters, we start with only two markets. In the first market, households buy and sell goods in exchange for money. The dollar cost in this market is the theoretical counterpart of the general price level. In the other market, households can borrow and lend. This credit or loan market establishes an interest rate, which borrowers must pay to lenders.

The introduction of the goods market allows people to specialize in production activities, a setup that adds to the economy's productivity. (Robinson Crusoe did not have this option.) The existence of the credit market means that a household's expenditure during any period can diverge from its income during that period. Thus, unlike Robinson Crusoe, a household with a given income has choices about consuming now versus later. Similarly, households can choose between working now versus later. We discuss these choices by considering incentives to save, that is, to accumulate assets that pay interest income. We stress the idea that a higher interest rate motivates people to save more; thereby, they consume less today and plan to consume more later. Similarly, we show that various forces can induce people to rearrange their work and production from one period to another.

In a later chapter (Chapter 6), we introduce a labor market on which labor services are bought and sold at an established wage rate. But to simplify the basic model, we do not include this market at the outset. Rather, we pretend that households work only on their own production processes; that is, each household owns its own business and provides the labor input for this business. For many purposes—such as studying the main determinants of aggregate output and work effort, the general price level, and the interest rate—this simplification will be satisfactory. But to explore some other topics—such as unemployment and wage rates—we have to deal explicitly with the labor market.

The analysis stresses the role of budget constraints, which ensure a balance between each household's sources and uses of funds. Although these budget conditions may seem tedious at times, it is important to keep these matters straight. Many serious errors in macroeconomic reasoning occur when economic theorists forget to impose the appropriate budget constraints in their models. We shall see that these conditions are especially important in evaluating temporary versus permanent changes in income, in studying the effects of interest rates on lenders and borrowers, and in evaluating the effects of money holdings. Also, when we introduce government policies in later chapters, we shall find it crucial to impose the government's budget constraint. Many errors in analyses of the government's expenditures and budget deficits result from a failure to impose this budget constraint.

Chapter 4 completes the discussion of microfoundations by exploring the incentives to hold non-interest-bearing paper money rather than financial assets that bear interest. The **demand for money** arises out of the process of carrying out transactions, which use money as a **medium of exchange**. Because households use money when they buy or sell goods or financial assets, it would require a great deal of planning and effort to hold little or no money. We then discuss how the quantity of money demanded depends on the price level, the interest rate, the level of income, and other variables.

MARKET-CLEARING CONDITIONS

We note in Chapter 5 that certain conditions must hold when we add up the actions of all households; for example, the total of goods sold by suppliers must equal the total bought by demanders. Similarly, the total amount loaned on the credit market must equal the total borrowed. We refer to conditions such as these as **aggregate-consistency conditions**. These conditions tell us something about how aggregate quantities must behave for the analysis to be internally consistent. Any reasonable macromodel must satisfy these conditions.

One way to ensure that the aggregate-consistency conditions hold is to assume that the various markets, such as those for goods and credit, always clear. Clearing means that the price level and the interest rate adjust simultaneously so that the aggregate demand for goods equals the aggregate supply, and the aggregate of desired lending equals the aggregate of desired borrowing. We use this **market-clearing approach** to satisfy the aggregate-consistency conditions in the basic model.

The idea that markets clear is closely related to the notion that private markets function efficiently. With cleared markets, it is impossible to improve on any outcomes by matching potential borrowers and lenders or by bringing together potential buyers and sellers of goods. Cleared markets already accomplish all of these mutually advantageous trades. We can see that market clearing is reminiscent of the optimizing behavior of individuals. On the one hand, people determine their individual choices of work, consumption, and so on to make themselves as well off as possible. On the other hand, market clearing means that the people who participate in and organize markets—and are guided by the pursuit of their own interests—do not waste resources and thereby end up achieving efficient outcomes. Market clearing is therefore the natural complement at the macro level to the microfoundations that underlie the model.

It is possible to satisfy the aggregate-consistency conditions without imposing market clearing in the sense that we have just described. One important idea is that imperfect information makes it impossible to make the best decisions about production and work at all times. We shall consider later some macroeconomic models that incorporate incomplete information (particularly in Chapter 19). But it is best to explore the workings of the economy under full information before going on to this advanced topic. Thus, we do not introduce incomplete information into the model at the outset.

Another alternative to market clearing is the **Keynesian model**. This model assumes that some prices, usually of labor services or commodities, are sticky and that some rationing of quantities bought or sold therefore comes into play. Sometimes this rationing takes the form of chronic unemployment and underproduction. More generally, the failure of markets to clear tends to generate inefficient results because some mutually advantageous trades do not take place. These kinds of "market failure" in the Keynesian model have led many economists to advocate corrective policy actions by the government.

The Keynesian model depends crucially on the assumption that prices are sticky. Thus, not surprisingly, the rationale for price stickiness has been the subject of substantial and still unresolved debate. In any case, the Keynesian theory has underlying it the market-clearing framework and therefore cannot be appreciated without first working through the logic of this framework. We therefore take up the Keynesian model (in Chapter 20) after the market-clearing analysis has been completed.

To summarize, the basic model relies on two key elements for making predictions about the behavior of quantities and prices in the real world. First, we use the model's microfoundations, which derive from the optimizing behavior of individuals subject to budget constraints. Second, we exploit the notion of market clearing, a process that reflects the efficient matching of potential buyers and sellers of goods, credit, labor services, and so on.

USING THE MARKET-CLEARING MODEL

Chapter 5 lays out the central theoretical apparatus used throughout the remainder of the book. After this point, the discussion amounts to extensions of the basic model to apply the reasoning to various topics in macroeconomics. The list of applications eventually includes supply shocks, inflation, business fluctuations, long-term economic growth, government expenditures, monetary and fiscal policies, international borrowing and lending, exchange rates, financial intermediation, incomplete information and rational expectations, and the Keynesian model.

We first use the model in Chapter 5 to study various disturbances that affect opportunities for production. Specifically, we assess the effects of supply shocks on output, employment, the price level, and the interest rate. We then relate the findings to some of the characteristics of U.S. business fluctuations that we explored in this chapter.

Chapter 6 brings in a labor market and allows for business firms as distinct economic units. In this extended model, we can show how the clearing of the labor market determines the wage rate and the quantity of employment. For most purposes, however, the extended model yields results that coincide with those in Chapter 5. We therefore return in most of the subsequent analysis to the simpler setting that neglects the labor market and considers only one type of economic unit. We can think of this unit as a combination of a household and a firm: this unit merges the consumption and working activities of households with the production and hiring activities of businesses. The main reason we use this device is that it simplifies the analysis without causing any mistakes.

Chapters 7 and 8 introduce the possibility of chronic rises in the general price level, that is, inflation. We look at inflation as primarily a monetary phenomenon. One theme is that inflation and monetary growth can be largely independent of the variations in output and employment, the "real" variables in the model. However, we do discuss some ways in which a higher rate of inflation can worsen the economy's real performance. The interaction of monetary phenomena with output, employment, and other real variables is a major issue in macroeconomics but one that is not fully resolved. In this book we deal first with simple models in which the interaction between monetary forces and the real variables is unimportant. Then we extend the analysis (in Chapters 17–20) to bring in more interesting possibilities for this interaction.

Chapters 9–11 apply the theory to business fluctuations and economic growth. Chapter 9 introduces investment, which is the accumulation of capital goods. We already noted that U.S. business fluctuations feature much greater variations in investment than in consumption. The theory can explain this pattern and other characteristics of business fluctuations as responses to shocks that affect technology or preferences. These types of disturbances have been the focus of an area of macroeconomic research called **real business cycle theory**. (The approach contrasts with monetary theories, which stress the effects of monetary disturbances on the economy.)

Chapter 10 expands the model to allow for unemployment. We view unemployment as arising from the problem of matching workers to jobs. Specifically, we relate the average level and dynamics of unemployment to the rates at which people find and lose jobs. Then we show how various economic forces influence the rates of job finding and job separation. We show, in particular, why unemployment rises during a recession.

Chapter 11 studies how investment shows up over the longer term as an increase in the stock of capital and thereby in economic growth. By allowing also for growth in population and for improvements in technology, we can apply the theory to an economy's long-term development. Accordingly, we can use the model to study the behavior of the major macroeconomic variables in the United States over the past century. In addition, we apply the theory to the growth experiences of the individual U.S. states, the regions of western Europe and Japan, and a large number of countries.

Chapters 12–14 bring in government expenditures, taxes, and public debt and thereby allow us to consider fiscal policies. First, we introduce government expenditures that are used to provide public services to consumers and producers. Then we consider how households react to income taxes and to transfer programs, such as social security. Finally, by introducing the public debt, we can evaluate the economic consequences of the government's financing its spending by budget deficits rather than taxes.

Chapters 15 and 16 extend the theory from the economy of one country to that of many countries, which interact on international markets for goods and credit. Chapter 15 simplifies the analysis by assuming that all countries use the same currency and quote prices in units of this currency. We can then readily apply the previous framework to analyze a country's **balance of international payments**. We explore, for example, how shocks to technology and fiscal policies influence a country's incentive to borrow or lend internationally.

Chapter 16 allows for different currencies and considers the determination of exchange rates. We consider the distinction between fixed and flexible exchange rates and discuss how exchange rates interact with interest rates and the balance of international payments.

Chapters 17–20 deal with interactions between monetary forces and real economic activity. Chapter 17 introduces financial intermediaries and studies the creation of deposits and the lending operations of banks and other institutions. The analysis stresses the role of intermediaries in promoting economic efficiency. Thus, a contraction in the amount of financial intermediation—such as that during the Great Depression and in other periods of financial crisis—tends to reduce the levels of production and employment. In addition, there are important effects of changes in financial intermediation on the general price level.

Chapter 18 explores the main pieces of empirical evidence that concern the interaction between monetary variables and the real economy. The theory can explain much of the evidence but not all of it. Specifically, using the model that we have developed up to this point, we cannot rationalize very large effects of purely monetary shocks on real economic activity. There is some evidence that these effects exist, although the evidence is not overwhelming.

Chapter 19 extends the market-clearing model to account for real effects of monetary disturbances. The new feature is that individuals have incomplete information about prices in various markets and about the overall monetary picture. When people do not observe something directly—such as the general price level—they are motivated to use their available information to forecast the unobserved variables as accurately as possible. This type of expectation is called *rational*, and hence, the approach is often called *rational-expectations macroeconomics*. In this setting monetary disturbances can affect real economic activity more or less as appears in the U.S. data on business fluctuations.

The theory in Chapter 19 has intriguing implications for monetary policy: the effects on real variables derive only from the erratic part of monetary policy, and the effects tend to be adverse. Thus, the main message is that monetary policy should be predictable rather than erratic.

Chapter 20 develops the model of business fluctuations that was stimulated by the research during the 1930s of the British economist John Maynard Keynes. This theory departs from the previous analysis by assuming that some prices do not adjust instantaneously to clear all markets. That is, the prices of goods or wages of labor are assumed to be sticky rather than perfectly flexible. We begin with a simple version of the Keynesian model, a version that brings out the idea that shocks to the economy can have multiplicative effects on output. Then we work out the **IS/LM model**, which is a popular extended version of this theory.

A basic conclusion from the Keynesian model is that recessions can result when monetary contractions or other disturbances lead to decreases in the aggregate demand for goods. There is more scope for active monetary and fiscal policies in this model than there was in the market-clearing framework.

For many years, the Keynesian model was the most popular tool of macroeconomic analysis. The popularity of this model has diminished since the late 1960s, however, especially at the frontiers of macroeconomic research. There are two main reasons for this decreased popularity. First, the Keynesian model does not deal very well with inflation or supply shocks, two problems that have been important since the late 1960s. Second, despite many attempts, economists have not found satisfactory ways to provide the Keynesian macromodel with internally consistent and plausible microfoundations. There is, in any event, another reason to postpone the consideration of the Keynesian model until late in the book: the model cannot be fully understood—and the distinctive features of it cannot be appreciated—until the market-clearing analysis has been worked out. Thus, whatever one's ultimate judgment about the usefulness of the Keynesian model, it is a great mistake to begin a study of macroeconomics with this model.

A NOTE ON MATHEMATICS AND ECONOMIC REASONING

This book does not use any advanced mathematics. Rather it relies on graphical methods and occasional algebraic derivations. Although calculus would speed up the presentation in some places, this technique is unnecessary for the main economic arguments. Students should therefore not find the book difficult on technical grounds.

What will be demanding from time to time is the economic reasoning. It is this aspect of economics that is the most difficult, as well as the most rewarding. Unfortunately, not all of this difficulty can be avoided if we wish to understand the economic events that take place in the real world. The feature that should help students to master the material is the use of a single, consistent model, which is then successively refined and applied to a variety of macroeconomic problems. Anyone who invests enough effort to understand the basic model will eventually see the simplicity of the approach, as well as the applicability to a wide variety of real-world issues. Conversely, anyone who fails to master the basic model will be in serious trouble later on.

ELEMENTS OF NATIONAL-INCOME ACCOUNTING

Up to this point, we have used terms such as *gross domestic product* (*GDP*), *consumer expenditure*, *investment*, the *general price level*, and so on without defining them precisely. Now, by looking at the **national-income accounts**, we develop the meanings of these terms. There are many difficult issues that arise in the construction of these accounts. We consider here only the basic concepts, which will be adequate for the subsequent analysis.

NOMINAL AND REAL GDP

We begin with the GDP. Nominal GDP measures the dollar value of all the goods and services that an economy produces during a specified time period. In 1996, for example, the nominal GDP in the United States was $7576 billion.

Consider the definition of nominal GDP one step at a time. The word *nominal* means that the GDP is measured in units of dollars, or, more generally, in units of some currency, such as pounds, marks, yen, and so on. For most goods and services—pencils, automobiles, haircuts, and so on—the dollar value is the price for which these items sell in the marketplace. However, governmental services—which include national defense, the justice system, and police services—are not exchanged on markets. These items enter into nominal GDP at their dollar cost of production.

It is important to understand that the GDP includes only the goods and services that an economy produces during a given time period: current GDP measures only current production. The construction and sale of a new house therefore counts in GDP, but the sale of a secondhand house (which was produced earlier) does not count. The GDP does include an estimate of the imputed rental income received on owner-occupied housing, that is, the rental income that would result if the housing were rented to others rather than used by the owner. This approach has not yet been followed for consumer durables, for example,

TABLE 1.2

THE CALCULATION OF NOMINAL AND REAL GDP

	1997A	1997B	1998A	1998B
Prices				
Butter	$2.00/lb.	$2.00/lb.	$3.00/lb.	$1.50/lb.
Golf balls	$1.00/ball	$1.00/ball	$1.10/ball	$0.89/ball
Quantities				
Butter	50 lb.	50 lb.	40 lb.	70 lb.
Golf balls	400 balls	400 balls	391 balls	500 balls
Nominal market values				
Butter	100	100	120	105
Golf balls	400	400	430	445
Nominal GDP	500	500	550	550
1997–98 average price				
Butter	$2.50/lb.	$1.75/lb.	$2.50/lb.	$1.75/lb.
Golf balls	$1.05/ball	$0.945/ball	$1.05/ball	$0.945/ball
Market values at 1997–98 average prices				
Butter	125.0	87.5	100.0	122.5
Golf balls	420.0	378.0	410.6	472.5
Total	545.0	465.5	510.6	595.0
Ratio to 1997 value	1.0	1.0	0.937	1.278
Chained real GDP, 1997 base	500.0	500.0	468.5	639.0
Implicit GDP deflator, 1997 base	100	100	117	86

the GDP does not include an imputed rental income on households' automobiles, furniture, and appliances. The GDP does now include an imputed rental income on government property.

The nominal GDP can be misleading because it depends on the overall level of prices, as well as on the physical amounts of output. The top part of Table 1.2 illustrates this problem. Think about a simple economy that produces only butter and golf balls. We show the hypothetical quantities and prices of these goods for 1997 in the first columns of the table. Notice that the nominal GDP for 1997 is $500. The columns la-

beled 1998A and 1998B show two possibilities for prices and outputs in 1998. Nominal GDP rises in both cases by 10% to $550. In case A, however, the production of both goods has declined, whereas in case B the production of both has increased. Thus, identical figures on nominal GDP can conceal very different underlying movements in production.

Economists construct a measure of real GDP to solve the problem of changing price levels. Until recently, the most common way to compute real GDP was to multiply the current quantity of output of each good by the price of that good in a base year. Then all of these multiples were summed up to get the economy's aggregate real GDP. If the base year is 1992, for example, then we refer to the resulting aggregate as "GDP in 1992 dollars" or as "GDP in constant dollars," because we use a set of constant (1992) prices. Similarly, we refer to nominal GDP as "GDP in current dollars," because it uses the prices of the current year.

Because the prices used in the calculation of real GDP do not vary from year to year, the method just described yields a reasonable measure for the changes over time in the overall level of production. One problem with this approach, however, is that it weights the outputs of various goods by their relative prices in the base year. These weights become less relevant over time as relative prices change, and the response of the Bureau of Economic Analysis had been to make frequent shifts in the base year used to calculate real GDP. A more accurate solution, called the chain-weighted method, has recently been adopted to get a more accurate measure of real GDP. The resulting variable is called **chain-weighted real GDP**.

The chain-weighted method starts by computing the average price of each good for two adjacent years, say 1992 and 1993. The quantities of each good produced are multiplied by these average prices and then summed for each year. The ratio of the sum for 1993 to that for 1992 gives the ratio of chain-weighted real GDP for 1993 to that for 1992. If we take 1992 to be the base year for the calculations, then the level of real GDP for that year is just the nominal GDP. Hence, the level of chain-weighted real GDP for 1993 on a 1992 base is the ratio of sums mentioned above multiplied by the nominal GDP for 1992.

We can proceed similarly to calculate the ratio of chain-weighted real GDP for 1994 relative to that for 1993 (by using the average of prices of all goods for 1993 and 1994). Then we multiply this ratio by the chain-weighted real GDP for 1993 to calculate the chain-weighted real GDP for 1994. This process can be repeated in this chainlike manner for each year to compute values after 1994 (or before 1992). Because it is more accurate than other approaches, we use real GDP calculated by this chained method throughout the book whenever the data permit.

The bottom portion of Table 1.2 illustrates this calculation, using 1997 as the base year. Consider the values of chain-weighted real GDP for the cases labeled 1998A and 1998B. These values differ substantially, although the values of nominal GDP are the same. In the 1998A example, real GDP falls below the 1997 level by 6.3%. This figure is a weighted average of the fall in butter production by 20% and that in golf ball production by 2.2%. Thus, real GDP gives a more accurate picture of the change in output than does the 10% increase in nominal GDP. Note also that the overall proportionate change is closer to that for golf balls than that for butter because golf balls account for a larger share of GDP in both years.

For the 1998B case, real GDP rises by 27.8% (a remarkable achievement for one year!). This figure is a weighted average of the rise in butter production by 40% and that in golf ball production by 25%. Again, the change in the golf ball sector counts for more than the change in the butter sector.

Although it reveals a lot about the economy's overall performance, the real GDP is not a perfect measure of welfare. Some of the problems with using real GDP as a measure of well-being are the following:

Aggregate GDP does not consider changes in the distribution of income across households.

The calculated GDP excludes a variety of nonmarket goods, among them legal and illegal transactions in the "underground economy," as well as services that people perform in their homes. For example, if someone cares for a child in the home, then GDP does not increase. But if the person hires someone to care for the child (and the transaction is reported to the government) or if the government pays for a day-care center to care for the child, then GDP increases.

⎯ The GDP assigns no value to leisure time.

Despite these shortcomings, we typically learn a great deal about an economy—in terms of short-run fluctuations and long-term development—by studying the changes in aggregate real GDP.

THE GROSS DOMESTIC PRODUCT—EXPENDITURE, PRODUCTION, AND INCOME

We can think about GDP in three different ways. First, we can consider the expenditures on domestically produced goods and services by different groups—households, businesses, all levels of government, and foreigners. Second, we can measure the production of goods by various industries—agriculture, manufacturing, wholesale and retail trade, and so on. Finally, we can calculate the incomes earned in the production of goods—compensation of employees, rental income, corporate profits, and so on. The important point is that all three approaches will end up with the same total for GDP. To see this, we take up each approach in turn, beginning with a breakdown by type of expenditure.

Measuring GDP by Expenditures

The national accounts divide GDP into four parts, depending upon who or what buys the goods or services. The four sectors are households, businesses, all levels of government, and foreigners. Table 1.3 shows the details of this breakdown for 1996. The first column lists values in current dollars and the second refers to chained real dollars in terms of the base year, 1992.

TABLE 1.3

EXPENDITURE COMPONENTS OF THE GROSS DOMESTIC PRODUCT FOR 1996

Category of Expenditures	Billions of Dollars	Billions of Chained 1992 Dollars
Gross domestic product	7576	6907
Personal consumption expenditure	5152	4691
Durable goods	632	611
Nondurable goods	1545	1442
Services	2978	2639
Gross private domestic investment	1164	1057
Fixed investment	1101	1042
Nonresidential	791	767
Residential	310	277
Change in business inventories	15	14
Government consumption and investment	1407	1271
Federal	523	467
State and local	884	805
Net exports of goods and services	−99	−114
Exports	855	826
Imports	954	940

Source: *U.S. Department of Commerce,* Survey of Current Business, *March 1997.*

The purchases of goods and services by households for their own consumption purposes is called **personal consumption expenditure**. This spending accounts for the bulk of GDP, for example, for $5152 billion out of a total $7576 billion or 68% of nominal GDP in 1992 (see Table 1.3).

The national accounts distinguish between purchases of consumer goods that will be used fairly quickly, such as toothpaste and various services, and those that will last for a substantial time, such as automobiles and appliances. The first group is called **consumer nondurables and ser-**

vices, and the second is called **consumer durables**. The important point is that consumer durables yield a flow of services in future periods, as well as currently. Table 1.3 shows the division of consumer expenditures among durable goods, nondurable goods, and services. Notice that purchases of consumer durables account for only 12% of overall consumer expenditure.

The second major category of GDP is **gross private domestic investment**. The "fixed" part of these investments comprises firms' purchases of new capital goods, such as factories and machinery. Note that business's capital goods are durables, which serve as inputs to production over many years. Thus, investment goods are similar to the consumer durables that we mentioned before. In fact, in the national accounts, an individual's purchase of a new home—which might be considered the ultimate consumer durable—is counted as a part of fixed business investment rather than personal consumer expenditure. For many purposes, we should add the other purchases of consumer durables to the national accounts' measure of gross investment to get a broader concept of investment.

Total gross private investment is the sum of fixed investment and the net change in business's inventories of goods. In 1996 this total investment equaled 15% of nominal GDP, or 24% if we include the purchases of consumer durables (see Table 1.3).

The third component of GDP is **government consumption expenditure and gross investment**. This category combines governmental consumption expenditures with public investment. It is possible, however, to get a breakdown into the two components. There are two points about the government sector that sometimes cause confusion. First, it includes all levels of government, whether federal, state, or local. Second, it includes the government's consumption and gross investment but excludes **transfer payments**. (Examples of transfer payments are social security benefits and welfare payments.) The idea is that transfers do not represent payments to individuals in exchange for currently produced goods or services. These expenditures therefore do not appear in GDP.

In 1996 government consumption and investment accounted for 19% of nominal GDP (see Table 1.3).

Some of the goods and services produced in an economy are exported to foreign users. **Exports** must be added to domestic purchases to compute the economy's total production (GDP). Foreigners also produce goods and services that are imported into the domestic country. **Imports** must be subtracted from domestic purchases to calculate GDP. The foreign component therefore appears in GDP as **net exports**: the spending by foreigners on domestic production (exports) less the spending by domestic residents on foreign production (imports). Notice that net exports may be either positive or negative. In 1996 this component was equal to −1.3% of nominal GDP. (Exports were 11.3% of GDP, and imports were 12.6%.)

Economists often omit net exports when they construct a macroeconomic model for a single economy. Then the model applies to a **closed economy** rather than an **open economy**, which includes the foreign sector. The rationale for assuming a closed economy is, first, to simplify the theory, and, second, at least for the United States, that exports and imports are small relative to GDP. (The share of foreign trade is, however, much higher now in the United States than it was 20 years ago.) We follow the closed-economy tradition of macroeconomics until Chapter 15, which allows for foreign trade. When we omit the foreign sector, we get the familiar division of GDP into three parts:

$$\text{GDP} = \text{Consumer expenditure} + \text{Gross private investment}$$
$$+ \text{Government consumption and investment}$$

One common error about national accounting arises because the spending on new physical capital is called "investment." This terminology differs from the concept of investment in ordinary conversation, a concept that refers to the allocation of saving among different financial assets, such as stocks, bonds, real estate, and so on. When we speak of a firm's investment, we refer to the purchase of physical goods, such as a factory. Do not be confused by these two different meanings of investment.

Another point about investment concerns **depreciation**. During any period, some of the existing stock of capital tends to wear out or depreciate. Thus, a part of gross investment merely replaces the old capital that has depreciated. The difference between gross investment (private plus public) and depreciation—called **net investment**—is the net change in the stock of capital goods. We shall discuss the difference between gross and net investment in Chapter 9. For now, note that the sum of consumption expenditures, *net* private investment, government consumption and *net* government investment, and net exports is called **net domestic product (NDP)**. The difference between GDP and NDP reflects the difference between gross and net investment, which is the amount of depreciation. Hence, we have the condition

$$NDP = GDP - \text{ Depreciation}$$

The NDP concept is useful because it measures output net of the amount needed to replace worn-out capital goods.

Measuring GDP by Production

Instead of breaking down GDP into the sectors that do the spending, we can look at a breakdown by the sectors that do the producing (and selling). Table 1.4 shows such a breakdown for 1994. In terms of shares of real GDP, the breakdown was 18% in manufacturing; 14% in wholesale and retail trade; 19% in services; 18% in finance, insurance, and real estate; 13% in production by government and government enterprises; 9% in transportation and public utilities; 4% in construction; 1% in mining; and 2% in agriculture.

In many cases a firm produces **intermediate goods**, which another business uses as an input. In order not to double count intermediate goods in GDP, the national accounts give each business credit only for its **value added** to production. The value added by a firm is the difference

TABLE 1.4

PRODUCTION COMPONENTS OF THE GROSS DOMESTIC PRODUCT FOR 1994

Category of Production	Billions of Dollars	Billions of Chained 1992 Dollars
Gross domestic product	6936	6609
Agriculture	118	118
Mining	90	97
Construction	269	253
Manufacturing	1197	1168
Transportation and public utilities	606	585
Wholesale and retail trade	1072	945
Finance, insurance, real estate	1274	1193
Services	1343	1250
Government	931	876
Statistical discrepancy	34	30
Rest of the world	−4	−3
Gross national product (GNP)	6932	6606

Source: *DRI data bank and U.S. Department of Commerce,* Survey of Current Business, *March 1997.*

between its revenues and the cost of goods that it buys from other firms. An example of an intermediate good is flour that a baker uses to make bread. The baker's value added is the market value of the bread less the value of the flour used to produce the bread. The amounts shown in Table 1.4 are the value added to production by each industry.

The last item shown in Table 1.4 refers to the rest of the world. This amount is the value added to production by the U.S. labor and capital that is used in other countries, net of the contribution of foreign labor and capital to domestic production. (The item is also called the *net factor income from abroad*.) For example, if U.S. residents own assets abroad (either financial assets or direct ownership of capital), then the returns on these assets are included in the value added by U.S. capital used in other countries. The returns on assets owned by foreigners in the United States appear analogously as a negative item.

The addition of the rest-of-the-world term to gross domestic product gives the total value added by factors owned by U.S. residents whether these factors are used in the United States or abroad. This total is called **gross national product** or **GNP**.

Measuring GDP by Income

The third way to look at GDP is in terms of the income earned in production. This concept is called **national income**. To make clear the relation between production and income, think of a simple closed economy that has one firm producing bread as the only final product and another firm producing flour as the only intermediate good. Suppose that the miller uses only labor to produce flour, and the baker uses labor and flour to produce bread. Sample income statements for these firms appear in Table 1.5. In this table the only sources of income are labor income and profits. Total nominal GDP, which is the market value of the bread, is $600. This amount also equals the total revenue of the baker. The income statement shows that this revenue divides up into

TABLE 1.5

DATA FOR CALCULATION OF GROSS DOMESTIC PRODUCT AND NATIONAL INCOME

Baker			Miller		
Revenue	Costs and Profits		Revenue	Costs and Profits	
Total revenue from sale of bread $600	Labor Flour Profit	$200 $350 $50	Total revenue from sale of flour $350	Labor Profit	$250 $100

TABLE 1.6

BREAKDOWN OF NATIONAL INCOME IN 1995

Category of Income	Billions of Dollars
National income	5814
Compensation of employees	4223
Proprietors' income	478
Rental income of persons	122
Corporate profits	587
Net interest	404

Source: *U.S Department of Commerce*, Survey of Current Business, *March 1997.*

$350 for the cost of flour, $200 for payments to labor (or, from the workers' standpoint, $200 of labor income), and $50 of profits (or return on capital). For the miller, the revenue of $350 goes for $250 of labor costs (or labor income) and $100 of profits. Thus, in this simple case, national income equals the total labor income of $450 plus total profits (return on capital) of $150, which equals the $600 of GDP. In this case, GDP also equals GNP, because there is no net factor income from abroad.

Table 1.6 shows the breakdown of national income in the United States for 1995: 73% of the total is compensation of employees, 8% is income of proprietors (owners of farms and small businesses), roughly 2% is personal rental income, 10% is corporate profits, and 7% is net interest income.

Three complications disturb the equality between GDP and national income in the real world. First, suppose that the baker uses some capital goods in the production process. As the capital wears out, the baker subtracts depreciation charges from profits. Hence, the total income for labor and profit equals the baker's total revenue, which equals GDP, less the depreciation charges. That is, national income equals NDP, which is GDP less depreciation.

A second adjustment arises because of sales and excise taxes, which are called "indirect taxes." These levies create a gap between the market price of a good—which includes the tax—and the revenue received by the producer. (The gap shows up as revenue for the government.) In the example from Table 1.5, if there had been a 5% sales tax on bread, then the consumer would have paid $630 for the bread, but the baker's total revenue would have remained at $600. National income would still be $600, but GDP (calculated at market prices) would be $630. Thus, national income for a closed economy equals GDP less depreciation and less these indirect taxes.

Finally, for an open economy, the net factor income from abroad is a source of national income but does not show up in GDP. Hence, the final result is that national income equals GDP less depreciation, less indirect taxes, plus the net factor income from abroad. Table 1.7 demonstrates this calculation using U.S. data for 1995.

Recall that the definition of national income includes only the amounts earned in the production of output. Economists also calculate the amount of income that people actually receive, a concept called **personal income**. This measure differs from national income for several reasons. First, only a portion of firms' profits are paid out as dividends to individuals. Second, personal income excludes the contributions paid for social insurance, because households do not receive these amounts directly as income. Next there are a series of adjustments to ensure that the amount of interest income in personal income corresponds to the amount that individuals receive. Finally, various transfer payments appear in personal income but not in national income. All of these adjustments are detailed in Table 1.7.

Economists also calculate the amount of income that households have left after paying personal taxes, a variable called **disposable personal income**. Table 1.7 shows the calculation of disposable personal income from personal income.

TABLE 1.7

DATA FOR CALCULATION OF GROSS NATIONAL PRODUCT, NATIONAL INCOME, PERSONAL INCOME, AND DISPOSABLE PERSONAL INCOME IN 1995 (BILLIONS OF DOLLARS)

Gross domestic product (GDP)	7254
Plus	
Receipts of factor income from the rest of the world	208
Less	
Payments of factor income to the rest of the world	215
Equals	
Gross national product (GNP)	7247
Less	
Depreciation	826
Equals	
Net national product (NNP)	6421
Less	
Indirect business taxes (and related items)	607
Equals	
National income	5814
Less	
Corporate profits	587
Contributions for social insurance	660
Wage accruals less disbursements	3
Plus	
Government transfer payments	1000
Net adjustment for Interest income	314
Personal dividend income	215
Business transfer payments	23
Equals	
Personal income	6115
Less	
Personal tax and nontax payments	794
Equals	
Disposable personal income	5321

Source: *U.S Department of Commerce*, Survey of Current Business, *March 1997*.

PRICES

One objective of macroeconomic theory is to explain the general level of prices and the changes in the price level over time. To use the theory, we need an empirical measure (or measures) of the general price level. The analysis of real and nominal GDP provides one such measure. The **implicit GDP price deflator** (or, more compactly, the GDP deflator) can be calculated as

$$\text{Implicit GDP price deflator} = \left(\frac{\text{Nominal GDP}}{\text{Real GDP}} \right) \times 100$$

It is conventional to multiply by 100 to obtain an index number that takes on the value 100 for the base year (for which nominal GDP equals real GDP).

If we use the chain-weighted method, as described in Table 1.2, to derive real GDP, then the resulting implicit GDP price deflator also reflects these chain weights. That is, the movements in the overall price index take account of the shifting composition of production over time.

For a concrete example, consider the data from Table 1.2. For the 1998A case, the GDP deflator is (Nominal GDP/Real GDP) · 100 = (550/468.5) · 100 = 117. Hence, the price of the average item rose by 17% from 1997 to 1998. This number is a weighted average of the increase in the price of butter by 50% and the increase in the price of golf balls by 10%. The price change for golf balls gets a larger weight than that for butter because golf balls account for a larger share of GDP in both years.

For the 1998B case in Table 1.2, the GDP deflator is (550/639) · 100 = 86. This fall in the price of the average item by 14% is a weighted average of the decrease in the price of butter by 25% and the decrease in the price of golf balls by 11%.

The formula for the implicit price deflator can be rearranged to see why we call it a price deflator. The rearranged equation is

Problems with the Consumer Price Index

The CPI has received a lot of attention in recent years because the dollar benefits paid under social security and a number of other government programs adjust automatically for changes in the CPI. The idea here is to maintain the real value of benefits paid even when the price level changes. Similarly, a number of features of the federal income-tax system, such as the bracket limits associated with each tax rate, change automatically with the CPI. (We shall discuss the details of the income-tax system in Chapter 13.)

Many economists think that the reported changes in the CPI overstate true inflation and, hence, that the adjustments of benefits and other items have been too large to keep things fixed in real terms. Naturally, this viewpoint has been controversial, because any repairs would have major consequences for federal transfer payments and tax collections. The idea that changes in the CPI have seriously overstated inflation was expressed in 1996 by the president's advisory commission on the consumer price index (see Boskin *et al.* [1996]). The conclusion they reached was that changes in the CPI exaggerate inflation on average by a hefty 1.1 percentage points per year.

One reason for the overstatement of inflation is called substitution bias. The idea is that changes in supply conditions shift the relative prices of various goods, and households respond by moving toward the goods that have become relatively cheaper. However, because the weights in the CPI were set in the past and do not change frequently, the index does not respond to changes in the patterns of purchases by giving more weight to the (cheaper) items that have become more important in the household's market basket of goods. This problem is pretty easy to fix by using the type of chain-weighting approach that we described before for the calculation of chain-weighted real GDP. The resulting chain-weighted GDP deflator, which we have already discussed in this section, is free from substitution bias because the weights change continually over time to reflect the shifting composition of GDP. The Bureau of Labor Statistics (BLS), which is responsible for calculating the CPI, was experimenting with the chain-weighting approach in 1997.

Another, more challenging, problem with the CPI involves quality change. Despite attempts to measure improvements in quality, these changes tend to be undercounted. Therefore, some of the price increases that are recorded as inflation should actually be viewed as rises in money spent to get better quality products. A full ↗

accounting for quality improvements would therefore lower the inflation rate. Some improved measurement has already been made along these lines, such as in automobiles, computers, and housing, and interesting proposals for measuring quality change have been made in the medical area.

A further, even more challenging, problem is that the CPI does not consider at all the effective reduction in the price level that comes from the introduction of new products, such as the personal computer or VCR. When the array of goods available expands, households are better off for a given dollar income (even if the new goods are initially "expensive"). Hence, households' real income rises, and the effective overall price level declines. However, economists have not figured out exactly how to adjust price indexes to capture this effect.

Many of the problems in the CPI, notably those due to quality change and new products, carry over to the GDP deflator. Therefore, to some extent, the overstatement of measured inflation corresponds to an understatement of the growth of the economy's gross domestic product; that is, too much of the change in the nominal GDP is attributed to inflation. Hence, the performance of economic growth would look somewhat better if price indexes were calculated more accurately.

$$\text{Real GDP} = \left(\frac{\text{Nominal GDP}}{\text{Implicit GDP price deflator}} \right) \times 100$$

Thus, we effectively divide or deflate the nominal GDP by the price deflator to compute the real GDP.

The implicit GDP price deflator is called "implicit" because it is not directly or explicitly calculated. Real GDP and nominal GDP are computed directly, and the GDP deflator is calculated by dividing the two as we have done. There are also explicit indexes of the general price level. Two important examples are the **consumer price index (CPI)** and the **producer price index (PPI)**, which is also called a wholesale price index. These are explicit indexes because they are calculated directly.

The CPI is based on a fixed market basket of consumer goods. Every few years the government takes a statistical survey to compile the base-year prices and expenditures on about 400 goods that are consumed by typical individuals. The expenditure shares serve as fixed weights until the next survey is taken. To calculate the CPI we first compute the ratio of the current market price of each good to its base-year price. Then we sum up over the ratios, weighting each by the share of the good in base-year expenditures. Typically, we also multiply the result by 100 so that the CPI for the base year is 100.

The PPI or wholesale price index is computed in a manner similar to that for the CPI. The PPI measures prices at an early stage of production: the "basket" consists of about 2800 items sold at wholesale. These goods are primarily raw materials and semifinished goods.[9] One shortcoming of the PPI is that it is too narrow a concept to reflect the general level of prices.

IMPORTANT TERMS AND CONCEPTS

acyclical Having no regular relation with the business cycle, that is, with detrended real GDP.

aggregate-consistency conditions Conditions on quantities that must hold when we add up the actions of all participants in a market—for example, the total of goods sold equals the total bought, and the total of funds lent equals the total borrowed. In the basic model, we use market-clearing conditions to ensure that the aggregate-consistency conditions are satisfied.

[9] *The CPI and PPI, which weight by the importance of goods in the base year, are examples of Laspeyres indexes of prices. In contrast, a price index that weights by the importance of goods in current market baskets is called a Paasche index of prices. The old-style GDP deflator, derived from the calculation of real GDP in which current production is evaluated at relative prices of the base year, turns out to be a Paasche index. For a discussion of Paasche and Laspeyres price indexes, see Edwin Mansfield (1985, pp. 105ff).*

balance of international payments The summary statement of a country's international trade in commodities, bonds, and international currency.

boom A period in which aggregate economic activity or real gross national product is high and rising.

budget constraint The equation relating the sources of funds in a period, such as income from the commodity market and initial assets, to the uses of funds in that period, such as consumption and end-of-period assets.

chain-weighted real GDP A method for constructing real GDP in which the relative-price weights continually adjust for the changing composition of production.

closed economy An economy isolated from the rest of the world.

consumer durables Consumable commodities purchased by households that last for a long time, such as automobiles, furniture, and appliances.

consumer nondurables and services Consumable commodities purchased by households that last for a short time.

consumer price index (CPI) A weighted average of prices of consumer goods relative to a base year.

countercyclical Moving in the direction opposite to the business cycle, that is, to detrended real GDP.

demand for money The amount of money that someone desires to hold, expressed as a function of the volume of spending, the interest rate, transaction costs, and other variables.

depreciation The wearing out of capital goods over time; often expressed as a fraction of the stock of capital.

disposable personal income   Personal income less taxes.

exchange rate   The number of units of the currency of a country that trade for one unit of another currency, such as the U.S. dollar.

exports   Goods that are produced by the residents of a country but are sold to foreigners.

general price level   The dollar price per unit of an aggregate of commodities.

gold standard   A system of international payments under which countries agree to buy or sell gold for a fixed amount of their currencies. The high point of this system was from 1890 to 1914.

government consumption expenditure and gross investment   Expenditures by government on consumption goods and capital goods. The consumption part includes an estimate of the imputed rental income on the stock of public capital.

Great Depression   The decline in aggregate economic activity in the United States that occurred from 1929 to 1933.

gross domestic product (GDP)   The market value of an economy's domestically produced goods and services over a specified period of time.

gross national product (GNP)   The total market value of the goods and services produced by the residents of a country over a specified period of time; GNP equals gross domestic product plus the net factor income from abroad.

gross private domestic investment   Total private expenditure on investment goods, including business spending on plant and equipment, the net change in business inventories, and residential construction. This total contains no adjustment for the depreciation of the existing capital goods.

implicit GDP price deflator The price index that relates the gross domestic product, measured in nominal terms, to real GDP.

imports Goods that are produced in foreign countries and purchased by the domestic residents of a country.

inflation rate The percentage change in a price index between two periods of time.

interest rate The ratio of the interest payment to the amount borrowed; the return to lending or the cost of borrowing.

intermediate goods Commodities that are purchased for resale or for use in the production and sale of other commodities.

IS/LM model The analytical tool used in Keynesian theory to study the simultaneous determination of aggregate output and the interest rate.

Keynesian model The theory developed by John Maynard Keynes that sought to explain aggregate business fluctuations. The failure of prices to adjust to clear markets is a central element of this model.

market-clearing approach The viewpoint that prices, such as the interest rate and the general price level, are determined to clear all markets, such as those for credit and commodities; that is, supply equals demand in each market.

medium of exchange The commodity or other item that people use as a means of paying for purchases; money.

microeconomic foundations The theoretical analysis of individual behavior that underlies the macroeconomic model of the economy.

money The usual means of payment or medium of exchange in an economy. Money also serves as a store of value. Money may take the form of paper currency, commodities, or deposits at financial institutions.

national income The income earned from aggregate production; gross national product adjusted for depreciation and sales and excise taxes.

national-income accounts The summary statement of gross national product and its components during a year.

net domestic product (NDP) Gross domestic product less depreciation.

net exports The difference between the value of exports and the value of imports.

net investment The change in the capital stock; gross investment minus the amount of depreciation.

open economy An economy that conducts trade with the rest of the world.

personal consumption expenditure Purchases of goods and services by households for use in consumption.

personal income Income received directly by persons; national income adjusted for undistributed corporate profits, social security contributions, transfer payments, and some other items.

procyclical Moving in the same direction as the business cycle, that is, with detrended real GDP.

producer price index (PPI) A weighted average of prices of raw materials and semifinished goods, relative to base-year prices.

real business cycle theory A theory of business fluctuations that relies on real disturbances rather than monetary shocks. This theory emphasizes shifts to the production function and usually assumes full market clearing and rational behavior of individuals.

real gross domestic product The gross domestic product (GDP) divided by a price index to adjust for changes in the average level of market prices; GDP in constant dollars.

recession A period of decline in the level of aggregate economic activity or real gross domestic product.

transfer payments Transfers of funds from government to individuals, such as welfare payments, that do not constitute payments for goods and services.

value added The increase in value of product at a particular stage of production.

wage rate The dollar amount paid to a worker in exchange for an hour of labor services.

MICROECONOMIC FOUNDATIONS AND THE BASIC MARKET-CLEARING MODEL

Work Effort, Production, and Consumption—The Economics of Robinson Crusoe

I n any economic analysis, the determination of work effort, production, and consumption depends on opportunities for production and on preferences about working and consuming. This basic interaction between opportunities and preferences shows up even in the simplest possible economy, which consists of isolated individuals, each of whom resembles Robinson Crusoe. In this setting, which we develop in this chapter, we can readily analyze the economy's responses to changed opportunities in terms of **wealth effects** and **substitution effects**. It turns out that the primitive environment of Robinson Crusoe contains the essence of choice problems that arise in complicated market economies. Therefore, the principal findings from this chapter remain valid when we extend the analysis in later chapters to settings that look more like modern industrialized economies.

We begin with a simple **production function**, which relates the quantity of output to the amount of work effort. This function determines the productivity of labor, which is the amount of extra output generated from more work. Next, we discuss preferences for consumption and leisure. Basically, people increase their work effort and accept less leisure only if they receive a sufficient addition to consumption.

PRODUCTION TECHNOLOGY

The basic theoretical model contains one type of economic unit, which we can think of as a combination of a household and a firm. This single unit combines the consuming and working activities of households with the producing and hiring activities of businesses. For most purposes, this abstraction will be satisfactory because some households ultimately own the private businesses. Further, by merging the functions of households and businesses, we achieve some major simplifications of the analysis. From now on we refer to this composite unit as simply a household.

Each household uses its labor effort as an input to production. Note that, to simplify matters, we do not yet consider stocks of capital as inputs to the production process. This chapter concentrates on the economic incentives that make people work more or less in order to produce and consume more or fewer goods.

Formally, the quantity of a household's commodity output per period, denoted by y, is a function of the quantity of labor input, l. We write this relation as

$$y_t = f(l_t) \tag{2.1}$$

where f is the household's production function, which specifies the relation between the amount of work and the quantity of goods produced. The subscript t, which denotes the time period, is omitted when no ambiguity results.

Because the model contains a single physical type of commodity, there is no ambiguity in measuring each household's output. The real-world counterpart of this output, when added up over all producers, is the gross domestic product (GDP). Many practical problems arise in using price indexes to add up goods that are physically different, but these difficulties do not arise in our simplified theoretical framework.

We assume in the basic model that people cannot store commodities from one period to the next, and thus we neglect inventories of goods. We can think of the commodities as perishable consumer goods. Examples include personal services, restaurant meals, and so on.

Work is productive in the sense that more work effort, l, yields more output, y. The extra output produced by one more unit of work is called the **marginal (physical) product of labor**, henceforth designated **MPL.** We assume **diminishing marginal productivity**, which means that each successive unit of work effort generates progressively smaller, but still positive, responses of output.

Figure 2.1, which is the graphical representation of equation (2.1), shows the relation of output to the quantity of labor input. Note that the curve goes through the origin, which means that output is zero when labor effort is nil. The positive slope of the curve (that is, of a straight line that is tangent to the curve) at any point indicates the additional output that results from extra labor input, which is the marginal product

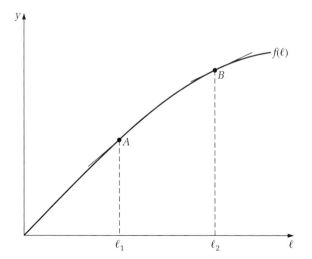

FIGURE 2.1

GRAPH OF PRODUCTION FUNCTION

The curve shows the level of function of the quantity of labor input. At point *A*, the slope of the tangent straight line equals the marginal product of labor when $l = l_1$. The same is true for point *B* where $l = l_2$.

FIGURE 2.2

RELATION OF MARGINAL PRODUCT OF LABOR TO LEVEL OF WORK

Because $l_1 < l_2$, the marginal product of labor at point *A* exceeds that at point *B*. That is, the marginal product of labor falls as work effort rises.

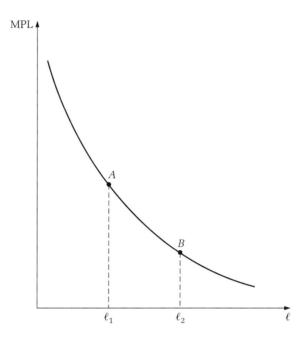

of labor. For example, at the employment level l_1, the MPL equals the slope of the straight line that is tangent to the production function at point *A*.

The shape of the production function in Figure 2.1 implies that the slope becomes less steep as work effort increases. This property reflects the diminishing marginal productivity of labor. For example, at the employment level l_2, which exceeds l_1, the slope of the tangent straight line at point *B* is smaller than that at point *A*. The full relation of the marginal product of labor, MPL, to the amount of work, *l*, appears in Figure 2.2. Note that the marginal product declines as work effort increases. We refer to the graph of MPL versus *l* as the *schedule* for the marginal product of labor. By a schedule, we mean the entire functional relation between MPL and *l*.

The curves in Figures 2.1 and 2.2 apply at some initial level of technology, that is, for a given production function $f(l)$. We show this production function again as the solid curve in Figure 2.3. The dashed

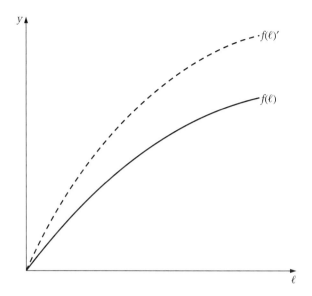

FIGURE 2.3

EFFECT OF AN IMPROVEMENT IN TECHNOLOGY ON THE LEVEL OF
PRODUCTION

The curve labeled $f(l)'$ corresponds to an improved technology, relative to the one labeled $f(l)$. This improvement raises the level of
output for a given amount of labor input.

curve in the figure shows the level of output for an improved technology,
denoted by $f(l)'$. The level of output is now higher at any given level of
labor input.

What is the effect of an improvement in technology on the marginal
product of labor? In general, a technological improvement may either
raise or lower labor's marginal product. For our purposes, we would
like to capture the typical or average response. Studies of production
functions at an economy-wide level suggest that, in the usual situation,
an improvement in technology raises the marginal product of labor at
any given level of work effort.

The construction of the curves in Figure 2.3 reflects the assumption
that an improvement in technology raises the marginal product of labor.
Namely, the curve labeled $f(l)'$—which corresponds to the improved
technology—is steeper than the initial curve at any level of work effort.
Recall that the slopes of the curves measure the marginal product of
labor, MPL, at each point. In Figure 2.4 we show explicitly that the
technological advance leads to an upward shift in the schedule for the
MPL.

FIGURE 2.4

EFFECT OF AN IMPROVEMENT IN TECHNOLOGY ON THE MARGINAL PRODUCT OF LABOR

The dashed curve corresponds to an improved technology, $f(l)'$, relative to the initial one, $f(l)$. The technological advance shifts upward the schedule for the marginal product of labor.

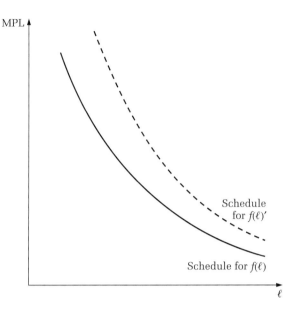

Schedule for $f(\ell)'$

Schedule for $f(\ell)$

TASTES FOR CONSUMPTION AND LEISURE

Suppose, as is true for Robinson Crusoe, that each person has no opportunity to exchange commodities or anything else with other households. In this case, each household's only option is to consume all the goods that it produces in each period. (Remember, there are no possibilities for storing commodities.) Then in the world of Robinson Crusoe we have

$$c_t = y_t = f(l_t) \tag{2.2}$$

where c_t is the amount of consumption in physical units. The equation says that each household's consumption equals its production, which depends on its quantity of work effort.

Consumption in each period is a source of happiness or **utility** for households. (Henceforth, we use the economist's standard jargon, *utility*.) Equation (2.2) implies that someone can consume more only if he or she raises production. Further, for a given technology, the quantity of goods produced, y_t, depends on the level of work effort, l_t. So the amount of work is the key decision that households make in this model.

In the real world, households have a lot of flexibility in their choices of work effort. For example, someone might work four hours per day or eight hours. A person can pick a job that requires lots of hard work or one that does not. Someone might work for only part of the year, as is often the case for construction workers and professional sports figures. From the perspective of a family, there is a decision on how many members participate in the labor force. There has, for example, been a strong increase over the last 40 years in the number of families with two full-time workers. One evidence of this trend is the growing rate of participation of women in the civilian labor force. This participation rate rose from 28% in 1940 to 59% in 1996 (while that for males declined from 84% to 75%).[1] In a longer time perspective, the amount of time spent at work depends also on the typical lengths of schooling and retirement.

We model this real-world flexibility on work effort by allowing people freely to choose their hours of work in each period. Thus, we neglect any constraints that, for example, permit people to work on some jobs for eight hours per day or four hours but not seven or two. This abstraction will be satisfactory when we think about the overall behavior of work effort for a large number of households. In this context the constraints tend to average out.

Households have a fixed amount of time in each period, which they can divide between work and leisure. By the term *leisure*, we mean to capture the full array of activities—other than work to produce goods—on which people spend their time. We assume that leisure time is intrinsically more enjoyable than time at work. In other words, leisure is a source of utility for households.

Suppose that we can define a function to measure the amount of utility that derives each period from consumption and leisure. The form of this **utility function** is

[1] *These figures, obtained from the DRI data bank, refer to persons aged 16 years or more (14 years or more for 1940) who are neither full-time students nor members of the military.*

$$u_t = u(c_t, l_t) \tag{2.3}$$
$${(+)}\ \ {(-)}$$

where u_t is the amount of utility (in units of happiness, which are sometimes called *utils*) that someone obtains for period t. We assume that the form of the utility function, u, is the same for all periods. The positive sign under the quantity of consumption, c_t, indicates that utility rises when consumption increases. The negative sign under work effort, l_t, signifies that utility falls when work effort rises (that is, when leisure declines). For convenience, we now drop the time subscripts and refer to period t's consumption and work as c and l, respectively.

We analyze a household's decisions on working and consuming by exploiting the central economic postulate of optimizing behavior. Each household opts for the levels of work and consumption that maximize utility in equation (2.3). Note, however, that this maximization is subject to the constraint from equation (2.2), which says that each household's consumption in any period equals its production for the same period. We want to use these facts to understand the household's selection of work and consumption.

To make progress in analyzing the household's choices, we must characterize further the utility function, which expresses people's tastes for consumption and leisure. A basic assumption is that the utility gained from an extra unit of leisure, relative to that from an extra unit of consumption, diminishes as the ratio of leisure to consumption rises. In other words, if someone has a lot of leisure but relatively little consumption, he or she is more concerned with adding to consumption rather than leisure. Consider the amount of extra consumption needed to compensate for the loss of a unit of leisure time. If a person starts with little consumption and a lot of leisure, it is important to add to consumption. Therefore, he or she is willing to work a lot more to get additional consumption. If the person is already working quite a bit and has a high level of consumption, leisure becomes more significant. Therefore, he or she is less willing to work more and give up leisure to obtain extra consumption.

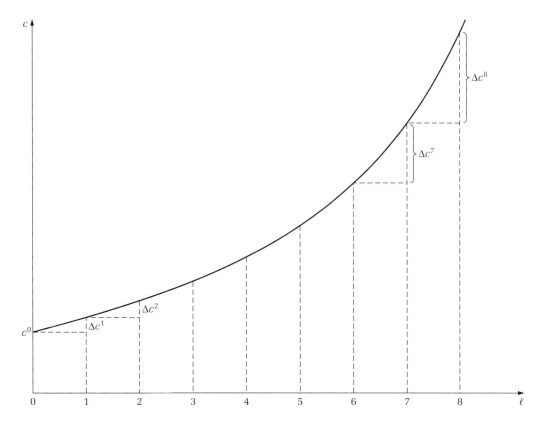

FIGURE 2.5

AN INDIFFERENCE CURVE FOR WORK AND CONSUMPTION

All points (l, c) on the curve yield the same level of utility, u^1. Hence, the household is indifferent among these pairs of work effort and consumption.

The curve in Figure 2.5 summarizes this discussion. At zero work effort, $l = 0$, the curve specifies a level of consumption, c^0, on the vertical axis. This amount of consumption, together with full-time leisure ($l = 0$), determines some level of utility from equation (2.3). Denote this level of utility by u^1. The curve shown in the figure connects this initial point to all other possible combinations of work and consumption that provide the same level of utility, u^1.

Suppose that the person works a positive amount, so that leisure becomes less than a full-time activity. For concreteness, assume that work is one hour per day, represented by $l = 1$ in Figure 2.5. By itself, this reduction in leisure lowers utility. But we want to know how much additional consumption would restore the original level of utility. Denote by Δc^1 the required amount of extra consumption. Then the new combination of work and consumption, where $l = 1$ and $c = c^0 + \Delta c^1$, yields the same utility as the initial pair, where $l = 0$ and $c = c^0$. Hence, the person is indifferent between these two pairs of work and consumption. We show that these two points yield the same level of utility by connecting them with the curve shown in the figure.

If the person works another hour—that is, $l = 2$—some additional consumption is again needed to maintain the level of utility. Figure 2.5 assumes that the required extra consumption is the amount Δc^2. Therefore, the point where $l = 2$ and $c = c^0 + \Delta c^1 + \Delta c^2$ again provides the same utility as the initial pair, where $l = 0$ and $c = c^0$.

We can continue this exercise as the amount of work rises. The result is the curve in Figure 2.5, which shows all pairs (l, c) that yield the same level of utility. Since people are indifferent among these pairs of work and consumption, the curve is called an **indifference curve**.

The previous discussion tells us something about the shape of an indifference curve. As someone works more, each additional unit of work requires a greater amount of extra consumption to maintain utility. Therefore, the size of each addition to consumption, Δc, is larger the higher is the associated number of work hours. Note, in particular, that $\Delta c^1 < \Delta c^2 < \cdots < \Delta c^7 < \Delta c^8$ in Figure 2.5.

At any point along the indifference curve, the slope of a tangent straight line indicates the increment in consumption that a person requires to make up for the loss of a unit of leisure. Each of the additions to consumption, Δc, that appear in Figure 2.5 approximates this slope in the vicinity of the corresponding level of work. For example, the amount Δc^2 is a good measure of the slope when the level of work lies between one and two hours per day. The previous results imply that the slope of the indifference curve rises as the amount of work, l, increases.

The slope of the indifference curve in Figure 2.5 indicates the amount of consumption that someone needs to make up for the loss of a unit of leisure. Put alternatively, if a worker receives more than this amount of consumption, he or she would be better off. For example, when someone is already working seven hours per day, he or she is willing to work an additional hour if consumption thereby rises by at least the amount Δc^8 in the figure. If it turns out that the extra hour of work increases consumption by an amount greater than Δc^8, economic reasoning predicts that the worker will work that extra hour. This viewpoint allows us to determine the number of hours that people actually work.

All points on the curve in Figure 2.5 yield the same level of utility u^1. But suppose that we look along the vertical axis and raise the consumption level above c^0; then utility increases. Corresponding to this higher level of utility, say u^2, we can construct another indifference curve. The new curve is similar to the one shown in the figure, but it lies wholly above this curve. That is, for any level of work, l, the amount of consumption, c, is higher. That is why the new indifference curve corresponds to a higher level of utility. (We can also say that for any level of consumption, c, the amount of work effort, l, is smaller along the new curve.)

Similarly, we could lower the level of consumption below c^0 along the vertical axis. In this case, we can start the construction of an indifference curve for a lower level of utility. As a general matter, we can define a whole "family" or "map" of indifference curves, each of which corresponds to a different level of utility. Figure 2.6 shows five of these curves, labeled by their levels of utility, where $u^1 < u^2 \ldots < u^5$. Along any curve the level of utility is constant. But as a person moves vertically from one curve to others—thereby raising consumption while keeping work fixed—the level of utility increases. We have already mentioned the central idea that the household wants to achieve the highest possible level

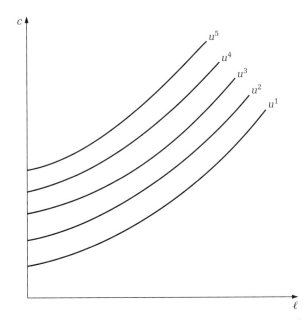

FIGURE 2.6

A FAMILY OF INDIFFERENCE CURVES FOR WORK AND CONSUMPTION

The level of utility rises as the household moves from the curve labeled u^1 to that labeled u^2, and so on.

of utility. Therefore, we can also say that the household's objective is to reach the highest possible indifference curve among the family of curves in Figure 2.6.

DECIDING HOW MUCH TO WORK

Suppose that a household begins from a particular combination of work and consumption, (l, c). Then we can consult Figure 2.6 to find the indifference curve to which this point corresponds. The slope of the indifference curve at this point indicates how much extra consumption, Δc, someone insists on to work an additional unit of time. To determine how much someone actually works, we combine the indifference curves with a description of people's opportunities for raising consumption when work effort rises. In the model, these opportunities come from the production function, which appears in Figure 2.1. The marginal product of labor, MPL, is the amount of extra output generated by an extra unit of work. Further, we know from equation (2.2) that each addition to output corresponds to an equal addition to consumption. The MPL is the addition to production—and therefore to consumption—that results from an extra unit of work. The slope of the indifference curve is the amount of extra consumption that a person needs to make up for less leisure time. Therefore, if the MPL exceeds the slope of the indifference curve, the person will be better off if he or she works more and uses the added output to expand consumption. However, as work rises, the MPL declines, and the slope of the indifference curve rises. Therefore, the increase in work lessens the initial excess of the MPL over the slope of the indifference curve. When the gap vanishes—that is, when the marginal product equals the slope of the indifference curve—it no longer pays to work more.

The results are in Figure 2.7. Consider the intersection of the production function, $y = f(l)$, with indifference curve u^2 at point D. At this position, the slope of the production function—which is the MPL— exceeds the slope of the indifference curve. An increase in work expands output, and hence consumption, by more than enough to maintain the

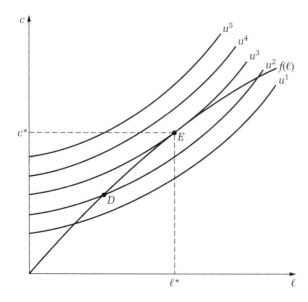

FIGURE 2.7

COMBINING THE INDIFFERENCE CURVES WITH THE PRODUCTION FUNCTION

The household moves along the production function, $f(l)$, to reach the highest possible indifference curve. This occurs at point E, where the production function is tangent to indifference curve u^3.

level of utility. Graphically, by raising work and moving along the production function beyond point D, a household intersects higher indifference curves and thereby raises utility.

Assume that work rises enough to reach point E in Figure 2.7. At this point the slope of the production function equals the slope of the indifference curve. We show this relationship graphically by drawing the production function, $f(l)$, as tangent to indifference curve u^3 at point E. Then we designate the associated levels of work and consumption as l^* and c^*. Notice that, at this point, a movement along the production function beyond point E intersects lower indifference curves. In other words, the extra output and consumption are now insufficient to make up for the loss of utility from extra work. Therefore, utility declines if work rises above the amount l^*.

To summarize, each household chooses the combination of work and consumption that maximizes utility. Therefore, the household selects the pair (l^*, c^*) at which the production function is tangent to an indifference curve.

SHIFTS IN THE PRODUCTION FUNCTION

We want to understand how people alter their work effort and consumption when there are changes in the opportunities for production. Here, we represent these changes by shifts of the production function, $f(l)$. Remember that we are examining the choices of work and consumption for a single period. So think here of changes in the production function that apply for that same period.

There are many examples of economic disturbances that alter production opportunities. For instance, the drought of 1988 reduced U.S. agricultural output and thereby amounted to a downward shift in the production function. The oil crises of 1973–74 and 1979 led to increases in the price of oil, which meant that users of energy had to give up more resources to carry out their production. From the standpoint of these users, the disturbance again looks like a downward shift in the production function, $f(l)$. On the other hand, discoveries of new technology—such as practical uses of electricity, nuclear energy, computer chips, and fiber optics—amount to upward shifts of the production function.

In analyzing the reaction of households to economic changes, we shall find it useful to place the responses into two categories:

━━━ wealth effects

━━━ substitution effects

A wealth effect (which economists also call an **income effect**) concerns the overall scale of opportunities. If a change allows people to obtain more of the things that provide utility, then wealth increases. A substitution effect refers to the relative ease or cost with which people can obtain the various items that provide utility. We might, for example, have a change in the possibilities for transforming more work (and, hence, less leisure) into more consumption. More generally, we could have a change in the relative costs of obtaining any two goods, such as bread and television sets.

We shall use the concepts of wealth and substitution effects extensively throughout this book. To begin we consider the wealth effects for the model that we have been analyzing. We assume throughout this discussion that people have a given pattern of tastes for consumption and leisure. Specifically, people's indifference curves, which appear in Figures 2.6 and 2.7, do not move around when the production function shifts.

WEALTH EFFECTS

As a general definition, a change raises wealth if it enables people to reach a higher level of utility. In contrast, wealth declines if the change forces people to a lower level of utility.[2] Unfortunately, this definition may be difficult to apply in some circumstances. We want to use the

[2] This viewpoint comes from John Hicks (1946, Chap. 2).

notions of wealth and substitution effects to assist in analyses of various economic changes, such as a harvest failure. In some cases, we do not know at the start whether a particular change will end up raising or lowering utility, so if we have to solve the whole problem to determine what happens to wealth, there may not be much point in using the concept.

We can usually test for the sign of the change in wealth by the following method. Start with a household's initial choices of work and consumption at the position (l^*, c^*) in Figure 2.7. Then see how the economic change alters opportunities in the vicinity of this initial point.[3] For example, the initial quantity of work effort, l^*, may allow the household to consume at a higher level than before. Then wealth surely increases (because the household can attain a higher level of utility). Alternatively, the initial level of work effort, l^*, may allow only a smaller quantity of consumption than before. In this case wealth probably declines.

Let's be more concrete about this method for the case of a shift to the production function. An increase in wealth arises if households can produce and consume more goods for the same amount of work effort. In the simplest case of a pure wealth effect, the production function shifts upward in a parallel manner. This shift means that more output is forthcoming for a given amount of labor input but that no change occurs in the slope of the production function at each level of work. That is, the marginal product of labor does not change at a given level of work. We show this case in Figure 2.8. In this case, the initial production function, $f(l)'$, parallels the old one, $f(l)$.

Recall that our previous case of a shift to the production function, as shown in Figure 2.3, involved changes in the slope of the function. For the moment we neglect this type of change because it brings in substitution effects. The parallel shift shown in Figure 2.8 is easier because it involves only a wealth effect.

How do people respond to an increase in wealth? We find the answer in Figure 2.9 by combining the change to the production func-

[3] *This general approach derives from the work of the Russian economist Eugen Slutsky. For a discussion (in the context of markets for goods), see Hal Varian [UPDATE] (1987, pp. 147–150).*

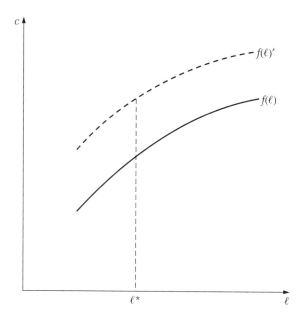

FIGURE 2.8

A PARALLEL UPWARD SHIFT OF THE PRODUCTION FUNCTION

The new production function, $f(l)'$, lies everywhere above the old one, $f(l)$. With this type of parallel shift, the two functions have the same slope at any given level of work effort.

tion with two of the indifference curves. The production function was initially tangent to an indifference curve at the point (l^*, c^*). Then, as mentioned before, the upward shift of the production function enables a household to reach a higher indifference curve. The new production function, $f(l)'$, is tangent to a higher indifference curve at the point $[(l^*)', (c^*)']$. The figure indicates that consumption increases—$(c^*)' > c^*$—and work effort decreases—$(l^*)' < l^*$. In other words, households respond to the increase in wealth by raising the quantities of both things that provide utility, consumption and leisure. We say that consumption and leisure are **superior goods** because the quantities of both rise in response to an increase in wealth. (Sometimes economists use the term **normal goods** instead of superior goods.) Alternatively, we can say that the wealth effect is positive for consumption and negative for work.

Generally, when there are many types of goods, we cannot be sure that the wealth effect is positive for all of them. Some goods

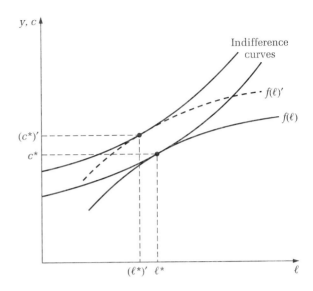

FIGURE 2.9

THE RESPONSE OF WORK AND CONSUMPTION TO AN INCREASE IN
WEALTH

The parallel upward shift of the production function motivates the
household to consume more and work less.

may be "**inferior**," which means that people desire less of them when
wealth rises. But when thinking about only two broad categories of
things that provide utility—consumption and leisure—we can be pretty
sure that both goods are superior. That is, some reasonable assumptions about the nature of preferences guarantee this result. Hence,
from now on, we assume that consumption and leisure are superior
goods.

It is not surprising that the wealth effect on consumption is positive.
Casual observation across families or countries immediately supports
this proposition. Similarly, we can look at the United States as the
economy has developed over time. It is no surprise that consumption
per person has grown along with the rise in output per capita.

The negative effect of wealth on work effort is somewhat harder to
verify. But it does show up in the long-run negative influence of economic development on average hours of work. In the United States, the
average hours worked per week for workers in manufacturing declined
from 55 to 60 in 1890 to about 50 in 1914, 44 in 1929, and 42 in 1996.[4]
Similarly, in the United Kingdom the average weekly hours of male man-

[4] The data are from U.S. Department of Commerce (1975,
pp. 168, 169) and Economic
Report of the President, 1992,
Table B–42. For a full analysis,
we should also consider changes
in labor-force participation. See
problem 2.10 at the end of the
chapter.

ual workers fell from 60 in 1850 to 55 in 1890, 54 in 1910, 48 in 1938, 47 in 1965, and 44 in 1994.[5]

If we look across countries at a point in time, we get some further indication of a negative wealth effect on work effort. For example, over the period 1953–60, the mean over ten industrialized countries for the average weekly hours in manufacturing was 43.9. (The ten are the United States, Canada, Switzerland, Sweden, New Zealand, the United Kingdom, Norway, France, West Germany, and the Netherlands.) But the mean over ten less-developed countries was 47.4. (These ten are Yugoslavia, Colombia, the Philippines, El Salvador, Ecuador, Guatemala, Peru, Taiwan, Egypt, and Ceylon.)[6]

The negative effect of economic development on average hours of work seems to weaken at high levels of development. In the United States the long-term downward trend in average hours worked per week in manufacturing apparently ended around World War II—the figure of 40.4 average hours per week for 1947 is nearly equal to that of 41.5 for 1996.[7] For male manual workers in the United Kingdom, the value of 47.0 average hours for 1965 is nearly equal to that of 47.6 for 1946. The value did decline, however, to 44.1 in 1994.

We have to go further with our economic analysis to explain the observations for the recent period. As mentioned before, we want to bring in substitution effects as influences on the choices of work and consumption.

SUBSTITUTION EFFECTS FOR WORK VERSUS CONSUMPTION

We started with a pure wealth effect where the production function shifted upward in a parallel manner, as shown in Figure 2.8. This change in technology allowed people to produce more goods for a given amount of work. There was no change, however, in the schedule for the marginal product of labor, MPL. This last condition is unrealistic, because technological advances tend to raise the MPL at each level of work.

[5] *The earlier data are rough averages from M. A. Bienefeld (1972, Chaps. 4, 5). Figures for 1938 and 1965 are from B. R. Mitchell and H. G. Jones (1971, p. 148). The value for 1986 is from Central Statistical Office, Annual Abstract of Statistics, 1996 edition.*

[6] *The data are in Gordon Winston (1966, Table 1). His study deals also with cross-county differences in labor-force participation.*

[7] *The available statistics refer, however, to hours paid by employers. The decline in hours worked may be greater than the data indicate because of the increasing importance of vacations and sick days. Also, more of a decline shows up when we look at the total private, non-agricultural economy. Here, average weekly hours worked in the United States fell from 40.3 in 1947 to 34.3 in 1991. But these data reflect partly the changing composition of the labor force, especially toward more female workers.*

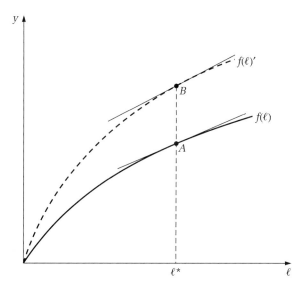

FIGURE 2.10

A PROPORTIONAL UPWARD SHIFT OF THE PRODUCTION FUNCTION

The new production function, $f(l)'$, is higher and more steeply sloped
than the old one, $f(l)$, at each level of work.

Suppose that we want to understand the effects on households'
choices from the type of upward shift to the production function that
appears in Figure 2.10. The new function, $f(l)'$, is proportionately higher
than the initial one, $f(l)$, at each level of work. Therefore, the slope of
the new curve exceeds that of the initial one at each level of work. This
change in slope brings in a substitution effect, which we now have to
consider.

The proportional shift in Figure 2.10 combines the parallel shift
in Figure 2.8 with a counterclockwise twist of the new function, $f(l)'$.
Recall that we already understand the pure wealth effects from the
parallel shift; therefore, we need only to study the consequences of this
counterclockwise twist of the production function to assess the type
of proportional shift that appears in Figure 2.10. Figure 2.11 isolates
this twist. Note that the new production function, $f(l)'$, is more steeply
sloped than the old one, $f(l)$, at each level of work. Hence, the twist
raises the marginal product of labor at any level of work.

Figure 2.12 shows the household's response to a twist of the production function. The initial function, $f(l)$, is tangent to an indifference

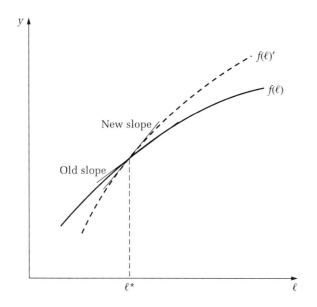

FIGURE 2.11

A TWIST OF THE PRODUCTION FUNCTION

At l^* the level of output is the same for the two production functions. However, the new function, $f(l)'$, is more steeply sloped than the old one, $f(l)$, at any level of work.

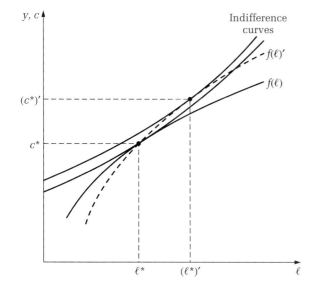

FIGURE 2.12

RESPONSE OF WORK AND CONSUMPTION TO A SUBSTITUTION EFFECT

The schedule for the marginal product of labor shifts upward when the production function shifts from $f(l)$ to $f(l)'$. The response is an increase in work—from l^* to $(l^*)'$—and a rise in consumption—from c^* to $(c^*)'$.

curve at the point (l^*, c^*). Since the new function, $f(l)'$, passes through this point, it would still be possible to work the amount l^* and consume the amount c^*. Households were happy initially to stay at this point because the MPL equaled the slope of the indifference curve, but the MPL is now higher. Therefore, more work now generates enough additional output (and consumption) to raise utility. That is, a movement along the new production function, $f(l)'$ in Figure 2.12, reaches higher indifference curves. Eventually, the household gets to one that is tangent to the new production function at the point $(l^{*\prime}, c^{*\prime})$. Then any more work would lower utility.

We have shown that a rise in the schedule for the marginal product of labor induces more work, $(l^*)' > l^*$, and more consumption, $(c^*)' > c^*$. Recall that a household always has the opportunity to work one more unit of time and use the additional MPL units of output to raise consumption. In terms of the two things that provide utility—leisure and consumption—households have the option to give up one unit of leisure in exchange for MPL extra units of consumption. When the schedule for labor's marginal product shifts upward, this deal becomes more favorable. That is, households now get more consumption, MPL, when they give up a unit of leisure. Or, to put this another way, consumption has become less costly relative to leisure. A rational person who wants to maximize utility finds it desirable to substitute toward the items that have become cheaper. In our example, this substitution effect motivates more consumption and less leisure (which means more work).[8]

COMBINING THE WEALTH AND SUBSTITUTION EFFECTS

We can now work out the full effects from a proportional upward shift of the production function, as shown in Figure 2.10. This change combines

[8] *Figure 2.12 shows that the household reaches a higher indifference curve. Therefore, the disturbance involves an increase in wealth as well as a substitution effect. Because the wealth effect is relatively unimportant, the example provides a close approximation to a pure substitution effect. To isolate the substitution effect exactly, we would have to include a small, parallel downward shift of the production function along with the twist shown in the figure. If this small shift were of the right size, then the household would remain on the initial indifference curve. But this minor modification would still leave people with higher levels of work effort and consumption. Thus, the elimination of the small wealth effect would not change any qualitative results.*

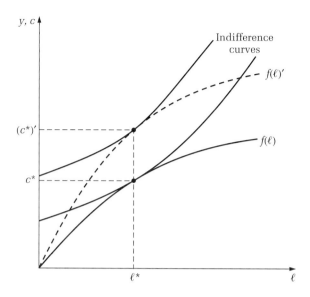

When the production function shifts upward proportionately, there is
an increase in consumption but an ambiguous change in work effort.

an increase in wealth with a substitution effect from the rise in the
schedule for the marginal product of labor.

Figure 2.13 shows the effects on the household's choices. Notice
that consumption increases, $(c^*)' > c^*$. The effect on work effort is, however, ambiguous. Let's consider the nature of this ambiguity. The positive
wealth effect leads to more consumption and more leisure and therefore
to *less* work. The substitution effect from the higher schedule for the
MPL implies more consumption and less leisure, which means *more*
work. Notice that the wealth and substitution effects reinforce themselves with respect to consumption but oppose each other with respect
to work and leisure. The proportional shift of the production function
leads to less work and more leisure only if the wealth effect dominates
the substitution effect. We cannot say in general which force will be more
important.

Let's use the perspective of wealth and substitution effects to reconsider the facts on work hours that we looked at before. Recall that over
the last 40 years or so, there has been no strong trend in average hours

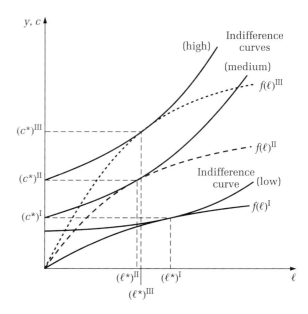

FIGURE 2.14

**EFFECT OF LONG-TERM ECONOMIC DEVELOPMENT ON AVERAGE
WORK HOURS**

The figure shows three levels of the production function as the economy develops from $f(l)^{I}$ to $f(l)^{II}$ to $f(l)^{III}$. The indifference curves in the corresponding regions are labeled low, middle, and high. Notice that work effort falls at early stages of economic development but changes little at more advanced stages.

worked per week in industry for the United States. There was, however, a major decline in average hours worked at earlier stages of economic development.

Suppose that we think of economic development as represented by a series of proportional upward shifts to production functions. Figure 2.14 picks out three stages of economic development: a low level where the production function (for the typical producer) is $f(l)^{I}$, a middle level at $f(l)^{II}$, and a high level at $f(l)^{III}$. We can think of the first curve as applying to the United States before World War I, the second curve as applying at the end of World War II, and the third as applying in 1998.

Consider the patterns for households' tastes that would be consistent with the data on average work hours. Imagine first an economy at a low level of development; that is, a situation in which the production function allows the typical person to reach only a low indifference curve. In this circumstance, people are likely to be willing to work long hours to maintain their consumption levels, even if their marginal products are low and although they are already working a lot. Diagrammatically, the indifference curve marked *low* in Figure 2.14 is extremely flat up to a high level of work effort. The flat slope means that people are willing to work a lot to gain a small amount of extra consumption. Notice that the first production function is tangent to the low indifference curve at the point $[(l^*)^I, (c^*)^I]$. Here, people work many hours but produce and consume relatively little because of the low level of the production function.

When production opportunities improve to the second level, $f(l)^{II}$, the production function is tangent to the indifference curve labeled *middle* at the point, $[(l^*)^{II}, (c^*)^{II}]$, in Figure 2.14. The figure shows this middle indifference curve with a slope that is higher and more steeply rising than that for the low indifference curve. This shape means that extra leisure has become more important relative to additional consumption. For this reason a reduction in hours worked, $(l^*)^{II} < (l^*)^I$, accompanies the rise in consumption, $(c^*)^{II} > (c^*)^I$. In this range of economic development, the negative wealth effect on work effort dominates the substitution effect.

Finally, the move from the second production function, $f(l)^{II}$, to the third, $f(l)^{III}$, corresponds to the case that we explored before in Figure 2.13. Here, the wealth and substitution effects roughly cancel to yield little change in work hours. But consumption again increases, $(c^*)^{III} > (c^*)^{II}$.

SUMMARY

In this chapter, households are isolated from each other and therefore behave like Robinson Crusoe's. There are no markets on which people can trade, and each household uses its own labor to produce goods by means of a production function. Because we treat goods as nonstorable, each household consumes what it produces.

We can express people's preferences in terms of their utility for consumption and leisure. Then we can translate these preferences into indifference curves for work and consumption. Basically, people work more only if they receive a sufficient addition to their consumption.

The combination of households' preferences with their opportunities for production determines the choices of work, production, and consumption. For convenience we analyze these choices in terms of wealth and substitution effects. An improvement in the production function increases wealth, which motivates less work and more consumption. That is, the wealth effect is positive for consumption and leisure.

The only substitution effect in the model involves the productivity of labor. If the schedule for labor's marginal product shifts upward, then households can obtain more consumption for an extra hour of work. Because consumption becomes cheaper relative to leisure, households work more to raise their consumption. In other words, they substitute away from leisure and toward consumption.

Toward the end, we use the apparatus to analyze the long-term behavior of work hours. Initially, as an economy develops, the increase in wealth motivates people to consume more and to work fewer hours per week. As the economy develops further, the substitution effect from labor's higher productivity tends roughly to offset the wealth effect. Hence, there is little change in work hours, but consumption continues to rise.

IMPORTANT TERMS AND CONCEPTS

diminishing marginal productivity A characteristic of the production function by which successive increments of an input yield progressively smaller increments in output.

income effect Another term for a wealth effect.

indifference curve A graph showing the combinations of two items, such as consumption and work effort, that yield the same level of utility.

inferior goods Goods for which the wealth effect is negative.

marginal product of labor (MPL) The increment of output obtained per unit increment of labor input while holding fixed any other inputs; the slope of the graph of the production function relating output to labor input.

production function The relationship between the quantities of output obtained and the quantities of inputs into production, such as labor and capital.

substitution effect The response of households to changes in the relative costs of obtaining any two goods, such as consumption and leisure.

superior goods (or normal goods) Goods for which the wealth effect is positive.

utility The level of happiness of a household, measured in units called utils. Utility increases with increases in either consumption or leisure.

utility function The relationship between the amount of utility obtained and the amounts of consumption and labor chosen by the household.

wealth effect The response of consumption and leisure (or labor) to changes in the household's opportunities for increasing utility. An increase (decrease) in wealth occurs when the household can raise (must reduce) consumption while leisure remains unchanged.

QUESTIONS AND PROBLEMS

MAINLY FOR REVIEW

2.1 What is a production function? How does it represent a trade-off that the individual *has* to make between work (and consumption) and leisure?

2.2 Distinguish between total product and marginal product. What are the implications for total product if marginal product is (a) positive and increasing, (b) positive and diminishing, and (c) negative?

2.3 What is a utility function? Show how to represent different levels of utility by a family of indifference curves. Can these curves shift in the way that the production function can?

2.4 Show how the slope of each indifference curve indicates the trade-off that the individual is willing to make between work (and consumption) and leisure. Explain why it may not be equal to the trade-off represented by the slope of the production function.

2.5 Suppose that to remain at the same level of utility an individual would have to receive one additional unit of consumption as compensation for one less unit of leisure. Would it be utility maximizing for the individual to work more if at that point the additional output obtained is more than one? if it is less than one? Restate your answer using the concepts of indifference curves and the production function.

2.6 Suppose there is an improvement in the production function. Assume that the improvement includes an upward shift in the schedule for the marginal product of labor. Will the individual work more to obtain more output; or work less, obtain the same or a greater amount of output, and enjoy more leisure than before? Explain your answer in terms of wealth and substitution effects. How does your answer change if either consumption or leisure is an inferior good?

PROBLEMS FOR DISCUSSION

2.7 Properties of a Specific Production Function

Suppose that the production function has the form

$$y = A \cdot \sqrt{l} + B$$

where y is output, l is labor input, A is a positive constant, and B is another constant, which may be positive, negative, or zero.

a. Graph the level of output, y, versus the quantity of labor input, l.

b. Is the marginal product of labor positive? Is it diminishing in l?

c. Describe the wealth and substitution effects from an increase in the coefficient A.

d. Describe the wealth and substitution effects from an increase in the coefficient B.

2.8 Effects of Shifts in the Production Function on the Choice of Work Effort

Assume again that the production function is $y = A \cdot \sqrt{l} + B$. What are the effects on a household's work effort, l, output, y, and consumption, c, from

a. an increase in the coefficient A?

b. an increase in the coefficient B?

2.9 Temporary versus Permanent Changes in the Production Function

Suppose that the production function shifts upward. Assume, as in Figure 2.8, that the shift is parallel, so that no change occurs in the schedule for labor's marginal product. Recall that we showed in Figure 2.9 that people respond by raising consumption and reducing work.

The improvement in the production function could be permanent—as in the case of a discovery of some new technology—or it might be temporary—as in the case of good weather for this period. What difference does it make for the results whether the change is permanent or temporary? That is, do we predict different responses of consumption and work effort in the two cases?

2.10 Changes in Labor-Force Participation

In the text we mentioned some variations over time in average hours worked per week. But we also see important changes in aggregate work effort that reflect shifts in labor-force participation. For example, people may alter their time spent at school or in retirement. Also, especially for married women in recent years, people may choose to work in the market rather than at home. Overall we can assess the changes in labor-force participation from the following table, which shows the ratio of the total labor force (including the military) to the adult population aged less than 65.[9]

Civilian Labor Force ÷ Population Aged 16–64 (%)	
1995	79
1990	78
1980	73
1970	67
1960	66
1950	65

Notice that labor-force participation rose sharply during the post–World War II period. Most of this change reflected the increased activity of women, especially married women, in the market sector.

What does our analysis of wealth and substitution effects say about this behavior of labor-force participation? (Think here of effects on a family that includes more than one potential worker.) Can we reconcile the rising rate of labor-force participation with the tendency of average hours worked per worker to stay constant or fall slowly? (Note: This question does not have a clear-cut answer!)

2.11 Productivity

A popular measure of productivity is the ratio of output (say, real GDP) to employment (say, worker-hours). In the graph of the production function

9 *The data are from the DRI data bank.*

88

that follows, this concept of productivity at the employment level l^{I} is given by the ratio $y^{\mathrm{I}}/l^{\mathrm{I}}$. Productivity at this point equals the slope of the dashed line that is drawn from the origin to intersect the production function at the employment level l^{I}.

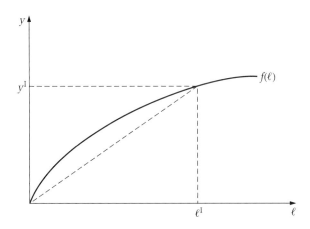

a. For the production function shown and for the employment level l, show graphically that productivity, y/l, always exceeds the marginal product of labor, MPL.

b. Consider a technological change that shifts the production function upward proportionately at all levels of l (as shown in Figure 2.10). What happens to the choices of work effort, l, and output, y? What happens to productivity, y/l? (Empirically, long-run economic development is associated with a sustained rise in output per worker-hour.)

c. Assume now that the form of the production function does not change. But suppose that people shift their tastes and become more willing to work. That is, at the initial levels of work and consumption, each person requires a smaller addition in consumption to give up a unit of leisure. What happens here to the choices of work effort, l, and output, y? What happens to productivity, y/l?

The Behavior of Households with Markets for Commodities and Credit

In the previous chapter, each household was like Robinson Crusoe: there were no possibilities for trade between one household and another. This chapter introduces two types of opportunities for exchange. First, there is a commodity market on which people can sell their outputs and buy those of others. On this market, the price level is the amount of money that exchanges for one unit of commodities. One important aspect of this market is that it allows people to specialize in their type of production. This specialization is a major element in efficient economic organization.

Second, there is a credit market on which households can borrow and lend. The interest rate determines the cost of borrowing and the return to lending. By using the credit market, people can avoid substantial fluctuations in their consumption even if their incomes vary a great deal from period to period. The effect of the interest rate on the time pattern of consumption and work is one of the key relations in this chapter.

THE COMMODITY MARKET

In the real world, people consume very little of most of the goods that they help to produce in the marketplace. For example, an auto worker's contribution to the output of cars is much greater than that worker's expenditure on cars. Typically, a person works on one or a few products and receives income from the sale of these products or from the sale of labor services, which help to create the products. This income is then spent on a wide range of consumer goods. As Adam Smith observed more than two centuries ago, people tend to specialize with respect to occupations and production activities. This specialization aids efficiency; in fact, the national output would be many times smaller if everyone participated in the production of all goods. In this case, people would learn each job badly and would spend most of their time shifting from task to task.

In the theoretical model, we want to capture the feature that individuals consume little of what they produce. To keep things workable, it is convenient to go to the extreme and assume that producers sell their entire output on a market on which people buy and sell commodities. Then sellers use their proceeds to buy other goods for consumption purposes.

The model would become unmanageable if we tried to keep track of the physical differences among many kinds of goods. Therefore, we continue to pretend that there is a single physical type of good, which households produce by one type of production process. As before, the production function is

$$y_t = f(l_t) \tag{3.1}$$

MONEY

Consider the sales and purchases of goods on the commodity market. We assume that it is inconvenient to trade one good directly for another. As economists have noted for hundreds of years, this form of **barter** exchange would require a person to find someone who wants exactly the goods that he or she has and has exactly the goods that he or she wants.[1] That is, it requires a **double coincidence of wants**. A general means of payments, such as money, avoids this problem. Buyers use money to purchase goods, and sellers receive money in exchange for goods. Thus, the problem of double coincidence of wants does not arise.

We assume, henceforth, that society has settled on a single form of money as a medium of exchange. The money in our model is analogous to paper **currency** issued by a government. At the present time, almost all governments issue currency. (One exception is Panama, which uses U.S. currency. Some others that lack their own paper money are Andorra, Greenland, Guadeloupe, Liechtenstein, and Luxembourg.) Money takes a paper form in the model, with no backing by gold or other commodities.

Historically, commodities such as gold and silver served as money. These precious metals possess attractive physical characteristics, which classical economists enumerated as indestructibility, homogeneity, divisibility, and cognizability.[2] But when paper money—such as U.S. dollar bills—replaces commodity money, these physical characteristics no longer enter into the analysis.

Money in our model is denominated in an arbitrary unit, such as a "dollar." We shall often refer to dollar amounts as **nominal** magnitudes. One important property is that, unlike some assets that we introduce later, money does not bear interest.[3]

Denote the dollar quantity of money that someone holds during period t by m_t. The aggregate quantity of money, denoted by M_t, equals the sum of the holdings by all individuals. (We adopt the convention of using a capital letter to represent an aggregate quantity.) For now, we assume that the aggregate quantity of money does not change over time.

THE PRICE LEVEL

Because goods are physically the same, we expect that all can be sold for the same number of dollars on the commodity market. The number of

[1] *The classic discussion of the difficulties with barter exchange is W. Stanley Jevons (1896, Chaps. 1–3). An interesting model of the evolution of specialized media of exchange appears in Robert Jones (1976).*

[2] *See W. Stanley Jevons (1896, Chap. 5) and—for an earlier discussion—John Law (1966 [1705], Chap. 1).*

[3] *Historically, it is rare for currency to pay interest. Some early forms of U.S. Treasury notes, such as those issued from 1812 to 1815, paid interest and also had some limited use as media of exchange. However, because no denominations below $100 were issued, these notes were used mostly as bank reserves. For a discussion, see Richard Timberlake (1978, pp. 13–17).*

dollars that people receive for each unit of goods sold is the dollar *price* of the good. We denote the price by P and measure it in units of dollars per good. Often, we refer to P as the general price level.

For a seller of commodities, the price P is the number of dollars obtained for each unit of goods sold. For a buyer, the price is the number of dollars paid per unit of goods. Since P dollars buy 1 unit of goods, $1 would buy $1/P$ units of goods. The expression $1/P$ is therefore the value of $1 in units of the commodities that it buys. Similarly, m exchanges for $(m) \times 1/P$ units of commodities. Whereas the quantity m is the value of money in terms of dollars, the quantity m/P measures the value of this money in terms of the quantity of commodities that it buys. Expressions like m/P are in units of commodities or in **real terms**. By contrast, a quantity like m is in dollar or nominal terms.

In the present chapter, we assume that people perceive the price level to be constant over time. (We drop this unrealistic assumption in Chapter 7, which begins the study of inflation.) Throughout the analysis, we assume that each household views itself as sufficiently small that it can buy or sell any amount of goods in the commodity market without influencing the established price. Economists call this **perfect competition**.

THE CREDIT MARKET

In the Robinson Crusoe model of Chapter 2, people had no way to shift resources over time. Goods could not be stored, and individuals could not borrow from others and repay these loans later. For now, we retain the assumption that goods cannot be stored, but we introduce possibilities for borrowing and lending on a credit market.

A person who makes a loan receives a piece of paper that indicates the terms of the contract. In our model we call this piece of paper a **bond**. The holder of a bond—the lender—has a claim to the amount owed by the borrower. Bonds in the model come in units of dollars. When someone buys 1 unit of bonds with $1 of money, he or she lends $1 on the credit market. If a person issues 1 unit of bonds in exchange for $1 of money, he or she borrows $1.

To simplify matters, pretend that all bonds have a maturity of one period. Each dollar unit of these bonds commits the borrower to pay the lender the **principal**, $1, plus interest, R, in the next period. The variable R is the interest rate, that is, the ratio of the interest payment, R, to the amount borrowed, which is $1. For the buyer of a bond, the interest rate is the return per period to lending; for the issuer of a bond, the interest rate is the cost per period of borrowing.

We assume that the credit market treats all bonds alike, regardless of the issuer. In other words, to keep things manageable, we assume that people do not differ with respect to their creditworthiness, the type of collateral that they put up for a loan, and so on. Accordingly, the interest rate, R, must be the same for all bonds. Further, any household is small enough to be able to buy or sell any amount of bonds without affecting the interest rate. Again, this is an assumption of perfect competition. We could extend this framework by bringing in various real-world complications, such as limitations on individuals' access to borrowing and the existence of bonds with various maturities.

Let b_t represent the number of bonds in dollar units that a household holds during period t. The amount of bonds may be positive or negative for an individual household. Notice, however, that for any dollar borrowed by one person, there must be a corresponding dollar lent by someone else. Hence, the *total* of positive bond holdings for lenders must exactly match the *aggregate* of negative bond holdings for borrowers. In the model we allow only one type of economic unit, households, to borrow and lend. In particular, we do not yet deal with governments, foreigners, financial institutions, or corporations as participants in the credit market. (We shall see later that the essential ideas do not change when we make these additions.) Therefore, in the model the *total* of bonds held by all households, denoted by B_t, must always be zero.

As noted before, b_{t-1} is the dollar amount of bonds that someone holds during period $t - 1$. In period t these bonds pay the interest, Rb_{t-1}, and principal, b_{t-1}. (Notice that the bonds bought or sold in period

$t - 1$ do not bear interest until period t.) Thus, the receipts from bonds are positive for lenders—for whom b_{t-1} is positive—and negative for borrowers. Recall that the aggregate stock of bonds for period $t - 1$, B_{t-1}, is zero. Therefore, the aggregates of interest and principal payments for period t must also be zero. The total of interest receipts always balances the total of interest expenses.

We measure **saving**, in the form of bonds, as the net change in someone's asset position, $b_t - b_{t-1}$. Note that this saving is a *flow*, which determines the *change* over one period in someone's *stock* of bonds. Saving is positive for some persons and negative for others. However, when we sum up across households, we know that $B_t = B_{t-1} = 0$. Therefore, the aggregate of saving in bonds, $B_t - B_{t-1}$, must also be zero in each period. In the aggregate, the additions to loans balance the additions to debts.

An individual's total of financial assets equals the sum of money and bonds, $m_t + b_t$. Recall that money holdings are nonnegative for all persons; that is, $m_t > 0$. (Only the government can issue money!) In the aggregate, since $B_t = 0$, the stock of financial assets equals the total money stock, M_t.

The change in an individual's financial assets, $(m_t + b_t) - (m_{t-1} + b_{t-1})$, is the total amount that an individual saves during period t. When summing up across all households, we know that $M_t - M_{t-1} = 0$ (because we are assuming that the total stock of money is constant), and $B_t - B_{t-1} = 0$. Therefore, the aggregate of total saving is zero at all points in time in the present model. (When we introduce investment in Chapter 9, this result will change.)

BUDGET CONSTRAINTS

BUDGET CONSTRAINTS FOR ONE PERIOD

Each household receives income from sales of output, y_t, on the commodity market. The quantity of output depends on the amount of labor input, l_t, through the production function, $y_t = f(l_t)$. Because the price of goods is P, the dollar income from selling output is Py_t. Recall that interest income from the bond market, Rb_{t-1}, is positive for lenders and negative for borrowers. Also, remember that people receive no interest income from their holdings of money.

Each household purchases the quantity of consumable goods, c_t, from the commodity market. Because the price of goods is P, the amount of consumption expenditure in dollars is Pc_t.

For a given total of financial assets, a household can use the credit market to exchange money for bonds, or vice versa, and thereby achieve the desired composition of assets between bonds and money. The amount held as bonds, b_{t-1}, determines the interest income or expense for period t. The motivation for holding money, which does not bear interest, derives from its convenience in carrying out exchanges. For expositional purposes, we shall defer our discussion of the demand for money until Chapter 4. For now, we just assume that people hold part of their assets as money.

We can express the equality between a household's total sources and uses of funds in the form of a budget constraint. The condition for period t is

$$Py_t + b_{t-1} \cdot (1 + R) + m_{t-1} = Pc_t + b_t + m_t \qquad \textbf{(3.2)}$$

The left side of equation (3.2) contains sources of funds, which include income from the commodity market, Py_t, the principal received on last period's bonds, b_{t-1}, the interest receipts from these bonds, Rb_{t-1}, and the amount of money held over from the previous period, m_{t-1}. The right side of the equation comprises uses of funds, which are consumption expenditures, Pc_t, holdings of bonds, b_t, and holdings of money, m_t. Because we treat the price level and interest rate as constants, these variables appear without time subscripts in the equation.

Rearrangement of equation (3.2) yields an expression for a household's nominal saving, which is the change over time in the dollar value of financial assets:

$$\text{Nominal saving} = \left(b_t + m_t\right) - \left(b_{t-1} + m_{t-1}\right) = Py_t + Rb_{t-1} - Pc_t \quad \textbf{(3.3)}$$

Nominal saving equals the income from producing and selling output plus interest receipts less consumption expenditures.

Households can leave saving intact by making simultaneous changes in income and consumption. For example, suppose that someone works more in period t and raises income, Py_t, by $1000. Then, if he or she also raises consumption spending, Pc_t, by $1000, saving does not change. Therefore, the budget constraint allows people to work more and raise consumption during any period, without altering the amounts of assets that they carry over to the future. This trade-off between consumption and leisure in a single period was the only choice available to Robinson Crusoe in the model from Chapter 2. The expanded model retains this option but also introduces possibilities that exploit the credit market. Specifically, individuals can vary current saving, which is the difference between income and expenditure. Thereby, people alter the amount of assets that they carry over to the future.

Recall that equation (3.3) specifies the saving for one household. As mentioned before, the total of this saving across households is zero. When we add up the right side of equation (3.3) over all households, we find that aggregate income equals aggregate spending, $PY_t = PC_t$. (Remember that the aggregate stock of bonds, B_{t-1}, is zero.) For Robinson Crusoe, the equality between production and consumption holds individually at every point in time. Now, because of the credit market, *some* people can consume more than their income (dissave), while others consume less (save). But it is still true for *the economy as a whole* that total output cannot depart from total consumption. (Recall that consumption is the only use for commodities in the present model.)

BUDGET CONSTRAINTS FOR TWO PERIODS

The previous discussion brought out the effects of current consumption and work on the assets that a household carried over to the future. We can clarify this process by studying choices over two periods.

The budget constraint from equation (3.2) holds for any period. For example, for period 1, the condition is

$$Py_1 + b_0 \cdot (1 + R) + m_0 = Pc_1 + b_1 + m_1 \qquad \textbf{(3.4)}$$

Now we shall find it convenient to assume that each household's money holdings are constant over time; that is, $m_1 = m_0$. Anyone who maintains a constant quantity of money carries out any saving or dissaving in the form of bonds. By making this assumption, we avoid a clutter of minor terms in the household's budget constraint over more than one period. But we shall return later (in Chapter 4) to reconsider the case in which money holdings change over time.

Using the condition $m_1 = m_0$, the budget constraint from equation (3.4) simplifies to

$$Py_1 + b_0 \cdot (1 + R) = Pc_1 + b_1 \qquad \textbf{(3.5)}$$

There is a similar one-period budget constraint for period 2:

$$Py_2 + b_1 \cdot (1 + R) = Pc_2 + b_2 \qquad \textbf{(3.6)}$$

The two budget constraints are not independent because b_1 appears as a use of funds in period 1 and as a source of funds in period 2.

We can combine the two one-period budget constraints into a single two-period budget constraint. First, solve equation (3.6) for b_1 to get

$$b_1 = Pc_2/(1 + R) + b_2/(1 + R) - Py_2/(1 + R)$$

Next, substitute for b_1 in equation (3.5) and collect terms into sources and uses of funds to get

$$Py_1 + Py_2/(1 + R) + b_0 \cdot (1 + R) = Pc_1 + Pc_2/(1 + R) + b_2/(1 + R) \qquad \textbf{(3.7)}$$

The sources of funds on the left side of equation (3.7) include the income from the commodity market for periods 1 and 2, Py_1 and Py_2, and the initial stock of bonds, b_0. The uses of funds on the right side involve the consumption expenditures over the two periods, Pc_1 and Pc_2, and the stock of bonds held at the end of the second period, b_2.

Observe how the incomes, Py_1 and Py_2, appear in equation (3.7). We divide next period's amount, Py_2, by the term $(1 + R)$ before adding it to this period's, Py_1. It is important to understand why incomes from the two periods, Py_1 and Py_2, are not just added together in the two-period budget constraint. Similarly, on the right side of equation (3.7), we divide next period's expenditure, Pc_2, by the term $(1 + R)$ before adding it to this period's, Pc_1. Again, we want to understand why we combine expenditures from different dates in this manner.

PRESENT VALUES

If the interest rate is positive—that is, $R > 0$—a given dollar amount of today's bonds translates into a larger number of dollars next period. Accordingly, individuals who can buy or sell bonds on the economy-wide credit market (that is, people who can lend or borrow) regard a dollar's worth of income or expenses differently depending on when it arises. Specifically, $1 received or spent earlier is equivalent to more than $1 later. Or, viewed in reverse, dollars received or spent in the future must be discounted to express them in terms that are comparable to dollars in the present.

Suppose, for example, that $R = 10\%$ per year. Assume that someone has $100 of income today but plans to spend these funds in the future. Then he or she can buy $100 of bonds now and have $110 available next year. Hence, $100 today is worth just as much as $110 next year. Equivalently, the $110 is discounted to correspond to the amount of today's income needed to generate $110 next year. We find this amount by solving the following equation:

Income needed today $\times\ (1 + 10\%) = \$110$

The required amount of current income is $\$110/1.1 = \$100$.

More generally, if we substitute any value of the interest rate, R, for 10%, the income for next period, Py_2, is divided by the term $1 + R$ to find the equivalent amount for this period. The result, $Py_2/(1 + R)$, is the **present value** of the future income. Economists call the term $1 + R$ the **discount factor**. When we discount by this factor—that is, when we divide by $1 + R$—we determine the present value of next period's income.

Equation (3.7) shows that we express the second period's income as a present value, $Py_2/(1 + R)$, before combining it with the first period's income, Py_1. Thus, the sum $Py_1 + Py_2/(1 + R)$ is the total present value of income from the production and sale of goods over periods 1 and 2. Similarly, we express next period's expenditure as the present value $Pc_2/(1 + R)$ before adding it to this period's spending, Pc_1. The sum $Pc_1 + Pc_2/(1 + R)$ is the total present value of consumption expenditures over periods 1 and 2.

THE HOUSEHOLD'S BUDGET LINE

The two-period budget constraint in equation (3.7) brings out the choices that a credit market offers to a household. Assume, for example, that a household raises today's spending, Pc_1, by $1000 and thereby cuts today's saving by $1000. This change reduces assets at the end of the first period, b_1, by $1000 (see equation [3.5]). For the second period, the household loses $1000 in receipts of principal from bonds and $100 in receipts of interest (assuming that $R = 10\%$). With $1100 less for the second period, the household can decrease next period's spending, Pc_2, by this amount to keep the final asset position, b_2, intact. Therefore, the increase in today's spending by $1000 balances against a decrease in next period's spending by $1100. More generally, the required decrease in spending for the next period, Pc_2, equals the increase in this period's spending, Pc_1, multiplied by the discount factor, $(1 + R)$.

To study the choices of c_1 and c_2 it is convenient to express everything in real terms by dividing through equation (3.7) by the price level,

P. If we rearrange terms to place those involving consumption on the left side, we get

$$c_1 + c_2/(1+R) = y_1 + y_2/(1+R) + b_0 \cdot (1+R)/P - b_2/[P \cdot (1+R)] \quad \textbf{(3.8)}$$

Note that each term in equation (3.8) is in real terms. For example, y_1 is period 1's real income from the commodity market, in the sense of indicating the number of commodity units that someone can buy during period 1 with the dollar income of Py_1.

Suppose that we fix the total of the items on the right side of equation (3.8) at some amount, which we can call x. So we can think of fixing the starting real value of bonds, $b_0 \cdot (1+R)/P$, the real present value of bonds carried over to period 3, $b_2/P \cdot (1+R)$, and the total present value of real income from the commodity market, $y_1 + y_2 /(1+R)$. Then we can rewrite equation (3.8) as

$$c_1 + c_2/(1+R) = x \qquad\qquad\qquad\qquad\qquad \textbf{(3.9)}$$

where $x = b_0 \cdot (1+R)/P - b_2/[P \cdot (1+R)] + y_1 + y_2/(1+R)$. Equation (3.9) makes clear that for a given quantity x, a household can change today's consumption, c_1, by making the appropriate adjustment in next period's consumption, c_2.

The straight line in Figure 3.1 shows the possibilities. If the household consumes nothing in the second period, so that $c_2 = 0$ (which would probably cause starvation and therefore be undesirable), then equation (3.9) says that today's consumption, c_1, equals x. Hence, the line in the figure intersects the horizontal axis at this point. Alternatively, if the household consumes nothing today, so that $c_1 = 0$, then the real present value of next period's consumption, $c_2/(1+R)$, equals x. In this case, next period's consumption is given by $c_2 = x \cdot (1+R)$. Therefore, the line in the figure intersects the vertical axis at this point.

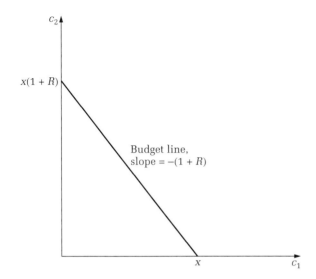

FIGURE 3.1

THE POSSIBILITIES FOR CONSUMING NOW VERSUS LATER

The budget line with slope $-(1 + R)$ shows the attainable combinations of consumption levels, c_1 and c_2. Along this line, the total real present value of expenditures over the two periods equals the fixed amount x.

The straight line in Figure 3.1 connects the value x on the horizontal axis to the value $x \cdot (1 + R)$ on the vertical. This **budget line** shows all the combinations of consumptions, c_1 and c_2, that satisfy the household's budget condition from equation (3.9). The important point is that the budget line shows the attainable pairs of consumption, c_1 and c_2, for a given real present value of spending over the two periods.

The slope of the budget line in Figure 3.1 is $-(1 + R)$. (The magnitude of the slope is the ratio of the vertical intercept, $x \cdot [1 + R]$, to the horizontal, x.) Along this line, a decrease by 1 unit in today's real spending, c_1, is matched by an increase of $(1 + R)$ units in next period's real spending, c_2. To put it another way, the interest rate R is the premium in future consumption for saving today rather than consuming.

So far, the analysis describes a household's opportunities for consuming in one period versus another. But we have not yet studied people's preferences for consumption at different dates. When we combine the opportunities with the preferences, we shall determine the actual choices of consumption over time. Thus, we now turn our attention to these preferences.

PREFERENCES FOR CONSUMING NOW VERSUS LATER

In Chapter 2 we derived indifference curves for consumption and work in each period. Now we want to think about choices over time; specifically, about consumption in period 1 versus consumption in period 2 and about work in period 1 versus work in period 2. To begin, suppose that the two work efforts, l_1 and l_2, are given. Then we want to construct indifference curves to show the household's attitude toward different combinations of the two consumption levels, c_1 and c_2. Figure 3.2 shows such a curve. For high levels of c_1 relative to c_2, such as at point A in the figure, a household is more interested in next period's consumption than this period's. Hence, a small increase in c_2 makes up for the loss of a unit of c_1. Thus, the curve in the figure has a relatively flat slope at point A. Similarly, the curve has a steep slope when c_1 is relatively low, as at point B in the figure. At any point, the slope of the indifference curve reveals the amount of next period's consumption needed to make up for the loss of a unit of current consumption.

As in Chapter 2, we can define a family of indifference curves, each applying to a different level of utility. Figure 3.3 shows three of these curves, labeled by their levels of total utility, where $U^1 < U^2 < U^3$.

CHOOSING CONSUMPTION OVER TWO PERIODS

The budget line in Figure 3.1 describes how households can use the credit market to shift between consumption now and consumption in

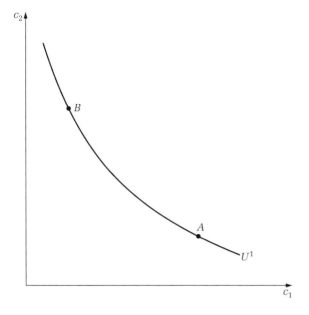

FIGURE 3.2

AN INDIFFERENCE CURVE FOR CONSUMPTION NOW VERSUS CONSUMPTION NEXT PERIOD

The household is equally happy with any combination of consumptions, c_1 and c_2, that lie along the curve. Today's consumption is high relative to next period's at point A and low relative to next period's at point B. Hence, the curve is steeper at point B than at point A.

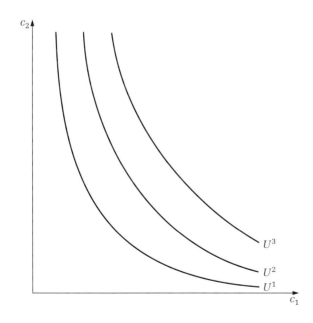

FIGURE 3.3

A FAMILY OF INDIFFERENCE CURVES FOR CONSUMPTION NOW VERSUS CONSUMPTION NEXT PERIOD

Along each curve, the level of utility is constant. Utility increases as the household moves from the curve labeled U^1 to that labeled U^2, and so on.

FIGURE 3.4

CHOOSING CONSUMPTION TODAY AND NEXT PERIOD

The choice of consumption levels, c_1^* and c_2^*, occurs at the tangency between the budget line and an indifference curve.

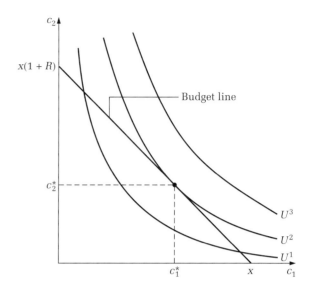

the next period. The family of indifference curves shown in Figure 3.3 describes people's willingness to exchange consumption now for consumption in the next period. If we combine the market opportunities from Figure 3.1 with the indifference map from Figure 3.3, we can determine the choices of consumption over the two periods.[4]

Figure 3.4 combines the budget line from Figure 3.1 with the indifference curves shown in Figure 3.3. Notice that the household moves along the budget line to reach the highest possible indifference curve. This occurs at the point of tangency, shown in the figure, at which the slope of the budget line equals the slope of an indifference curve. We label the corresponding levels of consumption for the two periods as c_1^* and c_2^*.

Recall that the slope of an indifference curve measures the bonus in next period's consumption needed to compensate for the loss of a unit of this period's consumption. In contrast, the slope of the budget line is $-(1 + R)$, which determines the premium, R, for saving more. At the point of tangency shown in Figure 3.4 the premium from saving more just balances the willingness to defer consumption. For this reason, any choice along the budget line other than the point (c_1^*, c_2^*) leads to lower utility. This result is clear geometrically from Figure 3.4.

[4] *This method comes from Irving Fisher (1930, especially Chap. 10). Interestingly, Fisher—who did his main work at Yale University—is one of the few macroeconomists who is popular today at both Yale and Chicago.*

To sum up, we combined people's opportunities (the budget line) with their preferences (the indifference curves) to determine the choices of consumption over two periods. These choices determined how much people save today. We can use this analysis to see how the time pattern of consumption and saving changes when there are shifts in the interest rate or other variables. The effects of changes in the interest rate turn out to be especially important for our subsequent macroeconomic analysis.

WEALTH AND SUBSTITUTION EFFECTS

As in Chapter 2, we can use the notions of wealth and substitution effects to analyze people's choices. In the present setting, wealth effects relate to the quantity previously denoted as x, which is the total present value of real consumption expenditures for periods 1 and 2. The important substitution variable for consuming now versus later, or for how much to save, is the interest rate, R.

WEALTH EFFECTS ON CONSUMPTION

Before, we found that parallel shifts of the production function implied pure wealth effects. These wealth effects show up here as shifts in the total real present value of expenditures, x, which is given by

$$x = c_1 + c_2/(1 + R) = y_1 + y_2/(1 + R) + b_0 \cdot (1 + R)/P - b_2/[P \cdot (1 + R)]$$

(3.10)

Also, recall that the amounts of real income from the commodity market come from the production function as $y_1 = f(l_1)$ and $y_2 = f(l_2)$.

Assume that the production function shifts upward for periods 1 and 2. Think of parallel shifts that do not change the schedule for labor's marginal product. Assuming for the moment that work efforts, l_1 and

FIGURE 3.5

WEALTH EFFECTS ON CONSUMPTION

The total real present value of consumption expenditures for periods 1 and 2 rises from x to x'. Consumption increases from c_1^* to $(c_1^*)'$ in period 1 and from c_2^* to $(c_2^*)'$ in period 2.

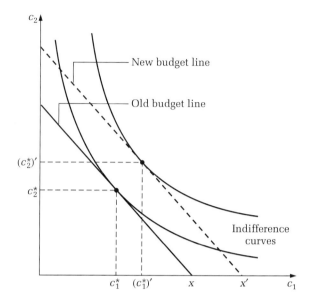

l_2, do not change, there are increases in the amounts of real income, y_1 and y_2. Now suppose that we hold constant the initial and final stocks of bonds, b_0 and b_2. Then the increases in y_1 and y_2 raise the total real present value of spending, x, from equation (3.10).

Figure 3.5 shows that the increase in the total real present value of spending generates a parallel outward shift of the budget line. (The slope stays the same because the interest rate does not change.) The new budget line allows the household to reach a higher indifference curve than before. Note that the new point of tangency between the budget line and an indifference curve occurs at higher levels of consumption for each period. Hence, the wealth effect is positive for c_1 and c_2—or, equivalently, c_1 and c_2 are both superior goods.

THE INTEREST RATE AND INTERTEMPORAL SUBSTITUTION

If the interest rate is R, each household faces the budget line that we label as "old" in Figure 3.6. Given the total real present value of spending

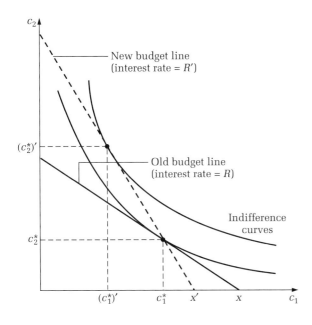

c_2

New budget line
(interest rate = R')

$(c_2^*)'$

Old budget line
(interest rate = R)

Indifference
curves

c_2^*

$(c_1^*)'$ c_1^* x' x c_1

FIGURE 3.6

EFFECT ON CONSUMPTION FROM AN INCREASE IN THE INTEREST RATE

When the interest rate is R on the old budget line, the household chooses the consumption pair (c_1^*, c_2^*). If the interest rate rises to R' on the new budget line, then the household opts for the pair $[(c_1^*)', (c_2^*)']$. Notice that the increase in the interest rate motivates people to choose a higher ratio of consumption next period to consumption this period.

for periods 1 and 2, the household selects the consumption pair (c_1^*, c_2^*). If the interest rate rises to R', then the new budget line is steeper than the old one. There are, however, many places that we could draw this new line in Figure 3.6. For present purposes, we want to isolate the substitution effect from a higher interest rate. If we held fixed the overall real present value of spending, x, then the new budget line would start from the value x on the horizontal axis but otherwise would lie to the right of the old budget line. But then the new budget line would allow the household to consume the same amount today, c_1^*, and more next period. Because wealth increases in this case, the shift would not be a pure substitution effect.

We can approximate a pure substitution effect by rotating the budget line around the point at which the household initially chose the levels of consumption. When drawn this way, the new budget line shown in Figure 3.6 intersects the old one at the point (c_1^*, c_2^*); the household therefore retains the option to buy this initial pair of consumptions. But

Empirical Evidence on Intertemporal Substitution of Consumption

Our theoretical analysis predicts that a higher interest rate motivates people to defer consumption from the present to the future. An empirical study by David Runkle (1991) isolated this effect by examining the behavior of food consumption from 1973 to 1982 for 1100 U.S. households. (The data come from the Panel Study on Income Dynamics [PSID], which is constructed at the University of Michigan.) Runkle found that an increase in the annual interest rate by one percentage point raised the typical family's growth rate of consumption by about one-half percentage point per year. (Runkle's estimates adjust the interest rate for inflation and taxes in ways that we shall explore in Chapters 7 and 13, respectively.) Economists have, however, been less successful at finding these types of effects in aggregate consumption data. For a discussion of this evidence, see Robert Hall (1989).

the household cannot increase either quantity without giving up some of the other.

Although the new budget line passes through the point (c_1^*, c_2^*) in Figure 3.6, the line is not tangent to an indifference curve at this point. Because the new budget line is steeper than the indifference curve, the premium to saving more, R', exceeds the amount needed to motivate more saving. It follows that the household would raise saving, that is, c_1 falls and c_2 rises. The new choices, labeled $[(c_1^*)', (c_2^*)']$ in the figure, correspond to the tangency between the new budget line and an indifference curve.[5] The important point is that the increase in the interest rate motivates people to raise future consumption, c_2, relative to current consumption, c_1. Equivalently, the rise in the interest rate induces households to save a larger fraction of current income.

[5] *Note that the household reaches a higher indifference curve. Hence, wealth increases, even though we rotated the budget line around the point at which the household initially chose consumption, (c_1^*, c_2^*). But it turns out that this wealth effect becomes negligible, relative to the substitution effect, when we look at smaller and smaller changes in the interest rate. So at least for small changes, we can neglect the wealth effect as a satisfactory approximation.*

Recall that the total real present value of spending over periods 1 and 2 is $c_1 + c_2/(1+R)$. Note again that we divide c_2 by the discount factor, $(1+R)$, before adding it to c_1. A rise in R lowers the cost of next period's consumption relative to that of current consumption because a person can obtain more units of consumption next period for each unit of current consumption forgone. It is this change in relative costs that motivates people to substitute future goods, c_2, for current ones, c_1. Economists call this mechanism an **intertemporal-substitution effect**.

CHOOSING WORK EFFORT AT DIFFERENT DATES

In Chapter 2 we studied the choice of work and consumption for a single period. There we stressed substitution effects from changes in the schedule for labor's marginal product. Also, we explored wealth effects from shifts in the position of the production function.

In this chapter, we have examined an individual's choices of consumption over time. But so far we have not considered the choices of work effort. If we combine the previous analysis of work and consumption with the present analysis of consumption over time, we shall understand how households choose work effort over time.

WEALTH EFFECTS ON WORK EFFORT

We can write the household's budget constraint for two periods as

$$f(l_1) + f(l_2)/(1+R) + b_0 \cdot (1+R)/P$$
$$= c_1 + c_2/(1+R) + b_2/[P \cdot (1+R)]$$

(3.11)

Note the substitutions $y_1 = f(l_1)$ and $y_2 = f(l_2)$ in the expression for the real sources of funds on the left side. Suppose that the production function shifts up in a parallel fashion for periods 1 and 2. For given amounts of work, l_1 and l_2, the real sources of funds increase on the left side of equation (3.11). As we saw before, households respond by raising c_1 and c_2.

Recall from Chapter 2 that people also react to more wealth by taking more leisure. Hence, the levels of work, l_1 and l_2, tend to decline rather than stay fixed. Macroeconomists usually stress the positive wealth effect on consumption but neglect the effect on leisure. However, the evidence on hours of work, which we reviewed in Chapter 2, indicates that this effect on leisure is important. For example, at early stages of economic development, the wealth effect is strong enough that average hours worked tend to diminish as an economy develops.

THE INTEREST RATE AND CHOICES OF WORK EFFORT

Figure 3.6 shows that an increase in the interest rate motivates households to reduce current consumption, c_1, and raise next period's consumption, c_2. Notice from the right side of equation (3.11) that an increase in R makes next period's consumption, c_2, cheaper relative to this period's, c_1. That is why people substitute toward c_2 and away from c_1 when R rises. But the same argument holds for leisure in the two periods. If someone takes leisure in period 2, he or she discounts the loss in output, $f(l_2)$, by the factor $(1 + R)$. Therefore, when R rises, the leisure from period 2 becomes cheaper relative to that in period 1. The conclusion is that an increase in the interest rate motivates people to substitute toward next period's leisure and away from this period's. Equivalently, this period's work, l_1, rises relative to next period's, l_2. Note also that the increase in l_1 reinforces the effect of the decrease in c_1 in raising current saving.

Overall, an increase in the interest rate has two types of inter-temporal-substitution effects. First, today's consumption, c_1, declines relative to next period's, c_2. Second, today's work, l_1, rises relative to next period's, l_2. Both effects—the reduction in current spending and the increase in current income—show up as an increase in current saving.

Empirical Evidence on Intertemporal Substitution of Work Effort

Macroeconomists typically stress the effect on saving that results from intertemporal substitution of consumption but neglect the effect from changes in work effort. There is, however, some evidence that intertemporal substitution of work effort is also important. George Alogoskoufis (1987b) found for U.S. data from 1948 to 1982 that an increase in the annual interest rate by one percentage point lowered the growth rate of work by about 0.6 percentage point per year. For British data from 1950 to 1982, the corresponding estimate (Alogoskoufis, 1987a) was about 0.2.

These results applied if aggregate work effort was measured by the total number of employees. If work effort was measured instead as hours worked per person, then the results were not statistically significant. Thus, these findings suggest that intertemporal substitution of work effort is more important for the number of workers than for hours worked per person. Thomas MaCurdy (1981) reports additional evidence that supports the importance of intertemporal substitution of work effort.

Thus, both responses reflect the positive response of an individual's desired saving to the return from saving, which is the interest rate.

BUDGET CONSTRAINTS OVER MANY PERIODS

Thus far, we have examined the behavior of households over two periods. To carry out this analysis, we had to hold fixed the amount of bonds that someone carries over to later periods. This amount is, in fact, not a given, because it depends on people's plans for consuming and earning income in the future. We now make this connection explicit by dealing with households' plans over many periods.

BUDGET CONSTRAINTS FOR ANY NUMBER OF PERIODS

Start with the two-period budget constraint from equation (3.7):

$$Py_1 + Py_2/(1+R) + b_0 \cdot (1+R) = Pc_1 + Pc_2/(1+R) + b_2/(1+R)$$

The final stock of bonds from the second period, b_2, determines the initial stock for period 3. Specifically, for period 3 the budget constraint is

$$Py_3 + b_2 \cdot (1+R) = Pc_3 + b_3$$

We can use this equation to solve out for the stock of bonds, b_2, and substitute the result into the two-period budget constraint to get the three-period budget constraint:

$$Py_1 + Py_2/(1+R) + Py_3/(1+R)^2 + b_0 \cdot (1+R)$$

$$= Pc_1 + Pc_2/(1+R) + Pc_3/(1+R)^2 + b_3/(1+R)^2$$

(3.12)

By now we see how to construct a budget constraint for any number of periods. The budget constraint for j periods is

$$Py_1 + Py_2/(1+R) + Py_3/(1+R)^2 + \cdots + Py_j/(1+R)^{j-1} + b_0 \cdot (1+R)$$

$$= Pc_1 + Pc_2/(1+R) + Pc_3/(1+R)^2 + \cdots + Pc_j/(1+R)^{j-1}$$

(3.13)

$$+ b_j/(1+R)^{j-1}$$

Notice that the previous examples of budget constraints are special cases of equation (3.13). For $j = 2$ we get the two-period budget constraint in equation (3.7) and for $j = 3$ we get the three-period constraint in equation (3.12).

Notice two things about the budget constraint for j periods in equation (3.13). First, the right side involves the stock of bonds, b_j, held at the end of period j. Second, we calculate the present value of income or expense for any period t by dividing by the factor $(1+R)^{t-1}$. This factor represents the accumulation of interest between period 1 and period t, that is, over $t - 1$ periods.

THE HOUSEHOLD'S PLANNING HORIZON

Suppose that a household is choosing today's consumption and work effort, c_1 and l_1. Typically, households make these choices in the context of a long-term plan that considers future levels of consumption and income. These future values relate to the current choices through the j-period budget constraint shown in equation (3.13). We can refer to the number j as the household's **planning horizon**.

How long is the horizon that people consider in making current decisions? Because we are dealing with households that have access to a credit market, a long planning horizon is appropriate. By borrowing or lending, people can effectively use future income to finance current spending, or current income to pay for future spending. When expressed as a present value, prospective incomes and expenses from the distant future are as pertinent for current decisions as are today's incomes and expenses.

Economists often assume that the planning horizon is long but finite. For example, in a class of theories called **life-cycle models**,[6] the horizon, j, represents an individual's expected remaining lifetime. If people do not care about things that occur after their death, then they have no reason to carry assets beyond period j. Accordingly, they set to zero the final asset stock, b_j, which appears on the right side of the budget constraint in equation (3.13). (We also have to rule out the possibility of dying in debt, which would correspond to $b_j < 0$.)

Researchers who use life-cycle models usually assume that the working span, which is the interval for which $l_t > 0$, is shorter than the length of life. In this case, people have retirement periods during which consumption must be financed either from savings accumulated during working years or from transfer payments. These transfers could come from the government (**social security**) or from children.

[6] *See Franco Modigliani and Richard Brumberg (1954) and Albert Ando and Franco Modigliani (1963).*

It is straightforward to define the anticipated lifetime—and thereby the finite planning horizon—for an isolated individual who has no concern for descendants. The appropriate horizon is, however, not obvious for a family in which the parents care about their children. (The children may also care about their parents!) In this context, the applicable horizon extends beyond someone's expected lifetime, and people would give some weight to the expected future incomes and expenses of their children. Further, since children care about the welfare of their children—should they have any—and so on for each subsequent generation, there is no clear point at which to terminate the planning period. Of course, this argument does not imply that anticipated incomes and expenses for the distant future count as much as those for a few years off. But by using present values, we already place a large discount on incomes and expenses from the distant future.

Instead of imposing a finite horizon, we can think of the household's plan as having an **infinite horizon**. There are two good reasons for proceeding in this way:

— First, if we think of the typical person as part of a family that has concerns about the members of future generations—children, grandchildren, and so on—into the indefinite future, then this setup is the correct one: it would be inappropriate to identify the horizon with the typical person's expected lifetime.

— Second, although it is not obvious at this point, an infinite horizon is the easiest framework to use.

BUDGET CONSTRAINTS FOR AN INFINITE HORIZON

When the planning horizon is infinite, the budget constraint includes the present values of incomes and expenses for the indefinite future. Then, using equation (3.13), we have

$$Py_1 + Py_2/(1 + R) + Py_3/(1 + R)^2 + \cdots + b_0 \cdot (1 + R)$$
$$= Pc_1 + Pc_2/(1 + R) + Pc_3/(1 + R)^2 + \cdots$$

(3.14)

We no longer terminate the sums for incomes and expenses at some finite date, j, as we did in equation (3.13). Notice also that the final stock of bonds, b_j, does not appear in the budget constraint. In effect, there is no "final" period to consider here.

For most purposes, we prefer to deal with the budget constraint in real terms. If we divide through equation (3.14) by the price level, P, then we get

$$y_1 + y_2/(1 + R) + y_3/(1 + R)^2 + \cdots + b_0(1 + R)/P$$
$$= c_1 + c_2/(1 + R) + c_3/(1 + R)^2 + \cdots$$

(3.15)

Equation 3.15 says that the present value of real income from sales to the commodity market over an infinite horizon, plus the real value of the receipts from the initial stock of bonds, equals the present value of real consumption expenditure over an infinite horizon. We shall use this form of the budget constraint when studying households' choices over many periods.

CHOICES OVER MANY PERIODS

Before, we discussed the choices of consumption over two periods, c_1 and c_2. Now we consider the entire path of consumption, c_1, c_2, c_3, ... In some of our previous discussion, we thought about a given total present value of real spending over two periods, $x = c_1 + c_2/(1 + R)$. Here we proceed analogously by looking at the total present value of real spending over an infinite horizon. Using the budget constraint in equation (3.15), we have

$$x = c_1 + c_2/(1 + R) + c_3/(1 + R)^2 + \cdots$$
$$= y_1 + y_2/(1 + R) + y_3/(1 + R)^2 + \cdots + b_0 \cdot (1 + R)/p$$

(3.16)

THE INTEREST RATE AND INTERTEMPORAL SUBSTITUTION

Given the total present value of real spending over an infinite horizon, a household can still substitute between c_1 and c_2. Just as before, for each unit of c_1 forgone, a household can obtain $(1 + R)$ additional units of c_2. But there is nothing special about periods 1 and 2. People can substitute in a similar manner between c_2 and c_3, c_3 and c_4, and so on. In general, if someone gives up 1 unit of c_t, the credit market allows him or her to raise c_{t+1} by $(1 + R)$ units.

Consider an increase in the interest rate, R. We know from before that this change motivates people to reduce c_1 relative to c_2. They do so because the higher interest rate makes today's consumption more expensive relative to the next period's. But the same reasoning applies to any pair of consumptions, c_t and c_{t+1}. An increase in R lowers c_t relative to c_{t+1}.

When we allow for variable work effort, we find that changes in the interest rate also have intertemporal-substitution effects on work and leisure. The generalization from the two-period model is that an increase in R motivates people to take less leisure in one period relative to that in the next period. That is, l_t rises relative to l_{t+1}.

Finally, note that a decrease in c_1 and an increase in l_1 both imply an increase in current saving. Thus, as in the two-period case, a higher interest rate motivates people to save more.

WEALTH EFFECTS

As before, wealth effects involve changes in the total present value of real spending, x, which is given in equation (3.16). Remember that the aggregate value of the initial stock of bonds, B_0, is zero. Therefore, if we think about the typical or average household, for which $b_0 = 0$, then wealth effects will arise only from changes in the present value of real income from the commodity market, $y_1 + y_2/(1 + R) + \ldots$. For a given amount of work effort in each period, these changes must involve shifts in the production function.

Permanent Shifts of the Production Function

Consider first the case in which the production function, $f(l_t)$, shifts upward in a parallel fashion for all periods. As examples, we can think of discoveries of new technologies or natural resources, that is, changes that create permanent improvements in productive capacity. Given each period's amount of work, l_t, each period's level of output, y_t, rises. Hence, the total real present value of spending, x, increases in equation (3.16).

As a generalization of the results for two periods, we find that the increase in the present value of real spending, x, leads to increases in consumption, c_t, for each period. Consumption in any period is a superior good, and the wealth effect is positive. Similarly, we find that more wealth leads to more leisure in each period. Therefore, an increase in wealth implies less work effort, l_t, at each date.

The Marginal Propensities to Consume and Save

Suppose that real income, y_t, rises by one unit in each period. One possibility is that consumption, c_t, also increases by one unit in each period. (This response would satisfy the budget constraint in equation [3.16].) If someone responds in this way, economists say that his or her **marginal propensity to consume**—defined as the change in consumption during a period relative to the change in that period's income—is one. Since consumption and income change by equal amounts in all periods, there is no change in saving for any period. In other words, the **marginal propensity to save**—defined as the change in saving for a period relative to the change in income for that period—is zero.

If income, y_t, changes by one unit in each period, as before, but a household increases current consumption, c_1, by less than one unit, then the current marginal propensity to consume is less than one. Correspondingly, the current marginal propensity to save is positive. Households must, however, use this extra saving to expand some future level of consumption. Hence there must be at least one subsequent period during which consumption, c_t, rises by even more than one unit.

Suppose that a household planned initially for a constant amount of consumption. Then the increase in period t's consumption, c_t, by more than one unit means that this consumption increases relative to today's, c_1. That is, consumption shifts away from the present and toward the future. We know that this type of shift is appropriate if the interest rate increases. But since the interest rate does not change here, the household would tend to maintain the relative amounts of consumption at different dates. For the case at hand, this balance results only if the household increases consumption in every period by one unit. Hence, if the improvement in the production function is permanent, then we predict that the marginal propensity to consume would be close to one. Correspondingly, the marginal propensity to save would be near zero.

Temporary Shifts of the Production Function

Suppose now that the parallel upward shift of the production function lasts only for the current period. So instead of discoveries of new technologies or resources, we can think of the effects of weather, temporary changes in the supply of raw materials, strikes, and so on.

If work efforts do not change, then the increase in real income occurs only in the current period. Households would like to spread this extra income over consumption in all periods. But to raise future consumption, households now have to raise current saving. Hence, current consumption, c_1, rises by much less than the increase in current real income, y_1. In other words, if the improvement of the production function is temporary, then the marginal propensity to consume is small, and the marginal propensity to save is positive and nearly equal to one.

Our findings about permanent and temporary changes of the production function correspond to Milton Friedman's (1957, Chaps. 2, 3) concept of **permanent income**. The general idea is that consumption depends on a long-term average of incomes—called permanent income—rather than just current income. If the change in income is temporary, then permanent income, and hence consumption, rise relatively little. Therefore, as in our discussion, the marginal propensity to consume out of temporary income is small.

Empirical Evidence on the Marginal Propensity to Consume

Empirical research provides strong evidence that the marginal propensity to consume out of permanent changes in income is much greater than that for temporary changes. Some of the clearest evidence comes from special circumstances in which there are windfalls of income, which people surely regard as temporary. One example is the receipt by Israeli citizens of lump-sum, nonrecurring restitution payments from Germany in 1957–58 (see Mordechai Kreinin, 1961, and Michael Landsberger, 1970). The payments were large, with a value that roughly equaled the average family's annual income. For this case, the data indicate that the typical family's consumption expenditure during the year of the windfall rose by no more than 20% of the amount received. Further, the measure of consumer spending includes purchases of consumer durables. Because these goods last for many years, we should view these purchases as partly saving rather than consumption. Therefore, the true marginal propensity to consume out of the windfall was much less than 20%.

Another example is the payment in 1950 to U.S. World War II veterans of an unanticipated, one-time life insurance dividend of about $175. At the time, this amount represented about 4% of the average family's annual income. In this case, the statistical estimates indicate that consumption rose by 30 to 40% of the windfall (see Roger Bird and Ronald Bodkin, 1965). But since the data again include purchases of consumer durables, the true marginal propensity to consume would be much lower than 30%.

More generally, statistical studies of consumer behavior indicate that the marginal propensity to consume out of permanent changes in income is large and not much different from one. In contrast, the marginal propensity to consume out of temporary income is only about 20 to 30% (see Robert Hall, 1989). Although this response to temporary changes is somewhat greater than that predicted by our theory, the important point for our analysis is that the response of consumer demand to permanent changes in income is much larger than that to temporary changes.

Wealth Effects from Changes in the Interest Rate

Thus far, we have looked only at intertemporal-substitution effects from changes in the interest rate. Now let's see whether a change in the interest rate leads to a wealth effect.

We can test for the effect on wealth by using the budget constraint, which is again

$$y_1 + y_2/(1+R) + \cdots + b_0 \cdot (1+R)/P = c_1 + c_2/(1+R) + \cdots$$

Abstract from the term that involves the initial stock of bonds, $b_0 \cdot (1+R)/P$, because this term will equal zero when we sum up over all households.

Suppose that we hypothetically hold fixed the paths of real incomes, $y_1, y_2, \ldots$, and expenditures, $c_1, c_2, \ldots$. Then consider the separate effects of an increase in R on the left and right sides of the budget constraint. The rise in R reduces the present values of real income, $y_1 + y_2/(1+R) + \ldots$, and real spending, $c_1 + c_2/(1+R) \ldots$. But the important question is which sum falls by the greater amount. If the present value of real spending falls by more, then the given path of real income would be sufficient to continue purchasing these goods and still have something left over. Then the household could increase consumption for some periods without necessarily decreasing it for others. Hence, wealth increases. The opposite conclusion applies if the present value of real spending falls by less than that of real income.

The budget constraint indicates that the terms that decline most with the rise in R are those that are most distant into the future. That is, the discount factor for period t is $1/(1+R)^{t-1}$, which is more sensitive to changes in R the higher the value of t. When R rises, the present value of real spending declines by more than that of real income if the path of spending is more heavily concentrated in the future than is the path of income. For the case in which the initial bonds, b_0, equal zero, this property applies for someone who has positive saving in most of the earlier years and negative saving in most of the later years. In other words, people who plan usually to be lenders experience an increase in wealth when the interest rate rises. Conversely, those who plan usually to be borrowers have a decline in wealth.

Although either situation may hold for an individual, neither case can apply for the average person. Because the aggregate stock of bonds is always zero in our model, we know that the average household is neither typically a lender nor typically a borrower. Therefore, in the aggregate, the wealth effect from a change in the interest rate is nil.[7] This result is important. It says that for aggregate purposes we can neglect wealth effects from changes in the interest rate, and we should focus on the intertemporal-substitution effects from these changes.

SHIFTS IN THE SCHEDULE FOR LABOR'S MARGINAL PRODUCT

A rise in the schedule for labor's marginal product typically accompanies an improvement in the production function. As we know, a higher schedule for labor's marginal product motivates people to work more. If the change is the same for each period, then work, and hence real income, rise by roughly equal amounts in each period. In this case the marginal propensity to consume would be close to one, and each period's consumption would increase by roughly the same amount as income. In other words, saving would not change.

A permanent improvement in labor's productivity means that consumption becomes cheaper relative to leisure at each date. Therefore, people work and consume more in every period. Because there are no changes in the relative costs of consumption or leisure for different periods, the responses in work and consumption tend to be the same in each period; hence, there are no effects on saving.

We should be careful to distinguish the substitution between consumption and leisure from the intertemporal-substitution effect. The intertemporal effect involves the cost of taking consumption or leisure

[7] *For further discussion of this result, see Martin J. Bailey (1971, pp. 106–108).*

in one period rather than another. For example, an increase in the interest rate motivates people to reduce today's consumption and leisure relative to future consumption and leisure. In contrast, the schedule for labor's marginal product determines the relative cost of consumption and leisure at a point in time. Therefore, a shift in this schedule induces changes in the relative amounts of consumption and leisure. But if the change in labor's productivity is permanent, then there are no intertemporal-substitution effects.

The results are different if the change in productivity is temporary. As an example, think of a gold rush or other temporary profit opportunity, which makes the reward for today's work effort unusually high. We can represent this case by shifting the schedule for labor's marginal product only for the current period. Then the new element is that today's leisure becomes more expensive relative to future leisure or consumption. Therefore, people have an incentive to expand today's work to increase future consumption and leisure. Thus, a temporary improvement of productivity stimulates saving: today's output rises by more than today's consumption.

SUMMARY

We introduced a commodity market on which people buy and sell goods at the price P. The existence of this market promotes economic efficiency because it allows producers to specialize.

We also introduced a credit market on which people borrow and lend at the interest rate R. By using this market, individuals can choose a time pattern for consumption that differs from that for income.

We began with a budget constraint over two periods but then extended the analysis to any number of periods. For most purposes, we can think of the behavior of households over an infinite horizon. We motivated the infinite planning period by thinking about a family in which parents care about their children, who care about their children, and so on.

An increase in the interest rate motivates households to shift away from consumption over the near term and toward that in the future. The opposite responses apply to work effort. These intertemporal-substitution effects mean that a higher interest rate motivates people to save more.

Improvements in the production function have wealth effects that are positive on consumption and negative on work for each period. If the shift is permanent, then the marginal propensity to consume is near one, and the marginal propensity to save is near zero. If the shift is temporary, then the marginal propensity to consume is small, and the marginal propensity to save is almost one. We also showed that a change in the interest rate has no aggregate wealth effect.

A permanent upward shift in the schedule for labor's marginal product raises work and consumption in each period but does not affect saving. In contrast, a temporary upward shift in the schedule raises current output by more than current consumption and thereby raises saving.

IMPORTANT TERMS AND CONCEPTS

barter Direct exchange of one good for another, without the use of money.

bond A contract that gives the holder (lender) a claim to a specified stream of payments from the issuer (borrower).

budget line A graph of the combinations of consumptions over two periods that satisfy the two-period budget constraint.

currency Non-interest-bearing paper money issued by the government.

discount factor The relative value of a dollar in different periods of time; for example, between one period and the next, the nominal discount factor is one plus the nominal interest rate.

double coincidence of wants   The situation required for barter to take place, in which the type and quantity of goods offered by one trader match those sought by the other trader.

infinite horizon   The household's planning horizon when plans extend into the indefinite future; a concept used in models that stress the role of intergenerational transfers.

intertemporal-substitution effect   The effect on current consumption (leisure) when the cost of future consumption (leisure) changes relative to that of current consumption (leisure).

life-cycle model   The theory of the choices of consumption and leisure that are made when the planning horizon is equal to the individual's expected remaining lifetime; it predicts that an individual will build up savings during working years and exhaust them during retirement years.

marginal propensity to consume   The effect of a change in income on consumption demand.

marginal propensity to save   The effect of a change in income on desired saving.

nominal   Measured in current dollar magnitudes; valued at current dollar prices; unadjusted for changes in the general price level.

perfect competition   The assumption that the individuals who participate in a market view themselves as sufficiently small that they can buy or sell any amount without affecting the established price.

permanent income   The hypothetical amount of real income that, when received constantly throughout the individual's planning horizon, has the same real present value as the actual flow of income; the per-period equivalent of the total present value of income. A temporary change in income entails a less than equivalent change in permanent income.

planning horizon The number of future periods that enter the household's budget constraint; the length of time for which the household plans consumption and leisure choices.

present value The value of future dollar amounts, after dividing by the discount factor.

principal of bond The amount borrowed, to be repaid at maturity.

real terms Measured in units of commodities; valued at base-year prices; dollar magnitudes that are adjusted for inflation by deflating by a price index.

saving The change in an individual's assets during a period of time.

social security Transfer payments made by government to households through social insurance programs such as old age and survivors' insurance and disability insurance.

QUESTIONS AND PROBLEMS

MAINLY FOR REVIEW

3.1 Why would individuals be interested only in the real value of consumption expenditures, income, and assets such as money and bonds? Would a fall in the dollar amount of consumption spending leave the individual worse off when it is accompanied by an equiproportionate fall in the price level?

3.2 Distinguish clearly between an individual's initial asset position and the change in that position. Which is affected by current consumption and saving decisions? Is an individual who is undertaking negative saving necessarily a borrower in the sense of having a negative position in bonds?

3.3 Derive the two-period budget constraint, and draw a graph of it. Why are there no terms involving money holdings on the side of sources of funds?

3.4 Show how taking a present value involves giving different weights to dollar values in different periods. Why is income in the present more "valuable" than income in the future? Why is consumption in the future "cheaper" than consumption in the present?

3.5 Review the factors that determine an individual's choice of consumption over two periods, c_1 and c_2, and show this choice graphically. Why is the individual best off when the budget line is tangent to an indifference curve?

3.6 What factors determine whether the marginal propensity to consume is less than one or equal to one? Can the marginal propensity to consume be greater than one?

3.7 Review the effects of the following changes on current consumption and work, distinguishing clearly between wealth effects and substitution effects.

a. A permanent parallel shift of the production function.

b. A change in the interest rate.

c. A temporary change in the marginal product of labor.

PROBLEMS FOR DISCUSSION

3.8 Discount Bonds

The one-period bonds in our model pay a single interest payment or "coupon" of $R and a principal of $1. Alternatively, we could consider a one-period discount bond like a U.S. Treasury bill. This type of asset has no coupons but pays a principal of $1 (or, more realistically, $10,000) next period. Let P^B be the dollar price for each unit of discount bonds, where each unit is a claim to $1 next period.

a. Is P^B greater or less than $1?

b. What is the one-period rate of interest on discount bonds?

c. How does the price, P^B, relate to this one-period rate of interest?

d. Suppose that instead of coming due next period, the discount bond comes due (matures) two periods from now. What is the interest rate *per period* on this bond? How do the results generalize if the bond matures j periods from now?

3.9 Financial Intermediaries

Consider a financial intermediary, such as a bank or savings and loan association, that enters the credit market. This intermediary borrows from some people and lends the proceeds to others. (The loan to a bank from its customers often takes the form of a *deposit*.)

a. How does the existence of intermediaries affect the result that the aggregate amount of loans is zero?

b. What interest rate would the intermediary charge to its borrowers and pay to its lenders? Why must there be some spread between these two rates?

c. Can you give some reasons to explain why intermediaries might be useful?

3.10 Wealth Effects

Consider the household's budget constraint in real terms over an infinite horizon, $y_1 + y_2/(1 + R) + \cdots + b_0 \cdot (1 + R)/P = c_1 + c_2/(1 + R) + \ldots$. Using this condition, evaluate the wealth effect of the following:

a. An increase in the price level, P, for a household that has a positive value of initial bonds, b_0. (The result has implications for the effects of unexpected price changes on the wealth of nominal creditors and nominal debtors.)

b. An increase in the interest rate, R, for a household that has $b_0 = 0$ and $c_t = y_t$ in each period.

c. An increase in the interest rate, R, for a household that has $b_0 = 0$, $c_t > y_t$ for $t > T$, and $c_t < y_t$ for $t < T$, where T is some date in the future.

3.11 Short-Term and Long-Term Interest Rates

Assume that $1 worth of one-period bonds issued at the end of period 0 pays out $(1 + R_1)$ during period 1, that is, the principal of $1 plus the interest payment of R_1. Assume that $1 worth of one-period bonds issued at the end of period 1 will pay out $(1 + R_2)$ during period 2. Suppose that people also market a two-period bond at the end of period 0. One dollar's worth of this asset pays out $(1 + 2R)$ during period 2. Lenders from date 0 to date 2 have the option of holding a two-period bond or a succession of one-period bonds. Borrowers have a similar choice between negotiating a two-period loan or two successive one-period loans.

a. What must be the relation of R to R_1 and R_2? Explain the answer from the standpoint of borrowers and lenders.

b. If $R_2 > R_1$, what is the relation between R (the current *long-term interest rate*) and R_1 (the current *short-term interest rate*)? The answer is an important result about the *term structure of interest rates*. (Greg Mankiw and Jeff Miron, 1986, studied this relation by looking at assets with three- and six-month maturities. They found that the U.S. data from before 1914 were more in line with the theory than were the data after 1914.)

3.12 The Household's Budget Constraint with a Finite Horizon

Consider the household's budget constraint for j periods from equation (3.13):

$$Py_1 + Py_2/(1 + R) + \cdots + Py_j/(1 + R)^{j-1} + b_0 \cdot (1 + R)$$

$$= Pc_1 + Pc_2/(1 + R) + \cdots + Pc_j/(1 + R)^{j-1} + b_j/(1 + R)^{j-1}$$

Assume that $y_t = 0$ for $t > T_1$, and $c_t = 0$ for $t > T_2$. Here, T_2 might represent the expected lifetime and T_1 the anticipated working span for an individual.

a. Assume that the household uses the planning horizon, $j = T_2$. Why might the household do this? What value would the household select for b_j? What does the j-period budget constraint look like in this case?

b. Discuss the pattern of saving, $b_t - b_{t-1}$, for the "retirement period," where $T_1 < t < T_2$. What can be said about saving for the typical working year, where $0 < t < T_1$? (This result concerns the *life-cycle* motivation for household saving.)

c. Suppose that the government forces people to retire earlier than they would otherwise choose. How would this action affect the choices of work effort, consumption, and desired saving for people who are still working but anticipating an earlier retirement?

d. Given that individuals care about their children (and parents), what difficulties arise in specifying a value for the finite planning horizon, $j = T_2$?

3.13 Permanent Income (optional)

The idea of permanent income is that consumption depends on a long-run measure of income rather than just on current income. Operationally, we can define permanent income to be the hypothetical, constant flow of income that has the same present value as a household's actual sources of funds.

a. Use the budget constraint in equation (3.15) to obtain a formula for permanent income. Explain the various terms in the formula.

b. What is the marginal propensity to consume out of permanent income?

c. If consumption is constant over time, what is the value of permanent income?

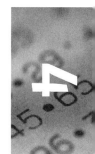

THE DEMAND FOR MONEY

The model contains two forms of financial assets, money and bonds. But so far, we have not analyzed how much money people hold or how these holdings change over time. We therefore carried out the analysis in the previous chapter under the assumption that each household maintained a constant stock of money. Whenever households changed their saving, they altered their holdings of bonds but not their holdings of money.

Now we provide the remaining building block in the model by explaining people's willingness to place part of their assets into money; that is, we explain the demand for money. We do this by setting up a simple model in which money is the medium of exchange and in which people economize on their costs of transacting by holding more money. For the most part, the results that we get from this simple model generalize to more complicated settings in which people hold money. The main point, which applies to the simplified model and to generalized settings, is that the demand for money is a crucial determinant of the price level.

THE NATURE OF A MONETARY ECONOMY

We assume, as mentioned in Chapter 3, that money is the sole medium of exchange in the economy. Trades occur between money and commodities and between money and bonds but not directly between bonds and commodities or between the commodities that different households produce.

We assume, in particular, that the interest-bearing bonds in the model are not money: these paper claims do not function as media of exchange.

There are several reasons for this limitation. First, the government may impose legal restrictions that prevent private parties, such as General Motors, from issuing small-size, interest-bearing notes that could serve conveniently as hand-to-hand currency. Further, the government may enact statutes that reinforce the use of its money. As an example, there is the proclamation that the U.S. dollar is "**legal tender** for all debts public and private."[1] Also, U.S. courts are more willing to enforce contracts that are denominated in U.S. dollars rather than in some other unit. Second, there are costs of establishing one's money as reliable and convenient. These costs include the prevention of counterfeiting, the replacement of worn-out notes, the willingness to convert notes into different denominations and possibly into other assets, and so on. Because of these costs, money would tend to bear interest at a rate lower than bonds. In fact, because of the inconvenience of paying interest on hand-to-hand currency, the interest rate on currency is typically zero.

We can relate our abstract concept of money to conventional measures of the money stock. The theoretical construct corresponds closely to currency held outside commercial banks. At the beginning of 1997, the amount of this currency in the United States was $397 billion, which amounted to 5.1% of the annual nominal gross domestic product (GDP). In other words, people held almost three weeks' worth of the GDP as currency in 1997.

[1] *Notice that this provision does not determine the price at which currency exchanges for goods. If the price level were infinite, what would the legal-tender property mean?*

The term *money* typically refers to a monetary aggregate that is broader than currency. One definition, called **M1**, attempts to classify as money the assets that serve regularly as media of exchange. This concept includes the checkable deposits that people hold at banks and some other financial institutions. The amount of these checkable deposits in the United States at the beginning of 1997 was $683 billion, or 8.9% of annual GDP. Therefore, M1—the sum of currency and checkable deposits—equaled $1080 billion at the beginning of 1997, or 14% of GDP. Put alternatively, M1 amounted to a bit more than seven weeks' worth of the GDP in 1997.

Still broader definitions of money add other kinds of deposits. For example, M2 ($3850 billion at the beginning of 1997) includes retail money-market mutual funds with initial investment less than $50,000, savings and small-denomination time deposits, and repurchase agreements. An even broader aggregate, M3 ($4966 billion at the beginning of 1997), encompasses retail money-market mutual funds with initial investment of $50,000 or more, time deposits in excess of $100,000, overnight and term liabilities issued by depository institutions, and Eurodollar accounts.

Table 4.1 shows data for 1995 on narrowly defined concepts of money for the major developed countries. The ratio of currency to annual GDP ranged from a low of 2% for Finland to a high of 11% for Spain. The definition of M1 is less homogeneous because the decision on which deposits to include and which to exclude is somewhat arbitrary. For instance, in the United States, some interest-bearing deposits at commercial banks are deemed to be checkable and are therefore included in M1, whereas others are excluded. In any event, the ratio of M1 to annual GDP ranged from a low of 16% for Austria to a high of 39% for Norway. (The value of 62% for the United Kingdom refers to M2.) As mentioned, we can readily identify the money in the theoretical model with currency, but the concept does not correspond precisely to broader monetary aggregates, such as M1 or M2. When we expand the theoretical framework (in Chapter 17) to incorporate

THE DEMAND FOR MONEY

TABLE 4.1
RATIOS OF MONEY TO GDP FOR SOME DEVELOPED COUNTRIES IN 1995

Country	Currency	Checkable Deposits	M1
Australia	.041	.138	.179
Austria	.061	.104	.164
Belgium	.054	.145	.199
Canada	.032	.141	.173
Denmark	.033	.268	.301
Finland	.023	.297	.320
France	.034	.204	.238
Germany	.072	.183	.254
Italy	.060	.281	.341
Japan	.096	.261	.357
Netherlands	.060	.212	.272
Norway	.046	.342	.388
Spain	.108	.167	.275
Switzerland	.092	.188	.280
United Kingdom	.028	.596[a]	.625[a]
United States	.057	.098	.155

Source: *International Monetary Fund*, International Financial Statistics, Yearbook, *1996, and Central Statistical Office*, Annual Abstract of Statistics, *1997.*

Note: *The ratio is the value of the monetary aggregate at the end of 1995 divided by the GDP for 1995.*

[a] *The U.K. data refer to M2 rather than M1, and the deposits include noncheckable types.*

financial institutions such as banks, we can deal with checkable deposits or other types of deposits. For now, however, we should think of money as currency. We also assume that the government has a monopoly in the issue of money (that is, currency) and that the interest rate on money is zero.

Given that people use money to transact, how much money should they hold? Suppose that everyone synchronized each sale of goods or bonds with an equal-sized purchase of some other good or bond. Then although people used money for all exchanges, they would end up holding virtually zero cash. But to hold this low average money balance, each person would have to spend a lot of effort on financial planning. He or she would have to synchronize the timing of sales and purchases and would have to carry out a large number of transactions. It is typically more convenient to allow receipts to accumulate awhile as cash before spending these funds or converting them into bonds. As Milton Friedman put it, money serves as a *temporary abode of purchasing power*. The general idea is that people can reduce their average holdings of cash only by incurring more costs. These costs are often called **transaction costs**, which refer to the expenses of carrying out trades, as well as the costs of making financial decisions.

Given the total of financial assets, a lower average cash balance means a higher average stock of bonds. Hence, by economizing on money, people earn more interest (or pay less interest if they are borrowing). The demand for money reflects the trade-off between transaction costs and interest earnings. In the next section we use a simple model to illustrate this trade-off and show how it determines the demand for money. Although the model is only an illustration, it nevertheless brings out the general forces that influence the demand for money.

A MODEL OF OPTIMAL CASH MANAGEMENT

Consider a retired person, who is living off previously accumulated assets. This person keeps financial assets primarily in bonds but holds some money to facilitate the purchases of consumer goods. For simplicity, assume that consumption expenditure is constant at the amount Pc dollars per year. (We assume here that the price level, P, does not change over time.) The retiree makes occasional withdrawals of funds from the stock of interest-bearing assets. Suppose that these withdrawals occur at the interval T. For example, if an exchange occurs every month, then $T =$ one-twelfth of a year. Equivalently, the frequency of exchange is 12 per year. Note that this frequency is the reciprocal of the period between withdrawals, $1/T$.

Each exchange of interest-bearing assets for money involves a transaction cost. There may be explicit brokerage changes, but, more likely, the main expense is the time and trouble for carrying out the transfer. If a person spends more time transacting, then he or she has less time available for work or leisure. Suppose that each exchange costs $\$\gamma$ (the Greek letter *gamma*), which includes the explicit costs and the dollar value attached to the time needed for the exchange. We assume a lump-sum transaction cost, which means that the charge is independent of the number of dollars withdrawn. If the retiree transacts at the frequency $1/T$ per year, then the total of transaction costs per year is the dollar amount $\gamma \cdot (1/T)$. Dividing by the price level, P, we find that the real transaction cost per year is

$$\text{Real transaction cost} = (\gamma/P) \cdot (1/T) \tag{4.1}$$

The term γ/P is the real cost per transaction.

When the retiree makes a withdrawal, he or she obtains the amount of money needed to meet expenses until the next withdrawal. In the present case, the money must cover the expenditures over an interval of length T. Since the person spends at the rate $\$Pc$ per year, the amount needed is PcT. The retiree spends these funds gradually to buy goods, running out of money when the time T has elapsed. At that point, he or she replenishes cash by making the next withdrawal from the stock of interest-bearing assets.

Figure 4.1 shows the time pattern of money holdings. Notice that a withdrawal of $\$PcT$ occurs at date 0. The retiree spends gradually at the rate $\$Pc$ per year and thereby just exhausts the stock of money at time T. Between dates 0 and T, the level of money is shown by the downward-

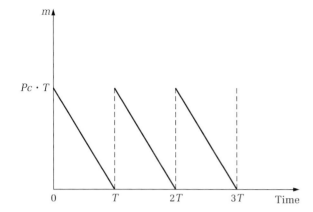

FIGURE 4.1

TIME PATTERN OF MONEY HOLDINGS

Money holdings reach a peak, *PcT*, just after each withdrawal. Then money declines gradually, reaching zero when it is time to make the next withdrawal. Notice that the withdrawals occur at the interval *T*.

sloping line in the figure. At date T there is another withdrawal of size $\$PcT$. Hence, money jumps upward—along the dashed line shown in the figure—to the level PcT. Then the money balance declines steadily again until the time for a new withdrawal at $2T$. This sawtooth pattern for money holdings keeps repeating with the peaks spaced at interval T.

Given the form of cash management from Figure 4.1, the average money balance is half the vertical distance to the peak:

$$\bar{m} = \frac{1}{2}PcT \tag{4.2}$$

where $\bar{m}$ denotes the average holding of money. If we divide by the price level, P, we can express the average holding of money in real terms as

$$\bar{m}/P = \frac{1}{2}cT \tag{4.3}$$

For a given total of financial assets in any period, an increase in the average money balance must imply a reduction in the average holdings of bonds and, hence, a decline in interest income. If the interest rate is R (per year), then the dollar magnitude of interest earnings forgone per year is the quantity $R\bar{m} = R \cdot (\frac{1}{2})PcT$. If all financial assets had been held as bonds, then the interest income per year would have increased by this amount. As usual, we can divide through by the price level to express this dollar magnitude in real terms. Therefore, the real amount of interest income forgone per year is given by

$$\text{Interest forgone in real terms} = R \cdot \bar{m}/P = R \cdot \frac{1}{2}cT \qquad \textbf{(4.4)}$$

[2] *The model is an example of the* inventory approach to money demand, *which was pioneered by William Baumol (1952) and James Tobin (1956). (The approach is often called the Baumol-Tobin model.) The two costs for holding money are analogous to those that arise when a firm holds an inventory of its product. The interest-forgone cost for money parallels the costs of forgone interest, storage, and depreciation, which apply to inventories of goods. The transaction cost for financial exchanges corresponds to the costs of restocking—that is, the transaction cost for ordering, shipping, and processing new goods from a supplier. More complicated models of inventories—whether of goods or money—stress the uncertainties in receipts and expenditures.*

There are two types of costs in our cash-management problem.[2] First, we can think of the interest forgone in real terms, $R \cdot \frac{1}{2}cT$, as a cost of holding money. We graph this cost versus the transaction interval, T, in Figure 4.2. Note that this cost is a straight line from the origin with slope equal to $R \cdot \frac{1}{2}c$. Second, there is the real transaction cost, which is given in equation (4.1) by $(\gamma/P) \cdot (1/T)$. This cost appears as a rectangular hyperbola in Figure 4.2. Transaction costs approach zero as the interval between transactions tends toward infinity and approach infinity as the interval tends toward zero.

We show also the total of interest and transaction costs in Figure 4.2. This curve is U shaped. Costs decline initially as the transaction interval rises above zero because transaction costs decline by more than interest costs increase. Eventually transaction costs do not fall as fast as interest costs rise. Therefore, total costs start to increase with increases in the interval, T. There is some amount of time between trips, denoted by T^* in the figure, that minimizes total costs.[3] Hence, a rational person chooses the interval T^*.[4]

[3] *The answer can readily be found from calculus. We want the value of T that minimizes total costs, $R \cdot \frac{1}{2}cT + (\gamma/P) \cdot (1/T)$. The result from setting the derivative with respect to T to zero is $T^* \sqrt{2(\gamma/P)/Rc}$. Since $\bar{m}/P = \frac{1}{2}cT$, the solution for T^* implies $\bar{m}/p = \sqrt{c(\gamma/P)/2R}$. The last result is sometimes called the square-root formula, because it relates $\bar{m}/P$ positively to $\sqrt{c}$.*

For later purposes, the important point is that the choice of transaction interval, T, determines the average holding of real money from equation (4.3) as the amount $\bar{m}/P = (\frac{1}{2})cT$. Therefore, a person's choice of transaction interval translates into that person's choice of an average holding of real money. Our main concern now is how various changes in the economy affect the transaction interval and, thereby, a person's average holding of real money.

There are three variables that determine the transaction interval, T^*, in the model: (1) the interest rate, R, (2) the real flow of expenditures, c, and (3) the real cost per transaction, γ/P. We can use graphical methods to study the effects of changes in any of these variables.

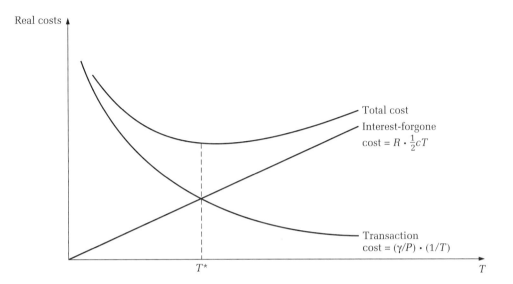

Real costs

Total cost
Interest-forgone
cost $= R \cdot \frac{1}{2}cT$

Transaction
cost $= (\gamma/P) \cdot (1/T)$

T^* T

FIGURE 4.2

COSTS OF CASH MANAGEMENT

The interest forgone by holding money, $R \cdot \frac{1}{2}cT$, increases with the period between withdrawals, T. Transaction costs, $(\gamma/P) \cdot (1/T)$, decline as the period rises. Total costs reach a minimum at the point T^*.

Figure 4.3 assumes an increase in the interest rate from R to R'. This change steepens the slope of the line that describes interest-forgone costs. In calculating total costs we find that the interest component has become more important relative to the transaction-cost component. Hence, we reach sooner the position at which increasing interest costs dominate over falling transaction costs. It follows that the minimum of total costs occurs at a shorter interval between withdrawals; that is, $(T^*)' < T^*$ in the figure.

We can interpret the result as follows. An increase in the interest rate makes it more important to economize on cash in order to avoid large amounts of forgone interest income. In our simple model, people can reduce average holdings of money only by transacting more frequently, that is, by shortening the period between financial exchanges, T. Although this process entails a higher transaction cost, people are

[4] *In our example, the period T^* turns out to equalize the two components of the total costs. That is, in Figure 4.2, the interest-forgone line intersects the curve for transaction costs at the point T^*. This property depends on the details of our example; it does not hold more generally.*

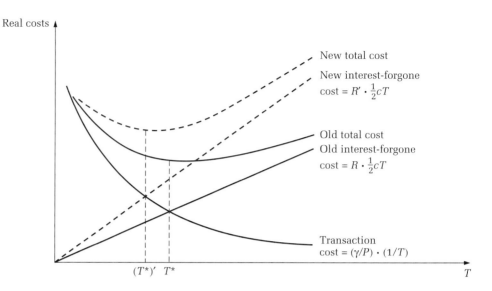

Real costs

New total cost

New interest-forgone
cost $= R' \cdot \frac{1}{2}cT$

Old total cost

Old interest-forgone
cost $= R \cdot \frac{1}{2}cT$

Transaction
cost $= (\gamma/P) \cdot (1/T)$

$(T^*)'$ T^*

T

FIGURE 4.3

EFFECT ON THE TRANSACTION INTERVAL OF AN INCREASE IN THE INTEREST RATE

An increase in the interest rate from R to R' steepens the line that describes interest-forgone costs. People respond by lowering the period between withdrawals from T^* to $(T^*)'$.

motivated by the rise in the interest rate to incur these costs. Hence, the rise in the interest rate, R, leads to a decline in the interval between transactions.

Recall from equation (4.3) that the average real money balance equals $\frac{1}{2}cT$. Since the increase in the interest rate lowers the period, T, it must also lower the average holding of real money. In other words, *a higher cost of holding money—a rise in the interest rate—reduces the real demand for money*. We shall use this important result many times in the subsequent analysis.

We can use a similar method to assess changes in the real flow of spending, c. A rise in the spending flow shifts the interest-forgone cost exactly as shown in Figure 4.3. Hence, someone with a greater annual flow of real expenditure chooses a shorter interval between withdrawals, T. This result follows because an increase in the real volume of spending, c, makes the interest-forgone cost more important relative to the transaction cost. Households with more real spending—typically, households with higher income—find it worthwhile to devote more effort to financial planning in order to economize on their cash.

Average real money balances equal the quantity $\frac{1}{2}cT$. For a given choice of transaction interval, T, a rise in real spending, c, increases average real money balances proportionately. But we have just shown that the period, T, declines as the volume of spending increases. This response means that a rise in real spending leads to a less-than-proportionate increase in the average holding of real money.[5] Sometimes economists refer to this result as **economies of scale** in cash holding. This property means that households with a larger scale of spending hold less money when expressed as a ratio to their expenditures.

Finally, we can consider an increase in the real cost of transacting, γ/P. We can show graphically that this change leads to a lengthening of the period between exchanges, T. People transact less frequently when the cost of each exchange rises. Because the period, T, lengthens, average real money balances, $\frac{1}{2}cT$, increase.

PROPERTIES OF THE DEMAND FOR MONEY

The results tell us the effects on average real money balances from changes in the interest rate, R, the real volume of spending, c, and the real cost of transacting, γ/P. We can summarize these findings in the form of a function, ϕ (the Greek letter *phi*), for average real money demanded:

$$\bar{m}/P = \phi(\ R,\ \ c\ ,\gamma/P) \qquad (4.5)$$
$$\quad\quad\ \ (-)\ \ (+)\ \ (+)$$

Again the signs indicate the effect of each independent variable on the dependent variable, $\bar{m}/P$.

To find the average money balance in nominal terms, we can multiply through equation (4.5) by the price level. Then we get

$$\bar{m} = P \cdot \phi(\ R,\ \ c\ ,\gamma/P) \qquad (4.6)$$
$$\quad\quad\ \ (-)\ \ (+)\ \ (+)$$

[5] *We can show that the decline in the transaction interval, T^*, is by a smaller proportion than the increase in real spending, c. Therefore, the average real money balance does rise on net. See footnote 3 for an exact result using calculus.*

Consider what happens if we double the price level, P, but hold fixed R, c, and γ/P. (Note that nominal spending, Pc, and the dollar cost of transacting, γ, double along with the doubling of the general price level.) These changes leave unaltered the curves in Figure 4.2, which describe the real cost of transacting and the real value of interest income forgone. Therefore, people do not change their choice of transaction interval, T. It follows that average *real* balances, $\bar{m}/P = \frac{1}{2}cT$, do not change in equation (4.5). But average *nominal* balances, $\bar{m} = \frac{1}{2}PcT$, double along with the doubling of the price level, as shown in equation (4.6).

THE AGGREGATE DEMAND FOR MONEY

For an individual household in our model, the level of real money follows a sawtooth pattern and varies between zero and the amount cT. Equation (4.5) determines the average level of real money, $\bar{m}/P = \frac{1}{2}cT$. Suppose that we sum up over many households, each of which has the same average real balance. Then, unless the timing of transactions is synchronized across households, this aggregation smooths out the sawtooth pattern. In particular, aggregate real money balances at any date look like an individual's average amount, $\bar{m}/P$, multiplied by the number of households.

We can write out a function, Φ (Greek capital *phi*), for aggregate real money demanded as

$$M/P = \phi(\underset{(-)}{R}, \underset{(+)}{C}, \underset{(+)}{\gamma/P}) \tag{4.7}$$

The function Φ looks like the individual's function ϕ in equation (4.5), but magnified to incorporate the adding up across many households. Similarly, the aggregate version of equation (4.6) for nominal money demand is

$$M = P \cdot \phi(\underset{(-)}{R}, \underset{(+)}{C}, \underset{(+)}{\gamma/P}) \tag{4.8}$$

GENERALIZATIONS AND IMPLICATIONS FOR MONEY DEMAND

Although we can complicate the theory of money demand in many ways, the properties that we derived from the simple model still tend to hold. That is because the simple model captures the basic trade-off that determines the demand for money: if people put more effort into transacting and financial planning, then they can lower their average holding of money. A lower money balance means, in turn, a greater amount of interest earnings. A person engages in various aspects of cash management up to the point at which the gain in interest income just compensates for the added transaction costs. Therefore, a basic result is that a higher interest rate motivates people to incur more costs in order to economize on money; hence, a higher interest rate reduces the demand for money.

An increase in the volume of real expenditures raises the benefits from financial planning. Therefore, although a higher level of spending means more money held, real money balances tend to rise less than proportionately with real spending. In the simple model, real spending corresponds to real consumption, C. Other components of spending, such as purchases of goods by businesses, also have a positive effect on the aggregate demand for money in a more general model.

The real demand for money rises less than proportionately with an increase in real spending if we hold fixed the real cost of transacting, γ/P. If we think about different households, then those with higher real income, and hence higher real spending, tend also to have a higher value of time. Since a major component of the transaction cost is the time wasted, the households with higher income likely have larger transaction costs. Since an increase in transaction costs means more real money held (see equation [4.5]), the higher-income households hold more money on this count. Therefore, this effect weakens the tendency for economies of scale in cash holdings. The more basic finding, which we rely on later, is that an increase in real spending raises the real demand for money.

The theory relates the demand for money in real terms to a set of real variables, which include the real flow of spending, the real costs of transacting, and the interest rate. A change in the general price level—with all the real variables held fixed—does not change the demand for money in real terms. Therefore, the nominal demand for money rises by the same proportion as the price level if all real variables do not change. For example, an increase in the price level by 10% raises the demand for nominal money, M, by 10%, so as to leave the real amount, M/P, unchanged.

In our simple model, the real transaction costs incurred per year, $(\gamma/P) \cdot (1/T)$, pertain to transfers from interest-bearing assets to money. More generally, transaction costs apply also to other forms of exchanges, such as the costs of buying commodities with money and the costs of making wage payments to workers.

We would want also to bring in the costs of financial planning and decision making. Typically, people who do more calculating manage to maintain a smaller average money balance and thereby achieve a greater amount of interest earnings. But this broader view of transaction costs does not alter the main conclusions with respect to the form of the functions for aggregate money demand in equations (4.7) and (4.8).

The costs of transacting change when there are technological innovations in the financial sector. For example, the use of computers by financial institutions makes it easier for customers to shift between money (defined as currency or checkable deposits) and alternative assets. These improvements tend to lower the demand for money. Similarly, the development of convenient checkable deposits in the late nineteenth and early twentieth centuries in the United States had a negative effect on the demand for currency (and a positive effect on the holdings of demand deposits).

The possibilities for economizing on money holdings are influenced also by the use of credit. It is easier to synchronize receipts and payments—and, thereby, easier to achieve a lower average money balance—when people buy with credit rather than cash. Credit also favors the use of checks rather than currency.

The Payments Period and the Demand for Money

Irving Fisher (1971, pp. 83–85) stressed the dependence of the demand for money on the period between payments of wages. The effects of this period are analogous to those for the interval between withdrawals from a financial asset. In particular, a shorter payments period reduces the average holding of real money balances. This effect is important during extreme inflations—for example, during the German hyperinflation after World War I. In such situations the cost of holding money becomes very high. Therefore, people incur more transaction costs—such as the costs of making more frequent wage payments—to reduce their average holdings of real money. For 1923, the final year of the German hyperinflation, an observer reported, "it became the custom to make an advance of wages on Tuesday, the balance being paid on Friday. Later, some firms used to pay wages three times a week or even daily" (Costantino Bresciani-Turroni, 1937, p. 303). Similarly, during the Austrian hyperinflation after World War I, "The salaries of the state officials, which used to be issued at the end of the month, were paid to them during 1922 in installments three times per month" (J. van Walre de Bordes, 1927, p. 163).

A broader model would bring in uncertainties associated with the timing and size of receipts and expenditures. An increase in these uncertainties tends to raise the average holding of money because people hold cash partly to guard against unexpected delays in receipts or unanticipated opportunities for purchases. Therefore, we anticipate that an increase in uncertainties about receipts and expenditures tends to raise the real demand for money. Although the introduction of uncertainty adds some important new effects, this generalization does not eliminate the types of influences on aggregate money demand that we summarized in equations (4.7) and (4.8).

THE VELOCITY OF MONEY

Economists often think of the relation between the average amount of money that someone holds, $\bar{m}$, and the amount of transactions carried out by that money. In our simple model, the dollar volume of transactions equals consumption expenditure, Pc. In a broader context, the dollar volume of transactions could be identified with GDP or with broader totals that include various kinds of intermediate expenditures. The ratio of transactions to the average money balance—measured as $GDP/\bar{m}$ if transactions are measured by nominal GDP—is called the **velocity of money**. The velocity is the number of times per unit of time, such as a year, that the typical piece of money turns over.

In our model, a person's average real money balance is given from equation (4.3) by $\bar{m}/P = \frac{1}{2}cT$. Therefore, velocity is $c/[\bar{m}/P] = 2 \cdot (1/T)$. Notice that the velocity of money depends directly on the frequency of exchange, $1/T$, between alternative financial assets and money. One variable that has an important effect on velocity is the interest rate, R. An increase in R motivates a higher frequency of financial exchanges, $1/T$, and therefore a higher velocity.

THE VELOCITY OF MONEY IN THE UNITED STATES

Figure 4.4 shows the velocity of money in the United States from 1889 to 1996. Velocity is defined here as the ratio of nominal GDP for the year to the annual average of the money stock.[6] The upper curve in the figure defines money to be the public's holding of currency. It is more common, however, to use the broader monetary aggregate, M1, which includes checkable deposits. Since these checkable deposits are an alternative to currency as a medium of exchange, we can readily apply our theory of the demand for money to the broader concept, M1, which is used for the lower curve in Figure 4.4.

The figure shows the tendency for velocity to rise since the end of World War II. This pattern applies whether we define money as currency

[6] *Although GDP is broader than consumer spending, it still covers only the final goods that an economy produces. Total transactions include intermediate exchanges, such as sales from suppliers to producers, from wholesalers to retailers, and so on. These trades are netted out in GDP. Also, a large and rapidly increasing volume of monetary exchange involves financial trades, such as purchases or sales of stocks and bonds. We do not have data on the total volume of transactions. We do know, however, the quantity of expenditures that are made by checks, called debits to demand deposits. For 1995, these debits totaled $397 trillion, which was 53 times the GDP of $7.5 trillion! The ratio of debits to GDP has increased dramatically in recent years—it was 31 in 1985, 16 in 1975, 8 in 1965, and between 5 and 7 from 1945 to 1960. The main reason for this change was the explosion of various types of financial transactions. (The data on debits are in issues of the* Federal Reserve Bulletin.*)*

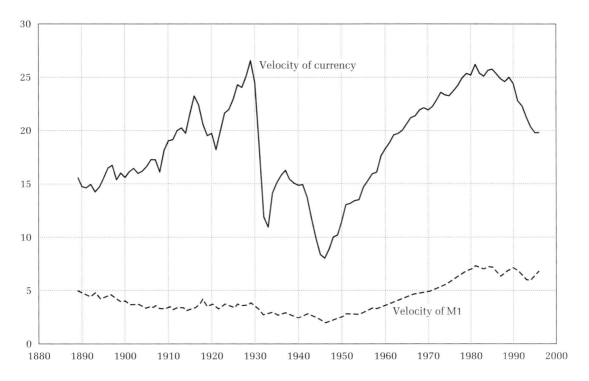

FIGURE 4.4

VELOCITY OF MONEY IN THE UNITED STATES, 1889–1996

The upper curve is the ratio of GDP for the year to the annual average of currency held by the public. The lower curve uses M1 rather than currency. (Prior to 1915, the numbers are based on the broader monetary aggregate, M2, which includes all deposits at commercial banks.) *Sources:* The monetary data are from Milton Friedman and Anna Schwartz (1970, Table 2); Board of Governors of the Federal Reserve System (1976, 1981); the *Federal Reserve Bulletin*, various issues; and DRI data bank.

or as M1. The pattern changed, however, after 1985: the velocity of currency fell from 25.7 in 1984 to 19.8 in 1996. The velocity of M1 fell from 7.2 in 1984 to 6.1 in 1994 before rising to 6.9 in 1996.

Two main factors account for the post–World War II behavior of velocity. First, interest rates tended to rise from 1945 until the early 1980s. For example, the interest rate paid on three-month maturity U.S. Treasury bills rose from 0.4% in 1945 to 2.9% in 1960, 6.5% in 1970, and a peak of 14.0% in 1981, but then declined to 7.5% in 1985 and 5.8%

in 1987. Since then, the rate rose to 8.1% in 1989, fell to a low point of 3.0% in 1993, and then rose to 5.0% in 1996. The rise in interest rates until the early 1980s motivated a reduction in real money balances in relation to the volume of real spending—hence, velocity increased. But the decline in interest rates after the early 1980s tended to reverse this pattern.

The second element is that technological advances in financial management enabled people to economize more easily on their money.[7] In our simple model, these developments appear as reductions in the real cost of financial exchanges, γ/P. These changes raise velocity because they induce people to switch from holdings of money to holdings of alternative financial instruments.

The velocity of currency rose over most of the period from 1889 to 1930. The important element here was the spread of checkable deposits as a convenient alternative to currency. It is interesting that the peak of currency velocity around 1930 actually exceeded the peak in 1985. Although there has been much talk recently about the economy's learning to dispense with currency, we see that there was actually less currency outstanding relative to the volume of consumer spending in 1930 than there was in 1985.

The broader monetary aggregate, M1, includes checkable deposits, which became increasingly popular from 1889 to 1930. Therefore, the velocity of M1 behaved very differently from that of currency during this period. There was, in fact, a small decline in the velocity of M1 from 1889 to 1930.

Major declines in the velocity of currency occurred during World Wars I and II. The demand for currency rises during wartime because there are more transactions with strangers, reduced desires to leave records of transactions from checking accounts (because of rationing, higher income taxes, and other legal restrictions on private activities), and increased demand for currency by foreigners (for a discussion, see Phillip Cagan, 1958). There was also a sharp decrease in the velocity of currency during the Great Depression. In this case, the major financial collapse lessened the attractiveness of alternatives to currency, including

[7] *Some of these advances— particularly the ready availability of money-market funds— were triggered by the rise in interest rates. Therefore, the second factor for explaining the rise in velocity is partly related to the first one.*

demand deposits. Therefore, the velocity of currency fell dramatically from 1930 to 1935.

The influences of the Great Depression and World War II led also to declines in the velocity of M1. There was, however, no noticeable effect during World War I.

EMPIRICAL EVIDENCE ON THE DEMAND FOR MONEY

Our simple model provides a number of conclusions about the factors that influence the demand for money. We can summarize the main results as follows:

— An increase in the interest rate, R, reduces the real demand for money.

— An increase in real spending, measured by real consumption or a broader construct, raises the real demand for money. In some cases, the increase in real money demanded is smaller in proportion than the increase in real spending; that is, there are economies of scale in the holding of money.

— An increase in the price level, P, say by 10%, raises the nominal demand for money by 10%; hence, the real demand for money does not change.

— An increase in real transaction costs, γ/P, raises the real demand for money.

We want to know how these propositions accord with the facts. During the post–World War II period there have been many statistical studies of the demand for money, so that a good deal of empirical evidence is available.[8]

[8] *For surveys of the evidence, see Steven M. Goldfeld and D. E. Sichel (1990), David Laidler (1985, Chap. 4), and John Judd and John Scadding (1982).*

The negative effect of interest rates on the demand for money is confirmed by investigators whether they measure money by M1 or currency. For example, in his classic empirical studies of the demand for money in the United States, Steven Goldfeld (1973, 1976) found that a 10% increase in interest rates (say, a rise from 10 to 11%) on time deposits and on commercial paper reduced the real demand for M1 in the long run by about 3%. Updated versions of this evidence appear in Goldfeld and Sichel (1990), and Fair (1987) reports similar findings for a number of OECD countries. In the U.S. results, the reduction in M1 reflected roughly the same proportionate declines in currency and in checkable deposits.[9]

Casey Mulligan and Xavier Sala-i-Martin (1996) observe that the negative effect of the interest rate on the demand for money involves two kinds of effects. First, a higher interest rate motivates people to transact more frequently between money and financial assets and, thereby, to reduce their money holdings along the lines of the model that we considered in this chapter. Second, if there is some cost in using interest-bearing assets at all—for example, for establishing a money-market account—then a rise in the interest rate would motivate more people to use these assets. When interest rates are very low, few people are motivated to economize on cash by using financial assets, and the sensitivity of money demand to the interest rate is small in magnitude. However, as the interest rate increases, people increasingly adopt the alternative financial assets, and the sensitivity of money demand to the interest rate increases. Their empirical evidence on individual holdings of checkable deposits and alternative financial assets bears out these ideas. At very low interest rates, say 2%, an increase in the interest rate by 10% is estimated to lower money demand by about 2%. But at an interest rate of 6%, an increase in the interest rate by 10% is estimated to lower money demand by around 5%.

There is strong evidence for a positive effect of real spending on the real demand for money and weaker evidence of economies of scale in this relation. Goldfeld found that an increase by 10% in real GNP led

[9] For the effects on currency, see Jack Ochs and Mark Rush (1983).

in the long run to an increase by 6 to 7% in the real demand for M1. (A somewhat larger response of M1 shows up if we consider a 10% increase in real consumer expenditure rather than real GNP.) The appearance of economies of scale—that is, a less than 10% response of real M1—turns out to reflect the behavior of checkable deposits. An increase by 10% in real GNP implies a long-run expansion of real currency by roughly 10%, but a rise in real checkable deposits by only about 6%.

Our model predicts that an increase in the price level raises the nominal demand for money by the same proportion. This proposition receives strong empirical support. Goldfeld found, for example, that an increase of the price level by 10% led to a 10% increase in the nominal demand for M1.

Finally, our theory predicts that a decrease in transaction costs lowers the demand for money. This effect has been important since the early 1970s because a variety of financial innovations have made it easier for people to hold less currency and checkable deposits. The innovations include automatic teller machines, the spread of credit cards, and various accounts that allow inexpensive computerized transfers between checkable and noncheckable deposits.

Most economists, when trying to estimate the demand for money, ignored these financial innovations. Until about the mid-1970s, the estimated equations seemed to work well in that their predictions about the demand for money were fairly accurate. However, most of the developments that substantially reduced transaction costs have occurred only since the mid-1970s. It is in this period that the estimates that ignored financial innovations started to fail. In particular, the actual amount of money that people held was substantially less than the amount predicted by earlier evidence. (This result has sometimes been referred to as "missing money.")

Michael Dotsey (1985) found that the volume of electronic funds transfers was a good proxy for the state of financial innovation. He showed, thereby, that recent financial innovations had a strong downward effect on holdings of checkable deposits.[10] Further, by

[10] *Differences in financial sophistication are also important when considering the demand for money across countries. For some empirical estimates over the long term, see Michael Bordo and Lars Jonung (1981).*

including his measure of financial innovation, he derived a money-demand equation that looked stable before the early 1970s and since. His fitted equation showed effects from interest rates and real spending that were similar to those, such as Goldfeld's, that included data only up to the early 1970s.

MONEY AND HOUSEHOLDS' BUDGET CONSTRAINTS

We want now to incorporate the discussion of money demand into our treatment of households' budget constraints. Recall the form of the budget condition for period t:

$$Py_t + (1 + R)\, b_{t-1} + m_{t-1} = Pc_t + b_t + m_t \qquad \textbf{(4.9)}$$

We simplified the analysis before by pretending that each household's money balance was constant over time: $m_t = m_{t-1}$. Then the money-balance terms on each side of equation (4.9) canceled, and terms involving money did not appear in the budget constraint over an infinite horizon. Now we want to reconsider this analysis when households can alter their holdings of money.

In our model of the demand for money, the cash position moved up and down during a period in accordance with the sawtooth pattern shown in Figure 4.1. For the purpose of constructing a budget constraint over an infinite horizon, it is satisfactory to neglect these ups and downs of money within a period. Hence, we now pretend that a household's money holding equals m_t during period t. This amount is constant during the period, but can change from one period to the next.

Suppose that a household starts with the money balance m_0 and plans to hold the amount m_1 in period 1. We allow m_1 to differ from m_0, but it is convenient to pretend for the moment that all future balances also equal m_1: $m_1 = m_2 = m_3 \ldots$. We can use the one-period budget constraint from equation (4.9) as we did in Chapter 3 to derive a budget condition that applies for any number of periods. For an infinite horizon, the result is

$$y_1 + y_2/(1 + R) + \cdots + b_0 \cdot (1 + R)/P + m_0/P$$
$$= c_1 + c_2/(1 + R) + \cdots + m_1/P$$

(4.10)

Equation (4.10) differs from equation (3.15) only by the addition of a monetary term on each side of the equation. The sources of funds on the left side now include the initial real money balance, m_0/P. This term makes sense because households can use their initial money to buy goods.

The uses of funds on the right side now include m_1/P, which represents the real money balance that the household plans to hold forever (because $m_1 = m_2 = \ldots$). The funds held permanently as money cannot also be spent on consumption: therefore, m_1/P shows up on the right side of equation (4.10) as a use of funds.

Suppose that a household's initial real money balance, m_0/P, rises, while the planned future real balance, m_1/P, does not change. The increase in real money is then equivalent to an increase in household wealth. We expect, therefore, that the household would increase consumption and leisure in all periods.

Suppose, alternatively, that m_1/P rises by the same amount as m_0/P. Equation (4.10) then shows that no resources are available for the household to raise consumption and leisure. The increase in m_0/P is just sufficient to maintain the expansion of m_1/P (forever). Nothing is left over for other purposes.

The important result is that consumer demand and desired leisure depend positively on the term, $m_0/P - m_1/P$. For a household that plans to maintain a constant real money balance—that is, $m_0/P = m_1/P$—the net effect is nil. Because the typical person will end up in this situation (in the market-clearing analysis of Chapter 5), this last result turns out to be important.

The same type of result holds if we allow m_t to vary after period 1. Instead of m_1/P, the right side of equation (4.10) contains a complicated average of the real money balances that the household plans to hold in all future periods. It remains true that an increase by one unit in all future values of m_t/P (for $t = 1, 2, \ldots$) raises the uses of funds on the right side of equation (4.10) by one unit. Therefore, if m_0/P and all future values, m_t/P, rise by the same amount, then the household would not change its choices of consumption and leisure.

THE REAL-BALANCE EFFECT

Consider the wealth effect from a change in the price level, P. Look at the household's budget condition in real terms from equation (4.10). Suppose that we hold fixed the levels of output, $y_1, y_2, \ldots$, and consumption, $c_1, c_2, \ldots$. Also, hold constant the interest rate, R, the planned level of *real* money balances, m_1/P, and the initial *nominal* money holding, m_0. Finally, think about the average person, for whom the initial bonds, b_0, equal zero.

Consider the effects on the left and right sides of equation (4.10) from a decline in the price level. Given our assumptions, nothing changes on the right side, which measures the uses of funds in real terms. The only effect on the left side (since $b_0 = 0$) is an increase in the real value of the initial money balance, m_0/P. Wealth therefore increases because people can use these higher initial real balances to raise consumption and leisure. The increase in wealth from a decline in the price level is called the **real-balance effect**.[11] As with other wealth effects, we predict that this one leads to increased consumption and leisure at all dates.

The real-balance effect operates only when there is a change in initial real money, m_0/P, relative to the planned future holdings, represented here by m_1/P. In most of our subsequent analysis, we shall look at situations in which the aggregates of actual and planned real money balances move by equal amounts. Then, as discussed before, there are equal changes to the left and right sides of the budget constraint in equation (4.10). In these cases, the change in real money balances

[11] *The effect has been stressed by many economists. See, for example, Gottfried Haberler (1939, especially Chaps. 8, 11), A. C. Pigou (1947), Don Patinkin (1948), and Robert Mundell (1971).*

will not involve net wealth effects on the aggregates of consumption and leisure.

The aggregate real value of bonds, B_0/P, is always zero and therefore cannot be affected by a change in the price level. A change in the price level nevertheless can have important distributional effects if some households are lenders and others are borrowers. Lenders, for whom $b_0 > 0$, benefit from a decline in the price level. They have more wealth and therefore tend to increase consumption and leisure. Borrowers, with $b_0 < 0$, lose from a decline in the price level and tend to reduce consumption and leisure.

We know that the aggregate effect from a decline in the price level on real bond holdings is nil because $B_0 = 0$. Our analysis also assumes that the increases in consumption and leisure for creditors balance the decreases for debtors. That is, we assume that the responses of creditors and debtors to changes in wealth are quantitatively about the same. In this case, we can neglect the distributional effects from price-level changes when we study the determinants of aggregate consumption and leisure. The distributional effects would, however, be central if we wanted to analyze the political pressures for changes in the price level: creditors would like lower price levels and debtors would like higher price levels.

TRANSACTION COSTS AND OTHER REAL EFFECTS OF MONEY

The specification of the household's budget constraint in equations (4.9) and (4.10) leaves out the transaction costs incurred in the process of cash management. In the simple model that we worked out before, these costs are given in equation (4.1) and should be added for each period as expenditure items on the right-hand side of equations (4.9) and (4.10). This approach is correct if the transaction costs represent literal purchases of goods and services—for example, banking services—that should be added to consumption spending to compute the household's total outlay on goods and services. (We would not want to include the transaction costs as consumption items because people do not get utility directly from banking services; the only reason that a household buys more of these services is to continue to carry out transactions while lowering the average holding of money.)

If the transaction costs represent wasted time that reduces the time devoted to work, then an increase in these costs would lower income in each period on the left-hand side of equations (4.9) and (4.10). Alternatively, if the wasted time leads to less leisure, then the budget constraints would be unaffected, but the household would be worse off because it has less leisure. The final conclusions on transaction costs will be similar in all these cases.

If we make the extension to include the transaction costs as literal purchases of goods and services, then the right-hand side of equation (4.10) would include the present value of these costs as a use of funds. Thus, for a given present value of the sources of funds on the left-hand side of the equation, a rise in the present value of the transaction costs subtracts from the present value of consumption that can be attained. In other words, an increase in the present value of transaction costs lowers the household's wealth. The conclusion is the same if transaction costs instead lower income or leisure in the various periods.

We know from before that the transaction costs incurred to economize on money holdings will rise if the interest rate, R, rises; if the real cost of transacting, γ/P, increases; and if the volume of transactions, C, rises. Thus, all of these changes will end up with negative wealth effects that reflect the increased use of resources to economize on the holding of money.

The transaction costs that we considered in our cash-management model involve the frequency of trips to the bank and are often called *shoe-leather* costs. This expression, intended literally to reflect the wearing out of shoes in the process of these bank trips, is meant to suggest that the costs are minor in normal times. In these situations, we may be able to neglect the wealth effects associated with money in our macroeconomic analysis. However, in more general specifications, the wealth effects associated with money could take forms that go beyond shoe-leather costs. For example, there are expenses incurred in making changes in prices, difficulties in dealing with uncertainty about the levels of future prices, and costs of adapting tax rules to changing price levels. We shall argue in Chapter 8 that these costs related to money may become important when inflation is high. Then the neglect of the wealth effects associated with money becomes problematic. In any event, the omission of these wealth effects is always an approximation at best.

SUMMARY

We explained in this chapter why people hold part of their financial assets as money rather than interest-bearing bonds. The explanation involves, first, the role of money (but not bonds) as a medium of exchange and, second, the extra transaction costs that arise when people economize more on their holdings of money. We showed that the average amount of real money held involves a trade-off between transaction costs and interest income forgone. A higher interest rate motivates people to incur more transaction costs in order to achieve a lower average real money balance.

Our theoretical model has the following major implications for the aggregate demand for money:

— An increase in the interest rate reduces the real demand for money.

— An increase in real spending raises the real demand for money, but possibly by a smaller proportion than the increase in spending.

— An increase in the price level raises the nominal demand for money by the same proportion.

— An increase in real transaction costs raises the real demand for money.

The empirical evidence generally supports these propositions.

We incorporated the holdings of money into households' budget constraints over an infinite horizon. If the planned future holdings of real money equal the initial holding, then there is no impact on the sources of funds net of the uses. In these cases, if we do not consider the transaction costs associated with money, then we do not have to worry about wealth effects from real money balances on the aggregates of consumer demand and leisure. However, the allowance for transaction costs implies that any change that raises the present value of these costs has, on this count, a negative wealth effect.

IMPORTANT TERMS AND CONCEPTS

economies of scale in the demand for money The property of the demand for money that the desired average real money holding increases less than proportionately with a rise in real income.

legal tender A characteristic of money, whereby its use as a medium of exchange is reinforced by government statute.

M1 The definition of money as the sum of currency plus checkable deposits plus travelers' checks; a measure of the volume of assets that serve regularly as media of exchange.

real-balance effect The effect of a change in wealth resulting from a change in the general price level; the wealth effect of a rise in the real value of money balances.

transaction costs Costs incurred in the process of making sales or purchases, such as brokerage fees or the cost of the time involved.

velocity of money The ratio of the dollar volume of transactions per period to the average money holding; the number of times per period that the average dollar turns over in making transactions.

QUESTIONS AND PROBLEMS

MAINLY FOR REVIEW

4.1 What are the costs of transacting between money and financial assets? (You may want to make a list and include such items as the cost of a trip to the bank and the time spent waiting in line.) How would the development of electronic teller services affect this cost?

4.2 Suppose that an individual's consumption expenditure is $6000 per year and that it is financed by monthly withdrawals of money from a saving account.

a. Depict on a graph the pattern of the person's money holdings over a period of one year. What is the average money balance?

b. Graph the pattern of money holdings when withdrawals of money are made only once in two months. Show that the average money balance is higher.

4.3 Refer to question 4.2. If consumption expenditure rises to $9000 per year and withdrawals continue to be made monthly, then what is the average money holding? Is it optimal for the frequency of withdrawals to remain the same when consumption increases? Explain.

4.4 What is the definition of the aggregate velocity of money? Use the concept of velocity to explain how a given aggregate quantity of money balances can be used to pay for a relatively large volume of consumption expenditure over a year.

4.5 Consider the following changes and state whether their effect on the real demand for money is an increase, a decrease, or uncertain:

a. A decrease in the interest rate.

b. An increase in real transaction costs.

c. An increase in real consumption.

d. An increase in the price level.

4.6 Consider again the changes listed in question 4.5, and describe their effect on velocity.

PROBLEMS FOR DISCUSSION

4.7 Transaction Costs and Households' Budget Constraints

Assume that the real cost of transacting between bonds and money, γ/P, rises.

a. How does this change show up in households' budget constraints? What is the effect on wealth?

b. We neglected transaction costs when considering households' choices of work effort, consumption, and saving. Suppose now that we bring in the wealth effect from part a. What then is the effect of an increase in the real cost of transacting, γ/P, on households' work effort, consumption, and saving?

c. Have we left out a new substitution effect in part b? Think about the choice between consumption and leisure. Consumption involves market exchange, which requires the use of money. But people can "buy" leisure without using money! So what substitution effect arises for consumption versus leisure when the real cost of transacting, γ/P, rises? How does this affect the answer to part b?

4.8 Further Aspects of Transaction Costs

In problem 4.7 we considered the effects of transaction costs on households' budget constraints. These costs might show up as purchases of financial services, for example, as brokerage fees or service charges by banks. Alternatively, transaction costs might just represent the time that it takes to go to the bank or to make a decision.

a. How do these two different views of transaction costs affect the way that the costs appear in households' budget constraints?

b. Do these differences affect our other answers to problem 4.7?

c. How should we think about the production of financial services? That is, how can we incorporate this "good" into the model?

4.9   Effects of the Payment Interval on the Demand for Money

Think of a worker with an annual income of $12,000. Suppose that he or she receives wage payments once a month. Consumption spending is constant at $12,000 per year. Assume that the worker holds no bonds; that is, he or she holds all financial assets in the form of money.

a. What is the worker's average money balance?

b. What would the average money balance be if the worker were paid twice a month instead of once a month?

c. What is the general relation between the average money balance and the interval between wage payments?

4.10   Effects of Shopping Trips on the Demand for Money

Assume again the conditions of problem 4.9 with workers paid once a month. But instead of carrying out consumption expenditures in a uniform flow, the worker now makes periodic shopping trips. At each trip he or she buys enough goods (for example, groceries) to last until the next trip.

a. If the worker shops four times each month, then what is the average money balance? Why is the answer different from that in part a of problem 4.9?

b. What happens if he or she shops only twice each month?

c. What is the general effect on the average money balance of the interval between shopping trips? Compare the answer with that for part c of problem 4.9.

d. Suppose that the cost of making shopping trips rises—for example, because of an increase in the cost of gasoline. How would this change affect the frequency of shopping trips? What does the result imply about the effect of an increase in the cost of shopping trips on the average real holding of money? How does this effect compare with the impact of financial transaction costs, γ/P, which we explored in the text?

4.11 Expenditures and the Demand for Money

a. Consider an increase in the aggregate of real spending, C. What is the effect on the aggregate demand for real cash balances, M/P? Notice that aggregate real spending can rise for two reasons. First, there could be an increase in everyone's real spending, with no change in the number of people. Second, there could be an increase in the number of people, with no change in each person's level of real spending. How does the response of aggregate real money, M/P, depend on which case applies?

b. What should happen to the velocity of money as an economy develops? (Take a look at Figure 4.4 to see the history of velocity in the United States.) In answering, be sure to specify what happens to the interest rate, R, and the real cost of transacting between money and interest-bearing assets, γ/P.

4.12 Effects of Other Variables on the Demand for Money

For given values of real income and spending, the interest rate, and real transaction costs, would you say that the following statements are true, false, or uncertain.

a. An agricultural society has lower real money demand than an industrial society.

b. Real money demand is higher in dictatorships than in democracies.

c. A country with a large fraction of elderly people has higher real money demand than a country with a small fraction of elderly.

d. A country with a higher literacy rate has lower real money demand.

(For evidence on these kinds of effects on money demand, see Lawrence Kenny, 1991.)

4.13 The Denominations of Currency (optional)

Consider how people divide their holdings of currency between large bills (say $100 and over) versus small ones. How would the fraction of the value of currency that someone holds as large bills change with

a. an increase in the price level?

b. an increase in a person's real income?

c. an increase in the interest rate?

d. a greater incentive to avoid records of payments (for example, to evade taxes or to engage in criminal transactions)?

Given these results, the facts for the United States are not so easy to explain. The fraction of currency held as large bills (denominations of $100 and over) stayed nearly constant—between 20 and 22%—from 1944 to 1970. Then the fraction rose steadily to around 60% in 1995. What do you think explains these numbers?

THE BASIC MARKET-CLEARING MODEL

In Chapter 2, we considered how isolated households chose their work effort and thereby their production of commodities. With no possibilities for trades with other households or for storing goods, each household's production was equal to its consumption. In Chapter 3, we allowed people to buy and sell goods at the price P and to borrow and lend at the interest rate R. With these market opportunities, a household could save or dissave, so that consumption and production were not necessarily equal in every period. The accumulation of saving over time determined a household's stock of financial assets, which could be held as money or bonds. Finally, by studying the demand for money in Chapter 4, we saw how people divided their assets between money and bonds.

In the discussion of a market economy in Chapter 3, we mentioned three conditions that must hold when we sum up over all households. First, since consumption is the only use for output in the model, total production, Y_t, equals total consumption, C_t. Second, because each dollar lent by someone on the credit market corresponds to a dollar borrowed by someone else, the aggregate stock of bonds, B_t, equals zero in every period. Finally, since the stock of money does not change over time, the total that people hold in each period, M_t, equals the given quantity, M_0. We shall refer to these three conditions as aggregate-consistency conditions.

AGGREGATE-CONSISTENCY CONDITIONS AND THE CLEARING OF MARKETS

How do we know that the totals of individuals' choices satisfy the three aggregate-consistency conditions? For example, on the commodity market, individuals think that they can sell, or *supply*, their desired quantity of goods, and also buy, or *demand*, their desired quantity. We need something to guarantee that the total of commodities supplied equals the total demanded.

Similarly, on the credit market, each person thinks that he or she can borrow or lend any amount at the going interest rate, R. For a particular interest rate, there is no reason that the total of desired holding of bonds, B_t, would be zero. But then we have an inconsistency because the total amount that people want to borrow does not equal the total that others want to lend. One way or another, the credit market has to balance the overall quantities of borrowing and lending.

Finally, with respect to money, each person believes that he or she can hold the quantity that he or she demands. Yet somehow the total of these demands must equal the given aggregate quantity of money.

The classical solution is that the interest rate, R, and the price of commodities, P, adjust to ensure that

— the total of commodities supplied equals the total demanded,

— the total of desired holdings of bonds is zero, and

the total of money demanded equals the aggregate quantity of money.

This viewpoint is called the market-clearing approach. In this approach the various prices, which are R and P in our model, adjust so that each market clears. By clearing we mean that the quantity supplied of each good—bonds, money, or commodities—equals the quantity demanded. When this condition holds simultaneously for every good, **general market clearing** applies.

When all markets clear, no one is unable to buy or sell commodities at the going price or unable to extend or receive credit at the going interest rate. Everyone can buy and sell as much as they want of each good at the market-clearing prices.

Recall that each household regards the interest rate, R, and the price level, P, as given. However, the aggregates of households' choices determine R and P to satisfy the market-clearing conditions. Hence, R and P cannot be independent of the aggregate of people's choices about bonds, money, and commodities. But any individual's transactions are assumed to be a small fraction of the totals on any market and therefore have a negligible effect on the market-clearing values of R and P. Hence, as a good approximation, each person can regard the interest rate and price level as determined independently of his or her behavior. Given this approximation, we can continue to use the analyses of individual choices that we worked out in Chapters 3 and 4.

As mentioned before, we need to ensure that the three aggregate-consistency conditions hold. But why do we use market clearing to ensure these conditions? This device amounts to assuming that private markets function to allocate resources efficiently. When the markets clear, it is impossible to improve on any outcomes by matching potential borrowers and lenders or by bringing together potential buyers and sellers of commodities. Cleared markets already accomplish all of these *mutually advantageous trades*. Thus, the assumption that markets clear is tied closely to the view that the individuals who participate in and organize markets—and who are guided by the pursuit of their own interests—end up generating efficient outcomes.

We could use some concept other than market clearing to ensure that the aggregate-consistency conditions hold. One alternative is the Keynesian model, in which some markets do not clear in the sense of our concept of cleared markets. Rather, some prices are sticky, and some rationing of quantities comes into play. For example, households may be unable to sell all of the goods or labor services that they desire at the going price. We shall explore this viewpoint in Chapter 20. But the subtleties of Keynesian arguments cannot be appreciated without first understanding the workings of a market-clearing model. Therefore, it is best to begin by studying a framework in which markets clear.

Economists often use the term *equilibrium* to signify market clearing. But because the concept of an equilibrium has been used in so many different ways in the economics literature, its meaning has become unclear. For example, some economists think of the Keynesian model as a *disequilibrium* framework, and others view it as a different concept of equilibrium. We shall avoid the terms equilibrium and disequilibrium in the discussion. But we should emphasize two ideas that are central to our thinking about markets. First, we have some aggregate-consistency conditions, which must be satisfied by any reasonable model. Second, we assume in most of the analysis that the interest rate and price level adjust to clear the markets. That is how we satisfy the aggregate-consistency conditions in the market-clearing model. We shall see later how the Keynesian model modifies the second idea but not the first one.

WALRAS' LAW OF MARKETS

Consider again a household that faces a given price level, P, and interest rate, R. Denote by y_1^s the quantity of goods that the household decides to produce and *supply* to the commodity market during period 1. By the amount supplied, we mean the quantity offered for sale at the going price. Similarly, let c_1^d represent the quantity of goods that a household offers to buy—or *demands*—from the commodity market. Finally, let b_1^d and m_1^d denote the household's planned stocks of financial assets for period 1; that is, b_1^d is the demand for bonds and m_1^d is the demand for money.

Suppose that a household carries over from period 0 the stocks of financial assets b_0 and m_0. Then the household's budget constraint in real terms for period 1 is

$$y_1^s + b_0 \cdot (1 + R)/P + m_0/P = c_1^d + b_1^d/P + m_1^d/P \qquad (5.1)$$

Summing up equation (5.1) over all households gives the aggregate form of the budget constraint for period 1:

$$Y_1^s + B_0 \cdot (1 + R)/P + M_0/P = C_1^d + B_1^d/P + M_1^d/P \qquad (5.2)$$

Since every dollar lent during period 0 must correspond to a dollar borrowed, we must have $B_0 = 0$. Using this condition and rearranging terms, equation (5.2) simplifies to

$$(C_1^d - Y_1^s) + (B_1^d/P) + (M_1^d/P - M_0/P) = 0 \qquad (5.3)$$

Equation (5.3) shows how the market-clearing model deals with the three aggregate-consistency conditions that we mentioned before. For period 1, these conditions are as follows:

— $C_1^d = Y_1^s$—the total demand for commodities equals the total supply.

— $B_1^d = 0$—any dollar that someone wants to lend corresponds to a dollar that someone else wants to borrow.

— $M_1^d = M_0$—people willingly hold the outstanding stock of money, M_0.

But look at equation (5.3). Suppose that the first two aggregate-consistency conditions hold, that is, $C_1^d = Y_1^s$ and $B_1^d = 0$. Then equation (5.3) guarantees that the third condition, $M_1^d = M_0$, holds also. In fact, if any two of the three conditions hold, then the third one must hold. Thus, we have to worry about satisfying only two of the three conditions for aggregate consistency. The third follows automatically from the aggregate form of households' budget constraints in equation (5.3). This result is called **Walras' law of markets**, in honor of the nineteenth-century French economist, Léon Walras, who pioneered the study of models under conditions of general market clearing. (Economists refer to his analysis as *general equilibrium theory*.)

We shall obtain the same results regardless of which pair of aggregate-consistency conditions we examine. Macroeconomists typically look at the condition for clearing the commodity market, $C_1^d = Y_1^s$, and at the one for money to be willingly held, $M_1^d = M_0$. We shall find it convenient to follow this practice. Remember, however, that the results would not change if we substituted for one of these conditions the condition that the credit market clear, $B_1^d = 0$.

CLEARING THE COMMODITY MARKET

We want to ensure that the aggregate quantity of commodities supplied, Y_1^s, equals the aggregate quantity demanded, C_1^d. We refer here to quantities for the current period, which is period 1, but it is convenient now to drop the time subscripts.

The previous analysis isolated several variables that influence the aggregate supply and demand for commodities, including the following:

— The interest rate, R. A higher rate implies intertemporal-substitution effects, which reduce current demand, C^d, and raise current supply, Y^s (by raising current work).

— Wealth effects from changes in the position of the production function. An increase in wealth raises demand, C^d, but lowers work effort. (This decline in work partially offsets the direct effect from an improvement in the production function on the supply of goods, Y^s.)

— Substitution effects from changes in the schedule for the marginal product of labor. An upward shift leads to an increase in supply, Y^s, (because people work more) and an increase in demand, C^d.

We can write out the condition for clearing the commodity market during the current period as

$$Y^s(\underset{(+)}{R}, \ldots) = C^d(\underset{(-)}{R}, \ldots) \qquad \textbf{(5.4)}$$

The function Y^s refers to the aggregate supply of commodities, and the function C^d refers to the aggregate demand. We indicate explicitly only the effects of the interest rate in these functions. The omitted variables in the functions, denoted by . . . , include the wealth and substitution effects that arise from changes in the production function.

Equation (5.4) deals with the summation over a large number of households. We would like to use this analysis even when households are not identical, for example, when they differ by productivity, age, tastes, initial assets, and so on. In some cases, the aggregation over different types of people will not cause major problems. For example, a change in the interest rate implies the same type of intertemporal-substitution effect for everyone. We can also handle shifts in production functions when these shifts are similar for all producers. However, some changes benefit some people and harm others. For instance, we discussed before how movements in the price level or the interest rate have positive or negative effects on wealth, depending on someone's status in the credit market. These types of changes shift the distribution of resources across households without changing the aggregate value of these resources. Economists call these kinds of changes **distributional effects**. Typically, we have no presumption about how distributional effects influence the aggregates of commodities supplied or demanded. So, as is customary in macroeconomics, we assume (hope) that we can neglect distributional effects for the purpose of aggregate analysis.

Recall some variables that do not influence aggregate supply and demand in equation (5.4). The aggregate quantity of bonds, B_0, is zero and therefore does not appear. We discussed in Chapter 4 the role of initial real money balances, M_0/P. We showed there that, as long as we consider only positions where $M_0/P = M_1^d/P$—which will hold when we have general market clearing—the level of real money balances has no net wealth effect in the aggregate. It follows that M_0/P—and the price level P itself—do not appear in equation (5.4).

We also mentioned in Chapter 4 that the present value of the transaction costs associated with cash management would enter as a negative item in households' wealth. The assumption here is that these costs are small enough to neglect for the purpose of studying the determinants of aggregate output, the interest rate, and so on. However, this assumption will be valid only as approximation. In particular, we note in Chapter 8 that this approximation is likely to be poor in the context of high inflation, where the costs of cash management can become large.

Finally, we demonstrated in Chapter 3 that a change in the interest rate, R, has no aggregate wealth effect. (A rise in R is good for people who are usually lenders but correspondingly bad for those who are usually borrowers.) Therefore, the effects of R shown in equation (5.4) refer only to intertemporal-substitution effects. For this reason, we know that a rise in R lowers current consumer demand, C^d, and raises current commodity supply, Y^s.

Because the interest rate has important influences on commodities supplied and demanded, we shall find it convenient to depict equation (5.4) graphically with R on the vertical axis. Figure 5.1 shows that the interest rate has a positive effect on aggregate supply, Y^s, and a negative

Why Does the Price Level Not Affect Commodities Supplied and Demanded?

It seems odd that the price level, P, would not appear in the condition for clearing the commodity market, equation (5.4). Intuitively, we would expect a higher price of commodities to discourage demand and encourage supply. Let's think about what happens when P rises. The production function, $f(l)$, does not change. Therefore, given l, a household's nominal income from sales of commodities, $P \cdot f(l)$, goes up along with P. But real income, $f(l)$, (obtained by dividing the nominal income by P) does not change. Since real income from production is the same, it is reasonable on this count that consumption demand (in real terms) and labor supply would not change.

We are also holding fixed the interest rate, R. Therefore, a once-and-for-all increase in the price level, P, does not affect the relative costs of consumption or leisure in different periods. That is, the change in P has no intertemporal-substitution effects.

For a given amount of nominal bonds, b_0, an increase in P would reduce the real amount, b_0/P.

This effect is bad for someone with positive bond holdings but correspondingly good for someone with negative bond holdings. The effect is nil in the aggregate because the total of bond holdings, B_0, is zero and because we neglect distributional effects.

Finally, the increase in P lowers M_0/P. Real wealth falls on this count, and households would respond by lowering consumer demand and raising labor supply. In Chapter 4 we called this mechanism the real-balance effect. We know, however, that in a position of general market clearing, households will be motivated to hold the existing money; that is, M_1^d/P will end up being the same as M_0/P. In this situation, we know from Chapter 4 that there will be no net wealth effect on consumption demand and labor supply. That is why we can ignore the real-balance effect when we think about positions of general market clearing. That is also why the price level, P, does not appear in equation (5.4).

FIGURE 5.1

CLEARING THE COMMODITY MARKET

Clearing of the commodity market, $C^d = Y^s$, occurs at the interest rate R^*. At this point the level of aggregate output is $Y^* = C^*$.

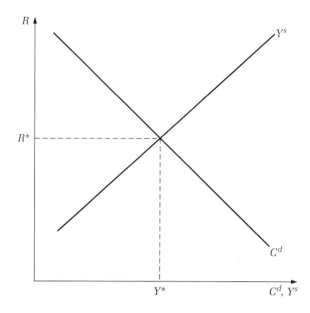

effect on aggregate demand, C^d. When R changes, the responses of supply and demand show up as *movements along the curves* in the figure. (We show the curves as straight lines only for convenience.)

The positions of the supply and demand curves in Figure 5.1 depend on the omitted elements, denoted by . . . , in equation (5.4). When any of these elements change—for example, because of a shift in the production function—the effects on commodity supply and demand show up as *shifts of the curves* in the figure. For given values of these elements, we can read off from the figure the value of the interest rate, R^*, that corresponds to the clearing of the commodity market, $Y^s = C^d$. Generally, we use an asterisk to signal that the value of a variable, such as $R = R^*$, derives from a market-clearing condition. Notice from the figure that the market-clearing level of output is the quantity $Y^* = C^*$.

Remember that each household's quantity of output, y, depends on the level of work, l, through the production function, $y = f(l)$. We assume that we can use an aggregate form of this relation

$$Y = F(L) \qquad (5.5)$$

The aggregate production function connects the aggregate amount of work, L, to the aggregate quantity of output, Y. Once we know the market-clearing level of output, Y^*, from Figure 5.1, we can use equation (5.5) to compute the corresponding level of aggregate work effort, L^*.

The market-clearing diagram in Figure 5.1 is the central graphical tool for the subsequent study of macroeconomic disturbances. Even when we complicate the model, we shall be able to use a version of this diagram to derive the main results. It is therefore worth reviewing the basic ideas behind this diagram. First, a higher interest rate stimulates the desire to produce and sell goods today but deters the desire to buy goods. These forces underlie the upward slope of the supply curve and the downward slope of the demand curve. Second, we determine the market-clearing values of the interest rate and the quantity of output by equating aggregate supply to aggregate demand.

THE QUANTITY OF MONEY EQUALS THE QUANTITY DEMANDED

The second aggregate-consistency condition requires the stock of money, M_0, to equal the aggregate quantity demanded during period 1, M_1^d. For convenience, we again drop the time subscripts.

In Chapter 4 we derived a function for the aggregate demand for money. When expressed in real terms—that is, as M^d/P—this demand depends negatively on the interest rate, R, and positively on the real amount of transactions, which we measure here by aggregate output, Y. Therefore, we can write the condition for money to be willingly held as

$$M = P \cdot \Phi(R, Y, \ldots) \qquad (5.6)$$
$$\quad\;\; (-) \;\; (+)$$

Note that the function Φ on the right side of equation (5.6) determines the demand for money in real terms, M^d/P. Therefore, $P \cdot L(R, Y, \ldots)$ is the nominal demand for money, M^d. The omitted terms, denoted by . . . , include any effects on real money demanded other than

FIGURE 5.2

THE DEMAND FOR MONEY EQUALS THE QUANTITY OF MONEY

The nominal demand for money is $M^d = P \cdot \Phi(R, Y, \ldots)$. For given values of Y and R, this demand is a straight line starting from the origin. The nominal quantity of money is the constant M. The amount of money demanded equals the quantity of money when the price level is P^*.

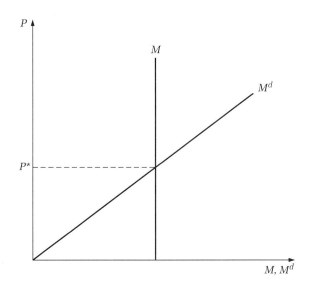

the interest rate and the level of output. For example, transaction costs would enter here.

Figure 5.2 shows graphically the equality between the quantity of money and the quantity demanded. We shall find it convenient to put the price level, P, on the vertical axis. Then the quantity of money is the constant M, which appears as a vertical line in the figure. The nominal demand for money is $M^d = P \cdot L(R, Y, \ldots)$. For given values of R and Y, this demand is directly proportional to P. Hence, we show it in the figure as a positively sloped straight line, starting from the origin. Notice that the quantity of money equals the quantity demanded when the price level is the value P^*.

GENERAL MARKET CLEARING

We want to determine the values of the interest rate, R^*, and the price level, P^*, that are consistent with the two aggregate-consistency conditions:

‗‗ The commodity market clears, as in Figure 5.1.

‗‗ The quantity of money equals the quantity demanded, as in Figure 5.2.

Remember from Walras' law that these two conditions ensure that the credit market clears, $B^d = 0$. Thus, it is appropriate to refer to R^* and P^* as the general-market-clearing values of the interest rate and the price level.

We can readily see the basic workings of the model. The market-clearing diagram from Figure 5.1 determines the interest rate, R^*, and the level of aggregate output, Y^*. We can substitute the values for R^* and Y^* into the money-demand function on the right side of equation (5.6). Then for a given quantity of money, M, Figure 5.2 determines the general-market-clearing value of the price level, P^*.

The procedure for solving the model is this simple because the price level does not appear in equation (5.4), which is the condition for clearing the commodity market. To put it another way, changes in P do not shift the curves in Figure 5.1. For this reason, we do not have to know the general-market-clearing value of the price level, P^*, when we determine the interest rate, R^*. We can just look at Figure 5.1 to determine R^*. Then, conditional on this result, we can use equation (5.6) and Figure 5.2 to solve out for P^*. The best way to clarify the workings of the model is to work through some examples, which are of substantial interest for their own sake.

SUPPLY SHOCKS

Economists use the term **supply shocks** to refer to sudden changes in the conditions of production. Adverse effects include harvest failures, strikes, natural disasters, epidemics, and political disruptions. The most important recent examples of supply shocks are the oil crises of 1973–74 and 1979, and to a lesser extent 1990. In fact, most economists became interested in supply shocks only after these dramatic changes in the market for oil.

For some reason—perhaps the sour disposition of economists—the term "supply shock" always refers to a negative effect on the supply of goods. But there can also be positive developments, such as technical innovations, bountiful harvests, or the sharp reduction in the price of oil in 1986. Our analysis applies to either favorable or unfavorable changes in productive conditions. As in some previous discussion, however, we shall find it important to distinguish temporary from permanent changes.

A TEMPORARY SHIFT OF THE PRODUCTION FUNCTION

Start with a temporary adverse change to the production function, say a shift that lasts for only the current period. As examples, we can think of the drought of 1988 that limited U.S. agricultural output and coal strikes that lowered production in Great Britain.

Consider first a purely parallel downward shift of the production function, as shown in Figure 5.3. This case is the simplest example of a supply shock because it does not alter the schedule for the marginal product of labor. Hence, there are no substitution effects from changes in the relative costs of consumption and leisure.

Effects on the Interest Rate and Output

One effect of the supply shock is that output decreases for a given level of work effort. On this count, the supply of goods, Y^s, falls.

Second, the disturbance reduces wealth. Because the change is short-lived, the wealth effects are small: we predict a small decrease of aggregate consumer demand, C^d, and a small increase of aggregate work effort. The increase in work implies a rise in goods supplied, Y^s. But since the wealth effect is weak, this increase offsets only a small part of the initial cutback in supply. Thus, the net effect is a decrease in aggregate supply, Y^s, which exceeds the small decline in aggregate demand, C^d.

Figure 5.4 shows the changes to the commodity market. Before the shift, the market cleared at the interest rate R^*. Then the disturbance

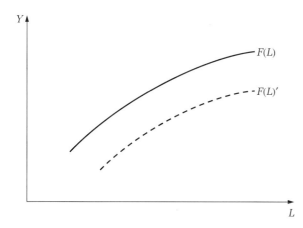

FIGURE 5.3

A PARALLEL DOWNWARD SHIFT OF THE PRODUCTION FUNCTION

We examine here a parallel downward shift of the production function from $F(L)$ to $F(L)'$.

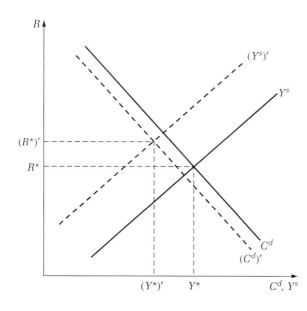

FIGURE 5.4

EFFECT OF A SUPPLY SHOCK ON THE COMMODITY MARKET

The temporary worsening of the production function lowers aggregate supply by more than demand. Therefore, clearing of the commodity market requires the interest rate to rise.

causes the aggregate supply curve to shift leftward from the one labeled Y^s to that labeled $(Y^s)'$. At the same time, the aggregate demand curve shifts leftward from the one marked C^d to that marked $(C^d)'$. As discussed before, the shift of the supply curve is larger than that of the demand curve. Hence, there is **excess demand** for commodities—$(C^d)' > (Y^s)'$—at the initial interest rate R^*. (In the opposite situation—a temporary favorable shift of the production function—there would be **excess supply** of commodities.)

The excess of goods demanded over those supplied means that, at the going interest rate, everybody would like to reduce his or her saving or borrow more. This desire arises because the worsening of the production function is temporary. Instead of cutting their consumption, individuals would like to absorb most of their temporarily depressed income by reducing current saving or by increasing current borrowing. People plan to repay their debts or build up their assets later when income is higher. But we know that not everyone can reduce saving or increase borrowing because aggregate saving must end up being zero. The interest rate has to adjust to make the aggregate of desired saving conform to the economy's possibilities: zero total saving. To put this point another way, the interest rate must change to clear the commodity market.

Figure 5.4 shows that the new interest rate, $(R^*)'$, exceeds the initial one, R^*. This rise in the interest rate eliminates people's desires to carry out negative aggregate saving. Equivalently, the increase in the interest rate lowers the quantity of goods demanded along the curve $(C^d)'$ and raises the quantity supplied along the curve $(Y^s)'$. At the new interest rate, $(R^*)'$, the commodity market again clears, that is, $(Y^s)' = (C^d)'$.

The new level of output, $(Y^*)'$, can be read off the intersection of the new supply and demand curves in Figure 5.4. Notice that the disturbance—the temporary worsening of the production function—leads to a fall in output. From the perspective of commodity demand, $(C^d)'$, it is clear that output must be lower: the decrease in wealth shifts the demand curve leftward, and the increase in the interest rate reduces the quantity demanded along the new curve, $(C^d)'$. It follows that aggregate demand—and, hence, output, which equals the quantity demanded—must decline overall.

From the standpoint of commodity supply, $(Y^s)'$, there is the initial leftward shift of the curve. Then the rise in the interest rate raises the amount supplied along the curve $(Y^s)'$. This increase in quantity supplied only partially offsets the initial decrease because supply and demand are again equal at the new interest rate, $(R^*)'$, and we have just shown that the quantity demanded is lower.

Effects on Work Effort

The forces that operate on work effort are closely related to those that affect consumer demand. The decline in wealth raises work and lowers leisure, and the rise in the interest rate reinforces these effects. Consequently, aggregate work effort rises and aggregate leisure declines. This result makes sense because the disturbance does not change the terms on which people can transform leisure into consumption; that is, the schedule for labor's marginal product does not shift. If the quantities of consumption and leisure change, then we would expect them to change in the same direction. In the present example, the aggregates of consumption and leisure both decrease.

The supply shock leads overall to less output and consumption, but to more work. Recall from the analysis in Chapter 2 that we reached similar conclusions when we confronted Robinson Crusoe with a downward shift of the production function. We might have expected some differences because people can use the credit market to borrow and lend in the present model, whereas Robinson Crusoe could not borrow and lend. But the interest rate adjusts in the market economy to ensure that the aggregate of desired saving is zero. The typical person therefore ends up saving zero, just like Robinson Crusoe. For this reason, we end up with similar predictions about the effects of a worsening of the production function on work effort, production, and consumption.

Remember from Chapter 1 that the reductions in output during recessions are regularly accompanied by declines in labor input, measured by employment or worker-hours. That is, labor input is a strongly procyclical variable. The present example does not fit this pattern because work effort moves in the direction opposite to output. In a later subsection we shall find that we can get the "right" pattern for work effort by allowing for a shift to the schedule for labor's marginal product.

Effects on the Price Level

To determine the price level, we use the condition that all money be willingly held. Recall that this condition is

$$M = P \cdot \Phi(\underset{(-)}{R}, \underset{(+)}{Y}, \ldots)$$

We know that the disturbance lowers aggregate output and raises the interest rate. Both changes reduce the real demand for money, which appears on the right side of the equation. Therefore, Figure 5.5 shows that the demand for money shifts leftward from the line labeled M^d to that labeled $(M^d)'$. Notice that the price level rises from the initial value P^* to the higher value $(P^*)'$. This change is necessary to restore equality between the amount of money demanded and the fixed quantity of money, M.

Note that shifts to the production function lead to movements in opposite directions for output and the price level; for example, an adverse shock lowers output and raises the price level. Recall from Chapter 1 that the general price level was, in fact, a countercyclical variable, at least from 1954 to 1996. The theoretical results therefore accord in this respect with the empirical pattern.

We can use the analysis to understand the effects on the U.S. price level from the oil crises of the last twenty years. Sharp increases in the price of oil, relative to that of other goods, occurred in 1973–74, in 1979–81, and in August 1990 with the start of the Persian Gulf crisis. Although oil crises do not directly affect production opportunities, the

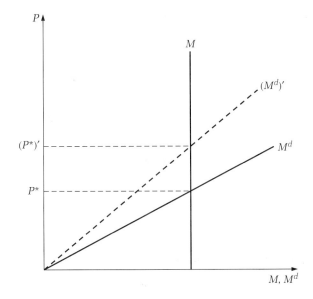

FIGURE 5.5

EFFECT OF A SUPPLY SHOCK ON THE PRICE LEVEL

The increase in the interest rate and the fall in output imply a leftward shift to money demand. The price level rises from P^* to $(P^*)'$ to restore equality between the amount of money demanded and the fixed quantity of money, M.

effects on U.S. businesses resemble those from downward shifts to production functions. Because oil is an important input to production, a cutback in the supply of oil—as reflected in an increase in its relative price—tends to deter the production of other goods. In addition, an increase in oil's relative price means that oil-importing countries, such as the United States, pay out more of their income to foreigners per unit of oil purchased. Therefore, for a given amount of work effort and production, an oil-importing country ends up with less income to spend on consumption.

Overall, the oil crises created adverse shifts of the type shown in Figure 5.4. (These changes apply if people perceived the increase in oil's relative price to be temporary.) Then we find that output falls, the interest rate rises, and the real demand for money declines. Hence, for a given quantity of money, the general price level increases. By similar reasoning, we find that the reductions in the relative price of oil in 1983–84, in 1986, and in 1991 after the end of the Persian Gulf War helped to hold down the overall level of prices in the United States.

We should not conclude that an increase in the relative price of any commodity leads to a rise in the general price level. By the general price level, we mean the number of dollars that it takes to buy a typical market basket of goods. This general level of prices can move up or down while some relative prices increase and some decrease. As an example, consider a poor harvest of grain that affects foreign countries but not the United States. The price of grain rises relative to the price of other goods. From the standpoint of the United States as an exporter of grain, the disturbance amounts to a temporary upward shift of the production function. Hence, there is an increase in real money demanded, which leads to a decline of the overall price level in the United States.

The Dynamics of Changes in the Interest Rate and the Price Level

We have figured out how a particular disturbance, such as a temporary worsening of the production function, changes the general-market-clearing values of the interest rate and the price level. We know that the aggregate-consistency conditions will not be satisfied unless we get to the new position of general market clearing. But we have not really explained how R and P move from one position of market clearing to another.

We mentioned before that a temporary worsening of the production function makes everyone want to save less at the initial interest rate. This decline in offers to lend funds relative to the offers to borrow tends to bid up the interest rate on loans. This reaction is consistent with the increase in the market-clearing value of the interest rate.

We noted also that the disturbance creates excess demand for commodities. It seems reasonable that suppliers would react to this excess demand by raising the price, P, at which they are willing to sell. This response accords with the increase in the market-clearing value of the price level.

The preceding sketch suggests that some plausible stories about market pressures would lead the economy toward the new position of general market clearing. Economists have, in fact, constructed some elaborate models of these dynamics. But it remains true that economists do not understand these processes very well. For one thing, it is difficult to explain how people behave along the way while the aggregate-consistency conditions do not hold.[1] But if we look only at positions in which these conditions hold, then we limit our attention to situations of general market clearing.

In the subsequent analysis, we focus on the characteristics of market-clearing positions. Along the way, we sometimes provide dynamic stories to motivate the changes in the price level and the interest rate. But these stories should be treated with caution, since they do not correspond to fully worked-out models. Our main propositions about the real world come from seeing how particular disturbances influence the conditions for general market clearing. This method usually provides answers that accord well with real-world observations. From an empirical standpoint, therefore, the lack of a formal dynamic theory of price changes may not be that much of a shortcoming.

Summarizing the Results

Let's review our findings for a temporary worsening of the production function. We found that this disturbance leads to cutbacks in output and consumption but to a rise in work effort. The interest rate and the price level rise.

Consider why the interest rate rises. Because everyone regards the fall in output as temporary, they would like to borrow funds to maintain their levels of consumption. Since not everyone can borrow at once, the interest rate increases to restore the balance between desired borrowing and lending. Anyone who lends funds in this depressed situation receives a premium in terms of a high rate of interest.

Consider why the price level rises. The decline in current consumption and output, combined with the rise in the interest rate, reduce the real demand for money. Because the quantity of money is fixed, the price level must rise for the amount of money demanded to equal this fixed quantity.

[1] *Walras thought of an auctioneer who adjusted various prices along the lines of our dynamic sketch, but no trades were concluded until all markets cleared. In this case, we would not have to worry much about how people behaved when markets did not clear. Of course, the device of an auctioneer who adjusts prices should not be taken literally for most markets. The more general idea is that buyers and sellers will manage quickly to establish prices that accord with the market-clearing conditions.*

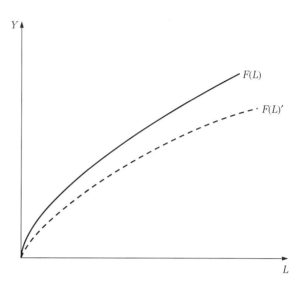

Including a Shift to the Schedule for the Marginal Product of Labor

We have just studied an example in which the production function shifted downward in a parallel fashion. In the typical case, however, the cutback in the production function would be accompanied by a worsening in the schedule for labor's marginal product. There may, for example, be a proportional downward shift of the production function, as shown in Figure 5.6: in this case, the marginal product of labor falls at a given level of work effort. We assume again that the change to the production function applies only for the current period; that is, people still perceive the disturbance to be temporary.

We again have the changes to the commodity market shown in Figure 5.4, but we have to add some new effects that concern the decrease in labor's marginal product. We discuss here *only* these new effects. The fall in productivity induces people to work less today, to increase current leisure, and to decrease current consumption. Because the worsening in production opportunities is temporary, people also want to shift toward current leisure and away from future leisure and consumption. That is, an intertemporal-substitution effect reinforces the reduction in today's work effort. The overall reduction in current work implies a reduction in the current supply of goods, Y^s, and a corresponding decline in current income. Households spread this fall in today's income over reductions in current and future consumption and future leisure. Current consumer demand, C^d, therefore decreases, but by only a small amount relative to the cut in current income.

To incorporate the new effects, we have to make modifications to Figure 5.4. First, we add a leftward shift to the supply curve, $(Y^s)'$. Second, we add a smaller leftward shift to the demand curve, $(C^d)'$. Notice that these changes do not alter the general configuration of the curves shown in Figure 5.4. Hence, we still conclude that output and consumption decrease, and the interest rate rises. Because of the fall in the schedule for labor's marginal product, these effects are all larger than before.

The only qualitative difference in the results concerns the behavior of work effort. We found before that work effort increased. Recall that this response reflected the decrease in wealth and the increase in the interest rate. But now people want to work less because of the fall in the marginal product of labor (MPL). Hence, it is now uncertain whether work effort rises or falls on net.

Think of this last result again in terms of a harvest failure. People want to work a lot today because output is low (the wealth effect) and because the interest rate is high (the intertemporal-substitution effect). But if the harvest failure makes additional labor today relatively unproductive, then people prefer to take leisure instead of work. People work less on net if the dominant effect is this substitution between work and leisure—the main concern then is to work relatively little when productivity is low, but to work hard and long when productivity is high. Labor input is then low along with output in response to an adverse shock and high along with output in response to a favorable shock. Recall from Chapter 1 that the U.S. economy exhibits this procyclical pattern for labor input.

Supply Shocks and the Interest Rate in Nineteenth-Century France

David Denslow and Mark Rush (1989) studied the effects of agricultural harvests on French interest rates over the period 1828 to 1869. This sample was attractive for several reasons: agriculture was a major part of output (roughly 50%), short-term fluctuations in agricultural output reflect mainly the influence of weather (which is a force from outside the economy and is therefore easy to interpret), the French economy had some aspects of an economy without international trade (as in our theoretical model), and good data are available. Denslow and Rush found that a temporary shortfall of wheat production had a statistically significant, inverse effect on the long-term interest rate in France: a 10% decline in the output of wheat raised the interest rate by 0.1 percentage point above the comparable interest rate in England. Thus, these results are consistent with our theoretical analysis.

When we look at the condition that money be willingly held, as shown in equation (5.6) and Figure 5.5, we again find that the disturbance raises the price level. Because output and the interest rate move by more than before, the increase in the price level is greater than previously.

A PERMANENT SHIFT OF THE PRODUCTION FUNCTION

Return to the case of a parallel downward shift of the production function, for which labor's marginal product does not change. But suppose now that this change is permanent rather than lasting for just one period.

The difference from the previous case concerns the size of the wealth effects. There is now a strong negative effect on consumer demand. Also, there is a strong positive effect on work effort, so that the

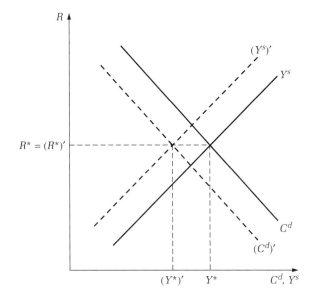

FIGURE 5.7

EFFECT OF A PERMANENT DOWNWARD SHIFT OF THE PRODUCTION FUNCTION ON THE COMMODITY MARKET

The permanent worsening of the production function reduces aggregate supply and demand by comparable amounts. Therefore, the interest rate does not change.

supply of goods falls by less than before. Recall that our analysis in Chapter 3 showed that a permanent shift in the production function had little effect on desired saving: people do not want to borrow more today because future income will be just as low as current income. It follows, for a given interest rate, that the decreases in commodities supplied and demanded would be roughly equal. We use the market-clearing diagram in Figure 5.7 to illustrate this case. Notice that the leftward shifts to the supply and demand curves are the same. Commodity supply still equals commodity demand at the initial interest rate, R^*, and the new market-clearing interest rate, $(R^*)'$, equals R^*.

Output and consumption again decline. Since the interest rate does not change, the reduction in consumer demand now reflects only the decrease in wealth. Similarly, the fall in wealth implies an increase in work effort.

Since output declines and the interest rate does not change, we know that real money demanded declines. We can therefore still use Figure 5.5 to see that the price level rises. Overall, the results for output and the price level resemble those that we found before when the change in the production function was temporary.

The major difference in results is the rise in the interest rate when the worsening of the production function is temporary but no change when the worsening is permanent. The interest rate is a signal that tells people the cost of using resources now rather than later. Specifically, a high interest rate attaches a high cost to current consumption and leisure, relative to future consumption and leisure. When the production function worsens temporarily, there is a scarcity of goods today relative to the future. A high interest rate makes sense in this situation because it makes people take today's relative scarcity into account when they decide how much to consume and work. Conversely, a permanent worsening of the production function means that fewer goods are available at all times; there is no shift in today's position relative to tomorrow's. The interest rate stays the same because there is no change in the cost of using resources today rather than tomorrow.

The results tell us something important about movements in interest rates. Interest rates change when there are economic disturbances that alter present conditions relative to prospective ones. Harvest failures, natural disasters, and major strikes fall into this category. As we stress in a later chapter, war may be empirically the most important example of a disturbance that has a temporary effect on the overall economy. In contrast, we do not predict that permanent shocks will generate large changes in interest rates. (*Warning*: The analysis has so far left out two important influences on interest rates: inflation and shifts to investment demand. We study inflation in Chapters 7 and 8 and investment in Chapter 9.)

As before, we can also include a downward shift to the schedule for the marginal product of labor. This extension does not change most of the results. We still predict that a permanent worsening of the production function has no effect on the interest rate. As in the analysis of a temporary shift, the response of work effort is ambiguous. The force that favors more work is the reduction in wealth, and the force that favors less work is the fall in labor's marginal product. Work effort again falls along with output if the dominant effect is the shift in labor's productivity.

CHANGES IN THE STOCK OF MONEY

In the previous examples, we deduced the change in the price level by examining the condition that money be willingly held. We found that changes in output and the interest rate altered the demand for real money balances. Then the price level changed to equate the nominal quantity of money demanded to the given nominal quantity of money. Essentially, we have dealt with changes in the demand for money while holding fixed the aggregate supply of nominal money, M.

Many economists have argued that changes in the quantity of money, M, are empirically the major source of variations in the price level. To study this linkage, we have to allow for changes in the stock of money. Therefore, we now construct a simple device that enables us to study these changes.

Think of a case in which the initial stock of money, M_0, and all subsequent stocks, M_t for $t > 0$, rise by the same amount. We consider, in other words, a permanent increase in the quantity of money. This change would arise if the government, on a one-time-only basis, printed up some extra money and gave it to people. In Chapters 7 and 17, we shall examine more realistic ways in which new money gets into the economy.

The condition for clearing the commodity market, $Y^s(R, \ldots) = C^d(R, \ldots)$, does not involve the level of the money stock, M. Therefore, we know right away that the change in the number of dollar bills outstanding does not alter the market-clearing value of the interest rate, R^*, or the levels of output and consumption, $Y^* = C^*$.

Consider again the condition that the money stock be willingly held:

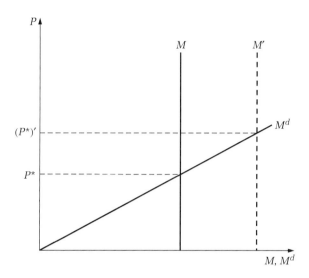

Figure 5.8

Effect of a Change in the Stock of Money

The quantity of money rises from *M* to *M'*. In order for this money to be willingly held, the price level rises from *P** to *(P*)'*.

$$M = P \cdot \Phi(\,R\,,\ Y\,,\dots)$$
$$(-)\ (+)$$

Since the interest rate and the level of output do not change, there is no change in the real demand for money, $\Phi(R, Y, \dots)$, which appears on the right side of the equation. Therefore, the line labeled M^d in Figure 5.8 does not shift. The figure shows, however, that the nominal quantity of money increases from M to M'. It follows that the price level rises from P^* to $(P^*)'$. In order for the change in the nominal amount of money demanded, M^d, to equal the change in the quantity of money, the price level must rise by the same proportion as the money stock. In other words, the real quantity of money, M/P, does not change. This result makes sense because the real amount of money demanded, $\Phi(R, Y, \dots)$, does not change.

We can, as before, outline a dynamic story that makes plausible the increase in the price level. At the initial level of prices, households have more money than they wish to hold, and they therefore try to spend the excess money on goods, leisure, and bonds. (The increased demand for bonds corresponds to the heightened demand for future goods and leisure.) These responses represent the real-balance effect. Remember that this effect operates when, as at present, households have more money than they plan to hold in the future. Since the real-balance effect raises the aggregate demand for goods above the supply, there is upward pressure on the price level.[2] Further, this increase in prices continues until the outstanding amount of money is willingly held. At this point, households no longer have excess money that they wish to spend, and there is no further pressure for the price level to rise.

THE NEUTRALITY OF MONEY

The results exhibit an important property that is called the **neutrality of money**. Once-and-for-all changes in the aggregate quantity of money affect nominal variables but leave real variables unchanged. For example, if the money stock doubles, then the price level doubles, as does the nominal value of production and consumption, $PY = PC$. But no changes occur in the real variables, which include output and consumption, $Y = C$, real money balances, M/P, and the quantity of work, L. The interest rate, R, also does not change. We should think of the interest rate as a real variable: it signals the cost of buying consumption or leisure today rather than tomorrow. In later chapters, we explore further aspects of monetary neutrality.

THE QUANTITY THEORY OF MONEY AND MONETARISM

The **quantity theory of money** refers to a body of thinking about the relation between money and prices. This viewpoint goes back hundreds of years, with some of the most interesting statements coming from David Hume, Henry Thornton, and Irving Fisher.[3] There are two common elements in these analyses. First, changes in the quantity of money have a positive effect on the general price level. Second, as an empirical matter, movements in the money stock account for the major longer-run movements in the price level.

[2] *We noted that households attempt to spend some of their excess money on bonds. This increase in the demand for bonds tends to drive down the interest rate. A lower interest rate causes excess demand for commodities and thereby reinforces the pressure toward higher prices. As the price level rises, the increase in the nominal demand for money reverses the pressure on the bond market and causes the interest rate to rise. At the new position of general market clearing—in which the quantity of money, the price level, and the nominal demand for money have all risen in the same proportion—the net change in the interest rate is nil.*

[3] *See Eugene Rotwein (1970), Henry Thornton (1978), and Irving Fisher (1971, Chaps. 2, 8).*

Some writers refined the quantity theory to apply to changes in the stock of money relative to changes in the quantity of goods on which people could spend their money. The last element corresponds in our model to the total output of goods, Y. But output is only one variable that affects the demand for real money balances. To go further, some quantity theorists stress that the price level increases when the quantity of money rises in relation to the real balances that people want to hold. Hence, most movements in prices would reflect movements in money if the variations in the nominal quantity of money are much greater than the fluctuations in the demand for real money balances.[4]

Sometimes economists identify the quantity theory of money with the statement that monetary changes are neutral. Then we have our previous proposition that shifts in the stock of money have proportional effects on the price level but no effects on real variables. Many quantity theorists regard this hypothesis as accurate in the long run but not for short-run variations in money. The quantity theory allows for the possibility that fluctuations in money have temporary effects on real economic activity. At this point, our model does not admit these short-run real effects of money, but we shall reexamine this matter in later chapters.

More recently, economists and journalists have used the term **monetarism** to describe a school of thought that is similar to modern versions of the quantity theory of money. As with most other terms that are common in the popular press, this one has been used in contradictory ways. But it is clear that monetarists regard the quantity of money as the major determinant of the price level, especially over the long run. Thus, monetarists stress control of the money supply as the central requirement for price stability. Also, monetarism allows for important short-term effects of monetary fluctuations on real economic activity. But monetarists typically regard these effects as unpredictable. Therefore, they argue that stable money is the best policy for avoiding erratic movements of the real variables.[5]

[4] *Milton Friedman stresses the stability of the demand for money as the hallmark of a modern quantity theorist. See Friedman (1956, p. 16).*

[5] *The term monetarism originates with Karl Brunner (1968). Brunner (p. 9) stresses three major features of the monetarist position: "First, monetary impulses are a major factor accounting for variations in output, employment, and prices. Second, movements in the money stock are the most reliable measure of the thrust of monetary impulses. Third, the behavior of the monetary authorities dominates movements in the money stock over business cycles."*

CHANGES IN THE DEMAND FOR MONEY

Our analysis determines the price level by looking at the condition that money be willingly held:

$$M = P \cdot \Phi(R, Y, \ldots)$$
$$ (-) \ (+)$$

We have just studied changes in the money stock: shifts in the quantity of money change the price level in the same direction. Earlier, we examined disturbances to the production function, which ended up changing output, Y, and the interest rate, R. With the money stock held constant, these changes affect the price level by shifting the real demand for money. Notice that the price level moves in the direction opposite to changes in the real demand for money.

An economy may experience changes in the demand for money that do not reflect movements in output or the interest rate. For example, in our model of the demand for money from Chapter 4, there may be changes in the cost of transacting between interest-bearing assets and money. These costs have declined significantly in recent years with the development of money-market funds, automated teller machines (ATMs), and other financial innovations. We predict that these types of changes reduce the demand for real money balances.

To represent this type of change, suppose that the real demand function for money, $\Phi(R, Y, \ldots)$, shifts leftward, as shown in Figure 5.9. The result is that the price level must rise for the nominal amount of money demanded to remain equal to the given nominal quantity, M. Hence, we predict that the financial innovations of recent years—which reduced the demand for real money balances—raise the price level for a given behavior of the nominal quantity of money. Notice also that these innovations lead to a lower level of real money balances, M/P.

In our model the change in the real demand for money—and the resulting change in real money balances—do not influence the condition

FIGURE 5.9

EFFECT OF A DECREASE IN THE DEMAND FOR MONEY ON THE PRICE
LEVEL

The demand for money shifts leftward from M^d to $(M^d)'$. The price
level rises from P^* to $(P^*)'$ to restore equality between the amount
of money demanded and the fixed quantity of money, M.

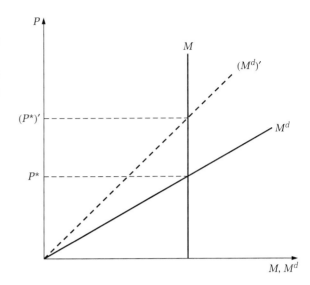

for clearing the commodity market, $Y^s(R, \ldots) = C^d(R, \ldots)$.[6] Therefore, these changes do not affect the market-clearing values of output or the interest rate.

SUMMARY

Any macroeconomic model must satisfy some conditions for aggregate consistency. In our context these are as follows: first, total output equals total consumption; second, any dollar that someone lends corresponds to a dollar that someone else borrows; and third, people hold the outstanding stock of money. We use the idea of market clearing to satisfy these conditions—the supply of commodities equals the demand, the aggregate demand for bonds is zero, and the amount of money demanded equals the quantity outstanding.

The households' budget constraints imply that the three aggregate-consistency conditions are not independent. Walras' law says that we can use any two of the three conditions. We focus on the condition for clearing the commodity market—that the supply of commodities equals

[6] *This property is only an approximation, because changes in real money balances go along with shifts in transaction costs, which would generally affect wealth and thereby the condition for clearing the commodity market.*

the demand—and on the condition that the stock of money be willingly held.

We constructed a market-clearing diagram to show how the condition for clearing the commodity market determines the interest rate and the level of output. The condition that money be willingly held determines the price level for a given nominal quantity of money.

We use the market-clearing apparatus to analyze supply shocks, which we represent as shifts to the production function. A temporary adverse shock lowers output, raises the interest rate and price level, and has an ambiguous effect on work effort. When the unfavorable shift to the production function is permanent rather than temporary, the main difference is that the interest rate does not increase. That conclusion follows because a higher interest rate signals the scarcity of goods today relative to later. When things get permanently worse, there is no reason for the interest rate to change.

Shifts in the nominal quantity of money are neutral in the model: the price level changes in the same proportion as money, but no real variables change. Shifts to the demand for money change the price level in the opposite direction. The only real variable that changes in this case is the quantity of real money balances.

IMPORTANT TERMS AND CONCEPTS

distributional effects Shifts in the distribution of resources across households, with no change in the aggregate of resources; changes such that some sectors in the economy gain at the expense of others.

excess demand A situation in which, at the prevailing price, the quantity demanded in a market exceeds the quantity supplied.

excess supply A situation in which, at the prevailing price, the quantity supplied in a market exceeds the quantity demanded.

general market clearing Simultaneous clearing of all markets.

monetarism A school of thought, based on the quantity theory of money, that changes in the nominal quantity of money primarily account for movements in the price level in the long run and for fluctuations in real economic activity in the short run.

neutrality of money The theoretical finding that once-and-for-all changes in the nominal quantity of money affect nominal variables, such as the general price level, but do not affect real variables, such as real gross national product.

quantity theory of money The theory that changes in the nominal quantity of money account for the majority of long-run movements in the general price level.

supply shock Changes that alter the supply of goods. Important sources of supply shocks are shifts to the production function, changes in marginal tax rates, and variations in the relative price of primary commodities, such as oil.

Walras' law of markets The finding that if all but one of the conditions for general market clearing hold, then the final one must hold as well; this result follows because households' budget constraints must be satisfied.

QUESTIONS AND PROBLEMS

MAINLY FOR REVIEW

5.1 How are transactions in different markets, such as consumption and borrowing, linked in individual budget constraints? How does Walras' law show that this linkage carries over to the markets as a whole?

5.2 How does a change in (a) the interest rate, (b) wealth, and (c) the production function affect the aggregate demand and supply of commodities? Describe the effects graphically, making sure to distinguish between *shifts in* and *movements along* the demand and supply curves.

5.3 Why is a change in the price level not effective in reducing excess demand or supply in the commodity market? Explain how a change in the price level can ensure that the outstanding quantity of money is held willingly.

5.4 Consider a parallel upward shift of the production function, which raises the aggregate supply of commodities. Use a graph to convince yourself that

a. if consumption demand shifts by an equivalent amount, then the interest rate does not change.

b. if consumption demand shifts by a smaller amount, then the interest rate declines.

5.5 Describe your results in question 5.4 in terms of the marginal propensity to consume. Which of the two possibilities is likely to hold when the shift in the production function is temporary?

5.6 What is meant by the neutrality of money? Explain its implications for the popular notion that an increase in the quantity of money reduces the interest rate.

5.7 Consider a decline in the transaction cost of converting financial assets into money. Describe its effect on (a) the price level, (b) the real quantity of money, and (c) velocity. Do these effects contradict the neutrality of monetary changes?

5.8 Walras' Law of Markets

a. Show how to derive Walras' law of markets (equation [5.3]) by using the households' budget constraints.

b. We seem to have three independent conditions for aggregate consistency: aggregate demand for bonds equals zero, $B_1^d = 0$; the money stock is willingly held, $M_0 = M_1^d$; and there is equality between commodities supplied and demanded, $Y_1^s = C_1^d$. Walras' law says that only two of these conditions are independent. Explain this result.

c. How do the number of independent conditions for aggregate consistency compare with the number of market prices that we have to determine in the model? By the term *market prices*, we mean to include both the price level, P, and the interest rate, R. (The interest rate is the price of credit.)

d. Write out Walras' law in the form of a sum of aggregate excess demands, $C^d - Y^s$, $M_1^d/P - M_0/P$, and B_1^d/P. What does the law say in this form?

5.9 Effects of a Change in Population

Assume a one-time decrease in population, possibly caused by an onset of plague or a sudden out-migration. The people who left are the same as those who remain in terms of productivity and tastes. The aggregate quantity of money does not change.

What happens to aggregate output, Y; work effort, L; the interest rate, R; and the price level, P?

5.10 Effects of a Change in the Willingness to Work

Suppose (in a magical, unexplained fashion) that all households change their preferences to favor consumption over leisure. That is, people raise their willingness to work. Assume that no change occurs in preferences for expenditures now versus later, so that aggregate desired saving does not change at the initial interest rate.

What happens to aggregate output, Y; work effort, L; the interest rate, R; and the price level, P? Can you think of some real-world events that might raise everybody's willingness to work?

(*Note*: We will be in trouble if we permit unrestricted fluctuations in preferences. A basic strength of the economic approach—and the basis for forming hypotheses that we can conceivably reject from observed data—is the assumption of stable tastes. Then we can analyze changes to production possibilities and other disturbances in terms of wealth and substitution effects, as we did in the text. In this manner, we end up with predictable influences on observable variables, such as output and the price level. But if tastes are unstable, then we can reconcile any observed behavior by invoking the appropriate shift in unobservable preferences. This capacity for explaining all data means that the model has no predictive value. Also, unaccountable shifts in preferences are more plausible for an individual than for the aggregate of households. Usually there is no good reason for everyone to become more eager to work at precisely the same time.)

5.11 Effects of a Shift in Desired Saving

Suppose that all households increase their preference for current expenditures over future expenditures. In particular, desired saving declines at a given value of the interest rate.

What happens to aggregate output, Y; work effort, L; the interest rate, R; and the price level, P?

(The note attached to problem 5.10 applies also to the change in tastes assumed in this problem.)

5.12 Temporary Changes in the Price Level

Consider again the analysis of a temporary worsening of the production function (Figures 5.4 and 5.5). We showed that the price level rises from its initial value, P^*, to a higher value, $(P^*)'$. But since the disturbance is temporary, the price level would return in later periods to the initial value, P^*. At least, this result would occur if nothing else changes, including the quantity of money.

So far, the analysis assumes that people expect the price level to remain constant over time. But we just showed that the current price level is above its expected future values when there is a temporary worsening of the production function. Think about how to modify the analysis to take account of expected future changes in the price level. (Do not spend too much time on this problem, since we shall study this topic in detail in Chapters 7 and 8.)

5.13 Consumption, Saving, and the Interest Rate (optional)

According to the theory, an increase in the interest rate motivates people to reduce current consumption relative to current income. Correspondingly, people increase current saving. Yet although a temporary downward shift of the production function leads to an increase in the interest rate, it does not lead to any change in the ratio of aggregate consumption to aggregate income (which equals one in this model). Also, there is no change in aggregate saving, which equals zero.

a. Explain these results.

b. Researchers often attempt to estimate the effects of a change in the interest rate on an individual's choices of consumption and saving. Many studies look at the relation between the interest rate and either the ratio of aggregate consumption to aggregate income or the amount of aggregate saving. What does the theory predict for this relation? Why does it not reveal the effect of a change in the interest rate on an individual's desire to consume and save?

c. The theory says that an increase in the interest rate motivates people to raise next period's consumption, c_2, relative to this period's, c_1. Suppose that we look at the relation of the interest rate, R_1, to the ratio of aggregate consumptions, C_2/C_1. Does this relation reveal something about the behavior of individuals?

d. Suppose that we want to use aggregate data to figure out the effects of the interest rate on an individual's choices of consumption and saving. What do the answers to this question suggest that we should look at?

5.14 The Dynamics of Changes in the Price Level

In the text, we examined a case in which the real demand for money declined. Then the price level increased, but the interest rate did not change.

a. Outline a dynamic story that describes the pressures for the price level to rise.

b. Does the interest rate stay fixed or move around while the price level adjusts in part a?

c. Can you tell a story in which the price level jumps immediately to its new market-clearing position rather than adjusting gradually in accordance with the sketch in part a?

5.15 A Currency Reform

Suppose that the government replaces the existing monetary unit with a new one. For example, the United States might shift from the old dollar to the Reagan dollar, which equals 10 old dollars. People can exchange their old currency for the new one at a ratio of 10 to 1. Also, any contracts that were written in terms of old dollars are converted at the ratio of 10 to 1 into Reagan dollars.

a. What happens to the price level and the interest rate?

b. What happens to the quantities of output, consumption, and work effort?

c. Do the results exhibit the neutrality of money?

5.16 Temporary versus Permanent Changes of the Production Function (optional)

Consider the parallel downward shift of the production function in

Figure 5.3. This type of change does not affect the schedule for labor's marginal product. Suppose first that this change is permanent.

a. We dealt with this type of disturbance for an isolated individual, Robinson Crusoe, in Chapter 2. We found that Crusoe reduced output and consumption but raised work effort. How do these results compare with those that we obtained in the present chapter, which includes markets for commodities and credit? Think of the typical or representative household: does that household's responses of output, consumption, and work effort differ from those of Robinson Crusoe?

b. Suppose now that the change to the production function is temporary. Compare again Robinson Crusoe's responses of output, consumption, and work effort with those of the typical household in the model from the present chapter.

c. For Robinson Crusoe, how do the responses of output, consumption, and work effort depend on whether the improvement to the production function is temporary or permanent? (Problem 2.9 in Chapter 2 deals with this matter.)

d. Put together the results from parts a, b, and c. They tell us how to compare temporary and permanent changes in the production function for the model in the present chapter, which includes markets for commodities and credit. How do the responses of output, consumption, and work effort for the typical household depend on whether the change in the production function is permanent or temporary?

THE LABOR MARKET

T o simplify matters, we assumed thus far that households used only their own labor to produce goods. In other words, we did not distinguish between households and firms. Now we make the analysis more realistic by introducing a market in which people exchange labor services. This market, known as the labor market, can be thought of as a place in which people supply and demand labor services. The people who buy labor services are the firms or employers in the economy. Those who sell services are the employees.

The clearing of the labor market—along with the clearing of the markets for commodities and credit—determines the aggregates of work and output. One objective of this chapter is to see how much the presence of the labor market and the existence of firms change the way that these aggregates are determined. For most macroeconomic questions, it turns out that the answer is "not much." Our previous simplified setting in which people work only on their own production processes is satisfactory for most purposes. The extensions in this chapter do, however, allow us to explore the determination of wage rates and the manner in which a labor market promotes economic efficiency. The extended framework will also be essential later when we study unemployment (in Chapter 10).

SETUP OF THE LABOR MARKET

Suppose, for simplicity, that everyone's labor services are physically the same. But instead of working on one's own production process, people now sell their labor services on the labor market. This market establishes a single wage rate, which we denote by w and measure in units of dollars per person-hour. (For convenience, we omit time subscripts here.) By the wage rate we mean that buyers of labor services pay w dollars for each hour that someone works for them. Correspondingly, sellers of labor services receive w dollars for each hour of work. As in our treatment of the commodity market, we assume that each individual buyer and seller regards the wage rate, w, as a given.

Denote by l^s the number of person-hours of labor services that a household supplies to the labor market during a period. Correspondingly, this household receives the dollar quantity wl^s of labor income.

Suppose that some of the households—who are inclined to be entrepreneurs—set themselves up as **firms**. These firms hire other people as workers. Let l^d denote the number of person-hours of labor services that a firm demands from the labor market. Correspondingly, the firm pays the dollar amount wl^d as wage payments to its workers.

Each firm uses its input of labor services, l^d, to produce commodities. The quantity produced and supplied to the commodity market is

$$y^s = f\left(l^d\right) \tag{6.1}$$

where f is again the production function. Since the goods sell at the price P, the firm's gross revenue from sales is Py^s. The firm's **profit** (or earnings) equals gross revenue less wage payments:

$$\text{Profit} = Py^s - wl^d = P \cdot f(l^d) - wl^d \tag{6.2}$$

Note that firms do not issue or hold bonds at this stage of the analysis. The potential to borrow becomes important in Chapter 9 when we allow for investment.

A firm's earnings go to the household or households that own the firm. We could introduce a **stock market**, on which people bought and sold the ownership rights in businesses. Then the profits would go to the current shareholders in the form of dividend payments. To keep things simple, we do not introduce a stock market and assume that the ownership rights in firms are distributed in an unspecified manner among the households.[1] In any event, it is important to note that all firms must be owned 100% by some households. Each household's total income now includes its share of profits from firms, as well as wage income, wl^s, and interest income.

THE DEMAND FOR LABOR

Think about a household that owns all or part of a firm. The household's utility depends on its consumption, c^d, and work, l^s. Hence, the firm's demand for labor, l^d, matters to the household-owner only through its effect on the firm's profit, which appears in equation (6.2). If the firm acts to benefit its owners—as we assume—then it sets its demand for labor, l^d, to maximize profit in each period.

An increase in labor input, l^d, has two effects on profit. First, an extra hour of work means that output, $f(l^d)$, increases by the marginal product of labor, MPL. Gross sales revenue therefore rises by the dollar amount, $P \cdot MPL$. Second, the wage bill increases by the dollar wage rate, w. Profit rises on net with an increase in labor input if the value of labor's marginal product, $P \cdot MPL$, exceeds w. To maximize profit a firm expands employment, l^d, up to the point at which the value of the marginal product just equals the wage rate, that is, until $P \cdot MPL = w$. If

[1] *The ability to buy and sell stocks in various businesses becomes more interesting if we allow for uncertainties about each firm's earnings. Then households have an incentive to diversify their holdings of stock across many types of businesses. Because we have not introduced these uncertainties, a stock market would not add much to the analysis.*

FIGURE 6.1

DEMAND FOR LABOR

Labor's marginal product, MPL, declines as the quantity of labor
increases. Producers set the demand for labor, l^d, at the point where
the marginal product equals the real wage rate, w/P.

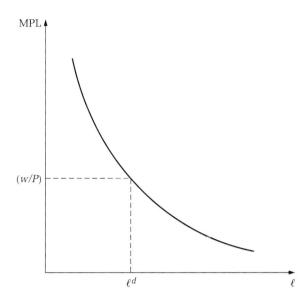

we divide through by the price level, then the condition that each firm
satisfies in every period is

$$MPL = w/P \qquad\qquad\qquad\qquad\qquad\qquad \textbf{(6.3)}$$

Notice that the right side of equation (6.3) is the **real wage rate**,
w/P. This variable is the quantity of commodities that someone can buy
with the dollar amount w. Equation (6.3) says that a producer chooses
the quantity of labor input, l^d, so that the marginal product, MPL, equals
the real wage rate. At that point, the last unit of labor contributes just
enough to output, MPL, so as to cover the extra cost of this labor in units
of commodities, which is the real wage rate.

Figure 6.1 illustrates the results. The curve shows the negative effect
of more labor input on the marginal product, MPL. Notice that firms set
their demand for labor, l^d, at the point where the marginal product equals
the real wage rate, w/P.

THE GAINS FROM EQUALIZING LABOR'S MARGINAL PRODUCT ACROSS FIRMS

At a point in time, each worker receives the same real wage rate because we assumed that all labor services are identical. Labor's marginal product therefore ends up being the same on all production processes. This result holds even if there are differences across firms in production functions or across households in their willingness to work. It is efficient to equalize these marginal products: otherwise the economy's total output could rise, without changing total work effort, by shifting workers from one place to another. The increase in output results if a worker moves from an activity where his or her marginal product is low to one where it is high.

There is no reason for workers' marginal products to be equal if a labor market does not exist. In our earlier model, in which people worked only on their own production processes, workers might end up with large differences in marginal products. Because one person could not work on another's production activity, there was no mechanism to equalize the marginal products.

Consider two isolated regions, A and B. The technology in A is primitive, and workers end up with the low marginal product and real wage rate, $MPL^A = (w/P)^A$. Region B is more advanced and ends up with a higher marginal product and real wage rate, $MPL^B = (w/P)^B$. Now suppose that an economy-wide labor market develops, and this market allows people from region A to work in region B and vice versa. As we set things up, the workers from the low-wage region A would migrate to region B. Then, by working with the better technology, these workers can produce more goods without working any harder. The movement of workers out of A and into B continues until the marginal products and real wage rates are equalized in the two regions. This equalization results partly through a higher marginal product in A (in which work declines) and partly through a lower marginal product in B (in which work increases). But for our purposes, the important point is that the opening up of the economy-wide labor market allows for an expansion of aggregate output without requiring an increase in total work effort. In that sense the economy operates more efficiently when the labor market exists.

As with the commodity and credit markets, we find that the existence of the labor market aids economic efficiency: this market exhausts all the potential gains from movements of workers from one place to another. Because everyone's marginal product and real wage rate end up being the same, there are no gains of this type that remain unexploited.

PROPERTIES OF THE DEMAND FOR LABOR

We can use Figure 6.1 to see how various changes affect the demand for labor. It follows at once that a decrease in the real wage rate, w/P, means a higher quantity of labor demanded. When the real cost of hiring workers decreases, firms expand employment until labor's marginal product falls by as much as the decrease in w/P.

An upward shift in the schedule for labor's marginal product—that is, an upward shift of the curve in Figure 6.1—leads to a greater quantity of labor demanded at any given real wage rate. Employment expands until the marginal product again equals w/P.

We can summarize the results by writing down a function for the aggregate demand for labor. This function takes the form

$$L^d = L^d(\underset{(-)}{w/P}, \ldots) \tag{6.4}$$

where the expression . . . again refers to characteristics of the production function.

Recall that each firm's choice of labor input determines its supply of goods through the production function, $y^s = f(l^d)$. Since the quantity of labor demanded with the real wage rate, we can write the function for the aggregate supply of goods as

$$Y^s = Y^s(\underset{(-)}{w/P}, \ldots) \tag{6.5}$$

LABOR SUPPLY AND CONSUMPTION DEMAND

The introduction of the labor market does not greatly alter our earlier analysis of work effort and consumption demand. The main modification concerns the household's choice between consumption and leisure at a point in time. In our previous model the schedule for labor's marginal product, MPL, tells people the terms on which they can substitute consumption for leisure. When someone works an extra hour on his or her own production process, he or she can use the additional output (of MPL units) to raise consumption. Now households sell their labor services at the real wage rate, w/P, rather than working on their own production. The real wage rate therefore indicates the terms on which people can substitute consumption for leisure. Someone who works an extra hour can use the additional w/P units of real income to expand consumption.

For a household, the real wage rate now appears where previously the schedule for labor's marginal product appeared. Specifically, an increase in the real wage rate motivates households to increase labor supply and consumption demand. But recall that the choice of labor demand by firms guarantees that the real wage rate equals the economy-wide marginal product of labor. Therefore, the effects from the real wage amount, ultimately, to corresponding effects from the schedule for labor's marginal product.

As before, wealth effects can arise from shifts in production functions. These effects show up first on firms' profits (and on stock prices if we had introduced a stock market). But it is important to remember that the profits go to the households that own the firms. Therefore, the shifts in production functions ultimately have wealth effects on households, as in our earlier model that ignored firms.

One new consideration is the wealth effect from a change in the real wage rate, given the position of the production function. An increase in w/P benefits the households that sell labor services. But this benefit is matched by an extra cost for the firms, which buy labor services. Since the firms are owned by households, the overall wealth effect on households from a change in w/P is nil. (There would be distributional effects if households differ by their relative amounts of wage and profit income. But we follow our usual practice of neglecting distributional effects on the aggregates of labor supply and consumption demand.)

The interest rate, R, has the same intertemporal-substitution effects as before. An increase in R motivates households to save more by reducing current consumption demand and raising current labor supply. An additional intertemporal-substitution effect arises if people anticipate variations over time in the real wage rate. Suppose, for example, that workers regard the current real wage rate as high relative to future values. Then they increase current labor supply and plan to reduce labor supply in the future. Before, we found similar effects if people anticipated changes in the schedule for labor's marginal product.

We can summarize the results in this section by writing down functions for the aggregates of labor supply and consumption demand. These functions take the forms

$$L^s = L^s(\underset{(+)}{w/P},\ \underset{(+)}{R},\ \ldots) \tag{6.6}$$

and

$$C^d = C^d(\underset{(+)}{w/P},\ \underset{(-)}{R},\ \ldots) \tag{6.7}$$

The omitted terms, denoted by . . . , include characteristics of the production function, as well as any elements that generate departures of expected future real wage rates from the current value.

CLEARING OF THE LABOR MARKET

The labor market clears when the aggregate supply of labor, L^s, equals the aggregate demand, L^d. Therefore, using equations (6.4) and (6.6), the

Empirical Evidence on the Response of Labor Supply to Time Variations in Real Wage Rates

We discussed in Chapter 3 the estimates of George Alogoskoufis (1987a, 1987b) for intertemporal-substitution effects on labor supply. Aside from the influence of interest rates, which we mentioned before, these studies also consider the response of labor supply to anticipated variations in real wage rates. For the United States, an increase by one percentage point per year in the expected growth rate of real wages raised the growth rate of the number of workers by about one percentage point per year. For the United Kingdom, the results showed less sensitivity of work effort to variations in real wages; an increase by one percentage point per year in the expected growth rate of real wages raised the growth rate of the number of workers by only about 0.4% per year. For both countries, the results were weaker if work effort was measured by hours worked per person rather than the number of workers: the relation between the expected growth rate of real wages and the growth rate of hours worked per capita was not statistically significant. This evidence therefore suggests that intertemporal substitution of labor supply in response to time variations of wages is more important for the number of people working than for hours worked per person.

Casey Mulligan (1995b) argued that it is hard to detect the intertemporal substitution of work from the household data used by Alogoskoufis and other economists because it is unclear when workers perceive the current real wage rate to be temporarily high or low. Mulligan therefore looked at a variety of alternative sources of evidence to assess the responsiveness of labor supply to anticipated variations in real wage rates.

Mulligan particularly focused on situations in which unusual events effectively created experiments that raised or lowered real wage rates in a temporary manner. One example is the Alaskan gas pipeline project, which began in 1974 and was completed in 1977. The project necessitated a dramatic—and clearly temporary—increase in construction labor, which was compensated by high—and temporary—real wage rates. Figure 6.2 shows the time patterns for the real wage rate (real hourly earnings in construction in Alaska) and work effort (average weekly hours of construction workers in Alaska). The key point is the sharp and temporary peak in both series during the building of the pipeline. The magnitude of the relation implies that a temporary rise of the real wage rate by 10% would increase labor ↗

supply by about 20%, which is much greater responsiveness than that reported by Alogoskoufis. (However, one special feature of this example is that many of the pipeline construction workers were migrants who came to Alaska to work specifically on this project. For this reason, the estimated relation does not reveal the response of labor supply for a fixed group of workers.)

Mulligan also looked at another Alaskan experiment, the cleanup of the *Exxon Valdez* oil spill in 1989. Figure 6.3 shows the patterns in the Alaskan transportation and public utilities industries (sectors especially affected by the cleanup operation) for real wages rates and average hours worked per week. The positive spikes in both series during the cleanup period provide an estimate of the responsiveness of labor supply to a clearly temporary increase in the real wage rate. The estimate in this case is that a temporary rise of the real wage rate by 10% would raise labor supply by even more than 20%. Thus, these nearly experimental situations suggest that workers are willing to expand their labor supply dramatically in response to temporary opportunities for high wage rates.

condition for clearing the labor market is

$$L^d(w/P, \ldots) = L^s(w/P, R, \ldots) \tag{6.8}$$
$$(-)(+)(+)$$

Recall that the terms denoted by . . . include characteristics of the production function.

As before, there are also conditions for clearing the commodity market and for ensuring that all money is willingly held. These conditions must hold along with equation (6.8) to ensure the clearing of all markets. When we take these conditions together, we shall be able to determine the nominal wage rate, w, as well as the interest rate, R, and the price level, P. In other words, we add one new market-clearing condition, equation (6.8), and thereby determine one more "price"—the price of labor services, w. For now, we focus on the new condition for clearing the labor market.

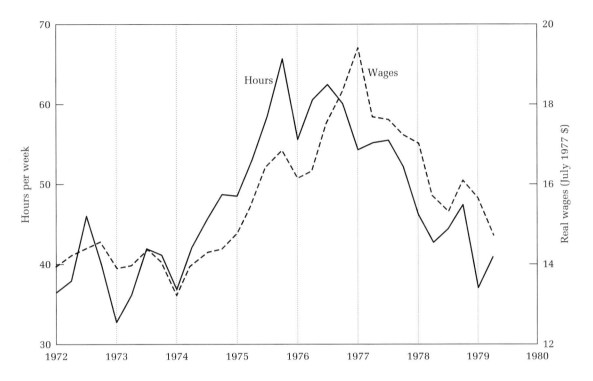

FIGURE 6.2

ALASKAN WAGE RATES AND HOURS DURING THE ALASKAN PIPELINE PROJECT

Note that real wage rates and average weekly hours worked in Alaskan construction were both high from 1973 to 1979 in response to the pipeline project. This behavior yields the estimate that a temporary increase by 10% in the real wage rate raises labor supply by about 20%.

Figure 6.4 shows the clearing of the labor market. For convenience, we place the real wage rate, w/P, on the vertical axis and labor demand and supply on the horizontal. The quantity of labor demanded by firms falls with w/P, and the quantity of labor supplied by households rises with w/P.

Notice from Figure 6.4 that the aggregates of labor demand and supply are equal when the real wage rate is $(w/P)^*$ and the level of work is L^*. We can think of this overall level of work effort as corresponding to aggregate **employment** (number of persons working) or to total hours worked

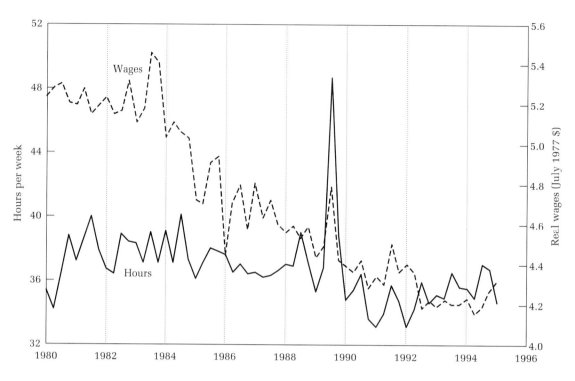

FIGURE 6.3

ALASKAN WAGE RATES AND HOURS IN RESPONSE TO THE *EXXON VALDEZ* OIL SPILL

Note that Alaskan real wage rates and average weekly hours worked in the transportation and public utilities industries were both unusually high in 1989 in response to the cleanup of the *Exxon Valdez* oil spill. This behavior yields the estimate that a temporary rise of the real wage rate by 10% raises labor supply by more than 20%.

by all persons. Figure 6.4 allows us to relate the market-clearing values of the real wage rate and employment (or total hours worked) to variables that shift either the labor-demand curve or the labor-supply curve. These variables include the interest rate, R, the forms of production functions, and prospective changes in the real wage rate. For example, an increase in the interest rate shifts the labor-supply curve rightward in Figure 6.4. Employment, L^*, therefore rises, and the real wage rate, $(w/P)^*$, declines.

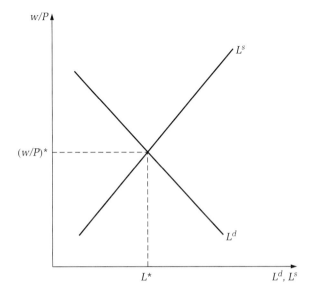

FIGURE 6.4

CLEARING OF THE LABOR MARKET

For a given value of the interest rate, R, and for a given form of the production function, the labor market clears when the real wage rate is $(w/P)^*$ and the quantity of work is L^*.

CLEARING OF THE COMMODITY MARKET

Using equations (6.5) and (6.7), we can write the condition for clearing the commodity market as

$$C^d(w/P,\ R\,,\ldots) = Y^s(w/P,\ldots) \tag{6.9}$$
$$\ \ \ (+)\ \ \ (-)\ \ \ \ \ \ \ \ \ \ \ \ \ \ (-)$$

We want to show that this condition is essentially the same as the one for clearing the commodity market in Chapter 5. That is, we want to demonstrate that the introduction of the labor market and firms leaves intact our previous analysis of the commodity market. This finding is important because it means that all of our results from Chapter 5 carry through to the extended model that includes a labor market.

Recall that the condition for clearing the labor market in equation (6.8) (and Figure 6.4) determines w/P. This condition implies that an increase in the interest rate, R, shifts the labor-supply curve rightward in Figure 6.4. Hence, w/P falls when R rises. We can use this result to substitute out for the real wage rate, w/P, in the condition for clearing the commodity market, equation (6.9). After substituting for w/P in terms of R, we get the simplified condition for clearing the commodity market:

$$C^d(\,R\,,\ldots) = Y^s(\,R\,,\ldots) \qquad\qquad \textbf{(6.10)}$$
$$\quad\; {\scriptstyle(-)} \qquad\qquad\; {\scriptstyle(+)}$$

As usual, the expression . . . includes characteristics of the production function.

Notice that w/P does not appear in equation (6.10) because we have replaced it by the various elements, including R, that determine the real wage rate. In particular, since Y^s depends on w/P in equation (6.9), and since w/P depends on R, Y^s depends indirectly on R. Therefore, when we solve out for w/P, Y^s depends directly on R in equation (6.10).

Let's examine in detail how the interest rate enters into the condition for clearing the commodity market in equation (6.10). Recall that an increase in R shifts the labor-supply curve rightward in Figure 6.4 and thereby causes a decline in w/P. This decline in w/P leads, as shown in equation (6.9), to an expansion of goods supply, Y^s. Therefore, the positive effect of R on Y^s in equation (6.10) picks up this channel of effects.

On the demand side, the change in the interest rate has two effects. First, from equation (6.9), an increase in R lowers consumer demand, C^d, for a given value of w/P. Second, because an increase in R leads to a lower value of w/P, there is a further decline in consumer demand. The negative effect of R on C^d in equation (6.10) picks up both channels of effect.

The important point is that equation (6.10) looks just like the condition for clearing the commodity market that we used in Chapter 5.[2] Because the condition for clearing the commodity market looks as it did before, we can still use our previous analysis to determine the interest rate and the quantities of output and work effort for each period. To see how this works, let's reconsider the example of a shift in the production function.

[2] *The only difference is that the labor market ensures that everyone's marginal product of labor, which equals the real wage rate, is the same. The equality of real wage rates arises only because we assumed, first, that everyone's labor services were physically identical and, second, that all jobs had similar working conditions. We could expand the analysis to deal with different levels of skills and different characteristics of jobs. Then we would find that real wage rates were higher for people who were more productive and on jobs that were less pleasant. But these considerations would not change the major macroeconomic results.*

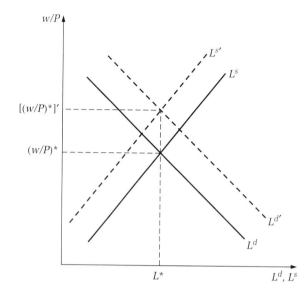

FIGURE 6.5

EFFECT OF AN IMPROVEMENT IN THE PRODUCTION FUNCTION ON THE LABOR MARKET

The permanent upward shift of the production function raises the demand for labor but lowers the supply. Therefore, the real wage rate increases, but the change in work is uncertain.

AN IMPROVEMENT IN THE PRODUCTION FUNCTION

Assume a permanent proportional upward shift of the production function. This change means that the level of aggregate output and the marginal product of labor increase for a given amount of aggregate work effort.

Figure 6.5 shows the effects on the labor market. Because the disturbance raises wealth, the supply of labor declines for a given value of w/P. Because of the upward shift to the schedule for labor's marginal product, the demand for labor rises for a given value of w/P. Hence, Figure 6.5 shows that the real wage rate increases, but the change in the quantity of labor is uncertain. As in some previous cases, the wealth effect suggests less work, but the improvement in productivity suggests more work. If the dominant element is the effect on productivity, then work effort rises in response to a favorable shock.

Figure 6.6 shows the effects on the commodity market. We use the market-clearing condition from equation (6.10), which takes account of the determination of the real wage rate from the labor market. Notice

FIGURE 6.6

EFFECT OF AN IMPROVEMENT IN THE PRODUCTION FUNCTION ON THE COMMODITY MARKET

The permanent upward shift of the production function raises the demand and supply of commodities by roughly equal amounts. Output therefore increases, but the interest rate does not change.

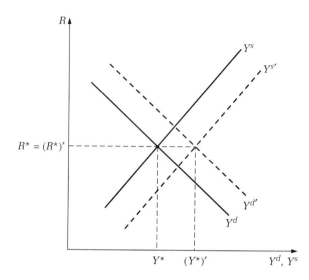

first the rightward shift in consumer demand. This shift reflects partly the wealth effect from the improvement in the production function and partly the substitution effect (toward consumption and away from leisure) from the rise in the real wage rate.

The supply of goods rises with the improvement in the production function but falls because of the increase in the real wage rate. Recall that the shift in the production function and the resulting change in w/P are permanent in this example. Therefore, the aggregate of desired saving would change little, if at all, at the initial interest rate. This result means that goods supply, Y^s, shifts rightward on net by roughly the same amount as C^d. We conclude from Figure 6.6 that output increases, but the interest rate does not change.[3]

An important observation is that the results coincide with those that we reached earlier, when people worked on only their own production processes. A permanent improvement in production opportunities raises aggregate output but has an ambiguous effect on work effort. Labor input is procyclical, as in the data, if the positive response of labor demand to the improvement in productivity dominates over the negative response of labor supply to the increase in wealth. Further, because the shift in the production function is permanent, there is no change in the interest rate.

[3] *Because the interest rate does not change, we do not have to modify the analysis of the labor market in Figure 6.5. Recall that this diagram applies for a given value of the interest rate.*

THE BEHAVIOR OF THE REAL WAGE RATE

The model predicts that the real wage rate would be procyclical: favorable shocks to the production function raise output and the real wage rate, whereas unfavorable shocks lower output and the real wage rate. Moreover, if the response of labor demand to the change in productivity dominates over the reduction in labor supply because there is more wealth, then labor input is also procyclical. The quantity of labor rises in booms along with the expansions of output and real wage rates. Similarly, these variables fall together during recessions.

The last results rely on the shifts in labor demand due to changing productivity in Figure 6.5. If the labor demand curve did not shift—because the production function did not change or because we allowed only for parallel shifts in the production function—then shifts in the labor-supply curve would trace out the fixed labor-demand curve. Since the labor-demand curve slopes downward, the quantity of labor and the real wage rate would have to move in opposite directions and therefore could not *both* be procyclical. This result is important because the data indicate that both variables are procyclical. To fit the theory to these facts we have to allow for shifts to labor demand that reflect changes in the productivity of labor.

We discussed in Chapter 1 the procyclical behavior of labor input, measured by employment or worker-hours. The dashed line in Figure 6.7 shows the U.S. real wage rate on a proportionate scale from 1959 to 1996. We measure the real wage rate by the ratio of average hourly earnings of production workers in manufacturing to the consumer price index (CPI). The solid line in the figure is a smooth trend line that filters out the longer-run movements of the real wage rate. (See the discussion of trend lines in Chapter 1.) Figure 6.8 plots the detrended real wage rate—the difference between the actual and trend values shown in Figure 6.7—against detrended real GDP. Recall that each of these detrended values represents a proportionate deviation from the long-run path. The real wage rate moves substantially around its trend but is less volatile than real GDP—the respective standard deviations are 0.011 and 0.018. The

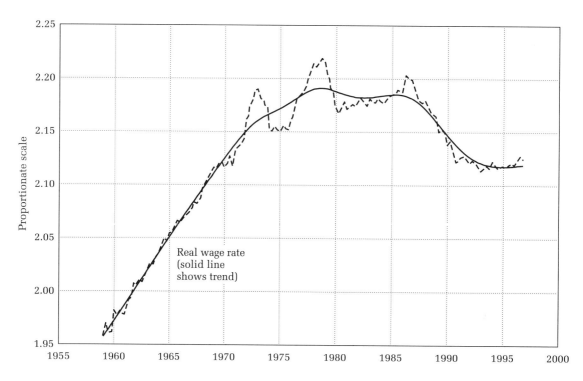

FIGURE 6.7

THE REAL WAGE RATE AND ITS TREND

The dashed line shows the real wage rate (average hourly earnings for production workers in manufacturing divided by the CPI, exclusive of shelter). The solid line is a smooth trend line for the real wage rate. See Chapter 1 for a discussion of the methodology.

[4] *The procyclical pattern for the real wage rate also shows up if we look at subperiods of the full sample. For example, the correlation of the detrended real wage rate with detrended real GDP is 0.62 from 1959 to 1972 and 0.51 from 1973 to 1996. The procyclical nature of the real wage rate would be even stronger if we were able to adjust for cyclical changes in the quality of the labor force. This*

real wage rate is clearly procyclical: the correlation of the detrended real wage rate with detrended real GDP is 0.55.[4] This pattern fits with the model's predictions and therefore provides some support for the theory.

In a long-run context, the development of an economy involves a series of permanent improvements to the production function of the sort depicted in Figures 6.5 and 6.6. Our analysis therefore predicts that

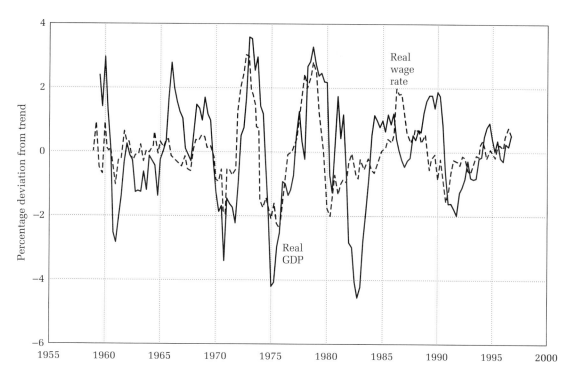

FIGURE 6.8

THE CYCLICAL COMPONENTS OF REAL GDP AND THE REAL WAGE RATE

The solid line shows the cyclical part of real GDP, and the dashed line shows the cyclical part of the real wage rate. The cyclical component of the real wage rate is the difference between the actual and trend values from Figure 6.7.

economic development leads to continuing increases in the real wage rate. This proposition accords with data for a large number of countries.

In the United States, the real wage rate shown in Figure 6.7—average real hourly earnings in manufacturing—grew at an average rate of 0.7% per year from 1959 to 1996. The figure shows, however, that real wage rates grew strongly from 1959 to 1973, at an average rate of 1.9% per year, and have not grown since. (The growth rate from 1973 to 1996 was −0.2% per year.) It is possible to look at a broader measure

[4] (continued) *average quality (measured by education, experience, or lifetime real wages) tends to rise during recessions because the lesser skilled workers typically lose jobs quicker than the more skilled. In addition, firms reduce their standards for hiring during booms. Because the average quality of the labor force is countercyclical, the real wage rate per unit of labor quality is more procyclical than the rate per worker-hour.*

of real labor compensation, one that applies to the entire economy and that includes some parts of fringe benefits.[5] This measure shows a small increase from 1973 to 1996—the average growth rate was 0.4% per year—but the dramatic decline in real wage growth after 1973 is still present. The behavior of real wage growth before and after 1973 mirrors the patterns in labor productivity. Output per worker-hour grew at 1.9% per year from 1959 to 1973 and by 0.8% per year from 1973 to 1996.

The diminished growth rate of labor productivity is well known and is often described as the **productivity slowdown.** However, the sources of this slowdown are not well understood. One interesting suggestion involves the overstatement of measured inflation, as discussed for the consumer price index in Chapter 1. If this inflation bias has increased over time (as can plausibly be argued), then the slowdown in real wage and productivity growth would be exaggerated in the data. That is, one way to explain the productivity slowdown is to argue that it has not occurred (or, at least, has been overstated)!

In addition to the movements in average real wages rates and overall productivity, there have been important changes especially in the 1980s in relative wages rates. Wages of workers with more education and experience have risen relative to those with less education and experience. These changes have shown up as increases in the inequality of wage incomes.

There is an ongoing controversy about the sources of the increases in wage inequality. One idea is that recent changes in technology, especially those that involve the growing importance of computers, have raised the demand for skilled workers relative to unskilled workers. This effect is called **skill-biased technological progress.** However, if this type of computer-based technological change has been important, then it becomes even more puzzling that overall productivity growth has been small. That is, we would have expected the computer revolution to contribute overall to rising productivity growth.

Another frequently advanced idea is that the growing importance of international trade—so-called **globalization**—has allowed U.S. firms

[5] *The data on real compensation per hour for the overall business sector are from Economic Report of the President, 1997, Table B–47.*

to specialize more in highly skilled industries, an effect that would also raise the relative demand for skilled labor in the United States. However, the evidence for this trade-based explanation of the changes in wage inequality does not seem to be convincing. For general discussions of the recent behavior of income inequality, see Lawrence Katz and Kevin Murphy (1992) and John Bound and George Johnson (1995).

NOMINAL WAGE RATES

To determine nominal wage rates and other nominal variables, we again consider the condition for money to be willingly held. This condition looks as it did in Chapter 5:

$$M = P \cdot \Phi(\,R\,,\ Y\,,\dots) \atop (-)\ \ (+)$$
(6.11)

The aggregate real demand for money, $\Phi(\cdot)$, would now include money held by firms as well as households. The form of this function would not, however, differ greatly from that in our earlier analysis: the amount of real money demanded still falls with an increase in the interest rate, R, and rises with an increase in output, Y.

The full market-clearing model now consists of equation (6.11) plus the conditions derived earlier for clearing the labor and commodity markets:

$$L^d(w/P,\dots) = L^s(w/P,\ R\,,\dots) \atop (-)(+)\ \ (+)$$
(6.12)

and

$$C^d(w/P,\ R\,,\dots) = Y^s(w/P,\dots) \atop (+)\ \ (-)(-)$$
(6.13)

We have already seen that equations (6.12) and (6.13) determine the real wage rate, w/P, the interest rate, R, and the levels of output, Y, and employment, L.

We showed in Chapter 5 that an increase in the quantity of money, M, was neutral. The price level, P, rose in the same proportion, but all real variables—including Y, L, R, and M/P—were unchanged. This property of monetary neutrality still holds in the model that includes a labor market. We should, however, add the real wage rate, w/P, to the list of real variables that do not change, and we should add the nominal wage rate, w, to the list of nominal variables that rise in the same proportion as the quantity of money.

To verify these results, remember that equations (6.12) and (6.13) determine R and Y. These variables then determine the real demand for money, $\Phi(\cdot)$. Given this real demand, equation (6.11) implies that an increase in M raises P in the same proportion. Real money balances, M/P, therefore do not change when there is a once-and-for-all shift in the nominal quantity of money.

Recall that equations (6.12) and (6.13) determine w/P and L. In fact, the real wage rate equals the marginal product of labor at this value of L. We can find the nominal wage rate, w, by multiplying the real wage rate, w/P, by the price level, P, which we have already determined. Notice that an increase in M raises P in the same proportion but does not change w/P. An increase in M therefore raises w (as well as P) in the same proportion.

THE LABOR MARKET IN THE MACROECONOMIC MODEL

Consider how the introduction of the labor market and firms affects our analysis. We have shown that these new features do not change the way that shifts to the production function affect the interest rate and the aggregate quantities of output and work effort. We also found that the extensions did not change the interaction between money and prices. In other words, our earlier simplification—which neglected the labor market and the existence of firms—allows us to get reasonable answers to many important questions. For most of the subsequent analysis, we shall therefore find it satisfactory to return to the simpler framework, which does not deal explicitly with the labor market or firms. The main place in which we reintroduce firms and the labor market is Chapter 10, which deals with unemployment.

SUMMARY

We introduced a labor market in which firms demand labor and households supply labor at a going wage rate. This market clears when the aggregate demand for labor equals the aggregate supply. One important aspect of a cleared labor market is that it equates each worker's marginal product to the real wage rate. This market therefore exhausts all the gains in output that can result by shifting workers from one production activity to another.

The requirements for general market clearing are that the labor market clear along with the markets for commodities and credit. In comparison with our previous analysis, we have added one new condition—that the labor market clear—and one new "price," the wage rate for labor services.

The inclusion of the labor market allows us to study the effects of various disturbances on the real wage rate. Shifts to the production function generate procyclical movements of the real wage rate, a pattern that fits the U.S. data. In a long-run context, the real wage rate will increase as an economy develops, a proposition that also accords with empirical evidence.

The conditions for determining the aggregate quantities of output and work, as well as the interest rate and the price level, turn out to be similar to those from before. For many purposes, we can therefore carry out the analysis by pretending, as before, that households work on only their own production processes. We must, however, consider firms and a labor market later when we study unemployment.

IMPORTANT TERMS AND CONCEPTS

employment The number of persons working at jobs in the market sector.

firm An economic organization that employs and supervises various factors of production and then sells its products to consumers or other firms.

globalization The increased tendency for production and other economic activities to be carried out on a worldwide basis.

productivity slowdown A reduction in the rate of growth of output per worker, thought to have occurred in the United States after the early 1970s.

profit The difference between revenues and costs for a firm.

real wage rate The value in real terms of the dollar amount paid for an hour of labor services.

skill-biased technological progress Technological change, possibly involving the increased use of computers, that tends to raise the demand for skilled labor relative to that for unskilled labor. This type of technological change is thought to underlie the rise in wage inequality during the 1980s.

stock market A market in which people trade shares of ownership in firms. The owners of stock receive the dividends paid out by firms.

QUESTIONS AND PROBLEMS

MAINLY FOR REVIEW

6.1 How does an increase in the real wage rate affect the demand for labor? Where does the assumption of diminishing marginal productivity of labor come in?

6.2 Consider two individuals, A and B; they have the same production function, but A has a greater willingness to work. If each individual is isolated on an island, who will work more? Who will have the higher marginal product? Show how total output can increase, with no increase in total labor, by exchanging labor services for goods between the two islands, that is, by opening up a labor market.

6.3 Suppose that the interest rate increases. How does this change affect the supply of labor and hence the real wage rate?

6.4 Explain why economic development tends to raise the real wage rate.

6.5 Suppose that the quantity of money, M, increases.

a. The increase in the nominal wage rate suggests that workers will be better off. Why is this not so?

b. The increase in the price level suggests that workers will be worse off. Is this correct?

PROBLEMS FOR DISCUSSION

6.6 The Labor Market and Efficiency

In the text we considered two isolated regions, A and B. The technology in A was inferior to that in B. Therefore, we found that the opening up of an economy-wide labor market led to higher aggregate output without requiring an increase in aggregate work effort. In this sense the new market improved the economy's efficiency.

a. Does the result mean that everyone is better off? In answering, consider the position of workers and firms (and the owners of firms) in both regions.

b. Does your answer suggest that some groups might oppose moves to free up markets, even when there would be gains in the aggregate? Can you think of any real-world examples of this phenomenon?

6.7 Walras' Law

a. When we introduce the labor market, what new aggregate-consistency condition arises?

b. Use the aggregate form of households' budget constraints to derive Walras' law of markets. How does the law differ from that in Chapter 5?

6.8 Wealth Effects from Changes in the Real Wage Rate

Suppose that the real wage rate, w/P, increases.

a. Why are there offsetting effects on wealth? What would you predict for the wealth effect on aggregate consumption demand and labor supply?

b. Suppose that most suppliers of labor own relatively little of the ownership rights in firms. What would you predict for the wealth effect on aggregate labor supply?

6.9 Temporary Shifts of the Production Function

Consider a temporary, parallel downward shift of the production function.

a. What are the effects on the interest rate, the real wage rate, and the quantities of output and employment?

b. Do the results differ from those in Chapter 5, where people worked only on their own production processes?

c. How do the answers change if the shift of the production function is proportional rather than parallel?

6.10 Short-Run Movements of the Real Wage Rate (optional)

Consider again a temporary, parallel downward shift of the production function.

a. Using the results from problem 6.9, what is the pattern of association between changes in the real wage rate and changes in the quantities of employment and output?

b. Assume, more realistically, that the schedule for labor's marginal product shifts downward. Assume, in particular, that this shift is large enough so that work effort declines. What then is the pattern of association between changes in the real wage rate and changes in the quantities of employment and output?

c. Suppose that business fluctuations result from temporary shifts of the production function. What do you predict for the cyclical behavior of real wage rates: do real wage rates move together with or inversely to output and employment? (There is some debate about the cyclical behavior of real wage rates. Most researchers find a procyclical pattern in the U.S. data since the 1950s: real wage rates tend to be high when output and employment are high.)

6.11 The Short-Run Behavior of Productivity (optional)

Suppose that we use the popular definition of labor productivity as the ratio of output to employment, Y/L.

a. How does this measure of productivity relate to the marginal product of labor?

b. Assume, as in problem 6.10, that business fluctuations result from shifts of the production function. How would productivity behave? In particular, is productivity high or low when output is high?

6.12 Determination of Stock Prices (optional)

Suppose that there are a fixed number of firms in the economy, each with access to the same production function, $f(l)$. Assume that the owner of a firm prints up and sells 100 ownership certificates (shares), each of which entitles the holder to 1% of the firm's profits. What would be the price of each share?

TWO

INFLATION

Thus far, we have simplified the analysis by holding fixed the general price level. Although this assumption was convenient, it conflicts dramatically with real-world experience. The typical pattern in most countries since World War II is that prices tend to rise over time; that is, there tends to be inflation. It is therefore important to modify the model to allow for the effects of changing price levels.

Chapter 7 begins by noting the empirical association between inflation and monetary growth. Then we discuss the important distinctions between actual and expected inflation and between nominal and real interest rates.

Chapter 8 incorporates the new tools into the market-clearing model. These extensions allow us to study the effects of monetary growth on inflation, interest rates, and other variables. One important finding is that fluctuations in monetary growth can be the principal source of variations in inflation. Nevertheless, these movements in monetary growth and inflation may have little to do with the behavior of real variables, at least if the inflation rate is not very high and variable.

An Introduction to Inflation and Interest Rates

$\boxed{\text{T}}$his chapter begins the study of inflation. By **inflation,** we mean a continuing upward movement in the general price level. The theoretical analysis suggests some possible sources of inflation. To sort out the possibilities, we shall find it convenient to think about the condition that all money be willingly held:

$$M = P \cdot \Phi(\underset{(-)}{R} , \underset{(+)}{Y} , \ldots) \tag{7.1}$$

One way for the price level to increase is through a downward movement in the real demand for money. For example, a permanent downward shift in the production function would lower aggregate output, Y, and thereby decrease the real quantity of money demanded. But notice that a single disturbance of this type creates a single increase in the price level rather than a continuing series of increases in prices. To generate inflation along this line, we would need a succession of downward shifts to the production function. There is no doubt that adverse shocks to the production function—such as oil crises, harvest failures, and strikes—can influence the general level of prices over short periods. But there is no evidence that these forces can account for inflation in the sense of persistent rises in prices. In fact, the typical pattern for most countries is one of growing output. Since this growth raises the real demand for money, we predict that prices would fall over time if the nominal stock of money, M, did not change.

There can also be reductions in the real demand for money that reflect increasing financial sophistication. In recent years, for example, many countries have developed financial instruments and procedures that make it easier for people to economize on money. In the United States in the post–World War II period, these financial innovations have led to a downward trend in the real demand for money. This element can account, however, for only a small amount of inflation: something like 1 to 2% per year is a reasonable estimate. Therefore, we cannot use this idea to explain the persistently high rates of inflation that prevailed in many countries from the late 1960s through the 1980s.

The remaining suggestion from the previous analysis is a link between inflation and increases in the quantity of paper money, M. At an empirical level it is clear, first, that the quantity of money often grows at a high rate over long periods of time and, second, that **rates of monetary growth** differ substantially across countries and over time for a single country. Monetary growth is therefore a good candidate as a source of inflation.

CROSS-COUNTRY DATA ON INFLATION AND MONETARY GROWTH

To assess the role of money as a determinant of inflation, consider the data for a large cross section of countries. Table 7.1 shows the experiences of 80 countries during the post–World War II period. The table reports the average growth rates of an index of consumer prices and money, defined as hand-to-hand currency. (The results are similar for the broader monetary aggregate, M1, which includes checkable deposits. However, because of differences in the nature of financial institutions, the meaning of M1 varies more across countries than does that of currency.) The table arranges the countries in descending order with respect to their average rates of inflation. Note the following:

- The average growth rates of prices and money are positive for all countries since World War II.

- The average growth rates are typically high. For example, the median inflation rate for the 80 countries is 8.4% per year, with 29 of them exceeding 10%. For the average growth rate of currency, the median is 11.5% per year, with 55 of the countries above 10%.

- There is a broad cross-sectional range for the average growth rates of prices and money. The average inflation rates vary from 91% for Brazil and 82% for Argentina (both of which have recently managed to attain much lower inflation rates) to 3% for Belgium, Singapore, and Germany. The rate for the United States is 4.4%. The growth rates of currency have a comparable range, varying from 96% for Brazil and 82% for Argentina to 3% for Belgium and 5% for Switzerland, France, and Denmark.

- The average growth rate of currency exceeds that of prices in almost all cases. That is, growth of real money balances is typical in the post–World War II period. The median growth rate of real currency across the 80 countries is 3.1% per year.

- Most significant, there is a strong positive correlation (0.99) across countries between the average rates of price change and the average rates of monetary growth.

TABLE 7.1

ANNUAL GROWTH RATES OF PRICES, MONEY, AND OUTPUT FOR 80 COUNTRIES IN THE POST–WORLD WAR II PERIOD (ARRANGED BY DECREASING ORDER OF THE INFLATION RATE)

	$\Delta P/P$	$\Delta M/M$	$\Delta M/M - \Delta P/P$	$\Delta Y/Y$	Time Span
Brazil	91.2	96.1	4.9	4.8	1960–94
Argentina	82.3	81.5	−0.8	2.2	1960–94
Peru	60.2	59.2	−1.0	3.1	1960–95
Bolivia	41.5	43.9	2.4	3.3	1960–95
Uruguay	41.2	44.7	3.5	1.9	1960–95
Chile	37.7	43.4	5.7	3.5	1960–95
Sierra Leone	33.8	30.3	−3.5	−2.8	1971–95
Israel	31.7	34.6	2.9	5.6	1960–95
Zaire	30.0	29.8	−0.2	2.4	1963–86
Turkey	27.9	30.2	2.3	5.4	1955–94
Ghana	26.0	25.2	−0.8	2.7	1960–95
Sudan	22.7	26.2	3.5	3.0	1960–95
Mexico	21.2	25.0	3.8	4.5	1960–95
Iceland	20.0	20.0	0.0	4.0	1960–95
Ecuador	18.2	30.9	12.7	5.0	1960–95
Colombia	17.7	22.2	4.5	4.6	1960–95
Somalia	17.2	21.7	4.5	1.8	1960–88
Nigeria	16.3	19.2	2.9	4.2	1960–95
Paraguay	14.9	17.5	2.6	4.7	1960–95
Jamaica	14.7	18.1	3.4	2.0	1960–94
Venezuela	13.8	16.6	2.8	3.6	1960–95
Costa Rica	12.6	16.5	3.9	4.6	1960–95
Dominican Republic	11.7	14.9	3.2	4.7	1960–95
Iran	11.5	19.2	7.7	3.4	1961–95
Madagascar	11.4	11.7	0.3	1.2	1962–95
Greece	11.3	14.9	3.6	4.1	1960–94
South Korea	10.6	19.3	8.7	8.1	1960–95
Philippines	10.6	13.6	3.0	3.9	1960–95

TABLE 7.1 *(CONTINUED)*

	$\Delta P/P$	$\Delta M/M$	$\Delta M/M - \Delta P/P$	$\Delta Y/Y$	Time Span
Syria	10.5	16.7	6.2	6.5	1960–90
El Salvador	9.8	10.7	0.9	3.3	1960–95
Egypt	9.7	13.4	3.7	6.0	1960–95
Guyana	9.4	16.0	6.6	0.9	1960–93
Gambia	9.1	11.5	2.4	3.9	1960–95
South Africa	9.1	14.2	5.1	3.1	1960–90
Spain	9.0	13.2	4.2	4.0	1960–95
Portugal	8.7	10.8	2.1	4.8	1960–95
Haiti	8.7	11.0	2.3	0.5	1960–95
Guatemala	8.7	11.5	2.8	3.9	1960–95
Nepal	8.5	14.9	6.4	3.3	1960–95
Trinidad and Tobago	8.4	8.8	0.4	1.9	1960–95
Mauritius	8.3	11.5	3.2	4.7	1963–95
Central African Republic	8.3	11.8	3.5	1.7	1960–95
Italy	8.1	9.1	1.0	4.6	1960–95
India	7.8	11.7	3.9	4.3	1960–95
New Zealand	7.7	8.4	0.7	2.5	1960–95
Honduras	7.7	11.1	3.4	3.9	1960–95
Pakistan	7.7	11.5	3.8	4.6	1960–95
Sri Lanka	7.6	12.0	4.4	4.0	1960–95
Ireland	7.5	9.9	2.4	4.3	1960–95
Congo	7.2	9.3	2.1	5.5	1960–95
United Kingdom	7.1	6.4	−0.7	2.3	1960–95
Gabon	6.9	10.0	3.1	5.6	1962–90
Cameroon	6.9	9.7	2.8	4.5	1960–90
Finland	6.6	8.4	1.8	3.1	1960–95
Ivory Coast	6.6	9.1	2.5	4.5	1962–90
Sweden	6.3	7.4	1.1	2.4	1960–95
Denmark	6.2	5.3	−0.9	2.7	1960–95

TABLE 7.1 (CONTINUED)

	$\Delta P/P$	$\Delta M/M$	$\Delta M/M - \Delta P/P$	$\Delta Y/Y$	Time Span
Australia	6.1	8.5	2.4	3.7	1960–95
Norway	6.0	6.4	0.4	3.7	1960–95
Senegal	5.9	12.2	6.3	3.0	1960–90
France	5.8	4.6	−1.2	3.3	1960–95
Chad	5.8	7.8	2.0	0.0	1960–95
Morocco	5.5	10.7	5.2	3.9	1960–95
Niger	5.5	8.9	3.4	3.1	1960–95
Tunisia	5.5	11.0	5.5	5.5	1960–90
Thailand	5.2	10.9	5.7	7.5	1960–95
Burkina Faso	5.2	11.0	5.8	2.7	1960–95
Canada	4.9	7.4	2.5	3.7	1960–95
Japan	4.8	10.4	5.6	5.4	1960–95
Togo	4.6	10.5	4.6	4.6	1962–90
Cyprus	4.5	9.5	5.0	5.3	1960–95
United States	4.4	7.3	5.8	3.1	1960–95
Netherlands	4.3	5.7	2.5	3.3	1960–95
Austria	4.2	5.8	5.6	3.1	1960–95
Saudi Arabia	4.1	12.7	5.9	6.1	1960–95
Switzerland	3.7	4.6	0.9	2.3	1960–95
Malta	3.6	9.6	6.0	6.2	1960–88
Germany	3.4	6.5	3.1	3.0	1960–95
Singapore	3.3	10.0	6.7	8.2	1960–95
Belgium	2.7	3.4	0.7	3.1	1960–95

Source: *International Monetary Fund*, International Financial Statistics.

Note: *All growth rates are annual averages for the sample periods shown in the right column. $\Delta P/P$ is the growth rate of consumer prices. $\Delta M/M$ is the growth rate of the stock of currency. $\Delta Y/Y$ is the growth rate of real gross domestic product.*

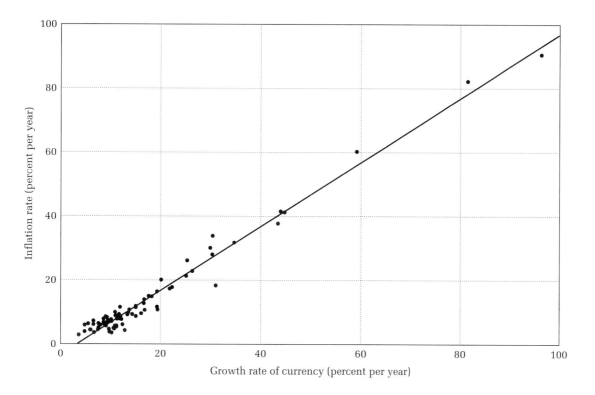

FIGURE 7.1

THE INFLATION RATE VERSUS THE GROWTH RATE OF CURRENCY FOR 80 COUNTRIES

The graph shows the positive relation between inflation and the growth rate of currency.

Figure 7.1 shows the positive association between inflation and the growth rate of currency. Each increase by one percentage point per year in the rate of monetary growth is associated with an increase by roughly one percentage point per year in the rate of inflation. The relation between inflation and monetary growth is, however, closer for the more extreme cases than for the moderate ones. For example, the association is less dramatic for countries in which the average rate of monetary growth is below 15% per year.

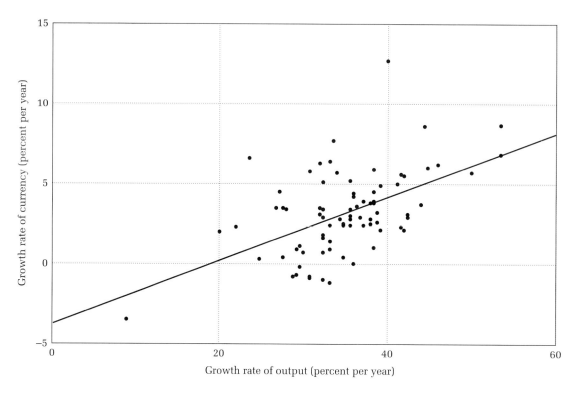

FIGURE 7.2

THE GROWTH RATE OF REAL MONEY BALANCES VERSUS THE GROWTH RATE OF OUTPUT FOR 80 COUNTRIES

The graph shows the positive relation between the growth rate of real currency and the growth rate of output.

If the growth rate of money exceeds the growth rate of prices, then real money balances, M/P, increase over time. Because money is willingly held at each date, the growth rate of real balances must equal the growth rate of real money demanded. Recall that our previous analysis of the demand for money suggested several factors that could lead to increases over time in the quantity of real money demanded. The most important is the growth rate of output. Table 7.1 shows the average growth rate of output for the 80 countries. Figure 7.2 graphs the growth rate of real money balances against the growth rate of output: the two are positively related (correlation $= 0.50$). In addition, the median growth rate of output, 3.8% per year, is close to that of real money balances, 3.1% per year. The positive effect of growing output on the growth of real money balances means that a country with a higher growth rate of output tends to have a lower rate of inflation for a given rate of monetary growth. Therefore, differences in the growth rates of output explain some of the imperfect association between monetary growth and inflation, as shown in Figure 7.1.

Another variable that influences the demand for money is the interest rate, R, which determines the cost of holding money. Other things equal, we predict that the average growth rate of real money balances will be lower for countries in which the interest rate has increased. Notice that the change in the interest rate, rather than the average level of the interest rate, matters here. Although researchers have verified this proposition for industrialized countries, we cannot demonstrate it for the substantial number of countries that lack organized securities markets on which interest rates are quoted.

We shall see in this and the next chapter that interest and inflation rates are closely related. In particular, increases in the inflation rate mean that money depreciates in real terms at a faster rate and, hence, that the cost of holding money is greater. It follows that an increase in the rate of inflation tends to reduce the real demand for money. We therefore predict that the average growth rate of real money balances will be lower for countries in which the inflation rate has increased. (Notice again that what matters here is the change in the inflation rate rather than the average level of the rate.) As examples, the sharp rises in inflation rates explain the negative growth rates of real money balances that show up in Table 7.1 for Zaire and Sierra Leone.

Overall, the cross-country data suggest a significant, positive association between monetary growth and inflation. This relation is even closer than it first appears if we consider additional variables, such as the growth rate of output and changes in interest rates and inflation rates, that affect the real demand for money.

U.S. TIME-SERIES DATA ON INFLATION AND MONETARY GROWTH

Table 7.2 reports data for the United States on the rate of CPI inflation and the growth rate of money (currency) for 1869–80, 20-year periods from 1880 to 1980, and 1980–96. Over the entire 127-year span, the average inflation rate was 3.1% per year, and the average growth rate of currency was 5.2% per year. Correspondingly, the average growth rate of real money balances was 3.1% per year. Notice that this figure accords with the average growth rate of output, which was 3.3% per year. (Again, the results are similar if we look at the broader monetary aggregate, M1, rather than currency.)

Although the time-series data for the United States do not provide the range of experience that appears in the cross-country sample, there are substantial differences in the various periods. For example, the average inflation rate was negative over three intervals: −2.1% for 1869–80 (the period preceding the U.S. adoption of the gold standard), −1.6% for 1920–40 (which includes the Great Depression), and −0.7% for 1880–1900 (the period that includes major contractions in the 1890s). The inflation rate exceeded 4% in three of the cases: 4.8% for 1960–80, 4.7% for 1940–60, and 4.6% for 1900–20. The world wars strongly influence the observations for the last two subperiods. For currency, the range of growth rates was from 2.0% for 1869–80 and 2.1% for 1920–40 to 7.2% for 1940–60 and 7.8% for 1980–96.

There is a positive association between monetary growth and inflation over the different periods. As in our previous analysis, we can explain some of the divergences between monetary growth and inflation by considering variables that affect the demand for money. These include

TABLE 7.2

U.S. Time Series Data on Inflation and Monetary Growth (average growth rates in percent per year)

	$\Delta P/P$	$\Delta M/M$	$\Delta M/M - \Delta P/P$	$\Delta Y/Y$
1869–80	−2.1	2.0	4.1	5.6
1880–1900	−0.7	3.0	3.7	3.2
1900–20	4.6	6.5	1.9	3.2
1920–40	−1.6	2.1	3.7	2.2
1940–60	4.7	7.2	2.5	3.6
1960–80	4.8	6.7	1.9	3.6
1980–96	3.7	7.8	4.1	2.5
1869–1996	2.1	5.2	3.1	3.3

Sources: *For the price level and real GNP or GDP, Figures 1.1 and 1.4. For money, Friedman and Schwartz (1970, Table 2); Board of Governors*, Federal Reserve Bulletin, *various issues; and DRI data bank.*

Note: *All growth rates are annual averages for the period shown in the first column. $\Delta P/P$ is the growth rate of the deflator for the GNP (GDP since 1959). $\Delta M/M$ is the growth rate of currency. $\Delta Y/Y$ is the growth rate of real GNP (GDP since 1959).*

the growth rate of output, changes in interest rates, and the development of financial institutions.

INFLATION AS A MONETARY PHENOMENON

Casual observation of two types of data—across countries and over time for the United States—suggests that we should consider seriously Milton Friedman's (1968b, p. 29) famous statement, "Inflation is always and everywhere a monetary phenomenon." We should, however, remember some important points. First, the analysis will not rule out effects of real disturbances, such as supply shocks, on the price level. We expect, however, that these effects will be more important for isolated episodes of price changes than for chronic inflation. Second, we should view the expression *monetary phenomenon* as incorporating variables that influence the real demand for money, as well as the nominal supply of money. Third, we would eventually like to know why monetary growth behaves differently in different countries and at different times. This question would require us to explore a number of new subjects, including governmental incentives to print more or less money. We sidestep the theory of money supply in this and the next chapter and look only at the consequences for inflation and other variables of a given, unexplained, time path of money. This type of analysis is crucial for an understanding of inflation, although it does not constitute a full study of the topic.

ACTUAL AND EXPECTED INFLATION

We now begin the process of incorporating inflation into the theoretical model. The inflation rate between periods t and $t + 1$ is defined as

$$\pi_t \equiv (P_{t+1} - P_t)/P_t \tag{7.2}$$

where π is the Greek letter *pi*. Notice that the inflation rate equals the rate of change of the price level between periods t and $t + 1$. By rearranging equation (7.2), we can solve out for the next period's price level as

$$P_{t+1} = (1 + \pi_t) \cdot P_t \tag{7.3}$$

Hence, prices rise over one period by the factor $1 + \pi_t$. Although we focus on rising prices—that is, positive rates of inflation—we can also consider declining prices. These cases are called **deflations**.

In making various decisions, such as the choice between consuming now or later, people want to know how prices will change over time. People therefore form forecasts or **expectations of inflation**. We use the symbol π_t^e to denote an expectation of the inflation rate π_t. Usually we think of someone as forming this expectation during period t. Because people already know the current price level, P_t, the expectation of inflation, π_t^e, corresponds to a forecast of the next period's price level, P_{t+1}.

In general, forecasts of inflation are imperfect: the actual rate of inflation is typically higher or lower than the average person's expectation. The forecast error—or **unexpected inflation**—is therefore usually nonzero. People do, however, have incentives to form their expectations *rationally*—making efficient use of the available information on past inflation and other variables—to avoid systematic mistakes. This rationality implies that unexpected inflation would not exhibit a systematic pattern of errors over time. For example, if unexpected inflation is positive this period, then it may be either positive or negative in the next period.

REAL AND NOMINAL INTEREST RATES

As before, let R_t be the interest rate on bonds. If a person buys $1 worth of bonds (with a maturity of one period) during period t, then he or she gets $(1 + R_t)$ as receipts of principal plus interest during period $t + 1$. The dollar value of assets held as bonds therefore rises over one period by the factor $1 + R_t$. We can think of the rate R_t as the dollar or **nominal interest rate**.

What happens over time to the real value of assets that people hold as bonds? If the price level is constant, as in previous chapters, then the real value of these assets also grows at the rate R_t. Thus, in a world of constant prices, the nominal interest rate, R_t, would also be the **real interest rate**, that is, the rate that determines the growth over time in the real value of assets.

If the inflation rate is positive, then equation (7.3) indicates that the price level rises over one period by the factor $1 + \pi_t$. Therefore, if the dollar value of assets rises over one period by the factor $1 + R_t$, then the real value of assets rises by the proportion $(1 + R_t)/(1 + \pi_t)$. Note that the numerator indicates that the dollars available next period grow by the factor $1 + R_t$, whereas the denominator recognizes that the price level is higher by the factor $1 + \pi_t$.

If households hold assets in the form of bonds, then the real value of these assets rises over one period by the factor $(1 + R_t)/(1 + \pi_t)$. We can define the real interest rate, r_t, to be the rate at which assets held as bonds grow in real terms. Hence, the real interest rate satisfies the condition

$$(1 + r_t) = (1 + R_t)/(1 + \pi_t) \tag{7.4}$$

It is the real interest rate, rather than the nominal rate, that determines the amount of extra consumption that someone can get in period $t + 1$ if he or she forgoes a unit of consumption in period t. If, for example, a person lowers c_t by one unit, then he or she saves P_t extra dollars (in the form of bonds) and thereby has an additional $P_t \cdot (1 + R_t)$ dollars to spend in period $t + 1$. This amount buys $P_t \cdot (1 + R_t)/P_{t+1}$ units of additional consumption in period $t + 1$. This term equals $(1 + R_t)/(1 + \pi_t)$, which is the same as $1 + r_t$ from equation (7.4).

The results imply that households will look at the real interest rate, not the nominal rate, when they decide how much to consume, work, and save in various periods. For this reason we want to explore further the meaning and measurement of the real interest rate.

We can obtain a more useful expression for the real interest rate, r_t, if we manipulate equation (7.4). Multiply through on both sides by the term $1 + \pi_t$, and simplify the result to get the condition

$$r_t + \pi_t + r_t\pi_t = R_t \tag{7.5}$$

Recall that we measure each variable—R_t, π_t, and r_t—as a growth rate per period, say, per month. If we think of interest and inflation rates that are no larger than, say, 20% per year, then the rates per month—R_t, π_t, and r_t—will be no greater than 2%. It follows that the interaction term, $r_t\pi_t$, will be very small in equation (7.5): less than $0.02 \times 0.02 = 0.0004$. We can therefore neglect this term and satisfactorily approximate the real interest rate as

$$r_t \simeq R_t - \pi_t \tag{7.6}$$

where the symbol $\simeq$ means approximately equal to.[1]

Recall that the nominal interest rate, R_t, determines how the dollar value of assets held as bonds grows over time. In contrast, the real interest rate, r_t, determines how fast these assets grow in real terms. Equation (7.6) says that the real interest rate, r_t, equals the nominal rate, R_t, less the rate of inflation, π_t. Thus, the real rate is lower than the nominal rate if the inflation rate is positive. Further, the real rate is positive only if the nominal rate exceeds the inflation rate. If the nominal rate is less than the inflation rate, then the real interest rate is negative. In this case the rise in dollar value at the rate R_t does not cover the rise in prices at the rate π_t.

ACTUAL AND EXPECTED REAL INTEREST RATES

We usually think of situations in which people observe the nominal interest rate on bonds, R_t. To calculate the **expected real interest rate** between periods t and $t + 1$, people have to subtract from R_t their expectation of inflation, π_t^e. The expected real interest rate, denoted by r_t^e, is then given by

$$r_t^e \simeq R_t - \pi_t^e \tag{7.7}$$

[1] *The approximation becomes better the shorter the length of the period (and becomes perfect as the length approaches zero). The length of the period actually plays no economic role in the model and we use these periods—discrete time—solely for convenience. We can therefore assume that a period is extremely brief and, hence, that equation (7.6) is accurate.*

Recall that the actual inflation rate, π_t, can be above or below its expectation, π_t^e. If inflation turns out to be surprisingly high—that is, $\pi_t > \pi_t^e$—then the real interest rate, r_t, is less than its expectation, r_t^e. In other words, if we combine equations (7.6) and (7.7), then the unexpected part of the real interest rate, $r_t - r_t^e$, is

$$r_t - r_t^e \simeq -(\pi_t - \pi_t^e) \tag{7.8}$$

Errors in forecasts of inflation, $\pi_t - \pi_t^e$, generate errors of the opposite sign in forecasts of the real interest rate.

It is possible to have institutional arrangements in which borrowers and lenders specify in advance the real interest rate, r_t, rather than the nominal rate, R_t. In this case the nominal payments for principal and interest adjust to compensate for inflation. These adjustments ensure that the actual real interest rate equals the prespecified value. People would then know the real interest rate in advance but would be uncertain about the nominal interest rate.

The financial arrangements in which people contract in advance for real interest rates are called **indexation** or **inflation correction**. These systems tend to exist in countries, such as Brazil and Israel, in which extreme inflation is chronic. Among the most advanced countries, the United Kingdom has been the leader since 1981 in issuing long-term indexed bonds of this type. We shall discuss the U.K. experience later in this chapter.

Other countries that have issued indexed bonds in recent years include Canada, Australia, New Zealand, Sweden, and Iceland. After many years of resisting economists' suggestions to use this kind of security, the U.S. government finally issued 10-year bonds indexed to the consumer price index in January 1997. (Many observers believe that Deputy Secretary of the Treasury Lawrence Summers—formerly a professor of economics at Harvard University—was instrumental in convincing the government to issue these kinds of bonds.) Economists do not know why private parties and governments typically prefer to borrow and lend at prespecified nominal interest rates rather than real rates.[2]

NOMINAL AND REAL INTEREST RATES IN THE POST–WORLD WAR II UNITED STATES

Table 7.3 shows the relation between nominal and real interest rates for the United States over the post–World War II period. The nominal rate, R_t, is the average for each year on three-month maturity U.S. Treasury bills (short-term U.S. government securities). The inflation rate for each year, π_t, is the rate of change of the general price level, measured by the consumer price index (CPI). The real interest rate for each year comes from the formula $r_t = R_t - \pi_t$.

The actual rate of inflation, π_t, may diverge substantially from the rate that people expected, π_t^e. In that case the real interest rate, r_t, differs from the expected rate, r_t^e. Because the expected real interest rate will be important for the subsequent analysis, we should make some effort to measure expected inflation.

Measures of Expected Inflation

Economists have employed at least three methods to measure expectations of a variable like inflation or the real interest rate:

1. Ask a sample of people about their beliefs.

2. Use the hypothesis of **rational expectations**, the idea that people's beliefs correspond to optimal predictions, given the available information. Then use statistical techniques to figure out these optimal predictions.

3. Use market data, such as interest rates or prices of financial contracts, to infer what people believe.

[2] *There have been some suggestions: (1) People use and hold money—an asset that is denominated in nominal units—making it desirable to borrow and lend in the same units. (2) The government enforces contracts in nominal units more diligently than contracts in other units. (3) The tax treatment of indexed bonds can be complicated. (4) It is hard to agree on a price index to use in making inflation corrections. Huston McCulloch (1980) suggested another reason: U.S. courts were unwilling to enforce indexing provisions on bonds after 1933. In that year Congress resolved not to honor the "gold clauses" that appeared in some previously issued bonds. These clauses—which were a form of indexing—committed borrowers to repay in a stated amount of gold rather than U.S. dollars. When the Congress voided these gold clauses, the courts interpreted the restriction as applying to all types of indexed bonds. Congress, however, rescinded this resolution in 1977, so the ban on indexed bonds no longer applies.*

TABLE 7.3

**INFLATION RATES, NOMINAL INTEREST RATES, AND REAL INTEREST RATES FOR RECENT U.S. EXPERIENCE
(PERCENT PER YEAR)**

	R_t	π_t	r_t	π_t^e	r_t^e
1948	1.0	0.4	0.6	1.2	−0.2
1949	1.1	−2.8	3.9	−4.0	5.1
1950	1.2	8.0	−6.8	−0.2	1.4
1951	1.6	4.3	−2.7	3.1	−1.5
1952	1.8	0.4	1.4	1.1	0.7
1953	1.9	0.7	1.2	−0.6	2.5
1954	1.0	−1.4	2.4	−0.9	1.9
1955	1.8	0.0	1.8	0.3	1.5
1956	2.7	3.5	−0.8	0.3	2.2
1957	3.3	3.4	−0.1	1.3	2.0
1958	1.8	1.3	0.5	0.1	1.7
1959	3.4	1.3	2.1	0.6	1.9
1960	2.9	1.6	1.3	0.7	2.2
1961	2.4	0.6	1.8	0.6	1.8
1962	2.8	1.3	1.5	1.0	1.8
1963	3.2	1.5	1.7	1.0	2.2
1964	3.6	0.9	2.7	1.0	2.6
1965	4.0	2.1	1.9	1.1	2.9
1966	4.9	3.2	1.7	1.7	3.2
1967	4.3	3.4	0.9	2.1	2.2
1968	5.3	3.8	1.5	2.8	2.5
1969	6.7	5.5	1.2	2.9	3.8
1970	6.5	4.3	2.0	3.6	2.9
1971	4.4	3.3	1.1	3.8	0.6
1972	4.1	3.7	0.4	3.3	0.8
1973	7.0	9.5	−2.5	3.6	3.4
1974	7.9	11.3	−3.4	6.2	2.7
1975	5.8	6.4	−0.6	6.7	−0.9

TABLE 7.3 *(CONTINUED)*

	R_t	π_t	r_t	π_t^e	r_t^e
1976	5.0	5.2	−0.2	5.6	−0.6
1977	5.3	5.9	−0.6	5.6	−0.3
1978	7.2	8.1	−0.9	6.2	1.0
1979	10.1	11.4	−1.3	7.6	2.5
1980	11.4	10.2	1.2	10.4	1.0
1981	14.0	7.6	6.4	9.7	4.3
1982	10.7	4.1	6.6	6.1	4.6
1983	8.6	4.0	4.6	4.5	4.1
1984	9.6	3.1	6.5	5.3	4.3
1985	7.5	3.2	4.3	4.2	3.3
1986	6.0	0.6	5.4	3.5	2.5
1987	5.8	3.7	2.1	3.5	2.3
1988	6.7	4.7	2.0	4.2	2.5
1989	8.1	5.1	3.0	5.0	3.1
1990	7.5	5.4	2.1	3.9	3.6
1991	5.6	2.2	3.4	3.7	1.9
1992	3.4	3.2	0.2	3.3	0.1
1993	3.0	2.3	0.7	3.3	−0.3
1994	4.0	2.8	1.2	2.8	1.2
1995	5.5	2.4	3.1	3.2	2.3
1996	5.0	3.2	1.8	2.7	2.3

Source: *The data are from DRI data bank. The variable π_t^e, from the Livingston survey, comes from the Federal Reserve Bank of Philadelphia. The figures are an average for each year of the six-month forecasts (from December of the previous year and June of the current year).*

Note: *The inflation rate, π_t, refers to the change in the CPI from January of each year to January of the next year. We use the figures that exclude the shelter component to avoid some problems of measuring mortgage interest costs. The nominal interest rate, R_t, is the average annual rate on secondary markets for U.S. Treasury bills with a three-month maturity. The real interest rate, r_t, equals $R_t - \pi_t$.*

The main shortcoming of the first approach is that the sample may not be representative of the whole economy. Also, economists have a better theory of how people take actions than of how they answer questions on surveys. Unlike in a market in which the participants back up their statements with money, it is less clear what it means when someone just expresses opinions about inflation or other variables.

The second approach, based on rational expectations, has produced some successes and some difficulties.[3] One problem arises in figuring out what information people have when they form expectations. Another concerns the choice among statistical models. In any event, the results about expected inflation from some of these studies do not differ in many respects from the survey findings that we consider below.

The third approach, which relies on market data, had limited success for measuring expected inflation until indexed bonds began to be issued in volume in the United Kingdom and other advanced countries.[4] The indexed bonds provide a market measure of real interest rates. For example, we can use the data to infer the market's expectation of real interest rates, r_t^e, that will prevail two or five years in the future. If nominal bonds also exist, then the market provides a corresponding measure of the expected nominal interest rate, R_t^e—for example, of the nominal rate anticipated to prevail two or five years in the future. The difference between the two observable rates, R_t^e and r_t^e, provides a market measure of the expected inflation rate, π_t^e, for the corresponding period—say, two or five years in the future.[5] (In practice, there are some complications to this procedure that involve tax considerations and riskiness of returns.)

The Bank of England has been using a variant of the method just described to compute the financial market's expectations about inflation over various future periods. This information about market beliefs is available since 1982 and has been used for several years by the Bank of England to formulate its monetary policy. The Federal Reserve in the United States will be able to make similar calculations once the U.S. government's indexed bonds have been around for a significant length of time.

[3] For uses of this approach to measure expected inflation, see, for example, James Hamilton (1985).

[4] One interesting source of data was the futures contract based on the CPI that was traded for awhile on the Coffee, Sugar & Cocoa Exchange. Traders on this market essentially bet on the value of the CPI in future periods. Then these traders won or lost money depending on the value that the CPI actually took later on. By looking at these bets, we can infer traders' expectations of future changes in the price level. For example, in February 1986, people anticipated an inflation rate of 4.5% for 1987 and 8.1% for 1988. By June 1986, however, the expected inflation rates had fallen to 4.4% for 1987 and 6.6% for 1988. The actual inflation rates—far below expectations as revealed by the CPI futures market—turned out to be 0.6% for 1986, 3.7% for 1987, and 4.6% for 1988. It is, unfortunately, impossible to bring these data up to date because insufficient trader interest prevented this futures market from operating.

Return now to the first approach, which uses survey data to measure expected inflation. Joseph Livingston, a Philadelphia journalist, began in 1946 to survey about 50 economists (fewer in the early years of the sample) for their forecasts of the CPI six to 12 months in the future. The variable denoted π_t^e in Table 7.3 is the average of the two six-month-ahead forecasts for each year, when expressed as the implied prediction for the annual rate of inflation.[6] The last column in Table 7.3 shows the corresponding value of the expected real interest rate, $r_t^e = R_t - \pi_t^e$.

INTEREST RATES AND EXPECTED INFLATION IN THE POST–WORLD WAR II PERIOD

One point to notice in Table 7.3 is that the nominal interest rate rose dramatically from the end of World War II until the early 1980s. The rate increased from 1% per year in 1948 to about 3% in the early 1960s, over 6% in the late 1960s, 10% in 1979, and 14% in 1981. The increase in the interest rates was not steady over this period: the rate declined from 3.3% in 1957 to 1.8% in 1958, from 6.5% in 1970 to 4.1% in 1972, and from 7.9% in 1974 to 5.0% in 1976. Further, despite the appearance of a generally upward drift in interest rates, it would not have been easy to forecast this "trend." In any event, someone who foresaw this pattern could have made a fortune by speculating on bond prices. After 1981, the interest rate fell dramatically to 6% in 1987 and 3% in 1992–93 before rising to around 5% in 1995–96.

Figure 7.3 plots the data from Table 7.3 on the nominal interest rate, R_t, the expected inflation rate, π_t^e, and the expected real interest rate, r_t^e. If r_t^e were constant, then R_t and π_t^e would move together on a one-to-one basis. Although r_t^e varied over time, the striking feature of the graph is the tendency for R_t and π_t^e to move in the same way. The same pattern holds for R_t and π_t, although π_t fluctuated more than π_t^e or R_t from year to year. In the subsequent analysis (in Chapter 8), we shall want to understand why nominal interest rates move roughly on a one-to-one basis with expected and actual inflation rates.

[5] *Eugene Fama (1975) suggested earlier that nominal interest rates were themselves good measures of expected inflation because he thought that expected real interest rates were roughly constant. But his estimated relationships broke down after the early 1970s when the expected real interest rate began to move around a lot. For some discussion of this topic, see Charles Nelson and William Schwert (1977).*

[6] *For a discussion of the Livingston survey, see John Carlson (1977).*

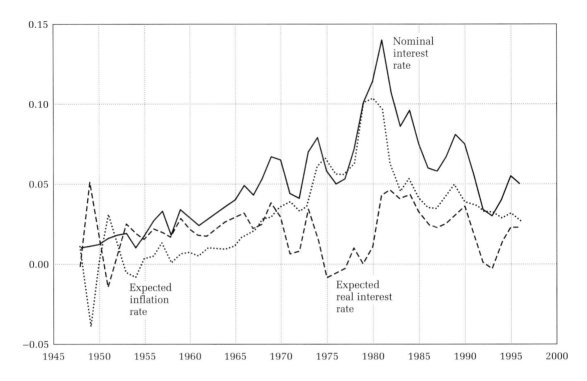

FIGURE 7.3

BEHAVIOR OF THE INFLATION RATE, NOMINAL INTEREST RATE, AND REAL INTEREST RATE IN THE UNITED STATES

The expected inflation rate and the nominal interest rate rose over much of the post–World War II period but fell after 1981. Expected real interest rates were unusually high from 1981 to 1984 but fell to around zero in 1991–92 before rising back to around 2% in 1995–96.

The behavior of expected real interest rates differs markedly from that of nominal rates. The expected real rate, r_t^e, showed no trend and fluctuated around a mean of 2% from 1950 to 1974. The rate fell to an average of 0.5% from 1975 to 1980, rose to an average of 4% from 1981 to 1984, and then fell to an average of 3% from 1985 to 1990. The rate declined to around zero in 1992–93 before rising to 2–3% in 1995–96.

Another fact to note from Table 7.3 is that deviations of actual from expected inflation, $\pi_t - \pi_t^e$, explain some of the behavior of actual real interest rates, r_t. Remember that, for a given value of r_t^e, the inflation surprise, $\pi_t - \pi_t^e$, reduces r_t one-to-one. As an example, surprise inflation—$\pi_t > \pi_t^e$—accounts for some of the smallest real interest rates. In 1950, the inflation rate of 8.0%—compared to the expected rate of -0.2%—was a surprise associated with the start of the Korean War. The real interest rate of -6.8% was therefore well below the anticipated rate of 1.4%. Similarly, for 1973–74, the inflation rates of 9.5% and 11.3%—compared to expectations of 3.6% and 6.2%—were surprises related to the first oil crisis. The real interest rates, -2.5% and -3.4%, respectively, were again well below expectations.

In a longer-run context, the average of the Livingston survey's measure of expected inflation from 1948 to 1980 was 2.4%, compared to an average for actual inflation of 3.7%. Correspondingly, the average expected real interest rate, r_t^e, of 1.8% was well above the average of the actual rate, r_t, of 0.5%. In other words, the persisting tendency—through 1980—of people to underpredict inflation is a partial explanation for why r_t averaged only slightly above zero.[7]

To use inflation surprises to explain high real interest rates, we have to search for unexpectedly low inflation. Mainly we find this pattern during the 1980s. The actual inflation rates for 1981, 1982, and 1984 were each about two percentage points below the expected values, whereas the actual for 1986 was about three percentage points below the expected. For this reason, the average of r_t from 1981 to 1986 was 5.6%, compared to an average for r_t^e of 3.8%. In other words, unexpectedly low inflation accounts for 1.8 percentage points of the high average for r_t from 1981 to 1986. In 1996, the actual and expected inflation rates were each around 3%, nominal interest rates were around 5%, and the actual and expected real interest rates were a little over 2%.

INTEREST RATES ON MONEY

We have discussed the nominal and real interest rates on bonds. But the same analysis applies to money once we specify that the nominal interest rate on money is zero, rather than R_t. Recall that the real interest rate on

[7] *Conceivably, the tendency to underpredict inflation up to 1980 means that the respondents to the Livingston survey were irrational. But this assessment depends heavily on hindsight. In fact, as mentioned in Chapter 1 and shown in Table 7.2, the high average inflation of the post–World War II period was a dramatic departure from the U.S. history during peacetime. Statistical models that forecast a lot better than the Livingston survey might not have been used by people who had access only to historical data. For a discussion of the rationality of the Livingston survey, see John Carlson (1977) and John Caskey (1985).*

Indexed Bonds in the United Kingdom

We mentioned before that indexed bonds adjust their nominal payments to provide a predetermined real interest rate. We can therefore use market information about indexed bonds to compute real interest rates. For bonds that are already issued, we can calculate the known real interest rate that will be paid over the maturity of a particular bond. We can also use the full array of bonds sold in the market to figure out the real interest rate that traders expect to prevail at any time in the future.

Although indexed bonds were first issued by the U.S. Treasury only in 1997,[*] there is a long enough history from the United Kingdom to assess their experience. The British government began in March 1981 to issue marketable bonds ("gilts") that linked the nominal interest payments and principal to a broad index of retail prices.[†] The figure shows nominal interest rates (calculated from conventional nominal bonds) and real interest rates (computed from indexed bonds) from March 1982 to January 1997. These values are market expectations in each year about the real rates that will prevail (over a six-month interval) two years in the future. Figure 7.4 also shows the expected inflation rate—over a six-month period

two years in the future—calculated as the difference between the expected nominal and real interest rates.

The expected real interest rate averaged 3.6% from March 1982 to January 1997 but varied considerably over time—from 2.0% to 5.2%. Thus, the expected real rate cannot be treated as a constant. Expected inflation fell from over 10% in early 1982 to just above 3% in early 1994, then rose to nearly 6% later in 1994 before declining to 3.4% in January 1997. This last figure for the United Kingdom is similar to the range of real rates, 3.3–3.5%, at which U.S. 10-year indexed notes were issued in the same month.

Because there are participants in the financial markets who can move readily between U.K. nominal or indexed bonds and U.S. nominal or indexed bonds, we would anticipate that the expected real interest rates on these assets would be similar. Otherwise, some people would switch to the bond that promised the higher real yield. This process of switching would continue until the prices of the bonds adjusted to keep the expected real interest rates close to each other.[‡]

One of the benefits from the existence of indexed bonds is the creation of market data on ↗

expected real interest rates and expected inflation. These data are not only nice for economic researchers but are also useful as a guide for monetary policy. In addition, indexed bonds provide convenient instruments for individuals and institutions to use as hedges against inflation risks. The assured real rate of return over the long run is especially useful for pension funds and insurance companies.

There is also a belief—based partly on the historical experience of the United Kingdom—that indexed bonds provide a relatively cheap form of finance for the government. (We shall consider debt finance in Chapter 14.) The validity of this argument is uncertain but did seem to be an important factor that convinced the U.S. Treasury to issue indexed securities in 1997.

---

* The famous economist Irving Fisher had his company, Cardex Rand, issue an indexed bond in the 1920s, but it was not very popular.

† Because the index linking involves a lag of eight months, the real yield varies somewhat with actual inflation. But as a first approximation, we can treat the real interest rate as known in advance.

‡ There are some elements that would allow for differences in expected real interest rates. First, the real returns on nominal bonds are riskier because of the uncertainty of inflation. Second, British indexed bonds have a favorable tax treatment because only the earnings corresponding to the real interest rate are taxable. In the United States, the inflation uplift part is taxed as interest income. Third, the U.K. bonds are tied to an index of U.K. prices, which may behave differently from U.S. prices. Finally, the data studied in Figure 7.4 apply two years in the future, whereas the U.S. Treasury bills considered in Table 7.3 have a maturity of three months.

any asset equals the nominal rate less the rate of inflation, π_t. The real rate for bonds is therefore $r_t = R_t - \pi_t$. Since money (currency) has a nominal interest rate of zero, the real interest rate is $-\pi_t$. Positive inflation means that the purchasing power of money erodes over time.

As with bonds, we can distinguish the expected real interest rate on money from the actual rate. The expected real interest rate on money is the negative of the expected inflation rate, $-\pi_t^e$.

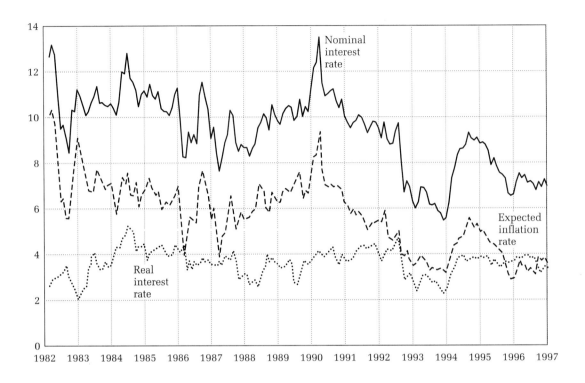

FIGURE 7.4

RATES ON U.K. BONDS

The nominal rates (from conventional bonds) and real rates (from indexed bonds) apply two years in the future for a six-month interval. The expected inflation rate is the difference between the nominal and real rates.

Remember that the money in our model is like currency, which pays a zero nominal interest rate. Most forms of checkable deposits now pay interest. For these types of "moneys," we would calculate the real interest rate just as we do for bonds: the real rate equals the nominal interest rate paid on deposits less the rate of inflation.

SUMMARY

We began by examining data on monetary growth and inflation across countries and over time for the United States. These data suggest that variations in monetary growth account for a good deal of the variations in inflation rates.

The real interest rate on bonds, r_t, equals the nominal rate, R_t, less the inflation rate, π_t. If a bond specifies the nominal interest rate in advance, then the expected real interest rate, r_t^e, depends inversely on the expected inflation rate, π_t^e. We examined the U.S. data since World War II on U.S. Treasury bills, the CPI inflation rate, and the Livingston survey of expected inflation. Over the long term, the nominal interest rate moved together with the actual and expected rates of inflation. The expected real interest rate averaged 2.0% from 1950 to 1974, 0.4% from 1975 to 1980, 4.3% from 1980 to 1984, 2.7% from 1985 to 1991, and 0.3% from 1992 to 1994. It equaled 2.3% in 1995 and 1996.

IMPORTANT TERMS AND CONCEPTS

deflation A sustained decrease in the general price level over time.

expectation of inflation The public's forecast of the inflation rate.

expected real interest rate The real interest rate that is expected to be earned (or paid) after adjusting the nominal interest rate by the expectation of inflation.

indexation A system of contracts in which payments are revised upward or downward according to increases or decreases in the general price level so as to keep the real value of payments independent of inflation.

inflation A sustained increase in the general price level over time.

inflation correction Another term for indexation.

nominal interest rate The amount paid as interest per dollar borrowed for each period; the rate at which the nominal value of assets that are held as bonds grows over time.

rate of monetary growth The percentage increase in the nominal quantity of money between two periods.

rational expectations The viewpoint that individuals make forecasts or estimates of unknown variables, such as the general price level, in the best possible manner, utilizing all information currently available.

real interest rate The rate at which the real value of dollar assets that are held as bonds grows over time; the interest rate on an asset after adjusting for inflation.

unexpected inflation The difference between the actual rate of inflation and the expectation of inflation; the forecast error made in predicting inflation.

QUESTIONS AND PROBLEMS

MAINLY FOR REVIEW

7.1 Monetarists hold that changes in the price level are primarily the result of changes in the quantity of money. Can this conclusion be based solely on theoretical reasoning? Explain.

7.2 Define the real interest rate. Why does it differ from the nominal interest rate in the presence of inflation?

7.3   Why does the actual real interest rate generally differ from the expected rate? How does this relation depend on whether bonds prescribe the nominal interest rate or the real interest rate?

7.4   Consider the Livingston survey of inflationary expectations. What are the pluses and minuses of using this type of information to measure expected rates of inflation?

PROBLEMS FOR DISCUSSION

7.5   Monetary Growth and Inflation

Suppose that the money-demand function takes the form

$$(M/P)^d = \underset{(+)\ (-)}{\Phi(Y,\ R,\ \dots)} = Y \cdot \underset{(-)}{\Psi(R)}$$

where Ψ is some function. This form says that an increase in real output by, say, 10%, raises the real demand for money by 10%.

a.   Is it possible that this form of the demand for money accords with our theory of money demand from Chapter 4?

b.   Consider the relation across countries between the average growth rates of money and prices. If the functional form for money demand shown in this question applies, how does the average growth rate of real output affect the relation between the growth rates of money and prices?

c.   What is the relation between the average growth rates of money and prices for a country in which the nominal interest rate, R, has increased?

d.   If the expected real interest rate is constant, what is the relation between the average growth rates of money and prices for a country in which the expected inflation rate, π^e, has increased? How does this result apply to countries for which we do not observe the nominal interest rate, R, on an organized credit market?

7.6 Statistical Relations between Monetary Growth and Inflation (optional)

Students who have studied econometrics and who have access to a statistical package on a computer should do the following exercise.

a. Use the data in Table 7.1 to run a regression of the inflation rate, ΔP, on a constant and the growth rate of money, ΔM. What is the estimated coefficient on money growth and how should we interpret it? What is the meaning of the constant term?

b. Run a regression of the growth rate of real money balances, $\Delta M - \Delta P$, on the growth rate of real output, ΔY, and a constant. Interpret the coefficient on ΔY.

c. Suppose that we add the variable, ΔY, to the regression run in part a. What is the estimated coefficient on ΔY, and how should it be interpreted?

7.7 Prepayments of Mortgages and Callability of Bonds

Mortgages typically allow the borrower to make early payments of principal, which are called *prepayments*. Sometimes the mortgage contract specifies a penalty for prepayments, and sometimes there is no penalty. Many state governments prohibit prepayment penalties on mortgages. (Lenders do, however, usually charge some fees for setting up a new mortgage.) Similarly, long-term bonds—although not most of those issued by the U.S. government—typically allow the issuer to prepay the principal after a prescribed date and with a specified penalty. When the bond issuer exercises this option to prepay, he or she is said to "call" the bond. Bonds that allow this option are said to be *callable* or to have a *call provision*.

a. When would a borrower want to prepay (or call) his or her mortgage or bond? Would we see more prepayments when nominal interest rates had unexpectedly increased or decreased?

b. From the late 1970s until 1982, banks and savings and loan associations were eager for their customers to prepay their mortgages. Why was this the case? Later on, the customers wanted to prepay. Why did they want to do so?

c. Suppose that there is an increase in the year-to-year fluctuations of nominal interest rates. (These fluctuations were particularly great from the mid-1970s through the early 1980s.) From the standpoint of a borrower, how does this change affect the value of having a prepayment option—that is, callability—in his or her mortgage or bond?

7.8 Rational Expectations and Measures of Expected Inflation
How would the hypothesis of rational expectations help us to measure inflationary expectations? What seem to be the pluses and minuses of this approach?

7.9 Indexed Bonds
Consider a bond that costs $1000. Suppose that the bond pays a year later the principal of $1000 plus interest of $100.

a. What is the nominal interest rate on the bond? What are the actual and expected real interest rates? Why is the nominal rate known but the real rate uncertain?

Suppose that someone issues an indexed bond, which adjusts the payments to compensate for inflation. For example, assume that the total amount paid a year later is the quantity $1100 \cdot (1 + \pi)$, where π is the inflation rate over the year.

b. What is the real interest rate on the indexed bond? Why is the real rate known but the nominal rate uncertain?

c. Can you think of other types of indexed bonds? Are the real and nominal interest rates both uncertain in some cases?

Money, Inflation, and Interest Rates in the Market-Clearing Model

|T| his chapter uses the market-clearing model to study inflation and nominal interest rates. For the main analysis we return to the setting from Chapter 5 that does not deal explicitly with a labor market or firms. As we saw in Chapter 6, this simplification will be satisfactory for most purposes. The basic approach will be to specify a given time path of the money stock, M_t. Then we figure out what time paths of the price level, P_t—and, hence, of the inflation rate, π_t—and of the nominal and real interest rates, R_t and r_t, will satisfy the conditions for general market clearing.

We shall focus on the consequences of different rates of anticipated inflation and monetary growth. Even when the inflation rate, π_t, varies over time, we assume that people forecast these changes accurately. Put another way, people have **perfect foresight** about future price levels, so that there is always equality between the actual and expected inflation rates, $\pi_t = \pi_t^e$. Accordingly, if people know the nominal interest rate,

R_t, then there is also equality between actual and expected real interest rates, $r_t = r_t^e$.

The analysis is limited because it does not address unanticipated inflation and monetary growth. (We shall explore these matters later.) But it is useful to study anticipated inflation as a separate topic. In particular, the changes in anticipated inflation explain the principal longer-term movements in U.S. nominal interest rates since World War II.

INCORPORATION OF INFLATION AND MONETARY GROWTH INTO THE MODEL

We want to incorporate into the model the new elements that were discussed in Chapter 7. These new features include inflation and the distinction between real and nominal interest rates. To analyze the link between monetary growth and inflation, we also have to extend the model to allow for changes in the stock of money.

For simplicity, we begin with situations in which the nominal interest rate, R, and the inflation rate, π, are constant over time. Therefore, the real interest rate, $r = R - \pi$, is also constant. Because we assumed equality between actual and expected inflation, $\pi = \pi^e$, there is also equality between actual and expected real interest rates, $r = r^e$.

MONETARY GROWTH AND TRANSFER PAYMENTS

We choose the simplest possible way to introduce monetary growth into the model: new money shows up as transfers from the government to households. (Later we shall see that the main results still hold for other, more realistic, methods of introducing new money into the economy.)

Denote by v_t the dollar amount of transfer that a household receives during period t. This amount need not be the same for everyone. The government finances the total of transfers, V_t, by printing and distributing new money. The change in the aggregate quantity of money, $M_t - M_{t-1}$, therefore equals the aggregate amount of transfers:

$$V_t = M_t - M_{t-1} \qquad\qquad\qquad \textbf{(8.1)}$$

Equation (8.1) is a simple version of a **governmental budget constraint**. The left side is total government expenditures, all of which take the form of transfers at this point. The right side shows government revenues. At present, this revenue derives solely from the printing of new paper money.

We can think of transfer payments as arising from a "helicopter drop" of cash.[1] Our public officials effectively stuff a helicopter full of paper currency and fly around dropping money randomly over the countryside. The transfer payments occur when people pick up the money. Despite the unrealistic flavor of this story, the only important aspect of it is that each person's transfer is independent of his or her level of income, previous amount of money holdings, and so on. Economists refer to these kinds of transfers as **lump-sum transfers**: the amount that someone receives is independent of his or her level of work effort, holdings of money, or other activities. Because the transfers are lump sum, an individual understands that changes in his or her holdings of money, m_t and m_{t-1}, have no impact on the size of his or her transfer, v_t.[2]

We have to modify households' budget constraints to include the transfer payments. Each household's budget constraint for period t is

$$P_t y_t + b_{t-1} \cdot (1 + R) + m_{t-1} + v_t = P_t c_t + b_t + m_t \qquad \textbf{(8.2)}$$

As before, the sources of funds on the left side include the dollar receipts from the commodity market, $P_t y_t$, plus the values of the bonds and money that were held last period, $b_{t-1} \cdot (1 + R) + m_{t-1}$. The new element is the dollar amount of transfer, v_t, which is an additional source of funds for a household. The right side of equation (8.2) contains the

[1] The original source of this popular story is reputed to be Milton Friedman (1969, pp. 4–5).

[2] The discussion assumes positive transfers, although we could deal with negative ones. Negative transfers are taxes, which can also be lump sum, that is, independent of individuals' levels of income, amount of money holdings, and so on. Whereas we view transfers as financed by a helicopter drop of cash, we can view taxes as collected by a giant vacuum cleaner.

same uses of funds as before: the nominal purchases of commodities, $P_t c_t$, plus this period's holdings of bonds and money, $b_t + m_t$. Notice that we date the price level, P_t, because it will no longer be constant over time. Since we assume that the nominal interest rate, R, is constant, we do not have to date it.

BUDGET CONSTRAINTS OVER AN INFINITE HORIZON

We showed in Chapter 4 that we did not have to concern ourselves with the presence of real money balances in households' budget constraints when we were interested in conditions for general market clearing. That conclusion remains valid here if we also take account of the transfer payments, V_t, which relate in the aggregate to the change in money balances from equation (8.1). The appendix to this chapter proves that the net wealth effect is nil in the aggregate for three types of monetary terms—initial real money balances, the interest forgone on the real money balances demanded in future periods, and the transfer payments received from the government. Basically, the starting real money balances plus the receipts of new money through transfer payments provide just enough resources, but no more, for the typical household to hold money in each period. There is nothing left over to spend on consumption or leisure.

We also showed in Chapter 4 that the present value of the transaction costs associated with cash management would appear as a negative item for households' wealth. That conclusion also remains valid here. However, we start by maintaining our previous assumption that these costs are small enough to ignore.

If we use this reasoning to neglect the various monetary terms that appear in equation (8.2), then the budget constraint expressed in nominal terms over an infinite horizon looks basically as it did before. Since we assume that the nominal interest rate, R, is constant, the constraint is

$$P_1 y_1 + P_2 y_2/(1+R) + P_3 y_3/(1+R)^2 + \cdots + b_0 \cdot (1+R)$$

$$= P_1 c_1 + P_2 c_2/(1+R) + P_3 c_3/(1+R)^2 + \cdots$$

(8.3)

The only new element in equation (8.3) is the dating of the price level.

Recall that we assume a constant rate of inflation, π. Therefore, the price levels for any two adjacent periods satisfy the condition $P_t = (1+\pi) \cdot P_{t-1}$. We can use this condition repeatedly to express each future level of prices in terms of the current price, P_1, and the inflation rate, π, to get the sequence:

$$P_2 = (1+\pi) \cdot P_1,$$

$$P_3 = (1+\pi)^2 \cdot P_1,$$

$$\vdots$$

If we substitute these results into the budget constraint from equation (8.3), then we get the revised condition

$$P_1 \cdot [y_1 + y_2 \cdot (1+\pi)/(1+R) + y_3 \cdot (1+\pi)^2/(1+R)^2 + \cdots] + b_0 \cdot (1+R)$$

$$= P_1 \cdot [c_1 + c_2 \cdot (1+\pi)/(1+R) + c_3 \cdot (1+\pi)^2/(1+R)^2 + \cdots] \qquad \textbf{(8.4)}$$

Notice that the next period's real income and spending, y_2 and c_2, enter multiplicatively with the factor $(1+\pi)/(1+R)$. But recall from Chapter 7 that the relation between real and nominal interest rates is $(1+r) = (1+R)/(1+\pi)$. The term in equation (8.4), $(1+\pi)/(1+R)$, is therefore equal to $1/(1+r)$. Hence, to express the next period's real income and spending, y_2 and c_2, as present values, we divide by the discount factor, $1+r$. This result makes sense because the real interest rate tells people how they can exchange goods of one period for those of another. In particular, it is the *real* interest rate, rather than the *nominal* rate, that matters here.

The same idea applies for any future period. For example, the real income and spending for period 3, y_3 and c_3, enter into equation (8.4) as a multiple of the factor $(1+\pi)^2/(1+R)^2$, which equals $1/(1+r)^2$. If we make all these substitutions into equation (8.4)—and also divide through by the current price level, P_1—then we end up with a simplified form of the budget constraint:

$$y_1 + y_2/(1+r) + y_3/(1+r)^2 + \cdots + b_0 \cdot (1+R)/P_1$$

$$= c_1 + c_2/(1+r) + c_3/(1+r)^2 + \ldots$$

(8.5)

(The nominal interest rate appears in the term $b_0 \cdot [1 + R]$ because this term is the nominal value of the bonds carried over to period 1.)

Equation (8.5) is the budget constraint in real terms over an infinite horizon. The new element is that the real interest rate, r, appears instead of the nominal rate, R, in the various discount factors.

INTERTEMPORAL-SUBSTITUTION EFFECTS

We discussed before how the interest rate has intertemporal-substitution effects on consumption, leisure, and saving. These effects involve the relative costs of taking consumption or leisure at one date rather than another. In making these comparisons an individual wants to know, for example, how much extra consumption he or she can get next period by reducing consumption this period. As we worked out before, an individual can save and thus transform each unit of consumption forgone this period into $1 + r$ units of added consumption for the next period. An increase in the real interest rate, r, motivates people to reduce current consumption and leisure to raise future consumption and leisure. In other words, a higher r motivates people to save more today. The important point is that the real interest rate matters here rather than the nominal rate. Thus, our previous discussions of intertemporal-substitution effects remain valid if we replace the nominal interest rate by the real rate. Recall that in this chapter we treat the real interest rate, r, as a known quantity. More generally, the expected real interest rate, $r^e = R - \pi^e$, is what matters for intertemporal-substitution effects. People do not shift their planned time paths of consumption and leisure, and, hence, their saving, unless they anticipate that the real interest rate will be either higher or lower. For intertemporal-substitution effects to arise, there must be a change in the nominal interest rate, R, relative to the expected rate of inflation, π^e.

INTEREST RATES AND THE DEMAND FOR MONEY

Recall that the demand for money involves a trade-off between transaction costs and interest forgone. Further, the interest forgone depends on the differential between the interest rate on bonds and that on money. Since the nominal interest rate on money is zero, this differential equals the *nominal* interest rate, R (and not the *real* interest rate, r). It follows that the demand-for-money function involves the nominal interest rate, R. Therefore, as in our previous analysis that neglected inflation, the function for the aggregate real demand for money takes the form

$$(M_t/P_t)^d = \Phi(\underset{(+)}{Y_t},\ \underset{(-)}{R},\ \ldots) \tag{8.6}$$

Notice an important point. It is the real interest rate, r, that exerts intertemporal-substitution effects on consumption and work. But it is the nominal interest rate, R, that influences the real demand for money.

MARKET-CLEARING CONDITIONS

We know from Chapter 5 how to express the conditions for general market clearing. First, the aggregate supply of goods, Y_t^s, equals the demand, C_t^d:

$$Y^s(\underset{(+)}{r_t},\ \ldots) = C^d(\underset{(+)}{r_t},\ \ldots) \tag{8.7}$$

Equation (8.7) shows the intertemporal-substitution effects from the real interest rate, r_t. As usual, this effect is positive on the supply of goods and negative on the demand. The omitted terms, denoted by . . . , include various aspects of the production function. Transaction costs associated with cash management would generally enter here through wealth effects, but we are assuming that these influences are small enough to neglect.

Second, we have the condition that all money be willingly held. We can write this condition for period t as

$$M_t = P_t \cdot \Phi(Y_t, R_t, \ldots) \tag{8.8}$$
$$(+) \ (-)$$

On the left is the actual quantity of money. On the right is the nominal demand for money, which depends positively on the price level, P_t, and aggregate output, Y_t, and negatively on the nominal interest rate, R_t. Any other factors that influence money demand, such as transaction costs, are denoted by the expression . . . in equation (8.8). We assume that these factors do not change over time.

THE SUPERNEUTRALITY OF MONEY

Before we explore the details of the link between monetary behavior and inflation, we can already see an important property from the condition for clearing the commodity market. Consider the underlying real factors in the model, which include the forms of production functions, the level of population, and the preferences of households. More generally, the transaction costs associated with cash management would also appear on this list, but we are assuming that these costs can be ignored. The various real elements enter into the demand and supply of commodities through the omitted terms, which we denote by . . . in equation (8.7). For given values of these elements, equation (8.7) determines the real interest rate, r_t, and the level of aggregate output, $Y_t = C_t$, at each date. If the underlying real elements do not change over time, then the market-clearing values of the real interest rate and output are constants.

The important point is not that the real interest rate and output are constant but rather that they are determined independently of the path of money. At least this result holds if we maintain the approximation that the transaction costs of cash management are small enough to neglect. Although changes in money will end up affecting the paths of the price level and the nominal interest rate, these monetary changes will, as an approximation, not affect some of the real variables in the model.

If all real variables are invariant with the behavior of money, then economists say that money is superneutral. The phrase **superneutrality of money** indicates an extension of another concept, the neutrality of money, which we discussed before. Neutrality of money means that once-and-for-all changes in the quantity of money affect nominal variables but not real variables. Superneutrality extends this idea from one-time changes in the stock of money to arbitrary variations in the entire path of money.

We know from before that money is neutral in the model. One point we want to consider in this chapter is whether money is superneutral. To the extent that money is not superneutral, we shall find some effects of money and inflation on real variables.

MONETARY GROWTH, INFLATION, AND THE NOMINAL INTEREST RATE

We want now to examine the details of the linkages among monetary growth, inflation, and the nominal interest rate. We carry out this analysis for given values of the real interest rate, r, and output, Y. By holding these variables fixed, we are making two types of assumptions. First, we use the property that anticipated variations in money and prices do not (as an approximation) affect the real interest rate and output. Second, we assume that no other shifts occur over time to the functions for aggregate commodity demand and supply. Generally, these types of changes would lead to movements in the real interest rate and output.

More specifically, the analysis neglects any systematic growth of output. Recall from Chapter 7 that countries with higher average growth rates of output tend to have less inflation for a given average growth rate of money. Although it is not hard to incorporate this feature into the analysis, we assume that output is constant to bring out the major points in the easiest possible way.

We can illustrate the main results by assuming a constant rate of monetary growth:

$$M_t = (1 + \mu) \cdot M_{t-1} \tag{8.9}$$

where μ (the Greek letter *mu*) is the monetary growth rate. Assume that equation (8.9) governs the behavior of money from the current date, $t = 1$, into the indefinite future.

We want to calculate the price level at each date, given that money grows at a constant rate. We already determined the real interest rate and output to equate aggregate commodity supply and demand in equation (8.7). Further, if these supply and demand functions do not shift over time, then the real interest rate, r, and output, Y, are constants. Given these results, the price level, P_t, must satisfy the condition that money be willingly held. Writing this condition in real terms, we have

$$M_t/P_t = \Phi(Y , R_t, \ldots) \tag{8.10}$$
$$\quad\quad\;\; (+) \;\; (-)$$

In Chapter 5 we found that once-and-for-all increases in the quantity of money raised the price level in the same proportion. It is therefore reasonable to consider the possibility that the price level, P_t, grows at the same rate as the money stock, M_t. In this case the inflation rate, π, is constant and equal to the rate of monetary growth, μ. So let's make this guess and see whether it accords with the condition from equation (8.10) that all money be willingly held.

If money and prices grow at the same rate, then the ratio of these two, which is the level of real money balances, M_t/P_t, does not change over time. Therefore, the amount of real money, which appears on the left side of equation (8.10), is constant.

Recall that the nominal interest rate, R_t, equals the quantity $r_t + \pi_t$. But we already know that the real interest rate is constant. Therefore, if the inflation rate is constant, then the nominal interest rate is also constant. This result means that the real demand for money, $\Phi(\cdot)$, which appears on the right side of equation (8.10), is constant. (Remember that output, Y, does not change over time.)

Since real money balances and the real amount of money demanded are each constant, we have only to be sure that the two constants are the same. This condition holds if we determine the current price level, P_1, to equate the amount of real money balances, M_1/P_1, to the real quantity demanded, $\Phi(\cdot)$. Then, since actual and desired real money do not vary over time, we can be sure that all money will be willingly held at each date: equation (8.10) holds in every period.

We have now verified that our guess—prices growing at the same rate as money—satisfies the conditions for general market clearing. This path of prices is therefore the one that will prevail in our market-clearing framework. To summarize, the results are as follows:

—— Prices grow at the same rate as the money stock, $\pi = \mu$.

—— Aggregate real money balances, M_t/P_t, are constant.

—— The nominal interest rate, R, is constant and equal to $r + \pi$.

—— The aggregate demand for real balances, $\Phi(Y, R, \ldots)$, is constant.

—— The current price level, P_1, equates the quantity of real money balances, M_1/P_1, to the real amount demanded, $\Phi(Y, R)$.

The results imply that the growth rate of money, μ, shows up one-for-one in the inflation rate, π, and in the nominal interest rate, $R = r + \pi$.

But recall that a higher nominal interest rate means a lower level of real money demanded. Therefore, a higher growth rate of money corresponds to a lower level of aggregate real money balances, M_t/P_t.

A SHIFT IN THE MONETARY GROWTH RATE

We can better understand the results by studying a change in the monetary growth rate. Suppose that the money stock has been growing for a long time at the constant rate μ. Further, assume that everyone expects this behavior to continue indefinitely. Hence, the inflation rate is the constant $\pi = \mu$, and the nominal interest rate is given by

$$R = r + \pi = r + \mu$$

We show this initial situation on the left side of Figure 8.1.

Consider how the quantity of money, M_t, behaves over time. We have the sequence

$$M_1 = (1 + \mu) \cdot M_0$$
$$M_2 = (1 + \mu) \cdot M_1 = (1 + \mu)^2 \cdot M_0$$

$$\vdots$$

Therefore, for any period t, the quantity of money is given by

$$M_t = (1 + \mu)^t \cdot M_0 \tag{8.11}$$

We shall find it convenient to graph the quantity of money, M_t, on a proportionate or logarithmic scale. Then each unit on the vertical axis corresponds to an equal proportionate change in a variable, say, a 1% change in the stock of money. Since money grows at the constant proportionate rate μ, the graph of money versus time is a straight line on a proportionate scale. Further, the slope of the line equals the growth rate, μ. The left side of Figure 8.2 therefore shows the quantity of money,

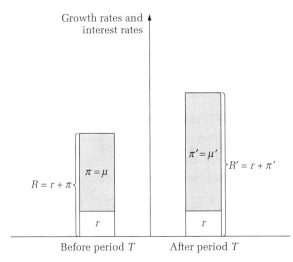

FIGURE 8.1

GROWTH RATES OF MONEY AND PRICES AND LEVELS OF INTEREST RATES: EFFECTS OF AN INCREASE IN THE MONETARY GROWTH RATE

Before period T, the growth rate of money is μ. Hence, the left side of the figure shows that the inflation rate is $\pi = \mu$, and the nominal interest rate is $R = r + \pi = r + \mu$. After period T, the growth rate of money is the higher value μ'. Consequently, the new inflation rate is $\pi' = \mu'$, and the new nominal interest rate is $R' = r + \pi' = r + \mu'$.

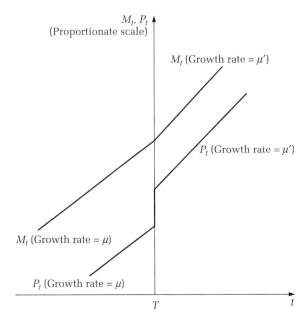

FIGURE 8.2

EFFECT OF AN INCREASE IN THE MONETARY GROWTH RATE ON THE PATH OF THE PRICE LEVEL

We show the behavior of money and prices before and after an increase in the monetary growth rate at date T. Notice that a jump in the price level occurs at date T.

MONEY, INFLATION, AND INTEREST RATES IN THE MARKET-CLEARING MODEL

M_t, as a straight line with slope μ.[3] We found before that the price level grows also at the constant rate $\pi = \mu$:

$$P_t = (1 + \pi)^t \cdot P_0 = (1 + \pi)^t \cdot P_0 \tag{8.12}$$

The left side of Figure 8.2 therefore shows the graph of the price level, P_t, as a straight line with slope μ. This line parallels the one for the stock of money, M_t.

Assume now that the growth rate of money rises from μ to μ' at some date T. Here, we think of this change as a surprise—before date T no one anticipated the acceleration of money. But, once it happens, we assume that everyone expects the new monetary growth rate, μ', to persist forever. Hence, we study here the consequences of a once-and-for-all increase in the rate of monetary expansion.

After the change in the monetary growth rate, the economy is in the same type of situation as before. The only difference is that the growth rate of money is μ', rather than μ. Therefore, we show on the right side of Figure 8.1 that the new inflation rate is $\pi' = \mu'$. We know, in addition, that the change in monetary behavior does not affect the real interest rate, which remains at the value r. The new nominal interest rate is therefore $R' = r + \pi' = r + \mu'$. Hence, the inflation rate and the nominal interest rate rise by as much as the increase in the monetary growth rate.

We show the levels of money and prices after date T on the right side of Figure 8.2. Because the growth rate of money rises after date T, the line for the money stock, M_t, has the slope μ', which exceeds the original slope. Note, however, that there is no immediate jump in the stock of money at date T; money just starts to grow faster at this point. Since prices grow at the rate $\pi' = \mu'$ after date T, the figure again shows the line for the price level, P_t, as parallel to that for the money stock. But notice an important complication in the graph of P_t in Figure 8.2: there is a jump in P_t at date T. Let's see why this jump takes place.

[3] We ignore the discrete length of periods in this graph. In effect, we treat this length as being extremely brief.

The acceleration of money at date T raises the nominal interest rate from $R = r + \mu$ to $R' = r + \mu'$. Recall that an increase in the nominal interest rate reduces the real demand for money. Hence, the existing amount of money will be willingly held at date T only if the actual real balances, M_T/P_T, fall by as much as the real demand. But there is no sudden change in the nominal quantity of money at date T, only an increase in the rate of growth. Therefore, real balances can fall to equal the smaller amount demanded only if there is an upward jump in the price level at date T.

We can say something about the size of the jump in the price level. The proportionate rise in the price level equals the proportionate fall in real money balances, which equals the proportionate decline in the real quantity of money demanded. Further, the magnitude of the decline in money demand depends on two things: first, the change in the nominal interest rate, which is $\mu' - \mu$, and second, the sensitivity of real money demanded to changes in the nominal interest rate. The jump in the price level is therefore greater the larger is the acceleration of money, $\mu' - \mu$, and the greater is the sensitivity of money demand to changes in the nominal interest rate.

The Increase in the Nominal Interest Rate

Let's think about why the acceleration of money at date T leads to a rise in the nominal interest rate. At date T, people learn that, henceforth, the government will pursue a more expansionary monetary policy. They know also that this policy means a rate of inflation, $\pi' = \mu'$, which exceeds the initial rate, $\pi = \mu$. Consider what the higher expected rate of inflation does at date T in the credit market. Borrowers now regard the old nominal interest rate, R, as a better deal. They hold this view because the real interest rate that they must pay has fallen from the value $R - \mu$ to the lower value $R - \mu'$. Hence, if the nominal interest rate did not change, borrowers would raise their demand for loans. On the other side, lenders see that their real rate of return has deteriorated.

Therefore, if the nominal interest rate did not change, lenders would decrease their supply of loans. A balance between loans demanded and supplied applies—that is, the credit market clears—only if the nominal interest rate rises.

The new nominal interest rate, R', exceeds the old one, R, by the increase in the inflation rate, $\mu' - \mu$. Lenders view this rise in the nominal rate as just sufficient to compensate them for the loss of purchasing power over time due to the higher inflation rate. Similarly, borrowers are willing to pay the higher nominal interest rate because they expect to repay their loans with more heavily deflated dollars. In other words, the increase in the nominal interest rate incorporates fully the change in expected inflation. Thereby, the acceleration of money and prices does not change the real interest rate, r.

The Jump in the Price Level

Consider now the intuition for why the price level jumps upward at date T. The sudden prospect of higher inflation and the consequent rise in the nominal interest rate lead to a fall in the real demand for money at date T. If the price level did not adjust, then people's actual real money balances, M_T/P_T, would exceed their desired amount. Consequently, everyone would attempt to spend his or her excess money by buying either goods or bonds. The rise in the demand for goods puts upward pressure on the price level, and the economy returns to a position of general market clearing only when the price level rises enough to equate actual and desired real money. This condition is the one that we used to determine the size of the jump in the price level in Figure 8.2.

Wage Rates

If we added a labor market to the model, then we would find that the real wage rate, w/P, and the quantity of employment, L, were independent of money: money is also neutral with respect to these two real variables. The path of nominal wage rates must therefore parallel the path of prices, which appears in Figure 8.2. This result means that nominal wages grow at the rate μ up to date T and at the higher rate μ' after date T. Further, the nominal wage rate would jump upward at date T.

Summarizing the Results for an Acceleration of Money

Let's summarize the results for a once-and-for-all increase in the growth rate of money (a decrease in the growth rate of money just reverses the signs of all effects):

— There are no changes in the real interest rate, the real wage rate, or the levels of output and employment.

— The inflation rate and the nominal interest rate (and the growth rate of nominal wages) rise by as much as the increase in the growth rate of money.

— The real demand for money and the actual quantity of real money balances decrease.

— The price level jumps upward to equate actual real money balances to the smaller quantity demanded.

Let's use these results to see whether money is superneutral, that is, whether the path of money matters for real variables. Recall that the path of money does not affect the real interest rate, the real wage rate, and the quantities of output and employment. However, because the acceleration of money raises the inflation rate, it also raises the nominal interest rate and thereby lowers the amount of real money demanded. The resulting fall in real money balances is one real effect of the change in monetary behavior. Anticipated monetary growth and inflation are therefore not superneutral in the model.

Underlying the decline in real money demanded is an increase in the transaction costs that people incur to economize on money. Since these costs absorb resources, the increase in these costs is an adverse real effect from the increase in monetary growth. Our analysis neglected any effects of transaction costs on households' choices of work effort, consumption, and saving. These kinds of effects are small in ordinary circumstances—that is, unless inflation is extreme—and we can safely ignore them in these contexts. But for very high inflation rates, such as those that we discuss later for the German **hyperinflation**, the resources spent on transaction costs can have significant effects on output, work effort, the real interest rate, and other real variables. The independence of real variables from anticipated monetary growth and inflation is therefore only an approximation, which is satisfactory when transaction costs are small.

Remember that the present analysis assumes perfect foresight about future price levels.[4] The model therefore features equality between actual and expected inflation and between actual and expected real interest rates. We saw in Chapter 7 that unexpected inflation has important effects on realized real interest rates. If inflation and real interest rates are uncertain, then there are a variety of real effects that would arise. We shall explore some of these effects in Chapter 19. For now, the important point is that the analysis deals only with anticipated inflation.

THE DYNAMICS OF INFLATION

Consider again the case in which monetary growth rises at date T from the initial value, μ, to the higher value, μ'. Let's think further about the transition from the initial rate of inflation, $\pi = \mu$, to the subsequent rate, $\pi' = \mu'$. Because the nominal interest rate increases, the level of real money balances decreases. For real money to fall, there must be a transition period during which prices rise by proportionately more than money. So far our analysis says that this transition occurs in an instant at date T by an upward jump in the price level. But in the real world there are a number of considerations that stretch out the transition. Here, we introduce some of these features to study some aspects of the dynamics of inflation.

[4] *The exception is the jump in the price level that accompanies the surprise acceleration of money at date T. The inflation rate (infinity) exceeds the expected inflation rate at this point.*

GRADUAL ADJUSTMENT OF THE DEMAND FOR MONEY

Return to the case in which people first learn at date T that money will be growing at a higher rate. Recall that the size of the jump in the price level at date T depends on the extent of the fall in real money demanded. Suppose now that people reduce their demand for money only gradually when the nominal interest rate increases. Then we may find only a small jump in the price level at date T. Most of the extra upward kick to the price level shows up only gradually as people reduce their real demand for money.

Recall that a person's real demand for money reflects some underlying decisions about the frequency of transactions, financial planning, and so on. If the nominal interest rate rises, then it is reasonable that people would take some time to modify these aspects of their behavior. Hence, in the aggregate, the real demand for money would decline gradually in response to an increase in the nominal interest rate.

Slow adjustment in the demand for money effectively spreads out the jump in the price level over a transition interval. When money accelerates at time T, the inflation rate reacts something like the solid line shown in Figure 8.3: the inflation rate, π_t, exceeds the new growth rate of money, μ', over an extended interval. The excess of π_t over μ' means that real money balances, M_t/P_t, fall over time to match the gradual decline in the real demand for money. Eventually, π_t approaches its new long-term value, μ': in the long run, the real quantity of money remains constant but at a lower level than initially.

ANTICIPATED CHANGES IN MONETARY GROWTH

Our analysis can deal with situations in which the growth rate of money either rises or falls. But, so far, we have assumed that the change in actual monetary growth coincides with the change in perceptions about future monetary growth. In other words, two things happen at date T in the previous examples. First, money accelerates or decelerates permanently.

FIGURE 8.3

EFFECT OF HIGHER MONETARY GROWTH ON INFLATION, INCLUD-
ING GRADUAL ADJUSTMENT OF THE DEMAND FOR MONEY

The growth rate of money rises from μ to μ' at date T. The solid
line shows that the inflation rate, π_t, stays above μ' for a while but
eventually approaches μ'.

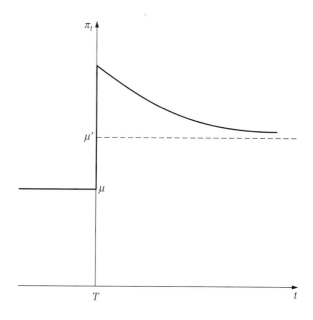

Second, people first learn at date T that this acceleration or deceleration
will occur.

People may receive advance information that allows them to forecast increases or decreases in monetary growth and inflation. This type
of information could derive from news about the prospects for war and
peace or from political changes that foreshadow changes in the monetary
regime. In the 1890s, for example, William Jennings Bryan campaigned
for president on a program of easy money (free coinage of silver). His
defeat probably lowered expectations of future monetary growth and inflation. Similarly, in 1980, the election of Ronald Reagan, rather than
Jimmy Carter, likely lowered expectations of future monetary growth and
inflation. Another example of advance information concerns the post–
World War I hyperinflation in Germany. People apparently anticipated
for several months before November 1923 that a **monetary reform** was
coming.[5]

If people forecast an acceleration or deceleration of money, then the
path of inflation differs from those already discussed. To avoid a great

[5] *Robert Flood and Peter Garber (1980) and Laura Lahaye
(1985) provide quantitative estimates for these expectations of
impending monetary reform.*

many complicated detail, the subsequent discussion just sketches the types of effects that arise.

Suppose that people learn currently that an acceleration of money is coming at the future date T. Then they know also that inflation rates and nominal interest rates will be higher in the future. When people know that the cost of holding money will rise after date T, they tend to reduce their demand for money before date T. Otherwise, they will get caught holding money at date T when the big increase in prices occurs. Thus, the expectation of future inflation has a negative effect on people's willingness to hold money today. This reduction in today's demand for money means that today's price level must rise. In other words, although the acceleration of money has not yet occurred, the expectation of a future monetary acceleration leads to a higher current rate of inflation. Finally, since this higher rate of inflation becomes anticipated, the nominal interest rate also rises before the acceleration of money.

The precise path of inflation depends on when people learn about the acceleration of money. But, as mentioned, the key point is that changes in expectations about future money can generate variations in inflation and the nominal interest rate that precede the changes in monetary growth. Thus, although the analysis stresses monetary factors as the source of inflation, significant divergences can arise in the short run between the growth rates of money and prices. These divergences are likely to be important in an environment in which a volatile monetary policy induces frequent revisions in forecasts of monetary behavior. Such an environment would also be marked by volatility in inflation rates and nominal interest rates.

To relate these ideas back to the German hyperinflation, the expectation of a monetary reform in 1923 would have caused people to anticipate a decrease in the future inflation rate (which actually occurred). This anticipation raised the real demand for money before the reform and served, thereby, to lower inflation before the reform took place.

THE TRANSITION FROM ONE INFLATION RATE TO ANOTHER

Let's stress a basic feature of the results concerning changes from one long-term inflation rate to another. Although jumps in the price level need not occur, an acceleration of money must involve a transition during which prices rise by proportionately more than money. This conclusion follows inevitably from the eventual decline in real money balances.

We can turn the results around to deal with a case in which money decelerates. Although a downward jump in the price level need not occur, the transition must involve a period in which prices grow by proportionately less than money. This result holds because the lower nominal interest rate raises the real demand for money.

Suppose, as an example, that the government reduces monetary growth permanently from 10% per year to 5%. Presumably, the objective of this policy is to reduce long-term inflation. Our analysis implies that there is a transition period during which the inflation rate is even less than 5% per year. There may, in fact, be deflation—falling prices—for awhile. Thus, in designing a monetary policy to end inflation, economic advisers have to think about the potential for very low or negative rates of inflation as a temporary side effect.

MONEY AND PRICES DURING THE GERMAN HYPERINFLATION

We can assess some of the theoretical results by examining the data on the post–World War I German hyperinflation. Here, we have something close to a laboratory experiment for studying the consequences of high and variable rates of monetary growth and inflation.[6] Over the period from 1921 to 1923, the rates of inflation ranged from near zero to over 500% per month! Further, the available data suggest that relatively small changes occurred in aggregate real variables, such as total output and

[6] *Not surprisingly, the topic has fascinated many economists. Two of the more important studies are by Costantino Bresciani-Turroni (1937) and Phillip Cagan (1956).*

employment. Hence, aggregate real money demanded would not be affected very much by changes in real spending.

When inflation rates are volatile, it is impossible to predict accurately the real interest rate on loans that prescribe nominal interest rates. This type of lending therefore tends to disappear during hyperinflations, such as the one in Germany. For this reason, when analyzing the demand for money during the German hyperinflation, we have no useful measures of the nominal interest rate. In this environment the best indicator of the cost of holding money comes directly from the expected rate of inflation, π^e. This rate tells people how much they lose by holding money rather than consuming or holding a durable good that maintains its value in real terms.

Table 8.1 summarizes the behavior of the monetary growth rate, μ, the inflation rate, π, and real money balance, M/P, in Germany from 1920 until 1925. In most cases the table indicates the average growth rates of money and prices over six-month intervals. The level of real money balances pertains to the ends of these intervals.

At the beginning of 1920 the growth rates of money and prices were already at the very high rate of about 6% per month. (When talking about hyperinflations, economists typically measure these rates per month rather than per year!) Then there was a deceleration of money to an average rate of less than 1% per month for the first half of 1921. Notice that, as the theory predicts, the growth rate of prices, π, fell by more than the growth rate of money, μ, when money decelerated. Correspondingly, real money balances increased by about 20% from early 1920 to early 1921. (The level of real money in early 1920 was roughly equal to that from before the war in 1913.)

In 1922 money accelerated dramatically to an average growth rate of nearly 30% per month toward the end of the year. During this period the growth rate of prices, π, exceeded that of money, μ. Hence, by late 1922, real money balances fell to about a quarter of the level prevailing in early 1920.

TABLE 8.1

MONETARY GROWTH, INFLATION, AND REAL MONEY BALANCES DURING THE GERMAN HYPERINFLATION

Period	μ^a	π^a	M/P (end of period)
2/20–6/20	5.7	6.0	1.01
6/20–12/20	3.0	1.1	1.13
12/20–6/21	0.8	0.1	1.18
6/21–12/21	5.5	8.4	0.99
12/21–6/22	6.5	12.8	0.68
6/22–12/22	29.4	46.7	0.24
12/22–6/23	40.0	40.0	0.24
6/23–10/23	233	286	0.03
Reform Period			
12/23–6/24	5.9	−0.6	0.44
6/24–12/24	5.3	1.4	0.56
12/24–6/25	2.0	1.6	0.57
6/25–12/25	1.2	0.4	0.60

Source: Sonderhefte zur Wirtschaft und Statistik, *Berlin, 1925*.

Note: *M is an estimate of the total circulation of currency. Until late 1923 the figures refer to total legal tender, most of which consists of notes issued by the Reichsbank. Later, the data include issues of the Rentenbank, private bank notes, and various "emergency moneys." However, especially in late 1923, many unofficial emergency currencies, as well as circulating foreign currencies, are not counted. The numbers are standardized so that the quantity outstanding in 1913 is 1.0. P is an index of the cost of living, based on 1913 = 1.0.*

[a] *Percent per month.*

During the first half of 1923 there was some letup in the acceleration of money, and money and prices grew together at the extraordinary average rate of 40% per month. Correspondingly, although the rate of inflation was enormous, the level of real money remained fairly stable. But late in 1923 the hyperinflation built to its climax with rates of monetary expansion of 300 to 600% per month for October–November. Again, the acceleration of money led to rates of inflation that exceeded the growth rates of money. Real money balances reached their low point in October 1923 at about 3% of the level for early 1920. If we neglect variations in aggregate real income from 1920 to 1923—which is satisfactory as a first-order approximation—then the reduction in real money implies a rise in velocity by more than 30-fold. In other words, if in 1920 people held the typical piece of currency for two weeks before spending it, then in October 1923 they held it for about half a day.

A major monetary reform occurred in Germany during November 1923. This reform included the introduction of a new type of currency, a promise not to print new money beyond a specified limit to finance government expenditures or for other purposes, some changes in government spending and taxes, and a commitment to back the new currency by gold.[7] In any event, there was a sharp curtailment in monetary growth and inflation after December 1923. For example, during 1924 monetary growth averaged 5 to 6% per month. But because of the deceleration of money after November 1923, the average inflation rate was even less—below 1% per month for 1924. Most dramatically, the quantity of real money balances rose from 3% of the early 1920 level in October 1923 to 56% of that level by December 1924.[8] (Much of the increase in real money arose as an infusion of new types of currency during the reform months of November and December 1923.)

In 1925 the growth rate of money fell to 1 to 2% per month, and the inflation rate remained at roughly 1% per month. Real money balances rose slowly to reach 60% of the early 1920 level by late 1925. Although the inflation rate remained low for the remainder of the 1920s, the level of real money did not reattain the early 1920 level. Perhaps this discrepancy reflects a long-lasting negative influence of the hyperinflation on people's willingness to hold money.

[7] For discussions of the reform, see Bresciani-Turroni (1937), Thomas Sargent (1982), and Peter Garber (1982). Sargent's analysis deals also with the ends of the hyperinflations in Austria, Hungary, and Poland in the early 1920s. He stresses the rapidity with which inflations can be ended once governments make a credible commitment to limit money creation in the long run.

[8] The biggest hyperinflation on record occurred in Hungary after World War II: the price level rose by a factor of 3×10^{25} over the 13 months from July 1945 to August 1946. In the stabilization period from August 1946 to December 1947, the inflation rate declined to about 15% per year, and real balances rose by a factor of 14. For a discussion, see William Bomberger and Gail Makinen (1983).

REAL EFFECTS OF INFLATION

SOME EFFECTS FROM UNANTICIPATED INFLATION

Our analysis in this chapter focuses on anticipated inflation. But let's note briefly some real effects that arise from unexpected inflation. During the German hyperinflation, one effect of this type was a substantial redistribution of wealth. Before the extreme inflation began, some households and businesses had nominal debts (including mortgages and other loans), and others held nominal assets. The hyperinflation—which was not anticipated at the time when people acquired these nominal debts and assets—wiped out most of the real value of claims that had a predetermined nominal value. Therefore, debtors gained while creditors lost. The general point is that unexpected inflation can have significant effects on the distribution of wealth.

The unpredictability of inflation reduces the willingness of people to enter into contracts that specify nominal values in advance. Thus, as we already noted, the usual types of bond and loan markets tended to disappear during the German hyperinflation and other extreme inflations. Although other kinds of markets may still function (such as a stock market and transactions denominated in foreign currencies in hyperinflation Germany or indexed bond markets in modern inflations), the loss of the traditional types of bonds and loans is an adverse real effect from unpredictable inflation. In particular, we would expect that the loss of these credit markets would hinder investment. Evidence discussed in Chapter 11 indicates that sustained inflation above a range of 15–20% annually does have a significantly negative effect on economic growth and investment.

EFFECTS OF ANTICIPATED INFLATION ON REAL MONEY BALANCES AND TRANSACTION COSTS

In the discussion of superneutrality of money, we mentioned that some real variables, such as aggregate output, were at least approximately independent of anticipated variations in money and the general price level. But even if aggregate output changes little, one real effect from an increase in expected inflation is the reduction of real money balances. During the German hyperinflation, this response was dramatic, with aggregate real money falling to about 3% of its initial level.

Corresponding to the increase in expected inflation and the reduction in real money, people expend more resources on transaction costs. Although we regard these costs as small in normal times, we cannot neglect them during extreme circumstances, such as the German hyperinflation. For example, people spent a significant portion of their time on the process of receiving wage and other payments once or twice per day and in searching rapidly to find outlets for their cash. Given these magnitudes, we would also predict that extreme inflation would have significant effects on aggregate output. For the German case, there is some evidence that the process of dealing with the severe inflation in late 1923 had adverse effects on aggregate output and employment.

THE REVENUE FROM MONEY CREATION

A different real effect from inflation involves the **government's revenue from printing money**. In our theory thus far, the government uses this income solely to finance transfers. More realistically, governments use the printing press to pay for a variety of expenditures.

Recall that the real amount of revenue for period t is the quantity $(M_t - M_{t-1})/P_t$. The condition $M_t = (1 + \mu) \cdot M_{t-1}$ implies that we can rewrite the expression for real revenue as

$$\text{Real revenue from printing money} = (M_t - M_{t-1})/P_t = \mu M_{t-1}/P_t \quad \textbf{(8.13)}$$

A higher value of μ implies a higher value of the inflation rate, π, which implies a higher value of the nominal interest rate, $R = r + \pi$. A higher growth rate of money therefore increases the cost of holding money: people forgo interest at a higher rate by holding money. For this reason, economists often refer to the government's revenue from money creation as the **inflation tax.** The government raises the tax rate on real money holdings when it raises μ and thereby raises R. We can also say that the higher value of π, caused by the higher value of μ, means that the real value of money declines at a faster rate.

Note from equation (8.13) that the real revenue from money creation is the product of the growth rate of money, μ, and a term that approximates the level of aggregate real money held, M_{t-1}/P_t. Recall that an increase in μ leads to a reduction in real money balances. Hence, if μ rises from, say, 10% per month to 20% per month—or by a factor of 2—then the government's real revenue increases if real money balances decline by less than 50%. This condition holds empirically except for the most extreme cases. During the German hyperinflation, for example, the condition was apparently not violated until the growth rate of money approached 100% per month between July and August 1923. Until then, the government successfully extracted more real revenue by printing money at faster rates.

In normal times for most countries, the government obtains only a small portion of its revenue from printing money. In 1996, for example, the Federal Reserve obtained $23 billion from this source. This amount corresponded to 1.5% of the total revenues of the U.S. government and to 0.3% of GDP. These figures are typical for the main developed countries.

In a few high-inflation countries, the revenue from money creation is more important. As an extreme example, for Argentina over 1960–75, money creation accounted for nearly half of government revenues and for about 6% of GDP. Some other countries in which the revenue from printing money has been important are Chile (5% of GDP over 1960–77), Libya (3% of GDP over 1960–77), and Brazil (3% of GDP over 1960–78).

During the German hyperinflation and in some other hyperinflations (such as Austria, Hungary, Poland, and Russia after World War I), money creation became the primary source of government receipts. The amounts obtained eventually approached 10% of GDP, which appears to be about the maximum obtainable from printing money. There was a close month-to-month connection in Germany between the volume of real government spending and the growth rate of the money supply.

The variations in monetary growth—and, hence, inflation—were driven in this case by shifts in real government spending (see Zvi Hercowitz, 1981). Much of the government spending over this period went to reparations payments associated with World War I. The reduction in these payments after November 1923 was therefore a major factor in the success of the German monetary reform.

SUMMARY

We introduced monetary growth into the model by allowing for governmental transfer payments. By considering the government's budget constraint, we found that the aggregate of these transfers equals the change in the stock of money.

We modified the households' budget constraints to include inflation. The main result is that these constraints involve the real interest rate, rather than the nominal rate. Similarly, the intertemporal-substitution effects on consumption and leisure depend on the real interest rate. When there is uncertainty about inflation, it is the expected real interest rate that matters in the budget constraints and for intertemporal-substitution effects.

The nominal interest rate, R, still determines the cost of holding money rather than bonds. Therefore, although the real interest rate matters for choices of consumption and work, it is the nominal rate that appears in the demand-for-money function.

We used the market-clearing model to analyze the interactions among monetary growth, inflation, and nominal and real interest rates. An important result is that—if transaction costs are neglected—the real interest rate, the real wage rate, and the aggregates of output and employment are invariant with anticipated variations in the quantity of money.

Money is, however, not superneutral in the model. (By superneutral, we mean that variations in the path of money have no real effects.) The behavior of money influences the level of real money balances, the nominal interest rate, and the volume of transaction costs. Further, the invariance of the real interest rate and aggregate output holds only as an approximation, which is reasonable when transaction costs are small enough to neglect. This approximation would not be valid at high rates of inflation.

An increase in the growth rate of money shows up in the long run as equal increases in the inflation rate, the nominal interest rate, and the growth rate of nominal wages. However, because the higher nominal interest rate reduces the real demand for money, there must be a transition interval during which the rate of inflation exceeds the growth rate of money. In a simple case the transition occurs in an instant as an upward jump in the price level. But if we bring in some realistic extensions of the model—such as gradual adjustment of money demand and foreknowledge of the acceleration of money—then we find a richer dynamics of prices during the transition. One general property is that the inflation rate exceeds the growth rate of money during the transition.

Similar results apply to a decrease in long-run inflation brought about by a decline in the growth rate of money. The process of reducing inflation involves a transition period with unusually low rates of inflation, which may be negative.

We illustrated some of the results by observing the dynamics of monetary growth and inflation during the post–World War I German hyperinflation. Higher rates of monetary growth led to lower levels of real money balances, whereas reductions in monetary growth had the opposite effect. We also discussed the effects of inflation on transaction costs and on the real revenue that the government obtains from printing money.

APPENDIX (OPTIONAL): THE WEALTH EFFECTS FROM THE MONETARY TERMS

We argued in Chapter 4 that we could neglect wealth effects associated with money if we ignore transaction costs. We now want to show that these wealth effects can still be neglected in the model that adds monetary growth and inflation.

Consider the household's budget constraint in nominal terms in equation (8.3). The first amendment when we consider the monetary terms is to add the initial nominal balance, m_0, as a source of funds on the left side of the equation.

The second change is that each household receives the nominal transfer, v_t, from the government in each period. The present value of these transfers should be added as a source of funds on the left side of equation (8.3).

If the household always held the constant *nominal* balance m_1 from period 1 onward, then we would modify the right side of equation (8.3) to include m_1 as a nominal use of funds. The constancy of nominal money balances is, however, unlikely in the presence of inflation. (Real money held would then decline steadily over time.) Suppose, instead, that the household adds the amount $m_2 - m_1$ to its money balance during period 2. This change in money enters into the budget constraint in the same way as period 2's nominal consumption expenditure, Pc_2. The quantity $m_2 - m_1$ would therefore be discounted by the factor $1 + R$ on the right side of equation (8.3). We can treat all future changes in money similarly: $m_3 - m_2$ like P_3c_3, and so on.

The budget constraint that extends equation (8.3) to include all the monetary terms is therefore:

$$P_1y_1 + P_2y_2/(1 + R) + \cdots + b_0 \cdot (1 + R) + m_0 + v_1 + v_2/(1 + R) + \ldots$$
$$= P_1c_1 + P_2c_2/(1 + R) + \cdots + m_1 + (m_2 - m_1)/(1 + R) + \cdots \quad \textbf{(8.14)}$$

The difference between the new sources and uses of funds in equation (8.14) is given by

$$v_1 + v_2/(1 + R) + \cdots - (m_1 - m_0) - (m_2 - m_1)/(1 + R) - \cdots \quad \textbf{(8.15)}$$

Each term that is being subtracted in (8.15) involves the change in nominal money, $m_t - m_{t-1}$. But recall from equation (8.1) that, in the aggregate, the change in nominal money, $M_t - M_{t-1}$, equals the government's nominal revenue, which equals the total nominal transfer to households, V_t. The expression in (8.15) therefore equals zero for the aggregate of households. In the aggregate, the additional sources of funds exactly match the additional uses. Therefore, if we follow our usual practice of neglecting distributional effects, then we can ignore any wealth effects from the monetary terms.

IMPORTANT TERMS AND CONCEPTS

governmental budget constraint   The equation showing the balance between total expenditures and total revenues of the government.

government's revenue from printing money   The real income that government obtains by increasing the quantity of high-powered money. In the United States this revenue accrues to the Federal Reserve and is subsequently transferred to the U.S. Treasury.

hyperinflation   A period with an extraordinarily high inflation rate, such as that in Germany after World War I.

inflation tax   The revenue that the government gets by printing money (and thereby causing inflation).

lump-sum transfer   A transfer payment from the government to an individual in which the amount paid does not depend on any characteristic of the recipient, such as income or wealth.

monetary reform   A fundamental change in the monetary system or in the formulation of monetary policy.

perfect foresight A situation in which expectations of inflation or of other variables are accurate, so that there are no forecast errors.

superneutrality of money The theoretical finding that a change in the pattern over time of monetary growth does not affect real variables, such as aggregate output and the real interest rate.

QUESTIONS AND PROBLEMS

MAINLY FOR REVIEW

8.1 Consider an individual who lives for two periods, earns a nominal income of $1000 in each period, and has zero initial and terminal assets. The nominal interest rate, R, on dollar loans is 15%, and the expected rate of inflation, π^e, between the two periods is 10%. Assume that the price level in the first period is 1.

a. What is the real value of period 1 income?

b. What is the maximum amount of dollars that could be borrowed in period 1? Find the real value of this amount, and add it to the real value of period 1 income to see the maximum amount of (real) consumption possible in period 1.

c. What is the price level in period 2? What is the real value of period 2 income?

d. What is the maximum amount of dollars that can be obtained in period 2 by saving in period 1? Find the real value (in period 2) of this amount and add it to the real value of period 2 income to see the maximum amount of (real) consumption possible in period 2.

e. As in question 3.3 of Chapter 3, plot a graph to show the consumption possibilities in the two periods.

f. What is the slope of the budget line that you drew in part e? Show that it is equal to $-(1 + R)/(1 + \pi^e)$.

8.2 Based on your answer to question 8.1, explain why $(1 + R)$ $/(1 + \pi^e)$, rather than $1 + R$, is the correct measure of the trade-off between real consumption in the two periods. In what situation would it be appropriate to use the nominal interest rate?

8.3 Distinguish between the measures of nominal saving given in equations (8.3) and (8.6). Explain why, when inflation is positive, the first measure is an overestimate of saving for a net lender (an individual for whom $b_{t-1} > 0$). Can we make a similar comparison for a net debtor (an individual for whom $b_{t-1} < 0$)?

8.4 Suppose that the commodity market clears at a real interest rate of 4%.

a. If the inflation rate is zero, what is the nominal interest rate? If the inflation rate is 10%, what is the nominal interest rate?

b. If the nominal interest rate did not go up by the same amount as the inflation rate, what would happen to the commodity market—that is, would there be excess supply or excess demand?

8.5 Which of the following statements is correct?

a. A constant rate of increase in the price level will lead to a continuous rise in the nominal interest rate.

b. A continuous increase in the inflation rate will lead to a continuous rise in the nominal interest rate.

8.6 What would be the effect on the nominal interest rate of each of the following events?

a. The announcement of a one-time increase in the money stock.

b. The announcement of a planned increase in the rate of monetary growth.

Why does the price level jump in both instances? Does the velocity of money increase in both cases?

8.7 Critically review the following statement: "The quantity theory of money predicts that the rate of inflation must equal the rate of monetary growth. In fact, the two are not equal; therefore the theory is wrong." How do factors such as anticipated increases in inflation or gradual adjustments in the demand for money alter the prediction? What about factors considered in Chapter 7, such as growth in output?

8.8 Can the government always increase its revenue by raising the rate of monetary growth? How does the answer depend on the response of real money demanded to the nominal interest rate?

PROBLEMS FOR DISCUSSION

8.9 Inflation and the Demand for Money
Suppose that households hold stocks of goods—for example, groceries—as well as money and bonds. Assume that these goods depreciate in a physical sense at the rate δ per year (δ is the Greek letter *delta*).

a. What is the "nominal interest rate" on holdings of these goods? Does this interest rate affect the demands for stocks of goods and money?

b. Assume that the nominal interest rate on bonds, R, does not change, but the expected inflation rate, π^e, rises. What happens to the demand for money?

Note: This problem shows that the demand for money can involve substitution between money and goods, as well as between money and bonds. The demand for money may therefore change with a shift in the expected inflation rate, even if the nominal interest rate on bonds does not change.

8.10   Wealth and Substitution Effects from Inflation (optional)

Suppose that the expected inflation rate, π^e, and the nominal interest rate, R, each increase by one percentage point. Thus, the expected real interest rate on bonds does not change.

a. What happens to the real demand for money?

b. Underlying this change in the demand for money, what happens to the real amount of transaction costs that people incur?

Assume now that we do not neglect the role of transaction costs in households' budget constraints.

c. What is the effect of higher inflation on people's wealth? How do consumption and leisure respond?

d. Does higher expected inflation also exert substitution effects on consumption and leisure? (Note that, unlike consumption, leisure does not require people to use money.) Therefore, what is the overall effect of higher expected inflation on consumption and leisure?

8.11   The Superneutrality of Money

a. What is the meaning of the term *superneutrality of money*?

b. Is money superneutral in the model? In particular, if the behavior of money changes, which real variables change and which do not change? Explain the factors that underlie these results.

8.12   Inflation and Saving (optional)

a. Suppose that we define a household's real saving to be the change in the real value of its assets: bonds and money. Use the household's budget constraint from equation (8.2) to derive an expression for real saving. Does real saving equal real income less real consumer expenditure? In the expression for real income, how do we measure the real interest income on bonds? In particular, does it involve the nominal interest rate, R, or the real interest rate, $R - \pi$? Is there also a term for real "interest income" on money?

b. Nominal saving equals real saving multiplied by the price level, P_t. What is the formula for nominal saving?

c. Suppose as an alternative that we define nominal saving to be the change in the nominal value of a household's assets held as bonds or money. (The standard national accounts follow this practice.) Compare the results with those from part b. What differences arise in the measurement of interest income on bonds and money?

d. Suppose that we define real saving to be nominal saving divided by the price level, P_t, where nominal saving is defined as in part c. Does this concept of real saving measure the change in the real value of assets? Compare the result with that from part a, which does measure the change in the real value of assets.

8.13 A Case of Counterfeiting

In 1925 a group of swindlers induced the Waterlow Company, a British manufacturer of bank notes, to print up and deliver to them 3 million pounds' worth of Portuguese currency (escudos). Since the company also printed the legitimate notes for the Bank of Portugal, the counterfeit notes were indistinguishable from the real thing (except that the serial numbers turned out to be duplicates of those from a previous series of legitimate notes). Before the fraud was discovered, 1 million pounds' worth of the "counterfeit" notes had been introduced into circulation in Portugal. After the scheme unraveled (because the duplication of serial numbers was discovered), the Bank of Portugal made good on the fraudulent notes by exchanging them for newly printed, valid notes. The bank subsequently sued the Waterlow Company for damages. The company was found liable, but the key question was the amount of the damage award. The bank argued that the damages were 1 million pounds (less funds collected from the swindlers). The other side contended that the bank suffered only negligible real costs in having to issue an additional 1 million pounds' worth of new money to redeem the fraudulent notes. (Note that the currency was a purely paper issue, with no promise of convertibility into gold or anything else.) Thus, the argument was that the only true costs to the bank were the expenses for the paper and printing itself. Which side do you think was correct? (The House of Lords determined in 1932 that 1 million pounds was the right measure. For discussions of this fascinating episode in monetary economics, see R. G. Hawtrey, 1932, and Murray Bloom, 1966.)

THREE

BUSINESS FLUCTUATIONS,
UNEMPLOYMENT,
AND ECONOMIC GROWTH

This part of the book considers the important problems of business fluctuations, unemployment, and economic growth. Chapter 9 extends the model to incorporate investment, which plays a key role in the short-term fluctuations of an economy. We then show how the model can explain why the bulk of business fluctuations show up as movements in investment. At this stage our model does not include the government's spending, taxes, and debt (which we take up in Chapters 12–14). Also, we do not allow any role for monetary disturbances as sources of changes in real economic activity. (We consider this topic in Chapters 17–20.) Thus, business fluctuations can arise in the model only because of supply shocks—that is, shifts in the production function—and, perhaps, from changes in preferences. Models that rely on these kinds of disturbances to explain economic fluctuations are called *real business cycle theories*. (Economists who use these models should perhaps be called "realists," as opposed to monetarists.) Such theories have been receiving a lot of attention recently from economists.[1] Later we shall build on the form of the analysis that we carry out here to understand business fluctuations that originate from movements in the government's spending, taxes, and debt or from monetary changes.

In Chapter 10 we show that fluctuations in economic activity involve variations in unemployment. As a related matter we discuss the average or "natural" rate of unemployment and show why it will be positive.

Chapter 11 takes up the longer-term aspect of investment, namely, its manifestation over time as the accumulation of productive capital. This accumulation plays a central role in long-term economic growth.

---

[1] *The term* real business cycles *originates with John Long and Charles Plosser (1983). For a general discussion and an extension to include monetary disturbances, see Robert King and Charles Plosser (1984) and Ben McCallum (1989).*

INVESTMENT AND REAL
BUSINESS CYCLES

S o far we have simplified matters by pretending that labor services were the only variable input to the production process. Now we want to be more realistic by including capital services as well. We shall think primarily of **physical capital**, such as machines and buildings used by producers. In the national accounts this category is called **producer's durable equipment and structures**.

We could broaden the concept of capital to include the goods held as **inventories** by businesses. We could add the capital held by governments, such as highways, schools, public buildings, and military hardware. We could include consumer durables, such as homes (called residential structures in the national accounts), automobiles, and furniture. We could go further to include **human capital**, which measures the effects of education and training on workers' skills and the effects of medical care and nutrition on workers' health. Although the general economic reasoning applies to human capital and to physical capital held by governments and households, we shall confine most of the analysis here to physical capital held by private businesses.

THE CAPITAL STOCK AND INVESTMENT
IN THE UNITED STATES

Figure 9.1 shows how a standard concept of physical capital evolved from the end of 1925 until the end of 1993. This concept, called **private fixed capital**, includes business's durable equipment and structures, plus residential structures. The data are in real terms; that is, they express the quantity of capital in terms of dollar values for a base year, which is 1987 in this case.[1]

Figure 9.1 shows the total of private fixed capital, as well as the breakdown between nonresidential and residential components. The residential part accounts for about half the total throughout the period. Note that private fixed capital excludes business inventories (which are not part of fixed capital), capital stocks owned by governments, and consumer durables other than homes. The figure shows separately the capital stocks held by households in the form of consumer durables (other than homes). The sum of these durables and the standard measure of fixed capital provides a broader measure of private fixed capital.

The various components of the capital stock grew throughout the post–World War II period. From 1946 to 1993, the average growth rate for the broad concept of private fixed capital was 3.6% per year. For the components, the average annual growth rates were 3.5% for business nonresidential capital, 3.3% for residential capital, and 5.4% for consumer durables. Consumer durables therefore rose relative to the other types of capital.

The capital stock behaved very differently before 1946. After growing for most of the 1920s (only partially shown in the figure), the overall stock and its components declined during the depressed years of the 1930s. Then, after some growth from the late 1930s until 1941, the capital stock declined again during World War II.

Changes in the capital stock correspond to fixed investment expenditures by firms or households. Figure 9.2 shows various categories of real fixed investment, expressed as ratios to real GDP (real GNP before 1959). The categories correspond to those for the capital stock in

[1] *The data refer to net capital stocks, as reported in U.S. Department of Commerce,* Survey of Current Business, *August 1994.*

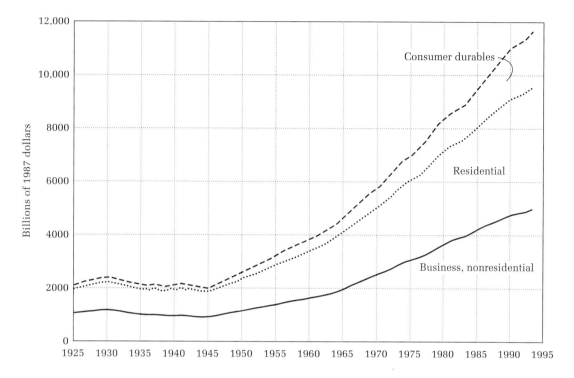

FIGURE 9.1

PRIVATE FIXED CAPITAL IN THE UNITED STATES, 1925–93

The solid line is real business, nonresidential capital. The dotted line adds real residential capital. The dashed line adds to the dotted line the real stock of consumer durables.

Figure 9.1. The investment numbers refer to actual expenditures and do not adjust for estimated depreciation of capital stocks. An allowance for the usual estimates of depreciation would not disturb the general nature of the time patterns shown in Figure 9.2.

The behavior of private investment will be a particular concern in our study of business fluctuations. The ratio to GDP of gross private fixed domestic investment (business nonresidential plus residential) averaged 15.2% from 1947 to 1996. But the values ranged from 12.5% in 1991–92 to 18.1% in 1979. Aside from the Korean War, the low values of this ratio pick out the principal recessions since World War II: 14.6% in 1958,

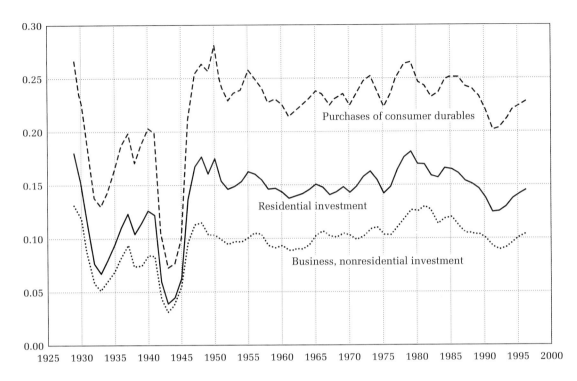

FIGURE 9.2

RATIOS OF FIXED PRIVATE INVESTMENT TO GDP

The dotted line shows the ratio of real business, fixed nonresidential investment to real GDP. The solid line adds the ratio of real residential investment to real GDP. The dashed line adds to the dotted line the ratio of real purchases of consumer durables to real GDP.

13.8% in 1961, 14.2% in 1975, and 12.5% in 1991. However, the ratio was relatively high, 15.9%, in the recession year of 1982.

For the broader category of gross private fixed domestic investment, which includes purchases of consumer durables, the ratio to GDP or GNP averaged 23.8% from 1947 to 1996. This ratio ranged from 20.2% in 1991 to 28.2% in 1950. As with the narrower concept of fixed investment, the troughs in this broader measure pick out the main recessions.

We see a stronger pattern of fluctuation in investment spending before World War II. The ratio for private fixed investment exclusive

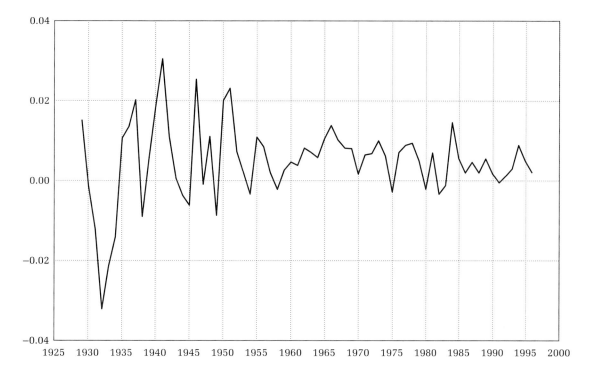

FIGURE 9.3

INVENTORY INVESTMENT AS A RATIO TO GDP

The graph shows the ratio of real business inventory investment to real GDP.

of consumer durables reached a low point of 6.7% at the trough of the Great Depression in 1933. After some recovery, the dip to a low point of 10.4% in 1938 corresponds to another recession. The lowest ratios of all—3.9% in 1943 and 4.5% in 1944—occurred during World War II. But we shall postpone our consideration of this wartime behavior until we study government expenditure in Chapter 12.

Business's investment spending also includes additions to stock of goods held as inventories of finished product or of goods-in-process. This inventory accumulation can be either positive or negative. Figure 9.3 shows the ratio of business's real inventory investment to real GDP. This ratio is extremely volatile, and, as with fixed investment, the low points tend to pick out the recessions. Real inventory investment was negative in the recession years of 1991, 1982–83, 1980, 1975, 1958, 1954, and 1949. Before World War II, inventory investment was negative during the recession years of 1938 and 1930–34.

REAL GDP AND ITS COMPONENTS DURING RECESSIONS

In this section we explore the behavior of real GDP, and especially of its private investment component, during economic downturns in the United States. If we examined times of economic upturn, we would reach similar conclusions, except that all signs would be reversed.

We already stressed in Chapter 1 that the investment components of GDP are volatile and strongly procyclical. Table 9.1 highlights the role of investment during the five most recent U.S. recessions: the trough quarters for real GDP are 1961.1, 1970.4, 1975.1, 1982.4, and 1991.4. The data in the table use the analysis from Chapter 1 of the detrended values for the various components of real GDP.

The key findings, shown in the last column of Table 9.1, are the following:

—— Broadly defined private investment accounts for the bulk of the fluctuations in real GDP, 93% on average. Thus, as a first approximation, explaining recessions amounts to explaining the sharp contractions in the private investment components.

—— Consumer spending on nondurables and services is relatively stable and accounts on average for only 24% of the shortfall of real GDP.

—— Government consumption and investment is not systematically related to recessions.

TABLE 9.1

CONSUMPTION AND INVESTMENT DURING RECESSIONS

Trough of Recession	1961.1	1970.4	1975.1	1982.4	1991.4	Mean
Shortfall of real GDP (billions of 1992 dollars)	64	117	162	214	122	—
Shortfall (%) in trend real GDP	2.8	3.3	4.1	4.4	2.0	3.3
% of shortfall in real GDP accounted for by:						
Personal consumption expenditures	26	29	46	41	80	44
Nondurables and services	13	6	29	20	50	24
Durables	13	3	17	21	30	21
Gross fixed private domestic investment	26	25	41	40	50	36
Nonresidential	10	15	11	21	30	17
Residential	16	10	33	19	20	19
Change in business inventories	57	47	42	35	−3	36
Government consumption and investment	6	4	−5	3	5	2
Net exports	−15	−5	−24	−19	−32	−19
Total private domestic investment[a]	96	95	100	96	77	93

Note: *The calculations are based on the detrended values for real GDP and its components, as discussed in Chapter 1.*

[a] *Purchases of consumer durables plus gross fixed private domestic investment plus change in business inventories.*

Net exports are countercyclical and account on average for −19% of the shortfall in real GDP (that is, the ratio of net exports to GDP is usually a little above trend during recessions).

We focus in this chapter on the behavior of private investment and consumption. We shall discuss government expenditure in Chapter 12 and net exports in Chapter 15.

CAPITAL IN THE PRODUCTION FUNCTION

We now begin to incorporate capital into the theoretical model. To keep things manageable, imagine that there is a single type of capital, which we can measure in physical units, for example, as a number of standard machines. Denote by k_{t-1} the quantity of capital that a producer has at the end of period $t-1$. Because it takes time to make new capital operational, we assume that the stock from period $t-1$ is available for use in production during period t. In other words, it takes one period for newly acquired capital to come on line.

The production function is now

$$y_t = f(\underset{(+)}{k_{t-1}}, \underset{(+)}{l_t}) \tag{9.1}$$

where the variable k_{t-1} is capital input and the variable l_t is labor input. In the real world there are variations in the **utilization rate** of capital. By the utilization rate we mean the fraction of total time that a piece of capital is used. A factory may operate, for example, for one shift per day or two, or it could be open or closed on weekends. We neglect these changes in utilization for the production function shown in equation (9.1). Here, we can think of the quantity of capital, k_{t-1}, as always operating for one standard-length shift per day.

The plus signs under the two inputs in equation (9.1) signify that each is productive at the margin. That is, an increase in either input, with the other held fixed, leads to more output. Remember that the marginal product of labor for period t, MPL_t, is the effect on output, y_t, from an extra unit of work, l_t. Note that we hold fixed the quantity of capital, k_{t-1}, when we measure the marginal product of labor.

We define the **marginal product of capital** in a parallel manner. This marginal product, MPK_{t-1}, is the response of output, y_t, when capital, k_{t-1}, increases by one unit, while the amount of work, l_t, does

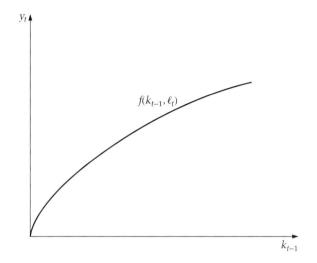

FIGURE 9.4

RESPONSE OF OUTPUT TO QUANTITY OF CAPITAL INPUT

The graph shows the effect on output, y_t, from a change in capital input, k_{t-1}. Here, the quantity of labor input, l_t, does not change.

not change. The dating on this marginal product shows that it relates to the quantity of capital, k_{t-1}, from the end of period $t-1$. Because of the lag in making new capital operational, this marginal product refers to the effect on output for period t.

We have discussed the diminishing marginal productivity of labor. Labor's marginal product, MPL_t, falls as the amount of work increases, at least if the quantity of capital does not change. Now we make a parallel assumption about the marginal product of capital. This marginal product, MPK_{t-1}, declines as the quantity of capital, k_{t-1}, increases, at least if the amount of labor does not change.

Figure 9.4 shows how output responds as a producer uses more capital with a fixed quantity of labor. The curve goes through the origin; that is, a producer gets no output if the capital stock is zero. The slope of the curve is the marginal product of capital, MPK_{t-1}. The slope is positive throughout but declines as the amount of capital increases. To stress this relationship, we show it explicitly in Figure 9.5.

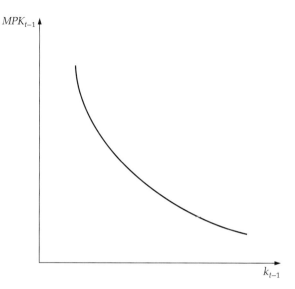

FIGURE 9.5

RELATION OF THE MARGINAL PRODUCT OF CAPITAL TO THE

QUANTITY OF CAPITAL

The graph shows that the marginal product of capital, MPK_{t-1}, declines as the amount of capital, k_{t-1}, increases.

INVESTMENT GOODS AND CONSUMER GOODS

Investment is the purchase of capital goods—machines or buildings—from the commodity market. In the real world, most private physical investment is carried out by businesses. But, as before, it is satisfactory not to distinguish firms from households. We can think of households in their role of producers as carrying out investment.

Capital goods generally differ physically from consumer goods. But to keep things simple, we continue to assume that there is only one type of good that people produce and exchange on the commodity market. One household buys this good for consumption purposes, and another (perhaps a business) buys it to accumulate more capital, that is, for investment purposes.[2]

As before, producers sell all of their output, y_t, on the commodity market at the price P_t. Households or firms buy these goods either for consumption, c_t, or investment, which we denote by i_t. Therefore, if

[2] *This setup is called a one-sector production technology. This specification, which appears in most macroanalyses, has only one process that allows producers to use inputs to produce goods. Some economists use a two-sector production model. Then there is one process for producing consumer goods and another for capital goods. There is, however, still only one physical type of capital and only one physical type of consumable.*

we think of households as doing the investment, a household's total demand for goods, y_t^d, equals the sum of consumption demand, c_t^d, and investment demand, i_t^d. Because all goods sell at the same price, suppliers do not care whether their goods are labeled as consumer goods or investment goods. We can therefore limit our attention to a producer's total supply of goods, y_t^s.

DEPRECIATION

Capital goods do not last forever, but rather tend to depreciate—or wear out—over time. We model this process in a simple form, where the amount of depreciation during period t is a constant fraction of the stock of capital, k_{t-1}, that is carried over from period $t-1$ and used during period t. If d_t denotes the amount of depreciation in units of commodities, then

$$d_t = \delta k_{t-1} \tag{9.2}$$

where δ (the Greek letter *delta*) is the constant rate of depreciation per period. To calculate the stock of capital, k_t, that is available for use in period $t+1$, we have to start with k_{t-1}, then add investment, i_t, and subtract depreciation, d_t:

$$k_t = k_{t-1} + i_t - \delta k_{t-1} \tag{9.3}$$

Two concepts of investment are commonly used:

——— Gross investment is the quantity of capital goods purchased, i_t.

——— Net investment is the change in the capital stock, $k_t - k_{t-1}$, which equals gross investment, i_t, less the amount of depreciation, δk_{t-1}.

Correspondingly, there are two concepts of output:

—— Gross product is the total amount produced, y_t.

—— Net product equals gross product less depreciation, $y_t - \delta k_{t-1}$. That is, net product is the quantity of goods produced less the amount of capital goods worn out during the process of production.

CHARACTERISTICS OF EXISTING CAPITAL

Remember that producers can call their output consumables or capital. But once a purchaser has put capital into place—for example, as a factory—it would be unrealistic to assume that these goods can be reclassified as consumables and then eaten up. Hence, we assume that the initial labeling choice as consumables or capital is irreversible: producers cannot consume their capital at a later date. They can, however, allow capital to depreciate and not replace it.

A second issue concerns the possibilities for moving capital goods from one production activity to another. Here we simplify the analysis by assuming that these movements are possible at negligible cost. This mobility of capital ensures that producers place all existing stocks in their most favorable use. Otherwise, someone could do better by shifting capital to another location. Recall also that we treat all units of capital as physically identical. Each unit must therefore end up with the same physical marginal product.

We shall sometimes find it convenient to think of resales of used capital. If a piece of capital has a low marginal product for one person, then he or she will find it advantageous to sell the capital to someone else. But since old and new capital are identical, the price of a unit of old capital during period t must equal that of new capital, which is P_t. We can therefore think of old capital goods as being sold along with new ones on the commodity market. Hence, we do not have to worry about a separate market for resales.

INVESTMENT DEMAND

Consider a producer's incentive to invest during period t. Recall that the stock of capital that will be available for production next period is the quantity

$$k_t = k_{t-1} + i_t - \delta k_{t-1}$$

At date t, the previous stock, k_{t-1}, and the amount of depreciation, δk_{t-1}, have already been determined by previous decisions. An increase by one unit in gross investment, i_t, therefore results in an increase by one unit in net investment, $i_t - \delta k_{t-1}$, and in the stock of capital, k_t. Hence, each producer decides how much to invest during period t by weighing the cost of this investment against the return from having more capital, k_t.

To raise investment by one unit, a producer must purchase an additional unit of goods from the commodity market at the price P_t. Hence, P_t is the dollar cost of an extra unit of investment.

There are two components of the return to investment. First, an additional unit of investment raises capital, k_t, by one unit. If we hold fixed the quantity of work for the next period, l_{t+1}, then next period's output, y_{t+1}, rises by the marginal product of capital, MPK_t. Since producers sell this output at the price P_{t+1}, the additional dollar sales revenue is $P_{t+1} \cdot MPK_t$.

Remember that the fraction, δ, of each unit of capital disappears after one period because of depreciation. The remaining fraction, $1 - \delta$, is still around. We can simplify the analysis by pretending that producers sell their old capital on the commodity market at date $t + 1$. (If they like, they can "buy back" this capital during period $t + 1$ to use for production at date $t + 2$.) Since goods sell at price P_{t+1} during period $t + 1$, the dollar revenue from the sale of used capital is $(1 - \delta) \cdot P_{t+1}$. Hence, this term is the second part of the return to investment.

Overall, an additional unit of investment costs P_t during period t and yields the amount $P_{t+1} \cdot (MPK_t + 1 - \delta)$ in period $t + 1$. The net dollar return on the investment is therefore $P_{t+1} \cdot (MPK_t + 1 - \delta) - P_t$. The ratio of this return to the number of dollars invested, P_t, determines the nominal rate of return to investment:

$$\frac{P_{t+1} \cdot (MPK_t + 1 - \delta) - P_t}{P_t} = (1 + \pi_t) \cdot (MPK_t + 1 - \delta) - 1$$

where $P_{t+1} = (1 + \pi_t) \cdot P_t$ and π_t is the inflation rate for period t.

The nominal rate of return from investment looks good or bad depending on how it relates to other returns. Specifically, households can earn the nominal interest rate, R_t, on bonds, or pay the rate R_t on debts to finance investment. If the nominal rate of return from investment exceeds R_t, then it pays to raise investment, that is, to buy more capital goods. But as the capital stock rises, diminishing marginal productivity implies that capital's marginal product, MPK_t, falls. This decline in the marginal product eventually reduces the nominal rate of return to investment enough to equal R_t. Producers then have no further incentive to expand investment.

Algebraically, investors act to satisfy the condition

$$(1 + \pi_t) \cdot (MPK_t + 1 - \delta) - 1 = R_t$$

where the left side is the nominal rate of return from investment. Recall, however, that the real rate of return on bonds, r_t, satisfies the relation $(1 + r_t) = (1 + R_t)/(1 + \pi_t)$. Using this condition, we can simplify the preceding result to the form

$$MPK_t - \delta = r_t \tag{9.4}$$

The left side of equation (9.4) is the **real rate of return from investment**—the gross return, MPK_t, less the rate of depreciation, δ.

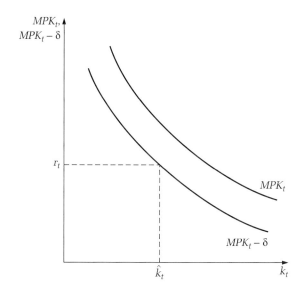

FIGURE 9.6

CHOICE OF CAPITAL STOCK

Producers aim for the quantity of capital, $\hat{k}_t$, at which the real rate of return from investment, $MPK_t - \delta$, equals the real interest rate, r_t.

Investors act to equate this return to the real rate of return on bonds, r_t. Any difference between these two rates makes it profitable to select either a higher or lower amount of investment. The amount of investment that households or firms choose therefore generates a marginal product, MPK_t, that equates the two real rates of return.

Figure 9.6 shows the results graphically. As the quantity of capital, k_t, rises, the marginal product, MPK_t, declines, as shown in the upper curve in the figure. The real rate of return from investment is the amount, $MPK_t - \delta$, shown by the lower curve in the figure. A producer chooses the quantity of capital, denoted by $\hat{k}_t$, at which the real rate of return from investment, $MPK_t - \delta$, equals the real interest rate, r_t.

Given the schedule for capital's marginal product, the **desired stock of capital**, denoted $\hat{k}_t$, depends on the real interest rate, r_t, and the depreciation rate, δ. Hence, we can write the desired stock of capital as the function

$$\hat{k}_t = \hat{k}(r_t , \ \delta , \ldots) \qquad \underset{(-) \ \ (-)}{}$$ **(9.5)**

323

The expression . . . represents the characteristics of the production function that affect the schedule for capital's marginal product. Note that an increase in r_t or δ means that the marginal product of capital, MPK_t, must be higher in equation (9.4). Therefore, for a given schedule of capital's marginal product, the desired stock of capital declines.

For given values of the real interest rate and the rate of depreciation, an upward shift in the schedule for capital's marginal product raises the desired stock of capital. We can show this result graphically by shifting the two curves upward in Figure 9.6.

Once we know the desired stock of capital, $\hat{k}_t$, we know also the choice of gross investment, i_t. Specifically, to attain the stock $\hat{k}_t$, a producer demands for investment purposes the quantity of goods i_t^d, where

$$i_t^d = \hat{k}_t - (1 - \delta)k_{t-1}$$

For given values of the starting capital stock, k_{t-1}, and depreciation, δk_{t-1}, gross **investment demand** varies one-to-one with changes in the desired stock of capital, $\hat{k}_t$. We can therefore use equation (9.5) to write out a function for gross investment demand as

$$i_t^d = \hat{k}(\underset{(-)}{r_t},\ \underset{(-)}{\delta},\ \ldots) - (1-\delta) \cdot k_{t-1} = i^d(\underset{(-)}{r_t},\ \underset{(?)}{\delta},\ \underset{(-)}{k_{t-1}}, \ldots) \qquad \textbf{(9.6)}$$

The implied amount of net investment demand is

$$i_t^d - \delta k_{t-1} = \hat{k}(\underset{(-)}{r_t},\ \underset{(-)}{\delta},\ \ldots) - k_{t-1} \qquad \textbf{(9.7)}$$

PROPERTIES OF INVESTMENT DEMAND

The main implications of the analysis for investment demand are the following:

▬ A reduction in the real interest rate, r_t, raises the desired stock of capital, $\hat{k}_t$, and investment demand.

An upward shift in the schedule for capital's marginal product, MPK_t, raises the desired stock of capital, $\hat{k}_t$, and investment demand.

Other things equal, investment demand declines if the previous stock of capital, k_{t-1}, rises. The phrase "other things equal" includes the various determinants of the desired stock of capital, $\hat{k}_t$.

An increase in the rate of depreciation, δ, lowers the desired stock of capital, $\hat{k}_t$. Net investment demand, $\hat{k}_t - k_{t-1}$, therefore declines. Gross investment demand equals $\hat{k}_t - (1 - \delta) \cdot k_{t-1}$. Because δ rises and $\hat{k}_t$ falls, the overall effect on gross investment demand is ambiguous.

Gross investment demand is positive if the desired stock, $\hat{k}_t$, exceeds the fraction, $1 - \delta$, of the initial stock, k_{t-1}. For an individual, negative gross investment means that the sales of old capital goods exceed the purchases of new ones. We assumed before that capital goods cannot be converted back into consumables; that is, we assumed **irreversible investment**.[3] One person's negative gross investment (net sales of capital goods) must therefore correspond to someone else's positive gross investment: when we aggregate over all producers, gross investment, I_t, cannot be negative. To put this result another way, the aggregate stock of capital, K_t, cannot fall below the initial stock, K_{t-1}, by more than the amount of depreciation, δK_{t-1}. Correspondingly, aggregate net investment, $K_t - K_{t-1} = I_t - \delta K_{t-1}$, can be negative only up to the amount of depreciation, δK_{t-1}.

Recall from Figure 9.1 that the capital stock declined during the Great Depression and World War II. At these times, private fixed net investment was negative. Our interpretation is that the aggregate desired stock of capital, $\hat{K}_t$, fell below the initial stock, K_{t-1}, during these years.

[3] *If producers are uncertain about future conditions—such as the future state of technology—then the irreversibility of investment becomes especially important. People are motivated to defer irreversible decisions, such as the initiation of investment projects, until the uncertainties are resolved. If the degree of uncertainty rises, then investment demand tends to fall. This element seems to underlie Keynes's (1935, Chap. 22) belief that investment demand is volatile and therefore causes variability of aggregate economic activity. For a discussion of irreversible investment, see Ben Bernanke (1983a).*

Absence of a Resale Market (optional)

We determined the choice of investment by pretending that producers resold the undepreciated portion of their capital, $(1 - \delta)k_{t-1}$, on the commodity market during period t. Then, if they desired, producers bought back investment goods in period $t + 1$, resold them in period $t + 2$, and so on. By pretending that producers resold their old capital, we can easily calculate the rate of return to investment over one period. But this device is artificial. Typically, a firm or household keeps a piece of capital for many years. The sale of used capital goods is unusual for most types of producers' equipment and structures, although it is common for residences and automobiles.

In most cases our analysis of investment goes through even if resales are impossible. In the previous setup, a producer resold the quantity of capital, $(1 - \delta) \cdot k_{t-1}$, during period t, and then bought back the desired stock, $\hat{k}_t$. The difference between purchases and sales is $\hat{k}_t - (1 - \delta) \cdot k_{t-1}$, which equals gross investment demand, i_t^d. If we consider producers who always have positive gross investment demand, then the potential for resale is irrelevant: someone with positive gross investment does not have to resell any capital. The producer just keeps the existing capital and then buys new goods in the amount i_t^d. In this case, there are no changes if we eliminate the possibility for resale.*

Remember that gross investment demand, i_t^d, equals net investment demand, $\hat{k}_t - k_{t-1}$, plus depreciation, δk_{t-1}. Therefore, for the previous results to hold, we do not need net investment demand to be positive for the typical producer. We need only to rule out net investment demand being so negative that it outweighs the positive amount of depreciation, δk_{t-1}.

For subsequent purposes, we assume that the previous analysis of investment demand is satisfactory. This analysis goes through if we allow resale of capital or if gross investment demand is always positive for every producer. But, of course, we shall also do okay as an approximation if—as seems plausible—gross investment demand is positive at most times for most producers.

---

* For a discussion of this issue and some related topics on investment, see Robert Hall (1977, especially pp. 71–74).

Gradual Adjustment of Investment Demand

The analysis assumes that producers purchase enough goods in a single period—which might be a year—to attain their desired stock of capital. That is, firms or households invest enough to close the gap between the capital carried over from the previous period, $(1 - \delta) \cdot k_{t-1}$, and the desired stock, $\hat{k}_t$.

We have ignored a variety of costs that arise when producers install new capital goods. To place new plant and equipment into operation, a business normally goes through a phase of planning and decision making, then a time of building and delivery, and finally an interval in which managers and workers familiarize themselves with the new facilities. Producers can speed up parts of this process but only by incurring extra costs. As examples, quicker decisions mean more mistakes, and faster service requires larger payments to workers and suppliers.

The costs for adjusting the levels of capital imply two types of lags in the investment process. First, a gap between the starting stock of capital, $(1 - \delta)k_{t-1}$, and the desired level, $\hat{k}_t$, stimulates higher investment over an extended interval. That is, since it takes time to build and install new plant and equipment, investors stretch out their purchases of new capital goods over an interval of time. Second, the higher capacity for production becomes available only after the investment project is completed. (We capture some of this element by assuming that this period's capital stock affects production for the next period.)

Although adjustment costs for investment are quantitatively important, we continue to ignore these costs as a simplification.* The main features of the analysis would not change if we brought in these complications.

---

* For discussions of adjustment costs in investment demand, see Robert Eisner and Robert Strotz (1963) and Robert Lucas (1967).

Quantitative Effects on Investment Demand

Since World War II, fixed net investment (exclusive of purchases of consumer durables) has averaged about 4% of the capital stock, K_{t-1}. Suppose that a change in the real interest rate, r_t, or in the schedule for capital's marginal product, MPK_t, lowers the desired stock of capital, $\hat{K}_t$, by 1%. The aggregate of net investment demand—over a period of, say, one year—would then decline by about 1% of the capital stock. If net investment demand were initially equal to 4% of the capital stock, then this change lowers it to 3% of the stock. Thus, a decline by 1% in the desired stock of capital translates into a fall by roughly 25% in net investment demand. Because one year's net investment is a small fraction—on the average about 4%—of the existing capital stock, small percentage changes in the desired stock generate large percentage changes in net investment demand. We should therefore not be surprised by two features of the U.S. data that we noticed before. First, because net investment demand is volatile, the fluctuations of investment cannot account for a large share of the cyclical movements of real GDP. Second, the desired stock of capital is sometimes low enough—such as during the Great Depression and World War II—so that aggregate net investment is negative.

INVESTMENT AND HOUSEHOLDS' BUDGET CONSTRAINTS

Remember that we can think of households, in their role as producers, as carrying out private investment expenditures. When we include investment as another use of funds in a household's budget constraint, we get the condition

$$P_t y_t + b_{t-1} \cdot (1 + R) + m_{t-1} + v_t = P_t c_t + P_t i_t + b_t + m_t \qquad \textbf{(9.8)}$$

As before, the left side shows the sources of funds, and the right side shows the uses. The new term is the expenditure for investment, $P_t i_t$, on the right side.

We have defined saving to be the change in the value of a household's assets, which could be held as bonds or money. In the presence of inflation, we have to distinguish the change in the real value of assets from the change in the nominal value: households would care about how the *real* value of their assets varies over time. We should define **real saving** accordingly to be the change in the real value of assets—the change in real bond holdings plus the change in real money balances. (**Nominal saving** can then be calculated by multiplying real saving by the price level.)

Aside from bonds and money, households now have another store of value—physical capital goods. (Remember that the households own the capital goods.) A household's total real saving is therefore the change in the real value of bonds and money plus the change in the quantity of capital:

$$\text{Real saving} = (b_t + m_t)/P_t - (b_{t-1} + m_{t-1})/P_{t-1} + k_t - k_{t-1} \qquad \textbf{(9.9)}$$

The last term in equation (9.9) is net investment. Hence, net investment is one component of real saving.

One way for a household to finance more net investment, $k_t - k_{t-1}$, is to raise real saving, which requires a cut in consumption or an increase in work effort (which would raise real income). But households can also finance investment by running down the real value of financial assets—bonds and money. A household (or business) can, for example, borrow to pay for additional capital goods. (A firm might borrow to finance a factory or a household might borrow to purchase a new home.) Hence, a household's or firm's decision to raise investment does not require a corresponding increase in that household's or firm's real saving.

From the standpoint of a single household or firm, the forces that influence net investment and real saving are different. Net investment demand expands, for example, with a fall in the real interest rate or an upward shift in the schedule for capital's marginal product. In contrast, a household's real saving increases when income is temporarily high or when the real interest rate rises.

If it were impossible to borrow and lend, then equation (9.9) would require each household's or firm's net investment to be financed only by that household's or firm's real saving. Producers could then exploit attractive investment opportunities only if they were willing to abstain from current consumption or leisure. The potential for running down financial assets or borrowing means that producers can undertake investments even if they are personally unwilling to save very much. In particular, the opportunities to borrow and lend ensure that all investment projects will be undertaken if the real rate of return to investment is at least as great as the real interest rate, r_t. Hence, the separation of individual decisions to invest from individual decisions to save promotes economic efficiency.[4]

What is the aggregate of real saving for households? Since the total stock of bonds, B_t, is still zero in each period, we find from equation (9.9) that

$$\text{Aggregate real saving} = M_t/P_t - M_{t-1}/P_{t-1} + K_t - K_{t-1} \qquad \textbf{(9.10)}$$

If we ignore the typically small part of real saving that consists of changes in aggregate real money balances, then equation (9.10) says that aggregate real saving equals aggregate net investment, $K_t - K_{t-1}$. Recall that individuals can invest by running down bonds or borrowing. But then others must be expanding their holdings of bonds, that is, lending. So for society as a whole, greater net investment does require greater aggregate real saving.

Because we did not allow in previous chapters for investment, we found that aggregate real saving must be zero (at least if we neglected changes in aggregate real money balance). Without investment, there is no way for the whole economy to save, that is, to change its real assets. But when the capital stock can vary, aggregate real saving can be nonzero: the economy can now adjust aggregate net investment to shift resources

[4] *Irving Fisher (1930, especially Chaps. 7, 11) stresses this feature of a market economy.*

from one period to another. These possibilities for shifting resources over time were present before for an individual, who could borrow and lend on the credit market at the real interest rate, r_t. When we add a variable amount of capital stock to the analysis, the total economy has opportunities for real saving that resemble those available to individuals on the credit market. These opportunities have important consequences for the analysis of market-clearing conditions.

CLEARING OF THE COMMODITY MARKET

There are still two aggregate-consistency conditions to satisfy: first, that the aggregate demand for commodities equal the supply and, second, that all money be willingly held. Because investment has major implications for the first condition but not the second, we focus on the condition for clearing the commodity market.

Clearing of the commodity market requires the aggregate supply of goods to equal the demand:

$$Y^s(\underset{(+)}{r_t},\ldots) = C^d(\underset{(-)}{r_t},\ldots) + I^d(\underset{(-)}{r_t},\ldots) \tag{9.11}$$

The left side of the equation shows the positive intertemporal-substitution effect from the real interest rate, r_t, on the aggregate supply of goods, Y_t^s. This response reflects the positive effect on work effort, L_t. The omitted terms in the function, denoted by . . . , include various characteristics of the production function, as well as the quantity of capital from the previous period, K_{t-1}.

The right side of equation (9.11) contains the two components of aggregate demand, consumption and gross investment. The real interest rate, r_t, has negative effects on consumer demand, C_t^d, and gross private investment demand, I_t^d. The omitted terms include the characteristics of the production function, as well as the quantity of capital, K_{t-1}, and the depreciation rate, δ.

FIGURE 9.7

CLEARING OF THE COMMODITY MARKET

The commodity market clears at the real interest rate r_t^*. Here, the
total output, Y_t^*, breaks down into C_t^* of consumption and I_t^* of gross
investment.

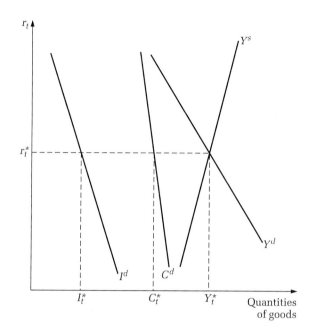

In Chapter 11, which considers long-term economic growth, it will
be important to keep track of how the aggregate capital stock changes
over time. Then we have to detail the role of the capital stock, K_{t-1}, in the
market-clearing condition from equation (9.11). But for now we assume
a given value of this stock. That is, we carry out a short-run analysis in
which changes in the stock of capital are small enough to neglect. This
setting is adequate to study the main role of investment during business
fluctuations.

Figure 9.7, which follows the approach developed in Chapter 5,
graphs the aggregates of commodities supplied and demanded against
the real interest rate, r_t. As before, the supply curve, Y^s, slopes upward, and the demand curve, Y^d, slopes downward. The figure breaks
down aggregate demand into its two components, consumption demand,
C^d, and gross private investment demand, I^d. Each of these curves
slopes downward versus r_t. We discussed before why investment de-

mand would be especially sensitive to variations in the real interest rate. Therefore, the figure shows the I^d curve with more of a negative slope than the C^d curve.

Figure 9.7 shows that the commodity market clears at the real interest rate r_t^*. Correspondingly, we label the level of output as Y_t^*. At this point, the uses of output break down between C_t^* of consumption and I_t^* of gross private investment.

REAL BUSINESS CYCLES

We want to use the model that incorporates investment to see whether we can generate the key features of business fluctuations that we discussed in Chapter 1. We proceed by considering the types of supply shocks—shifts to the production function—that we examined in Chapter 5. The main question is whether these kinds of shocks will generate the cyclical patterns that appear in the data. If the answer is yes, then we will have to conclude that real business-cycle models—theories that rely on these types of disturbances—should be taken seriously as frameworks for understanding business fluctuations.

We shall find it useful, as in Chapter 5, to distinguish temporary changes from permanent ones. Unlike in Chapter 5, however, we shall find it convenient to consider favorable shocks rather than unfavorable ones.

A TEMPORARY SHIFT OF THE PRODUCTION FUNCTION

Consider a temporary upward shift of the production function. To keep things simple, assume to begin with a parallel upward shift for period t. Then there are no changes in the schedules for the marginal products of labor, MPL_t, and capital, MPK_{t-1}. Also, we assume that there is no change in the schedule for the prospective marginal product of capital, MPK_t.

The improvement of the production function raises the aggregate supply of goods, Y_t^s, on the left side of equation (9.11). Wealth rises, but by only a small amount, because the increase in income is temporary. Consumer demand, C_t^d, therefore rises by a small amount, and work effort, L_t, falls by a small amount. This decrease in work offsets part of the increase in the supply of goods. Gross investment demand, I_t^d, does not shift because the schedule for capital's marginal product, MPK_t, has not changed.

Figure 9.8 shows the shifts to aggregate supply and demand. There is a rightward shift in supply and a smaller rightward shift in demand. In the figure the real interest rate labeled r_t^* is the one that cleared the market initially. At this real interest rate, the quantity of goods supplied now exceeds the quantity demanded: $Y_t^s > Y_t^d$. This excess supply arises because people react to the temporary abundance of production, and, hence, income, by raising their desired real saving. Thus, we can also say that the disturbance creates an excess of desired real saving over net investment demand.

The real interest rate must fall for the commodity market to clear: in Figure 9.8, the new market-clearing real interest rate, $(r_t^*)'$, is lower than the initial one, r_t^*. We can think of this decrease in the real interest rate as resulting from the excess of desired lending over desired borrowing.

Figure 9.8 shows that the new level of output, $(Y_t^*)'$, is above the initial amount, Y_t^*. This rise in output reflects partly an increase in consumption, $(C_t^*)' < C_t^*$, and partly a rise in gross investment, $(I_t^*)' < I_t^*$. (Since depreciation is fixed at the amount δK_{t-1}, the change in net investment equals that in gross investment.) Note that the fall in the real interest rate raises consumption and investment demand. In addition, the increase in wealth reinforces the expansion of consumer demand. Finally, the lower real interest rate and the rise in wealth imply that the quantity of work effort, $(L_t^*)'$, falls short of the initial amount, L_t^*.

Consider the quantitative responses of consumption and work. Because the wealth effect is weak, the changes in consumption and work

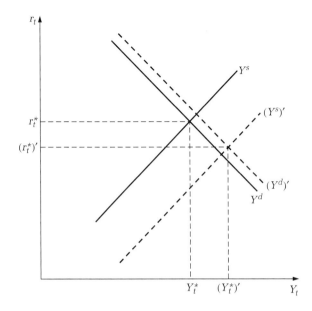

FIGURE 9.8

EFFECTS OF A TEMPORARY UPWARD SHIFT OF THE PRODUCTION FUNCTION

The rightward shift to aggregate supply, Y^s, exceeds the rightward shift to demand, Y^d. Hence, the real interest rate falls, and aggregate output rises.

will be large only if there is a substantial decline in the real interest rate, r_t. Consider what happens, however, if investment demand is highly responsive to r_t. (We discussed before why this outcome is likely.) In this case a small decrease in r_t is sufficient to equate desired real saving to net investment demand, that is, to clear the commodity market. Hence, most of the rise in output reflects an increase in investment, and there are only small changes in consumption and work.

An important conclusion is that fluctuations in investment partially insulate consumption from some types of temporary economic disturbances. When there is a temporary abundance of goods, everybody wants to save more or borrow less at the initial real interest rate. But if there are no possibilities for investment—the case that we considered in Chapter 5—then it is infeasible for everyone to save more or borrow less. The real interest rate therefore falls enough to make the total of desired real saving equal zero. Households must then make substantial adjustments in their consumption and work. When we introduce investment, it becomes possible for aggregate real saving to change. By raising aggregate net investment, the *economy* does what each individual would like to do at a given real interest rate. In fact, if investment demand is highly sensitive to the real interest rate, as we anticipate, then the bulk of the rise in output shows up as increases in investment and real saving. In contrast, consumption changes relatively little.

Notice that the results imply that investment will absorb most of the short-term fluctuations in real GDP. This conclusion accords with the evidence from Table 9.1 that broadly defined private investment accounts for about 90% on average of the shortfall of real GDP during recent U.S. recessions. The results also accord more generally with the observations from Chapter 1 that private investment is highly volatile and strongly procyclical. Similarly, the theory is consistent with the finding that consumer spending on nondurables and services is procyclical but is relatively stable and accounts on average for only a small fraction of the cyclical fluctuations in real GDP.

The Behavior of Employment

One feature of the results that conflicts with the data is the behavior of work effort. Labor input is procyclical, and recessions are invariably accompanied by declines in employment and worker-hours. But the analysis so far predicts that a temporary improvement to the production function leads to a small decrease in work.

Work effort falls in our example because we omitted a likely favorable effect of the disturbance on labor's productivity. As mentioned in some earlier cases, an upward shift of the schedule for labor's marginal product, MPL_t, usually accompanies a favorable shock to the production function. This change motivates people to raise work effort, L_t. In fact, because the improvement in productivity is temporary, there is also an intertemporal-substitution effect, which reinforces the tendency for work to rise.

The increase in work effort implies additional rightward shifts to commodity supply and demand of the sort shown in Figure 9.8. Hence, there is a larger expansion of output. There is also a larger decrease in the real interest rate and a correspondingly sharper increase in investment. Qualitatively, the main new finding is the tendency for more work to accompany the rise in output. Labor input therefore tends to be procyclical, as in the U.S. data.

The Cyclical Behavior of the Real Interest Rate

We have found that a temporary improvement to the production function lowers the real interest rate. If we considered a temporary adverse shock, then we would find that the real interest rate would rise. Thus, the analysis predicts that the real interest rate would be countercyclical— low rates in good times and high rates in bad times. To see how this prediction matches up with empirical evidence, we now consider U.S. data on the cyclical behavior of the real interest rate.

We argued in Chapter 7 that the real interest rate that matters for households' decisions is the expected rate: the nominal interest rate observed directly less the inflation rate that people anticipate. We can measure this expected real interest rate as in Chapter 7 by the three-month U.S. Treasury bill rate less an estimate of expected inflation for the corresponding three-month interval.[5] Our measure of expected inflation, available quarterly since 1959, is a statistical construct that represents the best forecast of inflation for each quarter that people could have generated, given the history of inflation observed up to the beginning of the quarter.[6] This measure does not differ greatly from the Livingston survey of expected inflation that we discussed in Chapter 7. (The Livingston survey is unavailable quarterly and is likely to be less accurate than the statistical construct.)

The dashed line in Figure 9.9 shows the expected real interest rate. The solid line, constructed by the method discussed in Chapter 1, is a smooth trend that reflects the longer-term movements of expected real

[5] *We thereby construct a short-term* expected real interest rate. *It is difficult to calculate* long-term *expected real interest rates because it is hard to measure long-term expected inflation.*

[6] *The data are an updated version of the series reported in Robert Barro and Xavier Sala-i-Martin (1990).*

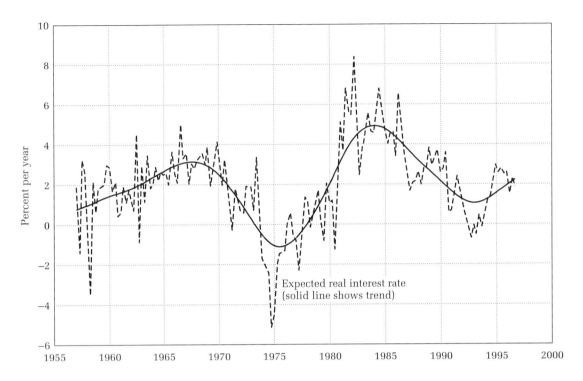

FIGURE 9.9

THE EXPECTED REAL INTEREST RATE AND ITS TREND LINE

The dashed line is the expected real interest rate (the three-month U.S. Treasury bill rate less the constructed estimate of expected inflation). The solid line is a trend line fitted to the expected real interest rate.

interest rates. Figure 9.10 plots the detrended value of the expected real interest rate—the difference between the actual and trend values—against detrended real GDP. The important observation for our purposes is that the expected real interest rate is weakly procyclical: the correlation with detrended real GDP is 0.26. In contrast, the model predicts that temporary shocks to the production function would generate a strongly countercyclical pattern of real interest rates. We therefore have to go further to try to reconcile the theory with the data.

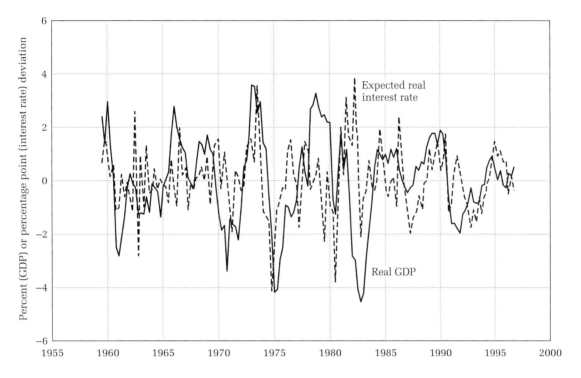

FIGURE 9.10

THE CYCLICAL BEHAVIOR OF THE REAL INTEREST RATE

The solid line is detrended real GDP, and the dashed line is the detrended value of the expected real interest rate (the difference between the actual and trend values from Figure 9.9).

A PERMANENT SHIFT OF THE PRODUCTION FUNCTION

One possible explanation for the conflict between theory and facts is that we allowed for only temporary shifts to the production function, whereas most shifts that occur in practice tend to persist over time. For example, a discovery of a new product or an innovation to production techniques would have a persisting effect on the economy. To see how the duration of the shift affects the analysis, we now consider the polar

FIGURE 9.11

EFFECTS OF A PERMANENT UPWARD SHIFT OF THE PRODUCTION

FUNCTION

A permanent upward shift of the production function implies that the
rightward shifts of demand and supply are roughly equal. Therefore,
output rises, but the real interest rate does not change.

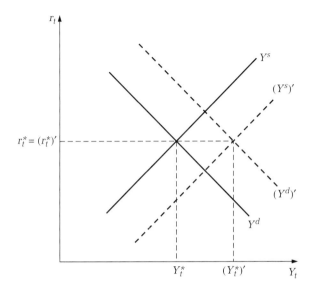

case of a permanent upward shift of the production function. But start
again with a parallel shift, which leaves unchanged the schedules for
the various marginal products.

When the favorable shock is permanent, the wealth effects become
important. There is a strong positive effect on consumer demand, C_t^d,
and a strong negative effect on work effort, L_t. Recall from our discussion in Chapter 5 (Figure 5.7) that this type of permanent change to the
production function exerts little net effect on desired real saving. Figure 9.11 shows, accordingly, that the rightward shift in demand equals
that in supply. This result still holds if we include a permanent upward
shift of the schedule for labor's marginal product, although the curves
shift by greater amounts.

The main point is that the supply of goods equals the demand at the
initial real interest rate, r_t^*. (Equivalently, net investment demand still
equals desired real saving.) This analysis therefore predicts that the real
interest rate will be acyclical, a finding that fits better than before with
the weakly procyclical behavior revealed by Figure 9.10.

Although the results for the real interest rate are better, the conclusions about investment and consumption are now unsatisfactory. Since the real interest rate does not change in Figure 9.11, investment stays at its initial value. All of the increase in output therefore reflects a rise in consumption. Thus, the model now predicts that investment would be acyclical, whereas consumption would be highly procyclical. As we know, this prediction conflicts dramatically with the data.

We cannot resolve the puzzle by mixing the results from the temporary and permanent cases to allow for shocks to the production function that persist for a while but not forever. As we move from the permanent to the temporary case, we enhance the procyclical response of investment and lessen the procyclical response of consumption—changes that achieve a better fit to the data. But we necessarily also introduce strongly countercyclical behavior of the real interest rate, a pattern that conflicts with the facts. The key element in the gap between theory and data turns out not to be the permanence of the disturbance but, rather, the invariance of the schedule for capital's marginal product. We therefore now consider the effects from changes in this marginal product.

SHIFTS TO THE PRODUCTIVITY OF CAPITAL

The previous examples dealt with disturbances that left unchanged the schedule for capital's marginal product, MPK_t. In these cases, there were no shifts to investment demand. Shocks to the production function tend, however, to shift the marginal products of the factor inputs, and we have already shown how the changes in labor's marginal product are crucial for generating the procyclical behavior of labor input. We now allow also for the likely shifts to capital's marginal product and, hence, to investment demand.[7]

Assume now an upward shift to the schedule for capital's marginal product, MPK_t. Recall that this marginal product refers to the output for period $t + 1$. To keep things simple, assume, for the moment, that no changes occur to the production function for period t. That is, we

[7] *John Maynard Keynes (1935, Chaps. 11, 12) stressed that shifts to investment demand, derived from changes in the perceived returns to investment, are a key element in business fluctuations.*

 INVESTMENT AND REAL BUSINESS CYCLES

341

FIGURE 9.12

EFFECTS OF AN INCREASE IN THE MARGINAL PRODUCT OF CAPITAL

The increase in the schedule for capital's marginal product raises investment demand. Therefore, the real interest rate and the level of output rise.

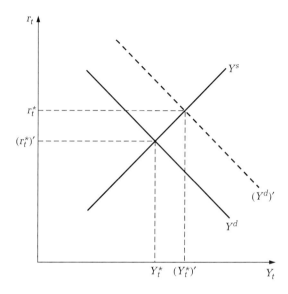

neglect the positive effects on the current supply of goods, Y_t^s, and the
effects from increased wealth.

Recall that the condition for clearing the commodity market is (with
time subscripts now omitted)

$$Y^s(\underset{(+)}{r},\dots) = C^d(\underset{(-)}{r},\dots) + I^d(\underset{(-)}{r},\dots)$$

Given our assumptions, the only effect from the disturbance is an
increase in gross investment demand, I^d, on the right side of the equation. Figure 9.12 shows accordingly a rightward shift of the aggregate
demand curve, Y^d, which reflects the rise in investment demand.

We see from the figure that the real interest rate and output increase.
Note that the expansion of output reflects the positive effect of the
higher real interest rate on work effort. The higher real interest rate
leads also to a fall in consumption. Investment therefore rises by more
than the increase in total output. Thus, this disturbance implies by
itself that the real interest rate, investment, and labor input would
be procyclical, whereas consumption would be countercyclical. Two

problems with these predictions are, first, that the real interest rate is not as strongly procyclical as this analysis would suggest and, second, that consumption is procyclical. To match these facts we have to combine the analysis from Figure 9.12 with the previous discussion of effects from shifts in the production function.

Return now to the shocks to the production function that we considered in Figure 9.8 for a temporary change and in Figure 9.11 for a permanent change. These kinds of disturbances tend to be accompanied by the sort of upward shift to the schedule for capital's marginal product, MPK_t, that we considered in Figure 9.12. We can fit the various business-cycle facts that we have been discussing if we mix the results from Figures 9.8 and 9.11—a case that applies if the disturbance persists for a while but not forever—and then also add the results from Figure 9.12. If we take the right mixture, then we get the following conclusions:

— The real interest rate can be weakly procyclical because the positive effect from the improvement in capital's productivity (Figure 9.12) typically outweighs the negative effect from the increase in desired real saving (Figure 9.8).

— Investment is procyclical because the direct effect from the shift to capital's productivity (Figure 9.12) outweighs the negative effect from the higher real interest rate. Because investment demand is highly sensitive to its determinants, including the marginal product of capital, the bulk of the fluctuations in output tend to show up in the investment component.

— Consumption is procyclical because the positive effect from more wealth (Figure 9.11) outweighs the negative effect from a higher real interest rate. Consumption can, however, account for only a small fraction of the overall movement in output: consumer demand responds little initially if the improvement to the production function is temporary (Figure 9.8), and the rise in the real interest rate reduces demand (Figure 9.12).

— Labor input is procyclical because the positive effects from labor's enhanced productivity and the higher real interest rate more than offset the negative effect from more wealth.

— The real wage rate is procyclical, as discussed in Chapter 6, primarily because the improvement in labor's productivity raises the demand for labor.

The main conclusion is that the model does pretty well in accounting for the broad features of business fluctuations that we have considered thus far. In later chapters we relate the model to the empirical behavior of additional variables, such as the unemployment rate (Chapter 10), the current-account balance (Chapter 15), and prices and money (Chapter 17).

SUMMARY

Private investment fluctuates proportionately by much more than total output, which fluctuates by more than consumption. For five recessions from 1959 to 1996, the shortfall in total private investment—gross fixed investment, changes in business inventories, and purchases of consumer durables—accounted on average for 93% of the shortfall in real GDP. In contrast, consumer expenditures on nondurables and services declined relatively little during these recessions.

We began the theoretical analysis of investment by introducing the stock of capital as an input into the production function. The marginal product of capital is positive but diminishes as the quantity of capital rises.

Gross investment is the quantity of capital goods that a producer buys from the commodity market. The total demand for goods is the sum of gross private investment demand and consumption demand. The change in a producer's stock of capital—or net investment—equals gross investment less depreciation. In the aggregate, gross investment cannot be negative. Aggregate net investment can be negative, and was in the United States for much of the 1930s and during World War II.

The real rate of return to investment is the marginal product of capital less the rate of depreciation. Producers determine their desired stocks of capital by equating this rate of return to the real interest rate. The desired stock of capital therefore rises if the real interest falls, if the schedule for capital's marginal product shifts upward, or if the depreciation rate declines. Small percentage changes in the desired stock of capital translate into large percentage changes in net investment demand. This property explains why investment expenditure is volatile.

The existence of the credit market means that a household's or firm's decision to invest does not require that household or firm to save. In the aggregate, however, real saving equals net investment (plus the change in real money balances). The existence of investment therefore allows the whole economy to change its amount of real saving.

We modified the market-clearing analysis from Chapter 5 to include gross private investment demand as a component of the aggregate demand for goods. We then used the modified framework to explore the effects from shocks to the production function. If we consider shocks that persist for a while but not forever and if we allow for shifts to the marginal products of labor and capital, then the model accords well with some observed features of business fluctuations. Specifically, the real interest rate is weakly procyclical, private investment is procyclical and accounts for the bulk of the fluctuations in output, consumption is procyclical but relatively stable, and labor input and the real wage rate are procyclical.

IMPORTANT TERMS AND CONCEPTS

desired stock of capital The stock of capital chosen by a producer, depending on factors such as the marginal product of capital, the real interest rate, and the depreciation rate.

human capital Skills and training that are embodied in workers and add to productivity.

inventories Stores of commodities held by businesses either for sale or for use in production.

investment demand The quantity of investment that is desired by firms and households, expressed as a function of the real interest rate, the depreciation rate, and the existing stock of capital.

irreversible investment The property that, once output has been used to form new capital goods, the process cannot be reversed by consuming the capital. Because investment is irreversible, uncertainty about the returns to investment can reduce or delay investment spending.

marginal product of capital (MPK) The increment of output obtained per unit increment in the input of physical capital, while holding fixed any other inputs.

nominal saving The current dollar value of real saving, calculated by multiplying real saving by a price index.

physical capital Capital inputs into production, such as machinery and buildings.

private fixed capital The sum of producers' durable equipment and structures and residential structures; a measure of the private capital stock that excludes business inventories and consumer durables other than homes.

producers' durable equipment and structures The measure of physical capital that includes machinery and buildings used in production.

real rate of return from investment The net real proceeds from investment over one period expressed relative to the real cost of the investment.

real saving The change in the real value of assets of a household or of the economy as a whole.

utilization rate The percentage of time that capital is used in production; for example, an increase in the number of shifts per day in a factory increases the utilization rate of machinery.

QUESTIONS AND PROBLEMS

MAINLY FOR REVIEW

9.1 What is meant by private domestic fixed investment? Does it include purchases of consumer durables? What about purchases of bonds?

9.2 Distinguish gross investment from net investment. When is net investment negative? Can gross investment be negative if capital goods cannot be resold?

9.3 Suppose producers expect inflation, that is, a higher price level in the next period. Will they want to increase their current purchases of capital goods? What if the nominal interest rate rises to reflect the higher expected inflation?

9.4 Does higher investment require higher saving on the part of an individual household or firm? For the economy as a whole, how do changes in the interest rate ensure that real saving rises to match an increase in investment?

9.5 Show graphically how the division of total output into consumption and investment is achieved through clearing of the commodity market. How does a temporary shift of the production function alter this division? Does your answer depend on the relative sensitivity of consumption demand and investment demand to changes in the interest rate?

9.6 Why does a decline in the productivity of capital reduce the interest rate? Could the interest rate fall so much as to leave the quantity of investment unchanged? Explain.

PROBLEMS FOR DISCUSSION

9.7 The One-Sector Production Function

In our model, output can be labeled as either consumables or capital goods. Economists call this a one-sector production function.

a. Why does the price of a unit of consumables always equal the price of a unit of capital in this model? What would happen if the price of consumables exceeded the price of capital goods, or vice versa?

b. Suppose that everyone wants to undertake negative gross investment; that is, everyone wants to resell old capital on the commodity market. Can the price of capital goods fall below the price of consumables in this case?

c. (optional) Consider a "two-sector model," in which different production functions apply to consumables and capital goods. Would the price of a unit of consumables always equal the price of a unit of capital goods in this model?

9.8 Inventory Investment

Businesses hold inventories of goods, partly as finished products and partly as goods-in-process and raw materials. Suppose that we think of inventories as a type of capital, which enters into the production function. Then changes in these stocks represent investment in inventories. (Typically, economists assume that the rate of depreciation on inventories is near zero.)

a. How does an increase in the real interest rate affect the quantity of inventories that businesses want to hold? What happens, therefore, to inventory investment?

b. Consider a temporary adverse shock to the production function. What happens to the amount of inventory investment? What do we predict, therefore, for the behavior of inventory investment during recessions?

9.9 The Investment Tax Credit

For most years from 1962 to 1986, some types of investment qualified for a credit against income taxes. Assume that this governmental program effectively refunds the fraction, a, of investment expenditures. How does the size of the refund percentage, a, influence producers' desired stocks of capital and, hence, their investment demand? (Assume that someone who resells capital has to return the investment credit on the amount sold.)

9.10 Capacity Utilization (optional)

One way for a producer to generate extra output is to use capital more intensively. That is, a producer can run more shifts per day or allow less down time for performing maintenance. Assume that more intensive utilization causes capital to depreciate faster.

a. How does a producer determine the best intensity of use for capital?

b. Show that an increase in the real interest rate, r_t, motivates producers to use their capital more intensively. What does this relationship imply for the effect of the real interest rate on the supply of goods, y_t^s?

9.11 The Ownership of Capital (optional)

In our model, the people who use capital also own the capital. Suppose that these people print up certificates, each of which conveys ownership rights to one unit of capital. These certificates can be sold to others (on a stock market). But instead of using the capital themselves, the buyers of these certificates may allow other people ("businesses") to use the capital. Then the users pay a fee to holders of certificates. This fee may be either a fixed rental or a share of the profits.

a. Why might it be a good idea to separate the ownership of capital from the use of that capital? (Remember that households or firms can already finance the purchase of capital by borrowing.) Why might it be a bad idea?

b. What determines the nominal and real value of the ownership certificates if each is a claim to one unit of capital?

c. In the real world why is the future real value of a certificate subject to great uncertainty? Specifically, why does the value depend on the fortunes of the company that issued it?

9.12 Investment Opportunities for Robinson Crusoe

In the market economy we found that investment takes the brunt of shocks to the production function. Suppose that we introduce opportunities for investment into the model of Robinson Crusoe, which we constructed in Chapter 2. How would Robinson Crusoe's investment and consumption respond to shocks to the production function? Are the results basically similar to those for the market economy?

Unemployment

W e have shown that an adverse shock to the production function can lead to a decline in labor input that accompanies the fall in output. Thus, measures of labor input, such as employment and worker-hours, are procyclical.

We have not yet discussed **unemployment**, which is the number of people who are looking for work but have no job. The sum of unemployment and employment is the **labor force**. People who neither have a job nor are looking for one are classified as **outside of the labor force**, and the ratio of the number unemployed to the labor force is the **unemployment rate**. A key empirical regularity, already discussed in Chapter 1, is that the unemployment rate is countercyclical: the correlation between the detrended unemployment rate and detrended real GDP is −0.90 (see Table 1.1). In this chapter, we want to explain why an adverse shock, which lowers output and employment, tends to raise the unemployment rate, and inversely for favorable shocks.

In the labor market of Chapter 6, the wage rate adjusted to equate labor supply and demand. Hence, anyone who sought work at the going wage rate was able to get a job: unemployment was always zero, and employment equaled the labor force.

Whereas unemployment refers to unsuccessful job seekers, the term **vacancies** describes the number of jobs that firms have been unable to fill. In the model of Chapter 6, the wage rate adjusted so that firms were able to hire their desired number of workers. Hence, vacancies were always zero, and employment equaled the firms' demand for workers.

Although this model of the labor market can account for some of the fluctuations in employment (that is, the labor force) and worker-hours, it cannot explain why the quantities of unemployment and vacancies are nonzero. The model therefore cannot tell us why unemployment and vacancies change over time. Given these deficiencies, it is also likely that the model is not yet satisfactory for understanding all of the movements in production and labor input. To get a full picture, we have to understand the variations in labor-force participation *and* the changes in the fraction of the labor force that have jobs. The present chapter focuses on the second element.

To explain unemployment and vacancies, we have to introduce some type of "friction" into the workings of the labor market. Specifically, we have to explain why people without jobs take some time to find and accept employment. Similarly, we have to see why businesses with unoccupied positions take some time to fill them. Thus, the key to unemployment and vacancies is the process of workers searching for jobs and businesses searching for workers.

In our earlier discussion, we simplified matters by treating all workers and jobs as identical. In this context, the process of search among workers and firms would be trivial. Thus, to make the analysis meaningful, we have to allow for differences among workers and jobs. We can think, in fact, of the labor market as operating to find good matches between jobs and workers. Because jobs and workers differ, this matching process is difficult and time-consuming. Unemployment and vacancies arise as aspects of this process.

The simple model of job matching developed in the next section has two main objectives. First, we want to explain why the levels of unemployment and vacancies are positive. Second, we want to see how these variables change over time and how they interact with the determination of production and labor input. We want, in particular, to understand why the unemployment rate is countercyclical.

A MODEL OF JOB FINDING

Consider a person who has just entered the labor force and is not yet employed, for example, a student who has just graduated from school and is seeking his or her first job or someone who is entering or reentering the labor force after raising a family. Suppose that this person searches for a position by visiting various firms. Each firm interviews job candidates to assess their likely qualifications for a position. As a result of each inspection, the firm estimates the value of the candidate's marginal product. To keep things simple, assume that the firm offers the person a job with a nominal wage, w, equal to this estimated value of marginal product. (We assume, only for simplicity, that the job entails a standard number of hours worked per week.)

The candidate must decide whether to accept an offer at the wage rate w. The alternative to taking a job is to remain unemployed and continue to search for another one.[1] More search pays off if a subsequent wage offer exceeds the initial one. The cost of turning down an offer is the wage income forgone while not working. The income forgone must, however, be measured net of any income that people receive because they are unemployed. This income includes **unemployment insurance**, which we shall discuss later, and any value attached to time spent not working (at "leisure"), rather than on the job.

In evaluating an offer, the first thing to determine is how it compares with others that might be available. In making this comparison, a job seeker would have in mind a distribution of possible wages,[2] given the person's education, experience, locational preferences, and so on.

[1] *We assume that it does not pay to accept a job and nevertheless keep searching. This assumption seems reasonable because the costs of getting set up in a job usually make it undesirable to take positions with short expected durations. Furthermore, it is likely (except for professors of economics) to be easier to search for jobs while unemployed.*

[2] *We assume, for simplicity, that the attractiveness of a job depends only on the wage paid. The basic results would not change if we expanded the model to consider an effective wage, which took account of working conditions, hours, job location, and so on.*

FIGURE 10.1

DISTRIBUTION OF WAGE OFFERS

The curve shows the chances of receiving wage offers of different sizes. The higher the curve, the more likely that wages of that size will be offered. Note that w^u is the income received while unemployed, and $\bar{w}$ is the reservation wage. Wage offers are accepted if they are at least as good as $\bar{w}$ and rejected otherwise.

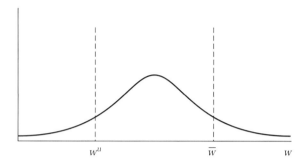

Figure 10.1 shows a possible distribution of wage offers. For each value of wages on the horizontal axis, the height of the curve shows the relative chance or probability of receiving that wage offer. For the case shown, the offers usually fall in a middle range of values for w. There is, however, a small chance of getting either a very high wage offer (in the right tail of the distribution) or an offer near zero.

Figure 10.1 shows the value w^u, which is the effective wage received while unemployed. We know right away that a person would reject any offer that paid less than w^u. For the case shown in the figure, w^u lies toward the left end of the distribution of wage offers. This construction implies that most—but not all—wage offers would exceed w^u. Given the position of w^u, a job seeker's key decision is whether to accept a wage offer when $w > w^u$ applies.

As mentioned before, a person may refuse a wage that exceeds w^u to preserve the chance of getting a still better offer (see note 1). But there is a trade-off because the job seeker then forgoes the income, $w - w^u$, while not working. The balancing of these forces generates what economists call a **reservation wage** (or sometimes an acceptance wage), denoted by $\bar{w}$. Wage offers below $\bar{w}$ are refused, and those above $\bar{w}$ are accepted. If a person sets a high value of $\bar{w}$, then he or she will probably spend a long time (perhaps forever) unemployed and searching for an acceptable job. In contrast, a low value of $\bar{w}$ (but still greater than w^u) means that the expected time unemployed will be relatively brief. The expected wage received while employed is, however, lower the lower is $\overline{w}$.

The optimal value of $\overline{w}$ depends on the shape of the wage-offer distribution in Figure 10.1, as well as on the value of w^u and the expected duration of jobs.[3] For our purposes we do not have to go through the details of the determination of the optimal $\overline{w}$. We can, however, note some properties that would come out of this analysis.

First, because some wage offers would generally be unacceptable—that is, $w < \overline{w}$ for some offers—it typically takes time for a job searcher to find an acceptable job. In the interim, the person is "unemployed" (although engaged in job search). Incomplete information about where to find the best job can therefore explain positive amounts of unemployment.

Second, an increase in the income while unemployed, w^u, motivates job seekers to raise their standards for job acceptance; that is, $\overline{w}$ increases. Given the distribution of wage offers in Figure 10.1, it becomes more likely that $w < \overline{w}$. Hence, wage offers are more likely to be rejected. It follows that job searchers tend to take a longer time to find a job when w^u increases. For a group of workers, an increase in w^u therefore lowers the **job-finding rate** and raises the expected **duration of unemployment**.

Third, suppose that the whole distribution of job offers becomes better. A favorable shock to firms' production functions might mean, for example, that marginal products of labor were all 10% higher than before. This kind of shock therefore shifts the distribution of wage offers in Figure 10.1 to the right. (The height of the curve at the old wage w is now the height at the wage $1.1 \cdot w$.) For a given reservation wage, $\overline{w}$, wage offers are, therefore, more likely to be in the acceptable range, $w > \overline{w}$. Hence, the job-finding rate rises, and the expected duration of unemployment falls.

A better distribution of wage offers also motivates people to raise their reservation wage, $\overline{w}$. If the income obtained while unemployed, w^u, does not change, however, then the first effect tends to dominate.[4] A shift to a better distribution of wage offers—generated, for example,

[3] For a discussion of models of job search that involve an optimal reservation wage, see Belton Fleisher and Thomas Kniesner (1984, pp. 477–507).

[4] If w^u and all wage offers were higher by 10%, the benefits and costs of accepting a job would not change. The job-finding rate and the expected duration of unemployment would therefore also not change. If we instead hold w^u constant—as we did in the text—then the net effect is equivalent to a fall in w^u. The net effect is, accordingly, an increase in the job-finding rate and a decrease in the expected duration of unemployment.

by a favorable shock to workers' productivity—raises the job-finding rate and lowers the expected duration of unemployment.

Fourth, a rise in the anticipated duration of a job makes it more attractive and thereby lowers the reservation wage, $\overline{w}$. This element creates an important dynamic aspect to the model because, in a full analysis, this expected duration would be higher the better the match was when the job was accepted. Therefore, if a person sets a higher standard for accepting a job offer today—by raising $\overline{w}$—the length of the current unemployment spell is likely to be greater. However, if a position is ever found, then it is likely to represent a good match that will produce a long-duration job. This enhanced duration will tend to reduce unemployment in the future (by lowering the rate of job separation, which is discussed in another section).

SEARCH BY FIRMS

Thus far, we have taken an unrealistic view of how firms participate in the job-search process. Firms received job applications, evaluated candidates in terms of likely marginal products, and then expressed wage offers.[5] This process does not allow firms to utilize the information that they have about the characteristics of their jobs, the traits of workers who are usually productive on these jobs, and the wages that typically have to be paid for such workers. Firms communicate this information by advertising job openings that specify ranges of requirements for education, experience, and so on, and also indicate a salary range. Such advertisements appropriately screen out most potential applicants and tend to generate more rapid and better matches of workers to jobs.

Although search by firms is important in a well-functioning labor market, the inclusion of this search leaves unaltered our major conclusions. In particular,

It still takes time for workers to be matched with acceptable jobs, so that the expected durations of unemployment and vacancies are positive.

[5] *Since the marginal product of most people on most jobs would be negative (for example, of a college professor as the chief executive officer of General Motors), we would have to allow wage offers to be negative. Usually, these negative offers would be unacceptable, so we can just as well think of no job being offered in such cases.*

—— An increase in workers' incomes while unemployed, w^u, lowers the job-finding rate and raises the anticipated duration of unemployment.

—— A favorable shock to productivity raises the job-finding rate and reduces the expected duration of unemployment.

JOB SEPARATIONS

Workers search for jobs that offer high wages, relative to perceived opportunities elsewhere, and employers search for workers with high productivity, given the wages that must be paid. Although workers and firms evaluate their information as well as possible, they often find out later that they made mistakes. An employer may learn, for example, that a worker is less productive than anticipated, or a worker may discover that he or she dislikes the job (or boss). When a job match looks significantly poorer than it did initially, firms are motivated to discharge the worker, or the worker is motivated to quit. These kinds of separations are more likely to occur the lower was the quality of the job match in the first place.

Separations also arise because of changed circumstances, even when firms and workers made accurate initial assessments of each other. An adverse shock to a firm's production function could, for example, lower its evaluation of a worker's marginal product and thereby lead to a discharge. If we distinguish the products of firms, then we would get a similar effect from a decline in the relative demand for a firm's product. Separations of this type are also sensitive to how good the job match was at the outset. If the match was not very strong to start with, then relatively small changes in production conditions or product demand would be sufficient to make the match mutually undesirable.

The cases just mentioned involve new information about the quality of a job match. But, in other cases, separations occur because jobs are known to be temporary at the outset. Examples include seasonal workers in agriculture or at sports facilities (or, for the example considered in Chapter 6, the employment of workers for the cleanup of the *Exxon Valdez* oil spill).

On the other side of the labor market, workers may experience changed circumstances with respect to family status, schooling, location, and retirement, as well as alternative job prospects. Some of these shifts are surprises, whereas others were predictable in advance. In either case, shifts in these household factors could induce a worker to quit a job.

The main point is that job separations occur for a variety of reasons. For a group of employed workers, we can identify factors that influence the **job-separation rate**. The rate is higher, for example, among inexperienced workers who are harder to evaluate initially or for younger persons who are likely to experience changes in family size or job preferences. The separation rate would also be higher in industries that are subject to frequent shocks to technology or product demand.

If there were no separations (and no new persons entering the labor force), then the process of job search would tend eventually to eliminate unemployment and vacancies. But the existence of separations means that the finding of new jobs is continually offset by the loss of old ones, that is, by the creation of new unemployment and vacancies. The level and change in unemployment and vacancies involves the interplay between job finding and job separation. We now illustrate this process with a simple example, which focuses on the number of people employed and unemployed.

JOB SEPARATIONS, JOB FINDING, AND THE NATURAL UNEMPLOYMENT RATE

Let L be the number of people employed and U the number unemployed. We assume here that the labor force, $L + U$, does not change over time. Hence, we do not allow for retirements or entry of new persons into

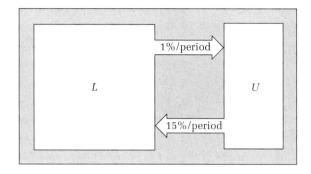

FIGURE 10.2

MOVEMENTS BETWEEN EMPLOYMENT AND UNEMPLOYMENT

In this example, 1% of those employed (L) lose their jobs each period. Simultaneously, 15% of those unemployed (U) find jobs each
period. The net change in the number unemployed during a period is
therefore $15\% \cdot U - 1\% \cdot L$. The change in the number unemployed
is the negative of the change in the number employed.

the labor force. Because of the reevaluation of jobs and workers, some
fraction of those employed experience a job separation in each period.
In Figure 10.2 the box labeled L denotes the number employed, and
the box labeled U shows those unemployed. The arrow from L to U
represents the number of job separations. If the labor force is constant,
and—unrealistically—if no job loser finds a new job immediately, then
all those who lose jobs move from category L to category U. For the
purpose of an example, assume that 1% of those employed lose their
jobs each period, that is, the job separation rate is 1% per period.

As discussed before, the other thing that happens each period is that
some fraction of those unemployed find jobs. In Figure 10.2 the arrow
pointing from U to L represents the number of unemployed persons who
find jobs during a period. Here (for the example to generate roughly the
right numbers), assume that 15% of those unemployed find work each
period. In other words, the job-finding rate is 15% per period.

We can work through the process of job separation and job finding to determine the numbers of people employed and unemployed.
Table 10.1 assumes that the labor force is fixed at 100 million people
(the actual size of the civilian labor force in 1996 was 134 million),
and the economy starts in period 1 with 90 million employed and 10
million unemployed. Thus, the unemployment rate is initially 10%. Of
the 90 million workers, 1%—or 0.9 million people—lose their jobs in
the first period. Simultaneously, 15% of those unemployed—1.5 million

TABLE 10.1

Period	Number Employed (L)	Number Unemployed (U)	Number Who Lose Jobs	Number Who Find Jobs	Net Change in Employment	Net Change in Unemployment
1	90.0	10.0	0.9	1.5	0.6	−0.6
2	90.6	9.4	0.9	1.4	0.5	−0.5
3	91.1	8.9	0.9	1.3	0.4	−0.4
4	91.5	8.5	0.9	1.3	0.4	−0.4
5	91.9	8.1	0.9	1.2	0.3	−0.3
6	92.2	7.8	0.9	1.2	0.3	−0.3
⋮	⋮	⋮	⋮	⋮	⋮	⋮
∞	93.8	6.2	0.9	0.9	0	0

Note: *We assume that the economy starts with 90 million people employed* (L) *and 10 million unemployed* (U). *Then, from Figure 10.2, 1% of those employed lose their job each period, and 15% of those unemployed find jobs. The net change in employment is therefore 15% · U − 1% · L. The change in unemployment is the negative of the change in employment. When the number employed reaches 93.8 million and the number unemployed reaches 6.2 million, the net changes in employment and unemployment are zero. Thus, the natural unemployment rate in this example is 6.2%.*

people—find jobs. Hence, the net change in employment during period 1 is 0.6 million. Correspondingly, unemployment falls by 0.6 million.

As the number of employed increases and the number of unemployed decreases, the quantity of job separations (1% of those employed) rises, and the quantity of job findings (15% of those unemployed) falls. The increase in employment therefore slows over time. The economy eventually approaches levels of employment and unemployment at which the number of job separations and findings is equal. Then, as long as the rates of job separation and job finding do not change, employment and unemployment are constant. In our example, the balance between job separations and job findings occurs when employment equals 93.8 million and unemployment equals 6.2 million, that is, when the unemployment rate is 6.2%. Therefore, in this model, we can say that the

natural unemployment rate is 6.2%. The economy tends toward this rate automatically, given the rates at which people lose and find jobs.

The model brings out some important points about the natural unemployment rate. First, although the unemployment rate eventually stays constant at this value, there is still a substantial amount of *job turnover*. Almost a million people lose and find jobs each period in the example when the unemployment rate is 6.2%. In this model—and in the real world—large flows from employment to unemployment, and vice versa, are a normal part of the operation of the labor market.

Second, the dynamics of employment and unemployment, as well as the value of the natural employment rate, depend on the rates of job separation and job finding. In the example these rates per period were set at 1% and 15%, respectively. More generally, our earlier analysis showed how the rates of job separation and job finding depended on various factors, such as a person's age and experience, the income available while unemployed, and the variability of an industry's supply and demand conditions. To see how these factors influence employment and unemployment, we want to consider alternative values for the rates of job separation and job finding.

Let σ (the Greek letter *sigma*) be the job-separation rate and ϕ (the Greek letter *phi*) the job-finding rate. The change in the number employed during a period, ΔL, is given by

$$\Delta L = \phi U - \sigma L \qquad\qquad\qquad \textbf{(10.1)}$$

Note that the first term, ϕU, is the number of unemployed who find jobs during a period, and the second term, σL, is the number of employed who lose jobs. Equation (10.1) says that the change in employment equals job findings less job separations.

Equation (10.1) implies that employment increases if job findings, ϕU, exceed job separations, σL. In the reverse case, employment decreases. To determine the natural levels of employment and unemployment, we set the change in employment, ΔL, to zero in equation

(10.1). Then, using the condition that the labor force, $L + U$, is fixed at 100 million, we find that

$$\phi U = \sigma L = \sigma \cdot (100 - U)$$

Solving this equation for the number unemployed, U, determines the natural values of unemployment and employment as

$$U = 100 \cdot \sigma/(\sigma + \phi) \tag{10.2}$$
$$L = 100 \cdot \phi/(\sigma + \phi)$$

The natural unemployment rate is therefore

$$u = U/100 = \sigma/(\sigma + \phi) \tag{10.3}$$

In our example, $\sigma = 0.01$ per period and $\phi = 0.15$ per period. Thus, $u = 0.01/0.16 = 6.2\%$, as we found before.

Equation (10.3) relates the natural unemployment rate to the rates of job separation, σ, and job finding, ϕ.[6] A higher rate of separation, σ, raises the natural unemployment rate, and a higher rate of finding, ϕ, lowers it. Thus, when we examine differences in natural unemployment rates—either over groups of people or over time—we should look for differences in the rates of job separation and job finding. People who lose jobs more frequently or have more trouble in finding jobs will be unemployed a larger fraction of the time.

MOVEMENTS IN AND OUT OF THE LABOR FORCE

Before applying the theory to data on unemployment rates, we can usefully extend the analysis to include movements in and out of the labor force. Conceptually, people are classified as outside of the labor force if they neither have a market job nor are currently looking for one. (Hence, the category includes full-time students and homemakers, who might reasonably think of themselves as "employed.") In practice, there are difficulties in distinguishing those outside the labor force from

[6] *For more thorough analyses of this type of model, see Robert Hall (1979), Chitra Ramaswami (1983), and Michael Darby, John Haltiwanger, and Mark Plant (1985).*

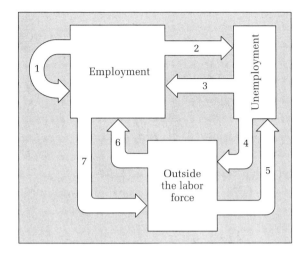

FIGURE 10.3

FLOWS OF PEOPLE AMONG THREE CATEGORIES: EMPLOYMENT, UNEMPLOYMENT, AND OUTSIDE OF THE LABOR FORCE

The diagram shows the possible movements from one category to another.

those unemployed: the distinction comes from people's answers to a survey question as to whether they are actively "looking for work" during a particular period. To some extent, the number classified as unemployed underestimates the true number, because some of those labeled as outside of the labor force would also like market jobs (at some wage rate!). But, on the other hand, many of those who call themselves unemployed are not actually interested in accepting employment on realistic terms.

For our purposes, the important new effects involve movements from inside the labor force to outside and vice versa. There are many good reasons for these movements, for example, when people retire, when they leave or reenter school, when they have changes in marital status or in the number and ages of children, or when the nature of the available jobs changes.

Figure 10.3 shows the possible transitions among the three categories, employment, unemployment, and outside of the labor force. (Notice that the flows labeled 2 and 3 are those that we studied before.) The list of possibilities is as follows:

1. A change in job, without becoming unemployed or leaving the labor force. (This type of shift is especially popular among sports figures

and professors of economics—but, more generally, over half of all job changes do not involve any unemployment; see Kim Clark and Lawrence Summers, 1979, p. 43.)

2. A loss of a job with a move to unemployment.

3. The finding of a job from the ranks of the unemployed.

4. A movement from unemployment to outside of the labor force; persons in this category are sometimes described as **discouraged workers**.

5. An entry or reentry to the labor force but initially unemployed.

6. An entry or reentry to the labor force with a job obtained at once (as in the case of most graduating majors in business and economics).

7. A loss of a job with a move outside of the labor force (a flow that includes permanent retirements, as well as withdrawals from the labor market to raise a family or return to school).

Total job separations are the sum of flows 1, 2, and 7, and total job findings are the sum of flows 1, 3, and 6. The difference between separations and findings is the change in employment. The change in unemployment is the sum of flows 2 and 5, less the sum of flows 3 and 4. Thus, because of the movements in and out of the labor force, the change in employment no longer coincides with the negative of the change in unemployment.

As before—but with greater complexity—people's tendencies to experience the various transitions shown in Figure 10.3 determine the levels of employment and unemployment over time. It is still true that employment tends to be lower the higher is the rate of job separation. Similarly, employment tends to be higher the greater is the rate of job finding. But the movements in and out of the labor force interact with these tendencies to lose and find jobs. For example, people who move frequently in and out of the labor force build up relatively little work experience. Hence, they tend to be the ones who are terminated first and hired last.

For unemployment, the new effects concern the possibilities for moving outside of the labor force. For example, the tendency for the unemployed to cease looking for work (flow 4 in Figure 10.3) reduces the number of persons counted as unemployed. But the tendency for people to shift from employment to outside of the labor force (flow 7) tends to raise unemployment. That is because, first, these people often become unemployed when they reenter the labor force (flow 5), and, second, they are more likely to lose a job later (flows 2 and 7).

THE BEHAVIOR OF U.S. UNEMPLOYMENT RATES

Table 10.2 shows unemployment rates for all civilian workers and for various categories of workers by age, sex, and race. The data are averages for five-year subperiods and the overall sample from 1948 to 1996. The average unemployment rate for all civilian workers for 1948–96 was 6.0%.

The average unemployment rates varied by demographic characteristics. Among persons 20 years and older, for example, the average rate for females was 5.4%, whereas that for males was 4.9%. (This difference by sex has largely vanished since the early 1980s.) For both sexes, the average unemployment rate declines by age until people reach at least their 50s. But the sharpest distinction applies to teenagers, who had an average unemployment rate of 16.3%, compared to 5.0% for those at least 20 years of age. For blacks and other minorities the average unemployment rate of 10.4% was roughly double that for whites of 5.1%.

The high unemployment rates from the mid-1970s to the mid-1980s contrasted with the growing ratio of employment to population. Table 10.3 shows the ratios of civilian employment to total population and to the population aged 16–64. The first ratio varied between 36% and 41% until the mid-1970s but then increased to 47% in 1988 and 48% in 1996. The second ratio stayed between 61% and 66% until the mid-1970s but then rose to 74% in 1990 and 75% in 1996.

TABLE 10.2

BEHAVIOR OF U.S. UNEMPLOYMENT RATES (PERCENT OF CIVILIAN LABOR FORCE WITHIN CATEGORY)

	All Civilian Workers	Males 20 Years and Older	Females 20 Years and Older	Teenagers (16–19)	White	Black and Other Minorities
1948–52	4.3	3.6	4.2	10.3	4.0	6.9
1952–57	4.3	3.6	4.2	10.8	3.8	7.9
1958–62	6.0	5.2	5.6	15.4	5.4	14.6
1963–67	4.6	3.3	4.6	14.8	4.1	8.6
1968–73	4.7	3.2	4.7	14.6	4.3	8.2
1973–77	6.7	5.0	6.6	17.5	6.1	11.8
1978–62	7.3	5.9	6.6	18.6	6.4	13.6
1983–87	7.5	6.6	6.6	19.0	6.5	14.1
1988–92	6.1	5.6	5.3	16.9	5.3	10.9
1993–96	6.0	5.3	5.3	17.7	5.3	10.3
1948–96	6.0	4.9	5.6	16.3	5.3	10.4

Source: *DRI data bank and* Economic Report of the President, *1997, Table B–40.*

Note: *The table shows the average civilian unemployment rate over the period indicated for various categories of workers.*

The growing employment ratios in recent years reflected mainly the rapid increase in the labor-force participation rate of women: this rate rose from 33% in 1948 to 43% in 1970, 52% in 1980, and 59% for 1994–96. In contrast, the participation rate for males declined slowly from 87% in 1948 to 83% in 1960, 80% in 1970, 77% in 1980, and 75% for 1993–96. Because of these changes, the fraction of the civilian labor force that is female rose from 29% in 1948 to 46% in 1996.

TABLE 10.3

BEHAVIOR OF U.S. EMPLOYMENT RATIOS

	Percent of Total Population	Percent of Population Aged 16–64
1948–52	39.8	61.1
1953–57	37.5	62.1
1958–62	36.1	62.0
1963–67	36.1	62.8
1968–72	38.4	64.0
1973–77	40.6	65.1
1978–82	43.4	67.5
1983–87	44.8	69.1
1988–92	47.0	72.8
1993–96	47.2	73.9
1948-96	40.9	65.9

Source: *DRI data bank.*

Note: *The table shows the ratio of civilian employment to the total population and to the population aged 16–64.*

CAUSES FOR THE DEMOGRAPHIC VARIATIONS IN UNEMPLOYMENT RATES

We can analyze the demographic disparities in unemployment rates by thinking about the determinants of the natural unemployment rates.[7] Differences in the natural rates reflect variations in the rates of job separation and job finding. We can compare the rates of job separation across the demographic groups by looking at data on the **duration of jobs**: persons with high rates of job separation end up with short-term jobs. To get information about job-finding rates, we can examine data on the

[7] *For discussions of empirical evidence in this area, see Theresa Devine and Nicholas Kiefer (1991).*

duration of unemployment. Persons who find jobs quickly end up with brief spells of unemployment.

The Duration of Jobs

The research on job tenure by Robert Hall (1980a, 1982), refined by Manuelita Ureta (1992), allows us to understand some of the differences in unemployment rates by age, sex, and race. First, most new jobs that people get do not last very long. For example, using data for 1978, 1981, and 1983, Ureta estimated that 55% of new jobs last less than one year, and only 15% last for five years or more. But as people get older and try a variety of jobs, most workers eventually find a good job match, which lasts for a long time. Using data for 1978, Hall estimated that by age 50 over 70% of all workers have been on their present job for at least five years. By age 40, about 40% of all workers are currently in a very long-term job, which will eventually last at least 20 years. These results mean that job separations (flows 1, 2, and 7 in Figure 10.3) are much more common for younger workers, most of whom have not yet found a long-lasting job match. This element therefore explains a good deal of the higher unemployment rate for younger persons, especially teenagers.

A lower average duration of jobs can also explain some of the higher average unemployment rate for women than for men. Ureta estimated— using the data for 1978, 1981, and 1983—that 52% of women who have jobs would eventually reach a tenure of at least 5 years on their job, and 17% would reach at least 20 years. The comparable figures for men were 64 and 30%, respectively. Historically, women moved in and out of the labor force (flows 4, 5, 6, and 7 in Figure 10.3) over their lifetime more often than men did. However, this distinction by sex has narrowed substantially since the early 1980s (see Farber, 1995). This observation is consistent with the elimination of the gap between the unemployment rates of men and women since the early 1980s (Table 10.2).

Surprisingly, the data indicate that blacks have roughly the same chance as whites to stay on a job for a long time. Ureta's estimate—based on the data for 1978, 1981, and 1983—is that 64% of blacks who have jobs would have an eventual tenure of at least 5 years on their current job, and 20% would reach at least 20 years. The figures for whites—58 and 25%, respectively—are comparable. However, some other data show that blacks are much more likely than whites to experience a job separation in any given month. Stephen Marston (1976, Table 4) estimates that this element accounts for about one-third of the higher average unemployment rate for blacks. If we put Marston's observations together with Ureta's, then the suggestion is that blacks have a strong tendency toward very short-term jobs although no less of a tendency to achieve jobs with a duration of at least five years.

The Duration of Unemployment

The other main element that determines the average unemployment rate is the duration of a typical spell of unemployment. The longer it takes for an unemployed person to find a job or leave the labor force (flows 3 and 4 in Figure 10.3), the greater will be the measured number of unemployed at any point in time.

The research by Kim Clark and Lawrence Summers (1979) provides some interesting information about the duration of unemployment. One point is that a large fraction of spells end within one month—the percentages were 79% for 1969, 60% for 1974, and 55% for 1975. (Note that 1975 was a year of deep recession, 1974 was an early stage of a recession, and 1969 was a strong boom.) Correspondingly, the average length of a spell is not very long—1.4 months in 1969, 1.9 months in 1974, and 2.2 months in 1975. But Clark and Summers argue that the importance of the long-term unemployed is more significant than these figures suggest. First, in determining the average number of people unemployed at any date, we effectively weight the frequency of each spell by its length. Therefore, although the average length of a spell in 1974 was only two months, it also turns out that spells of more than two months accounted for 69% of the number unemployed. Similarly, spells of six months or more still accounted for 19% of unemployment in 1974.

Second, roughly half of all spells of unemployment end in withdrawal from the labor force (flow 4 in Figure 10.3), rather than in employment (flow 3 in the figure). Then many of those who leave the labor force soon reappear as job searchers (flow 5 in the figure) and thereby count as a new spell of unemployment in the data. Clark and Summers argue that these spells of unemployment and the intervening periods outside of the labor force should be counted as long periods of unemployment. But many of these people (as well as some who never leave the labor force) may not be serious job seekers and should not be counted as unemployed in the first place. This ambiguity points out the fundamental problem of defining and measuring the concept of unemployment. It is easier to define and measure employment than unemployment.

Teenagers tend to find jobs or leave the labor force more quickly than do older persons. For 1974, for example, the average duration of unemployment for teenagers was 1.6 months, compared with just over 2 months for those over 20. The higher unemployment rate for teenagers therefore reflects mostly the short duration of their jobs, rather than a low rate of job finding.

For blacks, particularly those under 25, a greater difficulty in finding jobs accounts for a large part of their higher unemployment rate. Marston (1976, Table 4) estimated that this element accounted for two-thirds of the higher average unemployment rate for blacks from 1967 to 1973.

DETERMINANTS OF THE NATURAL UNEMPLOYMENT RATE

There is a long list of factors—especially government policies—that economists think influence the natural unemployment rate for the whole economy. We consider briefly some of the more important possibilities: unemployment insurance, the minimum wage, and labor unions.

Unemployment Insurance

The government's main program of **unemployment insurance** began in 1936. This program provides benefits to eligible persons who have lost their jobs and are currently "looking for work." Hence, those in the category labeled "unemployment" in Figure 10.3 are candidates for these benefits. Although the federal government plays some role, the main rules are set by the various state governments. A person's eligibility for benefits depends on a sufficient work history in a covered job.[8] (In 1995, roughly 95% of all civilian workers were in covered jobs— see *Economic Report of the President*, 1997, Tables B–34, B–42.) An individual's benefits run out after a period, which is usually between 26 and 39 weeks. But in times of recession, such as 1982–83 and 1991, the federal government tends to extend the period of eligibility.

Unemployment benefits are one component of the income, w^u, that a person gets by not working. The ratio of the potential benefits to the wage from a prior job is called the **replacement ratio**. This ratio has not changed dramatically since World War II: the ratio of the average weekly check from unemployment insurance programs to average weekly earnings for all nonagricultural workers increased from 39% in 1947 to 46% in 1996 (*Economic Report of the President*, 1997, Tables B–43, B–45). Over time, the main changes in the unemployment-insurance program have been extensions of coverage (especially to small firms and to employees of state and local governments) and increases in the allowable duration of benefits.

The existence of unemployment insurance makes the unemployed who are receiving benefits less eager to accept jobs or leave the labor force (flows 3 and 4 in Figure 10.3). The program also makes the employed persons who will be eligible for benefits more willing to accept job separations (flow 2 in Figure 10.3).[9] In particular, unemployment insurance motivates **temporary layoffs**, which are short-term job separations that occur during a period of slack production. Overall, a more generous program of unemployment insurance leads to a higher natural rate of unemployment.

Most empirical estimates of the effects of unemployment insurance in the United States rely on differences across states in the levels of benefits and in criteria for eligibility. Using these data, some researchers report that unemployment insurance raises the natural unemployment rate by between 0.5 and 1 percentage point.[10] Gary Solon (1985) noted

[8] *In some states people who quit their jobs or are fired for cause are eligible for benefits, whereas in others they are ineligible. It is, of course, often hard to tell who quits or is fired for cause. For a discussion of these issues, see Daniel Hamermesh (1977).*

[9] *This tendency diminishes if employers pay for the average benefits given to their ex-employees through a process called **experience rating**. With experience rating, a business that has a lot of job separations pays a larger amount into the fund that finances the unemployment benefits. This system therefore motivates employers to hold down their rates of job separation. There is some experience rating in the U.S. system of unemployment insurance, but not in the systems of most other countries. For a discussion, see Robert Topel and Finis Welch (1980).*

[10] *See, for example, Daniel Hamermesh (1977, p. 52) and Kim Clark and Lawrence Summers (1982, Table 10).*

that since 1979 unemployment-insurance benefits have been taxable for high-income families. He estimates that the reduction in effective benefits lowered the duration of insured unemployment for high-income persons by about 10%.

Lawrence Katz and Bruce Meyer (1988) focused on the duration of benefits. They estimated that an extension of allowable benefits by 1 week raises the mean duration of unemployment by between 0.16 and 0.20 week. An extension of benefits from 26 to 39 weeks—as in the 1982–83 and 1991 recessions—would therefore raise the average duration of unemployment by more than 2 weeks.

Many economists, such as Gary Burtless (1987) and Michael Burda (1988), argue that the generosity of the unemployment-insurance programs in some western European countries—especially the long period of eligibility for benefits—is one of the factors behind their persistently high unemployment rates. (In 1995, the unemployment rates were 23% in Spain, 17% in Finland, 13% in Ireland, 12% in France and Italy, 10% in Denmark, 9% in the United Kingdom, Sweden, and Belgium, 8% in Germany, and 7% in Portugal and the Netherlands, compared to 5.5% in the United States.) Richard Jackman, Richard Layard, and Stephen Nickell (1996) show, in a study of OECD countries, that higher unemployment-insurance benefits and a longer duration of benefits each raise the unemployment rate. In addition, they use information from OECD (1994) to assess the effects of employment protections in the form of notice and severance-pay requirements. They found that more of these protections tends to raise long-term unemployment (by reducing the incentives of firms to hire new workers and thereby making it harder for workers to find jobs) but may slightly lower short-term unemployment (presumably by curtailing the dismissal of existing workers).

Although there is evidence that unemployment insurance raises the unemployment rate, there is not much indication in the United States that these programs have become significantly more or less generous over the last two decades. It is therefore not easy to use the small variations in this program to explain much of the movement in unemployment rates from the 1970s to the 1990s.

The Minimum Wage

When considering determinants of the natural unemployment rate, economists often mention the **minimum wage**. Since 1938, the federal government has set minimum wage rates in covered industries. In 1946 this regulation covered about 57% of all nonsupervisory employees. But changes in legislation raised the coverage in the 1990s to around 90%.

Congress has changed the level of the basic hourly minimum wage numerous times since the initial choice of $0.25 in 1938. The minimum was $0.75 in 1950, $1.25 in 1963, $1.60 in 1968, $2.30 in 1977, $3.35 in 1981, $4.25 in 1991, $4.75 in 1996, and $5.15 in 1997. The ratio of the minimum wage to average hourly earnings ranged between 35 and 56% from 1950 to 1996. Although there is no clear trend, the ratio increased each time Congress enacted a new minimum but then declined gradually as average hourly earnings rose. For example, with no change in the minimum wage during the Reagan administration, the ratio fell from 46% in 1981 to 35% in 1989. The increases in the minimum wage in 1990 and 1991 raised the ratio to 41% in 1991, but it then fell to 37% in 1995. The rise in the minimum in 1996 brought the ratio back to 40%.

Research on the employment effects of minimum wages became a boom industry in the 1990s. Before that, the consensus was that a higher minimum wage had a small negative effect on overall employment. The key mechanism was that a higher minimum wage reduced the incentive of employers to hire low-productivity workers in sectors covered by the minimum. Empirically, researchers found that a higher minimum wage and greater coverage tended especially to reduce the employment of teenagers. The generally accepted estimate, until recently, was that an increase by 10% in the minimum wage lowered the quantity of teenagers employed by somewhat more than 1%.[11] There was also some indication of a negative effect on the employment of young adults aged 20–24 but no clear effect on older workers. In fact, because the minimum wage makes the labor of low-productivity workers artificially more expensive, it is likely that businesses would shift to more labor from high-productivity workers. Hence, labor unions tend to favor the minimum wage to protect

[11] *For a survey of the evidence collected up to the early 1980s, see Charles Brown, Curtis Gilroy, and Andrew Koehn (1982).*

their high-paid members from the competition of low-productivity, low-wage workers.

The happy consensus about the employment effects from minimum wages was shattered in the 1990s by the research of David Card (1992a, 1992b) and David Card and Alan Krueger (1994). They argued in a series of empirical studies that, instead of lowering employment of teenagers and other low-wage workers, higher minimum wage rates either had no effect or actually raised employment. One study by Card (1992a) found that the 1988 increase in California's minimum wage did not reduce its teenage employment relative to that in some other states in which the minimum wage was not increased. His other study (1992b) found that the 1990 rise in the federal minimum wage did not have a larger impact in the states with lower wages, where the heightened federal constraint should have been more important.

These results were interesting but they constituted just a couple of observations in the universe of the cross-state data. David Neumark and William Wascher (1992) used all the data and found the usual small, negative effect of a higher minimum wage on the employment of teenagers and young adults.

David Card and Alan Krueger (1994) studied the 1992 increase in New Jersey's minimum wage by using their own survey of employment before and after the change at fast-food restaurants in New Jersey and Pennsylvania (the control group for which the minimum wage did not change). Their key finding was that the rise in the minimum wage in New Jersey did not reduce the employment of fast-food workers there relative to that in Pennsylvania.

This New Jersey–Pennsylvania study has become, perhaps, one of the most criticized empirical analyses ever undertaken. Finis Welch (1995) convincingly criticized the underlying survey design, in which the researchers simply telephoned each restaurant before and after the change in the New Jersey minimum wage and then asked a "manager" about employment and wages. This procedure suggested that the data would be dominated by measurement error. David Neumark and William

Wascher (1995b) argued that the Card-Krueger findings emerged because employment happened to decline, on average, in the 74 places surveyed in Pennsylvania. The suggestion was that the outcome in Pennsylvania was likely to be dominated by measurement error and could not, therefore, serve as a useful control group for New Jersey. Neumark and Wascher also found that the results looked different if more accurate data from payrolls of the fast-food restaurants were substituted for the telephone survey information. In this case, the results showed the familiar small, negative effect of an increased minimum wage on fast-food employment. Finally, Dan Hamermesh (1995) noted that the 1992 shift in the New Jersey minimum wage had been enacted in 1990 and that employment of low-wage workers would likely have fallen before the law came into effect—for example, by reduced entry of fast-food businesses into New Jersey. In fact, New Jersey's growth of teenage employment was lower than Pennsylvania's before the 1992 increase in New Jersey's minimum wage.

On the more constructive side, David Neumark and William Wascher (1995a) assessed the effect of a higher minimum wage on teenage employment and teenage school enrollment. For teenagers who previously classified school as their major activity, a higher minimum wage tended to raise employment by inducing teenagers to leave school. For teenagers who were originally working but not in school, a higher minimum wage tended to reduce employment and raise idleness (out of school and not working). Thus, the effect of a higher minimum wage on teenage employment involved two offsetting forces—more work among persons previously in school and less work among those who were initially out of school. The overall effect was the usual, small negative effect on teenage employment.

The disturbing part of this Neumark-Wascher study is that, in addition to the small negative effect on overall teenage employment, a higher minimum wage also seemed to have adverse distributional consequences. The teenagers who lost jobs and became idle tended to be the most disadvantaged, notably blacks and Hispanics, who were initially not in school. Those who gained jobs or increased hours of work tended to be the more advantaged, notably nonblacks/non-Hispanics, who were initially in school but were induced to drop out to secure higher wage jobs. It is also questionable whether the higher employment of the second group—which required a drop in school enrollment—should be counted as a favorable aspect of the minimum wage. Thus, it becomes difficult to make the common argument that the minimum wage is a good idea because the small drop in overall employment is a price worth paying to reap the benefits on the distributional side. It appears that the distributional changes may, instead, be an additional cost of the program.

Even if the adverse effect of the minimum wage on teenage *employment* is clear, the effect on teenage *unemployment* depends also on the response of labor-force participation. Because a higher minimum wage reduces the chance of finding a job, it also reduces the number of teenagers who declare themselves as looking for work. This response lessens the tendency for a higher minimum wage to raise the measured unemployment rate of teenagers.

In any event, the behavior of the minimum wage cannot account for the high unemployment rates from the mid-1970s to the early 1980s. The reasons are, first, that the minimum wage did not increase relative to average hourly earnings and, second, that the higher unemployment rates over this period applied as much to older workers as to teenagers and young adults.

Labor Unions

Economists sometimes suggest that labor unions cause unemployment. Mostly, unions can raise real wage rates and hold down the levels of employment in covered industries. Correspondingly, there is a higher supply of labor and lower real wage rates in uncovered sectors. Unions can therefore create inefficiencies, which include the inappropriate distribution of work and production between covered and uncovered areas. Conceivably, more union power would also lead to reductions in aggregate employment and output. But it is less clear that unions have anything to do with the amount of *unemployment*: the adverse effects on total work may correspond mostly to reductions in the labor force.

We can look for effects of unions by observing the changes in unionization over time. The fraction of the civilian labor force that is unionized declined from a peak of 27% in the mid-1950s to 21% in 1980, 15% in 1986, and 15% in 1995 (U.S. Department of Commerce, *Statistical Abstract of the United States*, various years). We cannot, therefore, attribute the high unemployment rates from the mid-1970s to the early 1980s to an increase in unionization. (The principal increases in unionization were the rise from less than 3% to 6% at the beginning of the twentieth century, the rise from 7% to 15% in the mid-1930s, and the increase from 6% to 26% during World War II.)

EMPLOYMENT AND UNEMPLOYMENT DURING RECESSIONS

We showed in Chapter 9 that shifts to the production function could account for some characteristics of real-world business fluctuations. In particular, an adverse shock to the production function could generate a recession that featured declines in real GDP and labor input. Now we can use the apparatus from this chapter to see how supply shocks affect unemployment. We consider the case of a fixed labor force, so that changes in unemployment reflect inverse movements in employment.

Suppose that an adverse shock reduces the marginal product of labor for the typical worker and job. One effect, which we noted earlier, is that the job-finding rate, ϕ, declines. It does so because market opportunities—determined by labor's marginal product—have become poorer relative to the income received while unemployed, w^u. For the same reason, existing job matches become less mutually advantageous for firms and workers. Job separations therefore tend to increase, especially in the form of layoffs and firings by firms: hence, the job-separation rate, σ, tends to rise.

To see the effects on unemployment and employment, return to the example in which the labor force was fixed at 100 million persons and the job-finding rates were initially 15% and 1%, respectively. Table 10.4 assumes that the economy begins in period 1 at the natural unemployment rate, 6.2% in this example. Then the adverse shock to production functions—the force that initiates a recession—means that the job-separation rate rises from 1% to, say, 1.5%, and the job-finding rate falls from 15% to, say, 10%.

Although some people still find jobs, they are outnumbered by those who lose jobs. Hence, Table 10.4 shows that the unemployment rate rises steadily from 6.2% in period 1 to 9.4% in period 6. The number employed falls correspondingly from 93.8 million to 90.6 million.

Suppose that the temporary adverse shock to the production function lasts through period 5. As of period 6, the job-separation rate is again 1%, and the job-finding rate is 15%. Although some people still lose their jobs, they are now outnumbered by those who find jobs. The unemployment rate therefore falls gradually toward the natural rate of 6.2%, and employment rises correspondingly back toward 93.8 million.

We should stress two realistic features of recessions that emerge from this example. First, the buildup of a recession involves a period of gradually rising unemployment and falling employment. Second, even after an economic recovery begins, it takes a substantial period for the unemployment rate to return to its prerecession level.

In this example, with a fixed labor force, the dynamics of employment is just the reverse of that of unemployment. Further, if we abstract from changes in the stock of capital, then the movements in production would parallel those in employment. Although these patterns capture the broad features of business fluctuations, some elements are missing. First, hours worked per worker, especially *overtime* hours, are more flexible than numbers employed. Hours and output per worker therefore tend to fall in a recession (or rise in a boom) before the corresponding changes in employment. Second, businesses can change their utilization of capital and, hence, the volume of production. With a given number of worker-hours, a decrease in utilization during a recession shows up as a reduction in output per hour worked.[12] Third, the labor force can

[12] *A decrease in capacity utilization typically implies that fewer worker-hours would be required for current production. To the extent that worker-hours do not decline, firms are employing more labor than necessary for production. Economists have speculated whether this "excess" labor is underutilized (in that people work less intensively during recessions) or is, instead, used for activities that do not appear in measured output. Jon Fay and James Medoff (1985) found from a survey of 168 manufacturing firms that the typical firm reacted to a recession by assigning an additional 5% of work hours to maintenance and overhaul of equipment, training, and other activities that would not show up in measures of current output. Thus, there seems to be a significant diversion of labor during recessions to these productive, but typically uncounted, activities.*

TABLE 10.4

THE DYNAMICS OF EMPLOYMENT AND UNEMPLOYMENT DURING A RECESSION

Period	Job-Separation Rate (σ)	Job-Finding Rate (ϕ)	Number Employed (L)	Number Unemployed (U)	Number Who Lose Jobs	Number Who Find Jobs	Net Change in Employment
1	0.015	0.10	93.8	6.2	1.4	0.6	−0.8
2	0.015	0.10	93.0	7.0	1.4	0.7	−0.7
3	0.015	0.10	92.3	7.7	1.4	0.8	−0.6
4	0.015	0.10	91.7	8.3	1.4	0.8	−0.6
5	0.015	0.10	91.1	8.9	1.4	0.9	−0.5
6	0.01	0.15	90.6	9.4	0.9	1.4	0.5
7	0.01	0.15	91.1	8.9	0.9	1.3	0.4
8	0.01	0.15	91.5	8.5	0.9	1.3	0.4
9	0.01	0.15	91.9	8.1	0.9	1.2	0.3
10	0.01	0.15	92.2	7.8	0.9	1.2	0.3
⋮	⋮	⋮	⋮	⋮	⋮	⋮	⋮
∞	0.01	0.15	93.8	6.2	0.9	0.9	0

Note: *During the recession for periods 1 through 5, the job-separation rate is high—1.5% rather than 1% — and the job-finding rate is low—10% instead of 15%. Consequently, the unemployment rate rises from the natural rate, 6.2%, to 9.4% in period 6. When the job-separation and job-finding rates return to their normal values in period 6, the economy recovers gradually, and the unemployment rate approaches the natural rate of 6.2%.*

vary. Except for young persons, however—who tend to drop out of the labor force in bad times—there turns out to be little association of the labor force with the level of real economic activity (see problem 10.7).

SUPPLY SHOCKS, RECESSIONS, AND UNEMPLOYMENT

The theory shows how shocks to the production function could cause the high unemployment characteristic of recessions. We would like to know how much these recessions actually were the result of identifiable supply shocks. Although we cannot give a definitive answer to this question, there are some suggestive findings from empirical research.

Oil Shocks

James Hamilton (1983) documents the important role of oil shocks. Most economists believe that the dramatic increases in oil prices in 1973–74 and 1979–80 were important factors in the recessions of 1974–75 and 1980–82, respectively. Hamilton supports this view, but he also makes the surprising observation that the tendency "for oil price increases to be followed by recessions has in fact characterized every recession in the United States since World War II, with the single exception of the recession of 1960–61" (p. 229). The recession of 1957–58, for example, followed the increase in oil prices that stemmed from the Suez crisis, and the downturn of 1954 came after a rise in oil prices because of the Iranian nationalization of facilities. Hamilton's statistical results suggest that oil shocks have been important sources of high unemployment and low growth of real GDP. Moreover, the magnitude of the shocks for 1973–74 and 1979–80 likely explains why the two associated recessions—for 1974–75 and 1980–82—were the most severe of the post–World War II period. It is also noteworthy that the rise in oil prices at the start of the Persian Gulf crisis in August 1990 came at the beginning of the 1990–91 recession.

Sectoral Shifts

Aside from oil, economists have not been very successful in pinpointing identifiable supply shocks as regular elements in U.S. business fluctuations. It is possible nevertheless that an array of disturbances to productive conditions—which macroeconomists cannot identify directly—account for the recessions and booms. David Lilien (1982) pursued this idea by focusing on the changing composition of U.S. production. This composition has moved away from traditional areas of manufacturing, such as steel and automobiles, and toward high-tech industries and services. (The dominant movement earlier was from agriculture to manufacturing.) Lilien argues that the process of reallocating labor across sectors leads to high rates of job separation and therefore high rates of unemployment.[13] His empirical results (pp. 787–92) for the post–World War II United States show that periods of more rapidly changing industrial composition tend to be times of unusually high unemployment. Thus, the findings suggest that U.S. recessions derive in part from various shocks—such as technological innovations, changes in foreign competition, and variations in the relative prices of raw materials—that induce shifts in the composition of industry.

A number of economists have extended or questioned Lilien's conclusions. Katharine Abraham and Lawrence Katz (1986) argue that Lilien's results would emerge if only aggregate shocks matter but sectors respond differentially to the aggregate shocks. Prakash Loungani (1986) finds that, if the behavior of oil prices is held fixed, there is no longer much association in the U.S. data between changes in the composition of production and the unemployment rate. Loungani, Mark Rush, and William Tave (1990) show that the dispersion of stock prices across sectors has more explanatory power for unemployment than Lilien's measure, the dispersion of changes in employment. Stock prices may work better because these market valuations reflect the permanent implications of the various sectoral changes.

Steve Davis and John Haltiwanger (1996) show that recessions feature an unusually large volume of job reallocation, the sum of jobs created and jobs destroyed. Unemployment then emerges, as in Lilien, as a consequence of the frictions in the formation of new job matches. Davis and Haltiwanger demonstrate, however, that the process of reallocation is concentrated within sectors and therefore does not involve primarily the kinds of sectoral shifts that Lilien stressed. They also show that the jobs created and destroyed represent persistent changes in employment at the level of establishments. The changes in unemployment are, therefore, not concentrated in the temporary layoffs that are the focus of some theories, such as those that stress the role of unemployment insurance.

[13] *Our simple theory, summarized in equation 10.3, says that the natural unemployment rate is $\sigma/(\sigma + \phi)$. Thus, we predict an increase in the unemployment rate if the job-separation rate, σ, rises proportionately more than the job-finding rate, ϕ.*

Seasonal Fluctuations

Most macroeconomists attempt to eliminate seasonal effects by using **seasonally adjusted data** (provided by the U.S. Department of Commerce). The process of seasonal adjustment attempts to eliminate the normal fluctuations of a variable, such as real GDP, that occur from winter (the first quarter) to spring (the second quarter), and so on. Robert Barsky and Jeff Miron (1988) reached some interesting conclusions by focusing instead on the unadjusted numbers. First, the seasonal fluctuations in various quantities—such as real GDP, private consumption, private investment, and the amounts of employment and unemployment—are larger than the variations associated with typical recessions and booms. On a quarterly basis from 1948 to 1985, over 80% of the overall fluctuations in real GDP and over 60% of those in the unemployment rate were due to systematic seasonals (Barsky and Miron, 1988, Table 1). Furthermore, the seasonal patterns of comovement among GDP and its major components and between GDP and employment look similar to the comovements found in aggregate business fluctuations (ibid., Table 2). In the seasonal pattern, for example, private investment and consumption tend to move along with GDP, and investment is far more volatile than consumption. Miron (1988) shows that the results about seasonal behavior for the United States typically apply also to a sample of 25 industrialized or semi-industrialized countries.

The seasonal movements presumably reflect the influences of weather and holidays. To some extent we can think of these movements as regular shifts to technology (such as the effect of weather on the construction industry) and to some extent as systematic effects on preferences (such as the positive impact of Christmas on consumer demand and the negative influence of summer vacations on labor supply). Thus, the seasonal effects are analogous to the disturbances stressed in real business-cycle models: shocks to technology or preferences. The magnitude of the seasonal fluctuations shows that these types of disturbances can be quantitatively significant in the short run. In particular, this evidence weakens the argument of some economists that shocks to technology and preferences cannot be large enough to account for the observed magnitude of recessions and booms. Furthermore, the similarity of seasonal confinements to those in recessions and booms suggests that similar kinds of disturbances may underlie all of the observed fluctuations. The seasonal evidence therefore suggests that real business-cycle models provide a useful framework for understanding recessions and booms.

SUMMARY

When workers and jobs differ, it takes time for people to match up well with jobs. Workers search for positions with high wages (and other desirable characteristics), and businesses search for productive workers. During the process of search, some job seekers remain unemployed, and some positions remain vacant. The rate of job finding depends on such things as the income available while unemployed and the level and shape of the distribution of wage offers.

Because workers or firms make mistakes in their initial assessments and because circumstances change, existing jobs sometimes end. The job-separation rate depends on workers' characteristics—such as age and experience—and the variability of an industry's supply and demand conditions.

The dynamics of employment and unemployment depend on the rates of job separation and job finding. If these rates are constant, then the economy tends automatically to a natural rate of unemployment. This natural rate rises with an increase in the job-separation rate but falls with an increase in the job-finding rate. Movements in and out of the labor force also influence the natural unemployment rate.

We use this framework to analyze differences in average unemployment rates by age, sex, and race: these differences reflect underlying variations in the duration of jobs and of unemployment. Younger workers, for example, have much higher job-separation rates and therefore exhibit a higher average unemployment rate.

We found before that an adverse shock to the production function can generate a recession in which output and labor input decline. Now we show that this kind of shock also lowers the job-finding rate and raises the job-separation rate. Unemployment thereby rises during a recession.

The main direct evidence for cyclical effects of supply shocks involves changes in oil prices. Some results about sectoral shifts and seasonal fluctuations suggest, however, that shifts in technology and preferences—the types of disturbances stressed in real business-cycle theories—can be quantitatively important in the short run.

IMPORTANT TERMS AND CONCEPTS

discouraged workers Workers who leave the labor force following a period of unemployment.

duration of jobs The average length of time that a job is expected to last; the duration of jobs is inversely related to the job-separation rate.

duration of unemployment The length of time that a spell of unemployment is expected to last. The duration of unemployment is inversely related to the job-finding rate.

experience rating (for unemployment insurance) The feature of the U.S. program of unemployment insurance that taxes employers more heavily if they have a history of a higher job-separation rate.

job-finding rate The rate at which workers move from being unemployed or outside of the labor force to being employed.

job-separation rate The rate at which workers move from being employed to being unemployed or outside of the labor force.

labor force The total number of employed workers plus the number of unemployed.

minimum wage The amount below which the wage rate paid by a firm cannot legally fall.

natural unemployment rate The average unemployment rate that prevails in the economy, depending on the average rates of job separation and job finding.

outside of the labor force The classification of a person who is neither employed nor currently looking for a job.

replacement ratio (for unemployment insurance) The ratio of unemployment benefits to the prior wage earnings of a worker.

reservation wage The wage rate that is just high enough to induce someone to accept a job.

seasonally adjusted data Adjustment of quantities for normal seasonal variations. Seasonal adjustments are important for most national-accounts variables, such as real gross domestic product and its components, and also for monetary aggregates.

temporary layoffs Job separations in which the worker is usually rehired within a few months.

unemployment The situation of a worker who has no job and is looking for work.

unemployment insurance The government program of providing temporary benefits to workers who have lost their jobs and are currently unemployed.

unemployment rate The ratio of the number of unemployed workers to the total number of employed and unemployed workers; the fraction of the labor force that is unemployed.

vacancies The difference between the number of job openings at firms and the level of employment.

QUESTIONS AND PROBLEMS

MAINLY FOR REVIEW

10.1 What is the definition of the unemployment rate? Since it does not include workers who moved from "unemployment" to "out of the labor force," is it an underestimate of the amount of unemployment in the economy? Can you think of any reason that the unemployment rate overstates unemployment?

10.2 Suppose that a job seeker receives a wage offer, w, that exceeds his or her income while unemployed, w^u. Why might the person reject the offer?

10.3 Once a worker and a firm find a job match, why would they ever choose to end this match? List some elements that influence the rate of job separation.

10.4 What is the natural rate of unemployment? When would unemployment differ from the natural rate? Can the natural rate itself change over time?

PROBLEMS FOR DISCUSSION

10.5 The Job-Finding Rate

Discuss the effect on the job-finding rate and the expected duration of unemployment from the following:

a. An increase in unemployment-insurance benefits.

b. An increase in the minimum wage.

c. A technological shock that improves the available wage offers.

Consider a group of job seekers whose skills are hard to evaluate. For such people, the distribution of wage offers tends to have a wide dispersion. Would the job-finding rate be high or low for this group?

10.6 The Job-Separation Rate, the Job-Finding Rate, and the Natural Rate of Unemployment

Suppose that the labor force has 100 million people, of whom 92 million initially have jobs and 8 million are unemployed. Assume that the job-separation rate is 1% per period and the job-finding rate is 20% per period. Also, suppose that we can neglect movements in and out of the labor force. Trace out the path of employment and unemployment. What is the natural unemployment rate?

10.7 The Labor Force during Recessions

The data show little systematic response of the overall civilian labor force to recessions and booms. What response would you predict on theoretical grounds? (Hint: Think first about people's incentives to leave the labor force—that is, to stop looking for work—during a recession. Are there also incentives for some people to enter the labor force during bad times?)

The teenaged labor force declines during recessions. How can we explain this observation?

10.8 The Minimum Wage Rate

How does an increase in the minimum wage rate affect the employment of

a. high- and low-productivity workers in covered industries?

b. high- and low-productivity workers in uncovered industries?

What does a higher minimum wage rate mean for the unemployment rate of

a. teenagers?

b. all workers?

10.9 Vacancies and Unemployment (optional)

We considered in the text how an adverse shock to production functions could lead to higher unemployment (as well as lower employment and production).

a. What would this type of disturbance do to the number of job vacancies? How would the number of vacancies therefore relate to the level of real economic activity?

b. Consider a graph of unemployment versus vacancies. (Economists call such a graph a *Beveridge curve*, after the British economist William Beveridge.) What would you predict for the slope of this graph?

Economic Growth

This chapter considers three key determinants of long-term economic growth: the accumulation of capital, population growth, and improvements in technology. Capital should be viewed in a broad sense to encompass physical capital (machines and buildings), as well as human capital (improvements in the quality of labor due to education, training, and experience and also because of better health care and nutrition). We shall see that the accumulation of capital is an important element of growth but that the workings of diminishing returns imply that growth cannot go on forever just by adding to the capital stock. We shall also find that population growth can sustain growth in the level of output but not in the levels of product and income per capita. Finally, we shall work out the role of technological advances as a crucial mechanism for sustaining growth in the long run.

CHANGES IN THE STOCK OF CAPITAL

The previous chapter considered a production function that related a producer's output, y_t, to the previous period's stock of capital, k_{t-1}, and the quantity of labor input, l_t. We shall find it convenient for exploring long-term growth to neglect the one-period lag that we assumed before between increments to the capital stock and the use of this capital to produce goods. We also want to focus now on the aggregate of outputs and inputs. Therefore, we write the production function in aggregate form as

$$Y = F(\underset{(+)}{K}, \underset{(+)}{L}) \qquad\qquad\qquad (11.1)$$

where all variables refer to time t, but we omit the time subscripts on Y, K, and L for convenience.

We assume for now that overall population and aggregate labor input, L, are constant. We can therefore hold fixed L in equation (11.1) and focus on the relation between output, Y, and the capital stock, K. Figure 11.1 shows this relation (which we examined before in Figure 9.4). Recall that the positive slope of the curve at any point represents the marginal product of capital, MPK. As K rises (with L held fixed), the slope gets less steep because of the diminishing marginal productivity of capital.

The change in the economy's capital stock, ΔK, equals aggregate net investment, which equals gross investment less depreciation. As in Chapter 9, we assume that depreciation is the amount δK, where $\delta > 0$ is the depreciation rate.

Recall that aggregate net investment equals aggregate real saving (if we neglect changes in real money balances). We can define real **gross saving** to equal real saving plus depreciation. In the aggregate, real gross saving corresponds to gross investment or, equivalently, to the part of gross output, Y, that is not consumed. We now make the useful simplifying assumption that households set their real gross saving to

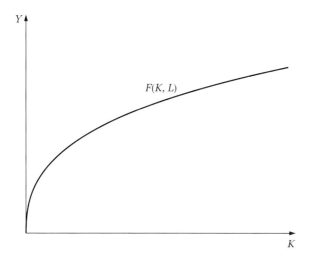

Y

$F(K, L)$

K

FIGURE 11.1

RELATION BETWEEN OUTPUT AND THE CAPITAL STOCK

The curve applies for a given quantity of labor input. The slope of the curve is the marginal product of capital, *MPK*. The slope declines as *K* rises because of diminishing marginal productivity.

equal the constant fraction, s, of gross output, Y. Then the change in the capital stock is given by

$$\Delta K = sY - \delta K = s \cdot F(K, L) - \delta K \qquad \textbf{(11.2)}$$

where s is the **saving rate**, which satisfies $0 < s < 1$.[1] Equation (11.2) says that net investment equals gross investment (and gross real saving), $s \cdot F(K, L)$, less depreciation, δK.

Figure 11.2 uses the graph of the production function from Figure 11.1 to illustrate the determination of net investment, ΔK. Gross investment, $s \cdot F(K, L)$, is the multiple s of the curve shown in Figure 11.1. Depreciation, δK, is the straight line from the origin with slope δ. Net investment is the difference between the two curves.

Figure 11.2 shows that net investment is positive for a range of capital stocks, $K > 0$. (If $K = 0$, then we assume that the economy cannot produce anything.)[2] But as K rises, diminishing returns set in, and the slope of the gross investment curve, $s \cdot F(K, L)$, gets flatter. Eventually— at the capital stock K^* shown in the figure—the curve gets flat enough

[1] *The model of economic growth that corresponds to equation (10.2) is called the Solow model and derives from the paper of Robert Solow (1956).*

[2] *This assumption leads to the chicken-and-egg problem of how any capital ever got produced. We could assume that people were born with a certain amount of human capital that enables them to produce something. This idea does not, of course, explain how the first person was created.*

ECONOMIC GROWTH

FIGURE 11.2

DETERMINATION OF THE CHANGE IN THE CAPITAL STOCK

The change in the capital stock equals net investment, which equals gross investment, $s \cdot F(K, L)$, less depreciation, δK. The change in the capital stock is positive if $K < K^*$.

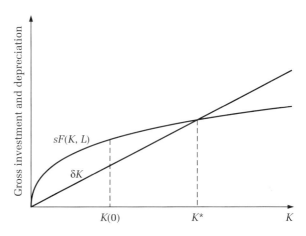

to cross the depreciation line, δK. At that point, gross investment just covers depreciation, and net investment, ΔK, equals zero.

Suppose, as an example, that the economy starts with the capital stock $K(0)$ shown in Figure 11.2. Gross investment exceeds depreciation at this point, and net investment, ΔK, is positive. The stock of capital, K, therefore rises over time, and the economy moves along the horizontal axis to the right of $K(0)$. This movement to higher values of K continues as long as ΔK is positive. That is, K increases over time as long as $K < K^*$, and K gradually approaches the value K^*. Once the capital stock gets to $K = K^*$, net investment becomes zero, and K no longer changes over time. The stock then stays fixed forever at K^*. For that reason, K^* is called the **steady-state** capital stock.[3]

Note that the capital stock, K, determines aggregate output, Y, from the production function shown in Figure 11.1, $Y = F(K, L)$, where L is a given quantity. An increase in K therefore translates into an increase in Y. It follows that Y grows over time whenever K grows, that is, as long as $0 < K < K^*$ in Figure 11.2. If the economy begins at $K = K(0)$, then Y starts at $Y(0) = F[K(0), L]$ and then grows because of capital accumulation. Eventually, K approaches K^*, and Y approaches its steady-state value, $Y^* = F(K^*, L)$. Thus, capital accumulation leads

[3] We reach the same conclusion if the economy starts with $K(0) > K^*$. Depreciation, δK, initially exceeds gross investment, $s \cdot F(K, L)$, in that case, and net investment, ΔK, is negative. Hence, K declines over time toward K^*. The steady-state capital stock, K^*, is stable in the sense that K approaches it for any starting value $K(0) > 0$.

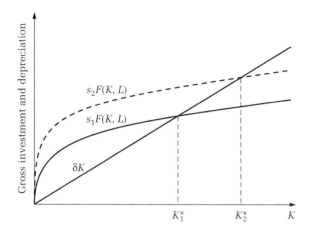

FIGURE 11.3

EFFECT OF AN INCREASE IN THE SAVING RATE

The rise in the saving rate from s_1 to s_2 raises the steady-state capital stock from K_1^* to K_2^*.

for a while—perhaps for a long time—to growth in output but cannot sustain growth in output forever. The workings of diminishing returns imply that growth vanishes in the long run.

Figure 11.3 shows that a higher saving rate shifts upward the $s \cdot F(K, L)$ curve and thereby raises K^*. A proportional upward shift in the production function, $F(K, L)$, would shift the $s \cdot F(K, L)$ curve upward in the same way as an increase in s. Therefore, K^* would again increase.

One way for $F(K, L)$ to shift upward is through a technological advance that raises the economy's productivity. However, better production possibilities for the private sector can also reflect improvements in public policies. For example, the government may provide better basic institutions that maintain property rights or deliver superior infrastructure services, such as transport and communications. These changes would also shift $F(K, L)$ upward and thereby have the effects shown in Figure 11.3.

Figure 11.4 demonstrates that a lower depreciation rate, which shifts the δK line downward, also leads to a rise in K^*. Thus, an economy has more capital and output in the long run if it saves a higher fraction of its output or has a better technology (higher $F[K, L]$ or lower δ).

FIGURE 11.4

EFFECT OF A DECREASE IN THE DEPRECIATION RATE

The fall in the depreciation rate from δ_1 to δ_2 raises the steady-state capital stock from K_1^* to K_2^*.

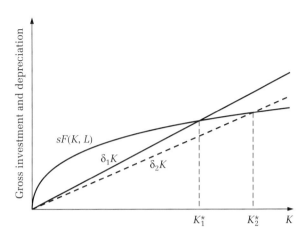

For some purposes, we want to use an algebraic determination of K^*, corresponding to the intersection between the $s \cdot F(K, L)$ and δK curves in Figure 11.2:

$$s \cdot F(K^*, L) = \delta K^* \qquad\qquad\qquad \textbf{(11.3)}$$

We can, for example, use equation (11.3) to assess the effect on K^* from an increase in the level of population and, hence, the aggregate labor input, L.

To study the effects from a change in L, we need to know what happens to output, $Y = F(K, L)$, when the two inputs, K and L, expand together. If K and L double, does the economy produce twice as much output, or more or less than twice the output? If output exactly doubles, then the production function exhibits **constant returns to scale**. Alternatively, there are **increasing returns to scale** or **decreasing returns to scale** if output more or less than doubles, respectively. The main reason that constant returns to scale would not apply is that some inputs that we have not considered, such as land, do not double when capital and labor double. Output then likely less than doubles when K and L double because the land gets more crowded. To put it another way, constant returns to scale in K and L are likely to be a reasonable approximation if land does not represent an important constraint on production possibilities. We assume for our analysis that fixed factors such as land are not so important and, hence, that constant returns to scale in K and L are a reasonable approximation.

Go back now to equation (11.3) and assume that the aggregate labor input, L, doubles. If K^* doubles, then $Y^* = F(K^*, L)$ would double because of constant returns to scale. Therefore, the left-hand side of equation (11.3) would double. Because δK^* on the right-hand side also doubles, equation (11.3) must still hold. We have therefore verified that K^* doubles if L doubles. We can also get this result qualitatively from Figure 11.3—an increase in L is another kind of change that leads to an upward shift in the $s \cdot F(K, L)$ curve.

We have found that a doubling of L leads to a doubling of K^*. Since both inputs double, Y^* must also double. More generally, K^* and Y^* change in the same proportion as L. Hence, a larger economy—with a greater population and, hence, a larger aggregate labor input, L—has a proportionately higher capital stock and level of output in the long run. To put this result another way, the steady-state quantities *per worker*, K^*/L and Y^*/L, are independent of L.

We can use Figure 11.2 to think about economies with different levels of L if we measure K^* and $K(0)$ as quantities per worker. The model then describes how capital per worker, K/L, rises from its initial value, $K(0)/L$, to its steady-state value, K^*/L. Correspondingly, output per worker, Y/L, rises from $Y(0)/L$ to Y^*/L.

Although this simple model cannot explain growth in the very long run, it can illuminate the process of growth over the transition from an initial position, $K(0)$ and $Y(0)$, to the steady-state position, K^* and Y^*. For reasonable specifications of the model, this transition turns out to take a long time—several generations, rather than several years. The properties of this transition therefore provide important insights about the growth of capital and output over a long period.

How Long Is the Transition Interval?

We found that the capital stock moves during a transition interval from its starting value, $K(0)$, to its steady-state value, K^*. A key determinant of the length of this transition interval is how rapidly the slope of $F(K, L)$ in Figure 11.1 flattens out as K rises, that is, how quickly diminishing returns to capital set in for given L. If the curve bends over rapidly, then it takes little time to reach K^*; that is, a relatively small change in K causes the $s \cdot F(K, L)$ curve in Figure 11.2 to intersect with the δK line. Conversely, if $F(K, L)$ bends over slowly, then it takes a long time. If diminishing returns to capital do not set in at all, then the $s \cdot F(K, L)$ curve in Figure 11.2 becomes a straight line, which never intersects the δK line. The steady-state capital stock, K^*, is then infinite and the transition interval is also infinite. (Capital and output, K and Y, can grow forever in this case.)

We should take a broad view of capital to include human, as well as physical, components. Education and experience and improved health are capital just as much as business plant and equipment are capital. We should then interpret L as the quantity of raw labor, that is, labor input that is not yet augmented by investments in human capital. The broad array of potential investments in physical and human capital suggests that the economy would not experience diminishing returns to capital very quickly. The steady-state value, K^*, would be finite—because diminishing returns would set in eventually—but could be very far from the typical starting value, $K(0)$. The transition interval is then finite, but long. A reasonable estimate from a full specification of the model is that it takes about 35 years—roughly a generation—to eliminate half of the gap between $K(0)$ and K^*.

CONVERGENCE

Consider a group of economies that has the same steady-state value, K^*, but different starting positions, $K(0)$. (Recall that we can allow for differences in L across economies by expressing K^* and $K[0]$ as quantities per worker.) In the model, K^* depends from Figure 11.2 and equation (11.3) on the position and slope of the production function, $F(K, L)$, and the saving and depreciation rates, s and δ. Thus, economies have similar values of K^* if they have access to about the same technologies—$F(K, L)$ and δ—and also have similar preferences about saving. Recall that we should think of $F(K, L)$ as reflecting public policies as well as the state of technology. Thus, these policies also have to be similar if economies are to have about the same values of K^*.

A key prediction of this model is that the initially poorer economies, with lower values of $K(0)$ and $Y(0)$, tend to catch up to the initially richer ones. The differences in capital stocks and outputs are gradually eliminated as each economy approaches the common steady-state values, K^* and Y^*. This tendency toward **convergence** means that the lower the starting values, $K(0)$ and $Y(0)$, the higher the average growth rate during the transition: the faster growth rate is the mechanism whereby the economies with lower starting values catch up to those with higher starting values. The model predicts, accordingly, that poor economies grow faster on average than rich economies.

For the development of a single country over time, the model predicts that growth rates will be high when capital per worker is low and will decline as capital per worker rises. Thus, we expect to find higher growth rates at early stages of development—such as in the nineteenth century for the United States—than at later stages.

A low value of capital per worker also implies a high marginal product of capital and therefore a high real interest rate, r. (Recall from Chapter 9 that investors equate capital's marginal product, MPK, to $r + \delta$.) It follows that the real interest rate would decline along with capital's marginal product as an economy develops.

POPULATION GROWTH

We already know that an increase in population, which leads to an increase in total labor input, L, causes the steady-state values, K^* and Y^*, to rise in the same proportion as L. Continuing growth of the population and the labor force lead to continuing expansion of L and, hence, of K^* and Y^*. For example, if L grows at 1% per year—a realistic number for recent U.S. experience—then K^* and Y^* also grow at 1% per year.[4] Since K and Y grow along with K^* and Y^* in the long run, population growth can sustain long-term growth in K and Y. Hence, the economy no longer tends to constant levels of capital and output if the population is continually expanding.

Suppose that the population grows at a constant rate, say 1% per year, and that aggregate labor input, L, also grows at 1% per year. The quantities K and Y then also grow in the long run at 1% per year. Since K grows at the same rate as L, the ratio K/L does not change in the long run. Similarly, Y/L is constant in the long run. Therefore, although population growth can sustain long-term growth in the levels of capital and output, it cannot sustain long-term expansion in capital per worker, K/L, or output per worker, Y/L.

If the growth rate of population is positive, then the main results from the previous discussion remain valid if we reinterpret everything in terms of quantities per worker (or per person). We must, for example, replace K and Y by K/L and Y/L, respectively. Instead of steady-state levels of variables, K^* and Y^*, we have to think about steady-state values of quantities per worker, $(K/L)^*$ and $(Y/L)^*$. Also, the statements about growth during the transition from $K(0)$ to K^*—now reexpressed as $K(0)/L(0)$ to $(K/L)^*$—translate into statements about growth of capital and output *per worker* or *per person*.[5] The previous results about convergence are correct if we say that countries with lower per capita levels of capital and output tend to have higher per capita growth rates. Similarly, the per capita growth rate for a country such as the United States

[4] *The labor force grows at a rate different from population if labor-force participation changes. For example, in recent years, the U.S. labor force rose relative to population because a larger fraction of women chose to work in the market. Two opposing forces were that people spent more time in school and tended to retire at earlier ages. In the long run, the growth of the labor force and, hence, aggregate labor input, L, depends on growth in population.*

[5] *The main complication arises in equation (11.2) if we want to interpret everything in per-worker terms, including the replacement of ΔK by the change in capital per worker, $\Delta(K/L)$. The new element is that an increase in L tends to reduce K/L for a given value of K. In L grows at the constant rate n, then a higher n means that gross investment per worker has to be higher to keep K/L from falling. In this sense, n is analogous to the depreciation rate, δ, which already appeared in equation (11.2). If fact, equation (11.2) remains valid when reexpressed in per-worker terms if we replace δ by $\delta + n$.*

would tend to decline over time as the per capita quantities of capital and output increased.

Finally, we should note that the discussion in this section allows the population growth rate to be positive, but does not consider how this growth rate is determined. We should be able to apply economic reasoning to determine population growth by thinking about the factors that influence fertility, mortality, and migration. Some classical economists, such as Thomas Malthus, David Ricardo, and Karl Marx, regarded population growth as a central element of economic analysis, although their theories did not stand up empirically. The discussion at the end of this chapter considers some recent work along these lines.

TECHNOLOGICAL PROGRESS

We already considered the effect of a one-time improvement in the technology. If the production function, $F(K, L)$, shifts upward in a proportional manner, then the $s \cdot F(K, L)$ curve shifts upward as shown in Figure 11.3. The result is that K^* increases. Steady-state output, $Y^* = F(K^*, L)$, then rises for two reasons: first, because the production function shifted upward, and second, because K^* rose. Note also that L is constant in this example. An improvement in the technology leads therefore to increases in the per-worker magnitudes, K^*/L and Y^*/L.

The results for a one-time improvement in technology suggest that the economy could sustain long-term per capita growth if the production function shifted upward continually. The technology would improve in this way if producers tended over time to discover new products and methods of production or if they learned to operate their existing methods more efficiently. Economists refer to this process of learning and discovery as **technological progress**. This kind of progress is, in fact,

FIGURE 11.5

THE APPROACH OF OUTPUT PER WORKER TO ITS STEADY-STATE PATH

The steady-state path, $(Y/L)^*$, features rising per capita product due to technological progress. Output per worker, Y/L, gradually approaches $(Y/L)^*$.

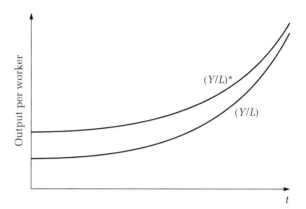

crucial to the long-term per capita growth that the U.S. economy has been able to sustain for two centuries. If the production function had remained fixed, then diminishing returns would have made it impossible to maintain per capita growth for so long just by accumulating more capital per worker. Technological progress, by allowing an escape from diminishing returns, enables the economy to grow in per capita terms, even in the long run.

The main results that we worked out before remain valid when the technology improves regularly over time. The major difference is that the per-worker quantities, K/L and Y/L, no longer tend toward fixed steady-state targets, $(K/L)^*$ and $(Y/L)^*$. We have to think instead about moving targets: for example, $(Y/L)^*$ might rise over time as shown by the upper curve in Figure 11.5, due to ongoing technological change. The actual output per worker, Y/L, then gradually approaches the moving target, $(Y/L)^*$, as shown in the figure. The approach of Y/L to $(Y/L)^*$ involves the accumulation of capital—that is, K/L adjusting toward $(K/L)^*$—just as in our previous settings.

In the long run, Y/L grows along the $(Y/L)^*$ path shown in Figure 11.5. The ratio of capital to labor, K/L, grows analogously along with $(K/L)^*$. Diminishing returns do not apply here, because the negative effect of a higher K/L on capital's marginal product is offset by technological progress. Capital's marginal product and the real interest rate therefore do not tend to fall along the steady-state path. (The marginal product and the real interest fall, as in the previous analysis, during the transition from Y/L to $[Y/L]^*$.)

The inclusion of technological progress affects some of the conclusions about convergence. The main new idea is that per capita growth rates are high not when Y/L is low in an absolute sense but rather when Y/L is far from $(Y/L)^*$, which is no longer constant over time. For a group of economies that have the same production function (and the same δ and s), the model still predicts that those with lower per capita product tend to grow faster in per capita terms. In fact, the learning and adaptation of advanced techniques provides another mechanism whereby the poorer places tend to catch up to the richer ones.

For the development of a single country over time, it is no longer necessarily true that the per capita growth rate would slow down as per capita product increased. If Y/L grows along with $(Y/L)^*$ in Figure 11.5, then the gap between $(Y/L)^*$ and Y/L does not change, and the per capita growth rate would not tend to decrease as Y/L rose. The theory says only that the per capita growth rate would fall if the spread between $(Y/L)^*$ and Y/L narrowed. An application to the United States suggests that the per capita growth rate should have been relatively high at early stages of development, perhaps for much of the nineteenth century. In the twentieth century, however, Y/L might have been close to $(Y/L)^*$— the steady-state path—and the per capita growth rate would not tend to fall as Y/L rose.

As with population growth, the discussion does not use economic analysis to explain the changes in technology. We would like, for example, to understand why producers carry out the research and development that leads to new products and better methods of production. We discuss at the end of this chapter some recent theories that attempt to explain technological progress.

The Behavior of the Saving Rate

We have assumed that the saving rate, s, does not vary as the economy grows. We now use our analysis of household behavior from earlier chapters to consider whether this assumption is plausible. For simplicity, we think about the effects in the framework that neglects technological progress. The same ideas would still apply, however, if we extended the analysis to incorporate this progress.

As the economy grows, K/L and Y/L rise toward their steady-state values, $(K/L)^*$ and $(Y/L)^*$. The increases in K/L and Y/L affect the saving rate through two channels: a substitution effect and a wealth effect. The substitution effect involves the real interest rate—recall that a higher rate gives households a greater incentive to defer consumption from the present to the future. As K/L rises, the decline in capital's marginal product, and hence in the real interest rate, reduces the incentive to defer consumption. This effect tends to lower the saving rate as the economy develops.

The wealth effect involves the behavior of Y/L and, hence, per capita real income. At early stages of development, real income is low in relation to the levels that will be attained later. The expectation of high future income—that is, the high ratio of long-run to current income—motivates households to consume more in relation to current income and, therefore, lowers the saving rate. As the economy grows and approaches the steady state, the ratio of current to future income rises. Hence, households are motivated to consume a smaller fraction of current income, and the saving rate tends to increase.

On net, the saving rate falls (or rises) as the economy develops if the effect from the declining real interest rate more (or less) than offsets the impact of growing real income. It turns out if one goes more deeply into models of saving behavior that the net effect can reasonably go in either direction. That is, there is no presumption that the saving rate will either fall or rise as an economy develops, and, moreover, the saving rate can plausibly remain roughly constant. Thus, our simplified framework that assumed a constant saving rate may be a reasonable approximation.

EVIDENCE FROM U.S. HISTORY

Table 11.1 contains data for the United States from the nineteenth and twentieth centuries on the growth rate of real gross national or domestic product (GNP or GDP), a measure of the real interest rate, and the ratios of real gross and net investment to real GNP or GDP. (The figures on GNP and investment for the nineteenth century are rough estimates.) The data are averages for the 20-year periods from 1840 to 1980 and for 1980–96. (Data are missing for 1861–68, and observations are excluded for the years around World War I, 1917–19, and World War II, 1941–46.)

A striking observation from the table is the absence of a long-term trend in the growth rate of real per capita product after around 1880. The six observations from 1880 to 1996 scatter around the mean of 1.6% per year. In contrast, the growth rates from 1840 to 1880 were higher than those that prevailed later.[6] For the full sample, the highest per capita growth rate, 3.3% per year, occurred in 1869–80 during the recovery from the Civil War. The lowest rates, 1.1% per year, were for 1880–1900 and 1920–40, periods that included lengthy depressions in the 1890s and 1930s.

The theory predicts declining per capita growth rates if an economy's output per worker, Y/L, is initially well below the steady-state path, $(Y/L)^*$ (see Figure 11.5). Thus, we can reconcile the theory with the facts if the U.S. economy began in 1840 with $Y/L < (Y/L)^*$ but had gotten close to the steady-state path by around 1880. We can then think of the U.S. economy as evolving since 1880 along a steady-state path in which the average per capita growth rate, 1.6% per year, was driven by technological progress. There is no tendency along this path for the per capita growth rate to rise or fall.[7]

The theory also implies that any decline over time in capital's marginal product would show up as a fall in real interest rates. To get a long time series on interest rates, we use the rate on prime commercial paper, a category that comprises short-term notes issued by established

[6] Note that the growth rates of population were very high in the 1800s, especially from 1840 to 1860. The pattern of high growth rates of output before 1880 is therefore more striking for the level of real GNP than for per capita real GNP.

[7] Note from Table 11.1 that there was a pronounced long-term decline in the growth rate of population, from 3.1% per year in 1840–60 to 1% per year for 1980–96.

TABLE 11.1

GROWTH RATES, INTEREST RATES, AND INVESTMENT RATIOS FOR THE UNITED STATES SINCE 1840

	Growth Rates (% per year)			Interest and Inflation Rates (% per year)[a]			Investment Ratios	
	Real GNP (GDP)	Population	Real GNP (GDP) per Capita	R	π	$r = R - \pi$	Gross Private Fixed Investment	Net Private Fixed Investment
1840–60	4.9	3.1	1.8	8.6	−0.5	9.1	—	—
1867–80	5.6[b]	2.3[b]	3.3[b]	6.7	−2.4	9.1	0.17[c]	0.09[c]
1880–1900	3.2	2.1	1.1	5.6	−0.7	6.3	0.19[d]	0.10[d]
1900–16	3.7	1.8	1.9	5.5	2.4	3.1	0.17	0.07
1920–40	2.2	1.1	1.1	3.3	−1.6	4.9	0.12	0.01
1947–60	3.1	1.7	1.3	2.3	2.5	−0.2	0.16	0.07
1960–80	3.6	1.2	2.4	5.9	4.8	1.1	0.15	0.06
1980–96	2.5	1.0	1.6	8.0	3.7	4.3	0.15	0.05

Sources: *For the data sources on real GNP (real GDP since 1959), see Figure 1.1 and Table 14.1.*

Notes: *The periods exclude the years around the three major wars, 1861–66, 1917–19, and 1941–46.*

R is the nominal interest rate on 4- to 6-month prime commercial paper. For 1857–89, the variable refers to 60- to 90-day rates, as reported in Macaulay (1938, Table 10). For 1840–56 the rates are Bigelow's estimates for the "New York and Boston money markets," as reported by Macaulay in Table 25. Interest rates since 1890 are in U.S. Department of Commerce (1975, p. 1001); Board of Governors, Federal Reserve Bulletin, various issues; and DRI data bank.

The inflation rate, π, is based on the GNP deflator since 1869 (GDP deflator since 1959). For the data sources, see Figure 1.4. Data on the price level before 1869 refer to the consumer price index, as reported in U.S. Department of Commerce (1975, p. 211).

The investment ratios equal real fixed, private, domestic investment divided by real GNP (real GDP since 1959). Data on investment for 1869–1928 are from Kendrick (1961, Tables A–I, A–III). Data since 1929 are from U.S. Department of Commerce (1986); U.S. Department of Commerce, Survey of Current Business, various issues; and DRI data bank.

[a]*Dates for the interest rate are 1840–59, 1867–79, 1880–99, 1900–15, 1920–39, 1947–59, 1960–79, and 1980–95. Thereby, the periods correspond roughly to those for the inflation rate.*

[b]*1869–80 (data on real GNP for 1867–68 are unavailable).*

[c]*1869–78.*

[d]*1879–1900.*

companies. (U.S. Treasury bills were first issued in 1929.) The real interest rate shown in Table 11.1 is the nominal interest rate less the inflation rate computed from the GNP or GDP deflator.[8] We use the actual real interest rate over periods of one or two decades to estimate the expected real interest rate.

Real interest rates from 1840 to 1880 (excluding the Civil War years) were very high, exceeding 9%, and remained above 6% from 1880 to 1900. For 1900–40 (excluding the years of World War I), the real rates averaged about 4%. After World War II, real interest rates were much lower, averaging less than 1% for 1947–80. In contrast, for 1980–96, the real interest rates averaged 4.3%, a value similar to that experienced before World War II.

The excess of the real interest rates in the nineteenth century—especially those from 1840 to 1880—over those of the twentieth century suggests a fall in capital's marginal product from one century to the next. The pattern during the twentieth century is less clear because the average of real rates from 1980 to 1996 was as high as those from the early years of the century. If we think of the real interest rates for the twentieth century as showing no long-term trend, then the results are consistent with rough stability of capital's marginal product over this period. We can again explain this behavior by arguing that the twentieth-century U.S. economy was evolving along a steady-state path, driven by technological progress. Although the ratio of capital to labor, K/L, rose over time, technological progress offset the tendency for diminishing returns. The theory is therefore consistent with the absence of a trend in capital's marginal product and, hence, in real interest rates during the twentieth century.

Table 11.1 also shows the ratios of gross and net fixed private investment to GNP or GDP. The gross numbers indicate a nearly constant ratio in the long run. The net figures suggest some long-term decline, corresponding to an increase in the ratio of depreciation to GNP or GDP. (However, given the errors in estimating depreciation, we should

[8] *Because the GNP deflator is unavailable for 1840–60, the inflation rate for this period is computed from the consumer price index.*

probably have more confidence in the gross numbers.) Recall that the theory of economic growth in this chapter assumed that the ratio of gross investment to output equaled a constant, s. Thus, the suggestion from the U.S. data is that this assumption may be a satisfactory approximation for long-run analysis. (The long-term stability of the gross investment ratio turns out, however, to hold much less well for other developed countries.)

To summarize, we can think of the U.S. economy as starting in 1840 with a low value of output per worker, Y/L, relative to the steady-state path, $(Y/L)^*$. The economy then went through a convergence interval in which the per capita growth rate and real interest rate were high, but declining over time. By the end of the nineteenth century, the economy had come close to the steady-state path. The economy evolved subsequently along this path: accordingly, the per capita growth rate and real interest rate showed no long-term trends during the twentieth century.

EVIDENCE ON CONVERGENCE FROM THE U.S. STATES AND REGIONS OF WESTERN EUROPE[9]

Figure 11.6 considers the growth of per capita income for 47 U.S. states or territories from 1880 to 1990. (The data for Oklahoma are unavailable because 1880 preceded the Oklahoma land rush.) The plot shows a remarkably strong inverse correlation between the average growth rate and the 1880 level of per capita income. That is, the initially poorer states grew significantly faster in per capita terms and thereby tended to catch up to the initially richer states.

Figure 11.7 depicts the convergence process in terms of the levels of average per capita income of the four regions: Northeast, South, Midwest, and West. The southern states tended to have low per capita incomes in 1880 (largely because of the Civil War) and high average growth

[9] This evidence comes from studies by Robert Barro and Xavier Sala-i-Martin (1991, 1992).

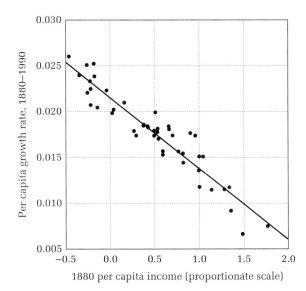

FIGURE 11.6

GROWTH OF PER CAPITA INCOME FOR U.S. STATES, 1880–1990

The average growth rate of per capita personal income, shown on the vertical axis, is inversely related to the initial level of per capita income, shown on the horizontal. (The horizontal axis uses a proportionate scale.)

rates thereafter.[10] The western states had high average incomes in 1880 (principally because of opportunities in mining), followed by low average growth rates. Thus, the figure shows that the average income levels for the four regions converged dramatically over the 110 years after 1880.

Although regional catch-up is part of the convergence story, the tendency for the poorer states to grow faster in per capita terms holds equally well within the regions. For example, the relatively poor eastern states, such as Maine and Vermont in 1880, tended to catch up to the relatively rich eastern states, such as Massachusetts and Rhode Island in 1880, about as fast as the typical southern state tended to catch up to the typical western or eastern state. Thus, the data for the U.S. states clearly reveal the convergence pattern predicted by the growth theory developed in this chapter.

We can also use the U.S. evidence to assess the speed of convergence. The pattern displayed in Figure 11.6 turns out to imply that the spread in levels of per capita income between the typical poor and rich

[10] *The average per capita income for 15 southern states was 51% of that for 21 eastern and midwestern states in 1880 and 86% in 1990. In contrast, before the Civil War in 1840, the available data (for a narrower concept of income) indicate that 11 southern states had an average per capita income that was 80% of that for 18 eastern and midwestern states. Thus, the southern states became markedly poorer than the northern states only because of the war.*

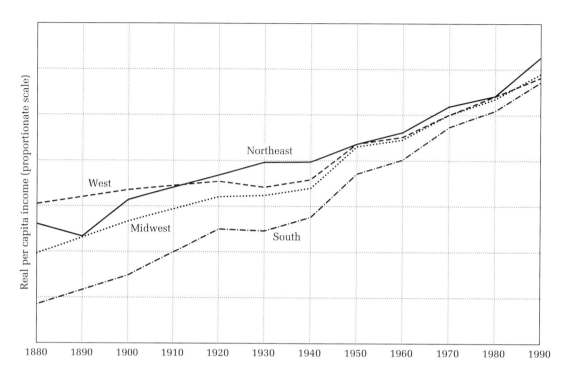

FIGURE 11.7

INCOME PER CAPITA FOR FOUR U.S. REGIONS

The spread of per capita personal income across the four regions narrowed substantially between 1880 and 1990.

state vanishes at roughly 2% per year. This speed of adjustment implies that the *half life* of convergence—the time that it takes to eliminate half of the initial gap—is about 35 years. For the states to get still closer together, say to eliminate three quarters of the initial spread, takes about 70 years. Figure 11.7 shows how these estimates of convergence times relate to the regional performance: although the level of per capita income in the South eventually got close to that in the other regions, it took about a century for this process to occur.

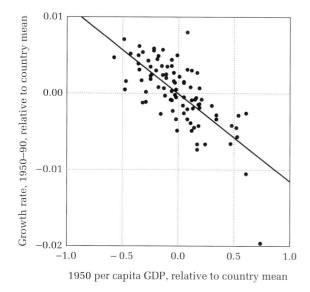

FIGURE 11.8

GROWTH OF PER CAPITA GDP FOR 90 EUROPEAN REGIONS, 1950–90

The growth rate of per capita GDP, shown on the vertical axis, is inversely related to the initial level of per capita GDP, shown on the horizontal. (The horizontal axis uses a proportionate scale.) See Figure 11.9 and Table 11.2 for a listing of the regions.

Figure 11.8 provides evidence on convergence for 90 regions of 8 western European countries from 1950 to 1990. (The data are for 11 regions in Germany, 11 in the United Kingdom, 20 in Italy, 21 in France, 4 in the Netherlands, 3 in Belgium, 3 in Denmark, and 17 in Spain: see Figure 11.9 and Table 11.2 for a listing of the regions.) Figure 11.8 shows that the average growth rate of per capita gross domestic product (GDP) on the vertical axis is inversely related to the 1950 level of per capita GDP, shown on the horizontal.[11] Thus, as with the U.S. states, the poorer regions grew faster in per capita terms than the richer regions and therefore tended to catch up in levels of per capita GDP. The results for the European regions also accord quantitatively with those for the U.S. states: the rate of convergence implied by Figure 11.8 turns out again to be about 2% per year.

[11] *The regional growth rates and levels of per capita GDP are expressed relative to the respective means for each country. The pattern shown in Figure 11.8 still appears if the country means are not subtracted out.*

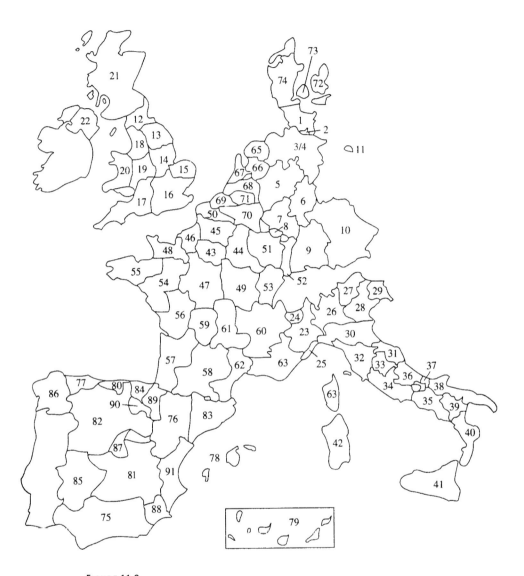

FIGURE 11.9

MAP OF EUROPEAN REGIONS

See Table 11.2 for the names of the regions. The map is adapted from Molle (1980, p. 20).

TABLE 11.2

LIST OF EUROPEAN REGIONS SHOWN IN FIGURES 11.8 AND 11.9

Germany	25.	Liguria	54.	Pays de la Loire	Spain
	26.	Lombardia	55.	Bretagne	
1. Schleswig-Holstein	27.	Trentino–Alto Adige	56.	Poitou-Charentes	75. Andalucia
2. Hamburg	28.	Veneto	57.	Aquitaine	76. Aragon
3. Niedersachsen	29.	Friuli-Venezia, Giulia	58.	Midi-Pyrénées	77. Asturias
4. Bremen	30.	Emilia-Romagna	59.	Limousin	78. Balears
5. Nordrhein-Westfalen	31.	Marche	60.	Rhône-Alpes	79. Canarias
6. Hessen	32.	Toscana	61.	Auvergne	80. Cantabria
7. Rheinland-Pfalz	33.	Umbria	62.	Languedoc-Roussillon	81. Castilla La Mancha
8. Saarland	34.	Lazio	63.	Provence-Alpes–Côte	82. Castilla-Leon
9. Baden-Württemberg	35.	Campania		d'Azur–Corse[a]	83. Catalunya
10. Bayern	36.	Abruzzi			84. Euskadi (Basque)
11. Berlin (West)	37.	Molise	Netherlands		85. Extremadura
	38.	Puglia			86. Galicia
United Kingdom	39.	Basilicata	65.	Noord	87. Madrid
	40.	Calabria	66.	Oost	88. Murcia
12. North	41.	Sicilia	67.	West	89. Navarra
13. Yorkshire-Humberside	42.	Sardegna	68.	Zuid	90. LaRioja
14. East Midlands					91. Valencia
15. East Anglia	France		Belgium		
16. Southeast					
17. Southwest	43.	Région Parisienne	69.	Vlaanderen	
18. Northwest	44.	Champagne-Ardenne	70.	Wallonie	
19. West Midlands	45.	Picardie	71.	Brabant	
20. Wales	46.	Haute Normandie			
21. Scotland	47.	Centre	Denmark		
22. Northern Ireland	48.	Basse Normandie			
	49.	Bourgogne	72.	Sjalland-Lolland-	
Italy	50.	Nord-Pas-de-Calais		Falster-Bornholm	
	51.	Lorraine	73.	Fyn	
23. Piemonte	52.	Alsace	74.	Jylland	
24. Valle d'Aosta	53.	Franche-Comté			

[a]*GDP data from Eurostat for Corse were combined with those for Provence-Alpes–Côte d' Azur.*

EVIDENCE ON CONVERGENCE ACROSS COUNTRIES

Figure 11.10 plots the growth rate of real per capita gross domestic product (GDP) from 1960 to 1990 for 114 countries against the level of real per capita GDP in 1960.[12] This data set includes most of the countries in the world: the main exceptions are most of the countries of eastern and central Europe and some smaller countries with missing data. (See Table 11.3 for a listing of the countries included in Figure 11.10.) The range of real per capita GDP in 1960 is from $250 for Ethiopia to $9800 for the United States (in terms of 1985 U.S. dollars).

Unlike the regional findings depicted in Figures 11.6 and 11.7, the diagram in Figure 11.10 reveals little relation between initial per capita GDP and the subsequent per capita growth rate. If anything, the initially poorer countries grew at a somewhat below-average rate from 1960 to 1990. Thus, these data do not conform to the convergence hypothesis that came from our theory of economic growth.

[12] *The data on real GDP are from Robert Summers and Alan Heston (1996). These data use internationally comparable price indexes to measure real GDP across countries.*

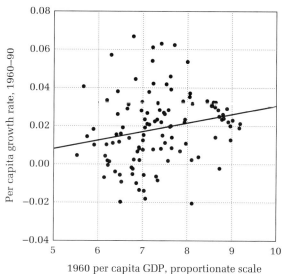

FIGURE 11.10

GROWTH OF PER CAPITA GDP FOR 114 COUNTRIES, 1960–90

The growth rate of per capita GDP, shown on the vertical axis, bears little relation to the initial level of per capita GDP, shown on the horizontal. (The horizontal axis uses a proportionate scale.) Table 11.3 lists the countries.

TABLE 11.3

LIST OF COUNTRIES IN FIGURE 11.10

1. Algeria	30. Rwanda	59. Bolivia	88. Thailand
2. Benin	31. Senegal	60. Brazil	89. Austria
3. Botswana	32. Seychelles	61. Chile	90. Belgium
4. Burkina Faso	33. Somalia	62. Colombia	91. Cyprus
5. Burundi	34. South Africa	63. Ecuador	92. Denmark
6. Cameroon	35. Sudan	64. Guyana	93. Finland
7. Cape Verde Islands	36. Swaziland	65. Paraguay	94. France
8. Central African Republic	37. Tanzania	66. Peru	95. Germany
9. Chad	38. Togo	67. Suriname	96. Greece
10. Comoros	39. Tunisia	68. Uruguay	97. Iceland
11. Congo	40. Uganda	69. Venezuela	98. Ireland
12. Egypt	41. Zaire	70. Bangladesh	99. Italy
13. Ethiopia	42. Zambia	71. Hong Kong	100. Luxembourg
14. Gabon	43. Zimbabwe	72. India	101. Malta
15. Gambia	44. Barbados	73. Indonesia	102. Netherlands
16. Ghana	45. Canada	74. Iran	103. Norway
17. Guinea-Bissau	46. Costa Rica	75. Iraq	104. Portugal
18. Ivory Coast	47. Dominican Republic	76. Israel	105. Spain
19. Kenya	48. El Salvador	77. Japan	106. Sweden
20. Lesotho	49. Guatemala	78. Jordan	107. Switzerland
21. Madagascar	50. Haiti	79. South Korea	108. Turkey
22. Malawi	51. Honduras	80. Malaysia	109. United Kingdom
23. Mali	52. Jamaica	81. Nepal	110. Yugoslavia
24. Mauritania	53. Mexico	82. Pakistan	111. Australia
25. Mauritius	54. Nicaragua	83. Philippines	112. Fiji
26. Morocco	55. Panama	84. Singapore	113. New Zealand
27. Mozambique	56. Trinidad and Tobago	85. Sri Lanka	114. Papua New Guinea
28. Niger	57. United States	86. Syria	
29. Nigeria	58. Argentina	87. Taiwan	

ECONOMIC GROWTH

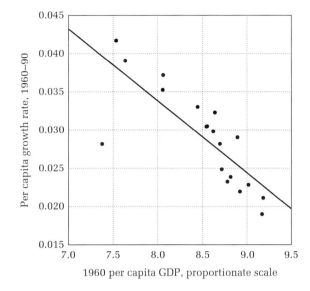

Figure 11.11 limits the sample to the 20 countries that were members of the Organization of Economic Cooperation and Development (OECD) by 1960.[13] Aside from having much higher average per capita GDP than the 114 countries considered in Figure 11.10, the OECD countries are more similar in terms of basic economic and political institutions. Figure 11.11 exhibits an inverse relation between the average per capita growth rate and the initial level of per capita GDP. Thus, a pattern of convergence does show up for this relatively homogeneous collection of well-off countries. The relation does, however, differ quantitatively from that found for the regions of the United States or western Europe in Figures 11.6 and 11.8. For the 20 OECD countries, the gap between poor and rich vanishes at about 1% per year, in contrast to the 2% per year found for the regions. Thus, although convergence appears among the OECD countries, the speed is slower than that for the regions.

In the first model that we considered, we derived the convergence hypothesis—poor economies growing faster than rich ones—by assuming that the various economies had the same steady-state values, K^* and

[13] *The 20 members of the OECD in 1960 were Austria, Belgium, Canada, Denmark, France, Germany, Greece, Iceland, Ireland, Italy, Luxembourg, Netherlands, Norway, Portugal, Spain, Sweden, Switzerland, Turkey, United Kingdom, and United States. Australia, Finland, Japan, and New Zealand became members a few years later.*

Y^*. Figure 11.2 and equation (11.3) showed that these values were the same if economies had the same production functions, $F(K, L)$, and also had the same depreciation and saving rates, δ and s. Recall also that for $F(K, L)$ to be the same we have to assume that the economies have similar public institutions and otherwise follow similar public policies.

In the extended models that allow for population growth and technological progress, the convergence hypothesis depends on each country having the same steady-state path, $(Y/L)^*$, shown in Figure 11.5. The poor grow faster per capita than the rich if poor and rich are approaching the same (moving) target. The target is the same, however, only if the economies are similar with respect to the available technology, the public policies followed, and the values of δ and s. The countries must also have the same rates of population growth and technological progress.

The notion that all these characteristics are roughly the same may be satisfactory as a first-order approximation in a long-run analysis of the U.S. states and the regions of countries in western Europe. However, the approximation would be inaccurate for the OECD countries and would be especially unreasonable for the heterogeneous collection of 114 countries. Thus, we should return to the theory to see how differences across economies in the steady-state path, $(Y/L)^*$, modify the convergence hypothesis.

The key idea is that per capita growth is higher the larger the gap between $(Y/L)^*$ and Y/L. Consider two countries, A and B, such that $(Y/L)_A$ is twice as large as $(Y/L)_B$. The poor country, B, grows faster than A if it has the same steady-state path as A. But if $(Y/L)^*_A$ were twice as large as $(Y/L)^*_B$, then the two countries would grow at the same rate. The point is that the theory implies a form of **conditional convergence**. The growth rate does not depend on the *absolute* value of Y/L, but rather on the value conditioned on the economy's own steady-state position. If a country has low per-worker output, but also has low per-worker product along the steady-state path, then the theory does not predict that this country will grow rapidly.

ECONOMIC GROWTH

415

One reason for a country to have a low value of $(Y/L)^*$ is that is has a low saving rate, s. It turns out that another reason for a low value of $(Y/L)^*$ is a high rate of population growth. A country also has a low value of $(Y/L)^*$ if it has access only to poor technologies, that is, if the level of the production function, $F(K, L)$, is low or if the technology does not improve rapidly over time.

Empirically, however, it seems that the most important reason for countries to have different target positions is that they differ with respect to public policies, broadly interpreted to include differences in basic institutions. For example, if governments fail to protect property rights, restrict trade, expend too many resources on unproductive activities, or provide poor infrastructure services such as transport and communication, then the country operates as if it had a low level of technology and, hence, a low value of $(Y/L)^*$.

The idea of conditional convergence can explain why convergence does not show up for the broad group of countries in Figure 11.10 but does arise for the more homogeneous subgroup of countries in Figure 11.11 and appears even more strongly for the regions of the United States and western Europe in Figures 11.6 and 11.8. The countries considered in Figure 11.10 differ substantially in terms of basic political and economic institutions and are therefore likely to vary considerably in their steady-state path, $(Y/L)^*$. The poor countries are, in particular, likely to be poor for good reason in the sense that the poverty reflects inadequacies of government policies or other factors that affect the willingness to save, invest, and work. Unfortunately, these kinds of adverse conditions tend to persist over time. Thus, although per-worker product, Y/L, is low in these countries, it does not tend to be systematically low in relation to the steady-state value, $(Y/L)^*$. This observation explains why the poor countries in Figure 11.11 do not grow on average at high rates.

If we shift the focus to a more homogeneous collection of economies, such as the OECD countries or, even more so, to the regions of the United States and western Europe, then the similarities of policies and institutions suggest that the steady-state values, $(Y/L)^*$, would be similar.

A low level of Y/L therefore signals a greater departure from $(Y/L)^*$. It follows that a simple pattern of convergence—the poor growing in per capita terms faster than the rich—shows up within these homogeneous groups. Moreover, the slower rate of convergence among the OECD countries than for the regions of the United States or western Europe can be explained by noting that the regions within a single country are likely to be more similar in terms of government policies and institutions than are the 20 OECD countries.

A further empirical challenge is to extend the analysis of growth across the broad group of countries considered in Figure 11.10 to isolate some of the factors that determine the steady-state path, $(Y/L)^*$. If we can hold constant $(Y/L)^*$, then the inverse relation between the per capita growth rate and the starting level of per capita product should emerge—that is, we should see conditional convergence in the data.

In a recent study of economic growth across countries (Barro, 1997), I explored the role of a number of explanatory variables, including measures of government policies. Once these variables are held constant, the relation between the growth rate of real per capita GDP from 1960 to 1990 and the level of real per capita GDP in 1960 looks similar to the results described before for the U.S. states and the regions of western Europe. The gap between a country's initial real per capita GDP and its own steady-state path vanishes at around 2–3% per year. This result from the cross-country data confirms the conditional convergence that is predicted by the theory.

It is important to recognize that these cross-country findings demonstrate convergence only in a very limited sense. A country tends to grow faster per capita if it starts farther below its own long-run target. This result does not mean that the typical less-developed country (LDC) in Africa, South Asia, or Latin America will tend to catch up to the currently prosperous countries. The long-run targets of these LDCs seem, on average, to be as low as their current actual positions; therefore, the LDCs on average are not growing at higher per capita rates than the prosperous countries.

The empirical results also provide indications about which kinds of government policies and other variables matter for a country's steady-state path, $(Y/L)^*$. This path appears to be lower the worse the maintenance of the rule of law and property rights, the less the country is open to international trade, the higher the share of government consumption expenditures in GDP, the lower the propensity to invest, the higher the tendency to have children and thereby have higher population growth, and the higher the long-run inflation rate. There is also evidence that a country tends to converge faster to its long-run target, $(Y/L)^*$, if it begins with higher stocks of human capital in the form of education and health. The effects on economic growth of these and other variables are currently the subject of intensive research.

RECENT THEORIES OF ECONOMIC GROWTH (OPTIONAL)

A serious deficiency of the theory is that the long-term growth rate depends entirely on factors—the rates of population growth and technological progress—that are not determined within the model. For long-term per capita growth, only the unexplained technological progress matters. In terms of the jargon used in the literature, the long-run growth rate is *exogenous*, that is, determined from outside. The framework does not provide a theory of long-run **endogenous growth** in which the long-term growth rate is determined by interactions within the model.

Research on theories of endogenous growth has been active over the last decade.[14] One area involves models of technological progress that are embedded into theories of economic growth. Another area considers theories of population growth that are integrated with models of growth. Still another strand of theory has dispensed with the idea of the diminishing productivity of capital. It is possible here only to sketch some of the basic ideas in the various approaches to endogenous long-term growth.

[14] *For a technical survey of this research, see Barro and Sala-i-Martin (1995).*

THEORIES OF TECHNOLOGICAL PROGRESS

For countries on the leading edge of technology, such as the United States, it is important to model the process of research and development, a process that leads over time to new and improved products.[15] The businesses that invest in research to come up with new ideas or better designs have to be compensated for their efforts. Typically, this compensation takes the form of exclusive, or at least preferred, access to the new products or methods of production for some interval of time. In some cases, the property rights in the new products or methods are enforced by patents, but, more often, the preferred access derives from secrecy or advantages from having moved first into a new area.

The economy's growth rate involves a trade-off in which inventions are encouraged by a greater private reward to discoveries, whereas efficiency—after inventions have already been made—dictates free access by many competitors to the available technologies. The results in these kinds of models have implications for desirable patent policy as well as for government subsidies of research efforts. If the private benefit from research falls short of the social benefits, then the amount of research and the consequent rates of technological progress and economic growth tend to be too low from a social perspective. For this reason, some of the models in this area rationalize a public subsidy to basic research (especially to research conducted by economists!).

For most countries, the important consideration is not discoveries of basic knowledge but rather the rate of absorption of the new methods that have been introduced by the leading countries. The advantages of being a follower—not having to invest resources in basic research—provides another force toward convergence across countries. That is, the poorer countries can grow faster because it is cheaper to adapt advanced techniques than to make one's own discoveries. Another point is that human capital is central to the ability to adopt new technologies. The tendency for growth rates across countries to be positively related to

[15] *Some important, but technically demanding, contributions in this area are by Paul Romer (1990) and Gene Grossman and Elhanan Helpman (1991, Chaps. 3 and 4).*

initial human capital may therefore reflect the enhanced capacity for using the technological advances that have been developed in other countries.

POPULATION GROWTH

Some theories of economic growth incorporate models in which parents choose their number of children and, hence, the growth rate of population.[16] The number of children per adult amounts to a form of investment. More investment of this type, that is, a larger number of children per adult, substitutes for other forms of investment, especially for resources spent improving the quality of each child. Hence, the theory predicts an inverse relation between fertility and the growth rate of per capita product: this relation reflects especially the negative linkage between fertility and the rate of investment in human capital. It is also possible, as in the classic analysis of Thomas Malthus (1809), to bring in a linkage between income and population growth that involves the response of health and mortality.

The empirical evidence across countries bears out some of the predictions about the role of population growth. For instance, there is a strong inverse association across countries between fertility rates and educational attainment, especially attainment of women. Moreover, for given education, the growth rate of per capita GDP is negatively related to the fertility rate.

CONSTANT-RETURNS MODELS

Diminishing productivity of capital seems natural if we define capital narrowly to include only machines and buildings. As this kind of capital rises in relation to the quantity of labor (and natural resources), we predict that capital's marginal product will fall. If we take a broader view of capital to include investments in persons, then the tendency for diminishing productivity is less obvious. The quantity of labor is no

[16] *See, for example, Richard Easterlin (1968), Gary Becker (1981), and Gary Becker and Robert Barro (1988).*

longer fixed, because the investments in humans effectively raise the quantity of labor available. We expect diminishing returns only if the number of bodies (or the quantity of natural resources) represents an important constraint on the production process.

We found before that an economy's long-term growth rate cannot be driven entirely by capital accumulation if capital's productivity is subject to diminishing returns. But the conclusions are different if diminishing productivity does not apply to capital, broadly construed. In this case, even without technological progress, capital accumulation can be sufficient to sustain long-term per capita growth.

One shortcoming of models without diminishing returns is that they do not predict the kinds of convergence results that we discussed before. In the constant-returns models, the growth rate does not depend on the starting level of per capita product. Thus, these theories do not accord with the empirical evidence, summarized earlier, that reveals absolute convergence for homogeneous groups of economies and at least conditional convergence for more heterogeneous groups. A promising research strategy is therefore to stick with the models that featured diminishing returns—although these diminishing returns likely set in slowly when human capital is considered—but extend them to include the theories of technological change and population growth that we sketched in this section. The diffusion of technology from advanced to follower countries is an important part of this framework.

SUMMARY

We began with a simple model in which economic growth depended on the accumulation of capital. The workings of diminishing returns imply that the capital stock and output approach fixed steady-state values; that is, growth vanishes in the long run. The steady-state levels of the capital stock and output are higher if the economy saves a larger fraction of its output, if producers have access to better technologies, and if governments follow more effective public policies. If the production function satisfies constant returns to scale in capital and labor, then the steady-state values of capital and output are proportional to the labor force.

The transition to the steady state features a declining growth rate of output and a falling real interest rate. These effects correspond to reductions in the marginal product of capital, due to diminishing returns. The model therefore predicts that an economy's growth rate of output will decline as it develops and approaches its steady state. If we consider a group of economies that have the same steady-state positions, then the initially poorer economies will grow faster and thereby converge toward the initially richer economies.

Continuing population growth leads to long-term growth of the levels of capital and output but not to long-term growth of the per capita quantities. The theory with population growth therefore predicts that the growth rate of per capita product will be inversely related to the initial level of per capita product. Some recent theories apply economic reasoning to the determinants of population growth.

Technological progress can offset the tendency for diminishing returns and lead thereby to long-term growth of per capita output. The per capita growth rate and the real interest rate still decline in the transition to the steady state. Once an economy reaches its steady state, per capita output rises steadily, but the growth rate and the real interest rate do not tend to decline. Recent theories try to explain the process of research and experience that leads to technological progress. Some of these theories also consider the diffusion of technologies from leading countries to followers.

The U.S. time-series data show that growth rates of real per capita output and real interest rates tended to decline during the nineteenth century but have shown no systematic pattern in the twentieth century. The theoretical interpretation is that the United States was converging toward its steady-state path during the nineteenth century and has been growing during the twentieth century along a steady-state path driven by technological progress.

The experiences of the U.S. states since 1880 and the regions of eight western European countries since 1950 show clear evidence of convergence in the sense of poorer regions growing faster than richer ones. This evidence indicates that the gap between the typical rich and poor region vanishes at roughly 2% per year. It therefore takes about 35 years to eliminate one-half of the initial gap.

The behavior across about 100 countries in the post–World War II period shows no tendency for the poor to grow faster per capita than the rich. We can explain this failure of convergence if we assume that countries differ in their steady-state positions because of differences in government policies, saving rates, and other factors. The data are consistent with conditional convergence in the sense that a country grows faster if it starts further away from its own steady-state position. In this interpretation, the typical less-developed country in Africa, South Asia, or Latin America did not grow rapidly from 1960 to 1990 because its low initial value of real per capita GDP was roughly matched by its low steady-state value.

IMPORTANT TERMS AND CONCEPTS

conditional convergence   The idea that poor countries grow faster than rich ones for given values of government policies, propensities to save and have children, and other variables.

constant returns to scale   The property of some production functions that a proportionate increase in all inputs results in an equiproportionate increase in output.

convergence   The tendency of a poor economy to grow at a higher rate per capita than a rich economy and thereby to catch up to the rich economy.

decreasing returns to scale The property of some production functions that a proportionate increase in all inputs results in a less than proportionate increase in output.

endogenous growth Long-run economic growth that is explained by the interactions within a model.

gross saving Saving measured without adjustment for depreciation of capital stocks. The total gross saving of an economy equals GNP less private consumption expenditure and government consumption.

increasing returns to scale The property of some production functions that a proportionate increase in all inputs results in a more than proportionate increase in output.

saving rate The ratio of saving to income. The gross saving rate is the ratio of gross saving (including depreciation of capital) to gross income.

steady state A situation in which the rate of growth of the economy is zero so that the capital stock, output, consumption, gross investment, and work effort are all constant. In a situation of steady-state growth, these variables grow at constant rates, rather than staying constant.

technological progress Improved knowledge about methods of production that shifts the production function upward.

QUESTIONS AND PROBLEMS

MAINLY FOR REVIEW

11.1 Does a positive saving rate, s, mean that the capital stock grows over time? Explain by referring to equation (11.2).

11.2 Consider the steady-state capital stock, K^*, determined from equation (11.3). How is K^* affected by the following?

a. An increase in the saving rate, s.

b. An upward shift in the production function, $F(K, L)$.

c. An increase in the depreciation rate, δ.

11.3 If labor input, L, doubles, why does equation (11.3) imply that the steady-state capital stock and output double? How does the result depend on constant returns to scale in the production function?

11.4 Explain why an increase in the capital stock, K, tends to reduce the growth rate of the capital stock, $\Delta K/K$, and the real interest rate. How do these results depend on diminishing returns to capital?

11.5 What is the meaning of the term convergence? How does absolute convergence differ from relative convergence?

11.6 For the United States, Table 11.1 shows that the real interest rate had no clear trend in the twentieth century. Does this result conflict with the theoretical prediction that the real interest rate would decline as the capital stock rose? What about the observation that the real interest rate declined substantially from 1840 to 1900?

11.7 For 114 countries from 1960 to 1990, the growth rate of real per capita GDP shows little relation to the level of real per capita GDP in 1960. Does this finding conflict with our theory of economic growth? How does this question relate to the concept of conditional convergence?

11.8 Constant Returns to Scale

Suppose that the production function, $F(K, L)$, satisfies constant returns to scale. This condition means that if we multiply the inputs, K and L, by any positive number, then we multiply output, Y, by the same number. Show that this condition implies that we can write the production function as $Y/L = f(K/L)$. (Hint: use $1/L$ as the number that multiplies the inputs, K and L.) What is the meaning of this result?

11.9 Growth with a Cobb-Douglas Production Function

Suppose that the production function takes the form $Y = F(K, L) = AK^\alpha L^{1-\alpha}$, where $A > 0$, L is the constant labor force, and $0 < \alpha < 1$. (This form is called a *Cobb-Douglas production function*, named after the former U.S. Senator and economist Paul Douglas and a mathematician associate, apparently named Cobb.)

a. Use equation (11.3) to work out formulas for the steady-state values, K^* and Y^*, when the production function is Cobb-Douglas.

b. What are the steady-state values of investment, I^*, and consumption, C^*?

c. Use equation (11.2) to work out a formula for the growth rate of the capital stock, $\Delta K/K$. Can you show that this growth rate declines as the capital stock rises?

d. With a Cobb-Douglas production function, we can write the growth rate of output as $\Delta Y/Y = \alpha \cdot (\Delta K/K) + (1 - \alpha) \cdot \Delta L/L$. (We can derive this result from calculus.) In the present case, $\Delta L = 0$. Use the answer from part c to work out a formula for the growth rate of output, $\Delta Y/Y$. Does this growth rate decline as K rises? Does it also decline as Y rises?

11.10 Effects of Saving Behavior on Convergence

Suppose that the gross saving rate, s, can change as an economy develops.

a. Is equation (11.2) still valid if s is the saving rate that applies at a point in time?

b. Suppose that s declines as an economy develops (because the saving rate is low when the marginal product of capital is low). How does this property affect the tendency for the growth rate of capital, $\Delta K/K$, to decline as the levels of K and Y increase? What does this behavior mean for the convergence property?

c. Suppose, instead, that s rises as an economy develops (because the saving rate is high when the level of income is closer to its steady-state value). What does this behavior mean for the convergence property?

11.11 Absolute and Conditional Convergence

Equation (11.2) implies that the growth rate of the capital stock is given by $\Delta K/K = sY/K - \delta$. Equation (11.3) implies that the (constant) gross saving rate satisfies the condition $s = \delta K^*/Y^*$. If we substitute out for s in the expression for the growth rate, then we get

$$\Delta K/K = \delta \cdot \left(\frac{Y/K}{Y^*/K^*} - 1 \right)$$

Note that Y/K is the average product of capital. For given L, this average product declines as K rises (because of diminishing productivity of capital).

a. Consider a group of economies that have the same steady-state values, K^* and Y^*. Does absolute convergence—poor economies growing faster than rich ones—hold for $\Delta K/K$?

b. Suppose that economies differ in their steady-state values, Y^*/K^*. Do we get conditional convergence for $\Delta K/K$ but not necessarily absolute convergence?

c. Do the results in parts a and b depend on the assumption that the gross saving rate, s, is constant?

11.12 Growth without Diminishing Returns

Suppose that the production function is $Y = AK$ (the so-called *AK model*), where A is a positive constant.

a. What is the condition for the change in the capital stock, ΔK, in equation (11.2)? What does the $s \cdot F(K, L)$ curve look like in Figure 11.2?

b. What is the growth rate of the capital stock, $\Delta K/K$, and output, $\Delta Y/Y$? Are these growth rates positive? Does the convergence property hold in this model?

c. Discuss how the results relate to diminishing returns to capital. Is it plausible that diminishing returns would not apply?

11.13 Effects of Population Growth (optional)

Suppose that population and the labor force grow at the constant rate n and that the gross saving rate is still the constant s.

a. Is equation (11.2) valid? Does the economy still tend toward constant steady-state values, K^* and Y^*?

b. Use equation (11.2) to derive the change over time in capital per worker, K/L. (Use the condition $\Delta(K/L) = \Delta K/L - (K/L) \cdot (\Delta L/L)$, where $\Delta L/L = n$. We can show from calculus that this condition holds exactly for infinitesimal changes.) Does K/L tend toward a constant, steady-state value, $(K/L)^*$? What determines this value? (Hint: problem 11.8 shows that if the production function, $F(K, L)$, exhibits constant returns to scale, then it is possible to write output per worker as a function only of capital per worker: $Y/L = f(K/L)$. That is, Y/L depends only on the ratio of K to L and is independent of the scale of the economy.)

c. Does population growth lead to growth of output in the long run? Does it lead in the long run to growth of per capita output?

11.14 Effects of Technological Progress (optional)

Suppose that technological change leads to steady improvements in the production function. We can represent these changes by including time, t, in the production function: $Y = F(K, L, t)$, where t has a positive effect on Y for given values of K and L. A simple form of technological progress operates by making each worker more productive. If L is constant, then the effective number of workers, denoted by $\hat{L}$, grows at the rate $x > 0$. We can write the production function in this case as $Y = F(K, \hat{L})$, where $\Delta \hat{L}/\hat{L} = x$. (This form of technical progress is called *labor augmenting*.) The effects are then formally similar to those from population growth, as discussed in problem 11.13.

a. Is equation (11.2) valid? Does the economy still tend toward constant steady-state values, K^* and Y^*?

b. Use equation (11.2) to derive the change over time in capital per effective worker, $K/\hat{L}$. (Use the condition $\Delta(K/\hat{L}) = \Delta K/\hat{L} - (K/\hat{L}) \cdot (\Delta \hat{L}/\hat{L})$, where $\Delta \hat{L}/\hat{L} = x$. We can show from calculus that this condition holds exactly for infinitesimal changes.) Does $K/\hat{L}$ tend toward a constant steady-state value, $(K/\hat{L})^*$? What determines this value? (Hint: problem 11.8 shows that if the production function, $F(K, \hat{L})$, exhibits constant returns to scale, then it is possible to write output per effective worker as a function only of capital per effective worker: $Y/\hat{L} = f(K/\hat{L})$.)

c. Does technological progress lead to growth of per capita output in the long run?

11.15 Economic Development and the Real Wage Rate

Assume that the real wage rate is determined on the labor market to equal the marginal product of labor.

a. Consider an economy with zero population growth and no technological progress. In the transition to the steady state, the capital stock rises. What happens during the transition to the real wage rate? How does the real wage rate behave in the steady state?

b. (optional) Consider an economy in which population grows at the constant rate n (see problem 11.13). Suppose that the capital-labor ratio, K/L, rises during the transition, but stays constant in the steady state. How does the real wage rate behave in this situation?

c. (optional) Consider an economy that experiences steady technological progress (see problem 11.14). Suppose, for this economy, that the capital-labor ratio rises during the transition *and* in the steady state. What is the behavior of the real wage rate in this economy?

11.16 Convergence and the Dispersion of Income (optional)

Consider a group of economies that satisfies our notion of absolute convergence: poor economies tend to grow faster than rich ones.

a. Does this convergence property imply that a measure of the dispersion of income, or income inequality, across the economies will necessarily narrow over time?

(This question is related to Galton's fallacy, an idea applied by Galton to the distribution of heights in a population. If a parent is taller than average, then the child tends to be taller than average but shorter than the parent. That is, there is some tendency for reversion to the mean, an effect that parallels the convergence tendency in our growth model. Does this reversion to the mean imply that the distribution of heights across the entire population becomes narrower over time? The answer is supposed to be no, but you have to explain why.)

b. For the U.S. states considered in Figure 11.6, a measure of the dispersion of per capita income across the states tended to decline for most of the period after 1880. The dispersion measure increased in the 1920s (a period that featured a collapse in agricultural prices) and also rose from the late 1970s to around 1990. Can you relate these observations to your answer from part a? (The behavior since the late 1970s is not well understood.)

c. We noted that absolute convergence does not hold for the 114 countries that we considered in Figure 11.10. For these countries, a measure of dispersion shows a mild increase from 1960 to 1990. How would you account for this outcome?

GOVERNMENT BEHAVIOR

Up to this point the government has not played much of a role in the model. In fact, all the government does is print money and give away the proceeds as transfer payments. In the real world, governments have important influences on the economy through various policies, including expenditures, taxes, transfer programs, regulations, and debt management. In this part of the book we consider the macroeconomic effects of these governmental activities.

Chapter 12 begins the study by considering government consumption expenditures and a simple form of tax revenues. With this extension we can analyze how government consumption affects real interest rates, the level of real gross domestic product, and the split of GDP between private and public expenditures. For the United States, short-run changes in government consumption have played a major role during wartime but otherwise have not been a central element in business fluctuations. The longer-term increase in the size of government has, however, crowded out private spending.

Chapter 13 introduces income taxes and transfers, activities that affect people's incentives to work, produce, and invest. We examine, in particular, the possibility—stressed by "supply-side economists"—that changes in tax rates have major effects on the level of economic activity.

Chapter 14 discusses the public debt and the related concept of the government's budget deficit. Although these issues have attracted a lot of attention in recent years, the major conclusion is that budget deficits have exerted only minor influences on the U.S. economy.

CHAPTER 12

GOVERNMENT CONSUMPTION AND PUBLIC SERVICES

T his chapter introduces government consumption and a simple form of tax revenues. Before considering these extensions to the model, it is useful to get some background by looking at data on government spending for the United States and other countries.

DATA ON GOVERNMENT EXPENDITURES

Figures 12.1 and 12.2 show the evolution of government spending in the United States from 1929 to 1996. Excluding the wartime experiences, total dollar government expenditures expressed as a ratio to nominal GNP (GDP since 1959) rose from 0.10 in 1929 to 0.19 in 1940, 0.23 in 1950, 0.29 in 1960, 0.33 in 1970, 0.34 in 1980, and 0.36 in 1996 (a comparable figure for 1902 is 0.07).

The pattern of steady rise in the importance of total government expenditures conceals the divergent movements in the major

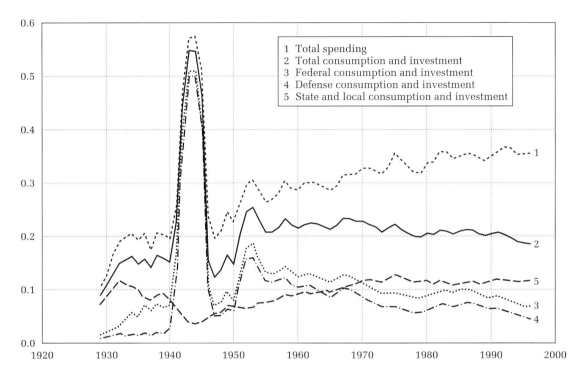

FIGURE 12.1

TOTAL GOVERNMENT SPENDING AND GOVERNMENT CONSUMPTION AND INVESTMENT

Expressed as Ratios to Nominal GDP (GNP before 1959)

underlying components. Figure 12.1 shows how government consumption and investment varied over time in the United States. Federal government consumption and investment rose from 0.02 relative to GNP (GDP since 1959) in 1929 to 0.07 in 1940 and—after World War II—to 0.08 in 1950. Following a rise to 0.12 in 1960, the federal ratio declined to 0.08 in 1979, before rising to 0.10 in 1986 and falling back to 0.07 in 1996.

Except during the Great Depression from 1933 to 1940, the dominant component of federal consumption and investment was defense spending. This spending was 0.028 relative to GNP in 1940 and 0.104 (relative to GDP) in 1960 but fell from there to a low point of 0.059 in

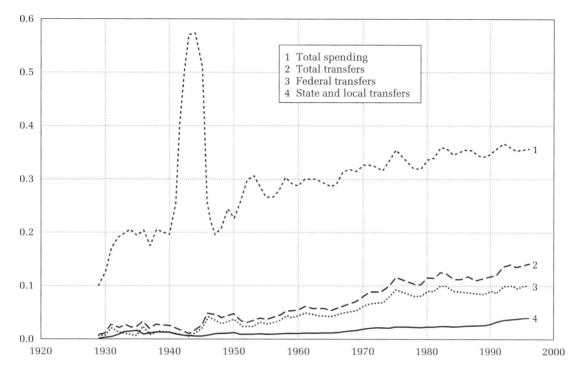

FIGURE 12.2

TOTAL GOVERNMENT SPENDING AND TRANSFER PAYMENTS

Expressed as Ratios to Nominal GDP (GNP before 1959)

1979; then this ratio rose to 0.075 in 1986 and fell to 0.046 in 1996. (As a fraction of total government expenditure, military spending declined from 36% in 1960 to 13% in 1996.) Figure 12.1 also shows the peaks in the defense ratio during wartime: 0.50 in 1943–44, 0.16 in 1952–53, and 0.10 in 1967–68.

State and local consumption and investment relative to GNP (GDP since 1959) was 0.07 in 1929 and 1950. Then this ratio rose to a peak of 0.12 in 1975 but subsequently remained relatively stable and equaled 0.11 in 1996. About half of the rise in this ratio from 1950 to 1975 took the form of increases in expenditures for education.

Figure 12.2 shows the behavior of transfers. Total transfer payments to persons rose from 0.01 relative to GDP in 1929 to 0.03 in 1940, 0.05 in 1950, 0.06 in 1960 (relative to GDP), 0.08 in 1970, 0.11 in 1980, and 0.14 in 1996. The state and local part of these transfers (which includes aid to families with dependent children) rose from 0.013 relative to GNP in 1950 to 0.033 (relative to GDP) in 1996. Thus, the main source of increase in the transfers' ratio came from the federal government—in particular, from the growing benefits paid through social security. For example, the expenditures for old-age, survivors, and disability—the main social security program—increased from 0.003 relative to GNP in 1950 to 0.046 relative to GDP in 1996. Over the same period, medicare expenditures rose from zero to 0.023 relative to GDP.

We can summarize the movements in U.S. government expenditures relative to GDP since the 1950s in terms of three major developments: a sharp drop in spending for the military (which was reversed in part after 1979), a roughly compensating increase in social security benefits, and a substantial rise in state and local spending (a major portion of which was for education) until the mid-1970s.

Table 12.1 shows the ratio of total government expenditures to GDP for 81 countries. The figures are averages from 1970 to 1985. The countries listed are those for which data are available on a broad concept of government expenditures. This concept is consolidated general government, which includes purchases of goods and services, transfer payments, and net interest payments by all levels of government. The ratios of government spending to GDP range from 11% for Paraguay and 12% for Guatemala to 77% for Israel and 54% for Sweden and the Netherlands. Aside from countries that have large defense expenditures, the ratios tend to be higher for the industrialized countries than for the less-developed countries. It appears to be economic development that leads to big government—especially in the form of large transfer payments—rather than vice versa!

TABLE 12.1

GOVERNMENT EXPENDITURES IN VARIOUS COUNTRIES

Country	Spending Ratio (%)	Country	Spending Ratio (%)	Country	Spending Ratio (%)
Argentina	27	Guatemala	12	Pakistan	24
Australia	34	Guyana	53	Panama	34
Austria	46	Iceland	36	Papua New Guinea	34
Barbados	31	India	20	Paraguay	11
Belgium	50	Indonesia	21	Peru	18
Bolivia	13	Iran	35	Philippines	13
Botswana	37	Ireland	48	Senegal	22
Brazil	26	Israel	77	Sierra Leone	23
Burkino Faso	14	Italy	44	Singapore	20
Burma	15	Japan	27	South Africa	28
Cameroon	19	Jordan	51	Spain	26
Canada	39	Kenya	27	Sri Lanka	31
Chile	32	Korea (South)	18	Swaziland	25
Colombia	15	Liberia	32	Sweden	54
Costa Rica	22	Luxembourg	41	Switzerland	34
Cyprus	27	Malawi	27	Syria	41
Denmark	52	Malaysia	33	Thailand	17
Dominican Republic	16	Malta	40	Tunisia	31
Ecuador	26	Mauritius	29	Turkey	23
Egypt	41	Mexico	22	Uganda	15
El Salvador	15	Morocco	32	United Kingdom	44
Fiji	26	Nepal	14	United States	35
Finland	39	Netherlands	54	Uruguay	23
France	43	New Zealand	34	Venezuela	24
Germany	46	Nicaragua	21	Yemen	35
Ghana	17	Norway	51	Zaire	35
Greece	36	Oman	50	Zambia	34

Note: *The table reports the ratio of government expenditure to gross domestic product. Government expenditure is total spending of consolidated general government. Data are averages from 1970 to 1985 from* International Monetary Fund, Government Finance Statistics *and* International Financial Statistics, *various issues.*

GOVERNMENT CONSUMPTION AND PUBLIC SERVICES

439

THE GOVERNMENT'S BUDGET CONSTRAINT

Let G_t denote the government's demand for commodities during period t. The G_t in the model corresponds in the national accounts almost to the category called government consumption. The one difference is that, since the major revision implemented in 1996, government consumption in the national accounts includes an estimate of depreciation on stocks of public capital. We shall abstract here from publicly owned capital and therefore from the depreciation of this capital. We also do not consider here public investment (which is included in the national accounts' total of government consumption and investment). Total real government expenditure in the model equals government consumption plus the real value of aggregate transfer payments, V_t/P_t. (We do not yet consider governmental interest payments.)

Thus far, we have assumed that the government's only revenue came from printing money. The real value of this revenue is the amount $(M_t - M_{t-1})/P_t$. Now we assume that the government also levies taxes on households. (The taxes could apply to firms, but remember that the households own the firms.) Let T_t be the aggregate dollar amount of taxes for period t. Then the real amount of tax revenues is T_t/P_t.

As before, the government's budget constraint equates total real expenditures to total real revenues.[1] We therefore have

$$G_t + V_t = T_t/P_t + (M_t - M_{t-1})/P_t \tag{12.1}$$

Our earlier formulation fits into equation (12.1) if we set government consumption, G_t, and taxes, T_t/P_t, to zero.

We assumed before that transfer payments were lump sum. This specification means that a household's real transfer, v_t/P_t, does not depend on that household's level of income, effort at soliciting transfers, and so on. Now we assume also that the taxes are lump sum. Hence, a household's real tax liability, t_t/P_t, is independent of that household's level or type of income, effort at avoiding taxes, and so on.

[1] In the U.S. economy the revenue from printing money accrues directly to the Federal Reserve, which then turns most of its profits over to the U.S. Treasury. For historical reasons, however, the national accounts treat the Fed as though it were a private corporation rather than part of the central government. The transfer of funds from the Fed to the Treasury therefore shows up in the national accounts as a tax on corporate profits. (We can almost feel sorry for the Fed, because its "profits" are taxed at nearly a 100% rate!)

In the real world, an elaborate tax law specifies the relation of some-one's taxes to his or her income, business profits, sales, holdings of property, deductions from taxable income, and so on. There are lots of things people can do—including hiring accountants, working less, un-derreporting income, and exploiting tax loopholes—to lower their obli-gations. These possibilities imply important substitution effects from the tax system on work effort, investment, relative demands for differ-ent goods (even including numbers of children), and so on. In general, people substitute in favor of the activities that lower their taxes.

In order to isolate the effects of government expenditures, we shall find it convenient initially to neglect these substitution effects from taxes. That is why we assume **lump-sum taxes**, which do not exert any substitution effects. (We bring in more realistic types of taxes and transfers in the next chapter.)

PUBLIC PRODUCTION

The government uses its outlays, G_t, to provide services to households and firms. We assume that the government provides these services free of charge to the users. In most countries public services include na-tional defense, enforcement of laws and private contracts, police and fire protection, elementary education and some parts of higher educa-tion, highways, parks, and so on. The range of governmental activities has typically expanded over time, although this range varies substan-tially from one state or country to another.

We could model public services as the output from the govern-ment's production function. The inputs to this function would be the government-owned stock of capital, labor services from public employ-ees, and materials that the government buys from the private sector. To simplify matters we take a different approach that neglects production in the public sector. We can neglect this production if we pretend that the government buys only final goods and services on the commodity mar-ket. In effect, the government subcontracts all of its production to the private sector. In this setup, public investment, publicly owned capital, and government employment are always zero. Ultimately, the introduction of governmental production would affect the main results only if the public sector's technology or management capability differed from that of the private sector. Otherwise, it would not matter whether the government buys final goods, as we assume, or instead buys capital and labor to produce things itself.

We assumed earlier that output could be labeled as consumables or capital goods. Now we introduce a third function for output: the government can purchase goods to provide public services to households and firms. As before, the suppliers of goods and services do not care whether the buyers use the goods for consumption or investment or to provide public services. The demanders of commodities—which now include the government—determine its use.

PUBLIC SERVICES

In our model we allow for two types of public services. The first type provides utility to households. Examples are parks, libraries, school lunch programs, subsidized health care and transportation services, and the entertaining parts of the space program. An important feature of these services is that they may substitute closely for private consumer spending. (If the government buys someone's lunch at school, then he or she does not buy his or her own lunch. But we have to be more subtle to find the private substitutes for the space program.)

The second type of service is an input to private production. Examples include the provision and enforcement of laws, aspects of national defense, government-sponsored research and development programs, fire and police services, and various regulatory activities. In some cases these services are close substitutes for private inputs of labor and capital. In other cases—including "infrastructure" activities such as the provision of a legal system, national defense, and perhaps highways and other transportation systems—the public services are likely to raise the marginal products of private factors.

In many situations a governmental program exhibits features of both types of services that we consider, but the mix varies across the range of programs. In our theory, however, we proceed as if there were only one type of governmental activity. This activity yields utility directly and also provides services to producers.

HOUSEHOLDS' BUDGET CONSTRAINTS

We have included real transfers, v_t/P_t, as a source of income for a household. Now we also have to subtract real taxes, t_t/P_t, to calculate real income after taxes. The budget constraint in real terms is now

$$y_t + b_{t-1} \cdot (1+R)/P_t + m_{t-1}/P_t + (v_t - t_t)/P_t = c_t + i_t + (b_t + m_t)/P_t$$

(12.2)

In making decisions, each household cares about the present value of real transfers net of real taxes, as given by

$$(v_1 - t_1)/P_1 + [(v_2 - t_2)/P_2]/(1+r) + \ldots$$

Consider the aggregate value of this expression. Each term involves the aggregate of real transfers net of real taxes, $(V_t - T_t)/P_t$. But we know from the government's budget constraint in equation (12.1) that this term equals the real revenue from money creation less government consumption; that is,

$$(V_t - T_t)/P_t = (M_t - M_{t-1})/P_t - G_t$$

(12.3)

If the money stock were constant, so that $M_t - M_{t-1} = 0$ holds in each period, then equation (12.3) would imply that the aggregate real value of transfers net of taxes, $(V_t - T_t)/P_t$, equals the negative of government consumption, $-G_t$. In the aggregate, households would therefore include the present value of government consumption, $[G_1 + G_2/(1+r) + \ldots]$, as a negative item when computing the overall present value of their resources. This result makes sense because the goods, G_t, that the government buys represents a part of the output stream that is not available for households. (As in the cases discussed in Chapter 4 and the appendix to Chapter 8, the results do not change if we include the various monetary terms.)

TEMPORARY CHANGES IN GOVERNMENT CONSUMPTION

We explore here the effects of government consumption on private consumption, private investment, and work effort. Consider an increase in the current level of public consumption, G_1. We shall find that the effects differ depending on whether the change is temporary or permanent. To begin with, think about a temporary change: G_1 rises, but households do not anticipate any changes in future values of G_t. Empirically, the most important example of this case is military spending during wars (if we think of the length of a period as corresponding to the expected duration of a war).

Recall that the government's budget constraint for period 1 is

$$G_1 + V_1/P_1 = T_1/P_1 + (M_1 - M_0)/P_1 \tag{12.4}$$

An increase in government consumption, G_1, must involve some combination of an increase in real taxes, T_1/P_1, a decrease in real transfers, V_1/P_1, or an increase in the real revenue from money creation, $(M_1 - M_0)/P_1$. Because we assume lump-sum taxes and transfers, our analysis of the real variables in the commodity market will be the same regardless of which combination we specify. For convenience, think of the extra government consumption as financed by more real taxes, T_1/P_1.

The higher current level of government consumption, G_1, means more public services of the two types mentioned before. First, there is a positive effect on utility during the current period (because we assume that people like the services that the government provides). Suppose that the public services substitute for some private consumption but not for leisure.[2] For example, if the government provides free libraries, parks, school lunches, or transportation, then households reduce their private spending in these areas. Use the parameter α (the Greek letter *alpha*) to measure the size of this effect. An increase in G_1 by one unit reduces aggregate private consumption demand, C_1^d, by α units.

It is plausible that the parameter α would decline as government consumption rises: as the amount of public services increases, the marginal unit would substitute less well for private spending. Notice, however, that the value of the parameter α does not necessarily indicate how valuable an extra unit of public services is. People might like these services a lot even if they do not substitute much for private spending, that is, even if α is small.

Some empirical work for the U.S. economy in the post–World War II period suggests that the parameter α is between 0.2 and 0.4.[3] That is, an extra unit of government consumption substitutes for between 0.2 and 0.4 unit of aggregate private consumption. We are therefore safe in assuming that α is positive but well below unity.

The second type of public service is an input to private production. Use the parameter β (the Greek letter *beta*) to measure the marginal product of public services. If the inputs of labor and capital do not change, then an increase in G_1 by one unit raises the aggregate supply of goods, Y_1^s, by β units.[4] We assume that β is positive but less than one. Diminishing marginal productivity of public services suggests that β would decline as G_t rose, for given inputs of capital and labor.

Net investment demand depends on the schedule for capital's marginal product, on the previous stock of capital, and on the real interest rate. We assume that public services do not affect the schedule for capital's marginal product; hence, there is no direct impact of government consumption on private investment demand. Any effects that arise must work through changes in the real interest rate.

[2] *We follow here the approach pioneered by Martin Bailey (1971, Chap. 9).*

[3] *See Roger Kormendi (1983) and David Aschauer (1985).*

[4] *David Aschauer's (1988) empirical results suggest important effects of this type from the government's contributions to "infrastructure" but not from other types of government expenditure. The infrastructure components include highways, airports, electrical and gas facilities, mass transit, water systems, and sewers.*

Recall that the present value of households' resources includes the negative of the present value of government consumption. (This term corresponds to the present value of taxes net of transfers.) Since the increase in government consumption is temporary, the present value of this consumption rises by only a small amount. The resulting fall in wealth reduces consumer demand and increases labor supply. These changes would reinforce the effects on consumer demand and goods supply that we have already mentioned. To focus on the temporary nature of the change in government consumption, we shall find it convenient to neglect these small wealth effects. The wealth effects will, however, become important when we consider permanent changes in government consumption.

CLEARING OF THE COMMODITY MARKET

Now we incorporate government consumption into the market-clearing conditions. Since the main new effects involve the demand and supply of commodities, we shall focus on the condition for clearing the commodity market. The new condition for period 1 is

$$\underset{(-)\ (-)}{C^d(r_1, G_1, \ldots)} + \underset{(-)}{I^d(r_1, \ldots)} + G_1 = \underset{(+)\ (+)}{Y^s(r_1, G_1, \ldots)} \tag{12.5}$$

The aggregate demand for commodities, Y_1^d, consists of private consumption demand, C_1^d, gross private investment demand, I_1^d, and government consumption, G_1. (Public investment demand would also enter here if we had included it in the model.) If private consumption and investment demand did not change, then aggregate demand would increase one-to-one with an increase in government consumption. But an increase by one unit in G_1 reduces consumer demand, C_1^d, by α units. Since there is assumed to be no effect on private investment demand, an increase by one unit in government consumption raises aggregate demand by $1 - \alpha$ units. (Recall that we assume $\alpha < 1$.)

An increase in G_1 by one unit raises the supply of goods, Y_1^s, by β units. (*Warning*: Our analysis assumes that taxes are lump sum. When we drop this unrealistic assumption in the next chapter, we introduce some important negative effects from governmental activity on the supply of goods.) If $\alpha + \beta < 1$, then the increase in aggregate demand, $1 - \alpha$, exceeds that in supply, β. This condition turns out to be important for figuring out the effects of a temporary increase in government consumption on the real interest rate.

Consider the inequality $\alpha + \beta < 1$. This condition says that, if government consumption expands by one unit, then households and firms get back less than one unit in the combined response from the substitution for consumer spending, α, and the increase in private output, β. One easy way to satisfy this condition is to assume that public services are useless: the government essentially buys up goods and throws them into the ocean. Although this assumption, where $\alpha = \beta = 0$, is popular (and appears implicitly in many macromodels), it may not be the most interesting way to model the functions of government!

But why does $\alpha + \beta < 1$ make sense? If $\alpha + \beta > 1$, then the typical household would benefit from an increase in public services, paid for by an increase in taxes. That conclusion follows because the amount that the typical household gets back—the value of the services that substitute for consumer spending, α, plus the value of the extra production, β— exceeds the additional taxes. Hence, if $\alpha + \beta > 1$, then it is plausible that the government would grow larger, and this expansion tends to reduce the values of α and β. It would, in particular, be popular for the government to expand at least until the condition $\alpha + \beta < 1$ was satisfied.

Figure 12.3 shows the effects of a temporary increase in government consumption on the commodity market. Without this increase, the market clears at the real interest rate r_1^*. Then the rise in G_1 increases the aggregate quantities of goods demanded and supplied. But since $1 - \alpha > \beta$, the rightward shift of the aggregate demand curve exceeds that of the supply curve. Therefore, at the real interest rate r_1^*, there is

The temporary increase in government consumption raises aggregate demand by more than supply. Therefore, the real interest rate and output rise.

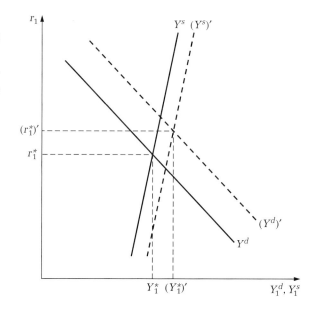

now excess demand for commodities. We conclude that the real interest rate increases to the value $(r_1^*)'$.

Figure 12.3 shows that output increases. There are two elements behind this increase. First, we assume that public services are productive. Second, the increase in the real interest rate motivates people to work more.

Consider now the composition of output. We know that government consumption rises. But private uses of output—for consumption and investment—decline. Consumer demand falls for two reasons. First, there is the substitution of public services for private spending. If we are talking about more military spending, however, then this effect is likely to be weak because the parameter α would be small. Second, the higher real interest rate induces households to postpone their expenditures. This second effect accounts also for the drop in private investment demand. Notice that the increase in government consumption **crowds out** private spending. Because of the higher real interest rate and the direct substitution of public services for consumer spending, the addition to government consumption induces consumers and private investors to spend less.

We suggested before that investment demand is especially sensitive to variations in the real interest rate. Therefore, unless the direct substitution of public services for consumer spending is strong, we predict that the temporary increase in government consumption will mostly crowd out private investment (including purchases of consumer durables), rather than consumption.

Since private consumption and investment decrease, the rise in total output is smaller than the increase in government consumption. Hence, the ratio of the change in output to the change in government consumption is positive but less than one. If the ratio were greater than one, then we would say that a change in government consumption has a multiplicative effect on output. But we do not get this sort of **multiplier** in the model. That is because the economy typically operates to buffer shocks rather than to magnify them. In particular, the rise in government consumption leads to decreases in private demands for consumption and investment and to an increase in work effort. Each of these responses serves to alleviate the initial excess demand for goods. (When we study the Keynesian model in Chapter 20, we shall reexamine the potential for a multiplier.)

Consider why the temporary increase in government consumption raises the real interest rate. The increase in spending, financed by a temporary increase in taxes, implies a temporary decline in households' disposable income. Since the shortfall in income is temporary, the marginal propensity to consume is small. Households therefore react mainly by reducing desired saving. When desired saving falls and investment demand does not shift, the real interest rate must increase.

The higher real interest rate is the signal that a wartime emergency is the right time for households to work harder, to produce more goods, and to reduce demands for private consumption and investment. In other words, the market uses the real interest rate to achieve the appropriate allocations over time for work effort, production, consumption, and investment.[5]

Our discussion refers to wars as cases in which government consumption is temporarily high. But we have ignored other aspects of major wars that can substantially affect the analysis. For one thing, we have neglected any negative effects of military reversals on productive capacity. These effects, an example of adverse supply shocks, would tend to reduce output. Another feature of wartime is the widespread use of rationing to hold down private demands for goods. Others are the military draft, confiscation of property, and appeals to patriotism to stimulate work and production. These mechanisms are examples of direct controls, which can substitute for a higher real interest rate as instruments for crowding out private spending and for stimulating work and production. These departures from free markets may not affect the general conclusions about the effects of wartime on the quantities of output, consumption, investment, and employment. But these controls may eliminate the increase in the real interest rate.

EVIDENCE FROM WARTIME EXPERIENCES

THE BEHAVIOR OF OUTPUT AND OTHER QUANTITIES

We can assess some effects of temporarily high government consumption by looking at the four most recent wars for the United States: World War I, World War II, Korea, and Vietnam. (We abstract from the Persian Gulf War because it was too brief to have much effect on government consumption.) For these cases we can reasonably neglect any direct effects of combat on productive capacity in the United States.

Table 12.2 describes the behavior of military spending, real GNP, and the major components of GNP during these episodes. (We use GNP for all the cases, because the recently constructed GDP values are

[5] *For some additional discussion of these effects, see Robert Hall (1980a).*

TABLE 12.2

THE BEHAVIOR OF OUTPUT AND ITS COMPONENTS DURING WARTIME

Peak Year of War Benchmark Year for Comparison	1918 1915	1944 1947	1952 1950	1968 1965
Excess real military spending (billions of 1982 dollars)	81.4	645.3	146.3	46.1
Excess as % of trend real GNP	16.8	66.2	11.4	2.0
Excess of real GNP (billions of 1982 dollars)	13.7	405.7	101.9	81.4
Excess as % of trend real GNP	2.8	41.6	8.0	3.6
Ratio to excess real military spending for the excess of				
Real GNP	0.17	0.63	0.70	1.77
Real personal consumption expenditures	−0.45	−0.08	−0.05	1.15
Durables	—	−0.04	−0.09	0.31
Nondurables and services	—	−0.04	0.04	0.84
Real gross private domestic investment	−0.19	−0.16	−0.26	−0.21
Other[a]	−0.19	−0.13	−0.01	−0.17
Excess of employment (millions)				
Total employment	2.1	8.4	1.5	2.5
Military personnel	2.7	9.9	1.9	0.7
Civilian employment	−0.6	−1.5	−0.4	1.8
Excess of total employment as % of trend value	5.3	14.8	2.4	3.2

Sources: *For World War II, the Korean War, and the Vietnam War, the data are from U.S. Department of Commerce (1986). For 1915 and 1918, the data on real GNP are those shown in Figure 1.1. Estimates for the components of real GNP use the data from Kendrick (1961, Tables A–I, A–IIa). The shares of real GNP shown in each year from Kendrick's data are applied to the figures on total real GNP to estimate values for real military spending, real personal consumption expenditures, and real gross private domestic investment.*

Note: *The method for calculating the excess or shortfall in each component is discussed in the text.*

[a] *Nonmilitary government purchases of goods and services and exports less imports.*

unavailable for the earlier three wars.) We contrast the behavior during the war years with that for a benchmark year; for example, we compare the peak year of the Korean War, 1952, with the benchmark year, 1950. Real military spending in 1952 was above the benchmark value[6] by $146 billion, an amount that equals 11% of trend real GNP for 1952. Real GNP in 1952 was $102 billion, or 8%, above its own trend.

Next, we calculate the ratio of excess real GNP and its various components to the excess of real military spending. For GNP the ratio in 1952 was 0.70. Hence—assuming that the boost in military spending was the major disturbance to the economy—this result supports the theory's predictions: a temporary increase in government consumption has a positive but less than one-to-one effect on output.

Since GNP rises by less than the increase in military spending, the nonmilitary components of GNP must decline overall. The figures shown for 1952 in Table 12.2 indicate that total private investment (gross private investment plus purchases of consumer durables) declined by the fraction 0.35 of the increase in military spending. In contrast, consumer expenditures for nondurables and services were actually higher by the fraction 0.04. Thus, the temporary excess of military spending crowded out only the investment part of private spending. Recall that the theory is consistent with this outcome, because military outlays would have little direct substitution for consumer spending.

The final rows of the table show the effects on employment. Total employment (numbers of persons working, including military personnel) in 1952 was above trend by 1.5 million, or 2.4% of the trend value. This total divided up between 1.9 million extra military personnel and 0.4 million fewer civilian workers. (We do not consider here the likely positive effects on hours and effort per worker.)

We apply a similar procedure for World War II. Because the economy had not yet fully recovered in 1940 from the Great Depression, we use 1947 as the benchmark year. Basically, the findings are similar to those from the Korean War except that the magnitudes are much larger. For example, the excess of real military spending in 1944 was $645 bil-

[6] *The benchmark value for 1952 is the actual value for 1950 adjusted by the average growth of real defense expenditure over a two-year period.*

lion, or 66% of trend real GNP. Real GNP was $406 billion, or 42%, above its own trend. Note that the ratio of excess GNP to excess military spending, 0.63, was similar to that for the Korean War.

For World War II, the excess military spending crowded out total private investment (gross private investment plus purchases of consumer durables) by a fraction of 0.20 and consumer purchases of nondurables and services by a fraction of 0.04. Total employment for 1944 exceeded its trend value by 8.4 million, or 15%. This total broke down into 9.9 million extra military personnel and 1.5 million fewer civilian workers.

For World War I, the excess of real GNP above trend in 1918 was only 0.17 times the excess of real military spending. This value is well below those estimated for the Korean War and World War II. The computations for World War I are, however, not so reliable because the underlying data on GNP are subject to substantial uncertainty.

We lack the data during World War I to break down consumption into durable and nondurable components. The results shown in Table 12.2 indicate that the excess military spending in 1918 crowded out gross private investment by the fraction 0.19 and personal consumer expenditure (which includes purchases of durables) by the fraction 0.45. The latter figure is much greater than that found for the Korean War and World War II. Finally, total employment in 1918 was above its trend by 2.1 million, or 5.3%. In this case there were 2.7 million extra military personnel and 0.6 million fewer civilian workers.

The results for Vietnam differ sharply from those for the other wars. To begin, using 1965 as the benchmark year, the estimate for the excess of real military spending in 1968 was only $46 billion, or 2% of trend real GNP. Thus, unlike the other cases, it is doubtful that the increase in military spending was the overriding influence on the economy in the middle and late 1960s.

The estimated excess of real GNP for 1968 was $81 billion or 4% of trend real GNP. Thus, the excess real GNP was 1.8 times the excess real military spending. Correspondingly, the total of the nonmilitary components of GNP were above trend in 1968. For example, the ratio to excess military spending was 0.10 for total private investment (gross private investment plus purchases of consumer durables) and 0.84 for the consumption of nondurables and services. Hence, the United States really was enjoying "guns and butter" at this time.

The most likely explanation for these results is that the economy was experiencing a boom in the 1960s that had little to do with the Vietnam War. This viewpoint is supported by the high growth rate of output in the period preceding the main increase in military spending. The average annual growth rate of real GNP was 5.1% from 1961 to 1965, compared with 4.3% from 1965 to 1968.

Suppose that we focus on the results for the Korean War, World War II, and World War I. Then there is an interesting comparison between the behavior of the economy during wartime booms and during recessions. The contrast concerns the relation between changes in total output and changes in private spending. Total output rises in wars but falls during recessions, whereas private spending declines in both cases. The wartime experiences are similar to recessions in that the major adjustments to private spending show up in the investment components. (World War I may be an exception, although the data are too unreliable to be sure.) As with the postwar recessions that we studied in Chapter 9 (Table 9.1), there are relatively small reductions in consumer purchases of nondurables and services during the Korean War and World War II.

Finally, let's stress the finding that temporarily high government consumption raises total output and employment. But, as predicted, the ratio of the excess real GNP to the excess in purchases is less than one.

THE BEHAVIOR OF REAL INTEREST RATES

The theory predicts that temporarily high government consumption, as in wartime, raises the real interest rate. We have to be careful, however, when matching up this prediction with the wartime behavior of interest rates. Recall that the previous theoretical analysis assumes that govern-

TABLE 12.3

INTEREST RATES DURING WARTIME

Period	π_t	R_t	r_t
1863–68	4.8	7.0	2.2
1918–23	2.7	5.8	3.1
1944–49	6.2	1.0	−5.2
1952–57	2.2	2.6	0.4
1968–73	5.2	6.6	1.4

Sources: *See Table 11.1.*

Note: *All values are averages, expressed at annual percentage rates, for the periods indicated. π_t is the inflation rate, based on the consumer price index for the period 1863–68 and on the GNP deflator for the other periods. R_t is the interest rate on four- to six-month prime commercial paper. $r_t = R_t − \pi_t$.*

ment consumption is temporarily high only for the current period. But during wars, military expenditures tend to build up for a while and then recede at the end of the war. Also, the length of the buildup and the timing of the war's conclusion (or who wins) are unknown at the outset.

One implication from the theory is that the average real interest rate should be high over the period from the peak of a war until some time after the war finishes. In line with this viewpoint, Table 12.3 reports averages of interest rates over six-year intervals, beginning with the peak year of each war. The figures therefore include between one and five years of peacetime after each war. Notice that the table considers the four wars that we just studied, plus the Civil War. In each case we calculate the average for the nominal interest rate on prime commercial paper over six-year periods. Then we compute real interest rates by subtracting the average rate of change of the GNP deflator. (For the Civil War, we lack data on the GNP deflator and therefore use the consumer price index.)

For the Civil War, the average real interest rate over the period 1863–68 was 2.2%. This rate was substantially less than the averages for 1840–60 and 1867–80, which were each 9.1%. For World War I, the average real interest rate over the interval 1918–23 was 3.1%. This value equaled the average for 1900–16 but was below that of 4.9% for 1920–40. For World War II, the average over the period 1944–49 was −5.2%, which was well below the averages of 4.9% for 1920–40 and −0.2% for 1947–60.

For the two most recent wars, Korea and Vietnam, the average real interest rates were 0.4% (for 1952–57) and 1.4% (for 1968–73), respectively. These values do not differ greatly from the average for 1947–80, which was 0.6%.

Overall, the results do not confirm a positive effect of wartime spending on real interest rates. The real interest rates were, if anything, below average during the wars.

For 1944–49, the substantially negative real interest rates reflect an overstatement of inflation because of the lifting of price controls. (General price controls did not apply to the earlier wars but were introduced to some extent during the Korean War.) The World War II controls kept the reported price levels below the "true" values from 1943 to 1945, so that inflation was understated for these years. As the controls were gradually eliminated from 1946 to 1948, the reported figures caught up with the true ones and inflation was overstated. My estimate is that, without controls, the inflation rate from 1944 to 1949 would have averaged 1.1% per year rather than the official value of 6.2%.[7] If the controls merely obscured the behavior of the actual price level, then the lower figure would be a reasonable estimate of the true inflation rate. Using this value, the average real interest rate for 1944–49 was −0.1% rather than −5.2%. This adjusted value of −0.1% is close to the average of real interest rates for 1947–60 (−0.2%). Thus, even with this adjustment for price controls, we would not conclude that the real interest rate was especially high during World War II.

[7] These estimates, based on the behavior of money and other variables, are reported in Robert Barro (1978b, p. 572).

The puzzle is, why did people work and produce so much during the wars if they were not motivated by high real interest rates? Casey Mulligan (1995a) has examined this question for World War II, and he finds that real wage rates were also not notably high (particularly when measured after tax—in the manner detailed in Chapter 13—because income-tax rates rose a lot). Thus, it seems that the wartime expansion of labor supply has to be motivated by factors other than narrow economic ones.

One idea is that people were patriotic, especially during World War II, and were therefore willing to work more without receiving pecuniary rewards. Another factor is the resort to aspects of a command economy, where governmental decrees on production, work, and expenditures substitute for free markets. Aside from the military draft, which applied to all the wars considered in Table 12.3, in the two world wars the government exerted direct pressures to work and produce and also rationed private consumption and investment. In other words, the command economy is in some respects a substitute for free markets with high real interest rates and high real wage rates. Although this argument may have some validity, it also implies that the data from U.S. wars may not be that helpful for testing the theoretical link between temporary government consumption and real interest rates.

We can get around some of these difficulties by looking at the long-term relation between wartime spending and interest rates in the United Kingdom. From the standpoint of scientific inquiry, Britain was very cooperative by fighting numerous wars, especially before 1815. Prior to World War I, these wars were not accompanied by the introduction of aspects of a command economy. Thus, unlike the U.S. case, we can be confident of predicting a positive effect of temporary wartime expenditures on real interest rates.

The solid line in Figure 12.4 shows a measure of temporary real military spending expressed as a ratio to trend real GNP.[8] The peaks correspond to the seven major wars for the United Kingdom over the

[8] *The details of this variable and further results are in Robert Barro (1987). For an earlier discussion of these data, see Daniel Benjamin and Levis Kochin (1984).*

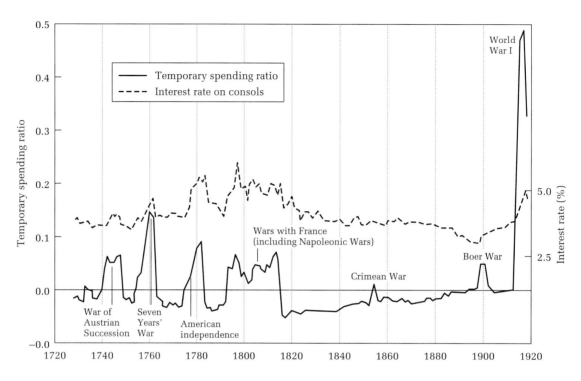

FIGURE 12.4

MILITARY SPENDING AND THE INTEREST RATE IN THE UNITED KINGDOM, 1730–1918

[9] *The data are for British consols, which are government bonds that pay a perpetual stream of coupons but have no maturity date. The results refer to nominal interest rates, whereas the theory applies to real interest rates. Over the period of study, however, the long-term inflation rate in the United Kingdom was close to zero. It is therefore likely that the positive relation between temporary spending and nominal interest rates also reflects a positive relation with real interest rates.*

period from 1730 to 1918. Notice that the high points for temporary spending were 50% of GNP in World War I (1916), 16% in the Seven-Years' War (1761), 9% during the War of American Independence (1782), and 7% during the Napoleonic Wars (1814).

The dashed line in the figure is the long-term nominal interest rate. The positive relation of this rate to temporary spending is clear visually and is also confirmed by statistical analysis: interest rates rose on average by 1.0 percentage point during the seven wars.[9] This change is large relative to the average level of rates, which was 3.5% from 1730 to 1918.

For some additional evidence, David Denslow and Mark Rush (1989) looked at the relation between long-term interest rates and temporary government expenditures in France from 1828 to 1869. They observed a positive relationship, which resembles the one found for the long-term British history. Thus, as with the long-term evidence for Britain, these findings for France are more in line with the theory than are the recent results for the United States.

PERMANENT CHANGES IN GOVERNMENT CONSUMPTION

The previous analysis applies to temporary changes in government consumption, such as in wartime. In other cases there are long-lasting shifts in the size of government. The data that we looked at before for the United States showed permanent increases in the ratio of government consumption to GNP or GDP during the 1930s and 1950s, but these ratios did not change a lot in the 1960s, 1970s, and 1980s.

We found before that a temporary increase in government consumption raised the aggregates of commodities demanded and supplied. But, as shown in Figure 12.3, the increase in demand exceeded that in supply. If the change in public consumption is perceived to be permanent, then the new element is that households anticipate a sizable increase in the present value of government consumption and, hence, in the present value of taxes net of transfers. The resulting fall in wealth reduces consumer demand and raises labor supply. These responses reduce the excess demand for goods. We shall find, in fact, that an increase in government consumption now raises the aggregates of commodities demanded and supplied by roughly equal amounts; that is, a permanent change in government consumption does not disturb the equality between demand and supply. Let's see why this is the case.

Consider first a simplified setting in which public services are useless ($\alpha = \beta = 0$) and labor supply is fixed. In this case, a permanent increase by one unit in government consumption effectively subtracts one unit from households' disposable income in each period. As with a permanent shift in the production function, the marginal propensity to

GOVERNMENT CONSUMPTION AND PUBLIC SERVICES

consume is close to one in this situation. Consumer demand therefore declines by about one unit; that is, one additional unit of public expenditure directly crowds out one unit of private consumer spending. Since government consumption is higher by one unit, the aggregate demand for goods does not change. With fixed labor supply and nonproductive public services ($\beta = 0$), the supply of goods also does not change. Therefore, *a permanent increase in government consumption leaves the aggregate demand for goods equal to the supply*. This result turns out to hold even if government services are productive ($\alpha \neq 0$ or $\beta \neq 0$) or if labor supply varies. A proof appears in the accompanying boxed section.

Figure 12.5 depicts the effects of a permanent increase in government consumption on the commodity market. Note that the demand and supply curves shift rightward by equal amounts. Therefore, aggregate demand still equals aggregate supply at the initial real interest rate, r_1^*. We conclude that a permanent expansion of government consumption has no effect on the real interest rate.

Figure 12.5 shows that output increases. This response reflects the productivity (β) of public services and a possible increase in labor supply. Labor supply tends to rise because of the decline in wealth, as

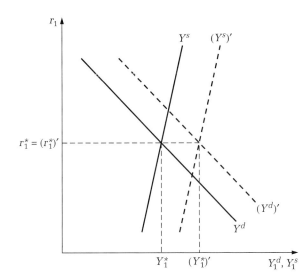

FIGURE 12.5

EFFECTS ON THE COMMODITY MARKET OF A PERMANENT RISE IN GOVERNMENT CONSUMPTION

The permanent increase in government consumption raises aggregate demand and supply by roughly equal amounts. Therefore, output increases, but the real interest rate does not change.

Results When Public Services Are Useful and When Labor Supply Varies (optional)

Suppose first that public services substitute for private consumer spending, that is, $\alpha > 0$. We know from before that the direct substitution between public and private spending implies that consumer demand declines by α units when government consumption increases by one unit. If $\alpha > 0$ and the rise in government consumption is permanent, then households effectively lose only $1 - \alpha$ units of disposable income in each period. The other α units provide services that households no longer have to buy on the market. The wealth effect therefore implies that consumer demand falls by about $1 - \alpha$ units. (The marginal propensity to consume is still close to one here.) If we add this response to the decline of consumer demand by α units, then we find that a one-unit increase in government consumption still leads to a decline by one unit overall in consumer demand. Thus, as in the case where $\alpha = 0$, the demand for goods remains equal to the supply.

Assume now that public services are productive, that is, $\beta > 0$. If government consumption rises permanently by one unit, then the supply of goods increases by β units in each period. Con-

sequently, households' income from production rises by β units in each period. Since the marginal propensity to consume is close to unity here, consumer demand also increases by about β units. In other words, the aggregates of goods supplied and demanded are each higher by β units. Hence, excess demand is still zero.

If $\alpha + \beta < 1$, then a permanent increase in government consumption reduces wealth and therefore motivates an increase in work effort. The higher work means an increase in the supply of goods and a corresponding rise in households' income from production. Since the marginal propensity to consume is close to unity, consumer demand rises by roughly the same amount. Therefore, although the rise in work effort means that goods supplied and demanded are each higher, it still follows that excess demand is nil. We have therefore shown that our basic result—a permanent change in government consumption leaves the aggregate demand for goods equal to the supply—holds even when public services are productive and labor supply is allowed to vary.

discussed in the boxed section. The increase in work effort may not occur, however, if government expenditures are financed by an income tax rather than a lump-sum tax. We consider more realistic types of taxes in the next chapter.

Consider next the composition of output. To begin, government consumption increases. Two forces lower consumer demand: first, public services substitute for private spending, and second, the reduction in wealth induces households to consume less. Private investment is constant because the real interest rate does not change.[10] Notice the difference from the case of a temporary change in government consumption. In that case the rise in the real interest rate crowded out both forms of private spending. Now, when the change in government consumption is permanent, the extra public outlays crowd out only consumer spending.

The decline in private consumption and constancy of private investment imply that total output increases by less than the rise in government consumption. That is, the ratio of the change in output to the change in government consumption is again positive but less than one. Thus, the model still does not have a multiplier.

Consider why the real interest rate increases when the rise in government consumption is temporary but does not change when the rise is permanent. A temporary increase in government consumption implies a temporary fall in households' disposable income, an effect that decreases desired saving. In contrast, if the increases in government consumption and taxes are permanent, then the decline in households' disposable income is also permanent. The marginal propensity to consume is therefore close to one, and the effect on desired saving is small. For this reason, the real interest rate does not change.

SUMMARY

We introduced government consumption as another use of output. To finance these expenditures and its transfer payments, the government

[10] *We are neglecting any effects on capital's marginal product, MPK, from the changes in government consumption, G, or the quantity of labor input, L.*

levies lump-sum taxes or prints money. The government uses its outlays on goods and services to provide a flow of public services. An additional unit of these services substitutes for α units of consumer spending and also raises production by β units. We assume the condition $\alpha + \beta < 1$, which means that households and firms get back directly less than the cost of an additional unit of public services.

A temporary increase in government consumption, as in wartime, raises aggregate demand by more than supply. Hence, the real interest rate and output increase. The crowding out of private investment and consumption means, however, that total output rises by less than the increase in government consumption: there is no multiplier.

Variations in government consumption play a major role during wartime but not in peace-time business fluctuations. The U.S. evidence from World War II and Korea supports the theory's predictions with respect to quantities. In particular, real output rises but by only 60–70% of the increase in real military spending. Thus, there is crowding out of private spending, especially investment. The U.S. data do not show a tendency for the real interest rate to rise during wartime. In contrast, the long-term data for Britain and France reveal a positive effect of wartime spending on interest rates.

A permanent increase in government consumption increases the aggregates of goods supplied and demanded by roughly equal amounts. Output therefore increases, but there is no change in the real interest rate. In this case, the crowding out of private spending falls entirely on consumption.

IMPORTANT TERMS AND CONCEPTS

crowding out (from government consumption) The decrease in private consumption and investment that results from an increase in government consumption.

lump-sum tax A tax paid by an individual to the government in which the amount paid does not depend on any characteristic of the individual, such as income or wealth.

multiplier The change in aggregate output per dollar autonomous increase in aggregate demand; assumed in simple Keynesian models to be positive and greater than one.

QUESTIONS AND PROBLEMS

MAINLY FOR REVIEW

12.1   What are the channels by which government consumption affects excess demand in the commodity market? How does it affect utility? Can you think of examples of public services that are not close substitutes for private consumption ($\alpha = 0$) but nevertheless provide utility?

12.2   Could government services be a substitute for leisure? If so, what additional channel of effect arises in the commodity market?

12.3   Why does the real interest rate rise as a result of a temporary increase in government consumption?

12.4   What is crowding out? Does it involve an intertemporal substitution effect alone? Could there be direct substitution of government spending for private investment?

PROBLEMS FOR DISCUSSION

12.5   Government Consumption in the National Accounts
The national accounts treat all of government consumption as part of real GDP. But suppose that the public services derived from this government

consumption, G_t, are an input to private production, that is, $Y_t = F(K_{t-1}, L_t, G_t)$. Then public services are an intermediate product—a good that enters as an input into a later stage of production. Hence, we ought not to include these services twice in real GDP—once when the government buys them and again when the public services contribute to private production.

a. Suppose that businesses initially hire private guards. But the government then provides free police protection, which substitutes for the guards. Assume that the private guards and police are equally efficient and receive the same incomes. How does the switch from private to public services affect measured real GDP?

b. How should we change the treatment of public services in the national accounts? Is the proposal practical?

[These issues are discussed in Simon Kuznets (1948, pp. 156–57) and Richard Musgrave (1959, pp. 186–88).]

12.6 Public Ownership of Capital and the National Accounts

When the government produces goods and services, the national accounts—until the revision in 1996—measured the contribution to GDP by the government's purchases from the private sector of labor, materials, and new capital goods. But the accounts neglected any contribution to output from the flow of services on government-owned capital. The accounts also did not subtract depreciation of this capital to calculate net product.

a. Under this old system, what happened to measured GDP if the government gave its capital to a private business and then bought the final goods from that business?

b. In the system introduced in 1996, the GDP includes an estimate of the flow of income generated by public capital. However, this income flow is assumed to equal the estimated depreciation of the public capital. How does this approach affect the answer to the question in part a?

12.7 The Role of Public Services

We assume that an additional unit of public services has two direct effects: first, it substitutes for α units of private consumption, and second, it raises production by β units.

a. Consider various categories of government expenditures, such as military spending, police, highways, public transit, research and development expenditures, and regulatory agencies. How do the parameters α and β vary across the categories? Are the parameters always positive?

b. Consider a permanent increase in government consumption. How do the sizes of the responses in output and consumption depend on the values of the parameters α and β? Explain the results.

c. Repeat part b for the case of a temporary increase in government consumption.

12.8 Prospective Changes in Government Consumption

During the current period, date 1, people find out that government consumption will increase permanently in some future period. There is no change in current consumption or in the paths of the money stock and real transfers.

a. What happens currently to the real interest rate and the quantities of output, private consumption, private investment, and employment?

b. What happens to the current price level and nominal interest rate?

c. Can you think of some real-world cases for which this question applies?

12.9 Effects of Government Consumption on the Real Wage Rate

Suppose that we include a labor market in the model.

a. What is the effect on the real wage rate from a temporary increase in government consumption?

b. What is the effect from a permanent increase in government consumption?

12.10 Government Employment during Wartime (optional)

In the model we assume that the government buys only final product from the commodity market. In particular, the government neither produces goods nor employs people. This assumption is basically satisfactory if the government's production function is similar to that of private producers. But the assumption is troublesome for wartime. Suppose, for example, that during World War II the government effectively removes 10 million people temporarily from the civilian labor force. But the government takes away no privately owned capital. Then, as before, assume that the government also temporarily raises its consumption of goods by a large amount.

a. Analyze the effects on the real interest rate and on the quantities of output, private investment, and private consumption. (How should we count the 10 million conscripts in the measure of output?) What happens to total and private employment?

b. If we include a labor market in the model, then what happens to the real wage rate?

12.11 The Price Level during the Korean War

With the start of the Korean War, the price level (GNP deflator) rose at an annual rate of 10% from the second quarter of 1950 to the first quarter of 1951. In contrast, the inflation rate was negative for 1949, 1.4% from the first quarter of 1951 to the first quarter of 1952, and 2.0% from the first quarter of 1952 to the first quarter of 1953.

The following table shows for various periods the inflation rate, π_t, the monetary growth rates, μ_t, for currency and M1, the growth rate of real government purchases of goods and services, ΔG_t, and the nominal interest rate on three-month U.S. Treasury bills, R_t. Can we use these data to account for the surge in the price level at the start of the Korean War? (This question does not have a definite answer!)

(*Hint*: Price controls were stringent during World War II. People may have expected a return to these controls under the Korean War in 1950.)

Year and Quarter	π_t	μ_t (M1)	μ_t (Currency)	ΔG_t	R_t
1949.1 to 1950.2	−0.3	1.8	−1.6	2.7	1.1
Start of War					
1950.2 to 1951.1	10.0	4.0	−0.5	24.6	1.1
1951.1 to 1952.1	1.4	5.3	4.7	27.9	1.6
1952.1 to 1953.1	2.0	3.2	4.5	9.2	1.8

Note: *All figures are in percent per year.*

12.12 The Optimal Level of Public Services (optional)

In the model a permanent increase in government consumption raises output but lowers private consumption and leisure. Recall that we used the condition $\alpha + \beta < 1$, where α measures the substitution of public services for consumer spending, and β is the marginal product of public services. We assumed also that the parameters α and β declined as government consumption rose.

a. What happens to the typical person's utility when government consumption rises permanently by one unit?

b. If the government wants to maximize the typical person's utility, then where should it set its consumption? What condition holds here for the parameters α and β?

c. Why is it not the right answer in part b to choose the level of government consumption that maximizes aggregate output (as measured by real GDP)?

d. Without working through the details, how does the analysis change if public services provide utility in other ways, that is, not only as a direct substitute for private consumer spending?

TAXES AND TRANSFERS

Thus far, we have taken an unrealistic view of governmental operations by assuming lump-sum taxes and transfers. In our model, the amount that a household or firm pays as taxes or receives as transfers has nothing to do with the household's or firm's income or other characteristics. In the real world, governments levy a variety of taxes and pay out a lot of transfers, but none of them looks like the lump sums in our theory. Generally, a household's or firm's taxes and transfers depend on its actions. But this dependence motivates changes in behavior. For example, income taxes deter people from working and discourage businesses from investing. Similarly, transfers to the unemployed or the poor may motivate people not to work. Overall, the system of taxes and transfers creates a variety of substitution effects on work effort, production, consumption, and investment. In this chapter we extend the theoretical analysis to incorporate some of these effects. But before considering the theory, it is useful to start with an overview of tax collections in the United States.

SOURCES OF GOVERNMENT REVENUES IN THE UNITED STATES

Figure 13.1 shows the breakdown of revenues by major types for the federal government since 1929. Individual income taxes have been a reasonably stable share of total federal revenues since World War II. For 1995, this share was 42%. The next component, corporate profits taxes, declined from about 25% of the total after World War II to 11% in 1995. Another item, levies for social insurance funds, have increased substantially since World War II. (The majority of these levies now go to social security, including medicare. The rest are mainly for unemployment insurance and government employees' retirement.) Notice that the total of payments into social insurance funds rose from 10% of all federal revenues in 1948 to 40% in 1995. Thus, in 1995, this category was about as large as the federal income tax on individuals. Another part of federal revenues is excise taxes, customs duties, and so forth, which fell from about 20% of the total after World War II to 6% in 1995. Finally, the Federal Reserve's payments to the Treasury—which correspond to the government's revenue from printing money—amounted in 1995 to 2% of total federal receipts. These proceeds from money creation were near zero before the mid-1950s.

Before World War II, the excise taxes and customs duties were relatively more important. These items were the major source of federal revenues before World War I. Individual income taxes began in 1913, except for some levies around the Civil War and in 1895. Corporate taxes started in 1909. Notice also that the levies for social insurance funds were small until the beginning of the unemployment insurance program in 1936 and social security in 1937.

Figure 13.2 shows a breakdown for the revenues of state and local governments. Property taxes were traditionally the largest component, but the share of this component fell from about 60% in the early 1930s to less than 40% after World War II and to 22% in 1995. In

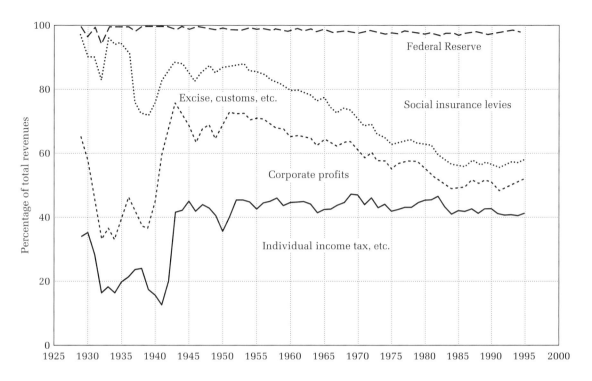

FIGURE 13.1

BREAKDOWN OF FEDERAL REVENUE

Figures are percentages of the total. Data for Figures 13.1–13.4 and 13.6 are from DRI data bank and U.S. Department of Commerce, *Survey of Current Business*.

the early period the relative decline in property taxes corresponded to the growth in sales taxes. These levies increased from 6% of state and local revenues in 1929 to 20% in 1941 but maintained a roughly constant share since World War II. More recently, state and local governments have turned to individual income taxes. This category constituted 4% of state and local receipts in 1929 and 1948 but then increased to 15% in 1995. The other category of state and local revenues that has become more important since World War II is federal grants-in-aid (transfers of funds from the federal government to state and local

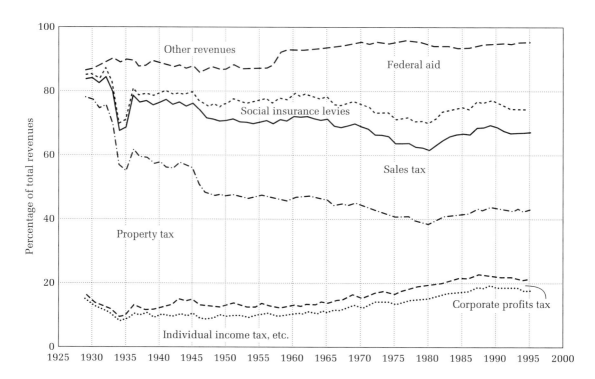

FIGURE 13.2

BREAKDOWN OF STATE AND LOCAL REVENUES

Figures are percentages of the total.

governments). These revenues climbed from 9% of the total in 1946 to 24% in 1978, then fell to 16% in 1987, but returned to 18% in 1995. (Federal grants-in-aid are primarily for welfare, medical care, transportation, education, housing, training programs, and general revenue sharing.)

Figure 13.3 shows the federal share of total government revenues. (Federal grants-in-aid are excluded here from total revenues.) Notice that the federal share was 34% in 1929, fell to a low point of 19% in 1932, but subsequently rose during the New Deal period to reach 49% by 1940.

FIGURE 13.3

FEDERAL RECEIPTS AS A FRACTION OF TOTAL GOVERNMENT RECEIPTS

After a peak of 80% during World War II, the share declined to 63% in 1975. For 1995, the fraction was 65%.

Figure 13.4 provides one measure of an overall tax rate, the ratio of total government revenues (excluding federal grants-in-aid) to GNP (GDP since 1959). The ratio rose from 11% in 1929 to 18% in 1940 and 25% in 1945. After a fall to 22% in 1949, the ratio increased slowly to 26% in 1960, 30% in 1969, and 31% in 1981. With the Reagan tax cuts, the ratio fell to 29% in 1983 but then returned to 30% for 1985–93 and to 31% in 1994–95.

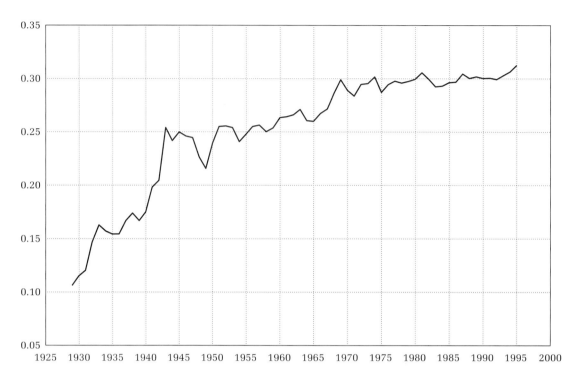

FIGURE 13.4

TOTAL GOVERNMENT RECEIPTS AS A RATIO TO GNP (GDP SINCE 1959)

TYPES OF TAXES

Notice that some taxes fall on income (individual income taxes, corporate profits taxes, and contributions for social security, which are levied on wage earnings), others on expenditures (excise and sales taxes), and some on holdings of property. But one way or another, the amount that someone pays depends on his or her economic activity: none of these levies looks like the lump-sum taxes in our theory.

FEDERAL INDIVIDUAL INCOME TAX

Consider now the complex, but fascinating, structure of the federal individual income tax. Begin by subtracting from a family's reported income the expenses for business purposes, deferred compensation through pension plans, and some other items to get **adjusted gross income**. Then take out either a standard deduction ($4000 for a single person, $6700 for a married couple in 1996) or the itemized deductions for some types of interest payments and taxes and a few other items. Then subtract the value of personal exemptions, which in 1996 was $2550 per dependent, including oneself, to get **taxable income**. (A complication—first introduced in the 1990 tax law in order to make it hard to figure out one's tax rate—is that the itemized deductions and dependency allowances are reduced in some ranges of high adjusted gross incomes as income rises.) Aside from any tax credits that apply, the law provides a schedule that relates the amount of tax to taxable income. (Marital status also matters here.) But it is important to note that the tax is not a constant fraction of taxable income; that is, it is not a **flat-rate tax**. Over most ranges of income, an increase in income (that is large enough to move someone into the next tax bracket) raises the **marginal tax rate**, which is the tax rate on an additional dollar of income. This setup is called a **graduated-rate tax**. (Sometimes it is called a "progressive tax," which seems to express someone's opinion about its merits. In contrast, a "regressive tax" system imposes a lower rate as income rises.)

Figure 13.5 shows the relation of the marginal tax rate and the **average tax rate** (the ratio of taxes to adjusted gross income) to a family's adjusted gross income. The graph applies in 1996 to a married couple who have two children and do not itemize deductions. (This assumption is unrealistic for high incomes, at which most people itemize deductions.) The graph therefore incorporates a standard deduction of $6700 and personal exemptions of $10,200. (However, to keep things

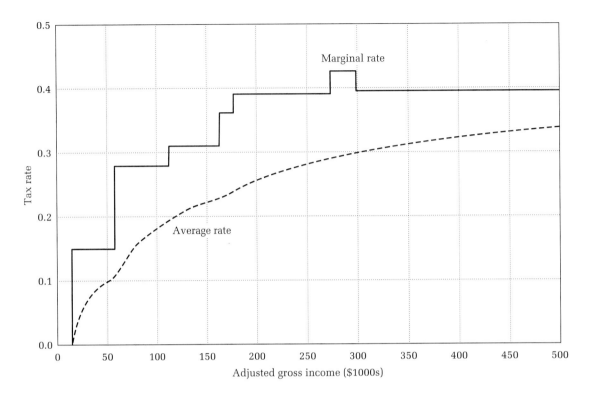

Figure 13.5

Marginal and Average Tax Rates for the Federal Individual Income Tax in 1996

The graph shows for 1996 the relation of marginal and average tax rates to adjusted gross income for a married couple with two children. We assume that the family uses the standard deduction.

interesting, the personal exemptions are phased out to zero as adjusted gross income rises from $177,000 to $300,000.) Note that the marginal tax rate is 0 for adjusted gross incomes between 0 and $16,000, 15% between $17,000 and $56,000, 28% between $57,000 and $113,000, 31% between $114,000 and $164,000, 36% between $165,000 and $176,000, 39% between $177,000 and $272,000, 43% between $273,000 and $299,000, and 39.6% for $300,000 and above. The funny looking notches in the figure derive from the phaseout of the personal exemptions. (For people who itemize deductions, the phaseout of these items would create more of these notches.)

Figure 13.5 also shows the average tax rate as a function of adjusted gross income. The average tax rate rises steadily with income but approaches 39.6%—the highest explicit marginal rate in the tax schedule—as income becomes very high. Recall that we have ignored itemized deductions and various devices that make income nontaxable. These elements strongly weaken the tendency for the average tax rate to rise as income increases.

The distinction between average and marginal tax rates is important for our analysis. *Average* tax rates determine how much revenue the government collects as a fraction of income: total revenue equals the average tax rate multiplied by the total amount of income. The effects of the tax system on people's choices depend, however, on *marginal* tax rates. These rates prescribe the fraction that the government takes from an additional dollar of income. In deciding how much to work, produce, and invest, households and firms take account of these marginal tax rates.

STATE AND LOCAL INCOME TAXES

Many states and some cities impose individual income taxes. Some of these tax systems have a graduated structure that resembles the federal system. In Vermont, for example, the tax is 25% of the federal levy. California and New York specify a schedule of marginal rates that rise from 0 to 9.3% and 0 to 6.85%, respectively. Other states have a flat rate of tax on income, except for a small exemption; for example, the rate is 3.0% in Illinois, 2.8% in Pennsylvania, and 5.95% (of "earned" income) in Massachusetts. Finally, there are a few states that have no income tax. For people who are looking for a place to move, these are Alaska, Florida, Nevada, South Dakota, Texas, Washington, and Wyoming. New Hampshire and Tennessee tax only some forms of property income.

SOCIAL SECURITY TAX

Another important form of tax (which the government amusingly calls a "contribution") is the levy on wage earnings and income from self-employment to finance social security. At present, almost all workers are covered by social security. The main exceptions are some government employees.

The social security tax is much simpler than the individual income tax. In 1996, for example, covered employees paid 6.2% of earnings up to a ceiling of $62,700 for old-age, survivors, and disability and paid 1.45% of earnings for medicare. Employers paid an equal amount. Thus, the combined marginal tax rate was 15.3% for labor earnings between 0 and $53,400 and 2.9% thereafter. This pattern of marginal rates implies that the average tax rate falls as earning increase beyond $62,700.[1] Except for the ceiling on earnings, the social security tax would amount to a flat-rate levy on labor income. The tax rates and ceilings have, however, increased substantially over time: in 1960 the rates were only 3% for each employee and employer, with an earnings ceiling of $4800.

CORPORATE PROFITS TAXES

Aside from taxing household income, governments also tax the net revenues of corporations. For large corporations in 1996, the federal marginal tax rate on taxable earnings was 35%. This rate had been close to 50% from the end of World War II until the 1986 tax reform (but a complicated "excess profits tax" applied also during the Korean War and World War II). From 1918 to 1938, the tax rates were between 12 and 15%.

We can think of the corporate profits tax as a levy on the capital owned by corporations. But since households own the corporations, the tax amounts ultimately to another levy on households' income from capital. In fact, the government taxes the earnings of corporations directly and then taxes them a second time when people receive dividends or

[1] In calculating effective marginal tax rates, we should deduct any extra benefits that someone gets because they pay the tax. Some parts of government revenue are therefore not a tax at all—these include charges for school tuition and hospitals, contributions to government employee retirement funds, and some other items. For individual income taxes, we treat this extra benefit as nil: even if people like public services, the amounts that they get do not depend on the individual taxes that they pay. For social security, there is some relation of an individual's benefits to that person's lifetime contributions to the program. Martin Feldstein and Andrew Samwick (1992) show that the effective marginal tax rate from the social security retirement program in 1990 varied from negative values to the full statutory rate of 11.2%. Young persons and dependent spouses face the highest marginal rates, whereas workers with dependent spouses, older workers, persons with low income, and persons with very high income (above the social security maximum) face the lowest rates.

capital gains. (Economists call this *double taxation.*) For the purposes of our analysis, we can think of adding the tax on corporate profits to individual income taxes to calculate an overall tax on the income from capital.

PROPERTY TAXES

The various state and local governments use a wide array of procedures to determine the taxes on houses, factories, and other property. We can think of the property tax as another form of tax on capital. For most purposes, we can therefore combine this tax with the individual income taxes and the corporate profits tax to find the overall tax on the income from capital.

SALES AND EXCISE TAXES

Many states and localities have general sales taxes and also special levies on gasoline, alcohol, tobacco, and other items. The federal government's excise taxes apply to petroleum products, alcohol, tobacco, automobiles, tires, and some other items.

An important feature of these taxes is that they apply to expenditures, rather than to income or wealth.[2] In the subsequent theoretical analysis, we shall focus on income taxes. Thus, in a broad sense, the analysis encompasses the types of taxes discussed in previous categories. But we should remember that sales and excise taxes operate in a different manner.

AN INCOME TAX IN THE THEORETICAL MODEL

We can evaluate the main effects of taxation by examining a simple form of income tax. Assume that a household's real taxes, t_t/P_t, are a fraction, τ, of its real taxable income. (τ is the Greek letter *tau.*) Hence,

[2] *Many other countries use a* value-added tax, *which amounts to a broad-based sales tax. Instead of applying to final sales, this levy depends on the value added to goods at various stages of production.*

for simplicity, we do not introduce a graduated-rate tax structure into the model but use instead a flat-rate tax. Also, we assume at this stage that the tax rate, τ, does not vary over time.

In the model—in which the households are the producers as well as the workers—we assume that a household's real taxable income equals its real net product, $y_t - \delta k_{t-1}$, plus real interest income, less an amount of **tax-exempt real income**, e_t.[3] Notice that we treat governmental transfers as nontaxable, which is accurate in most cases. Finally, we assume initially that there is no inflation, so that the real and nominal interest rates on bonds are equal: $r_t = R_t$. A household's real taxes are therefore given by

$$t_t/P_t = \tau \cdot (y_t - \delta k_{t-1} + r_{t-1}b_{t-1}/P_t - e_t) \tag{13.1}$$

If real taxable income is negative, then we assume that taxes are negative rather than zero.[4] We also assume that the tax parameters, τ and e_t, are the same for all households. In particular, we neglect any actions that individuals can take to affect either their marginal tax rate, τ, or their quantity of tax-exempt income, e_t. Since each household's marginal tax rate is τ, the average of these rates across households—the average marginal tax rate—is also τ.

Aggregate real tax revenues follow from equation (13.1) as

$$T_t/P_t = \tau \cdot (Y_t - \delta K_{t-1} - E_t) \tag{13.2}$$

where E_t is the aggregate amount of tax-exempt real income. (Remember that aggregate real interest payments, $r_{t-1}B_{t-1}/P_t$, equal zero.) The government's budget constraint in real terms follows from substitution for T_t/P_t in equation (12.1) as

$$G_t + V_t/P_t = \tau \cdot (Y_t - \delta K_{t-1} - E_t) + (M_t - M_{t-1})/P_t \tag{13.3}$$

Suppose that we take as given the amounts of government consumption, G_t, aggregate real transfers, V_t/P_t, and the real revenue from money

[3] *The formulation assumes that interest paid by borrowers reduces their taxable income one-to-one. This assumption was correct in most cases before the 1986 tax law for people who itemized deductions. The 1986 law placed more restrictions on the tax deductibility of interest payments.*

[4] *In the real world taxes can be negative because of the earned-income credit (a payment that the government gives to low-income families that have labor income) and because households and businesses can carry over some losses from one period to the next.*

creation, $(M_t - M_{t-1})/P_t$. Then, for a given amount of aggregate net product, $Y_t - \delta K_{t-1}$, the two tax parameters, τ and E_t, must be set so as to satisfy the government's budget constraint: the government has to generate enough tax receipts in each period to meet the expenditures that are not covered by printing money. We shall often think about changing the marginal tax rate, τ, and then allowing the exempt amount, E_t, to vary in order for equation (13.3) to hold. In that way we can isolate the substitution effect from a change in the tax rate. Note that we do not allow the government to borrow and lend on the credit market. That is, we wait until the next chapter to allow for budget deficits or surpluses.

HOUSEHOLDS' BUDGET CONSTRAINTS

From our analysis in previous chapters, each household's budget constraint in real terms is

$$y_t - \delta k_{t-1} + b_{t-1} \cdot (1 + r_{t-1})/P_t + m_{t-1}/P_t + v_t/P_t - t_t/P_t =$$
$$c_t + i_t - \delta k_{t-1} + (b_t + m_t)/P_t \tag{13.4}$$

Recall that we treat the households as carrying out the investment expenditures. We have also subtracted depreciation from both sides of equation (13.4), so that net product, $y_t - \delta k_{t-1}$, appears on the left, and net investment, $i_t - \delta k_{t-1}$, appears on the right. Notice that real taxes, t_t/P_t, subtract from the household's disposable funds on the left side.

Now substitute for real taxes from equation (13.1) into equation (13.4) and rearrange terms to get

$$(1 - \tau) \cdot (y_t - \delta k_{t-1}) + (1 - \tau) \cdot r_{t-1} b_{t-1}/P_t + (b_{t-1} + m_{t-1})/P_t$$
$$+ v_t/P_t + \tau e_t = c_t + i_t - \delta k_{t-1} + (b_t + m_t)/P_t \tag{13.5}$$

The first term on the left side equals net product or income, $y_t - \delta k_{t-1}$, less the tax on this income, $\tau \cdot (y_t - \delta k_{t-1})$. In other words, the after-tax income, $(1 - \tau) \cdot (y_t - \delta k_{t-1})$, enters into the household's budget constraint. Similarly, the after-tax real interest income, $(1 - \tau) \cdot r_{t-1} b_{t-1}/P_t$, appears on the left side of equation (13.5).

The uses of funds on the right side of equation (13.5) do not involve the tax rate. This result follows because we assume no tax on the expenditures for consumption or net investment. More generally, any sales or excise taxes would enter here.

TAX RATES AND SUBSTITUTION EFFECTS

We want to see how the presence of an income tax alters the various substitution effects on households. For this purpose we have to reconsider our concepts of the real interest rate, the marginal product of labor (or real wage rate), and the return to investment.

After-Tax Real Interest Rate

Households receive real interest at the rate r_t, but they pay the fraction τ of their receipts to the government. Hence, when measured net of tax, households earn interest at the rate $\tilde{r}_t \equiv (1 - \tau) \cdot r_t$. We refer to the variable $\tilde{r}_t$ as the **after-tax real interest rate**. Notice that this interest rate appears (for period $t - 1$) on the left side of equation (13.5).

In previous chapters we discussed the intertemporal-substitution effects that arise when the real interest rate changes. These effects still apply, but they refer now to the after-tax real interest rate. An increase in $\tilde{r}_t$ stimulates saving. The increase in saving reflects partly a reduction in current consumption demand and partly an increase in current work effort and the supply of goods.

After-Tax Marginal Product of Labor

When someone works an additional hour, he or she raises output, y_t, and, hence, income by the marginal product of labor, MPL_t. But households keep only the fraction, $1 - \tau$, of their extra income. Hence, the **after-tax marginal product of labor**, $(1 - \tau) \cdot MPL_t$, matters for the choices of work and consumption. (With a separate labor market, the after-tax real wage rate, $[1 - \tau] \cdot w_t/P_t$, would matter.)

Suppose that there is a given schedule for labor's marginal product, MPL_t, when graphed versus the amount of work, l_t. An increase in the tax rate, τ, lowers the schedule when measured net of tax, that is, as $(1 - \tau) \cdot MPL_t$. Households respond just as they would to a decrease in the schedule for labor's marginal product: they reduce work effort, the supply of goods, and consumption demand.

After-Tax Rate of Return to Investment

An increase in the stock of capital, k_t, by one unit raises next period's net product by the marginal product of capital less the rate of depreciation, $MPK_t - \delta$. Recall that this term is the real rate of return from an extra unit of investment. But owners of capital (households) now keep only the fraction $1 - \tau$ of this return. Therefore, the **after-tax rate of return to investment** becomes $(1 - \tau) \cdot (MPK_t - \delta)$. Producers determine their desired stock of capital, $\hat{k}_t$, by equating this after-tax rate of return to the after-tax real interest rate on bonds, $\tilde{r}_t$. Hence, the condition for the desired stock of capital is

$$(1 - \tau) \cdot (MPK_t - \delta) = \tilde{r}_t \tag{13.6}$$

Equation (13.6) implies that we can now write the function for the desired stock of capital, $\hat{k}_t$, as

$$\hat{k}_t = \hat{k}(\underset{(-)}{\tilde{r}_t}, \underset{(-)}{\tau}, \ldots) \tag{13.7}$$

As before, the term . . . represents characteristics of the production function that affect the schedule for capital's marginal product.

For a given tax rate τ, an increase in the *after-tax* real interest rate, $\tilde{r}_t$, on the right side of equation (13.6) raises the required after-tax return from investment. Hence, the desired capital stock falls. For a given value of $\tilde{r}_t$, a higher τ lowers the after-tax return from investment on the left side of equation (13.6). The desired capital stock therefore declines again. Finally, as in earlier cases, the desired capital stock rises if there is an upward shift in the schedule for capital's marginal product, MPK_t.

As before, the desired stock of capital, $\hat{k}_t$, determines a producer's gross investment demand:

$$i_t^d = \hat{k}(\underset{(-)}{\tilde{r}_t}, \underset{(-)}{\tau}, \ldots) - (1-\delta) \cdot k_{t-1}$$

$$= i^d(\underset{(-)}{\tilde{r}_t}, \underset{(-)}{\tau}, \underset{(-)}{k_{t-1}}, \ldots)$$

(13.8)

The new features concern the tax rate. First, the after-tax real interest rate, $\tilde{r}_t$, has a negative effect on gross investment demand. Second, for a given value of $\tilde{r}_t$, the tax rate, τ, has a separate negative effect on investment demand.

A CHANGE IN THE TAX RATE

Suppose that the income-tax rate, τ, increases. Aggregate real tax revenues are given from the tax law in equation (13.2) by $T_t/P_t = \tau \cdot (Y_t - \delta K_{t-1} - E_t)$. If the exempt amount, E_t, did not change, then real tax revenues would increase unless aggregate net product, $Y_t - \delta K_{t-1}$, fell by a great deal. Assume for the moment that this is not the case; that is, real tax receipts would rise if the exempt amount did not change.

Suppose that we hold constant the levels of government consumption, G_t, and aggregate real transfers, V_t/P_t, as well as the real revenue from money creation, $(M_t - M_{t-1})/P_t$. Then the government's budget constraint from equation (13.3) says that the amount of real taxes collected cannot change. If we raise the tax rate, then we have to increase the exempt amount, E_t, to keep real tax revenues the same. In effect, we raise the *average marginal tax rate*, represented by the parameter τ in the model, without changing the *average tax rate*. In the real world, for example, the government might increase various exemptions in the income-tax law but then raise all of the tax rates on taxable income to maintain the level of real revenues. Alternatively, the government could switch from one type of tax, such as the social security tax on wage earnings, to another, such as the individual income tax. Because the social security tax has a low average marginal tax rate, compared to the revenue that it collects, this change raises the average marginal tax rate while leaving unchanged the total of real taxes collected.

The important point is that, conceptually, we want to keep separate the effects of changes in the average marginal tax rate, τ, from those of changes in government consumption, transfers, or money creation. That is why we consider first the case in which the exempt amount varies along with the tax rate to keep fixed the volume of real tax revenues. Then we can also look at cases in which tax revenues do change, along with some combination of shifts in government consumption, transfers, or money creation.

Consider whether households' wealth changes when the tax rate, τ, increases or decreases. Remember that the aggregate of households' budget constraints involves the present value of aggregate real taxes net of transfers. This present value depends on the present value of government consumption. As long as we hold this last present value fixed, a change in the tax rate does not affect the aggregate present value of taxes less transfers and, therefore, would not seem to affect wealth. This result turns out to be a satisfactory approximation in most cases. We shall, however, see later that it is not exact. But, for now, we neglect any effects on wealth from changes in the tax rate.

CLEARING OF THE COMMODITY MARKET

Now we incorporate the various effects from the tax rate into the condition for clearing the commodity market. The condition for period 1 is

$$\underset{(-)\ (-)}{C^d(\tilde{r}_1,\ \tau\ ,\dots)} + \underset{(-)\ (-)}{I^d(\tilde{r}_1,\ \tau\ ,\dots)} + G_1 = \underset{(+)\ (-)}{Y^s(\tilde{r}_1,\ \tau\ ,\dots)} \qquad \textbf{(13.9)}$$

To avoid a clutter of terms, we do not write out explicitly some of the variables that influence consumer demand, investment demand, and the supply of goods. These include the initial capital stock, K_0, and the amount of government consumption, G_1.

One new feature is that the after-tax real interest rate, $\tilde{r}_1$, appears where the real interest rate, r_1, used to appear. Given the value of $\tilde{r}_1$, the tax rate, τ, has some separate effects. First, a higher tax rate lowers the schedule for the after-tax marginal product of labor, $(1 - \tau) \cdot MPL_1$, and thereby reduces the incentive to work. This response decreases goods supply, Y_1^s, and consumer demand, C_1^d. Second, a higher tax rate lowers the after-tax rate of return to investment, $(1 - \tau) \cdot (MPK_1 - \delta)$, and thereby reduces investment demand, I_1^d. Thus, in general, *a higher tax rate tends to depress market activity:* it reduces the demands for consumption and investment, as well as the supply of goods. These results follow because a household's tax liability rises when it engages in more market activity. A higher tax rate motivates people to substitute away from market activities and toward untaxed areas, such as leisure or the **underground economy**, in which income is not reported.

Figure 13.6 shows the clearing of the commodity market. The after-tax real interest rate, $\tilde{r}_1$, appears on the vertical axis. The horizontal axis shows the levels of commodity demand and supply.

EFFECTS OF A HIGHER TAX RATE

Assume that the income-tax rate rises permanently from τ to τ' at date 1. Figure 13.7 shows the effects on the commodity market. First, there is a leftward shift of the demand curve, reflecting the decreases in consumption and investment demand. Second, there is a leftward shift of the supply curve. Because the increase in the tax rate is permanent, we predict little response of desired real saving. That is, at the initial value of the after-tax real interest rate, the cutback in goods supply is roughly equal to the fall in consumption demand.[5] Since investment demand also declines, the overall fall in demand is greater than that in supply. Hence, Figure 13.7 shows that the increase in the tax rate creates an excess supply of commodities at the after-tax real interest rate that initially cleared the market. The after-tax real interest rate and the level of output therefore decline.

[5] *Recall that we hold constant aggregate real taxes. The change in the aggregate of desired saving therefore equals the change in goods supply, Y_1^s, less the change in consumer demand, C_1^d.*

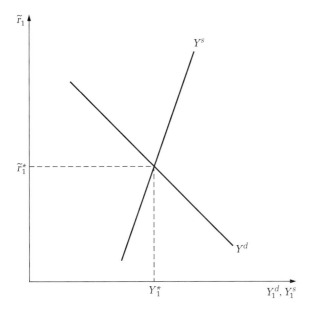

FIGURE 13.6

CLEARING OF THE COMMODITY MARKET

We graph the demand and supply of commodities versus the after-tax real interest rate, $\tilde{r}_1$.

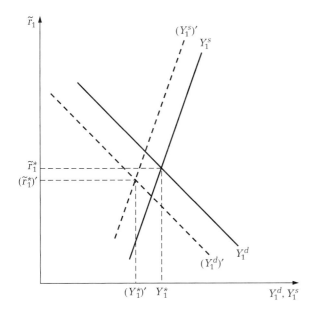

FIGURE 13.7

EFFECTS ON THE COMMODITY MARKET OF A HIGHER INCOME-TAX RATE

The increase in the income-tax rate from τ to τ' reduces the demand for commodities by more than the supply. Hence, output and the after-tax real interest rate fall.

We are, at this point, taking a short-run perspective in which the capital stock, K_0, is given. The fall in output therefore reflects a decrease in labor input, L. People work less in response to a higher tax rate because the government extracts a larger fraction of a marginal dollar of income.

Because government consumption does not change, the total of real private spending for consumption and investment must decline (to match the fall in output). Recall that the disturbance had no initial impact on desired real saving. The decline in the after-tax real interest rate reduces desired saving: therefore, real saving, and hence net investment, must decline overall. We can understand this result if we think of the drop in the after-tax real interest rate as a signal that the priority for using resources to accumulate capital has diminished. From the viewpoint of the private sector, the diminished priority for accumulating capital reflects the adverse effect of a higher tax rate on the after-tax rate of return to investment.

The effect on consumption is uncertain: the decrease in the after-tax real interest rate motivates more consumption, whereas the higher income-tax rate motivates less consumption. Thus, although total output falls, the higher tax rate may crowd out enough investment to avoid a decline in consumption in the short run.

LONG-RUN EFFECTS OF A HIGHER TAX RATE

We have shown that a permanent increase in the income-tax rate, τ, leads to less investment. This effect on investment in the short run suggests that the stock of capital would decline in the long run. To study this long-run effect, we have to use the dynamic analysis of capital accumulation and economic growth that we worked out in Chapter 11. We consider here only a sketch of these long-run effects.

We showed in Chapter 11 that the change in the capital stock is given by

$$\Delta K = s \cdot F(K, L) - \delta K$$

The Wealth Effect from a Change in the Tax Rate (optional)

We carried out the analysis under the assumption that the change in the tax rate left wealth unchanged. This assumption seems reasonable because we varied the amount of tax-exempt income, E_1, to hold constant the quantity of real taxes collected, T_1/P_1. But let's consider more carefully whether wealth changes.

As we discussed in Chapter 2, the effect of a disturbance on a household's wealth is positive or negative depending on whether the household can achieve a higher or lower level of utility. The increase in the tax rate that we have just considered ends up reducing the utility of the typical household. The effect on wealth is therefore negative rather than zero.

To see why, note first that someone who produces the quantity of output y_1 gets to keep only the portion $(1 - \tau) \cdot y_1$; the remainder goes as taxes to the government. Each household's contribution to the economy's output, y_1, therefore ex-

ceeds the contribution to that household's after-tax income, which is $(1 - \tau) \cdot y_1$.

In deciding how much to work and invest, households consider only the fraction $1 - \tau$ of the marginal products of their labor and capital. Hence, from a social perspective, people have insufficient incentives to work and invest.* An increase in the income-tax rate worsens this incentive problem and thereby causes work effort and output to fall further below their socially optimal levels. A higher tax rate therefore means that each household ends up with a smaller level of utility: each household is less wealthy.

We could modify the previous analysis to include a negative effect on wealth from an increase in the tax rate, but the general nature of the results would not change. For most purposes, we can therefore use the results that neglected the wealth effects.

TAXES AND TRANSFERS

---

* The fraction τ that goes to taxes reduces the required payments of all other taxpayers (by a very small amount per person). No individual takes these benefits to others into account when deciding how much to work and invest. Economists call this an external effect. This effect refers to the benefits that others get from one person's actions, when the person does not take these benefits into account.

where s is the gross saving rate or, equivalently, the ratio of gross investment to gross output. We have just demonstrated that a permanent increase in the income-tax rate, τ, lowers investment. This change enters into the long-run analysis as a decrease in the investment ratio, s.[6] We showed in Chapter 11 that a lower s leads in the long run to a smaller stock of capital, K.

EFFECTS OF A PERMANENT RISE IN GOVERNMENT CONSUMPTION UNDER INCOME TAXATION

In Chapter 12, we studied the effects of changes in government consumption when financed by lump-sum taxes. We shall see in Chapter 14 that temporary changes in government consumption, such as in wartime, tend to be financed by government borrowing, whereas permanent changes tend to be paid from taxes. The taxes are, however, unlikely to be lump sum and are more likely to resemble the income taxes that we have considered in this chapter. We should therefore reassess the consequences of a permanent shift in government consumption when financed by a change in income taxes.

We found in Chapter 12 that a permanent increase in government consumption reduced wealth and thereby raised work effort and output. If the public services were productive, then output also increased for given inputs of labor and capital. Private consumption decreased, but there were no effects on the real interest rate and private investment.

Suppose now that the permanent expansion of government consumption is paid by increased income taxes and is accompanied by an increase in the marginal income-tax rate, which we represent by the parameter τ. We found before that a higher income-tax rate tends to reduce work effort. This effect offsets the tendency of more government consumption to increase work effort: hence, the overall response of labor input is now ambiguous. This uncertainty about the change in labor input means that output could also rise or fall.

[6] *The higher tax rate also reduces the level of labor input, L, and therefore the level of output, Y, for a given stock of capital, K. We can show, however, that investment tends to fall as a fraction of output; that is, the ratio s declines. The capital stock falls in the long run partly because s has decreased and partly because L has declined.*

Recall that a permanent increase in government consumption had no effect on private investment, whereas a higher income-tax rate reduced private investment. A tax-financed increase in government consumption therefore leads to less private investment. This reduction of investment in the short run corresponds to a fall in the capital stock in the long run.[7]

THE RELATION BETWEEN THE TAX RATE AND TAX REVENUES

We combined a permanent increase in government consumption with a rise in the income-tax rate, τ, to generate more real tax revenues for each period, T_t/P_t. These revenues are given from the tax law as

$$T_t/P_t = \tau \cdot (Y_t - \delta K_{t-1} - E_t)$$

If we hold the exempt amount, E_t, constant, then real tax receipts increase with the tax rate only if output, Y_t, does not fall enough to reduce real taxable income, $Y_t - \delta K_{t-1} - E_t$, by proportionately more than the increase in the tax rate.

We can view the long-run movement in output, Y, in terms of the changes in the two productive inputs, K and L. We already found that a tax-financed increase in government consumption tends to reduce K but has an ambiguous effect on L. The variable K falls because producers get to keep only the fraction $1 - \tau$ of their output, and τ has increased. Similarly, L may fall because workers get to keep only the fraction $1 - \tau$ of their income. The tendency of Y to decline is therefore pronounced if private investment and labor input are highly sensitive to changes in the fraction of income, $1 - \tau$, that producers and workers keep for themselves.

The depressing effects of income taxation on capital and labor have to be very strong for tax revenues to fall when the tax rate rises. This outcome does, however, become more likely as the rate of tax,

[7] *This result follows because we assumed in Chapter 12 that a change in government consumption did not affect the schedule for the marginal product of capital, MPK. Some public services, such as infrastructure activities like highways and the maintenance of a legal system, tend to raise the marginal product of capital. In these cases, the effect on private investment in the short run is uncertain: the increase in MPK tends to raise investment, but the increase in the income-tax rate tends to lower it. The long-run effect on the capital stock is also ambiguous in this case.*

τ, increases. For example, when the tax rate is 10%, a 10% increase means that the new tax rate is 11%. The fraction of extra income that a producer or worker keeps, $1 - \tau$, falls accordingly from 90 to 89%, or by a percentage of 1.1%. In other words, a 10% increase in the tax rate translates into a decline by only 1.1% in the term, $1 - \tau$ that influences capital and labor. We therefore anticipate that a 10% increase in the tax rate would reduce real taxable income in the long run by much less than 10%.

Suppose that we consider higher starting values for the tax rate but continue to raise the rate each time by 10%. At a tax rate of 25%, a 10% increase (to a new rate of 27.5%) means that $1 - \tau$ falls from 75 to 72.5%, or by 3.3%. At a starting rate of 50%, a 10% increase lowers $1 - \tau$ from 50 to 45%, that is, by 10%. At the still higher rate of 75%, a 10% increase reduces $1 - \tau$ by 30%. Thus, the higher is the starting value of the tax rate, the greater is the proportional reduction of the term, $1 - \tau$, from a 10% increase in the tax rate. We predict therefore that the negative response of real taxable income to the tax rate becomes stronger as the rate of tax increases. At some point—but, surely, for a tax rate below 100%—we shall find that an increase in the tax rate reduces real taxable income by so much that real tax revenues fall.

Figure 13.8 shows the relationship between real tax receipts, T/P, and the tax rate, τ. (Think of this relation as applying in the long run, when capital and labor adjust fully to a change in the tax rate.) This relationship is called a **Laffer curve**, in honor of the economist Arthur Laffer. (For a discussion, see Don Fullerton, 1982.) When the tax rate, τ, is zero, the government collects nothing. As the tax rate rises above zero, tax revenues become positive—hence, the curve has a positive slope. As the tax rate continues to increase, however, the negative response of real taxable income becomes stronger. The slope of the curve therefore gets smaller as the tax rate rises, and the curve eventually becomes flat at the tax rate labeled τ^* in the figure. If the government raises the tax rate beyond τ^*, then revenues start to decline. In fact, as the tax rate approaches 100%, tax receipts approach zero. If the government wishes

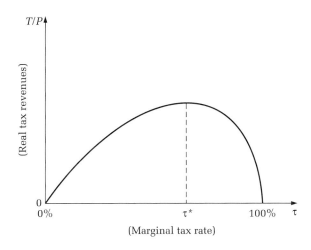

FIGURE 13.8

THE RELATION OF TAX RECEIPTS TO THE TAX RATE (A LAFFER CURVE)

Real tax revenue, T/P, initially rise with the tax rate, τ. Revenues reach their peak when the rate is τ^*. If the tax rate rises above τ^*, then revenues fall and approach zero as the tax rate approaches 100%.

to maximize its real revenues, it should not choose a tax rate of 100%. Rather, the value τ^* is the tax rate that maximizes receipts.

In 1980–81 some advocates of **supply-side economics** used a picture similar to that shown in Figure 13.8 to argue for an across-the-board cut in U.S. income-tax rates. These economists contended that the average marginal tax rate on income exceeded the value τ^*, so that a general cut in rates would yield a larger volume of real tax revenues. There is, however, no evidence that the United States has reached high enough tax rates for this result to apply.

The U.S. data do suggest that taxpayers at the upper end of the income distribution have been sufficiently sensitive to changes in marginal tax rates so that their income-tax payments have typically risen when their tax rates fell, and vice versa. Figure 13.9 shows the share of total income taxes paid in each year by taxpayers in the top 0.5% of the distribution for adjusted gross incomes (corresponding to incomes above $268,000 in 1994). For these taxpayers, the most important changes in tax policy are shifts in the top marginal tax rate. For instance, the period after 1981 featured a cut in the top marginal rate on unearned income from 70% to 50% in the 1981 law, a cut in the top rate on all forms of

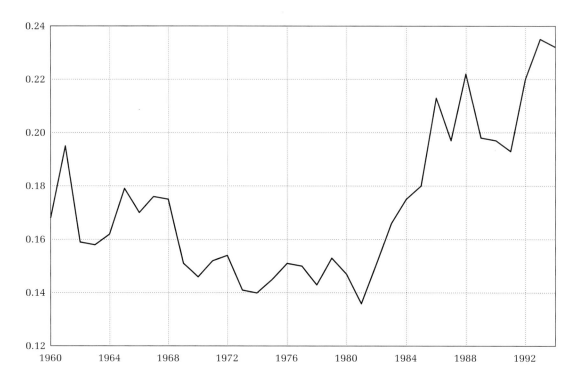

FIGURE 13.9

SHARE OF INCOME TAX PAID BY TOP 0.5% OF INCOME DISTRIBUTION

The graph shows the fraction of overall income taxes paid by taxpayers in the top 0.5% of the distribution of
adjusted gross incomes (incomes above $268,000 in 1994). The data were provided by Dr. Dan Feenberg of
the National Bureau of Economic Research.

income to 28% in the 1986 law (except that this law raised the rate on
long-term capital gains), an increase to roughly 31% in the 1990 law,
and a rise to around 40% in the 1993 law.

The first observation from Figure 13.9 is that the increase in the
reported taxable incomes of the rich after the enactment of the 1981
law was so great that the share of taxes paid by this group rose from
14% in 1981 to 18% in 1984–85. The share for 1986—21%—is inflated
by the surge in capital-gains realizations in anticipation of the rise in
the capital-gains rate for 1987. But the principal observation about the

1986 reform is that the share of taxes paid by the rich remained roughly constant—between 20 and 22% from 1986 to 1990—despite the sharp cut in the top marginal tax rate on most forms of income.

The rise in the top marginal rate in the 1990 law was followed by a small decline in the fraction of taxes paid by the rich—from 19.7% in 1990 to 19.3% in 1991. For the 1993 law, which also raised the top rate, the evidence is less clear. The share of taxes paid by the rich rose from 22.0% in 1992 to an all-time high of 23.5% in 1993; thus, the higher rate at the top—which was enacted in the middle of 1993 and effectively applied retroactively to all income for the year—likely did generate more revenue from the rich in the short run. However, this share fell in 1994 to 23.3% (a value that is a rough estimate because of the available data).

A study by Charles Stuart (1981) estimated that the maximum of tax revenues occurs in Sweden when the average marginal tax rate is about 70%. That is, he estimated τ^* to be about 70%. The actual value of the average marginal tax rate in Sweden reached 70% in the early 1970s and rose subsequently to about 80%. (Stuart took a broad view of taxes to go beyond the income-tax law.) Sweden was therefore operating on the falling portion of the Laffer curve during the 1970s.[8] Stuart attributed part of Sweden's relatively low growth rate of real per capita gross domestic product during the 1970s (1.7% per year) to this factor.

Lawrence Lindsey (1987) estimated the effect of the Reagan tax cuts from 1982 to 1984 on the tax payments by taxpayers in various income groups. He found that the reductions in tax rates lowered tax collections overall and for taxpayers with middle and low incomes. However, among taxpayers with the highest incomes (adjusted gross incomes in excess of $200,000), the increase of reported taxable incomes was sufficient to more than offset the decrease in tax rates. Lindsey estimated that the tax-rate cuts raised collections in this group by 3% in 1982, 9% in 1983, and 23% in 1984. Therefore, although U.S. taxpayers as a whole were not on the falling portion of the Laffer curve, the taxpayers with the highest incomes appeared to be operating in this range.[9]

[8] *A conceptually similar study by A. Van Ravestein and H. Vijlbrief (1988) estimated that the value of τ^* for the Netherlands in 1970 was also about 70%. The actual value of τ, as estimated by the authors, rose steadily after 1970 to reach 67% in 1985. Thus, the conclusion in 1985 was that the Netherlands was close to, but not beyond, the peak of the Laffer curve.*

[9] *The 1986 tax law raised tax rates on income from long-term capital gains. Some economists think that this tax rate was raised above the value that would maximize tax revenues; that is, a cut in the tax rate on capital gains might generate more tax receipts. Although this outcome is plausible, the empirical evidence on this issue is ambiguous.*

TRANSFER PAYMENTS

Suppose that the government raises the aggregate of real transfers, V/P, and finances these expenditures with more tax revenues, T/P. As in the case in which government consumption increases, the rise in real taxes typically requires an increase in the average marginal tax rate, τ. We have already discussed the adverse effects on work, production, and investment from an increase in the tax rate. Note especially that an increase in transfers, when financed by an income tax, is no longer neutral in the model.

If transfer payments are lump sum, as we have been assuming, then the analysis is finished. But lump-sum transfers make little sense. Generally, the point of transfer programs is to provide payments to persons in specified categories, for example, poor people, persons who have lost their jobs, old or sick people, farmers, college students, and others. But none of these transfers is lump sum: the amount depends in some way on a person's status.

Think about a welfare program, such as aid to families with dependent children (AFDC) or food stamps, in which the payments depend on a family's current or long-run income (as well as on the existence of dependent children). Individuals typically face a declining schedule of transfers, possibly subject to some discrete cutoff points, as a function of market income. The important point is that the negative effect of income on benefit payments works like a positive marginal tax rate. Because transfers are sometimes cut drastically when a family's income rises, these programs can imply high effective marginal tax rates on the earnings of low-income persons.

Suppose, again, that the government increases taxes to finance more welfare payments. We already noted the adverse effects on work, production, and investment that derive from the increase in the average marginal tax rate, τ. But the expansion of the welfare program means that low-income people stand to lose more benefits if they earn more market

The Earned-Income Tax Credit

We mentioned that transfer programs have substitution effects. For most welfare programs, these effects are adverse for labor supply because people receive the benefits only by working less or not at all. The earned-income tax credit (or EITC), which began in 1975 but expanded considerably in the 1990s, is different because people have to work to get the money. Therefore, this program may actually stimulate labor supply.

Under the EITC program in 1996, a family with two or more children received a 40% wage subsidy on earnings up to $8890 to yield a maximum credit of $3556. (People get this money even if it exceeds their income-tax liability for the year.) This feature of the program motivates labor-force participation. In 1996, the EITC remained constant for incomes between $8890 and $11,610 and was then phased out at a rate of 21% for earnings up to $28,495. The effect of this phaseout is to raise the marginal tax rate on earnings by 21 percentage points. This aspect of the program would be expected to lower work hours for persons with incomes in the relevant range.

A study by Nada Eissa and Jeff Liebman (1996) assessed the labor-supply effects from the increase in the EITC in the 1986 income-tax reform. Their key finding was that the labor-force participation of persons likely to be eligible for the credit—notably single women with children—rose by 2–3 percentage points relative to those persons unlikely to be eligible. Their study could not precisely estimate the effect of the EITC program on average work hours, but their evidence appeared to rule out a large reduction in these hours. Thus, the EITC program appeared to raise labor supply overall.

There are problems in the EITC program related to fraudulent claims and the necessity to pay for the credits through tax revenues. But at least the incentive effects from the program seem to be favorable for labor supply. Thus, there is good reason to favor this kind of mechanism for transferring income to the poor over more traditional welfare programs, such as aid to families with dependent children (AFDC) and food stamps.

income. That is, there is also an increase in the effective marginal tax rate for potential welfare recipients. Hence, the negative influences of this change on work and production reinforce the effects from the higher tax rate on market income.

In terms of dollar volume, the most important and rapidly growing transfer program in the United States and in most other countries is the payments to retirees and survivors under social security. We have already discussed the financing of these programs in the United States. From this standpoint, an expansion of social security leads to a higher marginal tax rate on income, τ, which has the usual adverse effects on work and production.[10] If people received social security benefits without restrictions, except for age,[11] then the distorting influences that arise from welfare programs would not apply. However, the U.S. system imposes a test on earned income: persons (now below age 70) who earn income above a specified amount experience a partial or total cutoff of social security benefits. This income test works like an income standard for welfare—namely, it imposes a high effective marginal tax rate on the potential recipients. Not surprisingly, researchers (such as Michael Boskin, 1977a) find that this income test motivates people to retire earlier than they would otherwise.

SUMMARY

In this chapter we expanded the model to include a simple form of income-tax law. The key parameters of this law are the marginal tax rate and the quantity of tax-exempt income. The marginal tax rate measures the extra tax that the government takes from an additional dollar of income. Households and firms take this marginal tax rate into account when deciding how much to work, produce, and invest. In contrast, the government's tax receipts equal the product of the average tax rate (total taxes divided by total income) and the amount of income.

[10] *Because the social security tax depends on labor income, not capital income, the effects on investment are different.*

[11] *Before 1961, recipients had to be over 65. Since 1961, there is an opportunity to receive reduced benefits at age 62. The 1983 law will eventually raise the basic retirement age from 65 to 67.*

Saving depends on the after-tax real interest rate, whereas work effort and investment depend on the after-tax marginal products of labor and capital, respectively. For a given total of real taxes collected, an increase in the marginal tax rate motivates people to substitute away from market activities, which are taxed, and toward leisure (or the underground economy). A higher tax rate therefore leads in the short run to less work, output, and investment and in the long run to a smaller stock of capital and lower levels of production and consumption.

When we combine a permanent increase in government consumption with a rise in the marginal tax rate, we change some of the results from the previous chapter. Because of the adverse effects of higher taxation, the short-run effects on labor input and output become ambiguous. Further, the higher tax rate leads in the long run to a lower stock of capital.

As the marginal tax rate rises, the quantity of real taxable income tends to fall. The sensitivity of this response becomes larger the higher is the tax rate. We can therefore draw a Laffer curve, which shows a diminishing effect of the tax rate on the quantity of real tax revenues. Eventually, the economy reaches a tax rate at which revenues are at a maximum. At that point, further increases in tax rates generate less real tax receipts. For Sweden, there is an estimate that this marginal tax rate is about 70%, which was reached and then surpassed in the early 1970s. The United States apparently has not yet reached this point. However, there is an indication that the richest taxpayers are sufficiently sensitive to their marginal tax rates that they typically paid less in income taxes when their marginal tax rates increased.

Transfer payments have allocative effects that resemble those from taxation. First, tax rates rise to finance the program, and second, larger transfer payments mean that the potential recipients stand to lose more benefits by earning income. On both counts, an increase in transfers tends to contract real economic activity.

IMPORTANT TERMS AND CONCEPTS

adjusted gross income Gross income less adjustments for tax purposes, such as business and moving expenses and deferred compensation through pension plans.

after-tax marginal product of labor The marginal product of labor less the tax levied on the resulting increase in product.

after-tax rate of return to investment The real rate of return from investment less the tax levied on the resulting increase in net product.

after-tax real interest rate The real interest rate less the tax paid on the interest earnings.

average tax rate The ratio of taxes to a measure of income.

flat-rate tax A kind of income tax in which the amount of tax is a constant fraction of taxable income.

graduated-rate tax A kind of income tax in which the marginal tax rate rises with taxable income.

Laffer curve A graph showing that tax revenues initially rise as the marginal tax rate rises but eventually reach a maximum and subsequently decline with further increases in the marginal tax rate.

marginal tax rate The fraction of an additional dollar of income that must be paid as tax. In a graduated-rate system, this tax rate varies in accordance with the level of income.

supply-side economics The study of the causes and effects of changes in the supply and productivity of factors of production. This approach emphasizes the negative effect of income taxes on the incentive to work.

taxable income Adjusted gross income minus the value of tax exemptions.

tax-exempt real income Income from production, interest earnings, or government transfers that is not liable for income taxes.

underground economy The collection of economic activities from which the income earned is not reported and therefore not taxed.

QUESTIONS AND PROBLEMS

MAINLY FOR REVIEW

13.1 Distinguish between the average tax rate and the marginal tax rate. Must the two be equal for a flat-rate tax?

13.2 Why must we hold tax revenue constant when studying the effect of a change in the tax rate? What wealth effects would operate if we did not?

13.3 Explain briefly why a rise in the tax rate reduces the after-tax real interest rate in the short run but raises the before-tax real interest rate in the long run. How does the latter affect the capital stock?

13.4 Ignoring wealth effects from an increase in the tax rate, does the quantity of work decline in the long run? Explain why.

13.5 Could an increase in the tax rate reduce real tax revenues? How does the answer depend on the response of labor supply to changes in the (after-tax) marginal product of labor?

13.6 Define supply-side economics. How could the economy benefit from lowering the tax rate? Include in the answer a discussion of the wealth effects of taxes.

PROBLEMS FOR DISCUSSION

13.7 The Flat-Rate Tax

Some economists advocate shifting from the graduated individual income tax to a flat-rate tax. Under the new system, there would be few deductions from taxable income, and the marginal tax rate would be constant. Because of the elimination of the deductions (sometimes referred to as loopholes), the average marginal tax rate would be lower than that under the current law.

a. What would be the effect of a shift to a flat-rate tax on output, employment, and investment?

b. How does the proposed flat-rate tax compare with the present social security tax?

c. How does the proposal relate to the changes in the 1986 tax law?

13.8 Subsidies

Suppose that the average marginal tax rate, τ, is zero. We mentioned that an increase in the tax rate, τ, above zero—with total revenues, T/P, held fixed—reduces the utility of the typical household.

a. Explain this result.

b. Does the result mean that a reduction in the tax rate below zero would be desirable? (A negative value of τ means that the government subsidizes production.)

13.9 Consumption Taxes (optional)

Instead of an income tax, suppose that taxes are levied on the quantity of consumption during each period. A household's real tax payments for period t are then given by the formula $t_t/P_t = \tau \cdot (c_t - e_t)$. (A comprehensive sales tax on consumables might operate in this manner.)

a. Write down the budget constraints for the government and the representative household.

b. What is the after-tax real interest rate?

c. How does the tax rate, τ, now enter into the functions for consumption demand, C^d, gross investment demand, I^d, and goods supply, Y^s?

d. What is the short-run effect (while the capital stock is held fixed) of an increase in the tax rate, τ? Consider, in particular, the responses of the real interest rate and the quantities of output, work effort, consumption, and investment. Compare the results with those for an income tax.

13.10 Effects of Inflation on a Graduated Income Tax

In 1985 a married couple in the United States paid income taxes in accordance with the following graduated table:

Range of Taxable Income	Tax Rate on an Extra Dollar of Taxable Income (marginal tax rate, %)
$ 3,540–5,719	11
5,720–7,919	12
7,920–12,389	13
12,390–16,649	16
16,650–21,019	18
21,020–25,599	22
25,600–31,119	25
31,120–36,629	28
36,630–47,669	33
47,670–62,449	38
62,450–89,089	42
89,090–113,859	45
113,860–169,019	49
169,020–	50

a. Suppose that each person's real income stays constant over time, so that inflation steadily raises everyone's nominal income. If the tax law shown had remain unchanged, what would have happened over time to the average marginal tax rate and to the total real tax collections?

b. Assume now that the dollar bracket limits that appear in the left column of the table are adjusted proportionately (or "indexed") over time for changes in the price level. What then is the effect of inflation on the average marginal tax rate and on total real tax collections? (This indexing rule applies in the United States as of 1985.)

13.11 Taxes, Inflation, and Interest Rates (optional)
Suppose that taxes are levied on nominal interest income and that the income-tax rate, τ, does not change over time.

a. What is the after-tax real interest rate on bonds? Consider a permanent increase in the monetary growth rate from μ to μ'. The acceleration of money is a surprise, but people anticipate that the higher rate of monetary expansion, μ', will continue forever.

b. Given the presence of the income tax, what is the effect of the increase in monetary growth on the inflation rate, π, the nominal interest rate, R, and the aggregate level of real money balances, M/P? (Assume that the income-tax rate, τ, is unaffected by inflation.)

c. Discuss the implications of the answer to part b for the relation between R and π.

13.12 Effects of Transfer Programs on Work
Discuss the effects on people's incentives to work of the following governmental programs:

a. The food stamp program, which provides subsidized coupons for purchases of food. The allowable subsidies vary inversely with family income.

b. A negative income tax. This program would provide cash transfers to poor persons. The amount of transfers is reduced as some fraction of increases in family income.

c. Unemployment compensation. People who work for a specified interval and who lose their jobs receive cash payments while unemployed (and "looking for work"). The benefits can last for six months or sometimes for longer periods. What difference does it make if businesses with histories of more layoffs have to raise their contributions to the unemployment-insurance fund? (A program that has this feature is said to be "experience rated.")

d. Retirement benefits under social security. What is the consequence of the income test, which reduces benefits to persons (of age less than 70) who earn income in excess of a specified amount?

The Public Debt

I n recent years, one of the hottest economic issues has been the **government's budget deficit** (which we shall define carefully later). At least from reading the newspapers, we might think that the economy suffers greatly when the government runs a large deficit. The most important task in this chapter will be to evaluate this view. As we shall see, the conclusions depart dramatically from those expressed in the newspapers.

Budget deficits arise when governments choose to finance part of their expenditures by issuing interest-bearing government bonds rather than levying taxes. The stock of government bonds outstanding is the interest-bearing part of the **public debt**. A budget deficit means that the quantity of public debt increases over time.

This chapter considers first the historical behavior of the public debt and government deficits. With these facts as a background, we extend the theoretical model to allow for public debt. Now the government can run budget deficits rather than levy taxes. We use the model to assess the effects of deficits on interest rates and other economic variables.

THE BEHAVIOR OF THE PUBLIC DEBT IN THE UNITED STATES AND THE UNITED KINGDOM

We can gauge the empirical significance of interest-bearing public debt by looking at the long-term history for the United States and the United Kingdom. Table 14.1 shows the behavior over the past two centuries of the central government's nominal interest-bearing public debt, denoted by B^g. The data for the United States are net of holdings of public debt by various agencies and trust funds, which are parts of the federal government. We think of the monetary authority—the Federal Reserve—as part of the central government and therefore net out the Fed's holdings of U.S. government bonds.[1] The table reports also the ratio of the public debt to nominal GNP (GDP for the United States since 1959). We show this ratio graphically for the United States from 1790 to 1996 in Figure 14.1 and for the United Kingdom from 1700 to 1995 in Figure 14.2.

For both countries the two main positive influences on the ratio of public debt to GNP are wartime and major economic contractions. Superimposed on these infrequent positive shocks is a regular pattern in which the ratio declines over time.

For the United States, the major peaks in the ratio of public debt to GNP occur at the end of the Revolutionary War (the value for 1784 was 0.33), the end of the Civil War (0.25 in 1865), the end of World War I (0.31 in 1919), and the end of World War II (1.07 in 1945). Smaller effects—which amount to pauses in the usual downward trend in the ratio rather than to actual increases—show up for the Spanish-American and Korean wars. Little impact appears, however, for the Vietnam War. (Recall from Chapter 12 that this war exhibited only a small excess of real military spending above trend.)

[1] For example, in September 1996, the gross amount of interest-bearing debt of the U.S. Treasury was $5225 billion. But $1447 billion of this total was held by various U.S. government agencies and trust funds and $391 billion by the Federal Reserve. The amount in private hands (including $300 billion with state and local governments) was therefore only $3396 billion.

TABLE 14.1

VALUES FOR PUBLIC DEBT IN THE UNITED STATES AND THE UNITED KINGDOM

	United States		United Kingdom	
	B^g ($ billion)	$B^g/(PY)$	B^g (£ billion)	$B^g/(PY)$
1700	—	—	0.015	0.22
1710	—	—	0.026	0.33
1720	—	—	0.039	0.57
1730	—	—	0.038	0.56
1740	—	—	0.033	0.44
1750	—	—	0.059	0.79
1760	—	—	0.074	0.91
1770	—	—	0.11	1.22
1780	—	—	0.12	1.01
1790	0.08	0.31	0.18	1.04
1800	0.08	0.18	0.28	0.78
1810	0.05	0.08	0.43	0.93
1820	0.09	0.11	0.57	1.32
1830	0.05	0.04	0.55	1.13
1840	0.00	0.00	0.56	1.01
1850	0.06	0.03	0.56	0.94
1860	0.06	0.01	0.59	0.69
1865	2.2	0.24	—	—
1870	2.0	0.25	0.59	0.51
1880	1.7	0.13	0.59	0.43
1890	0.7	0.05	0.58	0.37
1900	1.0	0.05	0.58	0.29
1910	0.9	0.03	0.70	0.29
1919	24.2	0.31	7.5	1.30
1920	23.3	0.27	7.9	1.21
1930	14.8	0.16	7.6	1.55
1940	41.2	0.41	9.1	1.18
1945	227.4	1.07	22.5	2.27
1950	198.6	0.69	27.0	2.03
1960	207.5	0.41	29.0	1.12

Table 14.1 *(continued)*

	United States		United Kingdom	
	B^g ($ billion)	$B^g/(PY)$	B^g (£ billion)	$B^g/(PY)$
1970	229.1	0.23	34.1	0.66
1980	616.4	0.23	96.3	0.42
1990	2288.3	0.41	192.5	0.38
1996[a]	3396.2	0.45	349.5	0.59

[a]*Figure for the United States is for September 1996. Figure for the United Kingdom is for March 1995.*

Notes: For the United States: B^g *is the end-of-year value (midyear value before 1916) of privately held, interest-bearing public debt of the U.S. federal government at nominal par value. The figures are net of holdings by the Federal Reserve and U.S. government agencies and trust funds. (They include holdings by some government-sponsored agencies and by state and local governments.) For the sources, see Barro (1978a, Table 1). Recent figures are from* Federal Reserve Bulletin.

P since 1870 is the GNP or GDP deflator (see Figure 1.4 of Chapter 1). Earlier data are based on wholesale price indexes, as reported in U.S. Department of Commerce (1975, p. 201).

Y is real GNP or GDP (see Figure 1.1). Estimates of real GNP for 1834–71 are unpublished data from Robert Gallman. Earlier figures are calculated from the growth rates of real output that are reported in Paul David (1967, Table 1) and Alice Jones (1980, Table 3.15).

For the United Kingdom: B^g *since 1917 is the central government's interest-bearing public debt at nominal par value. Before 1917 the figures are the accumulation of the central government's budget deficit, starting with a benchmark stock of public debt in 1700.*

P since 1830 is the GNP deflator (1980 = 1.0). Earlier data are wholesale price indexes.

PY since 1830 is nominal GNP. Earlier data are the product of P and an estimate of trend real GNP.

The sources for B^g are B. R. Mitchell and Phyllis Deane (1962), Mitchell and H. G. Jones (1971), and Central Statistical Office, Annual Abstract of Statistics, *various issues. Data on P and Y are from the preceding and also from C. H. Feinstein (1972), Deane and W. A. Cole (1969), and* International Financial Statistics, *various issues. Recent data pertain to March of each year.*

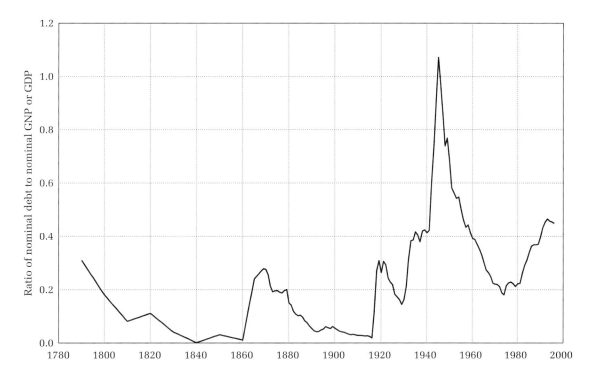

Figure 14.1

Behavior of the U.S. Public Debt, 1790–1996

The figure shows the ratio of the public debt to nominal GNP (GDP since 1959).

The positive effect of economic contraction on the ratio of public debt to GNP involves partly a negative effect on real GNP and partly a positive effect on public debt. A dramatic response to an economic downturn shows up during the Great Depression, during which the ratio of public debt to GNP rose from 0.14 in 1929 to 0.38 in 1933. Qualitatively similar behavior applies to less severe contractions: the ratio rose from 0.23 in 1979 to 0.31 in 1983, from 0.20 in 1973 to 0.23 in 1975, and from 0.039 in 1892 to 0.047 in 1894.

During peacetime, nonrecession years, the ratio of public debt to GNP tends to decline. This pattern applies to much of the (mostly peaceful) period after World War II: the ratio fell from 1.07 to a low point of

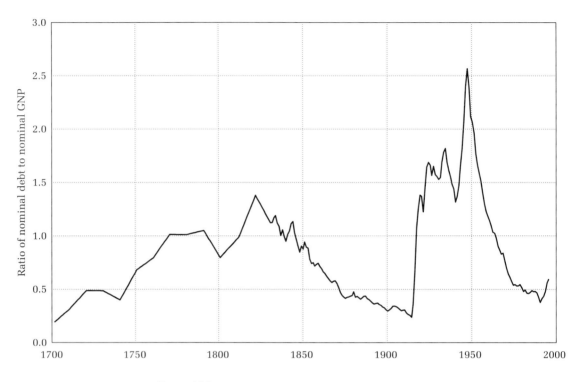

FIGURE 14.2

BEHAVIOR OF THE U.K. PUBLIC DEBT, 1700–1995

The figure shows the ratio of the public debt to nominal GNP.

0.18 in 1974. The ratio has, however, risen in most years since then, notably from 0.23 in 1981 to 0.45 in 1991. The ratio then remained at 0.45 in 1996. For the earlier peacetime periods aside from the Great Depression, the ratio fell from 0.31 to 0.14 between 1919 and 1929, from 0.24 to 0.02 between 1865 and 1916, from 0.11 to 0.01 between 1820 and 1860, and from 0.33 to 0.08 between 1784 and 1810. Notice also that the ratio for 1996, 0.45, is not remarkable by historical standards and is still below the values for the 1950s.

The experience of the United Kingdom is broadly similar to that for the United States. The major peaks in the ratio of public debt to GNP are again associated with wartime: 1.3 at the end of the Seven-Years' War in

1764, 1.2 after the War of American Independence in 1785, 1.4 after the Napoleonic Wars in 1816, 1.3 at the end of World War I in 1919, and 2.5 after World War II in 1946. It is noteworthy that the high points for the British debt in relation to GNP were more than twice as great as those for the United States. It is also interesting that the public debt amounted to more than 100% of annual GNP as long ago as the 1760s. Large amounts of public debt are not a modern invention!

Economic contractions again have a positive impact on the ratio of the debt to GNP. This response shows up especially for the United Kingdom during the depressed periods from 1920 to 1923 and from 1929 to 1933. The ratio of debt to GNP rose from 1.2 to 1.7 during the first interval and from 1.5 to 1.8 during the second.

Periods that involve neither war nor economic contraction typically display a declining pattern in the ratio of public debt to GNP. Again, this behavior applies as much to the post–World War II years as to earlier periods: the ratio declined from 2.47 in 1946 to 0.38 in 1990, before rising to 0.59 in 1995.

CHARACTERISTICS OF GOVERNMENT BONDS

In the model the government can now borrow funds from households by selling interest-bearing bonds. We assume that these government bonds pay interest and principal in the same way as private bonds, which are already in the model. In particular, we continue to simplify matters by pretending that all bonds have a maturity of one period.[2] In the main analysis we assume also that bondholders regard public and private debts as equivalent. Specifically, we do not treat the government as more creditworthy than private borrowers. In this case the government's bonds must pay the same nominal interest rate in each period, R_t, as that on privately issued bonds.

Our assumption about public and private bonds contrasts with our treatment of money. Because currency pays no interest, it seems that

[2] The average maturity of marketable, interest-bearing public debt in the United States was around nine years in 1946. This figure declined fairly steadily to reach a low point of about two and a half years in 1976. During much of this period, the U.S. Treasury was prohibited from issuing long-term bonds at interest rates that would have made them marketable. With the ending of this restriction, the average maturity rose to about six years in 1991 but fell to five years in 1996 (Economic Report of the President, 1975, Table C–73; 1997, Table B–86).

private enterprises would find it profitable to produce this stuff. In particular, the higher is the nominal interest rate, R_t, the greater is the gain from entering the business of creating currency. But because of legal restrictions or technical advantages for the government in providing a medium of exchange, we assume that the private sector does not issue currency.

With respect to bonds, we assume no legal restrictions on private issues and no technical advantages for the government in providing these types of securities. Hence, we do not allow the interest rate on government bonds to differ from that on private bonds. This assumption accords reasonably well with the U.S. data if we interpret private bonds as prime corporate obligations. For example, the market yield on six-month maturity U.S. Treasury bills averaged 6.2% from 1959 to 1996, while that on four- to six-month maturity prime commercial paper averaged 6.7%.[3] A similar comparison applies to long-term bonds.

Denote by B_t^g the aggregate dollar amount of government bonds outstanding at the end of period t. We still use the symbol b for privately issued bonds. An individual's total holdings of bonds for period t are now $b_t + b_t^g$. The aggregate of privately issued bonds is still zero, that is, $B_t = 0$. Hence, the aggregate quantity of bonds held by households now equals the public debt, B_t^g. We usually think of cases in which the government is a net debtor to the private sector, so that $B_t^g > 0$. The government may, however, become a creditor and hold net claims on the private sector.[4] We can represent this case by allowing for $B_t^g < 0$.

THE GOVERNMENT'S BUDGET CONSTRAINT

The presence of public debt alters the government's budget constraint in two respects. First, the dollar amount of net debt issue for period t, $B_t^g - B_{t-1}^g$, is a source of funds. (Notice that the simple rolling over or reissue of bonds as they come due is not a net source of funds. What counts is the difference between the stock outstanding at date t, B_t^g, and that outstanding in the previous period, B_{t-1}^g.) In this respect the printing of money and the printing of interest-bearing debt play the

[3] At least some of the positive differential between the yields on commercial paper and U.S. Treasury bills reflects two advantages of the government's notes: first, the interest payments are exempt from state and local income taxes, and second, the Treasury bills satisfy the requirement that commercial banks hold some amount of government bonds as backing for the government's deposits in these banks.

[4] The last time this became a serious possibility for the United States was around 1835. A major concern was the outlet for further governmental revenues once the national debt was fully paid off. (We do not have this problem anymore.) See the discussion in Davis Dewey (1931, p. 221).

same role in the financing of the government's expenditures. Second, the government's nominal interest payments, $R_{t-1}B_{t-1}^g$, appear as an expenditure. Recall that this term is zero for money.

The government's budget constraint in dollar terms for period t is now

$$P_t G_t + V_t + R_{t-1}B_{t-1}^g = T_t + (M_t - M_{t-1}) + (B_t^g - B_{t-1}^g) \qquad \textbf{(14.1)}$$

The two new terms are the government's interest payments on the left side, $R_{t-1}B_{t-1}^g$, and the net issue of debt on the right side, $(B_t^g - B_{t-1}^g)$. For simplicity, we return to the case in which transfers, V_t, and taxes, T_t, are lump sum.

THE GOVERNMENT'S DEFICIT

We can think of the government's saving or dissaving in the same way as for households. The national accounts define the government's nominal saving to be the change in the dollar value of the government's holdings of money and bonds. (This definition works if—as our model assumes—the government's investment is zero. Otherwise, net public investment would also be included in the government's saving.) Because we think of the government as issuing money and bonds, rather than holding them, an increase in money and bonds means that the government is dissaving. Economists use the term *surplus* to refer to positive saving by the government and the term *deficit* to refer to dissaving. (When saving is zero, the government has a **balanced budget**.)

Putting this terminology together, the nominal deficit, as measured in the standard national accounts, is

$$\text{Nominal deficit (national accounts)} = (M_t + B_t^g) - (M_{t-1} + B_{t-1}^g) \quad \textbf{(14.2)}$$

Combining the definition from equation (14.2) with the government's budget constraint from equation (14.1) leads to the usual expression for the nominal deficit:

Nominal deficit (national accounts) $= P_t G_t + V_t + R_{t-1} B^g_{t-1} - T_t$ **(14.3)**

That is, the nominal deficit equals nominal expenditures—for consumption, transfers, and interest payments—less tax revenues. This concept of the budget deficit, amounting to \$122 billion in 1996, is similar to the one that we often see in the newspapers.

The standard definition of the government's deficit in equation (14.2) does not take proper account of inflation.[5] As a parallel to our treatment for households, we would define the government's real deficit—that is, its real dissaving—to be the change in the real value of its obligations in the forms of money and bonds. The appropriate definition of the **real deficit** is therefore

Real deficit $= (M_t + B^g_t)/P_t - (M_{t-1} + B^g_{t-1})/P_{t-1}$ **(14.4)**

Multiplying through by the price level, P_t, the corresponding **nominal deficit** (the dollar value of the real deficit) is

Nominal deficit $= (M_t + B^g_t) - (1 + \pi_{t-1}) \cdot (M_{t-1} + B^g_{t-1})$ **(14.5)**

where $(1 + \pi_{t-1}) = (P_t/P_{t-1})$ was substituted on the right. A comparison of equation (14.5) with the national accounts' concept of the nominal deficit in equation (14.2) shows that the difference between the two measures is the subtraction of the term $\pi_{t-1} \cdot (M_{t-1} + B^g_{t-1})$. This term represents the reduction in the real value of the government's obligations due to inflation. If we want the real deficit (calculated by dividing the nominal deficit by the price level) to correspond to the change in the government's real obligations, then we have to deduct this term from the standard measure of the nominal deficit.[6]

The difference between the two measures of the deficit is large when the inflation rate is high. The choice of definition therefore matters a great deal for the high-inflation years from the late 1960s to the early 1980s. For the years before 1965 and since the middle 1980s, during which the inflation rate was typically low, the differences are much less significant.

[5] For a discussion of these effects from inflation, see Jeremy Siegel (1979).

[6] Note from equation (14.3) that the subtraction of $\pi_{t-1}B^g_{t-1}$ on the right side amounts to replacing the nominal interest rate, R_{t-1}, by the real rate, r_{t-1}. Similarly, the deduction of $\pi_{t-1}M_{t-1}$ corresponds to replacing the nominal interest rate on money, which is zero, by the real rate, which is $-\pi_{t-1}$. Thus, we effectively adjust for inflation by replacing nominal interest rates by real rates. Ideally, we would also adjust the measurement of the government deficit for changes in the market value of government bonds because of changes in interest rates. Robert Eisner and Paul Pieper (1984) and Robert Eisner (1986) make these adjustments and also consider changes in the market value of government assets, such as land and gold. Henning Bohn (1991) has gone further to include the unfunded pension liabilities for government employees and the anticipated liability for deposit insurance.

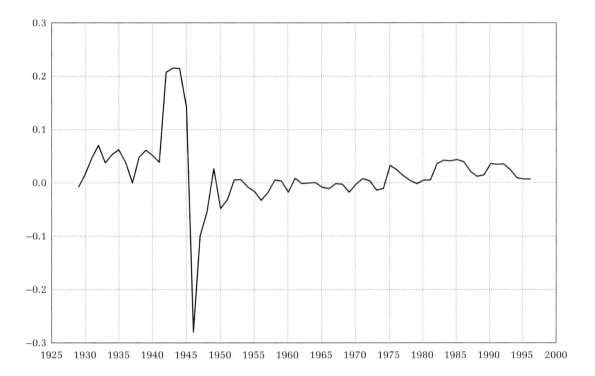

FIGURE 14.3

THE RATIO OF REAL FEDERAL DEFICITS TO REAL GDP

The real deficit is computed from equation (14.4), with B^g the stock of privately held public debt (measured as discussed in Table 14.1) and M the stock of high-powered money (currency outstanding plus reserves held at the Federal Reserve—see the discussion in Chapter 17). The values of B^g and M are divided by the GNP deflator (GDP deflator since 1990) for the fourth quarter of each year and then differenced from the prior year's value to get the real deficit. This value is then divided by the real GNP (GDP since 1990) for the year to get the ratio graphed in the figure.

[7] For 1946–47, the large negative real deficits reflect, first, decreases in the nominal debt, and, second, large increases in the reported price level. Much of these increases in the price level arose from the removal of price controls. Probably, the true price level rose more during World War II and less for 1946–47. (See the discussion in Chapter 12.) Hence, the true real deficits for 1946–47 were not as negative as those shown in the figure.

Figure 14.3 graphs the ratio of the inflation-adjusted real deficit to real GNP (GDP since 1990) from 1929 to 1996. Note, first, the positive relation between the real deficit and wars. This relation stands out for World War II: the real deficit exceeded 20% of real GNP from 1942 to 1944.[7] But there is also some effect during the Korean War for 1952–53 and, perhaps, during the Vietnam War for 1967–68.

The second important property is the positive relation between the real deficit and economic contraction. This pattern shows up strongly during the Great Depression: the real deficit exceeded 7% of real GNP in 1932. The real deficit also tended to be high during the post–World War II recessions—for example, in 1949, 1958–59, 1971, 1975–76, 1980–83, and 1990–92. The ratio of the real deficit to real GDP was 3.3% in 1975, 4.0% in 1982–83, and 3.6% in 1990–92.

Over the history of the United States, wartime spending and recession explain the bulk of real federal budget deficits. This relation appeared to break down, however, after 1983, when the Reagan tax cuts were not accompanied by comparable reductions in federal spending. From 1984 to 1986, the ratio of the real deficit to real GNP averaged 4.2% (see Figure 14.3), despite the strong economic recovery and the absence of wartime expenditure. But, partly because of changes from the 1986 tax law, which particularly raised taxes paid by businesses, the ratio fell to 1.4% in 1988–89. The increase in the ratio to 3.6% in 1990–92 reflected partly the effect of the recession and partly the temporary spending for the savings and loan bailout. With the economic recovery from 1992 to 1996, the real deficit fell to 0.7% of real GDP.

PUBLIC SAVING, PRIVATE SAVING, AND NATIONAL SAVING

Real public saving—if we neglect public investment—is just the negative of the real budget deficit; that is, from equation (14.4),

$$\text{Real public saving} = -(M_t + B_t^g)/P_t + (M_{t-1} + B_{t-1}^g)/P_{t-1} \qquad \textbf{(14.6)}$$

Real private saving—that is, real saving done by households—is given by

$$\text{Real private saving} = (M_t + B_t^g)/P_t - (M_{t-1} + B_{t-1}^g)/P_{t-1} + K_t - K_{t-1}$$

$$\textbf{(14.7)}$$

This result extends the measure of real saving from Chapter 9 to include the change in households' holdings of real government bonds.

The sum of public and private saving is called **national saving**. Equations (14.6) and (14.7) imply that this real saving by the entire nation is given by

$$\text{Real national saving} = K_t - K_{t-1} \tag{14.8}$$

Thus, the key result is that real saving for the overall economy must correspond to aggregate net investment. (If we had included public capital, then the change in this stock would add to the change in private capital on the right side of equation [14.8].)

PUBLIC DEBT AND HOUSEHOLDS' BUDGET CONSTRAINTS

As in Chapter 13, households care about the anticipated present value of real taxes. (Recall that we treat the taxes as lump sum at this stage.) We want to know how the outstanding stock of public debt and the government's current and prospective deficits affect the present value of real taxes.

To illustrate the main results, it is convenient to start with a number of simplifications. First, assume that the price level and aggregate money stock do not change over time. In this case the government obtains no revenue from money creation. Second, take as given the amount of government consumption, G_t, in each period. Third, suppose that aggregate transfers, V_t, are zero in each period. Finally, assume that the government starts with no interest-bearing debt: $B_0^g = 0$. We shall demonstrate later that the conclusions do not depend on these unrealistic assumptions.

Given our assumptions, the government's budget constraint in real terms for each period is

$$G_t + R \cdot B_{t-1}^g / P = T_t / P + (B_t^g - B_{t-1}^g) / P \tag{14.9}$$

Recall that the government starts with no interest-bearing debt at date 0. Therefore, if the government balanced its budget from date 1 onward—that is, if $B_t^g - B_{t-1}^g = 0$ in every period—then interest payments would always be nil. In this case, government consumption, G_t, would equal real taxes, T_t/P, at all times.

Suppose, instead of balancing its budget in period 1, that the government runs a deficit of $1, so that $B_1^g = 1$. Because we hold fixed government consumption, the budget constraint from equation (14.9) implies that this period's taxes, T_1, decline by $1. That is, we are considering a *deficit-financed tax cut*. The cut in taxes by $1 means that the aggregate of households' current disposable income rises by $1.

Assume now that the government wants to restore the public debt to zero from date 2 onward—that is, $B_2^g = B_3^g = \ldots = 0$. Then, in period 2, the government must raise taxes by enough to pay off the principal and interest on the $1 of debt that it issued at date 1. The taxes for period 2, T_2, rise accordingly by $1 + R$ dollars. Since the extra debt is paid off in period 2, taxes in subsequent periods do not change.

Overall, taxes fall by $1 during period 1 but rise by $1 + R$ dollars for period 2. The effect on the present value of real taxes is given by

$$(1/P) \cdot [-1 + (1 + R)/(1 + R)] = 0$$

Note that we discount the increase in next period's taxes of $1 + R$ dollars by the discount factor, $1 + R$. Hence, the net effect on the present value of real taxes is nil. Because there is no change in the present value of real taxes, the government's deficit during period 1 has no aggregate wealth effect for households. The shift from current taxes to a deficit would therefore not affect the aggregates of consumer demand and work effort. In this sense, households view as equivalent a current aggregate tax of $1 and a current budget deficit of $1. This finding is the simplest version of the **Ricardian equivalence theorem** on the public debt. (The theorem is named after the famous British economist David Ricardo, who first enunciated it.)[8]

[8] For discussions see David Ricardo (1957), James Buchanan (1958, pp. 43–46, 114–22), and Robert Barro (1989). Gerald O'Driscoll (1977) points out Ricardo's own doubts about the empirical validity of his famous theorem.

We can interpret the result as follows. Households receive $1 extra disposable income during period 1 because of the cut in taxes. But they also face $1 + R$ dollars of additional taxes during period 2. If households use the extra dollar of disposable income during period 1 to buy an extra dollar of bonds, then they will have just enough additional funds—$1 + R$ dollars—to pay the extra taxes in period 2. The tax cut during period 1 provides enough resources, but no more, for households to pay the higher taxes next period. That is why there is no aggregate wealth effect and no changes in consumer demand and work effort.

We can also interpret the results in terms of saving behavior. The budget deficit of $1 means that the government saves $1 less than before; that is, public saving falls by $1. Because households put all of their extra $1 of disposable income into bonds, private saving rises by $1. (In the case being considered, the marginal propensity to consume out of disposable income is zero, and the marginal propensity to save is one.) Because the rise in private saving exactly offsets the decline in public saving, the sum of the two—national saving—does not change.

To obtain the results, we assumed that the government paid off the entire public debt during period 2. To show that this assumption is unnecessary for the results, assume instead that the government *never* pays off the principal of $1 from the debt that it issued at date 1. Suppose that the government always balances its budget after the first period, so that $B_t^g - B_{t-1}^g = 0$ holds from period 2 onward. In this case, the stock of debt stays constant over time, so that $B_1^g = B_2^g = \ldots = 1$. But then the government must finance its interest payments of R dollars in each period. (Remember that these payments would have been zero if the government had not run a deficit during period 1.) These extra expenses mean that taxes, T_t, are higher by R dollars for *every* period after the first.

Taxes fall by $1 during period 1 but rise by R dollars for each subsequent period. The change in the present value of real taxes is now given by the expression[9]

THE PUBLIC DEBT

[9] *Use the condition for a geometric progression,* $(1 + z + z^2 + \ldots) = 1/(1 - z)$, *where* $z = 1/(1 + R)$. *The formula works if* $-1 < z < 1$, *a condition that holds here because* $R > 0$.

$$(1/P) \cdot \{-1 + R \cdot [1/(1+R) + 1/(1+R)^2 + \ldots]\}$$
$$= (1/P) \cdot \{-1 + [R/(1+R)] \cdot [(1+R)/R]\} = 0$$

Hence, the net change in the present value of real taxes is still zero.

We can think of this result as follows. Households receive \$1 of extra disposable income during period 1 because of the cut in taxes. But they also face an additional R dollars of taxes in each subsequent period. If households use the extra dollar of disposable income during period 1 to buy an extra dollar of bonds, then they receive \$1 more of principal and R dollars more of interest in period 2. If they use the interest receipts to pay the higher taxes, then households can again buy a bond for \$1. Continuing in this manner, households can always use the interest income to meet the extra taxes in each period. The tax cut during period 1 provides enough resources, but no more, for households to pay the stream of higher future taxes. That is why the net change in the present value of real taxes is again equal to zero. Hence, we still predict no changes in the aggregates of consumer demand and work effort. Equivalently, we still predict that private saving rises to offset the decline in public saving so as to maintain the total of national saving.

The basic conclusion is that shifts between taxes and deficits do not generate aggregate wealth effects. This result still holds if we drop many of the simplifying assumptions. If the initial level of public debt is nonzero, then the conclusion follows by considering the extra future interest payments and taxes that result from today's deficit. The results hold also if we superimpose an arbitrary pattern of transfers. Suppose, as an example, that the government reacts to higher future interest payments by reducing transfers rather than by raising taxes. Then we essentially add a new disturbance—equal decreases in future transfers and taxes—to the one that we already considered. Because this new disturbance has a zero aggregate wealth effect, the Ricardian result remains valid.

We can also allow for money creation and inflation. As one possibility, the government may react to higher future interest payments by printing more money rather than increasing taxes. In this case economists say that the government **monetizes** part of the deficit or monetizes part of the stock of public debt. Then we essentially add another new disturbance—an increase in future money creation and a decrease in future taxes—to the one that we treated before. We know that changes in money, which finance a cut in taxes, have no aggregate wealth effect. The budget deficit therefore still has no aggregate wealth effect. Monetization of the public debt does, however, have important implications for the behavior of prices. These effects work just like the increases in the quantity of money that we studied before: the monetization of deficits is inflationary.[10]

Finally, we can allow for nonzero deficits in future periods. As with a current deficit, these future ones do not generate any aggregate wealth effects. The aggregate wealth effect is still zero for any path of public debt. Hence, the aggregate of consumer demand does not react either to differences in the initial stock of real government bonds, B_0^g/P, or to variations in current or prospective government deficits.

Fundamentally, there is no aggregate wealth effect from budget deficits because they do not change the government's use of resources. The quantity of government consumption, G_t, is the amount of goods that the government buys during period t. Aggregate wealth effects therefore occur when there are changes in the present value of government consumption. But if we hold this present value constant, then there are no aggregate wealth effects from shifts between taxes and deficits.

THE EFFECT OF A DEFICIT-FINANCED TAX CUT

Recall that, with lump-sum taxes and transfers, the condition for clearing the commodity market is

$$C^d(\underset{(-)}{r_1}, \ldots) + I^d(\underset{(-)}{r_1}, \ldots) + G_1 = Y^s(\underset{(+)}{r_t}, \ldots) \qquad \textbf{(14.10)}$$

[10] Aris Protopapadakis and Jeremy Siegel (1987) carried out an empirical study of the relation of money growth and inflation to budget deficits and the stock of public debt. For ten industrialized countries in the post–World War II period, there was little relation between budget deficits or public debt and the rates of growth of money or prices.

We do not write out explicitly in these demand and supply functions the initial stock of capital, K_0, or the amount of government consumption, G_1. Also, recall that the previous analysis implies that the initial amount of real government bonds, B_0^g/P_1, does not matter for aggregate consumer demand, C^d, or goods supply, Y^s.

Suppose that the government cuts current taxes, T_1, and substitutes a corresponding increase in its interest-bearing debt, B_1^g. Assume that the government does not change its current or future consumption; thus, we are dealing with the pure effects from a budget deficit. Economists often refer to this type of action as stimulative **fiscal policy**. We found before that the replacement of current taxes by a deficit has no aggregate wealth effect. Hence, there are no effects on consumer demand or work effort. It follows that the tax cut has no impact on the condition for clearing the commodity market in equation (14.10). The real interest rate, r_1, and the quantities of output, Y_1, consumption, C_1, and investment, I_1, therefore do not change.

We can also think of the results in terms of desired saving and investment demand. Recall that the budget deficit stimulates an increase in desired private saving that exactly offsets the decrease in public saving. The budget deficit therefore has no effect on desired national saving. Because net investment demand also does not shift, the real interest rate does not have to change to maintain the equality between desired national saving and net investment demand.

The condition that money be willingly held in period 1 is

$$M_1 = P_1 \cdot \Phi(Y_1, R_1, \ldots) \tag{14.11}$$
$$\underset{(+)\ \ (-)}{}$$

Suppose that the government does not change the current money stock, M_1, or the path of prospective money stocks. Then the deficit-financed cut in current taxes has no effect on equation (14.11). Hence, the price level, P_1, and the nominal interest rate, R_1, do not change. Notice also that the inflation rate, π_1, and all future price levels are unaffected by the tax cut.

We have found that a deficit-financed tax cut does not stimulate the economy or affect interest rates. Since these results are controversial and important, we shall want to see later whether modifications of the model affect the conclusions.

OPEN-MARKET OPERATIONS

The inclusion of public debt in the model allows us to analyze **open-market operations**. An open-market purchase of securities occurs when the government—or a monetary authority like the Federal Reserve—buys government bonds with newly created money. In the opposite case there is an open-market sale of bonds for money. These open-market operations are the main way that the Federal Reserve actually affects the quantity of money in the United States. We shall want to see whether this realistic way of changing the quantity of money leads to results that differ from the unrealistic "helicopter drops" of money that we studied in Chapter 8.

Consider an open-market purchase during period 1, whereby the stock of money, M_1, increases by \$1, and the stock of government bonds, B_1^g, decreases by \$1. Assume that no subsequent changes in money occur; that is, there is a one-time increase in the quantity of money at date 1.

Table 14.2 shows that an open-market purchase of bonds amounts to the combination of two governmental policies that we have already examined. Suppose, first, that the government prints an extra dollar of money, M_1, and correspondingly reduces current taxes, T_1, by \$1. These changes are labeled as policy 1 in the table. Then suppose that the government raises taxes, T_1, backed up by \$1 and uses the proceeds to pay off \$1 of the public debt, B_1^g. These changes are called policy 2 in the table. The net effect of combining these two policies is to raise money by \$1, leave taxes unchanged, and reduce government bonds by \$1. Thus, we end up with an open-market purchase of bonds, policy 3 in the table.

TABLE 14.2

OPEN-MARKET PURCHASES OF BONDS AND OTHER GOVERNMENT POLICIES

Government Policy	Change in M_1	Change in B_1^g	Change in T_1
1. Print more money and reduce taxes	+$1	0	−$1
2. Raise taxes and retire public debt	0	−$1	+$1
3. Open-market purchase of bonds	+$1	−$1	0

Note: *An open-market purchase of bonds—policy 3—amounts to a combination of policies 1 and 2, which we have already studied.*

We know that policy 1 (more money and less taxes) raises the price level in the same proportion as the increase in the quantity of money. But, except for a reduction in the real amount of government bonds, there are no changes in real variables. We know that policy 2 (the fiscal policy in which taxes rise and public debt declines) has no effects except for another reduction in the real quantity of government bonds. By combining the two sets of responses, we find that an open-market purchase of bonds raises the price level and other nominal variables (other than the quantity of public debt) in the same proportion as the increase in the stock of money. Aside from the fall in the real amount of government bonds, there are no changes in real variables. Thus, the previous results about the neutrality of money still apply to open-market purchases or sales of bonds.

WHY DOES THE PUBLIC DEBT MATTER?

The results suggest that the public debt and government deficits do not matter much for the economy. But think about the parallel with private debt. The aggregate quantity of private debt is always zero, a result that also seems uninteresting. The possibilities for borrowing and lending are nevertheless important because they eliminate the need for individuals to synchronize their incomes and expenditures. The public debt plays a similar role. Because the credit market exists, the government need not match its receipts from taxes and money creation to its expenditures in each period.

The government's budget constraint from equation (14.1) implies that the real revenue from taxation and money creation for period t is

$$T_t/P_t + (M_t - M_{t-1})/P_t = G_t + V_t/P_t + R_{t-1}B^g_{t-1}/P_t - (B^g_t - B^g_{t-1})/P_t$$

$$(14.12)$$

Suppose that the paths for the government's consumption and transfers are given and that the initial stock of interest-bearing debt, B^g_0, is zero. If the government never issued any bonds, then its real receipts from taxes and money creation for period t would equal the given total of real expenditures for that period, $G_t + V_t/P_t$. The receipts have to be high or low whenever expenditures are high or low. The potential to issue debt gives the government more flexibility. The government can manage its issues of public debt to change its revenues for a period without changing the amount of expenditures for that period. By borrowing a lot when its expenditures are unusually large, for example, the government can lessen the need for abnormally high tax receipts or money creation at that time.

To bring out the main points, assume again that the stock of money is constant over time; that is, the government collects no revenue from money creation. The government's choices of public debt then dictate the timing of its real tax collections, T_t/P_t. For a given present value of taxes, the economy will respond to differences in the timing of collections only if the taxes are not lump sum. To see the nature of this response, let's reintroduce the type of income tax that we studied in Chapter 13. In this setting the aggregate real taxes for period t are given by

$$T_t/P_t = \tau_t \cdot (Y_t + R^g_{t-1}B^g_{t-1}/P_t - E_t) \tag{14.13}$$

where τ_t is the marginal tax rate and E_t is the amount of tax-exempt real income for period t. (Note that the interest payments on the public debt—which are taxable—appear in the aggregate of households' real taxable income.)

By managing the public debt over time, the government determines the behavior of real tax revenues, T_t/P_t, and thereby the marginal tax rates, τ_t, from equation (14.13). Consider the previous example in which current taxes, T_1, fall by \$1, and the public debt rises by \$1. Assume further that the government raises next period's taxes, T_2, by \$$(1 + R)$ to pay off the extra debt. Unless the government has gone beyond the point of maximum tax revenues on the Laffer curve, the changes in taxes collected show up as corresponding changes in the marginal tax rates: today's marginal tax rate, τ_1, declines, and next period's tax rate, τ_2, rises. These changes motivate households to shift their income toward the current period and away from the next period. Specifically, households raise today's work but plan to reduce work in the next period. This response operates like some intertemporal-substitution effects that we considered before.[11]

[11] Because the income-tax law applies to income rather than spending, there is no intertemporal-substitution effect on consumer demand.

[12] Investment demand may change, but this response depends on the change in the marginal tax rate for the time when the new capital stock is operational. If the changes in marginal tax rates are short-lived, then the direct effect on investment demand will be minor. For simplicity, we neglect this effect.

Figure 14.4 shows the effect on the commodity market during period 1. The increase in today's work effort appears as a rightward shift of the supply curve. Because today's demand does not change,[12] an excess supply of goods prevails at the initial after-tax real interest rate, $(\tilde{r}_1)^*$. Figure 14.4 shows, accordingly, that the after-tax real interest rate declines, and output increases. This extra output, which reflects increased work effort, shows up partly as more consumption and partly as more investment.

The counterpart of this period's lower marginal tax rate is a higher tax rate for period 2. Figure 14.5 shows that the changes to the market-clearing diagram are opposite to those found for period 1; in particular, the Y^s curve now shifts leftward. In comparison with the values that

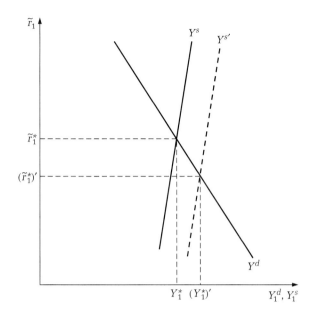

FIGURE 14.4

EFFECT ON THE COMMODITY MARKET OF A DEFICIT-FINANCED CUT IN TODAY'S MARGINAL TAX RATE

The marginal tax rate falls at date 1. The increase in today's supply of goods leads to an increase in output and a fall in the after-tax real interest rate.

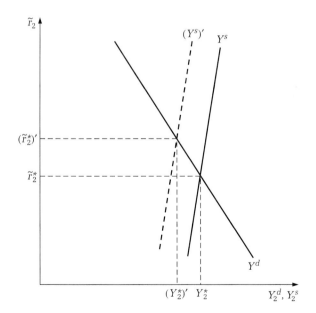

FIGURE 14.5

EFFECT ON THE COMMODITY MARKET OF A TEMPORARY INCREASE IN THE MARGINAL TAX RATE

During period 2, when the government pays off public debt, the marginal tax rate is higher. Therefore, output is lower and the after-tax real interest rate is higher.

would have arisen in period 2 with no changes in taxes, the after-tax real interest rate is higher, and output, work effort, consumption, and investment are all lower.

To summarize, when we consider income taxes, there are real effects from fiscal policy. A deficit-financed cut in today's marginal tax rate leads to increases in today's real economic activity. But the responses reverse later when the marginal tax rate is higher than otherwise. In our simple example, the higher future tax rate applies only to period 2. But, more generally, the higher tax rate could be spread over many periods. Then the tendency for real economic activity to decline would also be spread out into the future. Overall, fiscal policy turns out to be an instrument that can influence the timing of real economic activity. But, if the government uses this policy to stimulate output today, then the side effect is a reduction in output in the future.

THE TIMING OF TAXES

The government can manipulate its budget deficits to change the relative values of marginal tax rates for different periods and thereby influence the relative levels of output at different times. However, it would not be a good idea for the government randomly to make tax rates high in some periods and low in others. These types of fluctuations in tax rates cause unnecessary distortions because they give people the wrong signals in determining how to allocate work and production over time. Fortunately, the U.S. government has not behaved in this erratic manner; rather, the public debt has typically been managed to maintain a pattern of reasonably stable tax rates over time.

One example of this behavior concerns income-tax rates during recessions. Real government expenditures typically do not decline as much as aggregate output during a recession. (In fact, items such as unemployment compensation and welfare payments rise automatically.)

"Unpleasant Monetarist Arithmetic"

Thomas Sargent and Neil Wallace (1981) analyzed the effects from changes in the timing of the inflation tax. Consider a government that obtains a significant portion of its revenue from money creation. (Thus, the analysis applies especially to hyperinflations and to countries such as Argentina and Brazil that used to have high inflation.) Suppose that the government cuts current monetary growth in an attempt to reduce inflation. Assume, however, that the government does not change the current or prospective values for its real expenditures and tax receipts. In this case, the decrease in the current real revenue from printing money must correspond to an increase in interest-bearing public debt. Moreover, the financing of this higher debt later implies (with future real taxes and spending unchanged) that the future real revenue must come from additional money creation. In other words, the government is just rearranging the timing of the inflation tax; less occurs now and more occurs later.

Because future monetary growth rises, the contractionary monetary policy will be unsuccessful in generating a long-term decline in the inflation rate. Moreover, if people anticipate the increase in future monetary growth, then inflation may not even decline in the short run. That is because, as discussed in Chapter 8, the expectation of higher monetary growth in the future tends to raise the current inflation rate. Sargent and Wallace therefore conclude that a program to curb inflation by reducing monetary growth will be unsuccessful unless it is accompanied by a plan to offset today's lost real revenue from money creation by higher real taxes or lower real government expenditures.

To maintain a balanced budget, the government would have to raise tax rates when the economy contracts. But, instead of raising taxes, the government typically runs a real deficit during recessions.[13]

As another example, during wartime real government expenditures are much higher than normal, and real deficits are also especially high

[13] *Economists often estimate what the budget deficit would have been if the economy had been operating at a level of "full capacity" or "full employment." For discussions of the* **full-employment deficit**, *see E. Cary Brown (1956) and Council of Economic Advisers, Economic Report of the President (1962, pp. 78–82).*

at these times. The government thereby avoids abnormally high tax rates during wars. In this way the necessary increases in tax rates are spread roughly evenly over time. Tax rates rise somewhat during wartime but also rise afterward along with the higher interest payments on the accumulated debt.

THE CONVENTIONAL VIEW OF A DEFICIT-FINANCED TAX CUT

Our analysis of fiscal policy differs from that of most macroeconomic models. To see why, return to the case of lump-sum taxes, the type of taxes that most macromodels assume. For our analysis, the key point is that households regard as equivalent a current tax of $1 or a government deficit of $1. In particular, if the behavior of government purchases does not change, then shifts between taxes and deficits entail no aggregate wealth effects. In contrast, most macroeconomic models assume that a deficit-financed tax cut raises households' wealth even if there are no changes in government consumption. We shall look first at the results in this case and then examine briefly the arguments that some economists have made for a positive effect on aggregate wealth.

Suppose, again, that the government cuts current taxes by $1 and runs a deficit. If the tax cut makes people feel wealthier, then aggregate consumer demand rises, but work effort and the supply of goods fall. The excess demand for goods leads to a higher real interest rate and, thereby, to lower investment. Thus, this analysis predicts that government deficits raise real interest rates and **crowd out** private investment.

Another way to look at the results is that the increase in households' current disposable income leads partly to more consumption and partly to more desired private saving. In particular, because the marginal propensity to consume is positive, the marginal propensity to save is less than one. It follows that the increase in desired private saving offsets only a portion of the reduction in public saving. Thus, desired national saving declines, and the resulting excess of investment demand over desired national saving leads to an increase in the real interest rate.

According to this analysis, the decrease in net investment shows up in the long run as a decrease in the stock of capital. Some economists refer to this negative effect on the capital stock as a **burden of the public debt**. Each generation "burdens" the next one by leaving behind a smaller aggregate stock of capital.[14]

THE EFFECT OF A TAX CUT ON WEALTH

To reach the standard conclusions discussed in the preceding paragraphs, we have to argue that a tax cut makes people feel wealthier, even if the behavior of government consumption does not change. We consider here two of the more interesting justifications for this assumption—one concerning the finiteness of life and the other the imperfections of private loan markets. It is worth exploring these matters in any case, because they come up in other areas, as well as in the context of public debt.

Finite Lives

Suppose, again, that the government cuts current taxes by $1 and runs a deficit. We know that the government has higher interest payments and taxes in the future and that the present value of the extra future taxes equals $1. But assume that some of these taxes will show up after the typical person has already died. Then the present value of the extra future taxes that accrue during the typical person's lifetime falls short of $1. Hence, there is a positive effect on wealth (of persons currently alive) when the government replaces current taxes by a deficit.

Why is there an increase in wealth when people have finite lives? The reason is that the increase in wealth for the aggregate of current taxpayers coincides with a decrease for the members of future generations. Individuals will be born with a liability for a portion of taxes to pay interest on the higher stock of public debt. But these people will not share

[14] *For discussions, see James Ferguson (1964). Note especially the paper in that volume by Franco Modigliani, "Long-Run Implications of Alternative Fiscal Policies and the Burden of the National Debt."*

in the benefits from the earlier tax cut. If these future liabilities on descendants were counted fully by present taxpayers, then wealth would be unchanged.

Government deficits effectively enable members of current generations to die in a state of insolvency by leaving debts for their descendants. Current taxpayers experience an increase in wealth if they view this governmental shifting of incomes across generations as desirable. But, in fact, most people already have private opportunities for intergenerational transfers, which they have chosen to exercise to a desired extent. As examples, parents make contributions to children in the form of educational investments, other expenses in the home, and bequests. In the other direction—and especially before the growth of social security—children provide support for their aged parents. To the extent that private transfers of this sort are operative, the shift from taxes to deficits does not offer the typical person a new opportunity to extract funds from his or her descendants. Rather, the response to higher deficits would be a shift in private transfers by an amount sufficient to restore the balance of income across generations that was previously deemed optimal. In this case, the shift from taxes to deficits again has no aggregate wealth effect.[15]

As a concrete example, assume that a couple plans to leave a bequest with a present value of $5000 for their children. Then suppose that the government runs a deficit, which cuts the present value of the couple's taxes by $1000 but raises the present value of their children's taxes by $1000. Our prediction is that the parents use the tax cut to raise the present value of their intergenerational transfers to $6000. This extra $1000 provides the children with just enough extra funds to pay their higher taxes. Parents and children then end up with the same amounts of consumption and leisure that they enjoyed before the government ran its deficit.

Imperfect Loan Markets

The argument that taxes and deficits are equivalent assumes also that private and governmental interest rates are the same. In practice, however, the process of lending and borrowing involves transaction costs

[15] For a discussion of the interplay between public debt and private intergenerational transfers, see Robert Barro (1974). A different view is that parents use bequests to control their children's behavior rather than purely for altruistic reasons. For a discussion of this "strategic bequest theory," see Douglas Bernheim, Andrei Shleifer, and Lawrence Summers (1985).

for loan evaluations, collections, defaults, and so on. It is relatively easy to borrow if a person has a house, car, or factory to put up as collateral but much harder if a person, such as a student, just promises to repay a loan out of future labor earnings. The interest rates for borrowing are therefore high for persons with poor collateral.

Think of the world as divided into two groups. Group A consists of individuals or companies that lend or borrow at the same real interest rate, r, as the government. Group B comprises persons or businesses that would like to borrow at this interest rate but face higher borrowing rates. Let $\hat{r}$ be the real discount rate that someone from this group uses to calculate the present value of future incomes and expenses.[16] The rate $\hat{r}$ exceeds the real interest rate, r, for those from group A.

Suppose that the government cuts taxes and runs a deficit. The cut in taxes applies partly to group A and partly to group B. As before, the aggregate of future taxes increases. Let's assume that the division of these future taxes between group A and group B coincides with the division of the tax cut. (Otherwise, there is a distributional effect, which would require separate attention.) For group A, the present value of the higher future taxes equals the tax cut, and the wealth effect is nil. For group B, the present value of the extra future taxes is less than the tax cut because the discount rate $\hat{r}$ exceeds r. The members of this group are wealthier because the tax cut effectively enables them to borrow at a real interest rate, r, that is below their discount rate, $\hat{r}$. This cut in the effective borrowing rate motivates the members of group B to raise current demands for consumption and investment.

We have shown that a deficit-financed tax cut leads to an increase in the aggregate demand for consumption and investment (the demands from group A do not change, and those from group B increase). The rise in aggregate consumer demand means that the aggregate of desired private saving rises by less than the budget deficit; that is, desired national saving declines. Because investment demand (which went up) exceeds desired national saving (which went down), the real interest rate, r, must rise. This higher real interest rate crowds out current consumption and investment by the members of group A. In contrast, because of the initial

[16] *For someone who is borrowing at a high real interest rate, the discount rate $\hat{r}$ equals the borrowing rate. But if the borrowing rate is high enough (perhaps infinity), then a person may end up borrowing nothing even though he or she would be willing to pay a rate that was well above r. For such a person, the discount rate $\hat{r}$ is the highest real interest rate that he or she would be willing to pay on a loan.*

Empirical Evidence on the Macroeconomic Effects of Budget Deficits

Some important predictions from the standard analysis are that larger real government deficits lead to higher real interest rates, higher consumption, and lower national saving. There is little question that most government officials and news reporters, as well as many economists, believe that budget deficits raise real interest rates. Nevertheless, this belief does not have much evidence to support it. For example, Charles Plosser (1982, 1987) and Paul Evans (1987a, 1987b) carried out detailed statistical analyses of government deficits and interest rates for the United States and other industrialized countries. Their major finding was that budget deficits had no significant effects on nominal or real interest rates. Thus, their evidence contradicts the standard theory in which deficit-financed tax cuts make people feel wealthier.

Despite many empirical studies for the United States and other countries, it has proved difficult to reach definitive conclusions about the effect of budget deficits on consumption and national saving. One difficulty involves the direction of causation. Budget deficits often arise as responses to business fluctuations, government expenditures, and inflation. Because these variables interact with consumption and saving, it is hard to distinguish the effects of budget deficits on the economy from the effects in the reverse direction.

One empirical study by Chris Carroll and Lawrence Summers (1987) avoids some of these problems by comparing the saving rates in the United States and Canada. The private saving rates were similar in the two countries until the early 1970s but then diverged; for 1983–85 (the latest years in the study), the Canadian rate was higher by about six percentage points. After holding fixed some macroeconomic variables and aspects of the tax systems that influence saving, Carroll and Summers isolated a roughly one-to-one, positive effect of government budget deficits on private saving. This result accords with the Ricardian view.

The history of fiscal policy in Israel comes close to providing a natural experiment for studying the interplay between budget deficits and saving rates. The following figure shows the values from 1983 to 1987 for the national saving rate, the private saving rate, and the public saving rate. (In this case, real public saving equals ↗

public investment less the real budget deficit.) The pattern for the private saving rate roughly mirrors that for the public saving rate. The national saving rate is therefore relatively smooth.

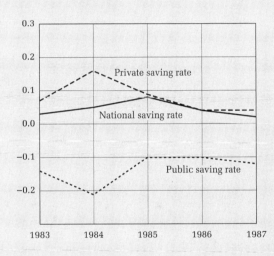

In 1983 the national saving rate of 13% corresponded to a private saving rate of 17% and a public saving rate of −4%. In 1984 the dramatic rise in the budget deficit led to a public saving rate of −11%. (A principal reason for the deficit was the strong adverse effect of the increase in the inflation rate on the collection of real tax revenues.) For present purposes, the interesting observation is that the private saving rate rose from 17% to 26%, so that the national saving rate changed little, actually rising from 13% to 15%. Then the Israeli stabilization program in 1985 eliminated the budget deficit (along with most of the inflation), so that the public saving rate increased from −11% in 1984 to 0 in 1985–86 and −2% in 1987. The private saving rate decreased dramatically at the same time—from 26% in 1984 to 19% in 1985 and 14% in 1986–87. The national saving rates were therefore relatively stable, going from 15% in 1984 to 18% in 1985, 14% in 1986, and 12% in 1987. Although one episode cannot be decisive in verifying or refuting a theory, it is interesting that this dramatic example from Israel reveals the roughly one-to-one relationship between budget deficits and private saving that the Ricardian view predicts.

stimulus to group B's demands, the consumption and investment of this group rise on net. Thus, the main effect of the budget deficit is a diversion of current expenditures from group A to group B.

In the aggregate, investment may rise or fall, and the long-term effect on the capital stock is uncertain. The major change, however, is a better channeling of resources to their ultimate uses: the persons from group B—who started with the high borrowing rates—command a greater share of current output. The deficit-financed tax cut ultimately induces the type-A people to hold more than their share of the additional public debt so as effectively to lend to the type-B people at the real interest rate r. This process works because the government implicitly guarantees the repayment of loans through its tax collections and debt payments. Loans between A and B therefore take place even though such loans were not viable (because of "transaction costs") on the imperfect private loan market.

This much of the argument may be valid, although it credits the government with a lot of skill in the collection of taxes from people with poor collateral. Even if the government possesses this skill, however, the conclusions do not resemble those from the standard analysis. In particular, in the analysis just presented, budget deficits are a good idea because they effectively improve the functioning of loan markets. In addition, despite the presence of imperfect credit markets, budget deficits do not necessarily reduce aggregate investment.

SOCIAL SECURITY AND SAVING

Retirement benefits paid though social security have expanded dramatically in the United States and most other countries. For example, the amounts paid out in 1993 for old age, survivors, and disability was 4.5% of GDP, compared to 3% in 1970, 2% in 1960, and less than 1% in 1950. Some economists, such as Martin Feldstein (1974), argued that this increase in social security reduced private saving. Because this effect could be quantitatively important, we want to examine it from the standpoint of our model.

The argument for an effect on saving applies when the social security system is not **fully funded**. In a funded setup, workers' payments accumulate in a trust fund, which provides later for retirement benefits. The alternative is a **pay-as-you-go system**, in which benefits to old persons are financed by taxes on the currently young. In this case, the people who are at or near retirement age when the program begins or expands receive benefits without paying a comparable present value of taxes. Correspondingly, the people from later generations pay taxes that exceed their expected benefits in present-value terms. (Most readers of this book are unfortunately in this last category.)

The U.S. system, like that of most countries, operates mainly on a pay-as-you-go basis.[17] Although the plan in 1935 envisioned an important role for the social security trust fund, the system has evolved steadily since 1939 toward primarily a pay-as-you-go operation.[18] Retirees increasingly received benefits that—in present-value terms—exceeded their prior contributions.

Consider the effects of social security in a pay-as-you-go system. We neglect here the substitution effects from the taxes and transfers because we already discussed these effects in the previous chapter. Now we look at possible wealth effects from an increase in retirement benefits, which are financed by higher taxes on workers.

The usual argument goes as follows. Old persons experience an increase in the present value of their social security benefits net of taxes. They therefore respond to the increase in wealth by consuming more. Young persons face higher taxes, offset partly by the expectation of higher retirement benefits. Because of this offset, the decrease in wealth for the young is smaller in magnitude than the increase for the old. Hence, the decrease in consumer demand by the young tends to be smaller in magnitude than the increase by the old. Aggregate consumer demand therefore tends to rise, or, equivalently, the aggregate of desired saving falls. The real interest rate increases accordingly, and

[17] Privatized arrangements, such as the present one in Chile, are fully funded, but no government trust fund is involved. For a discussion of this system, which many countries are trying to copy, see Jose Pinera (1996). See World Bank (1994) for an overview of social security systems throughout the world.

[18] For a discussion of the institutional features, see Michael Boskin (1977b) and Michael Boskin et al. (1987).

net investment decreases. In the long run, this decrease in investment shows up as a smaller stock of capital.

This argument for social security parallels the standard view of a deficit-financed tax cut. In both cases, the increase in aggregate consumer demand arises only if people neglect the adverse effects on descendants. Specifically, an increase in the scale of the social security program means that the typical person's descendants will be born with a tax liability that exceeds his or her prospective retirement benefits in present-value terms. If people take full account of these effects on their descendants, then the aggregate wealth effect from more social security is nil.

As in the case of a deficit-financed tax cut, more social security enables older persons to extract funds from their descendants. But, also as before, people value this change only if they give no transfers to their children and receive nothing from their children. Otherwise people respond to more social security by shifting private intergenerational transfers, rather than by changing consumption. In the United States, for example, the growth of social security has strongly diminished the tendency of children to support their aged parents.

On an empirical level, there has been a great debate about the connection of social security to saving and investment. First, Martin Feldstein (1974) reported a dramatic negative effect of social security on capital accumulation in the United States. But subsequent investigators showed that this conclusion was unwarranted.[19] Neither the long-term evidence for the United States nor that from a cross section of countries in recent years provides clear evidence that social security depresses saving and investment.

SUMMARY

[19] For a summary of the debate, see Louis Esposito (1978), the papers in the May 1979 issue of the Social Security Bulletin, and Dean Leimer and Selig Lesnoy (1982).

542

The ability to issue and retire interest-bearing public debt allows government expenditures to diverge in the short run from the sum of tax receipts and the revenue from printing money. Shifts between taxes and budget deficits affect the timing of tax collections but not their overall present value. Hence, for a given path of government consumption, this type of fiscal policy has no aggregate wealth effect. In the case of lump-sum taxes, the absence of a wealth effect implies that budget deficits do not affect the real interest rate or the quantities of investment and output. This result, called the Ricardian equivalence theorem, says that taxes and deficits have the same effect on the economy.

Budget deficits have real effects in the presence of an income tax. These effects concern the timing of taxes; changes in the timing exert intertemporal-substitution effects on work and production. It is desirable for the government to manage the public debt to avoid large random fluctuations in tax rates from period to period. This motivation accounts for the tendency of governments to run large real deficits during wars and recessions but to run real surpluses in "good times."

The standard view of deficit-financed tax cuts is that they make people feel wealthier. In this case, deficits would raise the real interest rate and crowd out investment. Sometimes economists rationalize the wealth effect from a tax cut by appealing to finite lives or imperfect capital markets. But an examination of these ideas suggests that they are unlikely to support the standard conclusions.

Finally, we note that social security is analogous to public debt. If debt-financed tax cuts have little effect on real interest rates and capital accumulation, then the same conclusion holds for an increase in the scale of social-security programs.

IMPORTANT TERMS AND CONCEPTS

balanced budget A situation in which there is no change in the real amount of money and bonds issued by government; zero real saving by government.

burden of the public debt The possible negative effect of the public debt on saving and investment and, hence, on the stock of capital available later.

crowding out (from government deficits) The decline in private investment that may result from a tax cut financed by a government budget deficit.

fiscal policy The choice of levels of government spending, taxation, and borrowing to influence the level of aggregate economic activity.

full-employment deficit The government deficit after adjusting for the automatic response of government spending and taxes to recession or boom; an estimate of what the deficit would be if the economy were operating at a full-employment level.

fully funded system (for social security) A system in which each individual's payments accumulate in a trust fund, and retirement benefits are paid out of the accumulated funds.

government budget deficit (or surplus) In real terms, the increase (or decrease) in the real value of the government's obligations to the private sector in the forms of money and bonds.

monetize the deficit Raise revenue to meet interest payments on government debt by increasing the quantity of money.

national saving The total saving carried out by the residents of a country; the sum of private and public saving.

nominal deficit The current dollar value of the government's real deficit.

open-market operations The purchase or sale of government securities by the Federal Reserve in exchange for newly created high-powered money.

pay-as-you-go system (for social security) A system in which benefits to retired persons are financed by taxes on the current working generation.

public debt The volume of interest-bearing government obligations to the public.

real deficit The change in the real value of the government's obligations to the public in the form of money and bonds.

Ricardian equivalence theorem The theoretical finding that, given the amounts of government consumption, an increase in current taxes has the same effect on the economy as an equal increase in the government budget deficit.

QUESTIONS AND PROBLEMS

MAINLY FOR REVIEW

14.1 What is the real deficit? Why does a rise in the inflation rate reduce the real deficit? Show how the real deficit is altered either by policy changes or by economic events, such as recessions.

14.2 Suppose that there is a temporary increase in lump-sum taxes. Is there any effect on households' wealth? Show how the typical household can use the credit market to offset the reduction in current disposable income.

14.3 Are government budget deficits inflationary? If so, do deficits affect the real interest rate? What about the nominal interest rate?

14.4 Why are open-market operations neutral?

14.5 Suppose that the government announces a reduction in income-tax rates to take place in some future period. What intertemporal-substitution effect will this announcement have on current work? What effect will it have on consumption?

14.6 Compare the effect of (a) government budget deficits and (b) social security on the tax liabilities of younger people. Why do the tax liabilities exceed expected future benefits in the case of social security?

PROBLEMS FOR DISCUSSION

14.7   The Aggregate Wealth Effect from a Deficit

Assume that taxes are lump sum. Suppose that the government cuts current taxes and runs a budget deficit. Then assume that the real public debt remains constant from period 2 onward. Also, the time paths of government consumption and real transfers do not change. Discuss the aggregate wealth effect that results from the government's current tax cut. How does this effect depend on the following considerations:

a.   Finite lifetimes?

b.   The existence of childless persons?

c.   Uncertainty about who will pay the higher future taxes?

d.   The possibility that the government will print more money in the future rather than raising taxes?

e.   The imperfection of private loan markets?

14.8   Effects of a Deficit-Financed Tax Cut

Assume that taxes are lump sum. Suppose, again, that the government cuts current taxes and runs a budget deficit. Discuss the effects for the current period on, first, the real interest rate and the quantities of output and investment and, second, the price level and the nominal interest rate, assuming that

a.   The paths of government consumption, real transfers, and money creation do not change.

b. The same as in part a, except that people expect the future growth rate of money to rise.

c. The same as in part a, except that people expect future real transfers to fall.

d. The same as in part a, except that people expect future government consumption to decline.

14.9 The Reagan Tax-Cut Plan for 1981

President Reagan's initial proposal in 1981 for cutting U.S. federal income-tax rates involved roughly a 23% overall reduction in rates. The full cut was to be phased in over a three-year period ending in 1983. The plan involved also gradual reductions over time in real government expenditures when expressed as a fraction of real GDP.

Consider an alternative plan that would have yielded the same present value of real tax revenues but that implemented the entire cut in tax rates in 1981. Assume that real government expenditures behave the same way as under Reagan's plan. Compare this plan with Reagan's with respect to the effects on work effort, production, and investment over the period 1981–83.

14.10 Social Security and Capital Accumulation

Suppose that the government introduces a new social security program that will make payments to covered persons when they retire.

a. What long-run effects do you predict on the stock of capital?

b. How does the answer depend on whether the social security program is fully funded or pay-as-you-go?

14.11 The Government's Stock of Gold

The U.S. Treasury's gold stock is held at the Federal Reserve. Mostly because of changes in the price of gold, the market value of these holdings rose from $12 billion at the end of 1970 to $92 billion at the start of 1997.

a. How would you modify the measure of the government's deficit to include these changes in the value of gold holdings?

b. Apply this reasoning more generally to the government's holdings of other commodities, capital goods, and land.

(Amusingly, the Federal Reserve values its gold holdings at the official price of $42.22 per ounce, rather than at the market price, which was around $350 per ounce at the beginning of 1997.)

14.12 Temporary Consumption Taxes (optional)

Suppose that taxes are levied on consumption rather than income. An individual's real tax for period t is then $t_t/P_t = \tau_t c_t - e_t$. Assume that the government runs a deficit during period 1 and cuts the marginal tax rate on consumption, τ_1. For subsequent periods, the marginal tax rates are higher than otherwise.

a. What is the impact of the tax cut on the quantity of goods demanded and supplied in period 1?

b. What is the effect during period 1 on the real interest rate, output, work effort, consumption, and investment?

THE INTERNATIONAL ECONOMY

Thus far, we have dealt with the macroeconomic performance of a single, closed economy and have neglected the interactions among countries on international markets. Most macroeconomists, especially those in the United States, focused until recently on this closed-economy framework. The justifications for this practice were, first, that the U.S. economy represented a large share of the world economy, which really is a closed economy; second, that a relatively small fraction of U.S. production and expenditure involved international trade; and finally, in a global context, that various restrictions inhibited the flow of goods and credit from one country to another.

Especially with the opening up of international markets over the last three decades, the practice of ignoring the rest of the world became increasingly unsatisfactory even for the large U.S. economy. For example, the ratio of U.S. real exports of goods and services to real GDP was 3% in 1959 but rose to 12% in 1996. The ratios of real imports of goods and services to real GDP rose over the same period from 5% to 14%. Aside from this greater volume of international trade, recent economic events have included large increases in U.S. borrowing from foreigners, substantial fluctuations in exchange rates, and important effects from world supply shocks, such as those affecting the market for oil.

This chapter and the next extend the model to allow for trade in goods and credit across national borders. With these extensions we will be able to analyze the international economic issues that have become important in recent years. We will be able, for example, to discuss the U.S. current-account deficit, which is almost as hot an issue as the U.S. budget deficit.

We shall find that our previous analysis of a closed economy applies to the macroeconomics of the world economy, whereas our earlier treatment of individuals carries over to the behavior of a small economy that operates on world markets. We can use this perspective to think about international borrowing and lending, changes in the prices of commodities such as oil, and the factors that determine a country's balance of international payments. Because the U.S. economy is so large, it is an intermediate case between the small economy and the entire world.

Aside from the parallels to the previous discussion, there are some entirely new issues that concern the determination of exchange rates among different currencies. As part of this analysis, we have to assess the linkages across countries of prices, interest rates, and monetary policies.

WORLD MARKETS IN GOODS
AND CREDIT

C onsider a world economy, within which the United States is one of many countries. From the perspective of the United States, we want to allow for the possibilities of buying goods from abroad or of selling goods to foreigners. That is, we will extend the analysis of the commodity market to include imports and exports. To carry out this extension, we begin with a number of unrealistic assumptions, which we will later relax. Assume first that the goods produced in each country are physically identical. In addition, suppose that transport costs and barriers to trade across national borders are small enough to neglect. (In this sense, the analysis applies when international markets are relatively open, as is true in the main for the industrialized countries in recent years.) Finally, pretend at this stage that, instead of using their own currency, all countries use a **common currency**, such as the U.S. dollar. The residents of each country hold U.S. dollars and quote prices in units of U.S. dollars.

Given these assumptions, goods in all countries must sell at the same dollar price P_t. Otherwise households and firms would want to buy all goods at the lowest price and sell all goods at the highest price. This result is the simplest version of the **law of one price**. At this point, we also abstract from inflation, so that the dollar price level in all countries is the constant P.

Suppose that each country has a central bank and that this bank holds a quantity of **international currency.** This currency could be pieces of paper denominated in U.S. dollars or other national or world units or could be a commodity such as gold. The precise form of the international currency is unimportant for our purposes, except that we assume that the nominal interest rate on this currency is zero.

Let $\bar{H}_t$ denote period t's world quantity of international currency, denominated in units of U.S. dollars. (An overbar means that the variable pertains to the entire world.) We assume, for simplicity, that $\bar{H}_t$ does not change over time: $\bar{H}_t$ equals the constant $\bar{H}$. The domestic central bank demands the real quantity H_t/P of this international currency to facilitate transactions between domestic residents and foreigners. (In the next chapter, we shall discuss further this demand for international currency.)

Assume that a single credit market exists in the world. If we abstract from differences in creditworthiness among borrowers, then the real interest rate, r_t, on this world credit market must be the same for lenders and borrowers from every country. When measured in U.S. dollars—that is, as future dollars paid per current dollar per year—the nominal interest rate is R_t. Because we abstract from inflation, the real interest rate, r_t, equals the nominal rate.

THE UNITED STATES AS AN OPEN ECONOMY

Consider the situation from the standpoint of the residents of a single country, which might be the United States. We refer to this country as the domestic or home country, and we refer to other countries as the rest of the world. Let Y_t represent the real gross domestic product (GDP), which is the total of goods and services produced domestically. Correspondingly, the dollar income from this source is the amount PY_t.

For the residents of a single country, the total of funds lent need no longer equal the total borrowed. Rather, the total amount lent on net by domestic residents corresponds to the total borrowed on net from this country by foreigners. Let B_t^f represent the net holding of foreign bonds by domestic residents at the end of period t. (For simplicity, we think of B_t^f as held by households, although the results would not change if the government held foreign claims or borrowed from abroad.) If $B_t^f > 0$, then the home country is a net creditor to the rest of the world, whereas if $B_t^f < 0$, then the country is a net debtor. Correspondingly, the amount $R_{t-1}B_{t-1}^f$ is the net interest income (positive or negative) for period t to domestic residents from abroad.[1]

If we add up for the entire world, then the total amount borrowed equals the total lent. Hence, the world aggregate for the net holding of foreign bonds, $\bar{B}_t^f$, is zero. This result for the world parallels the condition that we had before for a single country when we neglected foreigners. In our previous setting, an isolated country had no place to borrow from. Although this constraint no longer applies to an individual country, it still holds for the entire world (if we neglect the possibility of borrowing from Mars). Correspondingly, the world aggregate of net interest income from abroad, $R_{t-1}\bar{B}_{t-1}^f$, is also zero.

The net interest income from abroad is treated in the national accounts as the flow of income from the net ownership of capital held in foreign countries. It is therefore included in the accounts as part of the **net factor income from abroad**. This net factor income includes also labor income, corresponding to the earnings of domestic residents working in foreign countries less the earnings of foreigners working in the home country. We neglect this net labor income in our discussion: in this case, $R_{t-1}B_{t-1}^f$ equals the net factor income from abroad.[2]

If we ignore other sources of income from the rest of the world, such as transfer payments, then the total dollar income of domestic residents

[1] The variable B_t^f includes, more generally, not only interest-bearing securities but any other net claims of domestic residents on the rest of the world. It includes, for example, the ownership of capital located abroad, a form of capital that arises from **direct investment** in foreign countries. The term $R_tB_t^f$ encompasses the income from this ownership of capital.

[2] The net labor income from abroad is unimportant for most countries. It is, however, a significant negative item for Germany, which imports many foreign workers as *gastarbeiter*, and is also negative for the oil states of the Persian Gulf, such as Kuwait. The net labor income from abroad is a significant positive item for such countries as Pakistan and Turkey, which export workers to other places.

during period t is the gross national product (GNP), which equals gross domestic product (GDP), PY_t, plus the net factor income from abroad, $R_{t-1}B^f_{t-1}$. This total income can be spent in the following ways:

━━ Personal consumption expenditures, PC_t, on goods and services whether produced domestically or abroad.

━━ Gross private domestic investment, PI_t, which is the expenditure on capital goods located at home.

━━ Government consumption and investment, PG_t.

━━ **Net foreign investment**, which is the name given to the net acquisition of interest-bearing claims from abroad, $B^f_t - B^f_{t-1}$, plus any accumulation of international currency, $H_t - H_{t-1}$. The change in international currency is typically a small fraction of GNP and can usually be ignored.

The budget constraint for the home country is therefore

$$PY_t + R_{t-1}B^f_{t-1} = P \cdot (C_t + I_t + G_t) + (B^f_t - B^f_{t-1}) + (H_t - H_{t-1}) \qquad \textbf{(15.1)}$$

For a single economy in isolation (a closed economy), the gross domestic product, PY_t, must equal the total expenditure by domestic residents for goods and services, $P \cdot (C_t + I_t + G_t)$. When we open the economy to the rest of the world, we introduce some new items, which can create a divergence between the gross domestic product and the total of domestic expenditures on goods and services. The left side of equation (15.1) includes the net factor income from abroad, $R_{t-1}B^f_{t-1}$ (which adds to GDP to get GNP). The right side includes net foreign investment, which equals the net acquisition of interest-bearing claims, $B^f_t - B^f_{t-1}$, plus the accumulation of international currency, $H_t - H_{t-1}$.

The term $B_t^f - B_{t-1}^f$ is called the **balance on capital account** for the home country. If $B_t^f - B_{t-1}^f$ is positive, then there is an **outflow of capital**. (If it is negative, there is an **inflow of capital**.) An outflow of capital means that the home country acquires interest-bearing claims on foreigners and thereby provides funds for the foreigners to purchase goods and services.

Domestic residents have a total income of $PY_t + R_{t-1}B_{t-1}^f$ and a total expenditure on goods and services of $P \cdot (C_t + I_t + G_t)$. The difference between income and expenditure corresponds to saving by domestic residents in the form of additional assets acquired from the rest of the world and is called the **current-account balance**. Notice from equation (15.1) that

$$\text{Current-account balance} = PY_t + R_{t-1}B_{t-1}^f - P \cdot (C_t + I_t + G_t)$$

$$= \text{Net foreign investment} \qquad \textbf{(15.2)}$$

$$= B_t^f - B_{t-1}^f + H_t - H_{t-1}$$

This expression is the basic identity for the balance of international payments. The equation says that the current-account balance equals net foreign investment, which is the sum of the net capital flow, $B_t^f - B_{t-1}^f$, and the change in international currency, $H_t - H_{t-1}$. If the current-account balance is positive (or negative), then a country is said to have a **surplus** (or **deficit**) **on current account**. Notice that, as an accounting identity, a surplus on current account must have an offsetting financial transaction in the form of an increase in interest-bearing claims, B^f, or international currency, H.

Exports are the value of goods and services produced domestically that are sold to foreigners, and imports are the value of goods and services produced by foreigners that are bought by domestic residents. The difference between exports and imports, or net exports, is called the **trade balance**. The trade balance equals the total value of the goods and services produced domestically, PY_t, less the total value of domestic expenditures, $P \cdot (C_t + I_t + G_t)$. That is, the goods and services that are produced at home but not purchased at home must be moving on net— as net exports—to foreigners. The trade balance is positive or in surplus if exports exceed imports, and is negative or in deficit if imports exceed exports.

Equation (15.2) implies

$$\text{Current-account balance} = PY_t - P \cdot (C_t + I_t + G_t) + R_{t-1}B^f_{t-1}$$

$$= \textit{Trade } \text{Balance} + \textit{Net } \text{factor income} \quad \textbf{(15.3)}$$

$$\text{from abroad}$$

If we allowed for international transfers, such as foreign aid, then we would subtract the net transfers to foreigners on the right side of equation (15.3) to compute the current-account balance.

Consider a country that has experienced a current-account surplus for a long time and has therefore built up a substantial net asset position with respect to the rest of the world, B^f_t. The net factor income from abroad, $R_{t-1}B^f_{t-1}$, is positive, and equation (15.3) says that the current-account balance exceeds the trade balance. In other words, the country can now have a balanced current account even though its imports exceed its exports and, hence, its trade balance is in deficit. The country is paying for its excess imports with its net factor income from abroad.

We can get another perspective on international borrowing and lending by thinking about the home country's saving and investment. For this purpose, we want to break up the government's consumption and investment into its two parts:

$$G_t = GC_t + GI_t$$

where GC_t is government consumption spending and GI_t is government investment spending. Equation (15.3) shows that the current-account balance is $PY_t + R_{t-1}B^f_{t-1} - P \cdot (C_t + I_t + GC_t + GI_t)$. The expression $PY_t + R_{t-1}B^f_{t-1} - P \cdot (C_t + GC_t)$ is national saving, the part of GNP that is not spent on private consumption or government consumption. The current-account balance is therefore the difference between national saving and domestic (private plus public) investment; that is, if we denote national saving in dollar terms by S_t, then

$$\text{Current-account balance} = PY_t + R_{t-1}B^f_{t-1} - P \cdot (C_t + I_t + GC_t + GI_t)$$

$$= S_t - P \cdot (I_t + GI_t) \qquad \textbf{(15.4)}$$

Thus, a country runs a surplus on current account—and thereby lends funds abroad—when its national saving exceeds its domestic investment. Equation (15.4) also says that national saving, S_t, can be used either for domestic investment, $P \cdot (I_t + GI_t)$, or for net foreign investment, which equals the current-account balance.

Figure 15.1 shows the ratio of the U.S. current account balance to GDP or GNP from 1869 to 1995. (The ratio is to GNP until 1958 and to GDP thereafter.) Note that the current account was in deficit during the period from 1869 to 1896, except for 1894 and the years from 1876 to 1881. (The current account was also in deficit for most of the years from 1830 to 1868.) The deficit averaged 1.7% of GNP from 1869 to 1875 and 1.4% of GNP from 1886 to 1891.

The current account was in surplus for most years after 1896, averaging 0.7% of GNP from 1897 to 1914, 1.2% for the 1920s, and 0.4% for the 1930s. Because of World War I, the surplus on current account averaged 4.5% of GNP from 1915 to 1919. This surplus represented the substantial lending from the United States to its foreign allies. During World War II the account was in surplus in 1940–41 (averaging 1.3% of GNP) before the United States entered the war. After the United States entered, the account was in deficit from 1942 to 1945 (averaging −0.6% of GNP). For 1946–47, the current-account surplus averaged 3.1% of GNP.

From 1948 to 1976, the current account was typically in surplus but by an amount that averaged only 0.3% of GDP or GNP. Subsequently, there were deficits of 0.7% of GNP in 1977–78, followed by near balance in 1979–81, and a deficit of 0.3% of GDP in 1982. Then the current

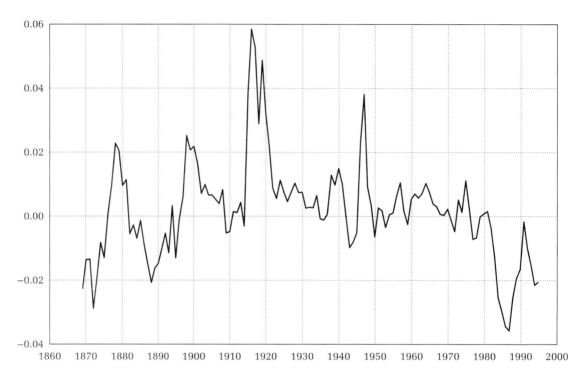

FIGURE 15.1

U.S. CURRENT-ACCOUNT BALANCE, 1869–1996

The figure shows the ratio to GDP (GNP prior to 1959) of the current-account balance. The data are from U.S. Department of Commerce (1975, 1986) and DRI data bank.

account shifted sharply toward deficit, reaching −3.6% of GDP in 1987. We have to go back to the 1880s and 1870s to find U.S. current-account deficits that were comparable in relation to GNP. After 1987, the current-account deficit diminished, reaching −1.5% of GNP in 1990 and virtual balance in 1991. Since then, the current-account deficit has risen to reach −2.5% of GDP in the third quarter of 1996.

Figures 15.2–15.4 highlight the main components of the current-account balance from 1959 to 1996. Figure 15.2 shows the ratio of the trade balance (nominal exports less nominal imports) to nominal GDP. The movements in this ratio are the main element in the variations in

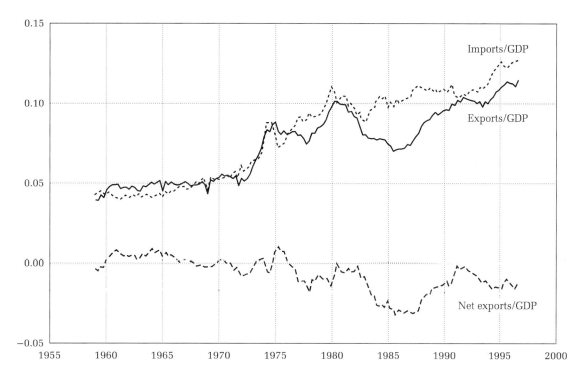

FIGURE 15.2

NOMINAL EXPORTS AND IMPORTS AS RATIOS TO NOMINAL GDP, 1959–96

The lower curve shows the ratio of the trade balance (nominal exports less nominal imports) to nominal GDP.
The upper curves show separately the ratios of nominal exports and imports to nominal GDP.

the current-account ratio, shown in Figure 15.1. Net exports declined, for example, from −0.6% of GDP in 1982 to −3.0% in 1987, then rose to −0.4% in 1991, but subsequently fell to −1.3% in 1996.

Figure 15.2 also shows how the trade-balance ratio breaks up into the ratios of nominal exports and nominal imports to nominal GDP. The most important observation here is the dramatic expansion of foreign trade over the post–World War II period: the export and import ratios in 1996 were 11.3% and 12.6%, respectively, compared to 4–5% in the late 1950s.

FIGURE 15.3

THE RATIO OF NET FACTOR PAYMENTS FROM ABROAD TO GDP, 1959–96

Figure 15.3 shows the ratio to GDP of net factor payments from abroad, the item that consists mainly of net capital income from abroad. These net payments were positive for most of the post–World War II period because the United States had accumulated net claims on the rest of the world. The net factor payments from abroad climbed to a peak of 1.4% of GDP in 1979–80. The shift toward a current-account deficit (Figure 15.1) meant that foreigners were accumulating net claims on the United States, a development that led to a gradual decline in the net factor payments from abroad: these payments fell to a small negative number (−0.1%) by 1996. The small value of net factor payments from abroad in 1996 suggests that the United States was roughly

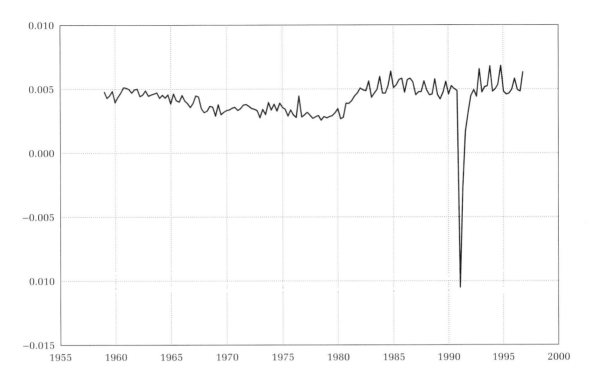

FIGURE 15.4

THE RATIO OF NET U.S. TRANSFERS ABROAD TO GDP, 1959–96

in balance with respect to its net claims on foreign countries. (It is hard to be precise because the data on net factor payments from abroad do not reflect exactly the market values of the various international assets and debts.)

Figure 15.4 shows the ratio to GDP of net transfers from the United States to the rest of the world. This ratio was positive for most of the post–World War II period and thereby tended to lower the current-account surplus. The ratio averaged 0.4% from 1959 to 1990. The temporary shift to a negative value in the first quarter of 1991 (−1.1%) reflected the payments from allied countries to the United States because of the Persian Gulf War. From then until 1996, the ratio averaged 0.5%.

THE ROLE OF THE INTERNATIONAL CREDIT MARKET

For an individual in a closed economy, the credit market allows for divergences between income and spending. For example, if a disturbance temporarily lowers someone's income, then he or she can borrow—or spend out of accumulated assets—to avoid a temporary decline in consumption or investment. Similarly, an individual can save most of a windfall of income to spread it over extra consumption in many periods.

When a closed economy experiences an economy-wide disturbance, such as a temporary decline in everyone's production opportunities, it is impossible for *everyone* to borrow more. In this case, the real interest rate adjusts so that the aggregate of desired borrowing equals the aggregate of desired lending. Hence, in a closed economy, the credit market cannot cushion spending against an economy-wide disturbance, even if it is temporary. (It is possible, in the short run, for a closed economy to avoid a cutback in aggregate consumption by accepting a decline in aggregate investment.)

A single country functions in a world credit market much as an individual functions in the credit market of a closed economy. Assume that the home country initially has a zero balance on current account. Then suppose that a temporary supply shock, such as a harvest failure or a natural disaster, makes everyone in the home country desire to borrow more at the initial real interest rate. (The assumption here is that the disturbance has little effect on investment demand.) If the home country's economy is small, then the world credit market can accommodate the increase in borrowing without significant changes in the world's real interest rate.

Now suppose that the supply shock applies to the entire world instead of just to the home country. Then the universal desire to borrow more cannot be satisfied. In these circumstances the real interest rate would rise on the international credit market to ensure that the world aggregate of desired borrowing equaled the world aggregate of desired lending.

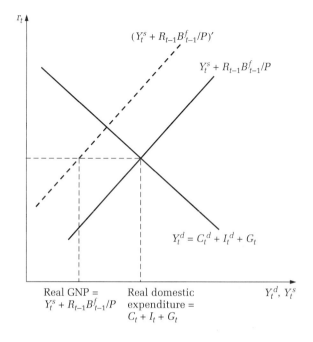

r_t

$(Y_t^s + R_{t-1}B_{t-1}^f/P)'$

$Y_t^s + R_{t-1}B_{t-1}^f/P$

$Y_t^d = C_t^d + I_t^d + G_t$

Real GNP = $Y_t^s + R_{t-1}B_{t-1}^f/P$ Real domestic expenditure = $C_t + I_t + G_t$ Y_t^d, Y_t^s

FIGURE 15.5

EFFECT OF A TEMPORARY SUPPLY SHOCK ON A SMALL OPEN ECONOMY

The supply shock lowers the domestic residents' aggregate supply of goods but has a negligible effect on demand. At the going world real interest rate, there is a fall in real GNP relative to real domestic expenditure. Consequently, the home country runs a current-account deficit, which corresponds to an inflow of capital from abroad.

Figure 15.5 illustrates the case of a temporary supply shock that applies only to the home country. The vertical axis plots the real interest rate, r_t, which prevails on the international credit market. For a small economy, which has access to the world credit market and exerts little effect on this market, it is appropriate to treat the real interest rate as a given. The downward-sloping solid curve in the figure shows the domestic residents' aggregate demand for goods, $Y_t^d = C_t^d + I_t^d + G_t$. As in our previous analysis of a closed economy, a lower real interest rate stimulates this demand.

The upward-sloping solid curve in the figure shows the domestic residents' aggregate supply of goods, $Y_t^s + R_{t-1}B_{t-1}^f/P$. This concept corresponds to real GNP, which is the total of goods produced by domestic residents.[3] As in previous analyses, a higher real interest rate raises the quantity of goods supplied.

[3] *This formulation views the net capital income from abroad as production carried out by domestic residents in foreign countries net of the production carried out by foreign residents in the home country. If we define supply in this way, then equality between supply and demand corresponds (if we neglect international transfers and net labor income from abroad) to balance on the current account.*

We draw the solid lines in the figure so that, at the given world real interest rate, the domestic residents' aggregate quantity of goods demanded, Y_t^d, is initially equal to the aggregate quantity supplied, $Y_t^s + R_{t-1}B_{t-1}^f/P$. Hence, real domestic expenditure on goods and services initially equals real GNP. It follows from equation (15.2) that the current account is in balance. Hence, if the home country's holding of international currency is constant ($H_t = H_{t-1}$), then the capital account is initially in balance ($B_t^f = B_{t-1}^f$).

Now suppose that a temporary supply shock reduces the home country's supply of goods but has a negligible effect on demand. (This situation applies for a temporary worsening of the production function if we neglect any effects on capital's marginal product.) The new supply curve is the one shown by the dashed line in Figure 15.5. At the going world real interest rate, r_t, the quantity of goods demanded by domestic residents now exceeds the quantity supplied. In the world economy this imbalance can be accommodated by the home country's borrowing from abroad. Then real domestic expenditure, $C_t + I_t + G_t$, equals the quantity of goods demanded, Y_t^d; real GNP equals the quantity of goods supplied, $Y_t^s + R_{t-1}B_{t-1}^f/P$; and the difference between the two is the real deficit on current account (see equation [15.2]). If there is no change in the home country's holding of international currency, then equation (15.2) says that the current-account deficit corresponds to a capital inflow from abroad, that is, to a negative value for the change in earning assets, $B_t^f - B_{t-1}^f$. Hence, a temporary supply shock induces the home country to borrow from abroad to avoid a cutback in current spending.

An example that fits well with this analysis is a harvest failure that affects agricultural output in a small country. The disturbance is largely temporary and has little effect on world credit and agricultural markets if the shock applies only to the one country. John Scoggins (1990) shows, for example, that shortfalls in the wheat harvest in Australia from 1931 to 1985 led to increases in Australia's trade deficit.

Notice that a worldwide supply shock would be different. In this case, the construction shown in Figure 15.5 applies to each country and, therefore, to the world aggregates of goods demanded and supplied. Consequently, the world real interest rate has to rise to clear the international credit market, that is, to equate the quantities of goods demanded and supplied in the world. The typical country then ends up at the point at which the new supply curve intersects the demand curve in Figure 15.5. At this point, there is a zero balance on the current account—as must always be the case, the typical country does not borrow from abroad.[4] Notice that this treatment of a worldwide disturbance, including the determination of the world real interest rate, corresponds to the type of analysis that we carried out before for a closed economy.

If a large country, such as the United States, experiences a supply shock, then we cannot neglect the effects on the world credit market even if the shock does not apply to other countries. We then reach conclusions that are a mixture of the two cases that we have just considered. The United States borrows from the rest of the world as suggested for a fixed real interest rate in Figure 15.5. But the pressure of this borrowing on world credit markets tends also to raise the real interest rate. This higher real interest rate induces other countries to run current-account surpluses and, thereby, to lend funds to the United States. Hence, an adverse shock to the production function in the United States leads to a higher real interest rate and, in the United States, to a current-account deficit. In other countries, it leads to current-account surpluses.

International borrowing can also arise from shifts to the aggregate demand for goods. We represent this case in Figure 15.6 by shifting the demand curve rightward while keeping the supply curve in place. One example of this kind of shift is an increase in private domestic investment demand, resulting from an upward shift to the schedule for the marginal product of capital, MPK.

As before, if the disturbance applies only to a small open economy, then it is appropriate to hold fixed the world real interest rate, r_t. At this given value of r_t, Figure 15.6 shows no change in real GNP but an increase in real domestic expenditure. The home country now borrows from abroad (runs a current-account deficit) to finance its higher level

[4] *It is important to remember that the world as a whole, and, hence, the typical country, cannot run a current-account deficit. Despite this basic constraint on the world economy, the errors and omissions in the international accounts make it difficult to verify this condition with actual data. For example, the numbers reported by the International Monetary Fund (International Financial Statistics, Yearbook, 1996) show a world current-account deficit of $138 billion in 1990 and $24 billion in 1995. These discrepancies are not fully understood but apparently relate to underreporting biases that affect exports more than imports. In addition, a few countries, such as Taiwan, are not included in some international agencies' concepts of the world.*

FIGURE 15.6

EFFECT OF A SHIFT IN DEMAND ON A SMALL OPEN ECONOMY

The positive shock to demand leads to an excess of real domestic expenditure over real GNP. Hence, the home country runs a current-account deficit.

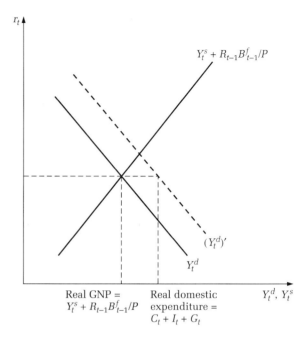

Real GNP = $Y_t^s + R_{t-1}B_{t-1}^f/P$

Real domestic expenditure = $C_t + I_t + G_t$

of investment. The ability to borrow from foreigners means that a small country with a favorable investment opportunity can pay for the investment boom without having to raise current production or curtail current consumption.

As with a supply shock, the results differ if the disturbance applies globally rather than just to the home country. Suppose, for example, that a technical innovation leads to an increase in private domestic investment demand in all countries. Then the construction shown in Figure 15.6 applies to the world aggregates of supply and demand. In this case the real interest rate, r_t, rises to ensure balance between the world totals of real GNP and real expenditure on goods and services. The world as a whole is a closed economy and, therefore, cannot finance an investment boom by borrowing from abroad. The expansion of world investment must come from either an increase in production (the movement along the supply curve in Figure 15.6) or a decrease in consumption.

An investment boom in a large economy, such as the United States, leads as before to a mixture of the results. The world's real interest rate rises, the United States runs a current-account deficit, and the other countries run current-account surpluses.

SECOND-ROUND EFFECTS FROM CHANGES IN NET FOREIGN ASSETS

We have, thus far, neglected the effects from changes in the current account on the stock of net foreign assets, B_t^f, and, hence, on the net factor income from abroad, $R_t B_t^f$. Consider again the case from Figure 15.5 in which the home country experiences a temporary supply shock. The decline in goods supplied and the negligible change in goods demanded meant that the country ran a current-account deficit. This deficit leads over time to a decline in net foreign claims, B_t^f.

Suppose, for example, that the current-account deficit is $1 billion per year and that the temporary supply shock, possibly a harvest failure, lasts for one year. At the end of the year, the economy returns to its preshock situation *except that the stock of net foreign assets is reduced by $1 billion.* The corresponding reduction in the net factor income from abroad, $R_{t-1} B_{t-1}^f$—by $50 million per year if the interest rate is 5%—amounts to a permanent reduction in the supply of goods, $Y_t^s + R_{t-1} B_{t-1}^f / P$. The reaction to this permanent decline in income (real GNP) would be a roughly one-to-one reduction of consumer demand, C_t^d. Hence, the current account is balanced when the supply shock is over, but consumption is permanently reduced. The shorter the duration of the supply shock, the less important is this long-run effect on consumption.

EXAMPLES OF INTERNATIONAL BORROWING AND LENDING

We can identify various situations in which a country borrows heavily on the world credit market. For Poland from 1978 to 1981, harvest failures and labor-force problems caused output to fall well below the anticipated average level of future output. An estimate of real product for Poland shows a decline of 14% from 1978 to 1981 (see Robert Summers and Alan Heston, 1988). Thus, the situation resembles that shown in Figure 15.5, in which external borrowing avoids a sharp decline in current real spending. The gross foreign debt of Poland reached $25 billion in 1981, about half of the country's annual output of goods and services.

Another example is Mexico, which made a major discovery of a natural resource, oil, in the early 1970s. By 1974, Mexico's oil prospects were great, but a significant volume of production had not yet occurred. In this situation, the increase in prospective income motivates an increase in consumption (and an expansion of marvelous government projects) before most of the oil revenue materializes. In addition, the oil discoveries motivated an increase of investment in oil-related industries. The case therefore corresponds to an increase in the aggregate demand for goods, as shown in Figure 15.6. The conclusion is that Mexico would borrow from abroad to finance its increase in current expenditures. In fact, Mexico's gross external debt rose from $3.5 billion or 9% of GDP in 1971 to $61 billion or 26% of GDP in 1981.[5] Of course, this type of foreign borrowing runs into trouble when, as in 1982–86, the relative price of oil falls unexpectedly, so that Mexico's income turned out to be lower than predicted.

As another example, consider a developing country that has a high marginal product of capital. This type of country borrows abroad to finance large amounts of investment and, thereby, high growth rates of output. The potential to borrow abroad means that a developing country's level of consumption need not be depressed drastically during the period of high investment.

One example of this behavior is Brazil, which sustained an average growth rate of per capita real gross domestic product of about 5% per year from 1971 to 1980. Over this period, Brazil's gross external debt grew from $6 billion, or 11% of GDP, to $55 billion, or 22% of GDP.

[5] The data on gross domestic product for Mexico and Brazil (mentioned later) are from International Monetary Fund, International Financial Statistics, 1982 Yearbook and April 1983. The figures on external debt are from Organization of American States, Statistical Bulletin of the OAS, vol. 4, nos. 1–2 (January–June 1982), Table SA–5, p. 30; and Morgan Guaranty Trust, World Financial Markets (February 1983), Table 2, p. 5.

For an earlier example of a rapidly developing country that borrowed heavily abroad, consider the United States. In 1890 the level of net foreign debt reached $2.9 billion, which amounted to 21% of GNP (see U.S. Department of Commerce, 1975, p. 869). Recall from Figure 15.1 that the United States was an international borrower for most years prior to 1890. Thus, the situation of the United States in the late nineteenth century was roughly comparable to that for Brazil in the 1970s.

Recall that borrowing from abroad reflects a shortfall of national saving, S, from domestic (private plus public) investment, $I + IG$. For Poland and Mexico, the borrowing reflected a drop in saving, which resulted from a decline in current income (Poland) or an increase in prospective income (Mexico). For Brazil and the nineteenth-century United States (and also for Mexico), the borrowing reflected the high value of investment demand.

In contrast, the countries that lend internationally are those with high desired saving—where current income is high relative to long-run income—or with relatively low investment demand. The international lenders include the mature industrialized countries, such as the United States through 1983 and Switzerland. Oil-exporting countries have also been major lenders, especially when the oil price rose rapidly in the middle and late 1970s. Saudi Arabia, for example, had a flow of oil income through 1981 that was high relative to the long-term prospective flow. The estimate for the net international investment position of Saudi Arabia (including international reserves) was about $145 billion in 1982 but declined to about $99 billion in 1986 because of the drop in oil revenues (see Economist Intelligence Unit, 1987).

It is important to recognize that the international credit market tends to be advantageous for borrowers and lenders. This market enables borrowing countries to spend more than their current income, a reasonable outcome in the cases we have mentioned. But the potential to lend abroad also permits countries that have a relatively large amount of desired saving to achieve higher rates of return than would be available domestically. Therefore, although there have been significant difficulties with defaults on foreign loans, we should not conclude that the existence of the international credit market is a bad idea overall.

We have, thus far, assumed a "perfect" world credit market, in which the real interest rate is the same for each country. As the residents of a country increase their borrowing—with the government of the country often doing the borrowing or guaranteeing the loans—there may, however, be an increasing risk of default. When a government borrows abroad, we particularly have to consider that "sovereignty" makes it difficult for foreign creditors to enforce loans. (Governments are sovereign in that they are above any meaningful international law: it is difficult, for example, for a creditor to foreclose on government property.) The increasing default risk implies that the real interest rate paid by a country tends to rise as the amount borrowed increases.[6] Consequently, a country (or an individual) has difficulty in using the credit market to smooth out spending when there are major fluctuations in income.

When we take account of this effect, we find that the results are a composite of those that we found before for a closed economy with those discussed in this chapter for a perfect world credit market. A temporary disturbance to a country's income then shows up partly as a change in that country's real interest rate and level of real expenditure and partly in the amount of borrowing from abroad. International borrowing buffers only a portion of the variations in a country's income.

THE CYCLICAL BEHAVIOR OF THE CURRENT ACCOUNT

We argued in Chapter 9 that shocks to the production function can generate cyclical patterns for closed economies that accord in many respects with empirical regularities. The type of disturbance that fit well was a proportional shock that affected the level of output and the marginal products of labor and capital. The effect on the production function had to persist for a while but not forever.

[6] For a discussion of these issues, see Jonathan Eaton, Mark Gersovitz, and Joseph Stiglitz (1986) and Jeremy Bulow and Ken Rogoff (1988).

This kind of shock to the production function was consistent with the following facts: investment and consumption are procyclical, but investment accounts for the bulk of the fluctuations in output; employment, worker-hours, labor productivity, and the real wage rate are procyclical; and the expected real interest rate is weakly procyclical. A procyclical pattern for the real interest rate arises if the boost to investment demand (for the case of a favorable shock) exceeds the increase in desired real saving as a result of the temporary expansion of income. Since the relative effects on investment demand and desired real saving can depend on the particulars of the disturbance, we would not expect to find a strongly procyclical pattern for the real interest rate. A weak procyclical pattern emerges if the average shock impinges more strongly on investment demand than on desired real saving.

Consider now what this type of shock to the production function implies for the cyclical behavior of the current-account balance in an open economy. We assume that the shock applies to the home country, but not to the rest of the world. (Any disturbance that affects all countries the same way cannot affect the current-account balance for the typical country.) We assume, in particular, that the world real interest rate does not change.

The key consideration, which also determined the cyclical behavior of the real interest rate for a closed economy, is whether the shock has a greater impact on investment demand or on desired real saving. Suppose, for the case of a favorable shock, that the increase of investment demand exceeds the rise in desired real saving that results from the temporary boost in income. This condition implies that a favorable shock to the production function leads in an open economy to a current-account deficit; that is, the current account will be countercyclical. As we mentioned before, however, the relative effects on investment demand and desired real saving depend on the details of the disturbance to the production function. We would therefore not expect to find a strongly countercyclical pattern for the current-account surplus. If the average

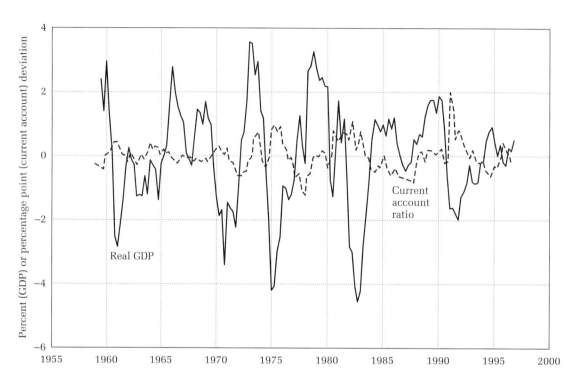

FIGURE 15.7

THE CYCLICAL COMPONENTS OF REAL GDP AND THE RATIO OF THE CURRENT-ACCOUNT SURPLUS TO GDP

The solid line is detrended real GDP, and the dashed line is the detrended value of the ratio of the nominal current-account surplus to nominal GDP.

disturbance affects investment demand more strongly than desired real saving—the condition that we assumed before for a closed economy—then the current-account surplus will be weakly countercyclical.

Figure 15.7 graphs the detrended ratio of the current-account surplus to GDP against detrended real GDP for the United States from 1959 to 1995. The current-account ratio does not have a strong cyclical pattern, but it does turn out to be weakly countercyclical: the correlation with detrended real GDP is −0.37. This finding is therefore consistent with the model that incorporates the kind of shocks to the production function that we have described.

Suppose now that the disturbances to the production function for the home economy are large enough to matter for the world credit market. This situation applies if the home economy is large or if the production conditions in other countries tend to be affected in the same direction (but by a smaller magnitude). We can then consider effects of disturbances to the production function on the current-account balance *and* the real interest rate. If a favorable shock has a greater impact on investment demand than on desired real saving, then the reaction will be partly a current-account deficit and partly a higher real interest rate. We therefore predict that the current-account surplus will be weakly countercyclical *and* that the expected real interest rate will be weakly procyclical. These patterns are the ones found in the U.S. data.

FISCAL POLICY IN THE WORLD ECONOMY

GOVERNMENT CONSUMPTION

We considered in Figure 15.6 the effect on a small open economy from a shift in the demand for goods. We know from Chapter 12 that an important source of increased demand is a temporary expansion of government consumption, perhaps related to wartime. Because government demand is high only temporarily, the present value of government consumption changes little. The disturbance therefore has only a small negative effect on wealth and, hence, only a minor impact on consumer demand. Given the small effect on consumer demand, the aggregate demand for goods rises on net relative to the supply, as shown in Figure 15.6. Consequently, the home country borrows from abroad to finance its temporary increase in government consumption. By borrowing, the country smooths out the reductions in private spending that are needed to pay for the extra government spending. A small part of the reduction in spending occurs while the government's expenditure is temporarily high. The rest of the cutback occurs in the future and corresponds to the payment of interest and principal on the accumulated foreign debt.

Suppose that the temporary government expenditures represent outlays during wartime. The international credit market then allows the combatant countries to borrow from neutrals and thereby moderate their short-run adjustments in consumption, investment, and leisure. Examples of this borrowing were the large loans from the United States to its allies during World Wars I and II, especially before the United States entered the wars. Shaghil Ahmed (1987b) studied these kinds of effects in the context of the long-term British history of wartime spending and trade balances. (Recall that we examined the data on British military spending in Chapter 12.) In line with the theory, Ahmed found a positive effect of temporary government expenditures on the trade deficit, especially from 1732 to 1830, a period that includes the major fluctuations in military expenditures (see Figure 12.4).

The wartime context suggests some serious limitations on the use of the world credit market. The possibility of a country's wartime defeat raises the probability of default and, thereby, drives up the real interest rate paid on loans. Consequently, a combatant country would find it difficult to pay for government expenditures without simultaneously cutting back on private spending or raising aggregate production.

The wartime example makes clear that the loan market is helpful only if combatants have noncombatants to borrow from. As in some examples that we considered before, a worldwide disturbance differs from a localized shock. In the case of a world war, there is no one abroad to borrow from. Then the worldwide incentive to borrow drives up real interest rates (if international loan markets remain open) but leaves the typical country with a zero balance on the current account. In Figure 15.6 this outcome corresponds to the intersection of the supply curve with the new demand curve at a higher value of r_t.

Recall from Chapter 12 that a permanent expansion of government consumption differs from a temporary increase. A permanent increase leads to a roughly one-to-one cutback in consumption demand and therefore has little effect on the aggregate demand for goods. It follows that permanent changes in government consumption do not lead to significant changes in the current-account balance. Countries tend to pay for permanent increases in the size of government by lowering private spending, rather than by borrowing from foreigners.

The invariance of the current account to permanent changes in government consumption makes sense if we think of borrowing from abroad as a way for a country to smooth out its adjustment to a temporary disturbance, such as a surge in government spending. The country pays for the spending partly through small reductions in current private spending but mostly through cutbacks in private spending at later times. This process works if the increase in government spending is temporary but breaks down if the increase is permanent. If the rise in government spending is permanent, then the balanced adjustment to the disturbance is a one-to-one reduction of private spending at each date. Because current private spending then falls by as much as current government spending rises, the country does not borrow from abroad. If the country borrows instead to finance a permanent expansion of government consumption, then it finds itself in even greater stress later: since the interest and principal on the debt must be repaid, private spending in future periods would have to decline by even more than the increase in government expenditures. (The assumption here is that the home country cannot continually surprise its foreign creditors by defaulting on its debts.)

TAX RATES

Recall that the current-account balance is the difference between national saving and domestic (private plus public) investment, $S - I - IG$. Changes in tax rates matter for the current-account balance if they influence desired national saving relative to domestic investment demand.

Effects on investment demand arise if the government changes the tax rate on income from capital. As an example, the Reagan tax cuts from 1981 to 1984 involved more favorable depreciation allowances and other changes that reduced the tax rate on income from capital. The predicted response is an expansion of investment demand and—for a given behavior of national saving—a move toward deficit on the current account.

Permanent changes in marginal tax rates on labor income have little impact on desired national saving, S, and therefore have little effect on the current-account balance. A permanent cut in marginal tax rates, for example, stimulates labor supply but raises consumer demand by an amount similar to the increase in labor income. Desired saving therefore changes little. It follows, for a given behavior of investment demand, that the current-account balance does not change.

Desired saving responds mainly to disturbances that affect the present relative to the future. For example, a temporary cut in the marginal tax rate on labor income would increase desired saving: the current supplies of labor and goods rise, but current consumption demand increases by only a small amount. This kind of change in tax rates therefore creates a surplus on the current account.

BUDGET DEFICITS

In Chapter 14 we spent a lot of time considering whether a deficit-financed cut in taxes affects consumer demand. (For present purposes, think of lump-sum taxes, which do not affect the incentive to work today rather than tomorrow.) In the Ricardian view, as long as the present value of government consumption does not change, households do not feel wealthier if current taxes decline. Consumer demand therefore does not change, and desired private saving rises one-to-one with the budget deficit. Equivalently, the increase in private saving exactly offsets the decrease in public saving, so that desired national saving, S, does not change. With no change in national saving—and no effect on investment demand—it follows that the current-account balance, $S - I$, does not change.

To understand this result, recall that the Ricardian view implies that the households in the home country absorb all of the government's additional debt. The budget deficit therefore does not induce residents of the home country to borrow more from foreigners, and the current-account balance does not have to change.

The standard view of budget deficits, which we also discussed in Chapter 14, starts with the assumption that a deficit-financed tax cut leads to an increase in consumer demand. Hence, desired private saving rises by less than one-to-one with the budget deficit, so that desired national saving, S, declines. One rationale for the increase in consumption demand is that finite-lived individuals feel wealthier when the government uses its budget deficit to shift tax obligations toward future generations.

In a closed economy the boost to the aggregate demand for goods leads to an increase in the real interest rate and to a fall of domestic investment. But an open economy can borrow from foreigners to pay for its increased demand for goods. We can again use Figure 15.6 to assess the effects. At the given value of the world real interest rate, r_t, real domestic expenditure rises because of the increase in consumer demand. On the production side, real GNP does not change. The gap between expenditure and GNP is the current-account deficit. Thus, when applied to an open economy, the standard analysis predicts that a budget deficit leads to a current-account deficit.

Many economists (and even more journalists) attributed the large U.S. current-account deficits of the mid 1980s to the effects of excessive budget deficits. Despite this consensus of opinion, a careful look at the evidence does not provide much support for a linkage between budget and current-account deficits.

The first column of Table 15.1 shows correlations between ratios of real budget deficits to real GDP and ratios of current-account deficits to GDP. The data are for ten major developed countries (Belgium, Canada, France, Germany, Italy, Japan, the Netherlands, Sweden, the United Kingdom, and the United States) over the period 1959 to 1989. For the

TABLE 15.1

CORRELATIONS BETWEEN THE RATIO OF THE BUDGET DEFICIT TO GDP AND THE RATIO OF THE
CURRENT-ACCOUNT DEFICIT TO GDP

Country	Correlation for Unadjusted Ratios	Correlation for Ratios Adjusted for Cyclical Variations
Belgium	0.24	−0.25
Canada	−0.15	0.02
France	0.23	0.09
Germany	−0.06	0.21
Italy	0.08	−0.43
Japan	−0.35	−0.24
Netherlands	−0.31	0.52
Sweden	0.29	0.01
United Kingdom	−0.22	−0.01
United States	0.55	0.64

Sources: *See Robert Barro and Xavier Sala-i-Martin (1990).*

Notes: *The data are from 1959 to 1989. The first column shows the correlation between the ratio of the real budget deficit to real GDP and the ratio of the current-account deficit to GDP. The second column shows the correlation after the two ratios are filtered for their normal relation with the movements in real GDP.*

United States, the correlation is positive: 0.55, a result that appears to corroborate the view that budget deficits caused the current-account deficits of the mid 1980s. Even for the United States, however, the correlation between the two deficit ratios is positive only because of the behavior since 1983. From 1959 to 1982, the correlation of the two ratios for the United States is virtually nil, 0.03.

For the other nine countries, the correlations shown in column 1 of the table are all over the map, ranging between −0.35 for Japan to 0.29 for Sweden. The overall impression is that the two deficit ratios are largely independent, and there is surely no indication that higher budget deficits lead regularly to higher current-account deficits.

It is possible that the normal cyclical behavior of the two deficits makes it difficult to isolate the effect of a budget deficit—run independently of business fluctuations—on the current account. We noted in Chapter 14 that the budget deficit was countercyclical: this deficit rises in recessions and falls in booms. In contrast, we showed earlier in this chapter that the current-account surplus was weakly countercyclical and, hence, that the current-account deficit would be weakly procyclical. Because the cyclical patterns—a countercyclical budget deficit and a procyclical current-account deficit—tend to create a negative correlation between the two deficits, it would be useful to purge the deficits of these cyclical influences to see whether the parts of the deficits that are not associated with business fluctuations are still related.

The second column of Table 15.1 presents the results of this exercise. The calculations first filtered out the normal reaction of the two deficit ratios for each country to the movements of real gross domestic product in that country.[7] The correlation between the filtered values was computed, and these values appear in the second column. For the United States, the correlation does go up, from 0.55 to 0.64. For the other countries, however, the correlations sometimes rise and sometimes fall: for Italy, for example, the correlation declines from 0.08 to −0.43, whereas for the Netherlands, it rises from −0.31 to 0.52. No clear patterns emerge overall, and we cannot conclude from this evidence that budget deficits systematically cause current-account deficits even after we take account of cyclical fluctuations.

Paul Evans (1988) carried out a more sophisticated statistical study of the relation between budget and current-account deficits in the post–World War II period in the United States, Canada, France, Germany, and the United Kingdom. His main conclusion, consistent with the findings presented in Table 15.1, is that the data are consistent with the Ricardian view that budget deficits do not cause current-account deficits.

[7] *The filtered part of each ratio is the part that cannot be explained by the current and four annual lags of the growth rate of real GDP.*

THE TERMS OF TRADE

We have assumed, thus far, that the home country and the rest of the world produced goods that were physically identical. Also, by neglecting transport costs, we assumed that all goods were **tradable** across countries. Continue to assume for now that all goods are tradable, but suppose that countries specialize in the production of different goods. For example, Chile produces a substantial fraction of the world's copper, whereas Brazil produces a large share of the world's coffee. Under these circumstances countries are affected significantly when the prices of their principal products change relative to the prices of other goods.

To keep things simple, pretend that the home country produces a single good (or market basket of goods) that sells at the dollar price P, whereas the rest of the world produces another good (or market basket of goods) that sells at the price $\bar{P}$. Then we want to study changes in the ratio, $P/\bar{P}$. If the ratio increases, then the home country's **terms of trade** improve. For each unit of goods that a home country produces and sells abroad (exports), it can now purchase more units of foreign goods (imports).

We have to modify the condition for the current-account balance to allow for differences between domestic and foreign prices of goods. To simplify the analysis, without affecting the main results, pretend that the entire gross domestic product, Y_t^s, is sold at price P and exported, and all of domestic expenditure (on private and government consumption and investment) is on imports of goods produced abroad and bought at price $\bar{P}$. Then the current-account balance is

$$PY_t^s + R_{t-1}B_{t-1}^f - \bar{P} \cdot (C_t^d + I_t^d + G_t) \tag{15.5}$$

The current-account balance is still the difference between national saving and domestic investment. But the dollar value of national saving is now $PY_t^s + R_{t-1}B_{t-1}^f - \bar{P} \cdot (C_t^d + G_t)$, and the dollar value of investment demand is $\bar{P}I_t^d$. The current account therefore depends on the two prices,

P and $\bar{P}$. For the purposes of discussion, assume that the current account has a zero balance at the initial values of P and $\bar{P}$.

Consider an improvement in the terms of trade—say, an increase in P for a given value of $\bar{P}$—that reflects a disturbance in the rest of the world. For example, Chile may enjoy an increase in the relative price of copper, or Brazil may experience a rise in the relative price of coffee. But since the disturbance originates from the rest of the world, Chile's capacity to produce copper or Brazil's to produce coffee does not change. We also assume, as is likely for the case of changes in coffee and copper prices, that people view the shift in P as temporary.

Suppose that the home country did not change its supply of goods, Y_t^s, or its demand for goods, $C_t^d + I_t^d + G_t$. Then equation (15.5) implies that the improvement in the terms of trade leads to a surplus on the current account. With an increase in P, the unchanged volume of real exports—corresponding here to total domestic production, Y_t^s—leads to a rise of export revenues, PY_t^s. Since import expenditures, $\bar{P} \cdot (C_t^d + I_t^d + G_t)$, are unchanged, the current account moves into surplus. (This result still holds if not all production is exported and if some of the expenditures are on domestic goods at price P, rather than on imports at price $\bar{P}$.)

The improvement in the terms of trade would, more realistically, motivate some changes in goods supplied and demanded. The effects on wealth are minor because the disturbance is temporary. The main responses that we have to consider involve substitution effects. For the moment let's neglect any effects on investment demand, I_t^d.

In deciding on work effort and production, households looked before at the marginal product of labor, MPL. The difference now is that producers sell all of their output at the domestic price, P, but buy goods for consumption at the foreign price, $\bar{P}$. An increase in $P/\bar{P}$ means that households obtain more in consumption for each unit of work and production. Therefore, just as in the case of an improvement in the schedule for labor's marginal product, an increase in $P/\bar{P}$ motivates an expansion of work effort and a corresponding rise in the supply of domestic goods, Y_t^s. This increase in supply reinforces the movement toward surplus in the current account.

An increase in $P/\bar{P}$ also motivates an increase in consumer demand. If the price change is temporary, however, then this response is weak. That conclusion follows because households would spread their temporarily high current income over more consumption in many periods. We still predict, therefore, that a temporary improvement of the terms of trade leads to a surplus on the current account.

Suppose now that the improvement in the terms of trade is permanent. The strong rise in wealth then motivates a substantial increase in consumption demand. In fact, there would now be little change in the home country's desired national saving, $PY_t^s + R_{t-1}B_{t-1}^f - \bar{P} \cdot (C_t^d + G_t)$. Hence, the current-account balance would not change: the expenditures on imports rise along with the receipts from exports. We predict therefore that a surplus on the current account accompanies a temporary improvement in the terms of trade but not a permanent improvement.

Consider now the effects on investment demand. Producers pay the price $\bar{P}$ for new capital goods (purchased as imports) but receive the price P for each unit of output. For a given schedule for the marginal product of capital, MPK, an increase in $P/\bar{P}$ makes investment more attractive. It follows that an improvement in the terms of trade stimulates investment demand.

The effect of an improvement in the terms of trade on investment demand depends on how long producers expect the improvement to last. If the change is temporary, then producers will not find it worthwhile to make much alteration to their investment plans. Because of adjustment costs for changing the stock of capital, investment demand will respond mainly to long-lasting shifts in the terms of trade.[8] Thus, we predict that investment demand will react little to a temporary improvement in the terms of trade but will respond positively to a permanent improvement. Consider, as an example, an increase in the price of oil. Oil producers would invest in new capacity if they expected the higher oil price to

[8] We mentioned the effects of adjustment costs on investment demand in Chapter 9. These costs were not crucial for the analysis in that chapter but are significant for distinguishing the responses of investment to temporary versus permanent changes in the terms of trade.

persist. But little investment would occur if producers thought that the price change was transitory.

We can now modify the previous analysis to include the responses of investment. A temporary improvement in the terms of trade raises desired national saving but has little effect on investment demand. Hence, as before, the current account moves toward surplus. A permanent improvement in the terms of trade has little effect on desired national saving but raises investment demand. We now predict accordingly that a permanent improvement of the terms of trade leads to a deficit on the current account. If we consider intermediate cases—in which the improvement in the terms of trade lasts for a while but not forever—desired national saving and investment demand would both increase. The effect on the current-account balance would therefore be ambiguous.[9]

As an empirical example of effects from changes in the terms of trade, consider the current-account balance of the major oil-exporting countries. Table 15.2 shows that the oil-exporters' current account was nearly balanced in 1972. Then the sharp increases in oil prices during 1973–74 led to a current-account surplus of $67 billion in 1974. From 1974 to 1978, the relative price of oil fell somewhat. But, more important, the growing perception that the relative price of oil would remain high motivated the oil-exporting countries to adjust their expenditures to their higher long-run incomes. By 1978 the current account was again nearly balanced but at much higher dollar levels of exports and imports—imports of the oil exporters went from $14 billion in 1972 to $95 billion in 1978. (Despite some concerns in the early 1970s about how the surpluses of the oil exporters would be "recycled," this concern proved to be unwarranted. The countries managed quickly to increase their expenditures on goods and services and thereby eliminated the surplus.)

The surprise increases in oil prices in 1979–80 again caused the oil-exporting countries to experience a large surplus on the current account—$102 billion in 1980. In this case, the upward adjustment of

[9] *For further analysis of effects from changes in the terms of trade, see Jeffrey Sachs (1981) and Jeremy Greenwood (1983).*

TABLE 15.2

CURRENT-ACCOUNT BALANCE OF MAJOR OIL-EXPORTING COUNTRIES

Year	Imports ($ billion)	Current-Account Balance ($ billion)
1972	14	3
1974	32	67
1976	64	38
1978	95	−2
1980	132	102
1982	163	−13
1984	127	−10
1986	98	−29
1988	104	−20
1990	114	14
1992	151	−24
1994	132	−9
1995	179	−5

Source: *International Monetary Fund,* International Financial Statistics, *various issues.*

expenditures on imports—to $163 billion—moved the current account to a small deficit by 1982. Then the sharp decline in the price of oil in 1986 led to a current-account deficit of $29 billion and to a reduction of imports to $98 billion. The deficit persisted until 1990, when the start of the Persian Gulf War produced an increase in oil prices and a current-account surplus of $14 billion. The decline in oil prices after 1990 led again to a small deficit on the current account.

NONTRADED GOODS

Thus far, we assumed that all goods were tradable across countries. But some items, such as services and real estate, are difficult to transport across national borders. Economists account for this phenomenon by including **nontraded goods** in the analysis.[10] Recall that the terms of trade refer to the price of tradables produced in the home country relative to the price of tradables produced in the rest of the world. Given the terms of trade, it is possible for the price of the home country's nontradables to change relative to the price of its tradables. In particular, since the nontradables do not enter into international commerce (by definition), the home country's relative price of nontradables and tradables tends to be more sensitive than the terms of trade to disturbances that originate at home. (In the extreme case of a closed economy, none of its goods enters into international trade, and only the domestic disturbances matter.)

Consider how the presence of nontraded goods affects the analysis of a change in the terms of trade. The main consideration is that an improvement in the terms of trade raises the price of the home country's tradables relative to its nontradables. This change motivates the home country to shift production, employment, and investment away from the nontradables sector and toward the tradables sector. Hence, the existence of nontradables reinforces the positive effect of the terms of trade on the production of tradables. The expansion in the tradables sector may go along, however, with a contraction of production and employment in the nontradables sector. Despite these new effects, it is important to note that the existence of nontradables does not affect our main predictions about the relation between the terms of trade and the current-account balance.

SUMMARY

We began by introducing international trade in goods and credit. These possibilities allow for the efficient specialization of production across countries and for an individual country's spending to diverge temporarily from its income.

The current-account balance equals national saving less domestic investment. A temporary supply shock in one country reduces desired

[10] *There are problems in implementing this idea because considerations such as transport costs mean that tradability is a relative matter. Although some goods enter more easily than others into international trade, with enough incentive, almost anything—including the services of workers—becomes a tradable good.*

saving and thereby leads to a deficit on the current account. Similarly, a surge in one country's investment demand generates a current-account deficit. If the shocks apply to the entire world, then there is no one abroad to borrow from. The world real interest rate therefore adjusts to equate the world aggregates of saving and investment. In this situation the typical country does not (and cannot) run a deficit on the current account. We showed that this type of analysis could account for some observed behavior of international borrowers and lenders.

If a shock to the production function affects investment demand by more than desired real saving, then the current-account surplus is countercyclical. We showed that this pattern shows up weakly in the U.S. data.

We used the framework to analyze various fiscal policies. A temporary increase in one country's government consumption, as in wartime, leads to a cutback in national saving and, therefore, to a current-account deficit. In contrast, a permanent change in a country's government consumption has little effect on national saving and the current-account balance. Even if temporary, an increase in government consumption does not cause a current-account deficit if the shift applies to all countries (as in a world war). The absence of potential lenders implies that the typical country maintains a zero balance on the current account.

A cut in the tax rate on capital income stimulates investment demand and thereby leads to a current-account deficit. In contrast, permanent reductions in marginal tax rates on labor income have little influence on desired national saving and the current-account balance. If these shifts in tax rates were temporary, they would have some impact on desired saving and the current account.

Budget deficits affect the current-account balance if these deficits alter desired national saving. In the Ricardian case, budget deficits do not affect desired national saving and, therefore, do not influence the current account. In some other approaches, a budget deficit lowers desired national saving and leads, thereby, to a deficit on the current account. We showed for ten developed countries that there was no regular relationship between budget and current-account deficits.

A temporary improvement in the terms of trade raises desired national saving and has little effect on investment demand. The current account moves accordingly toward surplus. In contrast, a permanent improvement in the terms of trade stimulates investment demand and has little effect on desired national saving. The current account therefore moves toward a deficit. Some evidence of the predicted linkages between the terms of trade and the current-account balance comes from the experience of the major oil-exporting countries.

IMPORTANT TERMS AND CONCEPTS

balance on capital account The net acquisition of interest-bearing assets from abroad.

common currency A regime in which all countries use the same currency and quote prices in units of this currency.

current-account balance The value of goods produced by domestic residents (including the net factor income from abroad) plus net transfers from abroad, less the expenditure by domestic residents on goods; if the current-account balance is positive (negative), then the current account is in surplus (deficit).

direct investment abroad Purchase of capital goods that are located in foreign countries.

international currency International media of exchange, such as gold or U.S. currency, held by central banks.

law of one price The condition that identical goods in different places must sell at the same dollar price.

net factor income from abroad Net income earned by the residents of a country from claims on foreign assets and from labor supplied to foreign countries.

net foreign investment The change in a country's net holdings of interest-bearing assets from abroad plus the change in its international currency.

nontraded goods Goods, such as services and real estate, that do not enter readily into international commerce.

outflow (inflow) of capital The positive (negative) balance on capital account for a country.

surplus (deficit) on current account A positive (negative) current-account balance.

terms of trade The price of a country's tradable goods expressed relative to the price of a market basket of the world's tradable goods; often approximated by the ratio of a country's export prices to its import prices.

tradable goods Goods that are actually exchanged or could potentially be exchanged with foreign countries.

trade balance The difference between the value of exports of goods and services and the value of imports of goods and services.

QUESTIONS AND PROBLEMS

MAINLY FOR REVIEW

15.1 Equation (15.2) states that the current account balance is identically equal to net foreign investment. If GNP or domestic expenditure changes, why is there a change in net foreign investment rather than a change in the real interest rate? What is the accompanying change in net exports?

15.2 Explain why an improvement in the terms of trade need not be associated with an increase in net exports.

15.3 Why is it infeasible for all countries to run a current-account deficit at the same time?

15.4 If a country runs a budget deficit must it also run a current-account deficit? How does the linkage between the two deficits depend on the relation between budget deficits and national saving?

PROBLEMS FOR DISCUSSION

15.5 Wealth Effects from Changes in the Real Interest Rate
Consider the wealth effects from a change in the world real interest rate.

a. What is the effect for a single country?

b. What is the aggregate effect for the world?

c. How do these results compare with our earlier findings for a closed economy?

15.6 Supply Shocks for a Single Country
Consider a supply shock that adversely affects the home country's production of tradable goods. Assume that the shock is temporary and that no significant change occurs in the terms of trade.

a. If the country can borrow from abroad at the world real interest rate, what happens to the home country's consumption and current-account balance?

b. How do the results differ if the home country cannot borrow from abroad?

c. Assume now that the domestic industries are owned primarily by foreigners. (In other words, domestic residents had diversified their ownership of assets internationally so as not to be too susceptible to local supply shocks.) How does this change affect the answers?

15.7 A Two-Country Model of the Current-Account Balance

Suppose that the world consists of two countries, A and B, that are roughly of the same size. Consider a temporary supply shock that affects the production function in country A but not in country B. What are the effects on the real interest rate and the current-account balances in the two countries?

15.8 Effects of Tax Changes on the Current-Account Balance

Discuss the effects on a country's current-account balance from the following changes in tax rates:

a. A permanent increase in the marginal tax rate on labor income.

b. A temporary increase in the marginal tax rate on labor income.

c. A permanent increase in the tax rate on consumption (say, a general sales tax on consumables).

d. A temporary increase in the tax rate on consumption.

e. A permanent cut in the tax rate on income from capital.

f. A temporary cut in the tax rate on income from capital.

15.9 A Change in the Terms of Trade

We considered in the text a change in the terms of trade that reflected a disturbance from the rest of the world. Suppose instead that a supply shock at home leads to an increase in the relative price of the home country's tradable goods. A harvest failure in Brazil would, for example, raise the relative price of coffee. What are the effects from this type of disturbance on the home country's

a. wealth and consumption of various goods?

b. current-account balance?

(*Hint*: Did you assume that the disturbance was temporary or permanent?)

15.10 Tariffs (optional)

Suppose that a small country levies a tariff on imports of a tradable good from abroad. If the good sells at price $\bar{P}$ abroad and if the rate of tariff is 10%, then domestic residents pay $1.1 \cdot \bar{P}$ for each unit of the good. If the tariff is permanent, then what are its effects on the home country's

a. consumption of the various tradable and nontradable goods?

b. production of tradables and nontradables?

c. balance on current account?

(*Hint*: What did you assume happened to the revenue collected from the tariff?)

Redo the analysis for the case in which the tariff is temporary.

EXCHANGE RATES

In the previous chapter we discussed international markets for goods and credit but said nothing about exchange rates. We could not discuss exchange rates because we assumed that all countries used a common currency, such as the U.S. dollar, and that all prices were quoted in units of this currency. To analyze exchange rates, we have to introduce different types of currency (dollars, yen, marks, etc.) and allow for prices to be quoted in these different currency units. This chapter makes the necessary extensions to consider these matters.

It is important to note that, even without discussing exchange rates, the previous chapter brought out various factors that influenced the current-account balance, including variations in the terms of trade. The extensions to include exchange rates do not invalidate any of these results. We shall find that some of the forces that affect the current-account balance lead also to movements in exchange rates. But the underlying shocks that cause countries to borrow or lend internationally will be the same as those that we studied before.

DIFFERENT MONIES AND EXCHANGE RATES

Suppose, as in the previous chapter, that the world's supply of international currency is fixed at the amount $\bar{H}$. We still assume that this currency is denominated in some nominal unit, such as the U.S. dollar, and that the nominal interest rate on international currency is zero.

In the real world, each country issues and uses currency in its own unit—such as dollars, pounds, and yen—instead of using a common currency. To allow for this fact, let M^i be the quantity of domestic currency for country i. We measure this money in domestic currency units, such as Japanese yen.

A typical setup is that the central bank of country i holds international currency, H^i, and then issues the domestic currency, M^i. Thus, we would have the simplified balance sheet for a central bank as shown in Table 16.1. The central bank's assets include international currency, H^i, foreign interest-bearing assets, and domestic interest-bearing assets, which include bonds issued by the home government. The holdings of domestic earning assets are called the central bank's **domestic credit**. The central bank's liabilities consist of domestic currency, M^i. (In practice, the liabilities also include deposits of financial institutions and governments held at the central bank. We discuss these deposits in Chapter 17.)

The domestic price level in country i, P^i, now expresses the number of local currency units, say yen, that exchange for a unit of goods. To start, think again of a case in which the goods produced in all countries are physically identical. Then the same product sells for P^i units of one currency (yen) in country i and for P^j units of another currency (say, German marks) in country j.

We now must introduce a new market, called an *exchange market*, on which people trade the currency of one country for that of another. For example, traders might exchange Japanese yen for U.S. dollars or for German marks. The exchange market establishes exchange rates among the various currencies. For convenience, we express all exchange rates

TABLE 16.1

SIMPLIFIED BALANCE SHEET OF A CENTRAL BANK

Assets	Liabilities
International currency, H^i	Domestic currency, M^i
Foreign interest-bearing assets	
Domestic interest-bearing assets (domestic credit)	

in terms of the number of units of domestic currency that trade for $1.00 (U.S.). For example, on April 25, 1997, 126 Japanese yen exchanged for $1.00, so that each yen was worth about 0.8 cent. Similarly, 1.72 German marks exchanged for $1.00, so that a German mark was worth about 58 cents.

The exchange rates for Japanese yen and German marks in terms of U.S. dollars determine the exchange rate between yen and marks. That is, 126 Japanese yen could buy $1.00, which could then be converted into 1.72 German marks. Hence, $126/1.72 = 73$ Japanese yen could buy one German mark. Thus, the exchange rate between yen and marks was 73 yen per mark. (In practice, traders can make these exchanges directly rather than going through U.S. dollars.)

Let ϵ^i (the Greek letter *epsilon*) be the exchange rate for country i: ϵ^i units of country i's currency (say, yen) exchange for $1.00. Alternatively, we see that the dollar value of one unit of country i's currency (1 yen) is $1/\epsilon^i$. Notice that a *higher* value of the exchange rate, ϵ^i, means that country i's currency is *less* valuable in terms of dollars because it takes more of country i's currency to buy $1.00.

For any two countries, i and j, we observe the exchange rates, ϵ^i and ϵ^j. These rates prescribe the number of units of each currency that trade

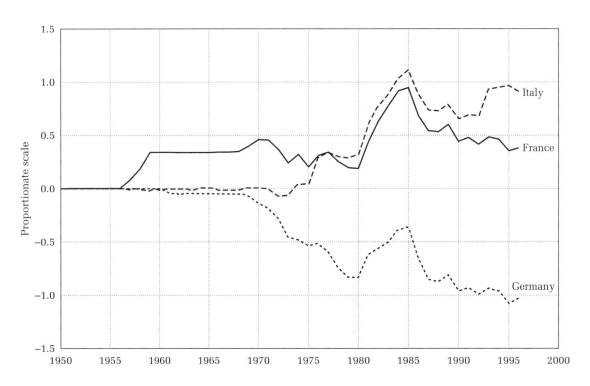

FIGURE 16.1

EXCHANGE RATES FOR FRANCE, GERMANY, AND ITALY

We show the proportionate (logarithmic) deviation of the exchange rate from the value that prevailed for each country in 1950. The exchange rates for 1950 were as follows: France, 3.5 francs per dollar; Germany, 4.2 marks per dollar; Italy, 625 lira per dollar. Data for Figures 16.1–16.6 are from International Monetary Fund, *International Financial Statistics, Yearbook,* various years.

for $1.00. Therefore, ϵ^i units of currency i (say, 126 Japanese yen) can buy ϵ^j units of currency j (say, 1.72 German marks). The exchange rate between currencies i and j—the number of units of currency i needed to buy one unit of currency j—therefore equals ϵ^i/ϵ^j ($126/1.72 = 73$ yen per mark). Alternatively, for one unit of currency i, traders can get ϵ^j/ϵ^i units of currency j.

Figures 16.1 and 16.2 show the exchange rates between six major currencies (those for France, Germany, Italy, Canada, Japan, and the

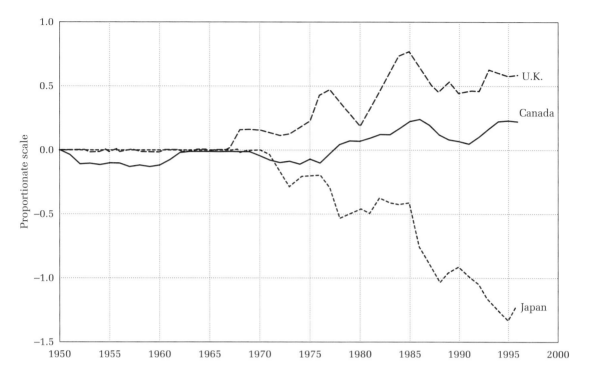

FIGURE 16.2

EXCHANGE RATES FOR CANADA, JAPAN, AND THE UNITED KINGDOM

See the note to Figure 16.1. The exchange rates for 1950 were as follows: Canada, $1.00 (Can.) per dollar (U.S.); Japan, 361 yen per dollar; United Kingdom, .357 pounds per dollar.

United Kingdom) and the U.S. dollar from 1950 to 1996. The figures show the proportionate deviation of the exchange rate for each year from the value that prevailed for the particular country in 1950. For example, in 1950, 3.50 French francs exchanged for $1.00, whereas in 1996, it took 5.12 French francs to buy $1.00. Figure 16.1 shows, accordingly, that the exchange rate for the French franc rose by 46% from 1950 to 1996. (Remember that the rise in the exchange rate means that the French franc became less valuable in relation to the U.S. dollar.)

PURCHASING-POWER PARITY

We are now ready to derive the central theoretical proposition of international finance. This result connects the exchange rate between two currencies to the price levels that prevail in the two countries.

Suppose again that we can think of all goods as tradable and physically identical. A resident of country i can use local currency to buy goods domestically at the price P^i or can exchange money into the currency of country j to buy goods at the price P^j. For each unit of currency i, a person gets $1/P^i$ units of goods domestically. Alternatively, by using the exchange market, he or she gets ϵ^j/ϵ^i units of currency j for each unit of currency i. Then, buying at the price P^j, the person gets $(\epsilon^j/\epsilon^i) \cdot (1/P^j)$ units of goods. For things to make sense, the two options *must* result in the same amount of goods: otherwise everyone would want to buy goods in the cheap country and sell goods in the expensive country. This idea is a version of the law of one price, a concept that we used in Chapter 15. Thus, it must be true that $1/P^i = (\epsilon^j/\epsilon^i) \cdot (1/P^j)$, or, after rearranging terms,

$$\epsilon^j/\epsilon^i = P^j/P^i \tag{16.1}$$

Equation (16.1) says that the ratio of the exchange rates for any two currencies, ϵ^j/ϵ^i, equals the ratio of the prices of goods in the two countries, P^j/P^i. This condition is called **purchasing-power parity (PPP)**. It ensures that the purchasing power in terms of goods for each currency is the same regardless of where someone uses the currency to buy goods.

Define the change of country i's exchange rate, $\epsilon^i_{t+1} - \epsilon^i_t$, to be $\Delta\epsilon^i$. Note that a positive value for $\Delta\epsilon^i$ means that country i's currency becomes *less* valuable over time in terms of dollars: it takes more of country i's currency to buy one dollar. We can say equivalently that country i's currency *depreciates* over time relative to the dollar. Conversely, if $\Delta\epsilon^i$

is negative, then country i's currency *appreciates* over time relative to the dollar.

The PPP condition implies that the rates of change of any two exchange rates are related to the inflation rates in the two countries. Equation (16.1) implies[1]

$$\Delta \epsilon^j / \epsilon^j - \Delta \epsilon^i / \epsilon^i \simeq \pi^j - \pi^i \qquad \textbf{(16.2)}$$

where π^j and π^i are the respective inflation rates. Equation (16.2) says that the higher a country's inflation rate, π^j, the higher the rate of depreciation of that country's currency, $\Delta \epsilon^j$. This equation is called the **relative form of PPP**, whereas equation (16.1) is called the **absolute form of PPP** (in the sense of involving levels of prices and exchange rates rather than changes).

Equations (16.1) and (16.2) apply when the prices, P^i and P^j, refer to the same tradable goods. But since we are often interested in the general levels of prices in different countries, let us try to think of P^i and P^j as the prices of market baskets of goods produced or consumed in countries i and j, respectively. We can, in practice, measure these prices by the deflators for the GDP or by consumer or wholesale price indexes. When we think of prices in this way, the PPP conditions need not hold exactly. One reason that the PPP conditions may fail in this context is that countries specialize in the production of different tradable goods, whose relative prices can change. Another reason is that countries produce and consume nontradable goods and services. Because nontradables cannot move from one country to another, the purchasing power of a currency in terms of nontradables may depend on where one buys them. Equation (16.1) therefore need not hold if P^i and P^j include prices of nontradables.

Suppose, as an example, that country j's terms of trade improve. That is, the prices of tradables produced in country j rise relative to the prices of tradables produced elsewhere. If P^i and P^j refer to market baskets of produced goods, then P^j / P^i must rise for a given ratio of the exchange rates, ϵ^j / ϵ^i, because the goods produced in country j have

[1] *Equation (16.1) implies*

$$\frac{\epsilon^j + \Delta \epsilon^j}{\epsilon^i + \Delta \epsilon^i} = \frac{P^j + \Delta P^j}{P^i + \Delta P^i}$$

where Δ denotes the change in a variable. If we multiply through and use the condition $\epsilon^j P^i = \epsilon^i P^j$ from equation (16.1), then we get

$$\Delta \epsilon^j \cdot P^i + \epsilon^j \cdot \Delta P^i \simeq P^j$$
$$\cdot \Delta \epsilon^i + \epsilon^i \cdot \Delta P^j$$

The approximation arises because we have neglected the terms $\Delta \epsilon^j \cdot \Delta P^i$ and $\Delta \epsilon^i \cdot \Delta P^j$, which involve products of changes. These terms approach zero if we consider very small intervals of time. We can rewrite the preceding expression as

$$\epsilon^j P^i \cdot (\Delta \epsilon^j / \epsilon^j + \Delta P^i / P^i) \simeq \epsilon^i P^j$$
$$\cdot (\Delta \epsilon^i / \epsilon^i + \Delta P^j / P^j)$$

Equation (16.1) implies that the terms $\epsilon^j P^i$ and $\epsilon^i P^j$ cancel. If we use $\pi^i = \Delta P^i / P^i$ and $\pi^j = \Delta P^j / P^j$ and rearrange terms, then we get equation (16.2).

Purchasing-Power Parity in Terms of the Big Mac

Since 1986, *The Economist* magazine has explored purchasing-power parity by looking at the cost of a simple product, McDonald's Big Mac hamburger, in various countries. The good is not perfectly tradable—because its provision requires local labor and land and because of differences in tax policies—but we would nevertheless predict that the ratio of prices across countries should relate to the exchange rates.

The Economist of April 12, 1997, reported that the prices of Big Macs and market exchange rates in April 1997 were as follows:

The Hamburger Standard

Country	Local Price of Big Mac	Local Price ÷ U.S. Price	Market Exchange Rate (local currency per U.S. $)	Over (+) or Under (−) Valuation of Local Currency (%)
Argentina	Peso 2.50	1.03	1.00	+3
Australia	A$ 2.50	1.03	1.29	−20
Austria	Sch 34.00	14.0	12.0	+17
Belgium	BFr 109	45.0	35.3	+28
Brazil	Real 2.97	1.23	1.06	+14
Britain	£1.81	0.75	0.61	+22
Canada	C$ 2.88	1.19	1.39	−14
Chile	Peso 1200	496	417	+19
China	Yuan 9.70	4.01	8.33	−52
Czech Republic	CKr 53.0	21.9	29.2	−25
Denmark	DKr 25.75	10.6	6.52	+63
France	FFr 17.5	7.23	5.76	+26
Germany	DM 4.90	2.02	1.71	+18
Hong Kong	HK$ 9.90	4.09	7.75	−47
Hungary	Forint 271	112	178	−37
Israel	Shek 11.5	4.75	3.38	+40
Italy	Lire 4600	1901	1683	+13

The Hamburger Standard, *continued*

Country	Local Price of Big Mac	Local Price ÷ U.S. Price	Market Exchange Rate (local currency per U.S. $)	Over (+) or Under (−) Valuation of Local Currency (%)
Japan	Yen 294	121	126	−3
Malaysia	M$ 3.87	1.60	2.50	−36
Mexico	Peso 14.9	6.16	7.90	−22
Netherlands	Fl 5.45	2.25	1.92	+17
New Zealand	NZ$ 3.25	1.34	1.45	−7
Poland	Zloty 4.30	1.78	3.10	−43
Russia	Roub 11,000	4545	5739	−21
Singapore	S$ 3.00	1.24	1.44	−14
South Africa	Rand 7.80	3.22	4.43	−27
South Korea	Won 2300	950	894	+6
Spain	Ptas 375	155	144	+7
Sweden	SKr 26.0	10.7	7.72	+39
Switzerland	SFr 5.90	2.44	1.47	+66
Taiwan	NT$ 68.0	28.1	27.6	+2
Thailand	Baht 46.7	19.3	26.1	−26
United States	US$ 2.42	1.00	1.00	0

If the PPP condition in equation (16.1) held exactly for Big Macs, then the ratio of the local price to the U.S.$ price would coincide with the market exchange rate (local currency per U.S.$). It is clear from the table that the price ratios and exchange rates are positively related, but not perfectly.

If the price ratio in a country exceeds the exchange rate, then Big Macs are relatively more costly to obtain in that country. Or, to put it another way, the market exchange rate overvalues the local currency by the percentage shown in the last column. The table shows that in April 1997 the cheapest places to buy a Big Mac—and, hence, the countries with the most undervalued currencies—were China, Hong Kong, Poland, and Hungary. The most expensive places—that is, the places with the most overvalued currencies—were Switzerland, Denmark, Israel, and Sweden. Similar patterns emerge if one constructs prices of a market basket of goods, not just Big Macs.

become more expensive relative to those produced in country i. The general point is that various real disturbances can shift the PPP condition in equation (16.1). Aside from changes in the terms of trade, some other factors that can affect this condition are changes in trade restrictions or transport costs, some aspects of tax policies, and various disturbances that shift the relative prices of traded and nontraded goods.

INTEREST-RATE PARITY

Suppose that there is a market-determined nominal interest rate in each country. The nominal rate in country i, R^i, will be expressed in units of its own currency; for example, as yen paid per year per yen lent out today.

Consider the Japanese interest rate from the standpoint of a person who is currently holding U.S. dollars. At date t the person can exchange $1.00 for ϵ_t^i units of Japanese currency. By lending in Japan at the interest rate R^i, the person receives $\epsilon_t^i \cdot (1 + R^i)$ units of yen at date $t + 1$. If he or she converts back to dollars using period $t + 1$'s exchange rate, ϵ_{t+1}^i, then the amount of dollars received is $\epsilon_t^i \cdot (1 + R^i)/\epsilon_{t+1}^i$. If we use the condition for the change in the exchange rate, $\Delta \epsilon^i = \epsilon_{t+1}^i - \epsilon_t^i$, then the quantity of dollars received becomes $(1 + R^i)/[1 + (\Delta \epsilon^i / \epsilon^i)]$, where $\Delta \epsilon^i / \epsilon^i$ is the rate of change of Japan's exchange rate with the U.S. dollar. Thus, if the exchange rate rises at a higher rate, then the dollar value of next period's holdings falls for a given value of Japan's nominal interest rate, R^i.

If there are no restrictions on the flows of assets across national borders (that is, no *capital controls*), then people can hold assets in any country. If a person chooses country i, then the dollar value of his or her holdings next period is $(1 + R^i)/[1 + (\Delta \epsilon^i / \epsilon^i)]$. But if this amount is not the same for all countries, then everyone would want to lend where the amount was greatest and borrow where it was smallest. Thus, as another implication of the law of one price—applied here to the returns on assets—the amounts must be the same for all countries:

$$(1 + R^j)/[1 + (\Delta\epsilon^j/\epsilon^j)] = (1 + R^i)/[1 + (\Delta\epsilon^i/\epsilon^i)]$$

We can use this result to derive a condition that is called **interest-rate parity**:[2]

$$R^j - R^i \simeq \Delta\epsilon^j/\epsilon^j - \Delta\epsilon^i/\epsilon^i \qquad\qquad \textbf{(16.3)}$$

The higher the rate of change of a country's exchange rate, $\Delta\epsilon^j/\epsilon^j$—that is, the more rapid the depreciation in value relative to the U.S. dollar—the higher must be that country's nominal interest rate, R^j.

The changes in the exchange rates would, in practice, not be known in advance. Then, as a first-order approximation, we would replace the variables $\Delta\epsilon^j/\epsilon^j$ and $\Delta\epsilon^i/\epsilon^i$ by their expectations to get[3]

$$R^j - R^i \simeq (\Delta\epsilon^j/\epsilon^j)^e - (\Delta\epsilon^i/\epsilon^i)^e \qquad\qquad \textbf{(16.4)}$$

Equation (16.4) says that a higher expected rate of change of the exchange rate, $(\Delta\epsilon^j/\epsilon^j)^e$, implies a correspondingly higher nominal interest rate, R^j.

A number of real-world considerations prevent interest-rate parity from holding exactly. These considerations include the tax treatment of interest income in different countries, effects from uncertainties about asset returns and exchange-rate movements, and governmental restrictions on international borrowing and lending. For the main developed countries, the departures from interest-rate parity are nonzero but tend to be small.

If purchasing-power parity holds in relative form, then equation (16.2) implies that the difference in the growth rates of the exchange rates, $\Delta\epsilon^j/\epsilon^j - \Delta\epsilon^i/\epsilon^i$, equals the difference in the inflation rates, $\pi^j - \pi^i$. In terms of expectations, the relative PPP condition is

$$(\Delta\epsilon^j/\epsilon^j)^e - (\Delta\epsilon^i/\epsilon^i)^e = (\pi^j)^e - (\pi^i)^e \qquad\qquad \textbf{(16.5)}$$

[2] *Multiply through by the term $[1 + (\Delta\epsilon^i/\epsilon^i)] \cdot [(1 + (\Delta\epsilon^j/\epsilon^j)]$. We get the interest-rate parity condition in equation (16.3) if we neglect the terms $R^i \cdot \Delta\epsilon^j/\epsilon^j$ and $R^j \cdot \Delta\epsilon^i/\epsilon^i$. As the length of the period diminishes, the approximation becomes more accurate.*

[3] *This result is an approximation because holders of assets would worry also about the degree of uncertainty attached to changes in exchange rates. For the major currencies, individuals can protect themselves, or hedge, against this uncertainty. Suppose, for example, that a U.S. resident holds a one-period bond denominated in German marks. Assume that the holder wants to know the dollar value of this asset one period from now. There is uncertainty about this value because no one knows today the next period's exchange rate between marks and dollars. A trader can eliminate this risk with a one-period futures contract on the German mark. The appropriate contract in this case (corresponding to going short on the mark) is one that guarantees the holder the price at which he or she will be able to sell marks for dollars next period.*

If we combine equation (16.5) with the interest-rate parity condition from equation (16.4), then we find that the expected real interest rates must be the same in countries i and j:

$$R^j - (\pi^j)^e \simeq R^i - (\pi^i)^e \tag{16.6}$$

For the main developed countries, expected real interest rates tend on the whole to move together,[4] a finding that supports equation (16.6) as a first-order proposition. The more detailed empirical evidence does, however, reveal significant divergences in expected real interest rates among these countries.[5] To explain these divergences we have to allow for departures from the relative PPP condition in equation (16.5). Recall that the PPP conditions need not hold if the price levels, P^i and P^j, refer to market baskets of goods produced or consumed in the two countries.

Suppose, for example, that the expected rate of inflation for country j is low relative to the expected rate of change of its exchange rate, all expressed in relation to country i:

$$(\pi^j)^e - (\pi^i)^e < (\Delta\epsilon^j)^e - (\Delta\epsilon^i)^e \tag{16.7}$$

Thus, instead of relative PPP from equation (16.5), the cost of obtaining goods in country j is expected to fall relative to that in country i.

If we use condition (16.7) together with the interest-parity condition from equation (16.4), then we get

$$R^j - (\pi^j)^e > R^i - (\pi^i)^e \tag{16.8}$$

Thus, the expected real interest rate is relatively high for the country in which people expect relatively low inflation, in the sense of condition (16.7).

It is plausible that goods in country j will become relatively cheaper over time if the relative cost of goods in country j is currently high, that is, if

$$P^j/P^i > \epsilon^j/\epsilon^i \tag{16.9}$$

[4] See Robert Barro and Xavier Sala-i-Martin (1990).

[5] See Robert Cumby and Maurice Obstfeld (1984) and Frederic Mishkin (1984).

This condition represents a departure from absolute PPP in equation (16.1). Condition (16.9) tends to lead to condition (16.7) because of the long-run tendency for absolute PPP to hold: if countries are relatively expensive today for buying goods, then they tend to become relatively less expensive over time.

We can also look at condition (16.9) as a statement that country j's currency is highly valued, that is, ϵ^j is low in relation to the PPP value, $\epsilon^i P^j / P^i$. We therefore conclude that *an overvalued currency is associated with relatively low expected inflation (in the sense of condition [16.7]) and, hence, with relatively high expected real interest rates (condition [16.8]).*

FIXED EXCHANGE RATES

Until the early 1970s and except during major wars, most countries typically maintained **fixed exchange rates** among their currencies. Figures 16.1 and 16.2 show that, from 1950 to the early 1970s, the exchange rates between six major currencies and the U.S. dollar moved infrequently and by small amounts compared to what came later. For the countries considered, the main exceptions to fixed exchange rates in this period were the fluctuations in the Canadian dollar rate until the early 1960s and some realignments in the rates for the French franc, German mark, and British pound.

We explored a simple but unrealistic system of fixed exchange rates in the previous chapter. In that setting all countries used a common currency, so that the fixity of exchange rates held trivially.

The fixed-rate regime that actually applied to the major developed countries from World War II until the early 1970s is called the **Bretton Woods System**.[6] Under this system, the participating countries established narrow bands within which they pegged the exchange rate, ϵ^i, between their currency and the U.S. dollar. Country i's central bank stood ready to buy or sell its currency at the rate of ϵ^i units per dollar. The German central bank (Bundesbank), for example, provided dollars

[6] *The system is named in honor of the meeting site, Bretton Woods, New Hampshire, where the regime was set up. For the details of this system, see James Ingram (1983, Chap. 9).*

for marks when people wanted to reduce their holdings of marks, and the reverse when people wished to increase their holdings of marks. To manage these exchanges, each central bank maintained a stock of assets in the form of U.S. currency or, more likely, in interest-bearing assets, such as U.S. Treasury bills, that could be readily converted into U.S. currency. Then the United States stood ready to exchange dollars for gold (on the request of foreign official institutions) at a fixed price, which happened to be $35 per ounce. Thus, by maintaining a fixed exchange rate with the U.S. dollar, each country indirectly pegged its currency to gold. (This setup is sometimes called a *gold-exchange standard*.)

Another example of a system of fixed exchange rates is the classical gold standard. Britain was effectively on the gold standard from the early eighteenth century until World War I, except for a period of suspension because of the Napoleonic Wars from 1797 to 1821. Britain returned to the gold standard in 1926 but departed from the system during the Great Depression in 1931. The United States was on the gold standard from 1879 until the trough of the Great Depression in 1933, when the dollar price of gold was increased from $20.67 to $35.00 per ounce. Earlier periods in the United States involved a greater role for silver in the context of a *bimetallic standard*. From an international perspective, the gold standard reached its high point from 1890 to 1914.

Under a gold standard, each country pegs its currency directly to gold instead of to a central currency, such as the U.S. dollar. An ounce of gold might, for example, be set at $20 in New York and at 4 pounds in London (roughly the values prevailing in 1914). Then the exchange rate between U.S. dollars and British pounds would have to be close to $5 per pound. Otherwise (subject to the costs of shipping gold), it would be profitable for people to buy gold in one country and sell it in the other. As with the Bretton Woods System, the classical gold standard would—if adhered to by the participants—maintain fixed exchange rates among the various currencies.

It is possible for countries to maintain fixed exchange rates in a regime that has no role for gold or another commodity. From 1979 to

1992, for example, several European countries in the **European Monetary System (EMS)** kept the exchange rates among their currencies fixed within fairly narrow ranges. This arrangement was called the **Exchange Rate Mechanism (ERM)**. Instead of using gold or U.S. dollars, the ERM used as an international money the **European Currency Unit (ECU)**, which is a basket containing specified amounts of various European currencies.

The Maastricht Treaty of 1991 envisioned the ERM as evolving by 1999 into a European monetary union with a common currency named in 1996 as the *euro*. However, the EMS weakened in 1992 when the United Kingdom (which had joined only in 1990) and Italy were forced to devalue. Then, in 1993, the admissible exchange-rate bands for the remaining countries were widened so much that the system could no longer be viewed as one of fixed exchange rates. The idea of a European monetary union was also politically unpopular in some countries, especially the United Kingdom and Denmark. Because of these difficulties, it was unclear as of 1997 whether the single European currency would ever come into existence.

To see the workings of a system with fixed exchange rates, start by letting P represent the dollar price of goods in the United States. Then, if the absolute PPP condition from equation (16.1) holds, country i's price level is

$$P^i = \epsilon^i \cdot P \qquad\qquad\qquad (16.10)$$

(Note in equation [16.1] that the U.S. dollar exchange rate with itself is unity.) If country i's exchange rate with the U.S. dollar, ϵ^i, is fixed, then the price level in country i, P^i, must maintain a constant ratio to the U.S. price level, P.

We can generalize the result by introducing deviations from absolute purchasing-power parity. As mentioned before, the reasons for these deviations include shifts in the terms of trade and a variety of other real disturbances. But we would retain the basic result; namely, a country cannot choose independently its exchange rate, ϵ^i, and its general price level, P^i. If absolute PPP tends to hold in the long run, then a fixed exchange rate means that a country's price level must maintain a given relation to the U.S. price level.

If the U.S. price level, P, changes, then equation (16.10) says that country i's price level, P^i, changes in the same proportion. In other words, any country that maintains a fixed exchange rate with the U.S. dollar experiences roughly the same inflation rate, π^i, as the U.S. rate, π.

Given fixed exchange rates, the interest-rate parity condition from equation (16.3) implies that country i's nominal interest rate, R^i, equals the U.S. rate, R. Thus, under fixed exchange rates, a single nominal interest rate would prevail in the world. (Again, differences in taxes and in riskiness of returns mean that this result would not hold exactly.)

THE QUANTITY OF MONEY UNDER FIXED EXCHANGE RATES

Before, when considering a closed economy, we stressed the relation between a country's quantity of money, M^i, and its price level, P^i. Yet we have determined a country's price level in equation (16.10) without saying anything about that country's quantity of domestic currency. Let us now investigate the relation between domestic money and prices in an open economy under fixed exchange rates.

It is still the case that the residents of country i demand a quantity of real money, M^i/P^i, which depends on variables such as domestic output, Y^i, and the world nominal interest rate, R. (We assume here that the residents of country i use and hold their own currency rather than that of other countries.) The condition that all domestic money in country i be willingly held is

$$M^i = P^i \cdot \Phi(Y^i, R, \ldots) \qquad \text{(16.11)}$$
$$ (+) \ (-)$$

If absolute purchasing-power parity holds, then we can substitute in equation (16.11) for the domestic price level as $P^i = \epsilon^i \cdot P$ from equation

(16.10). Then we get the condition for the domestic quantity of money:

$$M^i = \epsilon^i \cdot P \cdot \Phi(Y^i, R, \ldots) \qquad \qquad \textbf{(16.12)}$$

Given the exchange rate, ϵ^i, the U.S. price level, P, and the determinants of the real demand for money in country i, $\Phi(\cdot)$, equation (16.12) determines the nominal quantity of money, M^i, that must be present in country i. Hence, the quantity of domestic money *cannot* be regarded as a free element of choice by country i's central bank. If the central bank pegs the exchange rate at the value ϵ^i, then there is a specific quantity of money, M^i, that is consistent with this exchange rate.

To understand these findings, assume that the domestic price level, P^i, accords initially with absolute purchasing-power parity, as specified in equation (16.10), and that the quantity of domestic money, M^i, is the amount prescribed by equation (16.12). Then the quantity of money equals the amount demanded.

Now suppose that the monetary authority increases the quantity of domestic money, M^i, say, by an open-market purchase of government securities. In Table 16.2 we illustrate this case in step 1 by assuming that the domestic currency and the central bank's holdings of interest-bearing domestic assets each rise by $1 million.

Our previous analysis of a closed economy suggests that the increase in the quantity of domestic currency would raise the domestic price level, P^i. But then the price level in country i would exceed the value dictated by the PPP condition in equation (16.10). Hence, for a given exchange rate, goods bought in country i would become more expensive relative to goods bought elsewhere. In response, households and firms would move away from buying goods in country i and toward buying goods in other countries (or toward goods imported from country i). This reaction tends to keep the domestic price level, P^i, from rising; that is, the domestic price level stays in line with the prices prevailing in the rest of the world. But at this price level, domestic residents would be unwilling to hold the additional $1 million of domestic money, M^i.

EXCHANGE RATES

611

TABLE 16.2

EFFECTS OF OPEN-MARKET OPERATIONS ON THE CENTRAL BANK'S BALANCE SHEET

	Assets	Liabilities
Step 1	Domestic interest-bearing assets: +$1 million	Domestic currency, M^i: +$1 million
Step 2	International currency: −$1 million	Domestic currency, M^i: −$1 million

Note: *In step 1 the open-market purchase raises domestic currency by $1 million. But in step 2, the loss of international currency means that domestic currency declines by $1 million.*

Accordingly, people would return their excess domestic currency to the central bank to obtain U.S. dollars or other currencies. (Since the central bank pegs the exchange rate, ϵ^i, it stands ready to make these exchanges at a fixed conversion ratio.) Thus, in step 2 of Table 16.2, the quantity of domestic currency and the central bank's holdings of international currency each decline by $1 million.

Instead of reducing its holdings of international currency, the central bank could sell off other assets to get the international currency that people were demanding. The more general point, therefore, is that the return of domestic currency to the central bank causes the bank to lose some type of asset.

To complete the story, we must assess the central bank's reaction to its loss of international currency or other assets. As one possibility, the bank allows the domestic quantity of money, M^i, to decline. Then, as people return money to the bank, the domestic quantity of money falls back toward the level that is consistent with the PPP condition in equation (16.12). This automatic response of domestic money is a central element of the gold standard and other systems of fixed exchange rates.

As another possibility, when the automatic mechanism tends to reduce the quantity of domestic money, M^i, the central bank might offset this tendency, for example, by further open-market purchases of securities. When the bank acts this way, economists say that it attempts to **sterilize** the flow of international currency. By sterilization, economists mean that the central bank tries to insulate the quantity of domestic money, M^i, from changes in the bank's holdings of international currency or other assets. Eventually, this type of policy can lead to a sufficient drain on assets so that the central bank becomes unwilling or unable to maintain the exchange rate. That is, the central bank may no longer provide dollars at the fixed rate of ϵ^i units of domestic currency per dollar. Instead, there may be a **devaluation**, which means that the exchange rate rises above ϵ^i units of domestic currency per dollar. Thus, the tendency of central banks to sterilize the flows of international currency threatens the viability of fixed exchange rates.[7]

We should mention another possible reaction of government policy to the loss of central bank assets. Recall that this drain results in the present case from the central bank's excessive monetary creation, a policy that tends to make domestic goods more expensive relative to foreign goods. To counter this tendency, the home government might impose trade restrictions, which artificially raise the cost of foreign goods for domestic residents. Alternatively, the government might subsidize exports to make these goods cheaper for foreigners. The main point is that the government can interfere with free trade across national borders to prevent purchasing-power parity from holding. Thus, there are two types of potential ill effects from excessive monetary expansion under fixed exchange rates. One is the loss of international currency, an outcome that leads eventually to devaluation. But to avoid either devaluation or domestic monetary contraction, governments may interfere with free trade. In fact, the frequency of these interferences during the post–World War II period was a major argument used by opponents of fixed exchange rates (see Milton Friedman, 1968a, Chap. 9).

[7] The discussion in this and the following sections follows a viewpoint that is often called the **monetary approach to the balance of payments**. This approach was developed by Robert Mundell (1968, Part 2; 1971, Part 2). The early origins of this theory are in the eighteenth-century writings of David Hume; see Eugene Rotwein (1970).

WORLD PRICES UNDER FIXED EXCHANGE RATES

A system of fixed exchange rates, centered on the U.S. dollar, determines each country's price level, P^i, as a ratio to the U.S. price level, P (see equation [16.10]). To complete the picture, we have to determine the *U.S.* price level. This analysis is similar to the determination of the world price level in the common-currency system considered in Chapter 15. We have to equate the overall demand for international currency to the supply.

Suppose that all countries hold their international currency in the form of U.S. dollars (as was reasonably accurate under the Bretton Woods System). Then the total real demand for U.S. currency includes the holdings of U.S. residents plus the holdings of foreigners in the form of international currency. Given the dollar quantity of U.S. currency, M, we can determine the U.S. price level, P, in the manner of our closed-economy analysis. Specifically, a greater amount of money, M, means a higher U.S. price level, P, and a correspondingly higher price level, P^i, in each other country. Conversely, an increase in the real demand for U.S. currency—whether by U.S. residents or by foreigners—lowers the U.S. price level, P, and correspondingly reduces the price level, P^i, in each other country.

Under the international regime that prevailed after World War II, there were a number of factors that constrained the Federal Reserve's choice of the quantity of U.S. money, M. First, if the Federal Reserve pursued a monetary policy that was inconsistent with stabilization of the U.S. price level, P, then U.S. currency would become less attractive as an international medium of exchange. That is, other countries would not like it if their price levels—which were constrained to follow the path of the U.S. price level—grew too fast or fluctuated a great deal. Consequently, these countries might no longer find it desirable to peg their exchange rates to the U.S. dollar or to hold dollars as a form of international currency. This element constrained the expansion of U.S. money to the extent that the U.S. monetary authority wished to maintain the role of the U.S. dollar as the centerpiece of the international monetary system.

More important, the United States had a commitment to exchange U.S. dollars for gold at the rate of $35 per ounce. If the U.S. price level rose substantially, as it did during the late 1960s, then it would become attractive for foreign central banks to trade their dollars for gold. As it lost more and more gold, the United States would become unable to maintain the dollar price of gold. Eventually the system would break down, as it did at the beginning of the 1970s. Notably, Richard Nixon (the same president who gave us price controls and the 55-mile-per-hour speed limit) decided in 1971 that the United States would no longer provide gold to foreign central banks in exchange for U.S. dollars.

DEVALUATION

Return now to the situation of a typical country in a regime of exchange rates tied to the U.S. dollar. As suggested before, a country that typically pegs its exchange rate, ϵ^i, occasionally faces pressure to shift this rate. Consider, for example, a disturbance that tends to increase the domestic price level, P^i, relative to the U.S. price, P. The disturbance could be a rapid expansion of the domestic currency, M^i, or a decrease in the demand for country i's real money, M^i/P^i. The central bank tends in these circumstances to lose international currency or other assets. In response, the bank may raise the exchange rate, ϵ^i, that is, devalue the domestic currency in terms of the U.S. dollar.

A disturbance that tends to lower the domestic price level, P^i, relative to the U.S. price, P, implies gains in the central bank's assets. The bank is likely to react in this case by lowering the exchange rate, ϵ^i, that is, by appreciating the domestic currency in terms of the dollar. Economists call this change a **revaluation.**

Devaluations and revaluations typically do not involve long periods during which the central bank gradually loses or gains international currency. That is because the expectation of a shift in the exchange rate leads to **speculation**, a response that tends to hasten the central bank's actions. If people anticipate a devaluation, then they have an incentive to act in advance to exchange their domestic money at the central bank for international currency, which might be U.S. dollars. People react this way because they expect the domestic money to become less valuable relative to other monies. But since the speculative decline in the demand for domestic money leads to further losses of international currency by the central bank, the devaluation tends to occur sooner.

Figures 16.1 and 16.2 provide some examples of sudden devaluation and revaluation during the mainly fixed-rate period before the early 1970s. France devalued the franc by a total of 40% in 1957–58, Germany revalued the mark by 4% in 1961, and Britain devalued the pound by 14% in 1967.

Consider now the effects of a devaluation, that is, an increase in the exchange rate, ϵ^i. As noted before, this change may be a symptom of inflationary pressure, possibly caused by excessive expansion of the domestic currency, M^i. But let's consider here the effects of an autonomous devaluation, which is a devaluation that comes out of the blue, rather than as a response to changes in domestic money supply or demand.

If the domestic price level, P^i (measured, say, in terms of yen per unit of goods), did not change, then an increase in the exchange rate, ϵ^i (yen per dollar), means that goods in country i would become cheaper in terms of dollars. For a given U.S. price level, P, the demand for goods sold by country i would rise accordingly. This increase in demand suggests that the price level, P^i, would rise. This response would accord with the PPP condition, equation (16.10), which shows that a devaluation (a higher value of ϵ^i) leads to a higher domestic price level, $P^i = \epsilon^i \cdot P$.

If we treat the devaluation and the rise in the domestic price level as one-time events, then the higher domestic price level implies a greater demand for domestic money in nominal terms (see equation [16.11]). The rise in the nominal quantity of money, M^i, can come about in two ways. First, the central bank may create more money through open-market operations or other means. Second, if the central bank does not act, then individuals would bring international currency to the central bank to get more domestic currency. As the bank exchanges domestic for international currency, the quantity of domestic money, M^i, rises. Thus, a one-time devaluation tends to increase the central bank's international currency along with the increase in the quantity of domestic money, M^i.

Notice that there is a two-way direction of association between devaluation and the behavior of domestic prices and money. First, expansionary monetary policy creates pressure for devaluation. In this sense, domestic inflation causes devaluation. Second, a devaluation tends to raise domestic prices and money. In this sense, devaluation is itself inflationary.

Thus far, the analysis treats the changes in the exchange rate, ϵ^i, and the domestic price level, P^i, as one-time happenings. But, in practice, countries that devalue once tend to devalue again. This outcome makes sense if we think of devaluation as primarily a symptom of pressure for domestic inflation, in particular, as an indication that the domestic central bank is increasing the quantity of money at a rapid rate. Countries that act this way today are likely to continue this behavior later. Hence, a devaluation can create expectations of future increases in the exchange rate, ϵ^i. Then the interest-rate parity condition from equation (16.4) implies that the domestic nominal interest rate, R^i, would rise above that in the United States. This change reduces the real demand for country i's money, M^i/P^i; consequently, a devaluation of country i's currency may no longer generate an increase in country i's holdings of international currency.

FLEXIBLE EXCHANGE RATES

The international system of fixed exchange rates, centered on the U.S. dollar, broke down in the early 1970s. One reason for the breakdown was the excessive creation of U.S. dollars and the consequent rise in the U.S. price level after the mid-1960s. This inflation made it difficult for the United States to maintain convertibility of the dollar into gold at the rate of $35 per ounce. President Nixon decided in 1971 to raise the dollar price of gold and to curb flows of gold from the United States to foreign central banks. These actions signaled the end of the Bretton Woods System, whereby currencies were linked to gold through the U.S. dollar.

Since the early 1970s, many countries have allowed their exchange rates to vary or float more or less freely to clear the markets for foreign exchange. As is clear from a glance at Figures 16.1 and 16.2, the exchange rates of six major currencies with the U.S. dollar have fluctuated substantially over this period. Groups of countries, such as the European Monetary System from 1979 to 1992, maintained relatively fixed exchange rates among their currencies. Nevertheless, the important development since the early 1970s has been the increased reliance on **flexible exchange rates**. To study events in this period, we have to extend the analysis to consider the determination of exchange rates in a flexible-rate environment.

If the goods produced in various countries are physically identical, then the condition for absolute PPP, $P^i = \epsilon^i \cdot P$ from equation (16.10), still holds under flexible exchange rates. That is, the purchasing power of any currency in terms of goods is still the same regardless of where someone uses the currency to buy goods. Deviations from PPP can still arise from various disturbances, such as shifts in the terms of trade, changes in trade restrictions or transport costs, and so on.

A new result under flexible exchange rates is that country i's price level, P^i, is no longer tied to the U.S. price, P. Hence, country i's inflation rate, π^i, can also depart from the U.S. rate, π. The monetary authority of country i can now independently determine its domestic money supply, M^i, through open-market operations or other means. Given the quantity of domestic money, the domestic price level, P^i, is determined to ensure that this money is willingly held. This condition can be written by rearranging the terms from equation (16.11) as

$$P^i = \frac{M^i}{\Phi(Y^i, R^i, \ldots)} \qquad\qquad (16.13)$$

Note that, since country i's inflation rate can differ from the U.S. rate, country i's nominal interest rate, R^i, can also differ from the U.S. rate, R. The real interest rates, $R^i - \pi^i = r$, will, however, still be the same across countries if relative PPP holds.

The PPP condition, $P^i = \epsilon^i \cdot P$, implies that country i's exchange rate can be determined by substituting out for P^i from equation (16.13) to get

$$\epsilon^i = \frac{P^i}{P} = \frac{M^i}{P \cdot \Phi(Y^i, R^i, \ldots)}$$

The exchange rate, ϵ^i, is therefore determined by the monetary authority's choice of M^i and the values of Y^i, P (the U.S. price level), and R^i. (Note that R^i equals $r + \pi^i$, and π^i is the growth rate of P^i, which is determined from equation [16.13].)

Since $\epsilon^i = P^i/P$, we also know that the rate of change of country i's exchange rate with the U.S. dollar, $\Delta\epsilon^i/\epsilon^i$, must equal the difference between country i's inflation rate and the U.S. rate, $\pi^i - \pi$ (see equation [16.2]). This proposition turns out to fit the data well for countries with high average rates of inflation. Not surprisingly, these countries turn out also to be the ones that have maintained flexible exchange rates with the U.S. dollar over most years, even before the 1970s.

Table 16.3 reports the relative inflation rates (based on consumer price indexes) and growth rates of the exchange rate for some high-inflation countries, mainly over the period 1955–96. (The table covers the high-inflation countries for which data are available.) Notice that the difference between each country's average inflation rate and the U.S. rate, $\pi^i - \pi$, matches up closely with the average percentage change per year in the exchange rate, $\Delta\epsilon^i/\epsilon^i$. Thus, the relative form of PPP works well here.

TABLE 16.3

A COMPARISON OF INFLATION RATES WITH CHANGES IN EXCHANGE RATES FOR SOME HIGH-INFLATION COUNTRIES (PERCENT PER YEAR, 1955–96)

	$\pi^i - \pi$	$\Delta\epsilon^i/\epsilon^i$
Argentina	67.9	64.3
Brazil[a]	81.4	79.7
Chile	31.4	35.5
Colombia	12.4	14.6
Iceland	13.6	14.7
Indonesia[b]	7.0	7.1
Israel	23.6	23.9
Peru	48.3	45.7
Uruguay[c]	37.6	37.1

Sources: *The data on price levels (consumer price indexes) and exchange rates are from International Monetary Fund*, International Financial Statistics, *July 1997 CD-ROM release.*

Note: *The table shows each country's average inflation rate, π^i, less the average U.S. rate, π. These values match up closely with the average percentage change per year in the exchange rate with the U.S. dollar, $\Delta\epsilon^i/\epsilon^i$.*

[a]*1957–96*

[b]*1968–96*

[c]*1960–96*

Although each country can make independent choices about the quantity of money, it is important to recognize that flexible exchange rates do not isolate a country economically from the rest of the world. As long as the exchange-rate system allows free trade in goods and assets, the precise nature of the system does not have a great deal to do with the extent of international trade in goods and services or with the amount of international borrowing and lending. (We did, however, discuss the possibility that countries would resort to trade restrictions to defend a fixed exchange rate without having to undergo domestic monetary contraction.) The main results about international trade in goods and assets apply as well to a setting of flexible exchange rates as to one with fixed rates.

PURCHASING-POWER PARITY UNDER FLEXIBLE AND FIXED EXCHANGE RATES

Many economists have noted that purchasing-power parity seems to hold less well under the flexible exchange rates that have prevailed since the early 1970s than under the fixed rates that prevailed earlier for most countries. We already looked in Figures 16.1 and 16.2 at the behavior of exchange rates for six of the major developed countries. To see the implications for PPP, we have to adjust these exchange rates to take account of the divergent movements in domestic price levels.

Figures 16.3 and 16.4 show the price levels (deflators for the GDP or GNP) for the six countries from 1950 to 1996. Each price level is expressed as a ratio to the U.S. price level; that is, the values correspond to P^i/P from our previous discussion. The figures show for each year the proportionate deviation of the price ratio from the value that prevailed in 1950. For Germany in Figure 16.3, for example, the value for 1996 was about 20% below that in 1950 because the average German inflation rate from 1950 to 1996 was lower than that in the United States. For periods in which a country's inflation rate exceeded the U.S. value, the lines shown in Figures 16.3 and 16.4 rise over time.

Figures 16.5 and 16.6 show the ratio of the exchange rate, ϵ^i, to the relative price, P^i/P. As in previous figures, the numbers plotted represent the proportionate deviation from the value that prevailed in each country in 1950. If relative PPP held, then the numbers would all equal zero. Deviations in relative PPP show up as movements above or below zero in Figures 16.5 and 16.6.

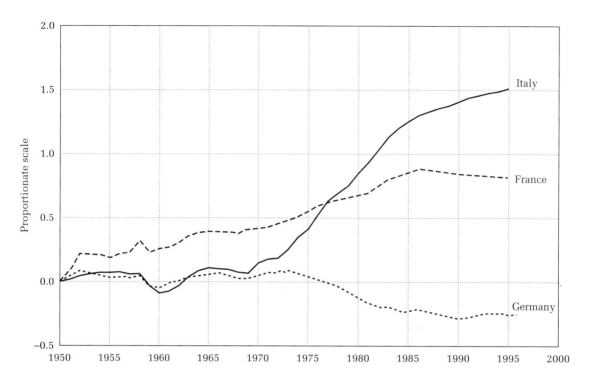

FIGURE 16.3

PRICE LEVELS FOR FRANCE, GERMANY, AND ITALY

Each price level (deflator for the GDP or GNP) is expressed as a ratio to the U.S. price level. The values shown are the proportionate (logarithmic) deviations from the value prevailing for each country in 1950. For sources, see the note to Figure 16.1.

Economists often call the ratio of ϵ^i to P^i/P—that is, $\epsilon^i \cdot P/P^i$—the **real exchange rate**. This ratio indicates the quantity of goods produced in country i that exchanges for one unit of goods produced in the United States. (A person can sell one unit of U.S. goods for P dollars, which can then be exchanged for $\epsilon^i P$ units of country i's currency. This much currency buys $(1/P^i) \cdot \epsilon^i P = \epsilon^i \cdot P/P^i$ units of country i's goods. This last term equals the real exchange rate.) A rise—that is, a depreciation—in the real exchange rate means that goods produced in country i have become cheaper relative to those produced in the United States. Or, to put

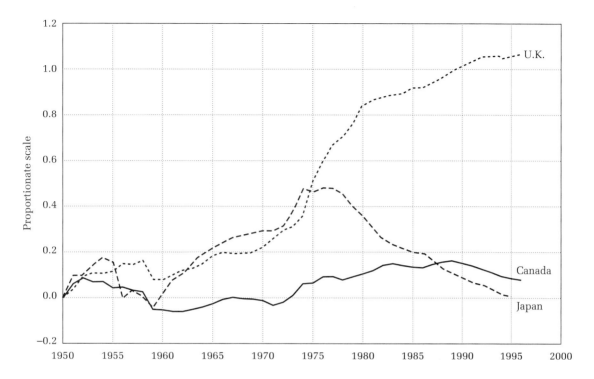

FIGURE 16.4

PRICE LEVELS FOR CANADA, JAPAN, AND THE UNITED KINGDOM

See the note to Figure 16.3.

it the other way, U.S. goods have become relatively more expensive. In order to distinguish it from the real exchange rate, economists sometimes refer to the ordinary exchange rate, ϵ^i, as the **nominal exchange rate**.

As an example, for Japan in Figure 16.6, the value of -0.30 for the real exchange rate in 1970 means that U.S. goods could be exchanged for only about 70% as much goods in Japan, compared to the situation that prevailed in 1950. Thus, Japanese goods became more expensive relative to U.S. goods from 1950 to 1970. Recall that the nominal exchange rate was fixed during this period (see Figure 16.2). The fall in the real exchange rate therefore reflected a *higher* average inflation rate in Japan

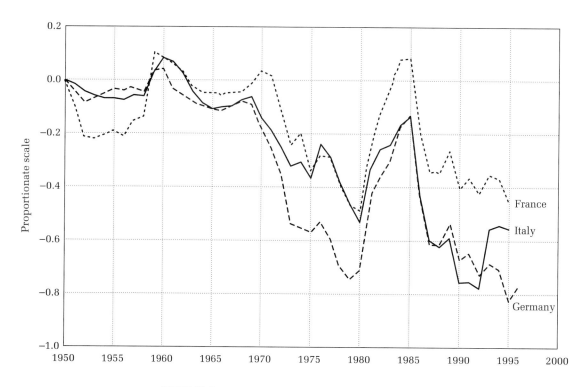

FIGURE 16.5

REAL EXCHANGE RATES FOR FRANCE, GERMANY, AND ITALY

The real exchange rate equals the nominal exchange rate, ϵ^i, divided by the ratio of price levels, P^i/P. The values shown are the proportionate (logarithmic) deviations from the value prevailing in each country in 1950. For the sources, see the note to Figure 16.1.

(4.5% per year from 1950 to 1970) than in the United States (3.0% per year); see Figure 16.4.

The real exchange rate for Japan continued to fall after 1970, so that Japanese goods exchanged for more and more U.S. goods, until reaching the value −0.99 in 1978. Then the rate rose back to −0.62 in 1985, before falling to −1.17 in 1988 and −1.35 in 1995. Since the mid-1970s, the Japanese inflation rate has been *lower* than that in the United States (see Figure 16.4). The periods of decline in the real exchange rate therefore reflected decreases in the nominal exchange rate (Figure 16.2).

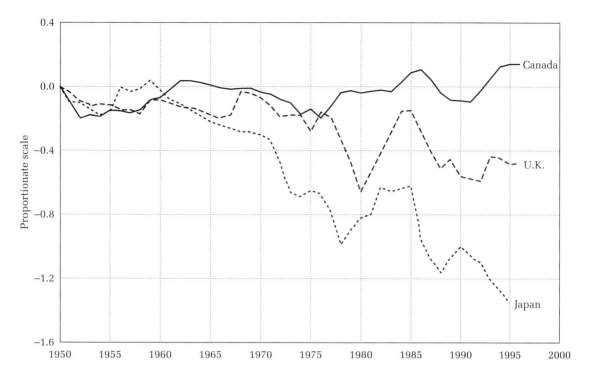

FIGURE 16.6

REAL EXCHANGE RATES FOR CANADA, JAPAN, AND THE UNITED KINGDOM

See the note to Figure 16.5.

The Japanese yen appreciated in nominal terms at an especially rapid rate from 1971 to 1973, 1976 to 1978, 1985 to 1988, and 1990 to 1995.

The European countries—France, Germany, and Italy in Figure 16.5 and the United Kingdom in Figure 16.6—experienced broadly similar patterns of real exchange rates. Each currency showed strong real appreciation from 1970 to 1980, followed by real depreciation until 1985, and a return to real appreciation from 1985 to 1987 and 1989 to 1990. The real exchange rates were reasonably stable from 1990 to 1996.

One interesting point, brought out by a comparison of Germany and Italy from 1970 to 1992, is that the real exchange rates behaved similarly even when the domestic price levels and nominal exchange rates moved in very different ways. For example, from 1970 to 1980, the Italian inflation rate averaged 8 percentage points per year more than that in the United States (Figure 16.3), and the Italian nominal exchange rate depreciated at an average rate of 3% per year (Figure 16.1). Thus, the real exchange rate for Italy *appreciated* at a rate of 5% per year (Figure 16.5). Over the same period, the average German inflation rate was 2 percentage points per year below that in the United States (Figure 16.3), and the German nominal exchange rate appreciated at an average rate of 7% per year (Figure 16.1). Thus, as with Italy, the real exchange rate for Germany appreciated by 5% per year (Figure 16.5). The real exchange rates for Germany and Italy also behaved similarly from 1980 to 1992, when the countries were part of the European Monetary System. However, the nominal depreciation of the Italian lira in 1992 (Figure 16.1) corresponded to a depreciation of Italy's real exchange rate relative to Germany's (Figure 16.5).

The lesson from the comparison between Germany and Italy from 1970 to 1992 is that very different patterns for nominal variables—domestic price levels, nominal exchange rates, and, it turns out, underlying rates of monetary growth—can coexist with similar patterns for real exchange rates. That is because the nominal exchange rates behaved sufficiently differently in Germany and Italy—especially during the 1970s—so as to offset the divergent trends in domestic price levels. Although the real exchange rates between each country and the United States have changed substantially since 1970, the suggestion is that some real disturbances—rather than the nominal policies that differed substantially between Germany and Italy—were at work. Economists have, unfortunately, not been so successful in isolating the important real disturbances.

We know for high-inflation countries, such as those studied before in Table 16.3, that differences in inflation rates explain most of the divergent movements in nominal exchange rates. For the six developed countries that we have been considering, the inflation rates are relatively moderate, and the fluctuations of inflation account for only a small part of the year-to-year variations in nominal exchange rates. Over the longer term, however, the differing behavior of domestic price levels does explain a large fraction of the movements in nominal exchange rates. From 1973 to 1996 for the six developed countries, the different movements in domestic price levels (shown in Figures 16.3 and 16.4) turn out to explain about 70% of the variations in nominal exchange rates (Figures 16.1 and 16.2).

Finally, note for Canada that the shifts in the real exchange rate were relatively mild (Figure 16.6). This outcome probably reflects the ease of moving goods and factors of production between Canada and the United States, as well as similarities in the types of goods produced. Figure 16.4 shows that the average Canadian inflation rate from 1950 to 1996 (4.3% per year) was similar to that in the United States (4.1% per year). The nominal exchange rate for the Canadian dollar therefore changed relatively little over this period (Figure 16.2).

Let us try to summarize some of the major facts about real exchange rates in the post–World War II period.[8] Some of these observations follow directly from Figures 16.1–16.6, and others come from more detailed statistical analysis of these and other data.

1. Real exchange rates, calculated by means of GNP or GDP deflators, have not been constant. The extent of fluctuations during the flexible-exchange-rate period from 1973 to 1996 turns out to be roughly twice as great as that from 1951 to 1972, when most nominal exchange rates were fixed.[9] Departures from relative PPP have therefore been important, especially since the early 1970s. There were, however, some substantial movements in real exchange rates in the earlier period when nominal exchange rates were fixed. Thus, fixed nominal exchange rates do not guarantee stability in real exchange rates.

2. The real exchange rates for Canada remained relatively stable even under flexible exchange rates. Thus, flexible nominal rates do not lead necessarily to large fluctuations in real exchange rates.

3. The past experience of movements in real exchange rates provides little guide to future changes. For example, the real depreciation of

[8] For a related discussion, see Michael Mussa (1979, pp. 10–27).

[9] The standard deviation of real exchange rates from 1973 to 1996 is about twice as large as that from 1951 to 1972.

the U.S. dollar against the European and Japanese currencies from 1970 to 1975 (Figures 16.5 and 16.6) would not have allowed us to predict the continuation of real depreciations from 1975 to 1980 (1975 to 1978 for Japan). Similarly, the real appreciation of the U.S. dollar from 1980 to 1985 would not have allowed us to predict the depreciations from 1985 to 1987 and from 1989 to 1990. People who state confidently that the U.S. dollar will rise or fall over some short-run horizon should not be taken seriously.

4. There is no clear connection between the behavior of real exchange rates and a country's experience with inflation or monetary growth. As an example, recall our comparison of Germany and Italy from 1970 to 1992. Probably we can think of the movements in real exchange rates as reflecting primarily real changes, involving the terms of trade, the relative prices of traded and nontraded goods, trade restrictions and tax policies, and so on. But the details of the links between these real variables and the real exchange rates have not been worked out empirically.

5. Supply shocks, such as the changes in oil prices, were unusually large from the early 1970s through the 1980s. These shocks imply shifts in the terms of trade and thereby in real exchange rates. Hence, the movement to flexible exchange rates is not responsible for all of the increased variability of real exchange rates since the early 1970s. (The increased importance of real shocks may make flexible exchange rates more attractive. Thus, the volatility of real exchange rates may help to explain why we have flexible exchange rates, rather than the reverse.)

6. Fluctuations in real exchange rates reflect market forces that no economist (or politician!) understands very well. With flexible exchange rates, these forces show up as variations in nominal exchange rates. Under fixed exchange rates, the forces exert pressure for change in domestic price levels and money stocks. Policymakers may resist these tendencies by carrying out offsetting monetary policies. Since these monetary actions cannot work in the long run, the ultimate reaction is likely to be restrictions on trade in goods and assets. Because of these restrictions, it may turn out that real exchange rates are less volatile under fixed exchange rates than under flexible rates. But because of the interferences with trade, the volume of international commerce would also be smaller. Although real exchange rates have been volatile since the early 1970s, it is important to remember that the volume of world trade increased substantially in comparison with the pre-1970 period. For example, in relation to GDP, the volume of U.S. international trade from 1972 to 1996 was roughly double that from 1948 to 1971.

EXCHANGE RATES AND THE CURRENT-ACCOUNT BALANCE

Exchange rates are often discussed in conjunction with the current account. A common argument, for example, is that the U.S. dollar has to depreciate in real terms in order for the U.S. current account to move toward a surplus. That is, U.S. goods have to become cheaper relative to foreign goods to eliminate an excess of imports over exports.

It seems plausible that a real depreciation of the dollar would deter imports and encourage exports. But suppose for the moment that the physical quantities of goods imported and exported did not change. Then a real depreciation of the dollar means that the current account would show a larger deficit. The reason is that importers have to pay more in terms of dollars (or in terms of goods produced in the United States) for each unit of foreign goods.

The offsetting force is that a fall in the relative price of U.S. products tends to lower the physical quantity of goods imported and raise the physical quantity of goods exported. The current-account balance moves toward surplus if these responses more than offset the adverse effect from having to pay more for each unit of goods imported.

To think about the net effect from a real depreciation of the dollar, recall that the current-account balance is the difference between national saving and domestic investment. The current-account balance moves toward surplus if national saving rises relative to domestic investment demand. To go further, we have to say something about where a shift in the real exchange rate came from.

To take a case that we considered before, suppose that a real depreciation of the U.S. dollar reflects an adverse shift in the U.S. terms of trade. That is, the tradable goods produced in the United States become less valuable relative to the tradable goods produced elsewhere. We discussed in Chapter 15 the response of the current-account balance to this kind of disturbance. If the shift in the terms of trade is temporary, then national saving falls, and domestic investment demand changes little. The current account moves accordingly toward deficit. If the shift is permanent, then national saving changes little, and investment demand declines. Hence, the current account moves toward surplus. The important point is that the real exchange rate depreciates in both cases, whereas the current account moves toward a deficit in one situation and toward a surplus in the other.

We could think of other reasons for a real depreciation of the dollar, such as a shift in the price of U.S. nontradables relative to U.S. tradables. Then we would find again that the current-account balance could move toward surplus or deficit. The general lesson is that a real depreciation of the U.S. dollar may go along with a move in either direction in the current-account balance: the results depend on the details of the disturbances that led to the decline in the dollar.

The U.S. data do not reveal any clear pattern in the relation between current-account balances and real exchange rates. From 1970 to 1980, for example, the U.S. dollar depreciated dramatically in real terms relative to most other major currencies (see Figures 16.5 and 16.6). Over this period, the U.S. current-account balance (Figure 15.1) averaged roughly zero and showed no regular pattern over time. From 1980 to 1985, the U.S. dollar appreciated in real terms, and the current-account balance moved toward a substantial deficit (3.0% of GDP in 1985). Then the U.S. dollar fell sharply in real terms from 1985 to 1987, and the current-account deficit rose to 3.5% of GDP. Finally, from 1987 to 1996, the

U.S. dollar changed relatively little in real terms. During this period, the current-account deficit fell to zero by 1991 but subsequently returned to 2% of GDP.

The overall indication is that movements in real exchange rates provide little or no information about what the current account is doing. This empirical observation is consistent with our theoretical reasoning because different underlying disturbances would lead to different patterns of association between the real exchange rate and the current-account balance.

Another point is that the real exchange rate is not a variable that is amenable to government policy. The nominal exchange rate can readily be influenced by governments, for example, by changing the growth rate of money in a setting of flexible exchange rates. Governments also choose whether to have a system with fixed or flexible exchange rates. But we should think of the real exchange rate as a relative price, specifically, as the price of U.S. goods relative to the price of foreign goods. Governments can influence the real exchange rate in the same way that they can affect other relative prices, for example, by restricting international trade in goods and assets or by tax policies (including tariffs and subsidies). If an economist urges the U.S. government to engineer a rise or fall of the U.S. dollar in real terms, then he or she is really advocating this kind of interference with market forces. Such advice is, unfortunately, rarely accompanied by a rationale for the necessary form of government intervention.

SUMMARY

Purchasing-power parity (PPP) connects a country's exchange rate with, say, the U.S. dollar to the ratio of that country's price level to the U.S. price level. In relative form, the PPP condition relates changes in exchange rates to differences in inflation rates. A variety of real factors, including changes in the terms of trade, shifts in the relative prices of traded and nontraded goods, and variations in trade restrictions and tax policies, can lead to deviations from PPP. Such deviations—corresponding to variations in real exchange rates—have been especially important since the early 1970s.

Interest-rate parity implies that differences in nominal interest rates across countries correspond to differences in expected rates of change of exchange rates. Differences in taxes and in riskiness of returns can lead to deviations from interest-rate parity, but these deviations are relatively small for the main developed countries. If purchasing-power parity holds in relative form, then interest-rate parity implies that expected real interest rates are equal across countries. If relative PPP fails, then expected real interest rates will diverge. We showed that a country with a highly valued currency—one that is expected to depreciate in real terms over time—tends to have a high expected real interest rate.

Examples of regimes with fixed exchange rates are the classical gold standard, the Bretton Woods System, the Exchange Rate Mechanism of the European Monetary System, and a world with a common currency. When the exchange rate is fixed to the U.S. dollar, a country's price level is determined mainly by the U.S. price level. Then, to satisfy the PPP condition, there is a specific quantity of money that is consistent with a country's chosen exchange rate. The flows of international currency tend to generate this quantity of money automatically. However, central banks sometimes sterilize the flows of international currency to maintain a higher quantity of domestic money. These actions tend to lead to devaluation of the currency or to trade restrictions. Inflation and devaluation are related in two ways: domestic inflation tends to cause devaluation, and devaluation can itself be inflationary.

Flexible exchange rates have been prevalent since the early 1970s. The flexibility of exchange rates leaves intact the main results about international trade in goods and credit: the conditions for purchasing-power parity and interest-rate parity apply in the same manner as before. Under flexible exchange rates, however, each central bank can make an independent choice of monetary growth and, hence, inflation.

U.S. real exchange rates do not have a regular pattern of association with the U.S. current-account balance. On theoretical grounds, the relationship depends on the underlying disturbance that caused the real exchange rate to change.

IMPORTANT TERMS AND CONCEPTS

absolute form of PPP The version of purchasing-power parity that involves levels of exchange rates and prices.

Bretton Woods System A system of international payments established after World War II in which each country pegged the exchange rate between its currency and the U.S. dollar. The United States exchanged dollars for gold at a fixed price ($35 per ounce), thus pegging the value of each country's currency to gold.

devaluation An action by the central bank of a country that raises the number of units of its currency that exchange for other currencies; a rise in the exchange rate.

domestic credit The total of the central bank's claims on the domestic economy. In the United States, the bulk of domestic credit takes the form of U.S. government securities held by the Federal Reserve.

European Currency Unit (ECU) A weighted average of all currencies of countries that belong to the European Union. The ECU is used as a currency unit by the European Monetary System.

European Monetary System (EMS) Arrangement whereby several European countries maintained nearly fixed exchange rates among their currencies. The system began in 1979 and pretty much broke down in 1992.

Exchange Rate Mechanism (ERM) The setup used by the European Monetary System (EMS) to maintain fixed exchange rates among the members' currencies.

fixed exchange rate A system in which countries peg the exchange rate between their currency and other currencies, such as the U.S. dollar. Examples of fixed-exchange rate regimes are the gold standard, the Bretton Woods System, the Exchange Rate Mechanism of the European Monetary System, and a setup with a common currency.

flexible exchange rate The system of international payments, prevalent since the early 1970s, in which countries allow the exchange rates for their currencies to fluctuate so as to clear the exchange market.

interest-rate parity The equalization of interest rates across countries, taking account of an adjustment for prospective changes in exchange rates.

monetary approach to the balance of payments Analyses of the balance of international payments and exchange rates that stress the quantity of money and the demand for money in each country.

nominal exchange rate The exchange rate between one currency and another. The term emphasizes the distinction from the real exchange rate, a measure that adjusts the nominal exchange rate for differences in national price levels.

purchasing-power parity (PPP) The condition that the ratio of the exchange rates for the currencies of any two countries must equal the ratio of the prices of goods in each country.

real exchange rate The exchange rate between two currencies divided by the ratio of the price levels in the two countries.

relative form of PPP The version of purchasing-power parity that involves changes in exchange rates and prices.

revaluation An increase in the value of a country's currency in terms of another currency, such as the U.S. dollar.

speculation (on exchange rates) Sale (or purchase) of a currency in exchange for another currency whenever a devaluation (or revaluation) is expected.

sterilization An action by the central bank of a country that prevents increases (decreases) in the amount of international currency from increasing (decreasing) the quantity of money in the country.

QUESTIONS AND PROBLEMS

MAINLY FOR REVIEW

16.1 Explain how the real exchange rate differs from the nominal exchange rate. Which rate is pegged in a system of fixed exchange rates? Can the government readily influence both rates?

16.2 Explain the conditions for absolute and relative purchasing-power parity in equations (16.1) and (16.2). How do these conditions relate to the behavior of real exchange rates?

16.3 Under fixed exchange rates, does the central bank have discretion over the money supply? Show how an attempt to exercise an independent monetary policy may result in devaluation or revaluation. Why might the attempt lead to trade restrictions?

16.4 Under flexible exchange rates, a country that has a persistently high rate of inflation will experience a steady increase in its exchange rate. Explain why this happens. Why might the central bank like this system?

16.5   We mentioned that examples of regimes with fixed exchange rates were the classical gold standard, the Bretton Woods System, and a setup with a common currency. Explain how each of these regimes would ensure fixed exchange rates.

PROBLEMS FOR DISCUSSION

16.6   Shifts in the Demand for Money

Consider an increase in the real demand for money in country i.

a.   Under a fixed exchange rate, what happens to country i's price level, P^i, and quantity of money, M^i? What happens to the country's quantity of international currency, H^i?

b.   Under a flexible exchange rate—with a fixed quantity of domestic money, M^i—what happens to the country's price level, P^i, and exchange rate, ϵ^i?

16.7   Monetary Growth under Flexible Exchange Rates

Equation (16.14) relates a country's exchange rate with the U.S. dollar, ϵ^i, to domestic money supply and demand. Suppose that a country raises its growth rate of money, μ^i, once and for all. Describe the effect of this change on the path of ϵ^i. (Assume that the U.S. price level, P, the world real interest rate, r, and the path of domestic output, Y^i, do not change.)

16.8   Flexible Exchange Rates and Inflation Rates

a.   Show, by using the condition for relative purchasing-power parity in equation (16.2), that the growth rate of the exchange rate, $\Delta\epsilon^i/\epsilon^i$, is approximately equal to the difference between country i's inflation rate, π^i, and the U.S. inflation rate, π.

b.   Using the IMF's *International Financial Statistics* (yearbook issue), calculate the values of $\Delta\epsilon^i/\epsilon^i$ and $\pi^i - \pi$ for some countries in the post–World War II period. (Pick some other than those appearing in Table 16.3.) What conclusions emerge?

16.9 Nixon's Departure from Gold in 1971

Under the Bretton Woods System, the United States pegged the price of gold at $35 per ounce.

a. Why did trouble about the gold price arise in 1971?

b. Was President Nixon right in eliminating the U.S. commitment to buy and sell gold (from and to foreign official institutions) at a fixed price? What other alternatives were there—in particular,

> **i.** What was the classical prescription of the gold standard?

> **ii.** The French suggested a doubling in the price of gold. Would that have helped?

16.10 Shipping Gold under the Gold Standard

Suppose that the price of gold is $5 per ounce in New York and 1 pound per ounce in London.

a. Assume that the exchange rate is $6 per pound. If a person starts with dollars in New York, then what can he or she do to make a profit? If the cost of transporting gold is 1% of the amount shipped, then how high does the exchange rate have to go above $5 per pound to make this action profitable?

b. Make the same calculations when the exchange rate is below $5 per pound, using the perspective of someone who starts with pounds in London.

(The results determine a range of exchange rates around $5 per pound for which it is unprofitable to ship gold in either direction. The upper and lower limits of this range are called *gold points*. If the exchange rate goes beyond these points, then it becomes profitable to ship an unlimited amount of gold. Can you show that the potential to ship gold guarantees that the actual exchange rate will remain within the gold points?)

16.11 Futures Contracts on Foreign Exchange

If a person buys a one-month futures contract on the German mark, then he or she agrees to purchase marks next month at a dollar exchange rate that is set today. The buyer of this contract goes "long" on the mark and does well if the mark appreciates (more than the amount expected) over the month. Similarly, the seller of a one-month futures contract agrees to sell marks next month at a dollar exchange rate that is agreed on today. The seller goes "short" on the mark and does well if the mark depreciates (more than expected) over the month.

Consider a German bond with a maturity of one month. This bond sells for a specified number of marks today and will pay out a stated amount of marks in one month. How can a person use the futures market to guarantee the dollar rate of return from buying the German bond and holding it for one month?

16.12 Changes in the Quantity of International Currency (optional)

Our analysis treated the quantity of international currency as the constant, $\bar{H}$. What modifications have to be made to allow for changes over time in this quantity? In answering, consider the following regimes:

a. International currency consists of U.S. dollar bills.

b. International currency is a pure bookkeeping entry, such as the European Currency Unit used by the European Monetary System.

c. International currency is gold.

16.13 Alternative Systems of Exchange Rates (optional)

In Chapter 15 we assumed a system with a common world currency. In this chapter we found that fixed exchange rates could be obtained by other means, such as a gold standard or an arrangement like the European Monetary System. We also found that exchange rates could be flexible rather than fixed. What seem to be the benefits and costs from the different setups? In particular,

a. Is it better to have fixed or flexible exchange rates?

b. Is it a good or bad idea for all countries to use a single form of currency?

(*Note*: This question is very difficult, and economists would not agree about the answer. In thinking about the issues involved, you might consider the following: Are there transaction benefits from having just one type of currency and just one unit for quoting prices? Do governments want to have independent monetary policies and perhaps to get revenue from printing money? Is it costly for governments or individuals to hold stocks of gold? Can we be sure that central banks will stick to their announced policies of fixed exchange rates? Is it useful in some respects for different countries to use different units for quoting prices? Is it true that real exchange rates have become more volatile since the early 1970s because of the move toward flexible exchange rates?)

16.14 Nontraded Goods and Real Exchange Rates (optional)

Suppose that each country produces some goods and services (such as haircuts and rents on buildings) that are not traded internationally. Assume that the price of nontraded goods in country i rises relative to the price of traded goods, but no change occurs in the relative price of nontraded and traded goods in the United States. What happens to country i's real exchange rate, $\epsilon^i/(P^i/P)$? (Assume that P^i and P are the GDP deflators for country i and the United States, respectively.)

In answering, note that the general price levels, P^i and P, include the prices of traded and nontraded goods. The law of one price says that the purchasing power of any currency should be the same for traded goods, regardless of where they are produced, but the same may not hold for nontraded goods.

Can you use the result to suggest an explanation for the movement in Japan's real exchange rate from 1950 to 1970 (see Figure 16.6)?

INTERACTIONS
BETWEEN THE MONETARY SECTOR
AND THE REAL SECTOR

Thus far, our analysis has stressed real factors, such as supply shocks, as sources of business fluctuations. The government can affect real variables by changing its purchases of goods and services or its tax rates, but there is little evidence that these fiscal actions have been major sources of business cycles in U.S. history. Many economists believe that monetary fluctuations—created mainly by governmental actions—have been a principal cause of these cycles. In this part of the book, we examine the theoretical and empirical foundations for these beliefs.

Chapter 17 studies commercial banks and other financial institutions that intermediate between lenders and borrowers. These financial intermediaries create deposits, which can be good alternatives to currency as means of payments. Through the effects on the demand for currency, changes in the nature of financial intermediation have an effect on the price level. We show also that financial intermediation can aid in the allocation of credit and thereby improve the economy's performance. Changes in the amount of financial intermediation—including those caused by shifts in governmental regulations—are therefore nonneutral. We still conclude, however, that purely monetary disturbances, such as those generated by open-market operations, are neutral.

In Chapter 18 we survey the various pieces of empirical evidence that concern the relation between nominal and real variables. We find that the theory can explain some of the evidence as reactions to supply shocks or to changes in the nature of financial intermediation. One observation that may conflict with our theory is the apparent sensitivity of real variables to purely nominal disturbances: there is some indication that money is nonneutral and plays a significant role in business fluctuations. It is therefore worthwhile to extend the theory to explain why monetary nonneutrality can be important.

Chapter 19 explores one type of model that generates this nonneutrality of money. This framework relies on incomplete information about prices. We retain the setting of cleared markets and assume that people form rational expectations about prices and other variables. Monetary surprises can lead in this setting to confusions between nominal and real disturbances and thereby to changes in real variables. In this way we explain some, but not all, of the observed linkages between money and business cycles. We go on to explore, first, the implications for monetary policy and, second, the possible empirical limitations of the approach.

Chapter 20 develops another model in which money can be nonneutral, the Keynesian theory of business fluctuations. This approach is an extension of the basic framework in which cleared markets are replaced by sticky prices and rationed quantities. As in Chapter 19, where people have incomplete information about prices, the Keynesian theory can explain some real effects of purely monetary disturbances. The two kinds of theories differ, however, in other respects, especially in regard to their implications for government policy. The discussion in Chapter 20 assesses the relative theoretical and empirical merits of the theories, although a final verdict is not yet available.

Financial Intermediation

U p to now the model treats money as currency, non-interest-bearing pieces of paper issued by the government. When we studied the demand for money in Chapter 4, we focused on the role of money as a medium of exchange. Households held money because they used it for purchases or sales of goods, bonds, and labor services. To reduce their average real money balance, households had to incur extra transaction costs, which might involve going more often to the bank or the store.

CHECKABLE DEPOSITS AND M1

We mentioned in Chapter 4 that currency is not the only medium of exchange in the real world. The most important alternative is checkable deposits. These deposits are now issued in the United States by various financial institutions, such as commercial banks and savings and loan associations. The holder of a deposit can purchase goods, bonds, and labor services by writing a check on his or her account. The check instructs the financial institution to transfer funds from the account of the check writer to that of another person. The important point is that checkable deposits are often preferable to currency as a medium of exchange.

The most popular definition of money, M1, attempts to classify together the assets that serve commonly as media of exchange. Thus, M1 is the sum of currency held by the public and checkable deposits. In the United States and most countries today, checkable deposits account for the bulk of M1. For example, in 1996, checkable deposits were 65% of M1 in the United States and 83% of M1 in Canada. (See Table 4.1 for a listing of the ratios of checkable deposits and M1 to GDP in various countries.)

Some economists have argued that "money" should also include deposits that are not checkable but can be converted readily into checkable form or into currency. The broader aggregate M2 includes consumer time deposits at various financial institutions, money-market deposit accounts, and some other items. Still broader monetary aggregates, such as M3, include additional types of financial assets. The problem is that once we go beyond the definition of money as common media of exchange, there is no clear place to draw the line. In the accompanying box we consider some interesting attempts to solve this problem by constructing indexes of monetary aggregates.

For our purposes, it is unimportant to settle on a precise definition of money. But we do want to extend the model to assess the economic consequences from the existence of various types of deposits and various kinds of financial institutions.

Deposits in the United States differ in the following ways:

Whether they can be withdrawn on demand at face value. This privilege applies to **demand deposits** and usually to **savings deposits**, which often have passbooks and legally allow for 30-days' notice of withdrawal. In contrast, **time deposits** have a stated maturity date, with some penalties typically attached to premature withdrawals.

Indexes of Money

Some economists have used an index-number approach to measure the money supply. The general idea is to construct an aggregate that weights different assets according to their "degree of moneyness." One approach, used by William Barnett, Edward Offenbacher, and Paul Spindt (1984), begins with the observation that people hold currency although it bears zero interest. Other assets, such as various kinds of deposits, provide fewer monetary services and therefore must pay positive interest rates to induce people to hold them. Then the general idea is to weight the quantities of various assets inversely to their interest rates (which are observable) and hence in direct relation to their amounts of monetary services (which are unobservable). Currency counts one-to-one as money, checkable deposits (which bear low but positive interest rates) count somewhat less that one-to-one, time deposits (which bear higher interest rates) count still less, and so on. Using this technique, Barnett et al. constructed a time series

of a weighted monetary aggregate, which behaves somewhat differently from M1 or other concepts.

One difficulty with the approach is that differences in interest rates among assets reflect characteristics other than monetary services. Also it is sometimes hard to measure the implicit interest rate from free services to holders of deposits. To get around these problems, Paul Spindt (1985) took a different approach. He made direct estimates of monetary services by observing how frequently the various kinds of assets were used in exchanges. Thus, currency and checkable deposits—which have high velocities—received a high weight for monetary services. In contrast, time deposits—which have low velocity—received a low weight as money. Using this procedure, Spindt calculated a time series for another weighted monetary aggregate, which showed somewhat different behavior from the aggregate of Barnett et al.

Whether people can write checks that instruct the financial intermediary to make payments to a third party. In the United States, all demand deposits are checkable.

— Whether they pay interest and at what rate.

— Whether they are insured by the federal government. Since 1980 this insurance applies to deposits up to $100,000 at most commercial banks, savings and loan associations, and mutual savings banks.

Households and firms decide how much to hold of the various deposits by considering the listed characteristics as well as the interest rate paid. The main point is that these deposits are often more attractive than either currency or bonds. By bonds, we mean interest-bearing obligations of governments, businesses, or households. By holding a bond, a household or firm lends funds directly to governments or to other households or firms. In contrast, deposits are liabilities of financial institutions. By holding a deposit, a household or firm lends funds to a financial institution. As we shall see, the financial institution then acts as an intermediary by lending its funds to governments or to other households or firms.

We want to understand why households and firms typically use the services of financial intermediaries rather than making loans directly. Then we can also see how the existence of financial intermediaries and the amount of financial intermediation affect the performance of the economy.

FINANCIAL INTERMEDIARIES AND THE CREDIT MARKET

Thus far in our model, the people who hold bonds make direct loans to others. A lender may, for example, hold a mortgage on someone's house, a loan collateralized by someone's car, or a loan to a business for investment purposes. But this type of direct lending is often inefficient. First, it requires households and firms to evaluate the creditworthiness of borrowers, a process that is often difficult. Second, unless individual households and firms hold portions of many different types of loans, they risk the loss of a large part of their assets when a single loan goes bad. But it is hard for a single household or business to diversify by holding lots of different loans. Finally, the form of claim that someone holds— say, a home mortgage—must match the form of the loan in terms of its maturity. In the case of a 20-year loan to a homeowner, the lender can cash in this claim only by selling it to someone else or by convincing the borrower to pay it off.

Financial intermediaries, such as commercial banks, can solve these problems.[1] First, these institutions are in a good position to evaluate and collect on loans and to assemble a variety of loans by type and maturity. The credit market works better when loans are evaluated and administered by financial specialists rather than by households and non-financial firms. Second, as we already noted, financial institutions can attract funds by offering deposits, which are desirable forms of assets for households and businesses. In normal times, during which financial institutions hold a sound, well-diversified portfolio of assets, the deposits are safe and easy to understand.

THE BALANCE SHEET OF A FINANCIAL INTERMEDIARY

A financial institution's deposits appear on the liabilities side of its balance sheet, and various loans appear on the assets side. Table 17.1 shows a typical balance sheet. To be concrete, the figures apply in 1996 to an actual commercial bank—Bank of Boston—which had total assets of $62.3 billion.

The main items on the asset side of the balance sheet are as follows:

Cash of $8.9 billion. This item includes currency (often called **vault cash**), deposits held on the books of the Federal Reserve, and amounts due from other banks. The total of currency and deposits held at the Fed is called **reserves**.

[1] *Other financial intermediaries are savings and loan associations, money-market funds, mutual savings banks, pension funds, investment companies, insurance companies, and the government's mortgage associations.*

TABLE 17.1

BALANCE SHEET OF BANK OF BOSTON, DECEMBER 31, 1996 (BILLIONS OF DOLLARS)

Assets		Liabilities	
Cash (includes deposits held at Fed		Checkable deposits	12.1
and other financial institutions)	8.9	Other deposits	30.5
Loans (net of loss reserve)	40.2	Borrowing from Federal Funds market	9.1
Securities	8.5	Borrowing from Fed	0
Federal Funds	0.0	Other liabilities	5.6
Other assets	4.7	Shareholders' equity	4.9
Total	62.3	Total	62.3

Loans of $40.2 billion. The principal items are commercial loans, mortgages, and installment loans.[2]

Securities of $8.5 billion. This category includes government bonds and short-term money-market instruments, such as commercial paper and certificates of deposit issued by other financial institutions.

Federal Funds of $0 billion. These are short-term (often overnight) loans to other financial intermediaries through the **Federal Funds market**. The interest rate charged on these loans is called the **Federal Funds rate**. Bank of Boston was a net borrower in the Federal Funds market.

The principal items on the liability side are the following:

Checkable deposits of $12.1 billion.

Other deposits of $30.5 billion.

[2] *In the United States there are legal restrictions on the types of earning assets that financial intermediaries can hold. For example, commercial banks cannot hold corporate stock.*

Borrowings from the Federal Funds market of $9.1 billion.

Borrowings from the Federal Reserve (also called the *Fed*), which are nil in this case. The Federal Reserve lends to financial institutions—principally commercial banks that are members of the Federal Reserve System—at the *discount window*. The interest rate charged on these loans is the Fed's **discount rate**.

Shareholders' equity of $4.9 billion. This "book value" is the sum of paid-in capital plus accumulated profits (as measured by accountants).

Reserves—Required and Excess

Financial intermediaries hold earning assets, by which we mean loans and securities, to obtain a flow of interest income. They hold physical capital and deposits at other financial institutions to carry out their business efficiently. What about cash? Because banks and some other depository institutions stand ready to convert their deposits into currency on demand, they keep some currency to meet the possible withdrawals of depositors. But in the United States in the post–World War II period, the main determinant of cash holdings by these institutions is the **reserve requirement** imposed by the Federal Reserve. (We shall discuss the Federal Reserve System later.) The Fed specifies the quantity of reserves that must be held against various categories of deposits. Legally the reserves can be held either as currency (vault cash) or as non-interest-bearing deposits on the books of the Federal Reserve. Before 1980, the Fed's requirements applied only to commercial banks that were members of the Federal Reserve System. However, the Monetary Control Act of 1980 extended the reserve requirements to all depository institutions (not including money-market funds) but at lower average percentages than before. The requirement at the beginning of 1997 was 10% of checkable deposits.[3] The Fed retains authority to change these requirements.

[3] *The requirement was only 3% of an institution's checkable deposits up to a total of $49.3 million. For further discussion of the Monetary Control Act, see Robert Auerbach (1985, Chaps. 6–8).*

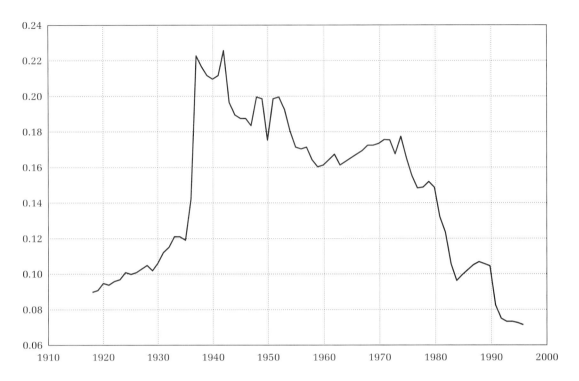

FIGURE 17.1

RATIO OF REQUIRED RESERVES TO CHECKABLE DEPOSITS

Data for Figure 17.1 and subsequent figures are from Board of Governors of the Federal Reserve System, *Banking and Monetary Statistics*, *1941–1970*; *Annual Statistical Digest*, *1970–79*; *Federal Reserve Bulletin*, various issues; and DRI data bank.

Figure 17.1 shows how the ratio of required reserves to checkable deposits behaved from 1918 to 1996. The main source of change in this ratio is shifts in legal requirements. However, some of the changes reflect shifts in the composition of deposits (between checkable and time or savings and among the categories of financial institutions). We shall discuss later some details and implications of shifts in the required-reserve ratio.

Instead of keeping non-interest-bearing cash, financial institutions prefer to hold assets that bear interest. Because these institutions can

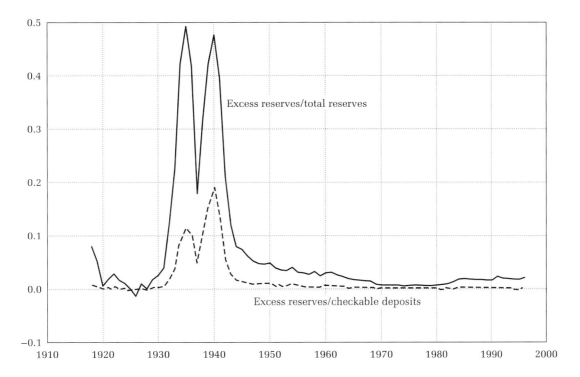

FIGURE 17.2
BEHAVIOR OF EXCESS RESERVES

shift rapidly in and out of short-term securities or the Federal Funds market, even a moderate interest rate induces them to keep very little reserves above the required amount. Economists use the term **excess reserves** for the difference between total and required reserves. Figure 17.2 shows that excess reserves were less than 1% of total reserves from 1969 to 1982, when interest rates were especially high, and were between 1 and 2% of total reserves from 1983 to 1996. At the lower interest rates that prevailed earlier during the post–World War II period, excess reserves were as much as 5% of the total. Notice also the large holdings of excess reserves from 1933 to 1941: the ratio of excess reserves to the total peaked at 49% and averaged 37%. This behavior reflects the financial crises of the Great Depression, as well as the extremely low interest rates on safe assets. (We shall discuss this period in detail later.)

Excess reserves provide funds that a financial institution can dip into during emergencies. By contrast, required reserves do not serve this purpose. For a given amount of deposits, a depository institution is not permitted to let its reserves fall below the required amount.

Deposits and Earning Assets

Suppose that a depository institution attracts an additional $100 of deposits. For concreteness, think about a checkable deposit for which the required-reserve ratio is 10%. Then the institution holds $10 out of the extra $100 as required reserves. The rest of the $100 may be divided as the institution chooses between loans and securities (which bear interest) or excess reserves (which do not bear interest).

The change in the institution's net earnings equals the interest on the additional earning assets, less the added costs of evaluating and collecting on loans or dealing in securities, less any extra costs of servicing the deposits (if no separate fees are charged), less the interest paid on the new deposits. For the institution to profit from this enterprise, it must be that the interest rate on deposits, call it R^d, is less than that on loans and securities, which we still call R. In particular, the spread, $R - R^d$, must cover the cost of the funds that the intermediary holds in non-interest-bearing form, the transaction costs associated with deposits and earnings assets, and some return on the capital invested in the business of being an intermediary. The total of these items represent the **costs of intermediation**. Competition among intermediaries would drive the interest rate on deposits high enough so that the spread, $R - R^d$, just covered the costs of intermediation.[4] It follows that the interest rate paid on deposits, R^d, would rise with the interest rate on loans and securities, R, and would decline with an increase in the costs of intermediation, such as a rise in the required-reserve ratio.

[4] *For further discussion, see Benjamin Klein (1974).*

Deposit Interest Rates and Financial Intermediation

The amount of deposits that households and firms want to hold—and, hence, the amount of funds that financial intermediaries have to loan out—depends on the interest rate on deposits, R^d. Deposits become more attractive relative to currency if R^d increases. (Note that the nominal interest rate on currency is fixed at zero.) Deposits become less attractive relative to bonds if the spread, $R - R^d$, rises.

Suppose, for example, that the required-reserve ratio declines as it did especially from 1980 to 1992 (see Figure 17.1). For a given value of R, our analysis of competition among financial intermediaries predicts that the deposit interest rate, R^d, would rise. Households and firms would therefore hold more deposits at the expense of currency and bonds. The increase in deposits means that financial intermediaries would expand their holdings of assets. Thus, we find that a lower reserve requirement leads, first, to more of M1 held as deposits rather than currency and, second, to more financial intermediation.

Regulation of Interest Rates on Deposits

From the 1930s until the early 1980s, the federal government regulated the interest rates that banks and other financial intermediaries could pay on deposits. With the Banking Acts of 1933 and 1935, the government prohibited interest payments on demand deposits.[5] This restriction stayed in force until the middle and late 1970s, when interest-bearing checking accounts began to develop. These mainly took the form of negotiable-order-of-withdrawal (or NOW) accounts. Of course, a negotiable order of withdrawal is just another name for a check. These types of accounts, which bear interest, began in New England in the mid-1970s and became available nationwide with the Monetary Control Act of 1980.

The Federal Reserve limited interest rates on time deposits through its **Regulation Q**. The ceiling rates on time deposits were high enough not to be binding at least until the 1950s. But the regulations were a significant constraint in the late 1960s, in much of the 1970s, and especially

[5] *The Glass-Steagall Act of 1933 also created legal separations between commercial and investment banks. The argument for this barrier was to avoid the conflicts of interest and excessive exposure to risk that were thought to arise when commercial banks participated in equity markets. Randall Kroszner and Raghuram Rajan (1994) evaluated this argument by examining the behavior of commercial banks in the underwriting of securities in the period before 1933. They found no evidence to support the conflict-of-interest hypothesis. In 1996 the Federal Reserve Board substantially loosened the constraints imposed by the Glass-Steagall Act, and it is likely that this regulation will be further weakened or eliminated in the future.*

from 1979 to 1982. Effective October 1983, however, the government removed the restrictions on the interest rates that institutions could pay on most time deposits.

What happens when the legal limit on deposits is below the interest rate that would otherwise be paid? One point is that the limits apply only to explicit interest. Institutions often compete for profitable deposits by providing services at below cost. The services that people receive by holding deposits amount to implicit interest, which substitutes for the explicit interest that the government prohibits. But despite the possibilities for evading restrictions on interest rates, we should not conclude that legal restrictions are irrelevant. Basically the implicit methods of paying interest tend to be less efficient than the explicit ones. That difference exists because there are limits to the services that banks can conveniently provide as close substitutes for explicit interest. (An offsetting consideration is that explicit interest is taxable, whereas free services typically are not.) As market interest rates rose from the 1950s to the 1970s, the ceiling rates on deposits made it increasingly difficult for the regulated institutions to compete for funds. In this case the regulation of interest payments meant that the deposit interest rate, R^d, offered by these intermediaries was lower than otherwise. Our previous analysis of deposit interest rates predicts some of the outcomes:

— People moved away from deposits and toward direct holding of assets such as bonds and mortgages. This process, which is the reverse of intermediation, is called **disintermediation**.

— New types of unregulated financial intermediaries arose, which attracted funds away from banks and other institutions. A primary example was money-market funds.

— The government eventually changed its regulations on deposit interest rates so that banks and other depository intermediaries could again compete effectively for funds. However, there are two remaining distinctions between money-market funds and other depository institutions. There are no reserve requirements on the money-market funds, and the shares in these funds are not insured by the federal government.

Borrowing from the Federal Reserve

From the start of the Federal Reserve System in 1914 until 1980, banks that were members of the system could borrow short-term funds at the discount rate from a Federal Reserve bank. With the Monetary Control Act of 1980, all depository institutions with checkable deposits can borrow from the Fed.

Borrowing from the Federal Reserve can be advantageous if the Fed's discount rate is below the rates at which financial institutions can otherwise borrow. Such borrowing may not always be desirable, however, even if the discount rate is relatively low. There are two reasons for that fact: first, the Fed examines banks more carefully when they borrow frequently at the discount window, and second, the Fed can refuse to lend to banks that ask "too often." In any case the lower the discount rate is, relative to market interest rates, the greater is the incentive for banks to borrow from the Fed.

Figure 17.3 shows the loans outstanding from the Fed to financial institutions. Notice that these borrowings were important during World War I and through the 1920s. The amount outstanding peaked at 13% of checkable deposits in 1920[6] and still amounted to 4% of these deposits in 1929, 3% in 1932, and 2% in 1933. Borrowings fell, however, to near zero for 1935–43. During the post–World War II period, some borrowing occurred, but the ratio of the amount outstanding to checkable deposits never exceeded 1%. For these years, the peaks in the ratio occurred in 1974 and 1984. For 1974, the average amount outstanding of $2.0 billion constituted about 1% of checkable deposits. Most of these loans were to the Franklin National Bank of Long Island, a large bank that engaged in questionable speculations and subsequently failed. For 1984, the average amount of $3.7 billion was again about 1% of

[6] *The borrowings of member banks actually exceeded their total reserves for 1919–21. For example, the average debt outstanding during 1920 was $2.5 billion, and the average amount of reserves was $1.8 billion.*

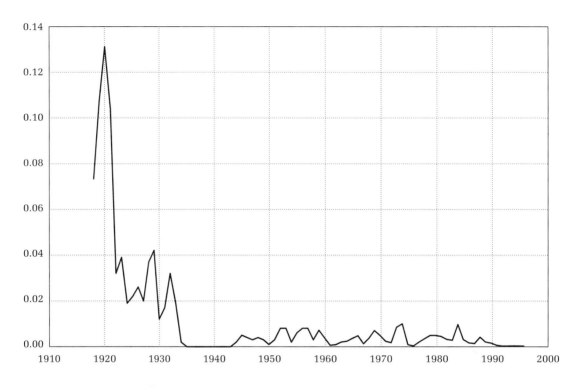

FIGURE 17.3

BORROWINGS FROM THE FEDERAL RESERVE AS A RATIO TO CHECKABLE DEPOSITS

checkable deposits. Most of these loans went to the Continental Illinois National Bank, also a large bank in trouble. Since 1991 the ratio has been near zero.

Figure 17.4 shows how the annual average discount rate at the New York Fed compares to the interest rate on four- to six-month maturity prime commercial paper. Although the two interest rates tended to move together, the discount rate typically has been lower than the commercial paper rate since World War II. The loans from the Fed therefore usually involved a subsidy to the borrower. In some years—1966–67, 1969–70, 1973–74, 1981, 1984, 1987–89, and 1994—the discount rate was more than a full percentage point below the commercial paper rate. Looking at

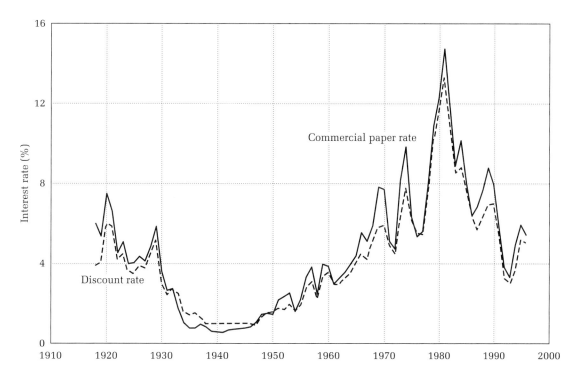

FIGURE 17.4

THE FED'S DISCOUNT RATE AND COMMERCIAL PAPER RATES

the earlier years, we see that the discount rate exceeded the commercial paper rate from 1932 to 1946 but was lower than the commercial paper rate during the 1920s and especially for 1918–20.

THE FEDERAL RESERVE SYSTEM

Since 1914 the Federal Reserve System has functioned as the central bank in the United States. There are 12 regional Federal Reserve banks, each of which was set up as a separate, quasi-private corporation. In the early days of the system, the 12 presidents of the regional banks served on the Governors' Conference, which had substantial influence over the Fed's policies. However, following the Great Depression and the Banking Act of 1935, the Governors' Conference was abolished, and the Fed's power was centralized in Washington, D.C. Since 1935 the main authority has resided with the **Board of Governors of the Federal Reserve System**. The seven members of this board are appointed by the president of the United States (and confirmed by the Senate) for staggered 14-year terms. The board is usually dominated by its chairman, currently Alan Greenspan, who is appointed by the president for a four-year term.

The Fed carries out its open market operations—purchases or sales of government securities in the open market—through the **Federal Open-Market Committee** (or **FOMC**). This important committee consists of the seven members of the Board of Governors plus the presidents of five of the regional banks (including the president of the New York bank and rotating membership among the other 11 banks). We shall discuss the FOMC when we deal later with open-market operations.

We have already mentioned that the Fed's activities include the setting of reserve requirements, the regulation of interest rates on deposits, and the lending to financial institutions at the discount window.[7] Now we want to focus on the Fed's instruments for controlling the quantity of money. We begin by looking at the balance sheet of the Federal Reserve System.

Table 17.2 shows the balance sheet at the end of 1996. The main items on the asset side are the following:

— Gold account of $11.0 billion (carried at the official price of $42.22 per ounce). The Fed holds this gold on behalf of the U.S. Treasury. In past years, when the United States was on the gold standard, variations in the quantity of gold resulted mainly from dealings with foreign central banks. Now there are changes if the Treasury auctions off gold or if there are adjustments in the official price of gold. (These changes in price occurred in 1933 and a few times in the 1970s.)

[7] *For discussions of the Federal Reserve System and its policy instruments, see Robert Auerbach (1985, Chaps. 14–16) and Milton Friedman (1960, Chap. 2).*

TABLE 17.2

BALANCE SHEET OF ALL FEDERAL RESERVE BANKS, DECEMBER 31, 1996 (BILLIONS OF DOLLARS)

Assets		Liabilities and Capital Account	
Gold account	11.0	Federal Reserve notes (currency)	426.5
Loans to depository institutions	0.1	Deposits of depository institutions	24.5
U.S. government and agency securities	428.8	U.S. Treasury deposits	7.7
Assets denominated in foreign currencies	19.3	Other deposits and liabilities	13.3
Special drawing rights account	10.0	Paid-in capital and surplus	9.1
Other assets	11.9		
Total	481.1	Total	481.1

Source: *Board of Governors*, Federal Reserve Bulletin, *March 1997*.

▬ Loans to depository institutions of $0.1 billion. These are the borrowings of depository intermediaries at the discount rate. The amount borrowed was unusually low in 1996.

▬ U.S. government and agency securities of $428.8 billion. As the balance sheet makes clear, the bulk of the Fed's assets are held in this form.

The sum of loans to depository institutions, U.S. government and agency securities, and some miscellaneous assets is called **Federal Reserve credit**. This amount represents the total of the Fed's claims on the government and the private sector. Note that the great bulk of Federal Reserve credit takes the form of U.S. government securities: unlike the central banks of many other countries, the Fed engages in little direct lending to the private sector.

The liability side of the Fed's ledger includes the following main items:

— Federal Reserve notes (currency) of $426.5 billion. At present, these notes are the only significant form of currency outstanding. At earlier times, currency was issued by the U.S. Treasury and—even earlier—by private banks.

— Deposits of depository institutions of $24.5 billion. These are the non-interest-bearing reserves of depository intermediaries.

— U.S. Treasury deposits of $7.7 billion. These deposits constitute the federal government's checking account, which is held at the Federal Reserve.

The total of federal reserve notes and deposits of depository institutions ($451.0 billion) is called the **monetary base** or **high-powered money** (or sometimes M0). This sum represents the total of the Fed's monetary liabilities (aside from those held by the U.S. Treasury or as foreign deposits). At the end of 1996, 95% of the monetary base took the form of currency, and only 5% consisted of deposits of depository institutions.

CONTROL OF THE MONETARY BASE

Open-Market Operations

In its early years of operation, the Federal Reserve focused on the discount window, which we shall discuss in the next subsection, rather than on open-market operations. Since the 1930s, however, open-market operations have become the principal instrument for controlling the monetary base.

Since 1935, decisions on open-market operations have been made by the Federal Open Market Committee (FOMC), an institution that we mentioned earlier. The directives of this committee are carried out by the trading desk of the New York Federal Reserve Bank. Although the directives to the trading desk are explicit in terms of quantities of government bonds to buy or sell, the FOMC's reports on its policy stance are often vague. Typically, these reports mention the "condition of the market" or targets for the interest rate on Federal Funds. But it is unclear how to relate these targets to the volume of open-market operations, which is what the FOMC actually controls.

In the early 1980s, the targets of Federal Reserve policy were expressed more in terms of monetary aggregates, such as M1 or M2, and less in terms of interest rates. As we shall see later, we can relate the behavior of monetary aggregates to changes in the monetary base and, hence, to open-market operations. It would therefore be meaningful to guide open-market operations by a target for a specified monetary aggregate. But there is not much evidence that the Federal Reserve has actually paid much attention to its announced targets (which it began to release in 1978 at the insistence of Congress).

It is interesting that the FOMC delays for 30–60 days the publication of its statements on open-market policy. The Fed believes that this secrecy helps it to maintain "orderly" securities markets. Anybody who can explain this reasoning deserves at least an A in the course![8]

Consider now the effect of open-market operations on the monetary base. In the case of an open-market purchase, the Fed writes a check to buy, say, $1 million of U.S. government securities. Suppose that the seller of the bonds is a commercial bank, which we call People's Bank. (We would end up with the same results if the seller were a household or, more likely, a large corporation.) The Fed credits this bank with $1 million more of reserves in the form of book-entry deposits at the Fed. At this point, the balance sheets of the Fed and People's Bank change as shown in Table 17.3. Notice that the Fed has $1 million more of assets in the form of government bonds. This amount balances the extra $1 million of liabilities, which show up as more deposits of depository institutions (in this case of People's Bank). Correspondingly, People's Bank has $1

[8] *The FOMC's secrecy has been challenged under the Freedom of Information Act, but the Supreme Court decided in favor of the FOMC. For a discussion, including the FOMC's defense of its secrecy, see Marvin Goodfriend (1986).*

TABLE 17.3

EFFECTS ON THE BALANCE SHEETS OF THE FED AND DEPOSITORY INSTITUTIONS FROM AN OPEN-MARKET PURCHASE OF GOVERNMENT BONDS

Assets	Liabilities
Federal Reserve	
U.S. government securities: +$1 million	Deposits of depository institutions: +$1 million
People's Bank	
Loans and securities: −$1 million	
Deposits at Fed: +$1 million	

million more of assets in the form of deposits held at the Fed but $1 million less of government bonds, a form of interest-bearing assets that are included in the bank's portfolio of loans and securities.

The balance sheets shown in Table 17.3 are not the end of the story because People's Bank probably does not want to keep $1 million more of non-interest-bearing reserves at the Fed. But let's hold off on this matter for now to focus on the behavior of the monetary base. The open-market purchase of securities shown in Table 17.3 raises the monetary base by $1 million, an increase that shows up initially as an extra $1 million in reserves held by depository institutions at the Fed. Note also that an open-market sale of securities would just reverse the process. If the Fed sells $1 million of U.S. government bonds, then the monetary base declines by $1 million.

In the United States, open-market operations involve government bonds, rather than private bonds, mortgages, shares in General Motors, and so on. That is the case because the Fed does not hold these types of private obligations. It would actually make little difference (except perhaps on political grounds) if the Fed switched from holdings of the public debt to holdings of private bonds. If this switch were made, then the private sector would end up holding more of the public debt but would owe correspondingly more to the Fed. The Fed would have more claims on the private sector but less on the U.S. Treasury. Overall, there would be no changes in the net positions of the private sector, the Federal Reserve, and the U.S. Treasury.

Loans to Depository Institutions

The Fed can also control the monetary base by varying the quantity of loans to depository institutions. The Fed can engineer these changes by shifting either the discount rate or other aspects of its lending policies to induce depository institutions to borrow more or less at the discount window. Suppose, for example, that People's Bank decides to borrow an additional $1 million from the Fed. Then the Fed records a loan of $1 million to People's Bank and also credits this bank with an extra $1 million of deposits. If People's Bank just holds these deposits at the Fed (perhaps because if would otherwise have fallen short of its reserve requirement), then the balance sheets of the Fed and People's Bank change as shown in Table 17.4.

TABLE 17.4

EFFECTS ON THE BALANCE SHEETS OF THE FED AND DEPOSITORY INSTITUTIONS FROM FED LENDING AT THE DISCOUNT WINDOW

Assets	Liabilities
Federal Reserve	
Loans to depository institutions: +$1 million	Deposits of depository institutions: +$1 million
People's Bank	
Deposits at Fed: +$1 million	Borrowing from Fed: +$1 million

Notice that the borrowings show up as $1 million more in loans to depository institutions on the asset side of the Fed's books. Simultaneously, on the liability side, there is an increase by $1 million in the deposits of depository institutions. There are corresponding changes on the books of People's Bank. The main point is that, as before, the monetary base rises by $1 million.

An increase in borrowings by depository institutions at the discount window is essentially the same as an open-market purchase of securities by the Fed. In both cases the monetary base increases. The only difference is that in one case (the open-market purchase) the Fed ends up holding more U.S. government bonds, whereas in the other (lending at the discount window), the Fed ends up with more loans to depository institutions. Correspondingly, People's Bank ends up holding fewer government bonds in the first case, and more debt to the Fed in the second. Overall, the difference amounts to a shift from the Fed's holding U.S. government bonds to the Fed's holding obligations on a private bank. But as mentioned before, these types of changes have no major consequences. The only significant difference concerns the subsidy that the Fed provides to depository institutions because the discount rate is typically set below market interest rates.

Economists often say that a shift in the discount rate is significant not for its direct impact on borrowings but rather as an announcement of the Fed's intentions. Over the longer term, the Fed moves the discount rate to match changes in market interest rates (see Figure 17.4). Hence, most of the movements in the discount rate are reactions to changes in the economy, rather than vice versa. But the timing and sometimes the amount of a shift in the discount rate are at the Fed's discretion. It is possible that some of these changes are a useful signal about the future behavior of the monetary base. No one has yet shown, however, that changes in the discount rate can actually help to predict the future quantity of the monetary base or other economic variables. The suggestion that shifts in the discount rate have an "announcement effect" is therefore an interesting, but unproven, idea.

Many economists think that the Fed should stop subsidizing borrowers; that is, it should set the discount rate at a penalty level above market interest rates. Of course, if the discount rate were actually a penalty rate, it would have to be above the rate at which an individual institution could otherwise borrow. For a risky bank like Continental Illinois in 1984, for example, the penalty rate would have to be well above the interest rate on commercial paper. But then, no institution would ever borrow from the Fed. Hence, the suggestion for a penalty discount rate amounts to a proposal for closing the discount window.

From the standpoint of controlling the monetary base, the existence of the discount window adds nothing to open-market operations. Thus, the argument for the Fed's lending to depository institutions comes down to the desirability of subsidizing selected financial institutions, presumably, mainly institutions that are in trouble. No one has yet come up with convincing arguments to justify this policy.

THE MONETARY BASE AND MONETARY AGGREGATES

Thus far, our discussion shows how the Fed can control the monetary base. But we already mentioned that the Fed might adjust the base to achieve a target value for a monetary aggregate, such as M1 or M2. Recall that these aggregates add various categories of deposits to the amount of currency held by the public. To study the relation between the monetary base and these monetary aggregates, we have to understand the behavior of deposits.

Return to the case shown in Table 17.3 in which the open-market purchase of government bonds raised the monetary base by $1 million. Instead of a single bank, consider now the effects on financial intermediaries as a whole. Table 17.5 shows that in step 1 these intermediaries have $1 million more of deposits at the Fed and $1 million less of loans and securities.

Suppose that the extra $1 million of deposits at the Fed are excess reserves, which the financial intermediaries do not wish to hold. Rather,

TABLE 17.5

EFFECT OF OPEN-MARKET PURCHASES OF BONDS ON THE FINANCIAL SYSTEM

	Financial Intermediaries (FIs)		Households		The Fed	
	Assets	Liabilities	Assets	Liabilities	Assets	Liabilities
Step 1:	Loans and securities: −$1 million Deposits at Fed: +$1 million				U.S. government bonds: +$1 million	Deposits of FIs: +$1 million
Step 2:	Loans and securities: +$1 million	Customer deposits: +$1 million	Deposits at FIs: +$1 million	Loans from FIs: +$1 million		
Step 3:	Loans and securities: +$900,000	Customer deposits: +$900,000	Deposits at FIs: +$900,000	Loans from FIs: +$900,000		

these institutions place these funds into earning assets. To be concrete, assume that they make an additional $1 million of loans to households. The results would be the same, however, if the intermediaries bought more securities. In any event, the recipients of the loans have an extra $1 million, which we suppose that they keep initially as deposits at a financial intermediary. Thus, the balance sheet of these intermediaries changes as shown in step 2 of Table 17.5. On the asset side, there is an additional $1 million of loans and securities, a change that offsets the initial decline by this amount. On the liability side, there is an added $1 million of customer deposits.

The recipients of the loan probably do not want to hold an extra $1 million of deposits. But as they spend these funds they are transferred to the accounts of others. Ultimately people are either induced[9] to hold an extra $1 million of deposits at financial intermediaries, or they are motivated to redeem all or part of this $1 million for currency (which the intermediaries stand ready to provide to depositors). For the moment, we shall ignore this important possibility of moving into currency. Then we eventually reach the situation shown as step 2 in Table 17.5.

The extra $1 million in customer deposits raises the required reserves of the financial intermediaries. For illustrative purposes, assume a reserve ratio of 10%, the value that applied at the end of 1996 to most checkable deposits. Thus, required reserves rise by $100,000. But then the financial institutions still have $900,000 ($1 million less the $100,000) of excess reserves. They therefore again place these funds into earning assets, which we assume take the form of loans. When people are motivated to hold these additional funds as deposits we arrive at step 3 in Table 17.5. Here, the intermediaries' loans and securities rise along with its deposits by another $900,000.

If we continue to work through this process, then we find that the deposits held at financial institutions rise by a large multiple of the expansion in the monetary base. Specifically, the deposits increase eventually by the amount $1 million $\cdot$ (1/0.10) = $10 million. In other words, the increase by $1 million in base money leads to an increase by $10 million in deposits. At this point, the intermediaries' required reserves are up by 0.10 $\cdot$ $10 million = $1 million; that is, the additional base money is all held as required reserves.

An important amendment to this **multiple expansion of deposits** concerns the households' demand for currency. Figure 17.5 shows the ratio of currency to checkable deposits since 1918. The ratio averaged 0.38 in the 1980s and 0.44 for 1990–96. For 1996, the ratio was 0.53. Using the value 0.4 as an illustrative value of this ratio, and assuming no changes in the relative attractiveness of currency and deposits, we predict that people will hold an additional 40 cents of currency for each extra dollar of deposits. Table 17.6 modifies the analysis to take account of currency. Now, with an extra $1 million of funds in step 2a,

[9] *As we show in the following section, the inducement derives in the present case from a higher price level.*

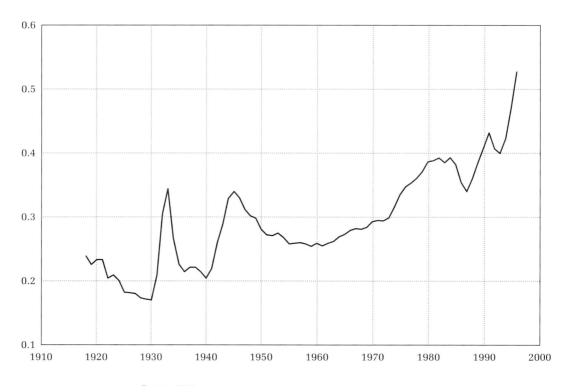

FIGURE 17.5

RATIO OF THE PUBLIC'S CURRENCY TO CHECKABLE DEPOSITS

the public is eventually motivated to hold (approximately) $700,000 more in deposits and $300,000 more in currency. As the public redeems deposits to obtain this extra currency, the financial intermediaries must get this currency by running down their deposits at the Fed. Thus, in step 2a, the liabilities of financial institutions show $700,000 more in customer deposits, and their assets show $300,000 less in deposits at the Fed. Notice that required reserves are now up by $70,000 (0.10 · $700, 000 of deposits) rather than the $100,000 in the previous step 2. But actual reserves are higher by only $700,000 rather than the previous $1 million. Thus, excess reserves are higher by $630,000 ($700,000 less $70,000) instead of the previous $900,000 ($1 million less $100,000). The

	Financial Intermediaries (FIs)		Households		The Fed	
	Assets	Liabilities	Assets	Liabilities	Assets	Liabilities
Step 1a:	Loans and securities: −$1 million				U.S. government bonds: +$1 million	Deposits of FIs: +$1 million
	Deposits at Fed: +$1 million					
Step 2a:	Loans and securities: +$1 million	Customer deposits: +$700,000	Deposits at FIs: +$700,000	Loans from FIs: +$1 million		Deposits of FIs: −$300,000
	Deposits at Fed: −$300,000		Currency: +$300,000			Currency: +$300,000
Step 3a:	Loans and securities: +$630,000	Customer deposits: +$450,000	Deposits at FIs: +$450,000	Loans from FIs: +$630,000		Deposits of FIs: −$180,000
	Deposits at Fed: −$180,000		Currency: +$180,000			Currency: +$180,000

"leakage" of funds into currency means that the financial intermediaries end up with less excess reserves than otherwise.

For the Fed, the additional currency outstanding of $300,000 corresponds to an equivalent reduction in the book-entry deposits of financial institutions. As shown in step 2a of Table 17.6, there is no change in the monetary base, which consists of currency plus the deposits of the financial institutions at the Fed. Thus, the monetary base remains higher by $1 million.

The rest of the analysis proceeds as before, except that some funds leak out to currency at each stage. We can find the ultimate position from the following set of equations, where the symbol Δ represents the change in the associated variable:

Δ(monetary base) = Δ(required reserves) + Δ(currency) = $1 million

Δ(required reserves) = $0.10 \cdot \Delta$(deposits)

Δ(currency) = $0.4 \cdot \Delta$(deposits)

Substituting the second and third conditions into the first leads to

$0.10 \cdot \Delta$(deposits) + $0.4 \cdot \Delta$(deposits) = $1 million

Solving for the change in deposits, we get the results:

Δ(deposits) = $1million/0.50 = $2,000,000

Δ(currency) = $0.4 \cdot \Delta$(deposits) = $800,000

Δ(required reserves) = $0.10 \cdot \Delta$(deposits) = $200,000

Thus, the incorporation of currency has a dramatic effect on the results. Instead of rising by $10 million, the deposits held at financial intermediaries end up increasing by only $2 million. Generally, the ultimate expansion of deposits is larger the smaller is the ratio of reserves to deposits (fixed at 0.10 in this case) and the smaller is the ratio of currency to deposits (0.4).

Given the changes in deposits and currency, we can calculate how an open-market operation affects various monetary aggregates. If we limit attention to checkable deposits (with a required-reserve ratio of 0.10), then the change in M1 is the sum of the changes in deposits and currency, or $2,800,000 in our example. Since an increase by $1,000,000 in high-powered money leads to an expansion by $2,800,000 in M1, we can say

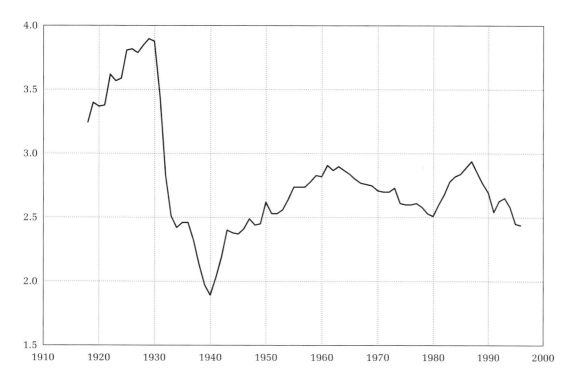

FIGURE 17.6

RATIO OF M1 TO THE MONETARY BASE (THE MONEY MULTIPLIER)

that the **money multiplier** (the ratio of M1 to the base) is 2.8. Generally, the money multiplier is higher the lower are the ratios of reserves and currency to deposits.

Figure 17.6 shows the behavior of the money multiplier from 1918 to 1996. This multiplier has been relatively stable since World War II, with a range of 2.4 to 2.9. This stability arises, however, only because of some long-term changes that happened to cancel. First, as shown in Figures 17.1 and 17.2, the ratios of required and excess reserves to checkable deposits declined from a total of 0.22 in 1950 to 0.07 in 1996. This change tended to raise the money multiplier. But second, as shown in Figure 17.5, the ratio of currency to checkable deposits rose from 0.26 in 1960 to 0.53 in 1996. This factor tended to lower the money multiplier.

The other striking feature of Figure 17.6 is the dramatic drop in the money multiplier from 3.9 in 1930 to 1.9 in 1940. This change reflected increases in the ratios of reserves and currency to checkable deposits. (We shall discuss the details of these changes later.)

EFFECTS OF FEDERAL RESERVE ACTIONS

THE NEUTRALITY OF OPEN-MARKET OPERATIONS

For a closed economy, we found in Chapter 14 that open-market operations were neutral. A one-time shift in the monetary base led only to proportional responses in the price level and other nominal variables (except for the quantity of public debt). This result applies also to an open economy under flexible exchange rates, as studied in Chapter 16. An additional result here is that the nominal exchange rate moves along with the other nominal variables.

These results do not change when we introduce financial intermediation. But we have to include as nominal variables the dollar quantities of the various deposits and reserves. Then we find that these nominal magnitudes rise along with the other nominal variables in proportion to the change in the monetary base. An open-market operation leaves unchanged the real quantities of deposits and reserves, the ratio of deposits to currency, the ratio of reserves to deposits, and so on.

Among the variables that do not change when there is a one-time open-market operation are the nominal interest rate on earning assets, R, and the nominal interest rate, R^d, paid on deposits. Because these interest rates are unchanged, households and firms would not alter their desired holdings of currency and deposits in real terms. Thus, the results are consistent with the unchanged real quantities of currency and deposits.

The financial intermediaries also end up in the same real position as before the open-market operation: there are no changes in the intermediaries' real quantities of deposits, reserves, and loans and securities. If these institutions held reserves initially only because of requirements—say, 10% of deposits—then the final holdings of reserves again equal the required amount.

THE AMOUNT OF FINANCIAL INTERMEDIATION

Financial intermediation is important because it facilitates the matching of borrowers and lenders, as well as the carrying out of transactions. The reflection of this process is the real quantity of deposits and the real quantity of loans and securities held by financial intermediaries. We can think of these real quantities as an indicator of the amount of financial intermediation in an economy.

The amount of financial intermediation depends on the benefits and costs. As mentioned before, the benefits relate to the efficient evaluation of loans, the diversification of assets by risk and maturity, and the convenience of deposits. The costs include the expenses of servicing deposits and loans, the return to capital in the intermediary business, and reserve requirements. If these costs of intermediation rise, then we predict that less intermediation will occur.

Suppose, as an example, that the Fed increases reserve requirements. Since financial intermediaries must hold more non-interest-bearing reserves for each dollar of deposits, these institutions end up paying a lower interest rate, R^d, on deposits. Households switch accordingly from deposits to currency or earning assets, and financial institutions end up with smaller real quantities of deposits and assets. Hence, there is less financial intermediation in the economy. Note that we would reach the same conclusion if, instead of assuming an increase in reserve requirements, we postulated a higher cost for financial intermediaries to service deposits or police loans. The economy ends up again with less financial intermediation.

When there is less financial intermediation, it becomes harder for resources to flow toward investors whose projects have the greatest marginal products or toward consumers who have the greatest desires to consume now rather than later. On both counts, the economy operates less efficiently. Typically this loss of efficiency shows up as smaller aggregates of the capital stock and output. But the principal conclusion is that less financial intermediation means a poorer match of resources to their ultimate uses.

To some extent, the costs of intermediation reflect the underlying expenses of policing borrowers and servicing deposits. We can think of these elements as part of the technology or production function that generates intermediating services. Then the amount of intermediation that results tends to be optimal, given this technology. But, as already noted, reserve requirements, government regulation of interest rates on deposits, and so on artificially raise the cost of intermediation. More restrictive policies—such as higher reserve requirements—tend to discourage intermediation, a response that leads to a less efficient allocation of resources.[10]

Financial Intermediation and the Price Level

The degree of financial intermediation also interacts with the determination of the price level. To see how this interaction works, recall how the price level is determined in a closed economy. (The results would be the same for an open economy under flexible exchange rates.) The key condition is the equation of the demand for money to the supply.

We now identify money with the monetary base, that is, as the sum of currency in circulation and the reserves held by financial institutions at the Fed. Suppose that the Fed controls the dollar quantity of base money, M, through open-market operations, as discussed earlier. Then the process of financial intermediation influences the price level because it affects the real demand for base money, M^d/P. For a given dollar quantity of base money, anything that raises the real demand leads to a fall in the price level. This effect works just like the various increases in the real demand for money that we considered in previous chapters.

[10] *For the argument that the financial industry should be fully deregulated, see Fischer Black (1970) and Eugene Fama (1983).*

Suppose again that the Fed raises the required-reserve ratio on deposits. For a given quantity of deposits, this change increases the demand for reserves by depository institutions. Therefore, on this count, the real demand for the monetary base goes up.

Some additional effects arise because the higher reserve ratio tends to reduce the interest rate paid on deposits. If households shift out of deposits and into currency, then the real demand for the monetary base increases further (because the demand for base money varies one-to-one with the demand for currency but varies only fractionally with the amount of deposits). If households move away from deposits and into earning assets, then the real demand for base money tends to decline (because the reduction in deposits reduces the real demand for reserves by financial institutions). Thus, the shifting of households' assets among deposits, currency, and earning assets has an ambiguous overall effect on the real demand for the monetary base.[11]

Because of the direct positive effect on the demand for reserves, we can be pretty sure that the overall effect of an increase in the required-reserve ratio is to raise the real demand for base money. For a given nominal quantity of base money, the rise in the real demand for base money means that the price level falls.

Historically, the main examples of large short-term variations in the real demand for base money involve banking panics and an experiment with changes in reserve requirements in 1936–37. It is therefore worthwhile to consider some details of these episodes.

Banking Panics

Banks and other financial intermediaries promise to convert their demand deposits into currency immediately at face value. These institutions typically also extend this instantaneous conversion privilege to savings deposits, for which some notice of withdrawal (usually 30 days) can legally be required. Intermediaries do not, however, hold nearly enough cash or liquid securities to allow for the simultaneous conversion of all deposits into currency at face value.[12] Even if the underlying

[11] *For further discussion of these types of effects, see James Tobin (1971a, 1971b).*

[12] *By liquid, we mean that little cost attaches to the quick sale of an asset. Thus, government bonds are liquid, but real estate is relatively illiquid. Loans that are costly to evaluate—such as those to local businesses and consumers—may also be illiquid.*

loans and securities are sound, financial institutions can get into trouble if too many customers want their cash at the same time. If people become concerned about a bank's ability to convert its deposits into currency at face value, then each individual has an incentive to get into line first to cash in. This incentive is especially great when the deposits are not insured by the government, as was the case in the United States until 1934. When many people attempt to cash in their deposits simultaneously, there is a "run on the bank." Sometimes a bank responds by temporarily *suspending* the privilege of converting demand deposits into currency. When such suspensions happen simultaneously at many banks or other financial institutions, economists say that a **banking panic** occurs.

The hallmark of a banking panic is a sudden increase in the demand for currency rather than deposits. As a response, banks and other intermediaries tend to increase their demands for excess reserves and other liquid assets to meet their customers' possible demands for cash. Overall, the banking panic leads to increases in the real demand for base money, partly in the form of the public's currency and partly as reserves of financial institutions. Hence, the previous analysis implies that a banking panic has two types of effects. First, it makes financial intermediation more difficult, a result that has adverse consequences for the efficient allocation of resources. Production and investment are, in particular, likely to decline. Then, second, unless there is substantial increase in the nominal quantity of base money, the sharp increase in the real demand for base money puts downward pressure on the price level.

Banking panics occurred fairly often in the United States before the Federal Reserve began operations in 1914. There were 12 episodes between 1800 and 1914 that are generally called banking panics. For the period after the Civil War, for which better data are available, the most severe crises occurred in 1873, 1893, and 1907. The panics typically exhibited increases in the ratios of the public's currency and banks' excess reserves to deposits. They also tended to show decreases in prices and in real economic activity. It is, however, hard to sort out the independent influence of the banking panics on output and other real variables. That task is difficult because, under the monetary system that was in place before the establishment of the Federal Reserve, poor economic conditions tended automatically to generate financial crises.[13] Economists think that these crises also made real economic conditions worse, but it is not easy to prove this proposition through statistical analysis.

A major reason for the creation of the Federal Reserve was the desire to moderate financial crises. One way that the founders of the Fed sought to promote financial stability was through the accommodation of seasonal demands for money. In this objective the Fed has been successful. The Fed's accommodation of seasonal variations in money demand have, for example, eliminated the seasonal pattern in nominal interest rates that applied before 1914 (see Jeffrey Miron, 1986). Whether this success helped to eliminate banking panics is unclear.

A more controversial idea—related to views on the role played by the Bank of England (see Walter Bagehot, 1873)—was that the Fed would serve as the **lender of last resort** through the operation of its discount window. When a financial crisis threatened, the lender of last resort would lend liberally to financial institutions at the discount rate, which would be set below market interest rates. In practice, direct lending by the Fed through the discount window was important during World War I and in the 1920s but has since become less significant.

During the 1920s, the Fed was successful in averting banking panics. It is likely, for example, that the sharp economic contraction of 1921 would have resulted in a banking panic under the pre–World War I monetary regime. The worst banking panics in U.S. history occurred, however, from 1930 to 1933 during the Great Depression. Milton Friedman and Anna Schwartz (1963, Chap. 7) argue convincingly that this financial crisis would have been much less severe if the Fed had not existed, because, under the earlier environment, the banks would not have relied on corrective measures from the Fed—actions that turned out not to materialize. The Fed failed, specifically, to act as a lender of last resort.

[13] *Phillip Cagan (1965, pp. 265ff.) argues that the banking panics have major elements that are independent of changes in business conditions. But Gary Gorton (1986) finds a close relationship between business failures and banking panics.*

Between 1930 and 1933 there was an unprecedented number of bank suspensions; roughly 9000 out of about 25,000 banks that existed at the end of 1929. In March 1933, President Franklin D. Roosevelt proclaimed a "banking holiday," which temporarily closed all the banks. About one-third of those that had existed in 1929 never reopened.

The banking panics from 1930 to 1933 led to sharp increases in the public's holdings of currency relative to deposits. Figure 17.5 shows that the ratio of currency to checkable deposits rose from 0.17 in 1930 to 0.34 in 1933. Similarly, the banking panics increased the ratio of excess reserves to checkable deposits from near zero in 1930 to 0.04 in 1933 and 0.12 in 1935 (see Figure 17.2). As mentioned before, these types of increases in the real demand for base money depress the price level if the nominal quantity of base money does not change.[14] Although the amount of base money increased from $6.6 billion in 1930 to $7.9 billion in 1933, this increase was insufficient to prevent a large decline in the price level: the GNP deflator fell at an annual rate of 7.9% over this period.

The reaction to the banking panics of the Great Depression was a substantial amount of banking legislation. The various regulations on deposit interest rates began at this time, and the Fed obtained the power to change reserve requirements. The principal innovation in 1934 was the creation of the Federal Deposit Insurance Corporation (FDIC), the institution that insures deposits at banks.[15] When the government guarantees the redemption of deposits, people lose most of their incentive to withdraw their funds when they are unsure about an institution's financial position. It therefore becomes harder for a bank run to start, or for one bank's problems to spread to others. There have, in fact, been no major banking panics since 1933. Accordingly, we no longer have this major source of instability in the real demand for base money and, hence, in the price level. We can be reasonably confident that this dramatic change from the earlier experience derives from the implementation of federal deposit insurance. On the negative side, the presence of federal deposit insurance reduces the incentives of financial institutions to use caution in accepting risky loans. This effect was especially great prior to 1991

[14] *The costs of financial intermediation also rise. Ben Bernanke (1983b) stresses this feature of banking panics during the Great Depression.*

[15] *The funds for this purpose come from a levy on the deposits of the insured banks. Formally, there is a ceiling—presently $100,000—for the size of insured deposits. But in practice the government seems to guarantee even the larger deposits. This practice was made explicit for the depositors of the Continental Illinois National Bank in 1984 and has been followed in most federal bailouts since that time.*

when an institution's premium charged for deposit insurance did not depend on its portfolio of loans. In particular, this non-risk-based insurance may account for the high incidence of problems in the 1980s in loans to real estate developers, oil explorers, and foreign governments. The federal government (and the U.S. taxpayer) ended up having to pay through the FDIC (and the parallel, now defunct, agency for savings and loan associations, the FSLIC) for much of this problem lending. Thus, federal deposit insurance likely caused the problem of banking panics to be replaced by the problem of greater incidence of insolvency for financial institutions.

In 1991, the Federal Deposit Insurance Corporation Improvement Act (FDICIA) enacted risk-based premiums for deposit insurance. The law also put into place a series of regulations and supervisory controls that were intended to decrease the likelihood of bank failures. However, there is no reason to think that this governmental system assesses risks properly—some observers argue that the new system makes credit from financial institutions artificially too expensive for some classes of borrowers. Perhaps a better system would be to rely on privately provided deposit insurance. Such a system would have the proper incentives to evaluate risks accurately.

Changes in Reserve Requirements in 1936–37

There were no changes in legal reserve requirements from 1917 until 1936. Then, mindful of the large quantity of banks' excess reserves (49% of total reserves and 12% of checkable deposits in 1935), the Fed decided to "mop them up" by sharply raising reserve requirements. The required-reserve ratio for member commercial banks in major cities other than New York and Chicago went, for example, from 10% of net demand deposits in 1935 to 15% in August 1936, 17.5% in March 1937, and 20% in May 1937. Overall, the ratio of required reserves to checkable deposits rose from an average of 12% in 1935 to 22% in 1937 (see Figure 17.1).

The Fed apparently believed that banks would hold required reserves instead of excess reserves and would make no major changes in their total reserves. But the massive holdings of excess reserves after 1933 (see Figure 17.2) reflected the banks' precautions in order to avoid the kinds of banking panics that occurred from 1930 to 1933. Thus, although the ratio of excess reserves to checkable deposits fell from 12% in 1935 to 5% in 1937, the banks then rebuilt this ratio to 10% in 1938 and 16% in 1939. Although the monetary base grew at an annual rate of 13% from 1937 to 1939, the GNP deflator declined over this period at an annual rate of 1.5%. We can attribute this behavior of prices to the growing demand for reserves by banks, a response that followed from the steep rise in required reserves during 1936–37.

Many economists also attribute the recession of 1936–38 to the Fed's steep increase in reserve requirements. Starting from the trough of the Great Depression in 1933, real GNP grew rapidly at the average rate of 9.6% per year until 1936. The average growth rate was near zero between 1936 and 1938 (before rising strongly at the average rate of 7.3% per year from 1938 to 1940). At this point, our theory predicts a real effect from the increase in reserve requirements only because of the adverse effect on financial intermediation, that is, on the matching of lenders and borrowers. We do not, in particular, predict real effects because of the depressing influence of higher reserve requirements on prices and other nominal variables. We shall, however, reexamine the important issue of linkages between nominal and real variables in Chapters 18–20.

Probably because of the economy's poor performance in 1936–38, the Fed has never again engineered a sharp short-run increase in reserve requirements. The legal requirements shifted many times between 1938 and 1996, but Figure 17.1 does not show any short-run movements in the required-reserve ratio that rival those of 1936–37. One notable development was the decline in the ratio from 15% in 1979 to 7% in 1996. This change reflected the spread of checkable deposits outside commercial banks and the reduced reserve requirements under the banking legislation of 1980 and in 1992. Prakash Loungani and Mark Rush (1991) have studied the full time series of changes in reserve requirements in the post–World War II period. They find that a reduction in these requirements tends to raise real economic activity.

SUMMARY

Financial institutions use the funds generated from deposits to make loans to households, businesses, and the government. The intermediation between deposit holders and borrowers is useful because it allows financial specialists to evaluate and collect loans. In addition, the process creates various types of deposits, which are convenient as stores of value and as media of exchange. The conventional definition of money, M1, adds those deposits that are checkable to the public's holding of currency. Thus, M1 attempts to measure the assets that serve as common media of exchange.

The amount of financial intermediation depends on the costs of intermediating; these costs include expenses for servicing deposits and loans, returns to capital in the intermediary business, and requirements to hold non-interest-bearing reserves. An increase in these costs—such as a rise in reserve requirements on deposits—leads to less financial intermediation. The adverse effects from the reduced intermediation include a greater difficulty of matching borrowers and lenders. These effects tend to show up as reductions in the quantities of investment and output.

The Federal Reserve controls the size of the monetary base (the sum of the public's currency and the reserves of financial institutions) mainly through open-market operations. In the United States these operations typically involve exchanges between base money and U.S. government bonds. The Fed's loans to financial institutions at the discount window affect the monetary base in a similar manner.

An increase in the monetary base leads to a multiplicative expansion of deposits and of monetary aggregates, such as M1. The money multiplier, which is the ratio of M1 to the base, is greater the smaller are the ratios of reserves and currency to deposits. The money multiplier has been reasonably stable since World War II, but fell sharply in the 1930s.

Open-market operations are still neutral in the model: they affect the price level and other nominal variables but do not change any real variables (aside from the private sector's holdings of real government bonds). Among the real variables that do not change are the ratios of deposits to currency and of deposits to reserves.

Given the quantity of base money, the price level depends inversely on the real demand for the monetary base. Historically for the United States, the major short-term movements in this demand stemmed from banking panics. These panics featured sharp increases in the public's demand for currency and in banks' demands for excess reserves. The implementation of deposit insurance in 1934 apparently eliminated banking panics but also increased the tendency for financial institutions to make risky loans and become insolvent.

IMPORTANT TERMS AND CONCEPTS

banking panic Simultaneous runs on many banks and financial institutions, featuring attempts by many depositors to convert their deposits into currency.

Board of Governors of the Federal Reserve System The seven-member group, appointed by the U.S. president, that makes most decisions of the Federal Reserve System.

costs of intermediation The total cost of operating a financial intermediary.

demand deposits Deposits held at a financial institution that can be withdrawn at face value without restrictions.

discount rate of Fed The interest rate charged on loans from the Federal Reserve to financial institutions.

disintermediation The decline in the use of the services of financial intermediaries that results when the public moves away from holding deposits toward direct holding of bonds and mortgages.

excess reserves The difference between the total reserves held by financial institutions and the amount required to be held under the reserve requirement of the Federal Reserve.

Federal Funds market The market for very short-term borrowing and lending between financial institutions, primarily commercial banks.

Federal Funds rate The interest rate on loans made in the Federal Funds market.

Federal Open-Market Committee (FOMC) A committee of the Federal Reserve that has responsibility for open-market operations.

Federal Reserve credit The sum of the Fed's holdings of loans to depository institutions, U.S. government securities, and miscellaneous assets. The total of the Fed's claims on the government and the private sector.

financial intermediaries Institutions that obtain funds from deposits made by individuals and make loans to households and businesses. Examples are banks, savings and loan associations, and money-market funds.

high-powered money The total amount of Federal Reserve Notes (currency) and non-interest-bearing deposits (reserves) held at the Fed by depository institutions; the monetary base.

lender of last resort The role of the central bank as a provider of loans to financial institutions during crises.

monetary base High-powered money.

money multiplier The ratio of M1 to the monetary base.

multiple expansion of deposits The effect of an increase in the monetary base on the volume of deposits held at financial institutions.

Regulation Q The legal limit (applicable in previous years) imposed by the Federal Reserve on the interest rate payable on time deposits and savings deposits held at banks.

reserve requirement The requirement imposed by the Federal Reserve that depository institutions must hold a certain quantity of reserves. For each category of deposits, the requirement is specified as a fraction of the amount of deposits.

reserves (of depository institutions) The total amount of currency and non-interest-bearing deposits at the Fed held by banks and other depository institutions.

savings deposits Deposits held at banks that usually allow funds to be withdrawn without penalty with a 30-day notice of withdrawal.

time deposits Deposits at banks and other depository institutions that have a stated maturity date and carry penalties for early withdrawal.

vault cash Currency held by a depository institution.

QUESTIONS AND PROBLEMS

MAINLY FOR REVIEW

17.1 What considerations limit the amount of excess reserves held by financial institutions? Explain how the volume of reserves can be less than the volume of deposits.

17.2 What factors account for the spread between the interest rate on earning assets and the interest rate on checkable deposits? Is an increase in the spread associated with a lower volume of deposits?

17.3 Show that for an increase in the monetary base to be matched by an equivalent increase in reserves and currency held by the public, there must be a multiplicative expansion of deposits. How much would deposits expand if the reserve requirement were 100%?

17.4 Why does the expectation of a bank failure give individuals an incentive to cash in their deposits? Show that this expectation can be a self-fulfilling prophecy. How does the provision of deposit insurance reduce the likelihood of this event?

17.5 Explain why a shift by households away from currency and toward checkable deposits would raise the price level.

PROBLEMS FOR DISCUSSION

17.6   The Fed's Discount Rate and Borrowing at the Fed

How does the volume of borrowing at the Fed depend on the discount rate and the interest rate on earning assets? Do the data shown in Figures 17.3 and 17.4 support the answer?

Suppose that the Fed lowers the discount rate and that borrowings by banks increase. Are the effects on the economy the same as those from an open-market purchase of bonds?

17.7   Reserve Requirements

Suppose that the Fed increases the required-reserve ratio on checkable deposits.

a. How does this change affect the real demand for base money?

b. How does it affect the price level?

c. How does it affect the nominal quantity of M1?

d. What real effects occur from the increase in reserve requirements?

Pretend now that the government imposes reserve requirements on something that has nothing to do with "money." The requirement could, for example, be on refrigerators—anyone who owns a refrigerator must hold $10 of non-interest-bearing reserves at the Fed.

How does this new policy affect the real demand for base money and the price level? What other effects arise (for example, on the number of refrigerators)? In what ways do the answers differ from those for the usual case in which the requirements apply to checkable deposits?

17.8 Vault Cash and Reserve Requirements

From 1917 until December 1959, vault cash did not count toward satisfying the Fed's reserve requirements. Part of it counted until November 1960, after which all of vault cash counted toward the requirements. Just before the change in 1959–60, vault cash at banks that were members of the Federal Reserve System was $2.2 billion, which amounted to about 2% of all checkable deposits.

If the monetary base did not change for 1960–61, how would the new treatment of vault cash affect the price level? (Base money declined from an average of $50.4 billion in 1959 to $50.0 billion in 1960 and $49.1 billion in 1961.)

17.9 Interest on Reserves Held at the Fed

At present, reserves held at the Federal Reserve bear no interest. Suppose that reserves were paid interest at a rate that was some fraction of the interest rate on commercial paper. If the quantity of base money stayed the same, how would this change affect the following:

a. The interest rate paid on checkable deposits?

b. The dollar amount of checkable deposits?

c. The price level?

d. The amount of intermediation in the economy?

e. The profits of the Federal Reserve (which go to the U.S. Treasury)?

17.10   Gold and the Monetary Base

Suppose that the U.S. Treasury receives $1 billion of gold from abroad. Then the Treasury deposits the gold at the Fed, so that the Fed's gold account and the Treasury's deposits at the Fed each rise by $1 billion.

a. What happens to the monetary base if the Treasury holds the extra $1 billion in deposits?

b. What happens if the Treasury spends the extra $1 billion and thereby restores its deposits to their initial level?

c. How can the Fed offset the effect of the gold inflow on the monetary base? (If it takes this action, then the Fed is said to "sterilize" the inflow of gold.)

d. Suppose that the government raises the official price of gold from $42.22 per ounce to the market price of around $350 (in 1997). The capital gain on the Fed's gold holdings (valued according to the official price of $42.22 at $11.0 billion at the end of 1996) would be credited to the Treasury's deposits at the Fed. What might this action do to the monetary base (which was $451 billion at the end of 1996)? What could the Fed do to keep the monetary base from changing?

17.11   Membership in the Federal Reserve System

Until 1980 only commercial banks that were members of the Federal Reserve System were subject to the Fed's reserve requirements. (There were also some services, such as check clearing and access to the discount window, that were provided free to members.) Membership was optional for banks with state charters but required for those with federal charters. (In 1980 only 30% of all commercial banks had national charters. But these institutions accounted for 55% of the deposits at commercial banks.)

FINANCIAL INTERMEDIATION

689

The fraction of state banks that were members of the Federal Reserve System declined from 21% in 1948 to 10% in 1980. Why do you think this decline occurred?

17.12 Runs on Financial Institutions

In the text we discussed runs on banks. How does the analysis differ if the run applies to other financial intermediaries, which do not offer checkable deposits? (This description would apply until the 1980s to savings and loan associations.)

17.13 Deposit Insurance (optional)

We discussed the role of federal deposit insurance, which has apparently prevented banking panics since 1933. A number of unresolved questions about this insurance are worth considering:

a. Could private companies satisfactorily provide insurance on deposits? Would the private sector end up providing the "right" amount of insurance? In particular, would private companies charge appropriately for this insurance in accordance with the riskiness of an institution's earnings? What problems can arise if the government provides the insurance but does not take proper account of risk? More generally, why is deposit insurance an area in which the government should be involved?

b. Is there a reason for the government to be in the insurance business for deposits but not for other things, such as corporate obligations? (The federal government has, in fact, gotten into the business of insuring the debt of doubtful borrowers—such as New York City and the Chrysler Corporation—as well as pension obligations and accounts at stockbrokers.)

The Interplay between Nominal and Real Variables — What Is the Evidence?

S|o far, our analysis has not stressed monetary variables as a source of fluctuations in real economic activity. Yet many economists think that movements in money and prices—that is, nominal disturbances—have a great deal to do with the short-term behavior of real variables, such as aggregate output and employment. In this chapter we concern ourselves primarily with the empirical evidence on this important issue. But first, let's summarize what our theory says so far about the interaction between nominal and real variables.

The theory predicts that changes in the monetary base are neutral. In particular, a one-time shift in the quantity of base money leads to proportional changes in the nominal variables but to no changes in the real variables. In a closed economy, the monetary change induces proportional responses in the price level, the nominal wage rate, and the dollar values of output, investment, and so on. In an open economy with flexible exchange rates, the nominal exchange rate would also change proportionately. But the important point is that there are no changes in the quantities of output and employment, the real interest rate, the real exchange rate, and so on.

We can also consider monetary disturbances in which the changes do not occur entirely at the present time. Then the anticipations of future monetary changes lead to complicated responses of the price level, as well as to shifts in the nominal interest rate. But the model still predicts no changes in the real variables. At least, the only exception in the theory concerns the transaction costs for moving between money and either goods or interest-bearing assets. Because changes in the nominal interest rate affect the real demand for money, some real effects occur through this channel. But these influences are usually viewed as too small to account for sizable fluctuations in aggregate real economic activity.

The results differ if monetary fluctuations reflect shifts in the cost of intermediation rather than changes in the quantity of base money. As examples, increases in reserve requirements or restrictions on the payment of interest on deposits raise the cost of intermediation, and a banking panic lowers households' willingness to hold deposits.[1] These cases are like reductions of the monetary base in that the price level and other nominal variables decline. But the higher cost of intermediation leads also to contractions of investment and output. Therefore, these types of disturbances move nominal and real variables in the same direction.

There are also real disturbances, such as the oil crises of 1973–74 and 1979–80, which we can represent as shifts to production functions.[2] An adverse shock reduces output and thereby lowers the quantity of real money demanded. For a given amount of base money, the price level rises. Hence, the price level moves in the opposite direction of output in this case.

In an open economy with fixed exchange rates, we found in Chapter 16 that it was not easy for the monetary authority to determine the quantity of base money once the exchange rate had been chosen. To sustain an increase in the monetary base (when this increase did not reflect a prior rise in the real demand for the base), governments had to restrict

[1] Banking panics are typically not independent of prior changes in business conditions. The potential for panics does depend, however, on some features of the financial structure. In particular, as discussed in Chapter 17, the implementation of federal deposit insurance in 1934 has apparently prevented panics since that time.

[2] For most purposes, we can include here changes in government consumption and shifts in taxes and transfers. For example, an increase in marginal tax rates is analogous to an adverse shift of the production function.

trade in goods or assets. Then it is not surprising that these restrictions—even if not the increase in base money itself—would have real effects.

Overall, the theory does allow for some relationships between nominal and real variables, but the sign of the interaction depends on the nature of the underlying disturbance. The key theoretical proposition, however, concerns monetary neutrality. Purely monetary disturbances—in the sense of changes in the monetary base—have no real effects. Although these monetary disturbances can create substantial variations in prices and other nominal variables, we still predict no important response in the aggregates of output, employment, and so on.[3]

Most economists regard the proposition of monetary neutrality as incorrect, at least in some short-run contexts. In fact, many researchers attribute a large portion of aggregate business fluctuations to monetary disturbances, which the theory says have no substantial real effects. The common view is that monetary expansion tends to stimulate real economic activity, and monetary contraction tends to cause recessions.

THE PHILLIPS CURVE

Economists often express their ideas about the relation between real and nominal variables in terms of the **Phillips curve** (named after the British economist A. W. Phillips). This curve is intended to summarize the relation between a measure of real economic activity, such as the unemployment rate or the departure of real GDP from its trend, and the departure from trend or growth rate of a nominal variable, such as the price level, nominal wage rate, or the stock of money. The basic notion behind the Phillips curve is that a burst of inflation (and more monetary growth underlying this inflation) brings about an economic boom that shows up as lower unemployment and higher real GDP. This idea was presented initially as an empirical, inverse relation between the unemployment rate and the rate of growth of nominal wages. But subsequently, researchers have often replaced the rate of wage change

[3] *The variations in prices lead to changes in the distribution of real assets. Specifically, nominal debtors gain from surprise inflation, and nominal creditors lose. But the theory does not allow for effects of these types of distributional shifts on the aggregates of output and employment. One possibility would be to extend the theory so that these distributional changes did have aggregate consequences.*

FIGURE 18.1

A SIMPLE PHILLIPS CURVE

The Phillips curve associates a lower value of the inflation rate, π, with a higher unemployment rate, u.

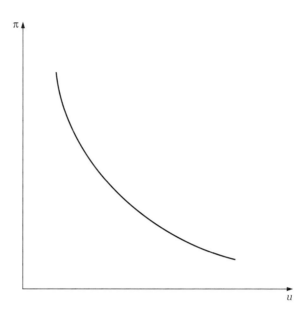

by other measures of nominal disturbances, such as the growth rate of prices or money. Figure 18.1 shows a simple version of the Phillips curve. In this figure, a lower inflation rate, π, is associated with a higher unemployment rate, u.

Economists sometimes argue that more inflation or more monetary growth results in lower unemployment and a higher growth of output only in the short run. The economy adjusts eventually to any established rate of inflation, so that the real variables no longer depend on the behavior of the nominal variables. Suppose that we think of the expected rate of inflation, π^e, as the rate of inflation to which the economy has adjusted itself. Then, as shown in Figure 18.2, it is only the surprise part of inflation, $\pi - \pi^e$, that would relate systematically (and presumably negatively) to the unemployment rate. This type of relation is called an **expectational Phillips curve** because the inflation rate enters in relation to the amount of expected inflation. One important property of this curve is that a given unemployment rate can coexist with any rate of inflation. An unemployment rate of 6% is consistent with an inflation rate of 0%,

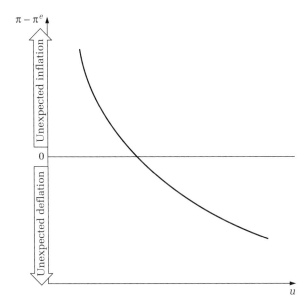

FIGURE 18.2

AN EXPECTATIONAL PHILLIPS CURVE

The expectational Phillips curve associates a lower value of unexpected inflation, $\pi - \pi^e$, with a higher unemployment rate, u. Thus, a given unemployment rate (say 6%) can coexist with any rate of inflation.

10%, 20%, and so on. If the inflation rate rises from 0% to 10% but the expected inflation rate rises by the same amount, then unexpected inflation, $\pi - \pi^e$, does not change. Therefore, if the expectational Phillips curve is correct, then this kind of increase in inflation has no significance for the unemployment rate.

If the expectational Phillips curve in Figure 18.2 applies, then we can view the simple Phillips curve in Figure 18.1 as holding for a fixed value of the expected inflation rate, π^e. When π^e changes, the curve in this figure shifts. Specifically, a higher value of π^e means that a higher inflation rate is associated with any given value of the unemployment rate.

We can view much of the macrotheorizing since the 1930s as attempts to explain versions of the Phillips curve and, as a related matter, the absence of monetary neutrality. This perspective applies as much to the Keynesian theory as to the more recent monetary theories of business fluctuations. But before we explore these theories, we should understand the nature of the facts that they are trying to explain. In particular, we want to know to what extent the Phillips curve—either the simple one or the expectational variety—and monetary nonneutrality are "facts." In this chapter we bring out the major pieces of empirical evidence that concern the interplay between nominal and real variables. Throughout this discussion, we look especially for findings that demonstrate the existence of the Phillips curve and the nonneutrality of money.

THE RELATIONSHIP BETWEEN UNEMPLOYMENT AND THE RATES OF CHANGE OF WAGES, PRICES, AND MONEY—LONG-TERM EVIDENCE FOR THE UNITED KINGDOM AND THE UNITED STATES

The term *Phillips curve* derives from studies of the relationship between unemployment and the growth rate of nominal wages carried out by A. W. Phillips (1958) and Richard Lipsey (1960). Lipsey's statistical analysis documented a significant inverse relationship between the unemployment rate and the growth rate of nominal wages in the United Kingdom in the late nineteenth and early twentieth centuries. The nature of his findings shows up in Figure 18.3, which plots the British data from 1863 to 1913. The growth rate of the nominal wage rate, $\Delta w/w$, appears on the vertical axis, and the unemployment rate, u, is on the horizontal. The curve shows a clear negative relationship, a finding that excited Lipsey and many subsequent researchers.

The inverse relation between unemployment and the growth rate of nominal wages does not hold up after World War I. The interwar period, 1923–39, exhibited exceptionally high unemployment rates: the average value of 14.3% contrasts with that of 4.7% from 1862 to 1913. But Figure 18.4 shows that there is no significant relation between the unemployment rate and the rate of change of wages over the period 1923–39.

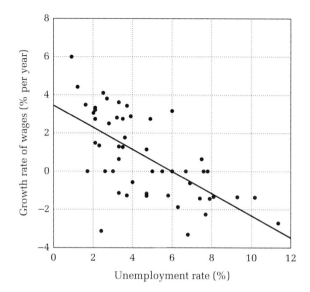

FIGURE 18.3

THE UNEMPLOYMENT RATE AND THE RATE OF CHANGE OF WAGES
IN THE UNITED KINGDOM, 1863–1913

Sources of data for Figures 18.3–18.5: The unemployment rate is from
B. R. Mitchell and P. Deane (1962), B. R. Mitchell (1980), and Central Statistical Office, *Monthly Digest of Statistics*, various issues.
The wage rate index is from B. R. Mitchell (1980), Department of Employment and Productivity (1971), and *Monthly Digest of Statistics*,
various issues.

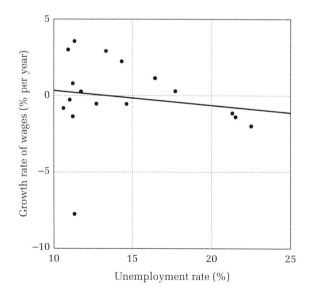

FIGURE 18.4

THE UNEMPLOYMENT RATE AND THE RATE OF CHANGE OF WAGES IN
THE UNITED KINGDOM, 1923–39

THE INTERPLAY BETWEEN NOMINAL AND REAL VARIABLES — WHAT IS THE EVIDENCE?

697

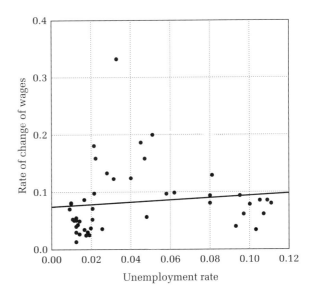

A different pattern of association between wage-rate changes and unemployment arises in the post–World War II period. For the years 1947–95, the relation between the unemployment rate and the rate of change of wages is significantly positive, as shown in Figure 18.5. In other words, the Phillips curve for the United Kingdom slopes in the "wrong" direction since World War II! The most notable change, however, from the pre–World War I period is the higher average growth rate of nominal wages: 8.5% per year for 1947–95 versus 0.8% for 1862–1913 (and −0.1% for 1923–39). In comparison with the period before World War I, the recent years involve mainly an increase in the average rate of wage change, with no significant difference in the average unemployment rate.

The results for the United Kingdom look basically similar if we replace the growth rate of nominal wages by the growth rate of either prices or a monetary aggregate. The only indication of an inverse relation between unemployment and the growth rate of a nominal variable— wages, prices, or money—appears in the years before World War I. Also,

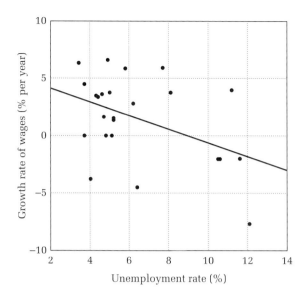

FIGURE 18.6

**THE UNEMPLOYMENT RATE AND THE RATE OF CHANGE OF WAGES
IN THE UNITED STATES, 1890–1913**

Sources of data for Figures 18.6–18.8: The unemployment rate is
from Figure 1.3. The wage-rate index is from Albert Rees (1959) and
Economic Report of the President, various issues. The recent data
include an adjustment for overtime pay.

for any of the nominal variables, the slope of the Phillips curve has the
wrong sign in the recent period.

The pattern of results for the United States resembles that for the
United Kingdom.[4] Figure 18.6 shows a significantly negative association
between the unemployment rate and the growth rate of wages from 1890
to 1913. Figure 18.7 shows the relationship over the interwar period,
1923–39. Although the slope is negative, this relation is not statistically
significant. Unlike the United Kingdom, the unemployment rates in the
United States were low during most of the 1920s. But for the 1930s, the
unemployment rates were similar in the two countries.

Figure 18.8 shows the absence of a significant correlation between
the unemployment rate and the growth rate of nominal wages for the
United States in the post–World War II period, 1947–96. Some weak indication of a positive relationship—that is, of a wrongly sloped Phillips
curve—shows up for this period for the United States if we replace the
growth rate of wages by that of either prices or a monetary aggregate,
such as M1.

[4] *Irving Fisher (1926) carried
out an early statistical study of
this type of relationship for the
United States, although he used
price changes instead of wage
changes. This study is reprinted
(under the cute title "I Discovered the Phillips Curve") in the*
Journal of Political Economy,
March/April 1973.

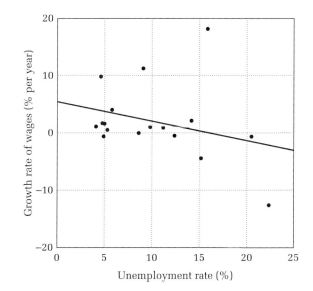

FIGURE 18.7

THE UNEMPLOYMENT RATE AND THE RATE OF CHANGE OF WAGES
IN THE UNITED STATES, 1923–39

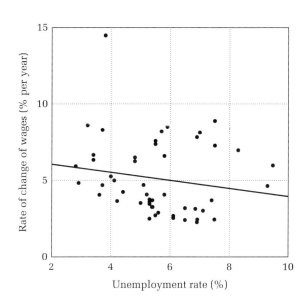

FIGURE 18.8

THE UNEMPLOYMENT RATE AND THE RATE OF CHANGE OF WAGES IN
THE UNITED STATES, 1947–96

A clear conclusion from the data is the absence of a stable relation between the unemployment rate—or, it turns out, real economic activity more generally—and the growth rates of nominal wages, prices, or money.[5] Thus, the sharply higher growth rates of the nominal variables since World War II, compared with those before World War I, correspond to little change in the average rate of unemployment (or in average growth rates of real GDP). Hence, we can firmly reject the notion of a Phillips curve, such as that shown in Figure 18.1, that is stable over the long term. At least in the long run, it is not true that more inflation leads to a lower unemployment rate or that to have low inflation a country must accept a high unemployment rate. We consider later more detailed evidence about the short-run relation between real and nominal variables.

CROSS-COUNTRY RELATIONS BETWEEN NOMINAL AND REAL VARIABLES

Suppose now that we look at average growth rates of real GDP for various countries[6] and compare these with the average growth rates of prices, money, and so on. If we look at averages over several decades, then the main variations across countries would reflect differences in the long-term average growth rates of real GDP, prices, money, and so forth. Hence, the relations among these variables should indicate how differences in the growth rates of the nominal variables associate in the long run with differences in the real growth rates.

Figure 18.9 uses data from 109 countries to relate the average growth rate of real gross domestic product from 1960 to 1990 to the average rate of consumer-price inflation over the same period. (Recall that we looked at similar data before in Chapter 7.) The upper panel in the figure indicates a weak negative relation between the output growth rate and the inflation rate.[7] This relation applies over a broad range of inflation, which includes rates as high as 100% per year. However, the bottom panel shows that the long-term relation between growth and inflation is

[5] *Formal statistical support for this proposition appears in Robert Lucas (1980) and John Geweke (1986).*

[6] *Because of differences in concepts and lack of data, it is hard to compare unemployment rates across countries.*

[7] *For detailed evidence on this relation, see Roger Kormendi and Phillip Meguire (1984) and Robert Barro (1997).*

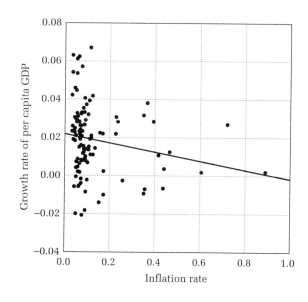

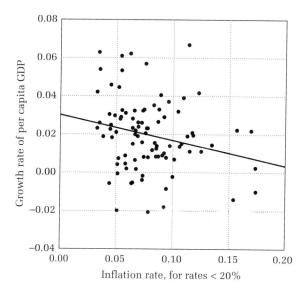

FIGURE 18.9

THE CROSS-COUNTRY RELATION BETWEEN THE GROWTH RATE AND THE INFLATION RATE, 1960–90

For 109 countries from 1960 to 1990, the upper panel shows a negative relation between the average growth rate of real per capita GDP and the average rate of CPI inflation. The bottom panel shows that the relation is still negative if we consider only inflation rates below 20% per year.

still weakly negative if we restrict attention to moderate inflation rates, in this case to values less than 20% per year. Similar conclusions apply if we relate the average growth rate of output to either the average growth rate of currency or the average growth rate of M1.

None of the cross-country evidence suggests that an economy has to accept a higher rate of inflation in the long run to attain a higher rate of economic growth. If anything, the evidence indicates that, in the long run, higher inflation and monetary growth come at the expense of higher economic growth.

THE CYCLICAL BEHAVIOR OF MONEY AND THE PRICE LEVEL

The evidence already presented suggests that nominal and real variables are not positively related—and may be inversely related—in the long run. We now want to look further at the short-run relation, specifically at the cyclical behavior of monetary aggregates and the price level. We begin with quarterly data for 1959–96, the period that we used before when we studied the cyclical behavior of real GDP and its components (in Chapters 1 and 9), of the real wage rate (in Chapter 6), and of labor input and unemployment (in Chapter 10). In the following section, we use the available annual data to examine the cyclical behavior of monetary aggregates and the price level from 1880 to 1940.

BEHAVIOR FROM 1959 TO 1996

The first column in the top part of Table 18.1 shows the volatility of various monetary aggregates and the price level (GDP deflator) for quarterly data from 1959 to 1996. The monetary aggregates are M1, real M1 (nominal M1 divided by the GDP deflator), M2, real M2, the monetary base, and the real monetary base. We measure volatility by the proportional standard deviation of the cyclical component, the same concept that we used before. For real GDP, for example, the standard deviation of the cyclical component is 1.7%, the value that appeared in Table 1.1. Table 18.1 shows that the various monetary aggregates have roughly the same volatility as real GDP; in each case, the standard deviation of the cyclical component of the real monetary aggregate is greater than that of its nominal counterpart. For the GDP deflator, the standard deviation of the cyclical part is 0.9%, about half that of real GDP.

The second column of the upper part of Table 18.1 shows the correlation of each cyclical component with the cyclical part of real GDP. For the nominal monetary aggregates, the correlations are 0.18 for M1, 0.34 for M2, and 0.35 for the monetary base. The correlations are stronger for the real counterparts: 0.36 for M1, 0.53 for M2, and 0.57 for the base. Thus, the monetary aggregates are all moderately procyclical, and the real values are more procyclical than the nominal ones.

Although money is procyclical, the price level (GDP deflator) is countercyclical: the correlation of the cyclical component with de-trended real GDP is −0.66. This result is consistent with the finding that the real monetary aggregates are more procyclical than the nominal ones.

Table 18.2 brings out the behavior of the monetary aggregates and the price level during the five recessions since 1959. The results are consistent with those shown in Table 18.1 in that the various monetary aggregates are typically below trend during the recessions (indicated by positive numbers in Table 18.2), whereas the price level is above trend (indicated by negative numbers). On average, the nominal aggregates were below trend during the recessions by 2.5% for M1, 2.0% for M2, and 2.0% for the monetary base. The corresponding figures for the real aggregates were 3.6%, 3.1%, and 3.0%. In contrast, the GDP deflator was 1.3% above its trend on average for the five recessions.[8]

The results on the nominal monetary aggregates for 1959–96 are consistent with the proposition that purely monetary changes—specifically, changes in the monetary base—have short-run effects in the same direction on real economic activity. The countercyclical behavior of the price level indicates, however, that monetary shocks cannot be

[8] *Earlier data for 1954 and 1958 also conform with this pattern for the post–World War II period.*

TABLE 18.1

CYCLICAL BEHAVIOR OF MONETARY AGGREGATES AND THE PRICE LEVEL

QUARTERLY DATA, 1959.3–1996.4	Standard Deviation	Correlation with Real GDP
Real GDP	.017	1.00
M1	.024	.18
Real M1	.028	.36
M2	.014	.34
Real M2	.020	.53
Monetary base	.015	.35
Real monetary base	.019	.57
GDP deflator	.009	−.66

ANNUAL DATA	1880–1940		1959–96	
	Standard Deviation	Correlation	Standard Deviation	Correlation
Real GNP or GDP	.057	1.00	.021	1.00
M1[a]	.073	.70	.031	.35
Real M1[a]	.050	.62	.039	.55
Monetary base	.070	.17	.023	.48
Real monetary base	.044	−.18	.030	.66
GNP or GDP deflator	.044	.27	.019	−.56

Note: *All variables are in proportional (logarithmic) units.*

[a]*Data are for M2 up to 1914 (for which data on M1 are unavailable) and for M1 thereafter.*

the principal disturbance that impinges on the economy. Changes that look like shifts to the production function—which move output and the price level in opposite directions—must be important. The evidence on the positive relation between money and output also does not address the question of whether shifts in money are causing changes in real

TABLE 18.2

MONETARY AGGREGATES AND THE PRICE LEVEL DURING RECENT RECESSIONS (PERCENTAGE SHORTFALL)

| | Trough Quarter for Real GDP | | | | | Mean for |
	1961.1	1970.4	1975.1	1982.4	1991.4	Five Recessions
Real GDP	2.8	3.4	4.2	4.5	2.0	3.4
M1[a]	0.9	1.5	1.8	2.7	5.4	2.5
Real M1[a]	1.3	2.3	3.3	4.7	6.4	3.6
M2[b]	1.4	4.5	3.4	1.7	−0.7	2.0
Real M2[b]	1.7	5.3	5.3	3.5	−0.1	3.1
Monetary base[c]	3.0	1.0	1.8	1.7	2.3	2.0
Real monetary base[c]	3.3	1.5	3.3	3.8	3.0	3.0
GDP deflator[d]	−0.7	−0.8	−2.1	−2.1	−1.0	−1.3

Note: *Real values are the nominal amounts divided by the GDP deflator. Negative numbers indicate that the cyclical component was positive during the recession. Data on M1, M2, and the monetary base are from Board of Governors of the Federal Reserve System,* Statistical Digests *and* Federal Reserve Bulletin. *The shortfall in real GDP comes from Table 9.1. The shortfalls in the monetary aggregates and the GDP deflator are relative to trend values. The trend values are computed as discussed in Chapter 1.*

[a] *Trough quarters for M1 and real M1 are 1960.4, 1970.2, 1976.3 (1975.4 for real M1), 1982.2, and 1991.1.*

[b] *Trough quarters for M2 and real M2 are 1960.4, 1970.2, 1974.4 (1975.1 for real M2), 1982.3 (1982.2 for real M2), and 1990.4.*

[c] *Trough quarters for the monetary base and real monetary base are 1961.2, 1970.4, 1976.1 (1975.4 for the real base), 1982.2, and 1991.4.*

[d] *Trough quarters for the GDP deflator are 1960.4, 1970.4, 1975.1, 1982.1, and 1991.1.*

economic activity or the reverse. We consider this problem of reverse causation in a later section.

BEHAVIOR FROM 1880 TO 1940

The left side of the bottom portion of Table 18.1 shows the volatility of real GNP, monetary aggregates, and the GNP deflator for annual data from 1880 to 1940. (Quarterly data are unavailable here.) The right side shows,

A Study of Price Surprises

An econometric study by Ray Fair (1979) analyzes the relation between surprise movements in the price level and the amount of real economic activity in the post–World War II United States. He focuses on the unemployment rate, u_t, as the measure of real economic performance. The statistical procedure estimates the relation between the unemployment rate and the surprise part of the price level, $P_t - P_t^e$, where P_t is the actual price level, and P_t^e is the price that the typical person expected for period t. In other words, the study estimates a form of an expectational Phillips curve.

Fair interprets the expected price, P_t^e, as the best forecast for the actual price, P_t, that people could have made with the data available through the previous period, $t - 1$, where the periods are treated as quarters of years. Fair uses statistical techniques to obtain a best fit between the actual price level, P_t, and the lagged values of a group of explanatory variables. Then he uses the fitted value from this relationship to proxy for the expected price, P_t^e, that is, for the best prediction of prices that could have been made from the assumed list of explanatory variables, when observed through date $t - 1$. Operationally, the constructed price surprise is similar to the cyclical component of the price level, the variable that we considered in Tables 18.1 and 18.2.

Fair finds no significant relation between the unemployment rate and the price surprise over the period 1954–73. When he adds data from 1974 to 1977—and thereby includes the effect of the 1973–74 oil shock on the 1974–75 recession—the estimated relation between price shocks and unemployment becomes positive. That is, the expectational Phillips curve has the wrong sign. This result accords with the finding in Table 18.1 that the GDP deflator was countercyclical from 1959 to 1996. If we look separately at the periods before and after 1973, then we find that the price level was countercyclical in both periods—the correlation with detrended real GDP was −0.58 from 1959 to 1972 and −0.70 from 1973 to 1996.

Ben Broadbent (1996) has recently reconsidered the relation between economy activity—measured in his case by real GDP—and price surprises. His study allows separately for supply shocks and thereby attempts to isolate the relation between price surprises and output that is driven by nominal disturbances. His study finds a weak positive effect from a surprisingly high price level on aggregate output. Roughly speaking, if the price level is surprisingly high by one percent, then output is raised by about 0.2 percent.

Studies of Unanticipated Money

I analyzed the real effects of monetary shocks in a number of papers (see Barro, 1978b). The starting point is the division of monetary growth into **anticipated** and **unanticipated** components. Conceptually, I identified the anticipated part with the prediction that could have been made by exploiting the historical relation between money and a specified set of explanatory variables. Unanticipated money is then the difference between the actual and anticipated amounts. Operationally, unanticipated money is similar to the cyclical component of a monetary aggregate, the concept that we used in Tables 18.1 and 18.2.

I estimated equations for real GNP and the unemployment rate over the post–World War II period to ascertain the real effects of anticipated and unanticipated changes in money. I found that unanticipated M1 growth had expansionary real effects that lasted over a one- to two-year period. Conversely, the anticipated parts of M1 growth did not have important real effects. Quantitatively, I estimated that a 1% rise in money above expectations raises next year's output by about 1% and lowers next year's unemployment rate by about six-tenths of a percentage point. Thus, unlike the price shocks that Fair studied—but more like the effects isolated by Broadbent—positive monetary surprises seemed to have significant expansionary effects on real economic activity.*

These findings are consistent with the procyclical behavior of the monetary aggregates shown in Table 18.1. However, this analysis still leaves open the possibility of reverse causation, that is, the possibility that money is responding positively to output rather than the other way around. In addition, other researchers, such as Chris Sims (1980), have found that money looks much less important for output when other variables, especially interest rates, are held constant.

---

* Studies of anticipated versus unanticipated money include C. L. F. Attfield, D. Demery, and N. W. Duck (1981), Roger Kormendi and Phillip Meguire (1984), Frederic Mishkin (1982), and Mark Rush (1986).

for comparative purposes, the results from 1959 to 1996 when annual data (for GDP) are used instead of quarterly data. Because information on M1 is available only since 1914 (when the Federal Reserve was founded), the data up to 1914 use the M2 concept of money.

The main contrasts between 1880–1940 and 1959–96 are, first, that the price level is procyclical in the earlier period (correlation with real GNP = 0.27) and countercyclical in the later one (correlation with real GDP = −0.56); second, that nominal M1 is more procyclical in the earlier period (0.70) than in the later one (0.35); and third, that the monetary base is less procyclical in the earlier period (0.17) than in the later one (0.48).[9] The differing behavior of the price level explains why the real monetary aggregates are more procyclical than their nominal counterparts in 1959–96, but less procyclical in 1880–1940.

One reason that nominal monetary aggregates such as M1 were more procyclical before World War II is that business contractions in this period were often accompanied by banking panics. These panics led to reductions in deposits relative to currency and bank reserves and thereby led to declines in M1 for a given quantity of high-powered money. Thus, although the nominal monetary base was only weakly procyclical from 1880 to 1940 (correlation of 0.17), nominal M1 (or M2) was strongly procyclical (correlation of 0.70).

If no monetary shocks occurred, then the positive effect of output on the real demand for money would tend to generate a countercyclical pattern for the price level. A procyclical pattern for nominal monetary aggregates tends, however, to induce a procyclical pattern for the price level. The observed behavior for the price level depends, therefore, on the strength of the procyclical pattern for money. In particular, the stronger procyclical pattern for nominal M1 (and M2) in the period 1880–1940 than in the period 1959–96 likely explains why the price level changed from procyclical before World War II to countercyclical after the war.

Table 18.3 shows the behavior of real GNP, the monetary aggregates, and the price level during the six principal recessions between 1880 and

[9] *Gold and silver coins and certificates accounted for roughly half of the monetary base through World War I and still retained a substantial role until 1933. The reserves held at the Fed appear in the monetary base after the start of the Federal Reserve System in 1914.*

TABLE 18.3

MONETARY AGGREGATES AND THE PRICE LEVEL DURING SIX RECESSIONS BEFORE WORLD WAR II

(PERCENTAGE SHORTFALL)

	Trough Year of Recession						
	1894	1908	1914	1921	1933	1938	Mean
Real GNP	4.3	3.6	4.4	9.3	18.7	9.9	8.4
M1 or M2[a]	3.5	3.6	9.9	−0.1	21.8	12.7	8.6
Real M1 or M2[a]	1.4	3.8	−2.4	3.4	10.0	13.0	4.9
Monetary base	−4.1	−7.5	13.2	−6.2	10.9	7.1	2.2
Real monetary base	−6.2	−7.3	0.9	−2.7	−0.9	7.3	−1.5
GNP deflator	3.4	1.1	4.3	−0.8	5.2	0.9	2.4

Note: Real values are the nominal amounts divided by the GNP deflator. Negative numbers indicate that the cyclical component was positive during the recession. For sources of data, see Figures 1.1 and 1.4 and Table 7.2. For the monetary base and M1, Friedman and Schwartz (1963).

[a] *Data are for M2 for the first three recessions (for which data on M1 are unavailable) and for M1 for the last three.*

1940. The shortfall of real GNP during the Great Depression of 1929–33—by 18.7%—dwarfs the post–World War II experiences shown in Table 18.2. The contractions of 1938 (9.9%) and 1921 (9.3%) were also more severe than any of those after World War II. The three earlier cases, 1894, 1908, and 1914, were similar in magnitude to the post–World War II recessions.

Four of the pre–World War II recessions—1892–94, 1906–08, 1914, and 1929–33—contained banking panics. Another one, 1937–38, involved the Fed's steep increase in reserve requirements. The 1920–21 episode occurred just after World War I. In this case, the monetary aggregates and the price level increased dramatically during the war but then fell sharply after 1920.

Table 18.3 shows that M1 or M2 was 8.6% on average below trend during the six recessions. The 1921 contraction is shown as an exception to the usual pattern, but this result is sensitive to the method for constructing the cyclical components. M1 fell by 10% from 1920 to 1921, but is estimated to be slightly above trend in 1921 because of the sharp runup in M1 from 1914 to 1920. In any event, the main observation—consistent with the finding in Table 18.1—is that M1 was typically below trend during recessions.

The monetary base was 2.2% on average below trend during the six recessions. The results vary, however, across the recessions. The monetary base was above trend in 1894, 1908, and 1921, but below trend in 1914, 1933, and 1938.[10] Thus, there is at most weak evidence for a positive link between the monetary base and real economic activity.[11]

Table 18.3 shows that the GNP deflator was typically below trend during the recessions, by 2.4% on average. The 1921 recession appears as an exception, but this result is again sensitive to the method for measuring the cyclical variables. The GNP deflator declined by 4% from 1920 to 1921, but the 1921 value is estimated to be above trend because of the high inflation rates from 1915 to 1920.

The observations from before World War II complement those from 1959 to 1996 in the sense of confirming the procyclical behavior of monetary aggregates such as M1 and M2. Shifts in the monetary base are, however, not systematically related to real economic activity in the earlier period. These data therefore do not provide much support for the idea that purely monetary changes—that is, shifts in the monetary base—affect real variables.

DOES MONEY AFFECT THE ECONOMY, OR IS IT THE ECONOMY THAT AFFECTS MONEY?

The evidence that money—the monetary base or aggregates such as M1—affects output positively in the short run comes, first, from the

[10] *The monetary base fell by about 10% from 1920 to 1921, mostly because of a sharp increase in the Fed's discount rate and a consequent reduction in the amount of borrowing by banks from the Fed. The monetary base is nevertheless estimated to be above trend in 1921 because of the sharp runup in the base from 1915 to 1920. The monetary base rose during the Great Depression from 1930 to 1933, but is estimated to be below trend in 1933 because the growth rate of the base was slower than its trend growth rate over the entire period from 1924 to 1933. Similarly, although the base grew from 1936 to 1938, the growth rate was less than the trend growth rate. Hence, the monetary base is estimated to be below trend in 1938.*

[11] *Mark Rush (1985) argued that shifts in the monetary base had little relation to real economic activity from 1885 to 1913.*

observation that the cyclical components of money and output are positively correlated and, second, from the observation (which is harder to document) that movements in money precede those in output. An important question is whether these observations imply that money affects output, or instead that money responds to changes in economic conditions. Economists often refer to the latter situation as one of **endogenous money**, that is, a situation in which the quantity of money is determined by economic forces rather than being set (*exogenously*) from outside.

A banking panic is one example of a situation in which the positive association between M1 and real economic activity seems to reflect mainly the response of money to the economy. For a given quantity of base money, a banking panic tends to contract the economy and also to lower the amount of M1. Moreover, since the response of M1 may be quicker than that of real GDP, the movement in M1 could precede the change in output. In any event, the change in the quantity of money is not the underlying causal element in this example.

In some previous cases, we considered changes in the real demand for base money while holding fixed the nominal quantity of base money. For example, a temporary supply shock reduces output and the real quantity of base money demanded. If the nominal quantity of base money does not change, then the price level would rise. But under some monetary systems, the monetary base would change automatically in these circumstances. Suppose, for example, that the monetary authority followed a price-level rule in which it tried to offset disturbances by reducing the monetary base whenever the price level tended to increase, and vice versa. Then a supply shock would result in lower output and also smaller quantities of the monetary base and M1. In the data we would find positive associations between output and the monetary base and between output and M1. But these associations would reflect endogenous responses of money rather than the impact of money on the economy.

The last example is important historically because monetary authorities tended to behave in the assumed manner under the gold standard or, more generally, in regimes in which the authorities attempt to fix the exchange rates between domestic and foreign currencies. (See the discussion in Chapter 16.) For present purposes, the important point is that these systems make money endogenous; in particular, they create a pattern in which the nominal quantity of money moves automatically in the same direction as the real demand for money. Because output has a positive effect on the real demand for money, the movements in output and nominal money would be positively correlated in these cases.[12]

The gold standard and fixed exchange rates have become less important in recent years, but monetary authorities still follow rules of behavior that make money (the monetary base, M1, and other aggregates) endogenous. Specifically, the nominal quantity of money tends to move in the same direction as the real demand for money; or, to put it another way, the variations in money tend to *accommodate* the movements in the demand for money. The point of this **monetary accommodation** is that it avoids changes that would otherwise have to occur in variables, such as the price level and the nominal interest rate, that influence the real demand for money. Suppose that the monetary authority has some objectives or targets for the path of the price level or the nominal interest rate. (**Interest-rate targeting** has, in fact, been an important part of the Federal Reserve's operating policy at least since World War II; see Marvin Goodfriend, 1987.) If the quantity of base money did not vary, then shifts in the real demand for money would tend to affect prices and nominal interest rates. To avoid or dampen these effects, the monetary authority could adjust the amount of base money to accommodate the shifts in the demand. But, as with the gold standard, this pattern of endogenous money generates a positive association between money and real economic activity. Again, the existence of this association does not demonstrate that money affects the real economy.

[12] *It is possible, but not inevitable, that the movements in nominal money would precede those in output. This timing depends on the precise specifications of the demand for money and the determination of output.*

Seasonal Fluctuations in Money

One straightforward example of endogenous money is the regular seasonal movements in the monetary base and M1. Before the founding of the Federal Reserve in 1914, there was a seasonal pattern in nominal interest rates; these rates tended, for example, to be higher than average in the fall of each year. One of the reasons given for the creation of the Fed was that it would eliminate this pattern by allowing the amount of currency outstanding to vary seasonally to accommodate the regular variations over the year in the real demand for money (see Carter Glass, 1927, p. 387). The Federal Reserve has, in fact, been successful in this regard. Almost since the Fed's inception, and especially since the end of World War II, there has been no important seasonal pattern in nominal interest rates.*

The counterpart of the elimination of the seasonal pattern in nominal interest rates was the introduction of substantial seasonal variation into the monetary base and M1. Robert Barsky and Jeffrey Miron (1988) document these seasonal patterns for the post–World War II period. They also show that the seasonal movements in the monetary base and M1 are positively correlated with the seasonal variations of real GNP; the most dramatic instances are the increases in all variables around Christmas and the reductions in all variables after Christmas. Probably all macroeconomists would accept the proposition that this seasonal behavior is an example of endogenous money. Money is high around Christmas because real activity is high and because the Fed allows the monetary base to expand at such times. Real activity is not high in December because the Fed capriciously expands the quantity of money at this time every year.

The seasonal evidence makes it clear that a positive association between money and output does not provide convincing evidence that money affects output. Some macroeconomists (such as Robert King and Charles Plosser, 1984) go further. They argue that the pattern of endogenous money that is so clear for seasonals applies also to the patterns that show up in business cycles. The reasoning is that, as with the Christmas season, the increase in the real demand for money during a boom induces the accommodating monetary authority to raise the nominal quantity of money at such times.

It is hard to evaluate this argument empirically. Without some additional information (such ↗

as knowledge about the effects of Christmas) it is hard to tell statistically whether the positive association between money and output that we found in Table 18.1 reflects the influence of money on output, or vice versa. In fact, this problem of sorting out the direction of causation among variables is the most difficult problem empirical economists face.

* For discussions, see Jeffrey Miron (1986), Truman Clark (1986), and Greg Mankiw, Jeffrey Miron, and David Weil (1987).

IMPLICATIONS OF THE EVIDENCE

If shocks to the monetary base have important consequences for business fluctuations, then this observation would conflict with our theory. Remember that the theory predicts that changes in the monetary base would be neutral, at least if we neglect transaction costs and distributional effects. In the next chapter we explore some extensions of the theory that allow for nonneutral effects from changes in the monetary base. In evaluating these extensions, we should keep in mind the empirical evidence. There is some suggestion that monetary nonneutrality is significant, but the evidence is not very strong.

SUMMARY

Much of the macrotheorizing since the 1930s can be viewed as attempts to rationalize a strong interplay between nominal and real variables, an interaction that shows up in various versions of the Phillips curve. We can view the Keynesian theory and more recent monetary theories of business fluctuations in this context. But before considering these theories, we should think about how much evidence there is to explain.

Neither the long-period evidence nor that from across countries suggests important positive effects on real variables from differences in the average growth rates of money, prices, or wages. In the long run, there is, if anything, a negative relation between economic growth and the rates of change of the nominal variables.

The data since World War II show that nominal money—the monetary base and monetary aggregates such as M1—are moderately procyclical. The price level is countercyclical, and, hence, real money is more procyclical than nominal money.

The data before World War II show only a weak procyclical pattern for the nominal monetary base. Monetary aggregates such as nominal M1 are, however, more procyclical than they are after World War II. This pattern probably reflects the role of banking panics in the earlier period. The strong procyclical pattern for nominal M1 likely explains why the price level was procyclical before World War II.

A positive association between money and output may indicate that money responds to the economy (endogenous money), rather than the reverse. The effects of banking panics on monetary aggregates such as M1 are one example of this kind of effect. More generally, a positive association between money and output arises whenever the monetary authority accommodates variations in the real demand for money with movements in the nominal quantity of money. This monetary behavior arises under the gold standard and also in systems in which the monetary authority targets the price level or the nominal interest rate. It is unclear at this point how much of the empirical association between nominal money—the monetary base or aggregates such as M1—and real economic activity can be explained by endogenous money rather than as effects of money on the economy.

If changes in the monetary base were nonneutral and quantitatively important, then our theory would be seriously incomplete. Some of the empirical evidence is consistent with the idea that money is nonneutral, but this evidence is not very strong. Therefore, although the nonneutrality of money deserves some attention, it is likely that economists have given it too much weight. The interplay between nominal and real variables is neither as large nor as pervasive as most people believe.

IMPORTANT TERMS AND CONCEPTS

anticipated money growth The public's forecast of the rate of monetary growth, based on the historical relationship between the quantity of money and economic variables.

endogenous money The automatic response of the quantity of money to changes in the economy. Money is endogenous under the gold standard or in regimes in which the monetary authority targets nominal interest rates or the price level.

expectational Phillips curve The relation between unexpected inflation and the unemployment rate. According to this curve, an unexpected increase in the inflation rate has a negative effect on the unemployment rate.

interest-rate targeting A setup in which the monetary authority attempts to keep a designated nominal interest rate close to a target value. In this regime, the quantity of money is endogenous.

monetary accommodation The response of the nominal quantity of money to a change in the nominal amount demanded. Accommodation tends to occur in regimes in which the monetary authority targets nominal interest rates or in other setups in which money is endogenous.

Phillips curve The relationship between nominal variables, such as the inflation rate, and real variables, such as the unemployment rate or the growth rate of aggregate output.

unanticipated money growth The difference between the actual amount of monetary growth and anticipated money growth.

QUESTIONS AND PROBLEMS

MAINLY FOR REVIEW

18.1 What is the theoretical link between the price level and real variables? What about between the inflation rate and real variables? Why do you think it might be important to distinguish between expected and unexpected inflation?

18.2 Consider the statement "Makers of economic policy face a cruel choice between unemployment and inflation." Is this statement supported by (a) theoretical results or (b) empirical findings on the Phillips curve?

18.3 How does the expectational Phillips curve explain the negative association between inflation and unemployment rates in the United States prior to World War I? Could the absence of this negative association in subsequent years be "explained" by shifts in the Phillips curve?

18.4 To what extent was the Great Depression (1929–33) accompanied by changes in the nominal and real quantities of money?

18.5 Explain why it is important to distinguish between shifts in the nominal quantity of money and shifts in money demand. What association would we expect between the price level and real output in periods in which both types of shifts occur?

18.6 What is the meaning of the term *endogenous money*? Under what circumstances would endogenous money generate a pattern in which money and output were positively correlated?

PROBLEMS FOR DISCUSSION

18.7 The Timing of Money and Output

Suppose that the data show that movements in money (say the monetary base) are positively correlated with subsequent movements in output. Does this finding imply that money affects the economy, rather than the reverse? If not, give some examples of endogenous money in which the movements of money precede those of output.

18.8 Seasonal Variations in Money

Suppose that the quantity of real money demanded is relatively high in the fourth quarter of the year and relatively low in the first quarter. Assume that there is no seasonal pattern in the expected real interest rate.

a. Suppose that there were no seasonal variations in the monetary base. What would be the seasonal pattern for the price level and the nominal interest rate?

b. What seasonal behavior for the monetary base would eliminate the seasonal pattern in the nominal interest rate? Is there still a seasonal pattern in the price level?

c. Suppose that there is a seasonal pattern for the expected real interest rate. Can the monetary authority affect this pattern? If not, can the monetary authority eliminate the seasonal behavior of the nominal interest rate? Is there still a seasonal pattern in the price level in this case?

18.9 Interest-Rate Targeting (optional)

Suppose that the Fed wants to keep the nominal interest rate constant. Assume that the expected real interest rate is constant, but the real demand for money shifts around (perhaps because of changes in output).

a. What should the Fed do to the quantity of money if the real demand for money increases temporarily? What if the real demand increases permanently?

b. How does the price level behave in the answers to part a? What should the Fed do if it wants to dampen the fluctuations of the price level?

c. In the real world the nominal interest rate moves around a lot. How can we incorporate this fact into the analysis?

MONEY AND BUSINESS FLUCTUATIONS
IN THE MARKET-CLEARING MODEL

I n the 1970s and 1980s, macroeconomists developed an information-based line of theory to provide a possible explanation of the role of money in business fluctuations. The approach is often called *rational expectations macroeconomics*, but we shall refer to it—somewhat more descriptively—as the *market-clearing model with incomplete information about prices*.[1]

It is important to stress that the theory developed in this chapter applies mainly to the interaction between monetary and real phenomena. Thus, the evidence surveyed in Chapter 18 indicates the potential scope for the theory. That evidence suggests something interesting to explain but does not imply that monetary shocks are the most important source of business fluctuations.

As with the previous analysis, this chapter relies on the conditions for general market clearing as its central analytical device. The approach also retains the assumption that households and firms behave rationally, even including the manner in which they form expectations of inflation and other variables. We introduce, however, a source of "friction" by allowing for incomplete information about prices. An important way in which people receive information—and thereby make their allocative decisions—is by observing prices of various goods. But it would be prohibitively expensive for individuals to observe all prices instantly. Households and firms therefore typically make do with partial knowledge about the prices of different goods, about wage rates in alternative jobs, and so on. In this situation, decisions often differ from those that they would make with full information.

Variations in money and the general price level make it difficult for households and businesses to interpret the limited set of prices that they see. Hence, when there is an increase in the general price level, a household or firm may mistakenly think that the price of its output has increased *relative* to other prices. Consequently, the household or firm tends to produce more goods than it would under full information. Because of these responses, we shall find that surprise increases in money and the general price level can lead to expansions in the aggregate level of real economic activity.

In this chapter we work out the details of a representative model from this line of macroeconomic theory. To bring out the role of incomplete information, we have to move away from the simplified model with an economy-wide market for commodities. Now we make things more realistic by including a variety of local markets on which households and firms buy and sell goods and services.

THE STRUCTURE OF A MODEL WITH LOCAL MARKETS

Consider again the model of a closed economy in which households produce goods and sell them on a commodity market. Assume now that, instead of being identical, products differ by physical characteristics, location, and so on. We now index commodities by the symbol z, which

[1] *For a survey of the research, see Ben McCallum (1979). See also the papers collected in Robert Lucas (1981). Two early papers that stimulated much of the subsequent work are Milton Friedman (1968c) and Edmund Phelps (1970).*

takes on the possible values 1, 2, . . . , q, where q is a large number. To be concrete and to simplify matters, we usually think of z as a location, that is, a "local market." But more generally, we could identify this index with various characteristics of goods, occupations, methods of production, and so on. Then the value $z = 1$ might signify the automobile industry, $z = 2$ the computer industry, and so on.

Because changes in job location or type of product entail substantial costs, people do not move very often from one place or line of work to another. To capture this idea in a workable model, we assume that each household produces and sells goods in only one location during each period. But there is mobility in the sense that people may change locations at some cost from one period to the next.

We now distinguish prices by location of product and by date, so that $P_t(z)$ is the price of goods of type z during period t. Thus, $P_t(1)$ might be the dollar price of a market basket of goods in Detroit and $P_t(2)$ the price of the same market basket in Pittsburgh. Correspondingly, the ratio, $P_t(1)/P_t(2)$, is the price of goods in location 1 relative to that in location 2. It is important to distinguish this *relative price* from the general price level, which we have stressed in previous chapters. By the general price level, P_t, we mean an average of the individual prices at date t.

To keep things manageable, we neglect any long-lasting differences across locations. That is, we ignore a variety of things that might make goods permanently more or less expensive in different places. (For example, a market basket of goods always costs more in Alaska than in New York.) Consequently, in the model, if the "local price," $P_t(z)$, exceeds the average price, P_t, then market z looks relatively favorable for sellers during period t. This situation attracts producers from elsewhere, and the expansion of goods supplied to market z tends to drive down the local price toward the general level of prices. Similarly, if the local price is lower than the average price, then producers move to other territory, and this process tends to bring the local price up to the general price level. Thus, there is a process of entry to and exit from local markets that keeps each local price reasonably close to the average price.

Because of this tendency for prices to converge, the long-run forecast of the price in any local market equals that for the average of the markets.

SUPPLY OF GOODS IN A LOCAL MARKET

At the beginning of period t, a producer in market z has the stock of capital $k_{t-1}(z)$. Correspondingly, the amount of goods produced at location z during period t is given from the production function as

$$y_t(z) = f[k_{t-1}(z), l_t(z)] \tag{19.1}$$

where $l_t(z)$ is the producer's work effort. Note that we again think of each household as working on its own production process, although we could extend the framework to include firms and hired workers.

The dollar revenue from sales equals output, $y_t(z)$, multiplied by the local price, $P_t(z)$. But households buy goods from many locations. As an approximation, the typical household pays the average price, P_t, for its purchases. In this case, a producer calculates the real value of the revenue from local sales—that is, the value in terms of the goods that can be bought—by dividing the dollar amount by the general price level, P_t. Hence, the real revenue from production is

$$[P_t(z)/P_t] \cdot y_t(z) = [P_t(z)/P_t] \cdot f[k_{t-1}(z), l_t(z)] \tag{19.2}$$

The term $P_t(z)/P_t$ is the price of goods sold in market z relative to the average price of goods. Notice that for a given amount of physical product, $y_t(z)$, an increase in the relative price, $P_t(z)/P_t$, means a greater real value of sales. (An increase in $P_t[z]/P_t$ looks like an improvement in the terms of trade, $P/\bar{P}$, from the model of international trade in Chapter 15.)

When deciding how much to work during period t, producers and workers looked before at the physical marginal product of labor, $MPL_t(z)$. (The index z means in this context that the marginal product applies to additional work and output in market z). To compute the effect on real sales revenue, producers must now multiply the change in physical product by the relative price, $P_t(z)/P_t$. Hence, the real value of labor's marginal product is $[P(z)/P_t] \cdot MPL_t(z)$.[2] An increase in the relative price looks to the producer just like a proportional upward shift in the schedule for labor's physical marginal product. Producers therefore react to changes in the relative price, $P_t(z)/P_t$, just as they did before to changes in the schedule for labor's marginal product.

Consider the response to a temporary increase in the relative price, $P_t(z)/P_t$. This change has the same effect as a temporary upward shift in the schedule for labor's marginal product. Producers therefore increase work effort, $l_t(z)$, and the supply of goods, $y_t^s(z)$. Recall that these responses involve two types of substitution effects: first, a shift away from leisure and toward consumption, and, second, a shift away from today's leisure and toward tomorrow's leisure. The second channel, which is an intertemporal-substitution effect, suggests that the current responses of work and production will be large.[3] As an example, we can think of the strong response of labor supply to the unusually high wages that firms offer during overtime periods.

Consider now the determination of investment demand. We can use the approach developed in Chapter 9 but amended for a model with local markets. Suppose that producers in market z buy capital goods from other markets at the *general* price level, P_t.[4] If capital, $k_t(z)$, rises by one unit, then next period's output, $y_{t+1}(z)$, increases by the marginal product of capital, $MPK_t(z)$. Since this output will sell at the *local* price, $P_{t+1}(z)$, revenues next period will rise by the amount $P_{t+1}(z) \cdot MPK_t(z)$. As before, we can pretend that producers sell their used capital at the *general* price, P_{t+1}.

If we neglect depreciation for simplicity, then the nominal rate of return to investment is $[P_{t+1}(z) \cdot MPK_t(z) + P_{t+1}]/P_t - 1$. If π_t is the inflation rate (for the general price level), then this expression becomes $(1 + \pi_t) \cdot \{[P_{t+1}(z)/P_{t+1}] \cdot MPK_t(z) + 1\} - 1$. As in Chapter 9, producers

[2] *With separate labor markets, a worker would look at the local dollar wage rate, $w_t(z)$, divided by the average price of commodities, P_t. The real wage rate, $w_t(z)/P_t$, is the value of the local wage in terms of the goods that it buys on the average commodity market. Firms would hire labor until the local marginal product, $MPL_t(z)$, equaled the local cost of labor, $w_t(z)$, expressed relative to the price of the firm's product, $P_t(z)$. That is, firms would satisfy the condition $MPL_t(z) = w_t(z)/P_t(z)$. The value of a worker's marginal product is therefore $[P_t(z)/P_t] \cdot MPL_t(z) = w_t(z)/P_t$. Thus, by responding to $w_t(z)/P_t$, labor suppliers ultimately react to the term, $[P_t(z)/P_t] \cdot MPL_t(z)$, that we used in the text. Because the answer is the same, we again simplify by not introducing firms or separate labor markets.*

[3] *The higher relative price, $P_t(z)/P_t$, increases wealth for sellers in market z but reduces wealth for buyers. Because the changes in relative prices are temporary, the wealth effects will be small. We neglect these wealth effects in order to focus on the main points.*

[4] *The main results still go through if we assume, more realistically, that producers must pay the local price, $P_t(z)$, for some of their purchases.*

invest enough to equate this rate of return to the nominal interest rate, R_t. (We still treat R_t as determined on an economy-wide market for credit.) Writing out this equation and simplifying leads to the condition for investment demand:

$$[P_{t+1}(z)/P_{t+1}] \cdot MPK_t(z) = r_t \qquad\qquad\qquad \textbf{(19.3)}$$

where r_t is the economy-wide real interest rate (defined by $1 + r_t = [1 + R_t]/[1 + \pi_t]$).

The condition for investment demand in equation (19.3) is the same as the one in Chapter 9, except that capital's marginal product, $MPK_t(z)$, is multiplied by the prospective relative price, $P_{t+1}(z)/P_{t+1}$. Thus, investment demand for period t rises with either an upward shift in the schedule for capital's marginal product or an increase in $P_{t+1}(z)/P_{t+1}$. Also, as before, investment demand falls with an increase in r_t. If actual and expected real interest rates can diverge (because of differences between actual and expected inflation), then it is the expected real rate, r_t^e, that has a negative effect on investment demand.

CONSUMER DEMAND

So far, we have examined the behavior of producers. Now we consider the incentives of consumers, who may come from elsewhere to purchase goods. The important point is that a higher relative price, $P_t(z)/P_t$, reduces consumption demand, $c_t^d(z)$. (Note that the index z refers to goods bought in market z, although the buyers may use the goods in other locations.)

CLEARING OF THE LOCAL MARKET

If we put the pieces of the analysis together, then the condition for clearing the local market is

$$Y_t^s(z)[P_t(z)/P_t, r_t^e, \ldots]$$
$${\scriptstyle(+)}{\scriptstyle(+)}$$

$$= C_t^d(z)[P_t(z)/P_t, r_t^e, \ldots] + I_t^d(z)[P_{t+1}(z)/P_{t+1}, r_t^e, \ldots]$$
$${\scriptstyle(-)}{\scriptstyle(-)}{\scriptstyle(+)}\phantom{/P_{t+1}, }{\scriptstyle(-)}$$

(19.4)

Here, we use capital letters to denote the total quantity of goods supplied or demanded in market z. Notice that a higher current relative price, $P_t(z)/P_t$, raises the supply of goods but lowers consumption demand. In addition, a higher prospective relative price, $P_{t+1}(z)/P_{t+1}$, increases investment demand.

We also include in the supply and demand functions the expected real interest rate, r_t^e. As before, an increase in r_t^e raises the supply of goods, $Y_t^s(z)$, but lowers the demands, $C_t^d(z)$ and $I_t^d(z)$.

Figure 19.1 depicts the clearing of a local commodity market. We put the current relative price, $P_t(z)/P_t$, on the vertical axis. The supply and demand curves in the figure assume a given value for the expected real interest rate, r_t^e, but assume that the prospective relative price, $P_{t+1}(z)/P_{t+1}$, moves along with the current relative price. The relative

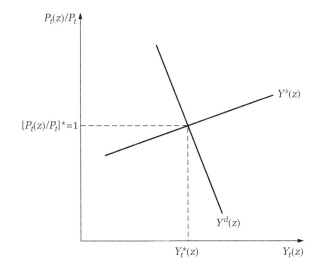

FIGURE 19.1

CLEARING OF A LOCAL COMMODITY MARKET

We show the dependence of commodity supply and demand on the relative price, $P_t(z)/P_t$, for a given expected real interest rate, r_t^e. For the average market, the market-clearing relative price is one.

price will tend to persist in this manner if the underlying disturbances to the local supply and demand curves tend to persist.

For the supply curve, the positive slope shows the response of the quantity supplied to a higher current relative price, $P_t(z)/P_t$. For the demand curve, the negative slope shows the reaction of the quantity demanded by consumers to the higher current relative price. This higher relative price tends, however, to be accompanied by an increase in $P_{t+1}(z)/P_{t+1}$, a change that stimulates investment demand. We assume that the net effect on the demand for goods is negative and therefore draw the demand curve with the conventional negative slope.

The intersection of the supply and demand curves determines the market-clearing values of the relative price, $[P_t(z)/P_t]^*$, and local output, $Y_t^*(z)$. For the average market—which, by definition, has not experienced unusual changes in its supply and demand curves—the market-clearing relative price must equal one; that is, $P_t^*(z)$ must equal the average price, P_t^*. The expected real interest rate, r_t^e, adjusts so that, in the average market, the quantity supplied equals the quantity demanded when $P_t(z)/P_t = 1$.

DISTURBANCES TO LOCAL MARKETS

We can imagine a variety of changes in tastes and technology that affect the clearing of a local market for goods: shifts in the numbers of producers, in production functions, in the numbers of demanders, and so on. Consider, as an example, an increase in local consumption demand, $C_t^d(z)$, due to an increase in the number of shoppers in market z or due to the popularity of some new or improved product, such as CD players or personal computers.

Figure 19.2 shows the effect on a local commodity market from the increase in consumer demand. The solid lines reproduce the supply and demand curves from Figure 19.1. The new demand curve is the dashed line, labeled $Y^d(z)'$, which lies to the right of the original curve. Note that we hold constant the expected real interest rate, r_t^e, a variable that

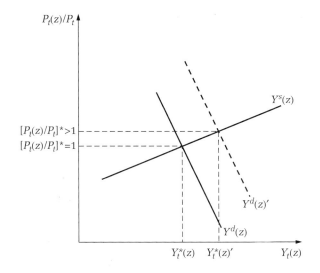

FIGURE 19.2

RESPONSES TO AN INCREASE IN LOCAL DEMAND

The change in consumer demand shows up as a positive shift to the local demand curve. Hence, the relative price and local output increase. Notice that the suppliers respond to the higher relative price by producing more goods (and by working harder). For the average market, the initial market-clearing relative price is one, and the new market-clearing relative price exceeds one.

would be determined in the whole economy, rather than in a single market.

Figure 19.2 shows that the current relative price and local output increase. The rise in the relative price motivates producers to work more and supply more goods. Thus, we can think of the high relative price as the signal that generates the unusually large volume of work and production. The high relative price persists over time and therefore stimulates current investment, $I_t(z)$. Consumption, $C_t(z)$, tends also to rise, despite the higher relative price, because of the initial boost to consumer demand. Finally, if the market-clearing relative price were initially equal to one—as is true for the average market—then the new relative price must exceed one.

Thus far, we have considered only the response of a local market to a local disturbance. Hence, we have not yet explained movements in the economy-wide totals of output and labor input. In the next section we show how a monetary disturbance may look, in each market, like a shift to local demand. Then output and labor input change just as they did in response to the shift in local demand that we just analyzed. When all markets respond this way, we end up with movements in the aggregate variables.

CHANGES IN THE STOCK OF MONEY

Consider a once-and-for-all increase in the quantity of base money, M_t. As in some cases that we explored before, this change might involve an open-market purchase of bonds by the Fed.

We found before for a closed economy that an increase in the quantity of money raised the general price level proportionately but left unchanged real variables such as aggregate output and employment. This conclusion still holds when there are a variety of locations in which households produce and trade goods. As in previous analyses, we can think of households as attempting to spend their excess real money balances on the goods in various markets. Then the price in each market, $P_t(z)$, ends up rising by the same proportion as the increase in money. The general or average price level, P_t, therefore moves one-to-one with the quantity of money, and the relative price in each market, $P_t(z)/P_t$, does not change. The level of output in each market, $Y_t(z)$, also remains the same. Thus, at this point, we still lack any connection between money and real variables.

IMPERFECT INFORMATION ABOUT MONEY AND THE GENERAL PRICE LEVEL

Now we make a crucial change in the setup to remove some information that individuals have about money and prices. The idea is that people know the prices of things that they recently bought or sold: they know the wage rate for their labor services (at least on the present job), the price of groceries at the local market, the rent on their apartment, and so on. Similarly, producers know a good deal about the costs of labor and other inputs, as well as the price of their own product. Producers and consumers have, however, much poorer knowledge about the prices of objects that they shopped for last year or perhaps have never examined.

We can model these ideas by assuming that sellers and buyers know the local price of goods, $P_t(z)$, but are less sure about the general or average price, P_t. The local goods represent the items that people have dealt with recently and for which they know the current price. The general price applies to other goods, which are potential alternatives to local product but for which people have a less accurate idea of the price.

As before, sellers and buyers in market z respond to their perception of the relative price, $P_t(z)/P_t$. But although they know the local price, $P_t(z)$, they are no longer certain about the general price level, P_t. We therefore have to analyze how people compute expectations of this average price under conditions of incomplete information. We rely on the concept of rational expectations, an idea that we mentioned in Chapter 7. This approach says that if people do not observe something directly, such as the current price level, then they form the best possible estimate of this variable given the information that they possess. In other words, people make efficient use of their limited data, so as not to commit avoidable errors.[5]

Consider the expectations that people have about prices for period t. Assume, for simplicity, that all markets look the same beforehand. That is, before period t, people cannot predict whether the price in market z, $P_t(z)$, will be higher or lower than the average price, P_t. Then, regardless of which market a person chooses to enter, we can focus on expectations of the general price level, P_t. To keep things manageable, pretend that everyone has the same information beforehand and therefore calculates the same expectation, which we denote by P_t^e.

The expectation of the general price level depends on past information and on knowledge about the workings of the economy. We can think of this expectation as incorporating information about the quantity of money and about variables that influence the aggregate real demand

[5] *The basic idea of rational expectations comes from John Muth (1961). For a discussion of applications to macroeconomics, see Robert Lucas (1977).*

for money. People can get useful information about these variables from lagged values of prices and money, from interest rates, and possibly from the government's announcements about monetary and fiscal policy. The expectation, P_t^e, therefore incorporates all of these elements.

CLEARING OF A LOCAL COMMODITY MARKET WHEN INFORMATION IS INCOMPLETE

For a given expectation of the general price level, P_t^e, people compute the **perceived relative price** for market z as $P_t(z)/P_t^e$. We assume that sellers and buyers react to this price ratio just as they did to the actual ratio, $P_t(z)/P_t$, in the model with complete information. Hence, an increase in the perceived relative price, $P_t(z)/P_t^e$, raises the supply of local goods, $Y_t^s(z)$, but lowers the consumer demand, $C_t^d(z)$.

We also continue to assume that a high relative price tends to persist and, therefore, that an increase in the currently perceived relative price, $P_t(z)/P_t^e$, raises the expectation of the relative price for the next period, $[P_{t+1}(z)/P_{t+1}]^e$. The increase in the prospective relative price raises investment demand, $I_t^d(z)$. We assume, as before, that the net effect of an increase in $P_t(z)/P_t^e$ on total demand, $Y_t^d(z)$, is negative.

Figure 19.3 shows the supply and demand in a local market when people do not observe the general price level. We assume a given expected real interest rate, r_t^e, and plot the perceived relative price, $P_t(z)/P_t^e$, on the vertical axis. As before, r_t^e is determined so that the average market clears when the price ratio, $P_t(z)/P_t^e$, equals one. That is, in the typical market, supply equals demand when the local price, $P_t(z)$, equals the expected price elsewhere, P_t^e.

CHANGES IN MONEY WHEN THERE IS INCOMPLETE INFORMATION

Consider again the effects of a once-and-for-all increase in the stock of money, M_t. We assume a surprise increase in money, one that people did not anticipate when they formed their expectation of prices, P_t^e.

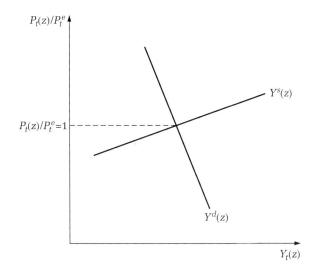

FIGURE 19.3

RESPONSE OF A LOCAL MARKET TO THE PERCEIVED
RELATIVE PRICE

A higher perceived relative price, $P_t(z)/P_t^e$, raises supply and lowers demand. The typical market clears when $P_t(z)/P_t^e = 1$.

Although this expectation was rational, it could not incorporate the effects from unanticipated changes in money.

Suppose, as before, that the local price, $P_t(z)$, rises in the typical market. (We can think, as usual, of people attempting to spend their excess money balances and thereby bidding up prices.) Since the expectation, P_t^e, is given, the rise in $P_t(z)$ implies an increase in $P_t(z)/P_t^e$. In other words, the typical person now thinks that he or she is located in a market in which the relative price is high. This belief must be incorrect, because the average across markets of the local prices, $P_t(z)$, always equals the general price level, P_t. But the surprise increase in money and prices—together with the lack of direct information about either the average price, P_t, or the quantity of money, M_t—means that the typical person underestimates the rise in the general price level. Thus, the typical person overestimates the relative price that he or she faces and reacts by raising goods supplied, $Y_t^s(z)$, and lowering goods demanded for consumption, $C_t^d(z)$. The rise in $P_t(z)/P_t^e$ also implies an increase in $P_{t+1}(z)/P_{t+1}^e$ and therefore an expansion of investment demand, $I_t^d(z)$.

For a given expected real interest rate, r_t^e, the typical market would clear at point A, where $P_t(z)/P_t^e = 1$. But the surprise increase in money and prices means that $P_t(z)/P_t^e > 1$, as shown at point B. Here, the quantity of goods supplied, $Y_t^s(z)$, exceeds the quantity demanded, $Y_t^d(z)$.

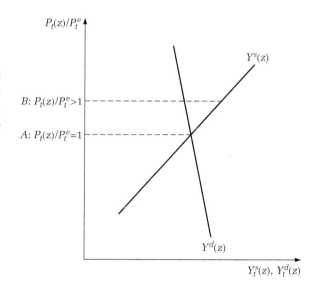

Point A in Figure 19.4 shows the price ratio, $P_t(z)/P_t^e = 1$, that would clear the typical local market. The surprise increase in money means, however, that the price in the typical market, $P_t(z)$, exceeds the expectation, P_t^e, as shown at point B in the figure. At point B, the supply of goods exceeds the demand. Something else therefore has to happen to clear the typical market.

Effects on the Real Interest Rate

Recall that the expected real interest rate, r_t^e, equals the nominal rate, R_t—which everyone observes on the economy-wide credit market—less the expected rate of inflation for the general price level, π_t^e. Thus far, we have not allowed for any effects of the monetary disturbance on r_t^e. But for a given value of r_t^e, Figure 19.4 shows that the supply of goods would exceed the demand in the typical market—in other words, excess supply of goods would apply in the aggregate. This aggregate excess supply will lead to a change in r_t^e.

Consider the results from the perspective of the typical commodity market. In Figure 19.5, the solid lines reproduce the supply and demand

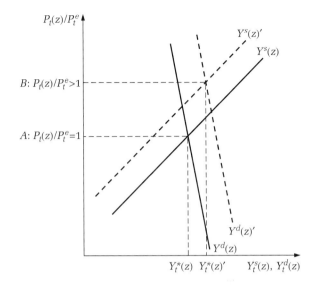

The solid lines for supply and demand come from Figure 19.4. The decline in the expected real interest rate, r_t^e, shifts the demand curve
rightward and the supply curve leftward. Hence, the typical commodity market clears where $P_t(z)/P_t^e > 1$.

curves from Figure 19.4. Note that excess supply of goods prevails along
the line labeled B, where $P_t(z)/P_t^e > 1$. This situation applies in the typical market after a positive monetary shock if the expected real interest
rate, r_t^e, does not change.[6] We therefore see that r_t^e has to decline—the
usual reaction to an economy-wide excess supply of goods—to clear the
typical market.

If r_t^e falls, then the demand curve shifts rightward, and the supply
curve shifts leftward, as shown by the dashed lines in Figure 19.5. Thus,
the fall in r_t^e motivates people in each market to consume and invest
more and to work and produce less. If we shift the curves by the right
amounts—that is, if we use the right amount of decline in r_t^e—then the
dashed lines intersect along the line labeled B. Although people still
perceive a high relative price in the typical market, this reduction in r_t^e
allows the market to clear.

Monetary Effects on Output, Work, and Investment

Figure 19.5 shows that output, $Y_t(z)$, rises in the typical market. The
sign of this change, which is ambiguous, involves several forces. First,

[6] We assume that people in all
commodity markets form the
same expectation, r_t^e. These expectations would actually tend
to diverge because people in different markets—who observe
different local prices—would
have different inflationary expectation, π_t^e. The basic results
would not change, however, if
we brought in this effect.

the high price ratio, $P_t(z)/P_t^e$, increases supply but reduces consumption demand. Second, the increase in the prospective relative price, $[P_{t+1}(z)/P_{t+1}]^e$, stimulates investment demand. Finally, the decrease in the expected real interest rate, r_t^e, boosts investment and consumption demand but discourages supply.

The presumption that output increases in the typical market depends on the positive effect from the prospective relative price, $[P_{t+1}(z)/P_{t+1}]^e$, on investment demand. If this response is large, then a positive monetary shock will raise investment, output, and work effort. Further, since this result applies to the *typical* market, it shows up also in the *aggregates* of investment, output, and work.

Let's review the process by which a surprise increase in money and prices leads to higher work, output, and investment. First, the general rise in prices looks to local suppliers like an increase in their relative price. They therefore work more and increase production, just as they would in response to a true expansion of local demand. In other words, the suppliers confuse the change in the general price level with the type of local disturbance that warrants an expansion of their real activity. (Recall that we considered this type of local disturbance in Figure 19.2.)

Second, since the increase in $P_t(z)/P_t^e$ makes people think that the local market will remain favorable to sellers for a while, people raise their expectations of the future relative price, $[P_{t+1}(z)/P_{t+1}]^e$. The higher value of this prospective relative price stimulates investment.

Finally, since the disturbance causes an excess supply of goods in the typical commodity market, the expected real interest rate, r_t^e, must decline. This response clears the typical market by raising the demand for goods and lowering the supply.

Overall, the expansion of work, output, and investment occurs because the typical household confuses a high general price level for a high relative price in its location. Although households strive to avoid these kinds of mistakes, the available information does not allow them to distinguish all changes in general prices from those in relative prices. Also, households have to weigh their mistaken reactions to changes in general prices against the potential errors from not responding to true shifts in relative prices. In most instances the local price, $P_t(z)$, accurately signals the reward for local production and investment. An overly cautious producer who fails to react to these signals—in order to avoid the mistaken responses to changes in the general price level—will also fail to exploit a variety of true opportunities for profit.

PERSISTING EFFECTS OF MONEY ON REAL VARIABLES

During recessions, variables such as output, employment, and investment tend to be depressed for periods of a year or more. We want to know therefore whether the theory can account for persisting effects of monetary disturbances on real variables. One possibility is that misperceptions about the general price level persist for a long time, such as a year or more. Then any real effects from these misperceptions would also persist. But this idea is implausible. We argued before that households would have incomplete information about prices in other markets, the general price level, and the aggregate quantity of money. But households presumably receive enough information about prices so that they would not make the same mistake in estimating the general price level for very long. Thus, it is unlikely that the persistence in these errors would be as long as the persistence of booms and recessions.

The theory does not require the confusions about prices to persist to explain the persistence in aggregate quantities. We showed, for example, that a positive monetary shock can lead to more investment. Then, perhaps a few months later, investors recognize that they confused an increase in the general price level for an increase in their relative price. But once producers have incurred the initial costs to initiate a project, it may not pay to terminate the project (even if the producers regret the start-up decision). Hence, investment demand may remain high even after the confusion about prices disappears. Moreover, the higher level of investment shows up later as more productive capacity, a change that tends to raise output and employment even after people learn the truth about past money and prices. Through this type of mechanism, a monetary disturbance can have a long-lasting influence on output and employment.

THE NEUTRALITY OF PERCEIVED CHANGES IN MONEY

The analysis in the previous sections applies to surprise changes in money and the general price level. It is important to recognize that the confusion between general and relative prices does not occur if households and firms understand fully the movements in money and prices. To see this point, suppose that everyone accurately anticipates a once-and-for-all increase in the quantity of money between dates $t - 1$ and t. Then the higher value of the money stock, M_t, shows up one-to-one as a higher rational expectation of the general price level, P_t^e. Hence, the increase of the price level in a typical market, $P_t(z)$, no longer represents a shift relative to expectations. Actual and expected prices increase in the same proportion, and the perceived relative price in the typical market, $P_t(z)/P_t^e$, does not change. The quantities supplied and demand in the typical market also remain the same; hence, the quantities of output and work and the real interest rate do not change. Fully understood movements in money and prices are therefore neutral, just as they were in our earlier models.

IMPLICATIONS FOR MONETARY POLICY

If changes in money can have real effects, it is natural to think about a systematic policy of varying the money supply to stabilize the economy. Specifically, economists often advise the Federal Reserve to accelerate money to bring the economy out of a recession. The theory developed in this chapter does not support this view of monetary policy.

We can think of monetary policy as a regular procedure for adjusting the quantity of money, M_t, in relation to the state of the economy. The monetary authority may, for example, expand money more rapidly than usual in response to a recession and hold down the growth rate of money in response to a boom. There is some evidence that the Federal Reserve has pursued this sort of countercyclical monetary policy since World War II.

What does the theory predict for the real effects of this type of policy? Given that the policy is in place, our best guess is that people take it into account when they formulate expectations of prices. If everyone knows that the Fed tends to inflate the economy in response to a recession, then households and firms raise their forecasts of money and prices accordingly. The expectation of prices, P_t^e, therefore incorporates the typical response of the Fed to the observed state of the economy. But this adjustment of expectations means that the Fed can affect money and prices in relation to people's expectations only when it departs from its usual practice. It follows that only the erratic part of the Fed's behavior has real effects. The systematic part of monetary policy—the acceleration of money in response to a recession and the contraction in response to a boom—does not create any confusions between general and relative prices. These kinds of monetary changes are therefore neutral in the model. Economists call this finding the **irrelevance result for systematic monetary policy**.[7]

A great many of the actual fluctuations in money are unpredictable, and the irrelevance result does not apply to these types of monetary movements. But we also cannot think of this erratic behavior as representing useful policy. Sometimes the changes are expansionary and sometimes contractionary but not in a way that systematically improves the workings of the economy.

STAGFLATION

Economists use the term **stagflation** to describe a situation in which inflation is either high or rising during a recession. During the recession of 1974–75, for example, the civilian unemployment rate reached a peak of 9.0% in May 1975, while the annual rate of change of the GDP deflator

[7] *For discussions of this result, see Thomas Sargent and Neil Wallace (1975) and Ben McCallum (1979).*

increased from 4% in 1972 to 9% in 1974–75. Similarly, during the recession of 1979–80, the unemployment rate peaked at 7.8% in July 1980, and the inflation rate rose from 8% in 1978 to 9% in 1980.

Although stagflation is a big problem for analyses based on the Phillips curve, this phenomenon poses no difficulty for the model developed in this chapter. First, there is no relation in the theory between the real variables and the perceived behavior of money and prices. Therefore, the increase in the average growth rates of money and prices from the late 1960s to the early 1980s—an increase that was presumably perceived by everyone—gives no reason to predict low unemployment rates. Second, the oil crises of 1973–74 and 1979–81 constituted supply shocks, disturbances that tend to raise the general price level for a given behavior of the money stock. Thus, we predict in these cases that a burst of inflation would accompany the shortfalls in output.

REAL EFFECTS FROM THE VOLATILITY OF MONEY

Thus far, expectations of prices, P_t^e, have depended only on information available before period t. Now we develop some interesting new results by allowing people to adjust their beliefs based on current information.

Recall that, during period t, producers find that goods sell locally at the price $P_t(z)$. If this price differs from P_t^e, then there are two possibilities. First, some local condition—such as a shift to demand in market z—caused the relative price of goods in this market to be either high or low. Second, the forecast of general prices may be inaccurate. That is, the general price level, P_t, may turn out to be either higher or lower than P_t^e. But by assumption, people cannot check things out directly by immediately sampling lots of prices in other markets or by observing a useful published index of current prices. Because the process of obtaining information is costly, sellers and buyers make do with incomplete knowledge about the prices of alternative goods. The observation of the local price, $P_t(z)$, does, however, convey some information about the current general price level, P_t, and we want to consider the nature of this information.

Suppose first that people can predict the general price level, P_t, with a high degree of accuracy. This situation applies if the monetary authority pursues a policy that usually provides for overall price stability. To carry out such a policy, the authority would have to avoid large random changes in the quantity of money, M_t. In this stable environment, people would not make significant adjustments to their expectations, P_t^e, when they observe the local price, $P_t(z)$. They would be confident that a movement of $P_t(z)$ signaled a change in the relative price, $P_t(z)/P_t$, rather than a movement in P_t. This high level of confidence in the monetary authority means, however, that people get fooled substantially on the rare occasions when monetary surprises are large. Even so, knowing they are right in the great majority of cases, suppliers and demanders will view changes $P_t(z)$ as an indication that $P_t(z)/P_t$ has changed and will therefore make substantial adjustments in their quantities supplied and demand. A surprise increase in money will therefore induce a large increase in output.

In contrast, consider an economy in which money is volatile and the general price level, P_t, often departs substantially from the forecast, P_t^e. In this setting people would be much less confident that a movement in $P_t(z)$ reflected a change in the relative price, $P_t(z)/P_t$. To a significant extent, they would believe that a high value of $P_t(z)$ signaled a higher than expected value of P_t. It follows that the perceived relative price, $P_t(z)/P_t^e$, and, hence, the quantities supplied and demanded would not be very responsive to observed changes in $P_t(z)$. A monetary shock would therefore have only a small effect on real variables.

The general conclusion is that *the greater is the historical volatility of money, the smaller is the real effect of a monetary shock*. This conclusion follows because a greater volatility of money makes people more inclined to associate observed increases in local prices with unexpectedly high general price levels. It is therefore harder for monetary shocks to fool people into thinking that relative prices have changed.

Incomplete Information about Prices and Money: Is It Significant?

A central element in the theory is that people do not observe immediately the general price level or the quantity of money. If people always knew the general level of prices—perhaps because they look regularly at a useful index, such as the CPI or the deflator for the GDP—then they would not confuse shifts in the general price level with changes in relative prices. Suppose, instead, that people observe quickly the quantity of money but not the general price level. Then—at least if they understand the economics taught in this book!—they can figure out the implications of the monetary movements for the general price level. They would therefore not confuse the monetary-induced parts of changes in the general price level with shifts in relative prices. But then the model predicts that the monetary changes would be neutral.

People can, in fact, observe quickly an index of prices (with a one-month lag for the CPI) or measures of monetary aggregates (with a one-week lag for M1 and the monetary base). Most people do not, of course, bother to collect and interpret these types of data. But, presumably, they choose not to do so because the information is of minor value to them.

Consider the usefulness of the available indexes of prices. One reason that they may not be very helpful is that each individual cares about a market basket of goods that differs substantially from the one used in the index. Then, in order to keep well informed about prices, people would have to take detailed samples from a variety of markets. Since this process is costly, people may sometimes make significant errors in their interpretations of observed prices.

A similar argument is that the data on monetary aggregates provide little useful information. Possibly because of seasonal adjustments and the arbitrariness in defining money, the reported measures bear little relation to the concept of money that matters in the theory. This argument leads, however, to a puzzle: the reported figures—on M1 and perhaps on the monetary base—seem to have a positive relation to real economic activity in the post–World War II period. If the data are meaningless, then it is hard to explain this relation. Alternatively, if the reported measures are important, then why would people not bother to observe them?

To put the various points together, it seems reasonable that ignorance about the general price level and the quantity of money can account for small and short-lived confusions about relative prices, because people would find it too costly ↗

to monitor continuously and interpret the behavior of general prices and the quantity of money. But it is unlikely that large or long-lasting confusions would arise. The costs of being misinformed about relative prices—and, therefore, making incorrect decisions about production, work, and investment—seem excessive relative to the costs of gathering the necessary information. Hence, this view suggests that monetary-induced confusions of general for relative prices can account for only small fluctuations in the aggregate economy. We cannot use this line of theory to explain the bulk of business fluctuations.

This conclusion is consistent with our findings about the cyclical characteristics of the principal macroeconomic variables. If monetary shocks were the main driving force behind business fluctuations, then the cyclical properties of some of the variables, such as the general price level, the real interest rate, and labor productivity, would differ substantially from the observed characteristics. We therefore conclude that business fluctuations must result primarily from other kinds of disturbances, such as the shifts to production functions that were stressed in previous chapters.

These propositions receive empirical support from some studies of various countries during the post–World War II period.[8] First, it turns out that monetary disturbances (measured by surprise movements in M1) have a positive relation to real GDP for most countries. As the theory predicts, however, the strength of this relation diminishes as a country's rate of monetary growth becomes less predictable. Countries such as the United States that display relative stability of money turn out to be the ones in which monetary shocks have a strong positive relation to real GDP. For places such as Argentina and Brazil, where monetary growth has fluctuated unpredictably, there is virtually no connection between monetary disturbances and real GDP.

We can also use the theory to explore the relation between monetary volatility and the signaling value of the price system. We already noted that greater fluctuations in money mean that perceived relative prices become less responsive to changes in local prices. This effect means that people make fewer mistakes when the changes in prices reflect surprises

[8] *See Roger Kormendi and Phillip Meguire (1984) and C. L. F. Attfield and N. W. Duck (1983).*

MONEY AND BUSINESS FLUCTUATIONS IN THE MARKET-CLEARING MODEL

743

in money and the general price level. But it implies that people make *more* mistakes when shifts in relative prices occur. More uncertainty about money and the overall price level means that observed prices become less useful as signals of changes in relative prices. Thus, the price system becomes less useful as a mechanism for channeling resources. The economy becomes less responsive to shifts in the composition of tastes and technology, shifts that require resources to move from one place to another.[9] Note especially that changes in the predictability of money are nonneutral. From this standpoint, the best monetary policy is the one that is the most predictable.

IMPLICATIONS OF THE MODEL FOR CYCLICAL FLUCTUATIONS

In previous chapters, such as Chapter 9, we worked out the model's predictions about cyclical behavior under the assumption that business fluctuations were driven by shocks to the production function. Consider now the alternative that the production function is stable and that business fluctuations are driven by monetary shocks. We can then use the analysis from this chapter to work out the implied cyclical characteristics of the principal macroeconomic variables.

Suppose that a value of money above trend corresponds to unexpectedly high levels of money (in the recent past) and vice versa. The model then predicts that an excess of money from its trend would lead to high levels of output, work effort, and investment (all relative to their trends). In other words, the theory predicts that money, labor input, and investment would be procyclical. These predictions accord with observed behavior in the United States.

The theory has, however, other predictions that are less satisfactory. A monetary shock leads, in the theory, to an increase in the general price level (relative to its trend) and to a fall in the expected real interest rate. The model therefore predicts that the price level would be procyclical and that the expected real interest rate would be countercyclical. These predictions conflict with the U.S. data (see Chapters 1 and 9).

[9] *For discussions of these types of adverse consequences of monetary uncertainty, see Friedrich Hayek (1945) and Henry Simons (1948).*

Since the production function was assumed to be stable and the capital stock cannot change greatly in the short run, the increase in labor input implies that the marginal and average products of labor would decline. The theory therefore predicts that labor productivity (output per worker-hour) and the real wage rate (which equals the marginal product of labor) would be low when the quantities of output and labor input were high. That is, labor productivity and the real wage rate would be countercyclical. These predictions conflict with the U.S. data (see Chapters 1 and 6).

These departures between theory and fact indicate that we cannot use the model, driven mainly by monetary shocks, to explain many of the features of business fluctuations. We can, however, fit the facts better if we reintroduce the shifts to the production function that we considered before. If business fluctuations are driven mainly by disturbances that can be modeled as shifts to the production function, then it is possible that monetary disturbances would also play a secondary role. The real effects of these monetary shocks could explain why money was procyclical. The observed cyclical behavior of the price level, real interest rate, labor productivity, and the real wage rate would also fit the theory if shocks to the production function were typically more important than monetary disturbances.[10]

RULES VERSUS DISCRETION

An exciting recent development in macroeconomics is the application of models of strategic behavior to the study of government policy. The initial inspiration for these ideas came from the distinction between anticipated and unanticipated monetary and price changes in the kinds of models that we have explored in this chapter. If only unanticipated money and unexpected changes in the price level matter for real variables, then policymakers who wish to affect real variables have an incentive to surprise people. But if individuals form expectations

[10] *We can also explain in this way the procyclical behavior of consumption. If only monetary shocks occur, then it is hard to explain why consumption and work effort move cyclically in the same direction.*

rationally, it is difficult to fool people systematically.[11] The resolution of these conflicting objectives involves the strategic interplay between the policymakers and the individuals in the economy. The nature of this interaction can be illustrated by working through a simple example about monetary policy.

Suppose that the monetary authority can use its instruments to achieve any desired rate of inflation, π. It would be more realistic to assume some error between the desired and actual inflation rate, but that change would not affect the basic results. The policymaker wants to reduce unemployment (or raise employment and output) but can do so only by creating a positive amount of unexpected inflation, $\pi - \pi^e$. This surprise inflation would correspond to a positive amount of unanticipated money growth. For a given expected rate of inflation, π^e, the unemployment rate decreases with π. (This result holds in the expectational Phillips curve shown in Figure 18.2 and in the model worked out earlier in this chapter.)

The monetary authority is assumed not to like inflation for its own sake; for given unemployment, the policymaker prefers an inflation rate of zero. Hence, for given π^e, an increase in π above zero entails a trade-off between the benefits of lower unemployment (or higher output) and the costs of higher inflation. The resolution of this trade-off determines the inflation rate, denoted by $\hat{\pi}$, that the policymaker selects.

The policymaker's selected inflation rate, $\hat{\pi}$, would generally depend on people's expected inflation rate, π^e. Write this dependence as the function, ψ (the Greek letter *psi*), that is,

$$\hat{\pi} = \psi(\pi^e) \tag{19.5}$$
$$(+)$$

If π^e is higher, then the monetary authority would have to set a correspondingly higher value of π to maintain the surprise, $\pi - \pi^e$. For this reason, the policymaker's choice, $\hat{\pi}$, tends to increase with π^e, as shown in equation (19.5). The graph of $\hat{\pi} = \psi(\pi^e)$ in Figure 19.6 makes two additional assumptions. First, $\pi > 0$ holds if $\pi^e = 0$; that is, the policymaker finds it worthwhile to inflate if people expect zero inflation.

[11] *Abraham Lincoln had a somewhat different view: "You may fool all of the people some of the time; you can even fool some of the people all of the time" (quoted in Alexander Mc-Clure, 1901, p. 124).*

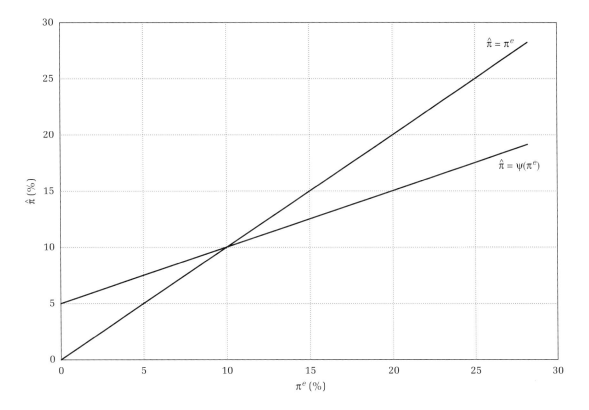

FIGURE 19.6

INFLATION IN A DISCRETIONARY REGIME

The line with the flatter slope shows the policymaker's choice of inflation rate, $\hat{\pi}$, as a function of the expected rate of inflation, π^e. The 45-degree line shows points where $\hat{\pi}$ equals π^e.

Second, the slope of the function, $\psi(\pi^e)$, is flatter than that of a 45-degree line—in other words, an increase in π^e raises $\hat{\pi}$ by less than one-to-one.[12]

Consider how an individual would form a rational expectation of inflation in this model. Suppose that each person knows everyone else's expectation, π^e, and also knows what the government is trying to do: set $\pi = \hat{\pi}$ to achieve a desired trade-off between unemployment and inflation. Then each individual can figure out the policymaker's choice, $\hat{\pi}$, and compute the rational expectation, $\pi^e = \hat{\pi}$. Thus, rational formation of expectations corresponds to the 45-degree line shown in Figure 19.6.

[12] *It is possible to show that this property holds if the cost attached at the margin to more inflation rises as the inflation rate increases.*

The intersection of the two lines in the figure determines the equilibrium inflation rate, $\pi^* = (\pi^e)^*$. This value satisfies two conditions: first, if $\pi^e = \pi^*$, then the policymaker—who is trading off the benefits of lower unemployment against the costs of higher inflation for a given value of π^e—will select the value $\hat{\pi} = \pi^*$, because this point lies on the line, $\hat{\pi} = \Psi(\pi^e)$. Second, the expectation, $\pi^e = \pi^*$, is rational because it is the best possible forecast of inflation. (In this model—but not in some extended versions—the forecast error is zero; that is, people have **perfect foresight**.)

We can clarify the nature of the results by thinking about some (made-up) numbers. Conjecture that $\pi^e = 0$. Facing this belief, the policymaker finds that the optimal choice for $\hat{\pi}$ is, say, 5%. But any individual can figure out, by knowing what the government is up to, that the policymaker would pick 5% inflation if everyone expected zero inflation. More generally, everyone knows that the government will engineer high inflation if people expect low inflation. Hence, $\pi^e = 0$ is an irrational expectation, and each individual would switch to $\pi^e = 5\%$.

If everyone expects 5% inflation, then the government would set $\hat{\pi}$ to be, say, 7%. Everyone would therefore switch to $\pi^e = 7\%$, an expectation that motivates the government to pick $\hat{\pi} = 8\%$, and so on. In the equilibrium, perhaps at 10% inflation, the government is motivated to pick $\hat{\pi} = \psi(10\%) = 10\%$, and people also expect inflation to be 10%. This result applies when the two lines intersect in Figure 19.6. At this point the government attaches such a high cost to additional inflation that it is not motivated to surprise people by choosing a still higher inflation rate. Hence, people regard 10% inflation as credible.

The unpleasant aspect of the equilibrium is that it entails a high inflation rate, $\pi = \pi^*$ in Figure 19.6, without any benefits from *surprisingly* high inflation. Since π^e is correspondingly high, the inflation surprise, $\pi - \pi^e$, is zero. Employment and output therefore receive no stimulus.

The economy would perform better with zero actual and expected inflation because the costs associated with inflation would be lower. In that case the inflation surprise, $\pi - \pi^e$, is again zero, but at least the inflation rate is low. It is clear, however, from Figure 19.6 that $\pi = \pi^e = 0$

is not an equilibrium in this model. If $\pi^e = 0$, then the policymaker would pick $\hat{\pi} > 0$, and—since people know that the policymaker would behave this way—$\pi^e = 0$ is inconsistent with rational expectations.

The high inflation result, $\pi = \pi^e = \pi^* > 0$, is often referred to as the outcome under **discretionary policy**. This outcome results if the policymaker can make no commitments or binding promises about future actions. In contrast, a policymaker who can make such commitments is thought of as operating subject to a **policy rule**. One simple form of rule specifies a constant rate of monetary growth or a constant rate of inflation (so-called **constant-growth-rate rules**). In the present setting, in which inflation is costly, the best thing that the monetary authority could do is to commit to zero inflation. (In other models the optimal rule would be more complicated.) With this commitment, $\pi = \pi^e = 0$ would be attainable and also superior to the discretionary result, $\pi = \pi^e > 0$.

Figure 19.6 illustrates the tension in a rule with low inflation. At $\pi^e = 0$, the policymaker really wants to renege on commitments and set $\pi = \hat{\pi} > 0$.[13] If this repudiation is feasible, then individuals presumably would have known it in advance and would not have maintained expectations of zero inflation. Then the equilibrium tends toward the discretionary one worked out before in Figure 19.6. To avoid this outcome, it is crucial that commitments be well enforced. They have to be strong enough so that policymakers cannot overturn them later even if they want to. To the extent that "sovereign power" makes such commitments infeasible, the outcomes tend to look more like the high inflation under discretion and less like the low inflation under rules.

An important point is that the high inflation result under discretion can arise even if the policymaker is well meaning and competent. The force that drives the result is the benefit from the inflation surprise. In the example just considered, this benefit arises, first, if an increase in surprise inflation reduces unemployment and, second, if the decrease in unemployment is desirable. The latter property holds if the private economy tends to generate unemployment rates that are too high on average. Two possible reasons for this market failure are the existence of income taxes and the availability of unemployment-insurance benefits.

[13] *The outcome where $\pi > \pi^e = 0$ is preferred to the rules solution, $\pi = \pi^e = 0$, as well as to the discretionary result, $\pi = \pi^e > 0$. However, $\pi > \pi^e$ is inconsistent with rational expectations in this model. The policymaker cannot systematically set inflation above expectations because it is infeasible to fool people consistently.*

(The Keynesian model, discussed in the next chapter, suggests that price or wage stickiness may be another reason that unemployment might be too high on average.)

Similar results about policy come up in many areas in which the policymaker would benefit by surprising people after the fact. Debtor countries may, for example, surprise creditors by defaulting on foreign debts, governments may surprise owners of capital by assessing high tax rates on existing capital (so-called *capital levies*), tax collectors may surprise people by announcing tax amnesties, governments may fail to honor patents after inventions have been made, and so on. In all of these areas, the surprise is tempting after the fact. But if people understand the government's incentives, then expectations before the fact will take account of the likelihood of subsequent policy actions. The equilibria then have undesirable properties: excessive inflation, too little foreign borrowing, low investment, poor tax compliance, and a low volume of inventions. To avoid these outcomes, governments would like to promise that they will resist the temptation to surprise people later. But the credibility of these commitments is a major problem.

There has been a lot of research on the applications of strategic behavior to government policy. A pioneering paper was written by Finn Kydland and Ed Prescott (1977). More recent developments, especially in applications to macroeconomics and monetary policy, are surveyed by Ken Rogoff (1989).

SUMMARY

A recently developed line of macroeconomic theory attempts to explain the role of money in business fluctuations. This approach retains the framework of market clearing and rational behavior but introduces incomplete information about prices to explain some real effects from monetary disturbances. Although people form expectations rationally, the incomplete information means that surprise increases in money and the general price level make producers in local markets think that the relative price of their output has risen. Monetary injections can thereby induce expansions in the quantities of production, work, and investment.

Perceived changes in money and the general price level do not lead to confusions about relative prices. The perceived parts of monetary changes are therefore still neutral. This result is consistent with the absence of a long-term relation of real variables to either monetary growth or inflation.

The systematic part of monetary policy causes no confusions about relative prices. The theory predicts accordingly that this part of policy has no significance for real variables. An increase in monetary uncertainty is nonneutral, however, because it alters the information that people receive by observing local prices. Since people recognize that monetary shocks are often large, the real variables become less sensitive to monetary disturbances. But because the observed prices become less useful as allocative signals, the allocation of resources becomes less efficient. Specifically, the economy becomes less responsive to variations in the composition of tastes and technology. Thus, the model's main lesson is that monetary policy should be predictable rather than erratic.

The theory is consistent with the procyclical behavior of money, labor input, and investment, but is inconsistent with the cyclical properties of the price level, the expected real interest rate, labor productivity, and the real wage rate. Also, because the costs of obtaining information about money and prices are not very large, the theory cannot plausibly explain major business contractions. The theory may, however, serve as a useful complement to real business-cycle models in which fluctuations are driven mainly by shocks to the production function.

IMPORTANT TERMS AND CONCEPTS

constant-growth-rate rule A rule for monetary policy in which a specified monetary aggregate grows at a constant rate.

discretionary policy A setup in which government policy is not restricted by prior commitments.

irrelevance result for systematic monetary policy The theoretical finding that a policy of changing the quantity of money in response to the state of the economy is predictable and therefore powerless to affect the economy.

perceived relative price The ratio of the observed price in a local market to the perceived general price level.

perfect foresight A situation in which expectations of inflation or of other variables are accurate, so that there are no forecast errors.

policy rule A rule or commitment for governmental actions with regard to money or other variables.

stagflation A situation in which a recession is accompanied by high and rising inflation.

QUESTIONS AND PROBLEMS

MAINLY FOR REVIEW

19.1 Explain why it is reasonable to assume that individuals have imperfect information about the general price level. What are the costs of collecting information about prices?

19.2 Explain what a relative price is. Is the real wage rate an example of a relative price? Show how a proportional increase in $P_t(z)$ and P_t^e leaves buyers and sellers unaffected.

19.3 What are the factors that might cause the relative price in a market to remain high for many periods of time? What are the factors that cause changes in the relative price to be offset in later periods? (Consider in your answer the changes in the capital stock and in the numbers of buyers and sellers.)

19.4 Can there be unexpected changes in the quantity of money when expectations are rational? If so, does a policymaker have the option of counteracting business cycles through surprise increases in money?

19.5 When expectations are rational, any errors made in estimating the price level will not persist. How then can we explain persistent deviations of aggregate output from trend?

PROBLEMS FOR DISCUSSION

19.6 Investment Demand in a Local Market

a. Suppose that producers in market z buy capital at the price P_t. What is the condition that determines investment demand if old capital sells next period at the price P_{t+1}?

b. What is the condition for investment demand if producers in market z buy capital locally at the price $P_t(z)$? How does the result depend on whether old capital sells the next period at price $P_{t+1}(z)$ or P_{t+1}?

19.7 Changes in the Predictability of Money

Suppose that the fluctuations of money become less predictable from year to year. What happens to the following:

a. The responsiveness of the perceived relative price, $P_t(z)/P_t$, to the observed local price, $P_t(z)$?

b. The effect of a given size monetary disturbance on output?

c. The allocation of resources?

19.8 Money and the Dispersion of Relative Prices (optional)

The local price, $P_t(z)$, differs across locations because each market experiences local shocks to supply and demand. (Think here of changes in the composition of tastes and technology.) Thus, the model generates a dispersion of relative prices across markets at each point in time. Suppose, as in problem 19.7, that the fluctuations in money become less predictable from year to year. Then what happens to the dispersion of relative prices across markets at a point in time?

(There is evidence that this effect is important during extreme inflations, such as the German hyperinflation, but not for the U.S. experience. See Zvi Hercowitz, 1982. For a survey of the related literature on price dispersion, see Alex Cukierman, 1983.)

19.9 Monetary Effects on Consumption (optional)

In the text we noted some shortcomings of the market-clearing model with incomplete information on prices. Here, we explore another problem, which concerns the behavior of consumption.

We argued that a positive monetary shock could increase output, labor input, and investment. Suppose, in fact, that work effort increases, so that leisure declines.

a. What must be the effect on consumption? (*Hint*: Does the monetary shock alter the terms on which people can substitute today's leisure for today's consumption?)

b. Would the results change if the monetary disturbance raised perceived wealth?

c. How do the theoretical results about consumption conform with the data on U.S. recessions?

19.10 Monetary Effects on Real Wage Rates (optional)

Another problem with the theory concerns the behavior of real wage rates. We explore this problem here.

Suppose that we allow each locality to have a labor market, on which the wage rate is $w_t(z)$. How would a surprise increase in money affect the real wage rate, $w_t(z)/P_t(z)$, in the typical market? (See footnote 2 for a suggestion on how to proceed.) How does the result compare with empirical evidence on the cyclical behavior of the real wage rate?

19.11 Revisions of the Monetary Data

a. Suppose that people observe the monetary base as it is reported from week to week. Then what does the theory predict about the effects of changes in base money on real variables?

b. The Federal Reserve often revises its data on money—especially M1—several months after the initial reports. (Mostly, these revisions arise because the Fed has to estimate the monthly figures on checkable deposits for some banks and other financial institutions.) What does the theory say about the economic effects of these revisions in the monetary figures? (Empirically, the revisions bear no relation to real economic activity.)

19.12 The Effects of Anticipated Policy

a. What is the irrelevance result for systematic monetary policy?

b. Does the result mean that the unpredictable parts of money do not matter?

c. Does the result mean that the systematic parts of all government policies are irrelevant? Consider, as examples, the following:

i. The unemployment-insurance program.

ii. A policy of raising government purchases during a recession.

iii. A policy of cutting income-tax rates during a recession.

19.13 The Fed's Information and Monetary Policy

Suppose that the Fed has a regular policy of accelerating money during a recession.

a. Why does the theory say that this policy does not matter?

b. If the Fed observes the recession before others do, then does the policy still not matter?

c. Suppose that the Fed knows no more about recessions than anyone else does. But the Fed also knows that real activity expands when monetary growth is surprisingly high. Thus, when the economy is in a recession, the Fed attempts to expand money by more than the amount people expect. What problems arise here? (*Hint*: Suppose that people understand that the Fed is pursuing this type of policy. What then is the rational expectation of monetary growth and inflation?)

19.14 Rules versus Discretion (optional)

Assume that the monetary authority's preferred inflation rate is zero, but the authority also wants to reduce unemployment by making inflation surprisingly high.

a. Show how the equilibrium inflation rate can be high. Is the rate surprisingly high? Does the result depend on the authority's having the "wrong" objective or on being incompetent?

b. Can the results improve if the policymaker has the power to bind himself or herself in advance to a specified inflation rate? If so, explain why this constraint (or rule) can improve matters.

c. Do you think that the policymaker's reputation may be a satisfactory substitute for a formal rule that prescribes future policies?

d. Can you think of some reasons, aside from possibly reducing unemployment, that a policymaker might like surprisingly high inflation?

The Keynesian Theory of Business Fluctuations

T he Keynesian theory was developed to understand the tendency of private enterprise economies to experience fluctuations in aggregate business activity. More specifically, Keynes's (1935) analysis sought to explain and suggest policy remedies for the prolonged depressions that occurred in the United States during the 1930s and in the United Kingdom during the 1920s and 1930s.

The Keynesian theory focuses on the process by which private markets match up suppliers and demanders. Notably, the theory assumes that prices on some markets do not adjust perfectly to ensure continual balance between the quantities supplied and demanded. Hence, unlike our previous models, some markets do not always clear. (The imbalance between supply and demand is often referred to as "disequilibrium," but we shall avoid that ambiguous term.) Because of the absence of general market clearing, output and employment typically end up below the efficient amounts. Although everyone could be made better off by an expansion of economic activity, the private market sometimes fails to generate this higher level of activity.

Keynesian models assume that there are constraints on the flexibility of some prices: the nominal wage rate or the dollar price of commodities responds only sluggishly to changes in market conditions. In extreme cases, the wage rate or price level is rigid, or at least fully determined from the past. Then current market forces have no influence on these prices. But economists' willingness to accept this type of assumption as reasonable has diminished. We shall therefore also consider the possibilities for introducing some flexibility of prices into the Keynesian model.

A SIMPLE KEYNESIAN MODEL

Keynes's analysis and some subsequent treatments[1] focused on "sticky" nominal wage rates and the resultant lack of balance between labor supply and demand. Prices for commodities were sometimes assumed to be perfectly flexible (leading to the so-called **complete Keynesian model**) but were more often treated also as sticky. In our framework, we can generate the basic Keynesian results without explicitly considering a separate labor market. Here, we treat as sticky the dollar price, P_t, for goods and services exchanged on the commodity market. (We return now to the case of an economy-wide market for goods and also assume a closed economy.) We should stress that the neglect of the labor market is purely a simplification. The same sorts of conclusions emerge if we choose instead to examine this market and postulate a sticky nominal wage rate.

Some early analyses assumed that prices were rigid. This assumption turns out to be unnecessary because the Keynesian framework can accommodate nonzero inflation rates. The crucial feature is not completely fixed prices but rather the failure of prices to clear all markets instantly. It is convenient, however, to begin with a model in which the

[1] *See Don Patinkin (1956, Chap. 13) and Robert Barro and Herschel Grossman (1976).*

price level is fixed. After we develop this model, we can allow for a nonzero inflation rate.

Start by writing down the standard conditions for general market clearing. For the commodity market, the condition for period t is

$$Y^s(\underset{(+)}{r_t}, \underset{(+)}{G_t}, \ldots) = C^d(\underset{(-)}{r_t}, \underset{(-)}{G_t}, \ldots) + I^d(\underset{(-)}{r_t}, \ldots) + G_t \qquad \textbf{(20.1)}$$

Recall that a higher quantity of government consumption, G_t, means a larger amount of goods supplied (because public services are productive) but a smaller amount of consumer goods demanded. We assume lump-sum taxes, although an income tax could also be considered. Equation (20.1) takes as given the stock of capital, K_{t-1}, and the characteristics of the production function.

Next we have the condition that money be willingly held:

$$M_t = P_t \cdot \Phi(\underset{(+)}{Y_t}, \underset{(-)}{r_t}, \ldots) \qquad \textbf{(20.2)}$$

where M_t is the nominal quantity of money for period t. As usual, the aggregate real demand for money depends positively on output, Y_t, and negatively on the interest rate, r_t. We enter the real interest rate, r_t, because with a fixed price level—and, hence, zero inflation—the nominal interest rate equals the real rate.

Equations (20.1) and (20.2) determine the general-market-clearing values of the interest rate, r_t^*, and the price level, P_t^*. We denote the associated general-market-clearing level of output by Y_t^*.

The departure for Keynesian analysis is that the fixed price level, P_t, differs from the general-market-clearing value, P_t^*. The standard Keynesian results emerge when the price level is excessive; that is, $P_t > P_t^*$. In this situation it will generally be impossible for the economy to attain full market clearing, as specified in equations (20.1) and (20.2). Consequently, we have to search for some concept other than supply equals demand to determine the interest rate and the level of output.

Think of starting from a position of general market clearing and then arbitrarily raising the price level above its market-clearing value. In this case, equation (20.2) can no longer hold at the general-market-clearing values of output, Y_t^*, and the interest rate, r_t^*. The excessive price level means that the quantity of money, M_t, would fall short of the aggregate quantity demanded. We can think of individuals as attempting to replenish their money balances, partly by selling bonds and partly by reducing consumer demand and leisure. The first channel suggests upward pressure on the interest rate. Since a higher interest rate raises Y_t^s and lowers $C_t^d + I_t^d$, an excess supply of commodities results. The second channel—whereby consumer demand and leisure decline—reinforces this effect. Thus, the excessive price level leads to an excess supply of goods.

THE RATIONING OF SALES

How does the commodity market operate under conditions of excess supply? That is, what happens when, at the going price P_t, the total of offers to sell goods exceeds the overall willingness to buy? Normally, economists would predict a decline in the price level, but that mechanism is ruled out by assumption. We therefore have to study the commodity market when excess supply prevails but the price level cannot fall.

Some type of rationing rule must allocate sales when there is an imbalance between the quantities supplied and demanded. The usual mechanism assumes two properties. First, no supplier or demander can be forced to sell or buy more than he or she desires, a condition that follows from the principle of *voluntary exchange*. Second, trade proceeds as long as some seller and some buyer are both made better off; that is, the market ensures the execution of all mutually advantageous exchanges, given that the fixed price P_t applies to all trades. The first condition means that the total quantity of goods sold, Y_t, cannot exceed the smaller of aggregate supply and demand; otherwise, some involuntary sales or purchases would occur. The second condition guarantees that the amount sold is at least as great as the minimum of aggregate supply and demand; if not, some mutually advantageous trades at price P_t would be missed. Thus, the combination of the two properties ensures that output is determined by the **short side** of the market, as expressed by the condition

$$Y_t = \min(Y_t^s, Y_t^d) \tag{20.3}$$

where min denotes the minimum of the variables in the parentheses.

Note that we deal here with the rationing of sales on the commodity market. In a more general Keynesian framework, we would include also the rationing of jobs—that is, sales of labor services—on a separate labor market. The people who seek jobs but cannot find them are considered to be **involuntarily unemployed**.

Under conditions of excess supply—$Y_t^s > Y_t^d$—output is determined by aggregate demand, Y_t^d, which defines the short side of the commodity market. The typical demander therefore experiences no difficulty in finding goods to purchase from the eager suppliers. However, the representative supplier faces an insufficiency of buyers for the products that he or she offers for sale at the price P_t.[2] Thus, we have to reconsider households' decisions in the presence of this constraint. These modifications play an essential role in Keynesian analysis.

In the standard model of a competitive market, individual sellers and buyers are able to transact any amount desired at the going price. But this condition cannot hold for all suppliers when an excess supply of goods prevails. Here, we want to specify the constraint that confronts an individual supplier of goods. We assume that the total quantity of real sales available, Y_t, is somehow apportioned by a nonprice mechanism among the sellers, who offer the larger quantity, Y_t^s. In other words, some kind of rationing process assigns each producer the quantity of real sales, y_t. Notice that we consider a ration on sales rather than on purchases. A ration on purchases would apply if goods were in excess demand.

[2] *In a disaggregated setup, excess supply could appear in some markets and excess demand in others. The standard Keynesian model applies when the great majority of markets experience excess supply.*

We assume that each producer regards his or her real sales limit, y_t, as a given, in the same way that they take as given the price level, P_t, and the interest rate, r_t. We do not allow an individual to take any actions that would influence the size of the ration. We exclude, for example, such possibilities as greater search for buyers, black-market activities that could involve price cutting, overstatement of the true sales offers to secure a larger individual ration,[3] and so on. Basically, the allowance for these features would amount to relaxing the constraint of the fixed price, P_t.

THE CHOICE OF WORK EFFORT

The production function implies

$$y_t = f(k_{t-1},\ l_t,\ G_t) \qquad\qquad (20.4)$$
$$(+)\ \ (+)\ (+)$$

We assume that the ration is an effective constraint on sales, in the sense that $y_t < y_t^s$ applies for the typical producer.[4] The level of output, y_t, is then a given to the producer rather than something that he or she can choose.

Given the quantity of capital, k_{t-1}, and the level of government consumption, G_t, the amount of work, l_t, is the minimum amount necessary to produce the assigned level of output, y_t. The production function from equation (20.4) therefore determines l_t for given values of y_t, k_{t-1}, and G_t. We can write the quantity of work as the function

$$l_t = l(y_t,\ k_{t-1},\ G_t) \qquad\qquad (20.5)$$
$$(+)\ \ (-)\ \ \ (-)$$

For given values of the other inputs, l_t varies directly with y_t, as shown by the graph of the production function in Figure 20.1. For any value of y_t on the vertical axis, we can read off l_t on the horizontal. Note that more output means more labor input. With a labor market included, more

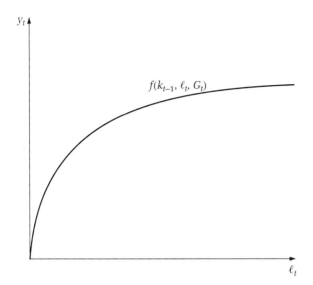

$f(k_{t-1}, \ell_t, G_t)$

y_t

ℓ_t

FIGURE 20.1

DETERMINATION OF LABOR INPUT

The graph of the production function shows the effect on output of more labor input, given the quantities of capital and government consumption. For a given level of output on the vertical axis, the graph determines the quantity of work on the horizontal. Notice that more output means more labor input.

work also means less involuntary unemployment. Increases in either of the other inputs, k_{t-1} and G_t, mean that less work is needed to produce a given amount of output; hence, l_t declines in equation (20.5).

In the model without sales constraints, households set the level of work to equate the marginal product of labor to the value placed on an extra unit of leisure time. But an effective restraint on sales means that work effort is smaller than otherwise. Because of diminishing marginal productivity, labor's marginal product now exceeds the value placed on an extra unit of leisure. Households would like to work and produce more, if only the goods could be sold at the going price. But the constraint on sales prevents the expansion of work and production. We can also say that the constraint on sales means that the economy operates inefficiently. Everyone could be made better off if work and production were higher, as they would be if all markets cleared. But in the Keynesian model, where the commodity market (and the labor market) do not clear, these efficient adjustments are assumed not to occur.

THE KEYNESIAN CONSUMPTION FUNCTION

The restraint on sales means that households receive less real income than they would otherwise. In our model, where the households are also the producers, each household's current real receipts from the commodity market equal the real sales ration, y_t. If prospective real sales equal the current value, then variations in y_t have a one-to-one effect on future real incomes. The effect of y_t on consumption demand would then be roughly one-to-one. If the constraint on sales is temporary, then the effect of y_t on consumption demand would be smaller.

In the more realistic case in which workers are employed by firms, an imposed limit on sales implies that firms have lower employment than otherwise. In this setting, the reduction in households' income involves partly less wages and partly less profits (since some households own the businesses). These shifts in income lead to adjustments in consumption demand, as in the simpler model in which firms and households are not distinguished.

The main point is that an increase in current output, y_t, has a positive effect on consumer demand. Hence, the consumption function, now denoted by $\hat{c}^d$, takes the form

$$c_t^d = \hat{c}^d(\underset{(+)}{y_t},\ \underset{(-)}{r_t},\ \ldots) \tag{20.6}$$

Notice that the interest rate, r_t, still has a negative intertemporal-substitution effect on current consumer demand.

The expression in equation (20.6) is called the **Keynesian consumption function**. The distinctive feature of this function is the presence of the quantity of real sales or real income, y_t. In our previous analysis, households chose consumption by considering wealth effects, the real interest rate, the possibilities for substituting between consumption and leisure, and the nature of their preferences. But now there is a separate effect from the given level of real sales in the commodity market. Anything that raises the quantity of real sales and, hence, real income, y_t, spills over to increase consumption demand.

Another argument that economists sometimes use to derive the Keynesian consumption function concerns the credit market. Up to now we have assumed that this market allows households to borrow or lend any amount that they desire at the going interest rate, r_t. An alternative view is that households cannot borrow readily unless they have good collateral, such as a house, car, or business, to secure the loan. In particular, because of the costs of collection and customer evaluation, households cannot usually borrow based solely on a promise to repay out of future labor income. Economists describe as **liquidity constrained** a person who would like to borrow at the going interest rate to raise current consumption but cannot obtain a loan (at a "reasonable" interest rate). People in this situation would alter their consumption demand, c_t^d, virtually one-to-one in response to changes in their current income, y_t. Therefore, this viewpoint can also explain why the variable y_t appears on the right side of equation (20.6) for some consumers. We shall try to evaluate the importance of liquidity constraints later on.

DETERMINATION OF OUTPUT IN THE KEYNESIAN MODEL

Putting together the results thus far, we can write the level of aggregate demand in the form

$$Y_t^d = \hat{C}^d(\underset{(+)}{Y_t}, \underset{(-)}{r_t}, \ldots) + I^d(\underset{(-)}{r_l}, \ldots) + G_t$$

where $\hat{C}^d$ is an aggregate version of the Keynesian consumption function, and I^d is the investment demand function, which we have studied previously. Recall that the price level exceeds its general-market-clearing value—$P_t > P_t^*$—and goods are therefore in excess supply. Output is demand determined in this situation, as follows:

$$Y_t = Y_t^d = \hat{C}^d(Y_t, r_t, \dots) + I^d(r_t, \dots) + G_t \qquad \textbf{(20.7)}$$
$$\phantom{Y_t = Y_t^d = \hat{C}^d(}{\scriptstyle(+)}\ {\scriptstyle(-)}{\scriptstyle(-)}$$

Equation (20.7) is the key relation in the Keynesian model. It says that output, Y_t, equals aggregate demand, Y_t^d. But the tricky aspect is that the consumption part of aggregate demand is itself a function of output. Thus, equation (20.7) says that the level of output (and, hence, income), Y_t, determines a level of demand, Y_t^d, that is, in turn, equal to output.

An important element in the determination of output is the responsiveness of aggregate consumer demand to variations in output, that is, the aggregate marginal propensity to consume out of changes in current real income, Y_t. Typically, this marginal propensity is between zero and one, with the value approximating one when people view a change in output as permanent. We denote the marginal propensity to consume by ν (the Greek letter *nu*).

Consider an extreme version of the Keynesian model in which the interest rate, r_t, as well as the price level, P_t, is fixed. Later on, we shall allow r_t to be flexible. Figure 20.2, which is called the **Keynesian-cross diagram**, shows how equation (20.7) determines the level of output for a given r_t. The line labeled Y_t^d shows the dependence of aggregate demand on the level of output, Y_t. Note that I_t^d and G_t in equation (20.7) do not depend on Y_t. The slope of the Y_t^d line therefore reflects only the positive effect of Y_t on C_t^d. The slope of the line equals the marginal propensity to consume, ν, which is positive but less than one. (We show Y_t^d as a straight line only for convenience.)

The 45-degree line in Figure 20.2 indicates positions for which output, Y_t, equals the level of demand, Y_t^d. Equation (20.7) therefore holds when the aggregate demand curve intersects the 45-degree line. We denote the level of output at this intersection by $\hat{Y}_t$. The Keynesian model

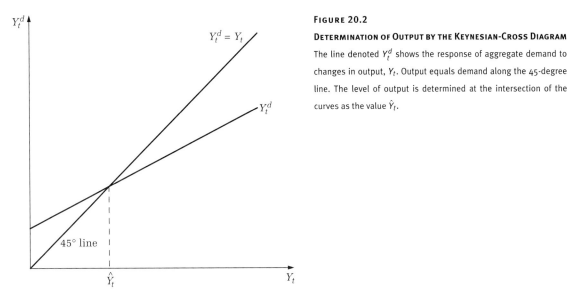

FIGURE 20.2

DETERMINATION OF OUTPUT BY THE KEYNESIAN-CROSS DIAGRAM

The line denoted Y_t^d shows the response of aggregate demand to changes in output, Y_t. Output equals demand along the 45-degree line. The level of output is determined at the intersection of the curves as the value $\hat{Y}_t$.

with a given interest rate (and price level) predicts that the economy's output will be this quantity $\hat{Y}_t$.

The Multiplier

To illustrate the determination of output, consider an increase in aggregate demand, Y_t^d. This increase could apply to either consumption demand or investment demand. The Keynesian model usually focuses, however, on shifts to investment demand that reflect changing beliefs about the marginal product of capital.[5]

The increase in aggregate demand leads to an increase in output, Y_t. (Recall that, with excess supply of goods, output is demand determined.) The increase in output means more real income and, hence, a *further* increase in aggregate demand. This change leads to another rise in output and, thereby, to more demand, and so on. Because each successive increase in output is smaller than the one before, the process does not lead to an infinite expansion of output. Rather, the ultimate rise in output

[5] *Keynes attributed a large part of these disturbances to* animal spirits, *by which he meant spontaneous shifts in optimism or pessimism. These shifts caused businesses to alter their expectations for the profitability of investment. See Keynes (1935, Chap. 12).*

FIGURE 20.3

THE MULTIPLIER

Aggregate demand increases by the amount *A*. The figure shows that the response of output, $\Delta\hat{Y}$, exceeds the initial expansion of demand. The geometry implies that $(\Delta\hat{Y} - A)/\Delta\hat{Y} = v$, so that $\Delta\hat{Y} = A/(1 - v)$. The term $1/(1 - v)$ is the multiplier.

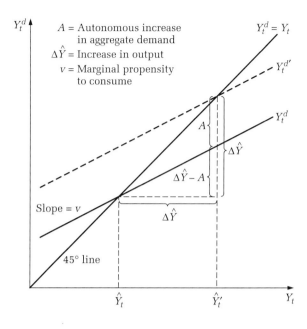

is a finite multiple of the initial expansion of demand. To calculate the exact change, we can use the Keynesian-cross diagram.

In Figure 20.3, the aggregate demand curve is initially the one labeled Y_t^d. The intersection with the 45-degree line determines the level of output, $\hat{Y}_t$. Then an **autonomous increase in demand** of size *A* shifts the aggregate demand curve upward to the one labeled $Y_t^{d'}$. (By autonomous, we mean that the change comes from outside of the model rather than being explained by the theory.) The level of output, $\hat{Y}_t'$, corresponds accordingly to the new intersection with the 45-degree line.

The geometry of the Keynesian-cross diagram in Figure 20.3 reveals the relation between the initial and final levels of output, $\hat{Y}_t$ and $\hat{Y}_t'$. Let $\Delta\hat{Y}$ be the change in output, $\hat{Y}_t' - \hat{Y}_t$, and observe the smaller right-angle triangle with base $\Delta\hat{Y}$. The slope of the line marked with an arrow equals the marginal propensity to consume, *v*. Since the vertical side of the triangle is of length $\Delta\hat{Y} - A$, the slope satisfies the relation

$$v = (\Delta \hat{Y} - A)/\Delta \hat{Y}$$

It follows that the change in output is given by

$$\Delta \hat{Y} = A/(1 - v) \tag{20.8}$$

Thus, output changes by a multiple of the autonomous shift in demand, A. The *multiplier* is the term $1/(1 - v)$, which is positive and greater than one. Note that the higher is the marginal propensity to consume, v, the larger is the multiplier. Also, for the analysis to make sense—that is, for the ultimate expansion of output to remain finite—the marginal propensity to consume must be less than one, as we have assumed.

We can better understand the source of the multiplier by deriving equation (20.8) in an alternative manner. The autonomous increase in demand leads initially to an increase in output by the amount A. Then the rise in real income by the amount A leads to an increase in aggregate demand by the quantity vA. The additional increase in output of size vA causes demand to rise further by the amount $v \cdot vA$. In other words, there is a continuing sequence in which each round's increase in output is the amount v multiplied by the previous round's increase. It follows that the full increase in output comes from summing up all the rounds:[6]

$$\Delta \hat{Y} = A + vA + v^2 A + \ldots = A \cdot (1 + v + v^2 + \ldots) = A/(1 - v) \tag{20.9}$$

This result coincides with the one shown in equation (20.8).

We should stress two points about the derivation of the change in output, $\Delta \hat{Y}$. First, we assume that excess supply of goods prevails throughout and, hence, that producers never hesitate to meet extra demand with more output. Second, the discussion mentions a sequence of rounds only for the purpose of exposition. In the basic model, we do not allow any time to elapse while households adjust demand or production. An autonomous increase in demand therefore leads immediately to the full multiplicative response of output, as shown in equation (20.9).

[6] *The formula for a geometric series implies that* $1 + v + v^2 + \ldots = 1/(1 - v)$ *if* $-1 < v < 1$.

More generally, we could include some dynamics whereby output adjusts gradually toward the value dictated by the Keynesian-cross diagram in Figure 20.3.

Before going on, let's work out a third way to look at the multiplier. We can rewrite the condition for determining output from equation (20.7) as

$$Y_t - \hat{C}^d(\underset{(+)}{Y_t}, \underset{(-)}{r_t}, \ldots) = I^d(\underset{(-)}{r_t}, \ldots) + G_t \tag{20.10}$$

The left side is the sum of desired private saving plus taxes. Equation (20.10) says that the level of output is determined so that desired private saving plus taxes equals investment demand plus government consumption. (Equivalently, if we moved G_t to the left side of equation [20.10], then the equality would be between desired national saving and investment demand.)

Suppose that an autonomous increase in demand means that the right side of equation (20.10) rises by the amount A. (Equivalently, part of this change could show up as an increase in consumer demand and, hence, as a decrease in the left side of the equation.) If taxes do not change, then output must rise enough to generate a matching expansion of desired saving on the left side of the equation. Since the marginal propensity to consume is v, the marginal propensity to save is $1 - v$. The change in saving is therefore $(1 - v) \cdot \Delta\hat{Y}$. Since this extra saving must balance the autonomous increase in demand, A, it follows that $\Delta\hat{Y} = A/(1 - v)$. This answer for the change in output coincides with those found in equations (20.8) and (20.9).

The multiplier is a distinctive feature of the Keynesian model and would not arise under conditions of general market clearing. To see this point, assume an autonomous increase in aggregate demand, Y_t^d, with no shift in aggregate supply, Y_t^s. In a market-clearing setting, as in Chapter 5, we know that the real interest rate, r_t, rises to clear the commodity market. Since the increase in r_t reduces Y_t^d, output must rise by less than the autonomous increase in demand. (Remember that consumer demand does not depend directly on output in the market-clearing model.) Thus, the market-clearing model features a *dampener* rather than a multiplier.

THE DETERMINATION OF EMPLOYMENT

For a given level of output, Y_t, the amount of work, L_t, is the minimum amount necessary to produce this quantity of goods. That is, using an aggregate version of equation (20.5):

$$L_t = L(\underset{(+)}{Y_t}, \underset{(-)}{K_{t-1}}, \underset{(-)}{G_t}) \qquad\qquad \textbf{(20.11)}$$

For given values of the capital stock and government consumption and for a given form of the production function, anything that leads to a change in output leads to a change of the same sign for employment. The previous discussion showed that an autonomous increase in aggregate demand led to a multiplicative expansion of output. Now we find that an increase in employment accompanies the rise in output. Employment is therefore procyclical in this example.

Recall that the analysis applies in the range in which goods are in excess supply. Since the marginal product of labor exceeds the value attached to leisure time, people eagerly work more whenever it becomes feasible to sell more goods. If we introduced a separate labor market with a sticky nominal wage, then we would find that suppliers of labor, who face rationing of jobs, readily accept more work whenever the employers raise their demands. In this setting, the amount of involuntary unemployment corresponds to the gap between the aggregate supply of labor, L_t^s, and the quantity of work. Thus, increases in employment show up as decreases in involuntary unemployment. Unemployment is therefore countercyclical.

THE KEYNESIAN INVESTMENT FUNCTION

Because of the multiplier, small disturbances to the aggregate demand for goods can be magnified into sizable fluctuations in aggregate output. For example, a small cutback in investment demand could generate a recession in which real GDP and consumption fall significantly below trend. In the data, however, typical recessions feature large shortfalls in investment with relatively small contractions in consumer expenditures on nondurables and services. Recessions do not usually involve small reductions of investment that are accompanied by major declines in consumption. To explain these aspects of the data, we have to modify the Keynesian model to include a direct effect of economic conditions on investment demand.

Recall that, with excess supply of goods, producers reduce their inputs of labor services. Thereby the marginal product of labor exceeds the value of leisure time. Similar reasoning suggests that producers would cut back on their inputs of capital services. That is, when sales are rationed, producers reduce their desired stocks of capital. Thereby the marginal product of capital (less the depreciation rate) exceeds the real interest rate. The main point is that a reduction in the available real sales leads to a smaller desired stock of capital and, hence, to less investment demand.

We can write the **Keynesian investment function** as

$$i_t^d = \hat{i}^d(\underset{(+)}{y_t}, \underset{(-)}{r_t}, \ldots) \tag{20.12}$$

The Keynesian investment function includes the level of output, y_t, and thereby looks similar to the Keynesian consumption function in equation (20.6). Actually, what matters for desired capital and therefore for investment demand is the prospective quantity of real sales and output, y_{t+1}. A cutback in current output, y_t, reduces investment demand, i_t^d, to the extent that prospective output, y_{t+1}, also declines.

THE INVESTMENT ACCELERATOR

The Keynesian investment function is related to the **investment accelerator**, a concept that was discussed frequently in the early literature on business cycles. The main difference is that the accelerator relates investment demand to the change in output, whereas the investment demand function in equation (20.12) involves the level of output or, more precisely, the prospective amount of output, y_{t+1}. Recall that the level of the capital stock, k_{t-1}, appears with a negative sign among the omitted terms of the investment demand function in equation (20.12). If we allowed for changes over time in the quantity of capital, then we could generate a dynamic relation for investment. This relation turns out to resemble the accelerator. For an analysis of a model with an accelerator and a multiplier, see Paul Samuelson (1939).

The formal analysis of the determination of output and employment does not change when we introduce the Keynesian investment function. The only difference is that we have to redefine the parameter v to be the **marginal propensity to spend**, which is the total effect of a change in current output, y_t, on the demand for goods, y_t^d. This total effect is the sum of the marginal propensity to consume and the **marginal propensity to invest**. The latter term is the impact of a change in output, y_t, on investment demand in equation (20.12). For the analysis to go through, the marginal propensity to spend, v, must be less than one.

Recall that the multiplier in equation (20.8) is the expression $1/(1 - v)$. The term $1 - v$ is now one minus the marginal propensity to spend, rather than the marginal propensity to save. If the marginal propensity to spend, v, is less than one, then the term $1 - v$ is positive.

The new results concern the composition of output during business fluctuations. The Keynesian investment function implies that an autonomous contraction of demand can lead to a major decline of investment. At least this response follows if the contraction lasts long enough for prospective output, y_{t+1}, to decline.

If a recession does not persist long enough to have a major effect on the present value of income, then the cutback in current output, y_t, has only a minor impact on consumer demand, c_t^d. Most of the shortfall in output could then show up as less investment rather than less consumption. In other words, the Keynesian model can now be consistent with this important feature of recessions in the real world.

We mentioned before that liquidity constraints, whereby some people cannot borrow readily at the going interest rate, could be a basis for the Keynesian consumption function. But if such constraints were important, then we would expect recessions to exhibit major shortfalls in consumer expenditures on nondurables and services. In fact, the data show relatively little fluctuation in these categories of spending. The components that decline proportionately more during recessions are—aside from business investment—the purchases of consumer durables, including residential housing, automobiles, and furniture. These goods are relatively easy to buy on credit because durables serve as good collateral for loans. This observation therefore suggests that liquidity constraints do not play a key role in U.S. business fluctuations.

IS/LM ANALYSIS AND THE ROLE OF THE INTEREST RATE

Our previous analysis, which includes the multiplier, shows how to determine the level of output for a given interest rate. As long as there is excess supply of goods, the condition for determining output is, repeating equation (20.7),

$$Y_t = Y_t^d = \hat{C}^d(\underset{(+)\ (-)}{Y_t,\ r_t,\ \ldots}) + \hat{I}^d(\underset{(+)\ (-)}{Y_t,\ r_t,\ \ldots}) + G_t \qquad \textbf{(20.13)}$$

Our assumption to this point that the interest rate, r_t, is a given means that the analysis is seriously incomplete. We now want to go further to consider the determination of r_t in the Keynesian model. To carry out this analysis, we have to reintroduce the condition that all money be willingly held. This condition is, repeating equation (20.2),

$$M_t = P_t \cdot \Phi(\underset{(+)}{Y_t}, \underset{(-)}{r_t}, \dots) \qquad \textbf{(20.14)}$$

Given that the price level, P_t, is fixed by assumption, equations (20.13) and (20.14) determine the interest rate and the level of output. (Recall that, with no inflation, the real and nominal interest rates coincide.) Notice that equation (20.13) determines Y_t for a given value of r_t. A change in r_t would affect aggregate demand, Y_t^d, and thereby the level of output. What we want to do now is figure out the value of Y_t that corresponds to each value of r_t. That is, we want to trace out the combinations of r_t and Y_t that are consistent with the equality between output and aggregate demand, as specified in equation (20.13).

An increase in the interest rate lowers aggregate demand on the right side of equation (20.13). As with any decline in demand, the level of output falls. Therefore, if we map out the combinations of r_t and Y_t that satisfy equation (20.13), we get a downward-sloping relationship. Following standard notation, we label as **IS** the curve in Figure 20.4 that shows this relation.[7] Along the IS curve, the interest rate and the level of output are consistent with the equality between output and aggregate demand.

Consider now the condition that money be willingly held, as specified in equation (20.14). Given the quantity of money, M_t, and the price level, P_t, this condition defines another array of combinations for the interest rate and output. We want to trace out the pairs of r_t and Y_t that are consistent with this condition. Since a higher value of Y_t raises the demand for money on the right side of equation (20.14), r_t must rise to lower the demand for money back to the given level, M_t. Hence, when we map out the combinations of r_t and Y_t that satisfy equation (20.14),

[7] *The terminology IS refers to the equation of investment demand to desired saving. Recall from equation (20.10) that the condition $Y_t = Y_t^d$ is equivalent to an equality between investment demand (plus government purchases) and desired private saving (plus taxes). The apparatus in Figure 20.4 comes from John Hicks (1937).*

FIGURE 20.4

USE OF IS/LM CURVES TO DETERMINE OUTPUT AND THE INTEREST RATE

The IS curve shows the combinations of Y_t and r_t that satisfy the condition $Y_t = Y_t^d$. The LM curve shows the combinations that induce people to hold all the existing money, M_t. Thus, the levels of output and the interest rate correspond to the intersection of the two curves.

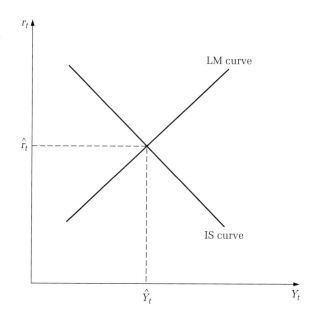

we determine an upward-sloping relationship. The curve designated **LM** in Figure 20.4 shows this relation.[8] Along the LM curve, the interest rate and the level of output are consistent with the condition that all money be willingly held.

The intersection of the IS and LM curves in Figure 20.4 picks out the combination of output and the interest rate—labeled $\hat{Y}_t$ and $\hat{r}_t$—that satisfies the two necessary conditions: output equals aggregate demand, and all money is willingly held. As long as the price level is fixed, the Keynesian model predicts that the level of output will be the amount $\hat{Y}_t$ and the interest rate will be the value $\hat{r}_t$. Hence, we can use the IS/LM apparatus to analyze the determination of output and the interest rate in the Keynesian model. Because of the popularity of the Keynesian model, the IS/LM diagram has been the principal analytical tool for many macroeconomists since the 1950s.

[8] *The letter L is often used to denote the demand-for-money function; hence, the terminology LM refers to the equation between the demand for money, L, and the quantity of money, M.*

VARIATIONS IN OUTPUT AND THE INTEREST RATE

To bring out the role of the interest rate, consider again an autonomous increase in aggregate demand. If the interest rate did not change, then output would rise multiplicatively. However, the expansion of output increases the demand for money above the given quantity M_t. Households' attempts to move out of bonds and into money imply that the interest rate must increase to restore balance on the credit market. This increase in the interest rate reduces the demand for money, but it also decreases the aggregate demand for goods. Hence, the overall effect on output is less than the full multiplicative amount. In fact, the increase in output may fall short of the autonomous expansion of demand. In other words, the increase in the interest rate may make the multiplier be less than one in the Keynesian model (as it is for sure in the market-clearing model).

Figure 20.5 uses the IS/LM apparatus to show the results. We reproduce the solid lines from Figure 20.4. The boost to aggregate demand appears as a rightward shift in the IS curve; that is, output increases for a given value of the interest rate. The size of this shift is the change in aggregate demand, A, times the multiplier, $1/(1 - v)$. Since the LM curve does not shift in this example, the figure shows that output and the interest rate rise. The increase in output is, however, less than the full multiplier amount, which equals the rightward shift of the IS curve.

For a given amount of government purchases, it is clear that total private spending for consumption and investment increases. But because of the rise in the interest rate, it is possible that one of these components would decline. Suppose, for example, that the autonomous disturbance is an increase in investment demand. The rise in output stimulates consumer demand, but the increase in the interest rate depresses this demand. Thus, consumption may fall along with the expansion of output and investment. Similarly, if the autonomous change applies to consumer demand, then investment may decline.

FIGURE 20.5

**KEYNESIAN ANALYSIS OF THE EFFECT OF AN INCREASE IN AGGRE-
GATE DEMAND ON OUTPUT AND THE INTEREST RATE**

The increase in aggregate demand shifts the IS curve rightward. The
size of the shift is the autonomous rise in demand, A, times the multiplier, $1/(1 - v)$. Output and the interest rate increase, but the rise
in output falls short of the full multiplier amount, $A/(1 - v)$.

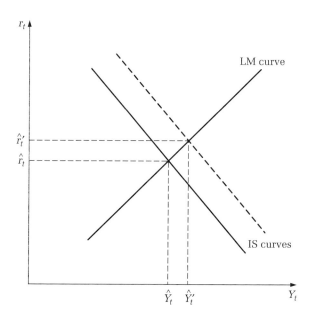

FISCAL POLICY IN THE KEYNESIAN MODEL

The government can influence aggregate demand directly by changing
the level of its consumption, G_t. Suppose that the government raises consumption by one unit and finances this extra spending with lump-sum
taxes. Consider the case in which the rise in purchases is temporary,
so that wealth effects are small. As in the analysis from Chapter 12,
consumer demand falls by a fraction of the increase in government consumption. Thus, aggregate demand expands, but by less than one unit.
In terms of the IS/LM diagram, the disturbance can again be represented
by Figure 20.5.[9] Now the rightward shift of the IS curve equals some
fraction of the increase in government purchases, times the multiplier,
$1/(1 - v)$. Notice that output and the interest rate increase. But the increase in output is again less than the full multiplier amount.

The effects of more government consumption on private spending
are uncertain. The expansion of output stimulates private demands, but
the higher interest rate reduces these demands. In addition, there is the

[9] *This diagram applies if the
change in government purchases
has no direct effect on the demand for money. Otherwise,
there is also a shift of the LM
curve.*

direct negative effect of government consumption on private consumer spending. Recall that empirically for the United States, a temporary burst of wartime expenditure tends to crowd out investment but has little effect on consumer expenditures for nondurables and services.

Another type of fiscal policy is a reduction in taxes, financed by issue of more government bonds. Economists often argue that this policy is expansionary in the Keynesian model. But to get this answer, we have to assume that deficit-financed tax cuts make people feel wealthier. Then the stimulus to consumer demand shifts the IS curve rightward, as shown in Figure 20.5. Given this shift, there would again be increases in output and the interest rate.

Because of the higher future taxes, it can still be true (as in Chapter 14) that a deficit-financed tax cut has no aggregate wealth effect on consumer demand. Since the IS curve does not shift, output and the interest rate would not change. In other words, the Ricardian theorem, which states that taxes and deficits are equivalent, can remain valid within the Keynesian model.

If households treat a tax cut as a signal of more wealth, then the Keynesian model predicts an expansion of output. Because production and employment are constrained initially by lack of demand, the typical household ends up better off in this situation. Thus, households actually do end up being wealthier. But this result has nothing to do with tax cuts as such. In the Keynesian model, *anything* that makes people feel wealthier generates the increases in output and employment that actually make them wealthier. (Think about what would happen in this model if we assumed that households felt poorer when they saw a tax cut.)

CHANGES IN THE PRICE LEVEL

Recall that the starting point for the Keynesian model was the excessive price level, $P_t > P_t^*$. If the price level declines toward its general-market-clearing value, P_t^*, then the basic constraint on the economy relaxes. We anticipate, therefore, that the level of output, $\hat{Y}_t$, would rise toward its

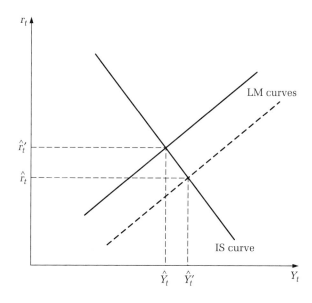

FIGURE 20.6

KEYNESIAN ANALYSIS OF THE EFFECT OF A DECREASE IN THE PRICE LEVEL ON OUTPUT AND THE INTEREST RATE

A decrease in the price level shifts the LM curve rightward. The interest rate falls, and the level of output rises.

general-market-clearing value, Y_t^*. To see how this relationship works, we can use the IS/LM diagram.

Recall from equation (20.14) that the LM curve shows the combinations of r_t and Y_t that equate the amount of money demanded to the given quantity of money, M_t. A decline in the price level lowers the nominal demand for money, $M_t^d = P_t \cdot \Phi(r_t, Y_t, \ldots)$. To restore equality with the given supply of money, we need changes in r_t or Y_t that raise the real demand for money, $\Phi(r_t, Y_t, \ldots)$. Hence, the LM curve shifts rightward, as shown in Figure 20.6.

Notice that the new LM curve intersects the unchanged IS curve at a lower interest rate, $\hat{r}_t' < \hat{r}_t$, and a higher level of output, $\hat{Y}_t' > \hat{Y}_t$. We can understand these changes by recalling that a lower price level reduces the nominal demand for money, $M_t^d = P_t \cdot \Phi(r_t, Y_t, \ldots)$. Households' attempts to exchange their excess money for bonds tends to depress the interest rate, a change that leads to greater aggregate demand for goods and, hence, higher output.

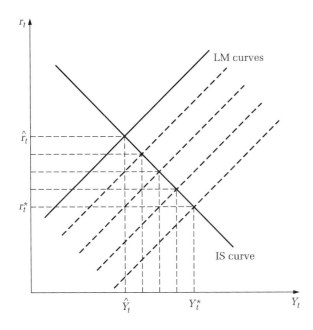

FIGURE 20.7

EFFECTS OF DECLINES IN THE PRICE LEVEL TO THE GENERAL-MARKET-CLEARING VALUE, P_t^*

Each decrease in the price level shifts the LM curve rightward. The interest rate falls, and the level of output rises. When the price level reaches its general-market-clearing value, P_t^*, the interest rate and output attain their general-market-clearing values, r_t^* and Y_t^*.

Consider a sequence of reductions in the price level from its initial value toward the general-market-clearing value, P_t^*. Each reduction in the price level shifts the LM curve rightward as shown in Figure 20.7. Correspondingly, the interest rate falls, and the level of output rises. When the price level falls to the value P_t^*, the interest rate will have fallen to its general-market-clearing value, r_t^*, and output will have risen to its general-market-clearing value, Y_t^*.

Once the price level reaches P_t^*, further reductions in the price level would not generate more increases in output, because the commodity market shifts at this point to excess demand, $Y_t^d > Y_t^s$, rather than excess supply. Then the suppliers no longer produce the quantity demanded but rather produce the lesser amount, Y_t^s. Recall that the IS curve assumes that producers accommodate demand fully: $Y_t = Y_t^d$. The curve is therefore inappropriate when there is excess demand for goods.[10]

[10] *Under excess demand it is purchases of goods and services, rather than sales, that have to be rationed. For a theoretical discussion, see Robert Barro and Herschel Grossman (1976). For empirical applications to the previously centrally-planned economies of eastern and central Europe, see David Howard (1976) and Richard Portes and David Winter (1980).*

CHANGES IN THE QUANTITY OF MONEY

Assume again that the price level is fixed above its general-market-clearing value, so that $P_t > P_t^*$. Consider an increase in the quantity of money, M_t, perhaps resulting from an open-market purchase of bonds. Since P_t is fixed, equation (20.14) implies that the real amount of money demanded, $\Phi(r_t, Y_t, \ldots)$, must go up for the additional money to be willingly held. The increase in M_t therefore works just like a reduction in P_t. We can again use Figure 20.6 to analyze the effects. The rightward shift of the LM curve leads to a lower interest rate and a higher level of output.

We can interpret these results by noting that the quantity of money, M_t, rises above the amount demanded at the initial values of the interest rate, $\hat{r}_t$, and output, $\hat{Y}_t$. As before, households' efforts to exchange excess money for bonds lead to a lower interest rate and, hence, to higher output.

The important finding is that an increase in the quantity of money is a substitute for a reduction in the price level toward the general-market-clearing value. One way to correct for an excessive price level, $P_t > P_t^*$, is for prices to fall. But an alternative is to raise the stock of money and thereby increase the general-market-clearing level of prices, P_t^*. Monetary expansion closes the gap between P_t and P_t^* by raising P_t^* rather than by lowering P_t.

SHIFTS IN THE DEMAND FOR MONEY

Notice from equation (20.14) that a reduction in the real demand for money, $\Phi(r, Y, \ldots)$, works exactly like a decrease in the price level. Both changes lead to an excess of money, M_t, over the amount demanded, M_t^d. If the demand for money falls—for example, because of a financial innovation—then the LM curve shifts rightward as shown in Figure 20.6. This change leads again to a decrease in the interest rate and an expansion of output.

These results follow because the decline in the demand for money raises the general-market-clearing value of the price level, P_t^*. From this perspective, a decrease in the real demand for money works in the same way as an increase in M_t. Both changes reduce the spread between P_t and P_t^* by raising the value of P_t^*.

IS/LM ANALYSIS AND GENERAL MARKET CLEARING

The IS/LM framework is designed to bring out the interaction between monetary phenomena (the LM curve) and real phenomena (the IS curve). In the Keynesian model, the main source of this interaction is the stickiness of the general price level (or the nominal wage rate). It was for this reason that the IS/LM apparatus was helpful when we studied various disturbances in the context of a fixed price level.

Suppose that we return to a setting of general market clearing, where the price level is flexible. Then Figure 20.7 shows how we could use the IS/LM diagram to find the general-market-clearing values of the interest rate, r_t^*, and output, Y_t^*. The apparatus is cumbersome, however, because disturbances typically imply shifts of the IS and LM curves, as well as changes in the position of the market-clearing price level, P_t^*. The model that we developed in Chapter 5 is much easier in the context of flexible prices.

THE SUPPLY SIDE IN THE KEYNESIAN MODEL

The Keynesian model—whether the simple version we have been studying or more sophisticated versions—views aggregate demand as the central determinant of output and employment. The analysis pays little attention to aggregate supply. In formal terms, the neglect of the supply side arises because the postulated excessive price level, $P_t > P_t^*$, means that excess supply of goods and services prevails. The model assumes, in other words, that productive capacity and the willingness to work do not represent effective constraints on output. Only the willingness to spend limits the extent of economic activity in this model. This perspective explains why Keynesian analyses typically pay little attention to some matters that are important in a market-clearing framework: shifts to the production function, variations in the stock of capital, effects of the tax system on the willingness to work, and so on.[11] The neglect of these elements became embarrassing with the supply shocks of the 1970s. In fact, the failure to handle supply shocks was one of the major elements that led many economists to look for alternatives to the Keynesian model.

INFLATION IN THE KEYNESIAN MODEL

Thus far, we have assumed in this chapter that the price level was fixed. This assumption is unsatisfactory, especially for present-day economies, where inflation rates are typically positive and often highly variable over time. Since the Keynesian model does not rely on market-clearing conditions to determine the price level, we need some other mechanism to replace the assumption that prices are rigid. The usual device is an ad hoc adjustment relationship, whereby the price level moves gradually toward its general-market-clearing value, P_t^*. Recall that the condition $P_t > P_t^*$ corresponds to an excess supply of commodities. An adjustment of the price level toward its market-clearing value, P_t^*, means accordingly that prices decline when goods are in excess supply and rise when goods are in excess demand.

One simple form of a price-adjustment rule is

$$\pi_t = \lambda \cdot (Y_t^d - Y_t^s) \qquad \qquad \textbf{(20.15)}$$

where λ (the Greek letter *lambda*) is positive. The higher the parameter λ, the more rapidly prices adjust to an imbalance between supply and demand. Sometimes economists regard the reaction of prices to excess demand as different from that to excess supply. Prices are thought to rise quickly in the face of excess demand but to fall sluggishly when there is excess supply. This asymmetry would support the Keynesian focus on

[11] *The Keynesian model considers these factors to the extent that they influence investment or consumption demand. Also, the supply of labor services matters when computing the amount of involuntary unemployment.*

cases in which the price level exceeds its market-clearing value. But the reason for this asymmetry in the price-adjustment relation has not been well explained.

As it stands, the price-adjustment formula in equation (20.15) has some problems. First, inflation is nonzero only if the commodity market does not clear, that is, if $Y_t^d \neq Y_t^s$. But the theory should allow inflation and cleared markets to coexist. Second, as a related matter, inflation is negative in the Keynesian case in which goods are in excess supply. Thus, we cannot use equation (20.15) to incorporate positive inflation into the Keynesian analysis.

Recall that equation (20.15) implies that the price level, P_t, moves toward the general-market-clearing price, P_t^*. But monetary growth or some other factors can lead to continuing changes in P_t^*. It seems reasonable that P_t would respond to expected changes in P_t^* as well as to the gap between P_t and P_t^*. If we define π_t^* to be the expected rate of change of P_t^*, then we might modify equation (20.15) accordingly to the form

$$\pi_t = \lambda \cdot (Y_t^d - Y_t^s) + \pi_t^* \qquad \textbf{(20.16)}$$

Equation (20.16) says that inflation, π_t, exceeds the anticipated rate of change of the market-clearing price, π_t^*, when there is excess demand and is below π_t^* when there is excess supply. Thus, the actual price level, P_t, tends to approach the target, P_t^*, even when the target moves over time.

Note that equation (20.16) is consistent with nonzero inflation when the commodity market clears. A high rate of anticipated monetary growth implies, for example, high values for π_t^* and π_t. If π_t^* is positive, then π_t can be positive even when goods are in excess supply. Hence, positive inflation can exist in the Keynesian model.

We now have the following general description of a recession. First, there is some adverse shock to aggregate demand, perhaps stemming from an autonomous decline in firms' desires to invest. Then output, employment, and investment (and probably consumption) fall below their general-market-clearing values, and the unemployment rate increases. The shortfalls in quantities persist because prices (and wages) do not adjust downward immediately to reestablish general market clearing. In other words, although prices are no longer rigid, they are still sticky. But equation (20.16) says that the inflation rate, π_t, falls below the rate of change of the market-clearing price, π_t^*, and P_t falls relative to P_t^*. The resulting increases in real money balances[12] lead to decreases in interest rates and, hence, to expansions of aggregate demand and output. In this way, the economy tends to return gradually to a position of general market clearing.

The role for active policy in the Keynesian model appears as a substitute for the economy's automatic, but sluggish, reaction through price adjustment. Expansions in the growth rate of money (monetary policy) or increases in government purchases (fiscal policy) can spur aggregate demand. Thereby, the model says that the recovery from a recession can be quickened.

CYCLICAL PROPERTIES OF THE KEYNESIAN MODEL

In the Keynesian model, the cyclical properties of the major macroeconomic variables depend on whether disturbances impinge mostly on the IS curve or the LM curve. Consider first shocks to the IS curve due to changes in investment demand. An expansion of this demand leads (from Figure 20.5) to increases in output, investment, and the expected real interest rate. The change in consumption is ambiguous (the rise in income suggests more consumption, but the higher real interest rate suggests less consumption). The quantity of labor input rises along with output, and the unemployment rate falls. Since the production function has not shifted and the capital stock changes little in the short run, the rise in labor input means that labor productivity declines. To

—

[12] *The discussion assumes that the growth rate of the market-clearing price, π_t^*, reflects an equal growth rate for the quantity of money. The growth rate of money therefore exceeds that of prices.*

The Aggregate Supply–Aggregate Demand Model

Two problems with the usual Keynesian model are, first, that it does not allow for effects on output from shifts in aggregate supply and, second, that it determines the price level only by means of an ad hoc price-adjustment relation, such as equation (20.16). The **aggregate supply–aggregate demand (AS-AD) model** was developed as an attempt to resolve these difficulties. Although the AS-AD model has substantial shortcomings, we discuss it here because it has become popular in many textbooks.

We have already learned from Figure 20.6 that a reduction in the general price level, P_t, leads in the Keynesian model to an increase in output, Y_t. This quantity equals the amount demanded, Y_t^d. We can use this result to determine the possible combinations of P_t and $Y_t = Y_t^d$ that can prevail. The curve labeled AD (for aggregate demand)* in the following figure shows these combinations. As P_t declines toward its market-clearing value, P^*, the level of output rises toward its market-clearing value, Y^{*}.[†]

The upward-sloping curve labeled AS (for aggregate supply) in the figure reflects the supply behavior that we discussed in Chapter 19. Suppose that people have a given expectation, P_t^e, of the price level for period t. If P_t rises for given P_t^e,

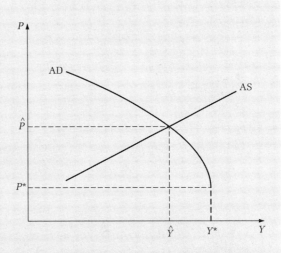

then producers are motivated to raise the quantity of goods supplied, Y_t^s. Similarly, if we introduced a separate labor market and interpreted P_t as the nominal wage rate, then workers would supply more labor when the wage rate rose relative to the expected wage rate. We showed in Chapter 19 that we can get these responses of supply in a model with localized markets if people have incomplete information about the general price level. The AS curve reflects these ideas: an increase in P_t, for given P_t^e, leads to an increase in Y_t^s.

If $P_t^e = P^*$, the market-clearing value, then the quantity supplied, Y_t^s, would equal the market-clearing value, Y^*, when P_t equaled P^*. In this case, the AS curve would pass through the ↗

point (Y^*, P^*) in the accompanying figure and would therefore intersect the AD curve at this point. The construction in the figure assumes instead that $P_t^e > P^*$. The quantity supplied, Y_t^s, is therefore below Y^* if $P_t = P^*$.

In the AS-AD framework, the price level is assumed to be determined at the value denoted $\hat{P}$ where the AS and AD curves intersect. The corresponding level of output is the amount $\hat{Y}$. This quantity equals the amount demanded, Y_t^d, determined along the AD curve, and also equals the quantity supplied, Y_t^s, determined along the AS curve.

Since $\hat{Y}_t < Y^*$ in the figure, we know from supply behavior that $\hat{P}_t < P_t^e$. (Recall that $Y_t^s = Y*$ if $P_t = P_t^e$.) As time passes, P_t^e presumably adjusts downward toward the actual price, $\hat{P}_t$. The fall in P_t^e causes the AS curve to shift rightward: the quantity supplied is higher for a given P_t if P_t^e declines. Thus, $\hat{Y}_t$ rises and $\hat{P}_t$ falls over time. The economy tends thereby toward the market-clearing position, (Y^*, P^*).

The attractive feature of the AS-AD model is that output responds to shifts to supply or demand. An expansion of aggregate demand, represented by a rightward shift of the AD curve, leads to increases in Y_t and P_t. An increase in aggregate supply, corresponding to a rightward shift of the AS curve, causes an increase in Y_t and a decrease in P_t. These changes refer to short-run situations in which the expectation, P_t^e, can be held

fixed. In the long run, the adjustment of P_t^e moves the economy back to the market-clearing position, (Y^*, P^*).

The main problem with the AS-AD framework is that the various pieces of the analysis are contradictory. The AD curve reflects the underlying IS/LM model, and the key to this model is the presence of excess supply of goods (and labor). The excess supply reflects, in turn, the assumed stickiness of prices (and wages) at excessive levels. In the AS-AD model, described in the figure, the adjustment of the price level to the value $\hat{P}$ eliminates the excess supply of goods. The key features of the IS/LM model—such as the Keynesian consumption and investment functions and the workings of the multiplier—do not apply in this situation.

The AS curve assumes that producers (and workers) can sell their desired quantities at the going price, P_t. That is why the quantity supplied rises when P_t increases relative to P_t^e. This setup is inconsistent with the Keynesian idea—present in the IS/LM model and therefore in the AD curve—that producers and workers are constrained by aggregate demand in their ability to sell goods and services.

It is possible to interpret the AD curve as applying to the IS/LM model when the price level has adjusted to ensure general market clearing, as in Figure 20.7. The market-clearing value of output, Y_t^*, in this figure depends, however, on ↗

monetary disturbances because the quantity sup-plied is a function of the price surprise, $P_t - P_t^e$. In this case, the AS-AD model has no Keynesian features and is equivalent to the market-clearing framework with incomplete information about the general price level, that is, the model worked out in Chapter 19. In the AS-AD framework, however, the effects of unanticipated changes in the price level, $P_t - P_t^e$, are allowed to operate only on the supply side. The model ignores the effects of per-ceived relative prices on consumption and invest-ment demand.

We have available, at this time, two internally consistent models that allow for significant inter-actions between monetary and real variables. The IS/LM model achieves this interaction by assum-ing that the price level is typically too high and adjusts only gradually toward its market-clearing value. The market-clearing model from Chapter 19 gets this interaction by assuming that people have incomplete information about the general price level. The AS-AD model does not seem to provide a third, or hopefully superior, model.

* The notation "aggregate-demand curve" is unfortunate because the AD curve is not a demand curve in the usual sense. The curve shows the combinations of P_t and Y_t that are consistent with the condition $Y_t = Y_t^d$. The level of Y_t shown along the curve therefore equals the quantity demanded, but only because the actual quantity produced has already been equated to this demand.

† If P_t fell below P^*, then excess demand for goods would result. We have not studied the determination of output under conditions of excess demand, but an analysis of this situation indicates that output would fall below Y^* (see Robert Barro and Herschel Grossman, 1976). Output is maximized not by making P_t as low as possible, but by setting it equal to its market-clearing value, P^*.

determine the effect on the real wage rate we would have to introduce a labor market. The usual assumption in the Keynesian analysis is that the real wage rate is not closely tied to the marginal product of labor and, hence, that the cyclical pattern of the real wage rate is ambiguous. Finally, the price-adjustment relation (equation [20.16]) implies that the inflation rate rises.

If we considered a shock to the IS curve that reflected a boost to con-sumption demand, then the only difference concerns the composition of output between consumption and investment. Consumption would rise, unambiguously, in this case, whereas the change in investment would be uncertain.

Thus, for shocks to the IS curve, the predictions of the Keynesian model for cyclical behavior are as follows:

—— Procyclical variables: investment (probably), consumption (probably), labor input, expected real interest rate, price level.

—— Countercyclical variables: unemployment rate, labor productivity.

—— Acyclical or uncertain variables: real wage rate, quantity of money.

A comparison with the observed cyclical characteristics that we have discussed before for the United States suggests the following evaluation. To fit the dominant role of investment in observed fluctuations we would have to assume that shocks to investment demand were more important than those to consumption demand. (It also helps if investment demand is more sensitive than consumption demand to changes in output.) In the data, the expected real interest rate is only weakly procyclical; hence, shocks to the IS curve, which predict a strong procyclical pattern, cannot be the whole story. The price level appears to be countercyclical, a conflict with the predictions. Labor productivity is procyclical, another conflict. The real wage rate is procyclical, whereas the model makes no prediction about this variable. Finally, we have assumed thus far that the quantity of money remained constant while the IS curve shifted.

Turn now to shifts in the LM curve due to changes in the quantity of money. An increase in money leads (from Figure 20.6) to increases in output, investment, and consumption, and to a decrease in the expected real interest rate. Labor input rises, and the unemployment rate falls. Labor productivity declines, the change in the real wage rate is uncertain, and the inflation rate rises. In comparison with the results for IS shifts, the differences are that investment and consumption are both clearly procyclical, the expected real interest rate is countercyclical, and the quantity of money is procyclical. We can therefore explain the weakly procyclical behavior of the expected real interest rate in the data by arguing that shocks to the IS and LM curves both occur, but that those to the IS curve are typically more important. The effects from shocks to the LM curve can also make the model consistent with the observed procyclical pattern for monetary aggregates.

Overall, the main conflict between theory and facts concerns the predictions that the price level will be procyclical and that labor productivity will be countercyclical. The failure to generate a prediction about the real wage rate is another shortcoming.

The price level is procyclical in the model because output always follows aggregate demand, and an increase in demand leads to a higher inflation rate. The price level can be countercyclical only if a shock to aggregate supply leads to higher output and a lower inflation rate. But in the Keynesian model that we have examined, output is demand determined and is therefore invariant with shifts to supply. This shortcoming motivated some economists to develop a Keynesian model in which shifts to aggregate supply affected output. The boxed section describes this aggregate supply–aggregate demand (AS-AD) model, but argues that it leads to logical inconsistencies.

Some economists have tried to explain the incorrect predictions about labor productivity by arguing that employment and worker-hours are inaccurate measures of labor input. In a recession, firms maintain most of their workers and paid worker-hours although the workers expend less effort than they do during a boom. (This effect is sometimes called **labor hoarding**.) Moreover, during recessions, a larger fraction of workers' effort is devoted to maintenance and other activities that do not show up in measured output (see footnote 12 in Chapter 10 for further discussion). These considerations suggest that labor productivity is underestimated in recessions (when labor input is exaggerated and output is undervalued) and overestimated in booms. Hence, true productivity may be countercyclical, as predicted by the theory.

An alternative, perhaps more plausible, view is that measured labor productivity *and* real wage rates are procyclical because workers really are more productive in booms than in recessions. This perspective accords with real business-cycle models in which the booms and recessions are themselves caused by shifts to the production function and, hence, to productivity.

STICKY PRICES AND NEW KEYNESIAN ECONOMICS

All the novel features in the Keynesian analysis, as summarized by the IS/LM model, derive from the assumption that prices (or wages) are sticky. The key postulate is that prices do not fall quickly when there is excess supply of goods. Among other things, this assumption delivers the following results:

- Output is determined by aggregate demand; supply-side elements play no important role.

- There may be a multiplier connecting autonomous shifts in aggregate demand to the responses of output.

- Whenever people feel wealthier and raise consumer demand, the expansions of output and employment actually make them wealthier.

- There are real effects from changes in the quantity of money.

- There is a desirable role for active monetary and fiscal policies.

Given all the results that follow from sticky prices, it is not surprising that economists have tried to provide a rationale for this stickiness.

In fact, the provision of this rationale has been the central mission of a field called **new Keynesian economics**, which began in the mid-1980s. For a survey of this area, see David Romer (1993).

One common feature of new Keynesian models is imperfect competition in the product market. Each producer of goods is viewed as a monopolist in the provision of its specialized good or service. Hence, as with any monopolist, the price of the good would be set above the marginal cost of production. Therefore, if for some reason the price were held fixed, then the producer would be happy to respond to an increase in demand by raising the quantity produced and sold, because, with price above marginal cost, profits rise with the quantity produced (at least as long as marginal cost does not rise too much). Thus, this part of the analysis supports the Keynesian idea that output would be driven by fluctuations in the demand for goods.

There are two major shortcomings in this analysis. First, the monopoly element has to be introduced on the selling side of the market, rather than on the buying side. For goods and services, this assumption seems reasonable, because we tend to think of firms as sellers, and the firms may be large enough to have some market power in their specialized activities. However, the assumption that monopoly prevails on the selling side of markets looks less reasonable if we consider the labor market, which is the traditional focus of Keynesian analysis. If a firm has monopoly power in its purchases of labor services, then it would set the wage rate below the marginal product of labor. If the wage rate were held fixed for some reason, then the firm would be happy to respond to an increase in the supply of labor by hiring more workers, because profit rises with employment when the marginal product of labor is above the wage (at least if the marginal product does not fall by too much). Thus, this analysis would have shifts in employment driven by fluctuations in the supply of labor rather than the demand. In this case, the main results would be opposite to those implied by standard Keynesian models.

The other difficulty, which has received much attention in the new Keynesian literature, is that the results still hinge on the assumption that prices do not adjust rapidly when economic disturbances occur. In this case, the main argument has been that small costs for changing prices—often called **menu costs**—may be sufficient to explain the lack of rapid adjustment. The idea is that an individual price setter, such as a firm, may benefit only a small amount over some range from adjusting price to its preferred value. Therefore, even a small menu cost would be sufficient to explain the failure to adjust prices very often. But because one firm's "incorrect" price matters for other firms in a setting of imperfect competition, it is also possible that the macroeconomic consequences from the lack of price adjustment could be serious. That is, small menu costs could somehow be magnified to explain substantial market failure at the aggregate level. Although some of the models that embody this idea are ingenious, it seems fair to say that the argument does not work well quantitatively. In particular, if output and employment fall below their market-clearing levels to a significant extent, then the cost to an individual firm from having the wrong price becomes large and cannot be explained by a small menu cost. Hence, small costs for changing prices still do not seem to be capable of explaining large departures of output and employment from their market-clearing levels.

LONG-TERM CONTRACTS

Before the advent of new Keynesian economics, models with **long-term contracts** were sometimes used to explain the stickiness of prices or wages. This approach recognizes that buyers and sellers often form long-term relationships rather than dealing exclusively on auction markets, such as wholesale markets for agricultural commodities, organized securities markets, and so on. For example, the associations between employers and workers or between firms and their suppliers often extend over many years. These types of continuing interchanges frequently involve formal—though more often implicit—contractual obligations between the parties. Some presetting of prices—or, more likely, of wages—may be one feature of these contracts.[13]

Prior agreement on prices or wages may allow one party, which might be a group of workers, to shift some risk from themselves to the

[13] *Some major papers in this area are Donald Gordon (1974), Costas Azariadis (1975), Martin Baily (1974), and Herschel Grossman (1979).*

other party, say a large corporation. An automobile company may, for example, shield its workers from some of the fluctuations in the demand for (U.S.) cars. This setup is desirable if the company is in a better position than the workers to assume risks, perhaps because the company has better access to insurance and other financial markets.

The presetting of some prices may also prevent one person from demanding "unreasonable" terms, *ex post*. A firm might, for example, lower the wage rate after an employee had incurred significant costs in moving to a job. Similarly, a builder might raise the price for a construction project at a time when delays became prohibitively expensive. In these cases the market for builders, workers, and employers may be competitive beforehand but more like a monopoly later. Some of these problems can be avoided by entering into prior contractual arrangements about prices and other considerations. Some economists have used the contracting approach to rationalize the stickiness of prices or wages in Keynesian models.[14] Suppose, as an illustration, that two parties agree on a price, P, over the life of a contract.[15] In some cases the chosen price will be the best estimate of the average market-clearing price during the contract, P^*, given the information available at the outset. Unanticipated events, such as monetary disturbances, lead, however, to departures of the price from its market-clearing value. When the contract expires, the parties will agree to a new price, which equals the anticipated market-clearing price over the next period.

At any point in time, there is an array of existing contracts, which specify prices that likely depart somewhat from market-clearing values. If there has been a recent monetary contraction, for example, then the typical price will be above its market-clearing value (with the reverse holding for monetary expansion). As more people renegotiate contracts, the average price adjusts gradually toward the average market-clearing value. We can, in other words, use this model to rationalize a price-adjustment relation of the form of equation (20.16):

$$\pi_t = \lambda \cdot (Y_t^d - Y_t^s) + \pi_t^*$$

[14] *See, for example, Jo Anna Gray (1976), Stanley Fischer (1977), and John Taylor (1980).*

[15] *The contracting theory actually motivates the presetting of a relative price or a real wage rate rather than a dollar price or wage. Yet most contracts in the United States are not explicitly "indexed," that is, do not contain automatic adjustments of nominal prices or wages for changes in the general cost of living. Firms and workers apparently find it convenient to frame their contracts in terms of the standard unit of account— the dollar—even when inflation is moderately high and variable. But inflation does tend to produce contracts with shorter durations.*

The gradual response of the average price to excess demand corresponds to the process of recontracting, and the anticipated rate of change of the market-clearing price, π_t^*, reflects the known factors that negotiators take into account when setting prices or wages at the start of contracts. Note that an excessive price—corresponding to an excess supply of goods and services—is no more likely than too low a price. The price-adjustment relation would be symmetric and would therefore not support the Keynesian focus on excessive price levels.

Although the contracting viewpoint may rationalize a process of gradual price adjustment, there are difficulties in using this analysis to explain Keynesian unemployment and underproduction. The Keynesian results emerge when prices or wages are above market-clearing values *and* when the quantities of output and employment equal the smaller of supply and demand. Recall that this short-side rule for determining quantities accords with voluntary exchange on an impersonal market. But the rule is not generally sensible in a long-term contract, which is now the theoretical basis for sluggish price adjustment.

In an enduring relationship, in which long-term contracts arise, firms and households do not have to change prices or wages every instant to get the "right" behavior of quantities. Workers can, for example, agree in advance that they will work harder when there is more work to do—that is, when the demand for a firm's product is high—and work less hard when there is little work. Unlike in an auction market, these efficient adjustments in work and production can occur even if wages do not change from day to day. (For large short-term increases in work, contracts may prescribe overtime premiums or other types of bonuses.) The important point is that stickiness of wages does not necessarily cause errors in the determination of the levels of employment and production.

Similarly, suppose that inflation is sometimes higher than expected and sometimes lower. Firms and workers know that inflation—if not accompanied by some real changes—does not alter the efficient levels of work and production. It is therefore reasonable to agree on a contract that insulates the choices of quantities from the rate of inflation. Over many

Some Empirical Evidence on the Contracting Approach

Two empirical studies provide some evidence about the contracting approach. Shaghil Ahmed (1987a) used a data set for 19 industries in Canada over the period 1961–74. He used these data because an earlier study by David Card (1980) calculated the amount of indexation—that is, automatic adjustment of wages for general inflation—in each industry's labor contracts. (Indexation ranged across the industries from zero to roughly 100%.) According to theories in which contracts are the basis for the Keynesian model, industries with little indexation should show substantial responses of real wages and, hence, of employment and output, to nominal disturbances. Industries with lots of indexation would be affected little by nominal disturbances.

Ahmed found that nominal shocks—computed from unanticipated changes in money or some other nominal variables—had positive effects on hours worked in most of the 19 industries. These results are consistent with some other findings that we discussed in Chapter 18 for the United States and other countries. The important point for present purposes, however, is that the extent of an industry's response to nominal disturbances

bore no relation to the amount of indexation in that industry. Those with lots of indexation were as likely as those with little indexation to respond to nominal disturbances. This finding is damaging to theories that use long-term contracts as the basis for the Keynesian model.

Mark Bils (1989) studied labor contracts for 12 manufacturing industries in the United States. He reasoned that if the signing of new contracts was important, then he should find unusual behavior of employment and real wages just after these signings. His results were mixed. On the one hand, some industries, especially motor vehicles, turned out to exhibit significant changes in employment subsequent to new labor agreements. Prior changes in employment tended to be reversed just after a new contract. These results, although applying only to a few industries, provide some support for the contracting approach. On the other hand, Bils did not find any corresponding changes in real wage rates after new labor contracts were signed. Since these changes in wage rates are central to the contracting approach, it is difficult to reconcile this part of Bils's findings with that approach.

periods, where the effects of unanticipated inflation on real wage rates tend to average out, both parties to a labor contract would benefit from this type of provision. (When inflation gets very high and unpredictable, however, firms and workers prefer either to index wages to the price level or to renegotiate contracts more frequently.)

One important lesson from the contracting viewpoint is that stickiness of prices or wages need not lead to underproduction and unemployment. Within a long-term agreement, it is unnecessary for prices and wages to move all the time to attain the general-market-clearing values of output and employment. Thus, stickiness in prices and wages no longer tends to generate Keynesian results. Rather than supporting the Keynesian model, the perspective of long-term contracting demonstrates that output and employment can be determined efficiently—as if prices and wages always adjusted to clear markets—even if prices and wages are sticky.

SUMMARY

In the Keynesian model the price level (or the nominal wage rate) exceeds the market-clearing value. The resulting excess supply of goods and services means that output is determined by aggregate demand. Correspondingly, there is underproduction and unemployment.

In the simplest Keynesian model, in which the interest rate is given, an increase in aggregate demand leads to a multiplicative expansion of output. The increase in demand could reflect an autonomous shift to investment or consumption demand or could come from an increase in government purchases. The expansion of output is accompanied by increases in employment, investment, and consumption. If we include the Keynesian investment function and the dependence of consumption on long-run income, then the model can match the empirical observation that investment is more volatile than consumption.

The IS/LM analysis shows how to determine the interest rate along with the level of output. In this model, an increase in aggregate demand may no longer have a multiplicative effect on output: the increase in the interest rate crowds out the demands for consumption and investment.

In the Keynesian model, a decrease in the price level implies more real money balances and a lower interest rate. The fall in the interest rate stimulates consumption and investment demand, and this increase in demand leads to an expansion of output and employment. Similarly, an increase in the quantity of money or a cutback in the demand for money leads to a lower interest rate and thereby to higher levels of output and employment.

We can incorporate inflation into the Keynesian model by using a price-adjustment formula that relates inflation positively to the excess demand for goods. When the commodity market clears, the inflation rate equals the anticipated rate of change of the market-clearing price. This mechanism allows the price level to fall, relative to the market-clearing value, during a recession. The resulting increases in real money balances lead to decreases in the interest rate and to increases in aggregate demand. Thus, the economy adjusts automatically toward the market-clearing levels of output and employment. In the Keynesian model, active monetary and fiscal policies can speed up this gradual process of automatic adjustment.

The Keynesian model can account for many observed features of business fluctuations. Shocks to the IS curve have to be more important than shocks to the LM curve in order to generate a weakly procyclical pattern for the expected real interest rate. The Keynesian model predicts, incorrectly, that the price level would be procyclical and that labor productivity would be countercyclical. The model also makes no clear prediction about the cyclical behavior of the real wage rate.

Some novel features of the Keynesian analysis are the following:

- Output is determined by aggregate demand; supply-side elements play no important role.

- There may be a multiplier connecting autonomous shifts in aggregate demand to the responses of output.

━━━ Whenever households feel wealthier and raise consumer demand, the expansions of output and employment actually make them wealthier.

━━━ There are real effects from changes in the quantity of money.

━━━ There is a desirable role for active monetary and fiscal policies.

These features follow from the assumption that prices are sticky downward. Most macroeconomists use sticky prices as a proxy for the coordination problems that characterize the private sector's reaction to fluctuations in aggregate supply and demand and to shifts in the composition of tastes and technology. But when economists model these problems in terms of incomplete information, costs of moving, and so on, the Keynesian features that we listed do not tend to emerge.

An interesting rationale for sticky prices concerns long-term contracts. Each (explicit or implicit) contract specifies a wage or price over an interval of time. Then the gradual process of recontracting means that the average wage or price adjusts gradually toward the average market-clearing value. Although this perspective may account for sticky prices, it is less successful in explaining the Keynesian predictions about quantities, because sensible agreements would allow for efficient adjustments of work and production even if wages or prices do not change from day to day. Thus, the existence of long-term contracts does not explain the type of unemployment and underproduction that arises in Keynesian models.

IMPORTANT TERMS AND CONCEPTS

aggregate supply–aggregate demand model An approach that combines the Keynesian IS/LM model with a condition that determines the price level to equate the aggregates of supply and demand.

AS-AD model   Aggregate supply–aggregate demand model.

autonomous change in demand   An unexplained shift in the aggregate demand for commodities.

complete Keynesian model   A version of the Keynesian theory that assumes sticky nominal wage rates but a perfectly flexible general price level.

investment accelerator   The positive effect of changes in output on investment demand.

involuntary unemployment   The inability of workers to obtain employment at the prevailing market wage; a feature of Keynesian theory.

IS curve   A graph used in Keynesian theory to show the combinations of aggregate output and the interest rate that satisfy the condition that aggregate output equals the aggregate demand for commodities.

Keynesian consumption function   The dependence of consumption demand on income and the interest rate; a central element of Keynesian theory.

Keynesian cross diagram   The graph in the Keynesian model that depicts the determination of the level of aggregate output for a given interest rate.

Keynesian investment function   The dependence of investment demand on output and the interest rate; an important element of Keynesian theory.

labor hoarding   The tendency of firms to retain their workers during a recession in which production and sales decline. Labor hoarding may explain the tendency for measured labor productivity to fall in recessions and rise in booms.

liquidity constraint The negative effect on consumer demand from the inability to borrow at the "going" interest rate.

LM curve A graph used in Keynesian theory to show the combinations of aggregate output and the interest rate that satisfy the condition that the demand for money equals the given quantity of money.

long-term contracts Agreements between buyers and sellers or between firms and workers that specify the terms of exchange over a number of periods.

marginal propensity to invest The effect of a change in output on investment demand.

marginal propensity to spend The effect of a change in income (or output) on the total demand for goods, whether for consumption or investment.

menu costs Costs of a lump-sum type that must be paid to adjust a nominal price or wage. New Keynesian models rely on these costs to rationalize the sluggish adjustment of prices or wages.

new Keynesian economics Models that attempt to explain the role of sticky prices and aggregate demand in the Keynesian framework. The new models incorporate elements of imperfect competition and allow for menu costs of changing prices.

short-side rule (for determining quantities) The condition that the quantity of output or sales in a situation of excess demand or excess supply is determined by the lesser of the quantity demanded and the quantity supplied.

QUESTIONS AND PROBLEMS

MAINLY FOR REVIEW

20.1

a. Contrast the form of consumption demand in the Keynesian model with that in Chapter 5. Why does a change in current income not affect consumption demand in the market-clearing model?

b. Make the same comparisons for investment demand.

20.2 What is involuntary unemployment? Are the temporary layoffs of workers on long-term contracts an example of involuntary unemployment?

20.3 How does output adjust to ensure the aggregate-consistency condition for the commodity market (equation [20.7])? Would this result apply if goods were not in excess supply?

20.4 Explain how an increase in the quantity of money reduces the real interest rate in the Keynesian model. Why does this effect not arise in the market-clearing model?

20.5 What is the output multiplier for an increase in government purchases? Discuss how the size of the multiplier is affected by the following:

a. Whether government purchases are tax financed or deficit financed.

b. Any increases in the interest rate.

c. Whether government purchases are temporary or permanent.

20.6 Assume that the price level is fixed at a level that is "too high." Show in this case that the interest rate and output must adjust to ensure the condition that all money be willingly held. Can the interest rate be too high as a result? How does a downward adjustment of the price level bring down the interest rate and eliminate excess supply of commodities?

PROBLEMS FOR DISCUSSION

20.7   The Paradox of Thrift

Suppose that people become "thriftier" and thereby decide to save more and consume less.

a.   For a given interest rate, what happens to the quantities of output and employment? What happens to the amount of private saving? (*Hint*: What happens to the quantity of investment?) If the amount of private saving falls when people become thriftier, then there is said to be a *paradox of thrift*.

b.   Redo the analysis when the interest rate is allowed to adjust. What happens now to the amount of saving? Is there a paradox of thrift?

c.   Can there be a paradox of thrift in the market-clearing model, in which the price level is also allowed to adjust? What accounts for the differences in results?

20.8   The Multiplier

Consider an autonomous increase in investment demand.

a.   Why is there a multiplicative effect on output if we hold fixed the interest rate?

b.   Is there still a multiplier when the interest rate adjusts? How does this answer depend on the magnitudes of the following:

    i.   The sensitivity of aggregate demand to the interest rate?

    ii.   The sensitivity of money demand to output?

iii. The sensitivity of money demand to the interest rate?

20.9   Perceived Wealth in the Keynesian Model

Suppose that the president of the United States makes a speech and announces that we are all wealthier than we previously thought. If we all believe the president, then what does the Keynesian model predict for the changes in output, employment, and "wealth"? Explain these results and contrast them with the predictions from the market-clearing model.

20.10   A Change in Inflationary Expectations

Consider an (unexplained) increase in inflationary expectations, π^e.

a.   How does this change affect the IS curve?

b.   How does it affect the LM curve? (Recall that money demand depends on the nominal interest rate, $R = r + \pi^e$.)

c.   What happens to the level of output, the real interest rate, and the nominal interest rate? Explain these results and contrast them with those from the market-clearing model. (*Hint*: How does the change in inflationary expectations compare to an autonomous shift in the demand for money?)

20.11   Extreme Cases in the IS/LM Analysis

Consider the following extreme cases (which have sometimes been suggested, but have not been supported empirically).

a.   Suppose that money demand is insensitive to the interest rate. What does the LM curve look like? In this case what is the effect on output and the interest rate from a disturbance that shifts the IS curve?

b.   Suppose that money demand is extremely sensitive to the interest rate (sometimes called a *liquidity trap*). How does the LM curve look in this case? What is the effect now from a shift in the IS curve?

c. Suppose that the interest rate has a negligible effect on aggregate demand. How does the IS curve look in this situation? What are the effects from a shift in the LM curve?

d. Finally, suppose that aggregate demand is extremely sensitive to the interest rate. Draw the IS curve, and describe the effects from a shift in the LM curve.

20.12 Stagflation in the Keynesian Model

Suppose that we define stagflation as an increase in inflation during a recession.

a. Assume that a recession stems from an autonomous decline in aggregate demand. Can we get stagflation from this disturbance in the Keynesian model?

b. Is there some other way to generate stagflation in the Keynesian model?

20.13 The Cyclical Behavior of the Real Wage Rate (optional)

Consider a positive shock to the IS curve. We showed that output and the inflation rate would rise in the Keynesian model. What happens over time to the nominal wage rate and therefore to the real wage rate? What are the implications for the cyclical behavior of the real wage rate?

BIBLIOGRAPHY

Abraham, Katharine G., and Lawrence F. Katz. 1986. "Cyclical Unemployment: Sectoral Shifts or Aggregate Disturbances." *Journal of Political Economy* 94 (June): 507–22.

Ahmed, Shaghil. 1987a. "Wage Stickiness and the Nonneutrality of Money: A Cross-Industry Analysis." *Journal of Monetary Economics* 20 (July): 25–50.

Ahmed, Shaghil. 1987b. "Government Spending, the Balance of Trade and the Terms of Trade in British History." *Journal of Monetary Economics* 20 (September): 195–220.

Alogoskoufis, George S. 1987a. "Aggregate Employment and Intertemporal Substitution in the U.K." *Economic Journal* 97 (June): 403–15.

Alogoskoufis, George S. 1987b. "On Intertemporal Substitution and Aggregate Labor Supply." *Journal of Political Economy* 95 (October): 938–60.

Ando, Albert, and Franco Modigliani. 1963. "The 'Life-Cycle' Hypothesis of Saving: Aggregate Implications and Tests." *American Economic Review* 53 (March): 55–84.

Aschauer, David A. 1985. "Fiscal Policy and Aggregate Demand." *American Economic Review* 75 (March): 117–27.

Aschauer, David A. 1988. "Is Public Expenditure Productive?" Presented at conference of National Bureau of Economic Research, Cambridge, MA, July.

Attfield, C. L. F., D. Demery, and N. W. Duck. 1981. "A Quarterly Model of Unanticipated Monetary Growth, Output and the Price Level in the U.K." *Journal of Monetary Economics* 8 (November): 331–50.

Attfield, C. L. F., and N. W. Duck. 1983. "The Influence of Unanticipated Money Growth on Real Output: Some Cross-Country Estimates." *Journal of Money, Credit and Banking* 15 (November): 442–54.

Auerbach, Robert D. 1985. *Money, Banking and Financial Markets,* 2nd ed. New York: Macmillan.

Azariadis, Costas. 1975. "Implicit Contracts and Underemployment Equilibria." *Journal of Political Economy* 83 (December): 1183–1202.

Bagehot, Walter. 1873. *Lombard Street.* New York: Scribner Armstrong & Company.

Bailey, Martin J. 1971. *National Income and the Price Level,* 2nd ed. New York: McGraw-Hill.

Baily, Martin N. 1974. "Wages and Employment under Uncertain Demand." *Review of Economic Studies* 33 (January): 37–50.

Barnett, William A., Edward K. Offenbacher, and Paul A. Spindt. 1984. "The New Divisia Monetary Aggregates." *Journal of Political Economy* 92 (December): 1049–85.

Barro, Robert J. 1974. "Are Government Bonds Net Wealth?" *Journal of Political Economy* 82 (November/December): 1095–1118.

Barro, Robert J. 1978a. "Comment from an Unreconstructed Ricardian." *Journal of Monetary Economics* 4 (August): 569–81.

Barro, Robert J. 1978b. "Unanticipated Money, Output and the Price Level in the United States." *Journal of Political Economy* 86 (August): 548–80.

Barro, Robert J. 1987. "Government Spending, Interest Rates, Prices and Budget Deficits in the United Kingdom, 1730–1918." *Journal of Monetary Economics* 20 (September): 221–47.

Barro, Robert J. 1989. "The Ricardian Approach to Budget Deficits." *Journal of Economic Perspectives* 3 (Spring): 37–54.

Barro, Robert J. 1997. *Determinants of Economic Growth: A Cross-Country Empirical Study.* Cambridge, MA: MIT Press.

Barro, Robert J., and Herschel I. Grossman. 1976. *Money, Employment and Inflation.* Cambridge: Cambridge University Press.

Barro, Robert J., and Xavier Sala-i-Martin. 1990. "World Real Interest Rates." *NBER Macroeconomics Annual 1990.* Cambridge, MA: MIT Press.

Barro, Robert J., and Xavier Sala-i-Martin. 1991. "Covergence across States and Regions." *Brookings Papers on Economic Activity,* no. 1, pp. 107–82.

Barro, Robert J., and Xavier Sala-i-Martin. 1992. "Convergence." *Journal of Political Economy* 100 (April): 223–51.

Barro, Robert J., and Xavier Sala-i-Martin. 1995. *Economic Growth.* New York: McGraw-Hill.

Barsky, Robert B., and Jeffrey A. Miron. 1988. "The Seasonal Cycle and the Business Cycle." Unpublished, University of Michigan, July.

Baumol, William J. 1952. "The Transactions Demand for Cash: An Inventory Theoretic Approach." *Quarterly Journal of Economics* 66 (November): 545–56.

Becker, Gary S. 1981. "The Demand for Children." In *A Treatise on the Family.* Cambridge, MA: Harvard University Press.

Becker, Gary S., and Robert J. Barro. 1988. "A Reformulation of the Economic Theory of Fertility." *Quarterly Journal of Economics* 103 (February): 1–25.

Benjamin, Daniel K., and Levis A. Kochin. 1984. "War, Prices and Interest Rates: Gibson's Paradox Revisited." In Michael D. Bordo and Anna J. Schwartz, eds., *A Retrospective on the Classical Gold Standard, 1821–1931.* Chicago: University of Chicago Press.

Bernanke, Ben S. 1983a. "Irreversibility, Uncertainty, and Cyclical Investment." *Quarterly Journal of Economics* 98 (February): 85–106.

Bernanke, Ben S. 1983b. "Non-Monetary Effects of the Financial Collapse in the Propagation of the Great Depression." *American Economic Review* 73 (June): 257–76.

Bernheim, B. Douglas, Andrei Shleifer, and Lawrence H. Summers. 1985. "The Strategic Bequest Motive." *Journal of Political Economy* 93 (December): 1045–76.

Bienefeld, M. A. 1972. *Working Hours in British Industry.* London: Weidenfeld and Nicolson.

Bils, Mark. 1989. "Testing for Contracting Effects on Employment." Rochester Center for Economic Research, working paper no. 174, January.

Bird, Roger C., and Ronald G. Bodkin. 1965. "The National Service Life Insurance Dividend of 1950 and Consumption: A Further Test of the 'Strict' Permanent Income Hypothesis." *Journal of Political Economy* 73 (October): 499–515.

Black, Fischer. 1970. "Banking and Interest Rates in a World without Money." *Journal of Bank Research,* Autumn, pp. 9–20.

Blinder, Alan S. 1980. "Inventories in the Keynesian Macro Model." *Kyklos* 33, no. 4: 585–614.

Bloom, Murray T. 1966. *The Man Who Stole Portugal.* New York: Charles Scribner's Sons.

Board of Governors of the Federal Reserve System. 1976. *Banking and Monetary Statistics, 1941–1970.* Washington, DC.

Board of Governors of the Federal Reserve System. 1981. *Annual Statistical Digest, 1970–1979.* Washington, DC.

Board of Governors of the Federal Reserve System. *Federal Reserve Bulletin,* various issues.

Bohn, Henning. 1991. "Budget Deficits and Government Accounting." Unpublished. Wharton School, University of Pennsylvania.

Bomberger, William A., and Gail E. Makinen. 1983. "The Hungarian Hyperinflation and Stabilization of 1945–1946." *Journal of Political Economy* 91 (October): 801–24.

Bordo, Michael D., and Lars Jonung. 1981. "The Long-Run Behavior of the Income Velocity of Money in Five Advanced Countries, 1870–1975: An Institutional Approach." *Economic Inquiry* 19 (January): 96–116.

Boskin, Michael J., ed. 1977a. *The Crisis in Social Security.* San Francisco: Institute for Contemporary Studies.

Boskin, Michael J. 1977b. "Social Security and Retirement Decisions." *Economic Inquiry* 15 (January): 1–25.

Boskin, Michael J., chairman (with Ellen R. Dulberger, Zvi Griliches, Robert J. Gordon, and Dale Jorgenson). 1996. *Toward a More Accurate Measure of the Cost of Living, Final Report to the Senate Finance Committee from the Advisory Commission to Study the Consumer Price Index.* Washington, DC: U.S. Government Printing Office, December.

Boskin, Michael J., Laurence J. Kotlikoff, Douglas J. Poffert, and John B. Shoven. 1987. "Social Security: A Financial Appraisal across and within Generations." *National Tax Journal* 40 (March): 19–34.

Bound, John, and George Johnson. 1995. "What Are the Causes of Rising Wage Inequality in the United States?" *Federal Reserve Bank of New York Policy Review,* January, pp. 9–17.

Bresciani-Turroni, Costantino. 1937. *The Economics of Inflation.* London: Allen and Unwin.

Broadbent, Ben. 1996. "Monetary Policy Regimes and the Costs of Discretion." Unpublished. Harvard University.

Brown, Charles, Curtis Gilroy, and Andrew Koehn. 1982. "The Effect of the Minimum Wage on Employment and Unemployment: A Survey." *Journal of Economic Literature* 20 (June): 487–528.

Brown, E. Cary. 1956. "Fiscal Policy in the Thirties: A Reappraisal." *American Economic Review* 46 (December): 857–79.

Brunner, Karl. 1968. "The Role of Money and Monetary Policy." Federal Reserve Bank of St. Louis, *Review,* July, pp. 9–24.

Buchanan, James M. 1958. *Public Principles of Public Debt.* Homewood, IL: Irwin.

Bulow, Jeremy, and Kenneth S. Rogoff. 1988. "Sovereign Debt: Is to Forgive to Forget?" Unpublished. Stanford University, February.

Burda, Michael. 1988. "Reflections on 'Wait Unemployment' in Europe." Economic Policy Panel, London, April.

Burtless, Gary. 1987. "Jobless Pay and High European Unemployment." In Robert Lawrence and Charles

Schultze, eds., *Barriers to European Economic Growth.* Washington, DC: Brookings Institution.

Cagan, Phillip D. 1956. "The Monetary Dynamics of Hyperinflation." In Milton Friedman, ed., *Studies in the Quantity Theory of Money.* Chicago: University of Chicago Press.

Cagan, Phillip D. 1958. "The Demand for Currency Relative to the Total Money Supply." *Journal of Political Economy* 66 (August): 303–28.

Cagan, Phillip D. 1965. *Determinants and Effects of Changes in the Stock of Money, 1875–1960.* New York: Columbia University Press.

Card, David. 1980. "Determinants of the Form of Long-Term Contracts." Princeton University working paper no. 135, June.

Card, David. 1992a. "Do Minimum Wages Reduce Employment? A Case Study of California, 1987–89." *Industrial and Labor Relations Review* 46 (October): 38–54.

Card, David. 1992b. "Using Regional Variation in Wages to Measure the Effects of the Federal Minimum Wage." *Industrial and Labor Relations Review* 46 (October): 22–37.

Card, David, and Alan Krueger. "Minimum Wages and Employment: A Case Study of the Fast-Food Industry in New Jersey and Pennsylvania." *American Economic Review* 84 (September): 772–93.

Carlson, John A. 1977. "A Study of Price Forecasts." *Annals of Economic and Social Measurement* 6 (Winter): 27–56.

Carroll, Chris, and Lawrence H. Summers. 1987. "Why Have Private Savings Rates in the United States and Canada Diverged?" *Journal of Monetary Economics* 20 (September): 249–79.

Caskey, John. 1985. "Modeling the Formation of Price Expectations: A Bayesian Approach." *American Economic Review* 75 (September): 768–76.

Central Statistical Office. *Annual Abstract of Statistics.* London, various issues.

Central Statistical Office. *Monthly Digest of Statistics.* London, various issues.

Chaudhury, Ajit K. 1979. "Output, Employment and Inventories under General Excess Supply." *Journal of Monetary Economics* 5 (October): 505–14.

Clark, Kim B., and Lawrence H. Summers. 1979. "Labor Market Dynamics and Unemployment: A Reconsideration." *Brookings Papers on Economic Activity,* no. 1, pp. 13–60.

Clark, Kim B., and Lawrence H. Summers. 1982. "Unemployment Insurance and Labor Market Transitions." In Martin N. Baily, ed., *Workers, Jobs and Inflation.* Washington, DC: Brookings Institution.

Clark, Truman A. 1986. "Interest Rate Seasonals and the Federal Reserve." *Journal of Political Economy* 94 (February): 76–125.

Cukierman, Alex. 1983. "Relative Price Variability and Inflation, a Survey and Further Results." *Carnegie-Rochester Conference Series on Public Policy* 19 (Autumn): 103–58.

Cumby, Robert, and Maurice Obstfeld. 1984. "International Interest Rate and Price Level Linkages under Flexible Exchange Rates: A Review of Recent Evidence." In John F. O. Bilson and Richard C. Marston, eds., *Exchange Rate Theory and Practice.* Chicago: University of Chicago Press.

Darby, Michael R. 1976. "Three-and-a-Half Million U.S. Employees Have Been Mislaid: Or an Explanation of Unemployment, 1934–1941." *Journal of Political Economy* 84 (February): 1–16.

Darby, Michael R., John C. Haltiwanger, Jr., and Mark W. Plant. 1985. "Unemployment Rate Dynamics and Persistent Unemployment under Rational Expectations." *American Economic Review* 75 (September): 614–37.

David, Paul A. 1967. "The Growth of Real Product in the United States since 1840." *Journal of Economic History* 27 (June): 151–97.

Davis, Steve J., and John Haltiwanger. 1996. *Job Creation and Destruction.* Cambridge, MA: MIT Press.

Deane, P., and W. A. Cole. 1969. *British Economic Growth, 1688–1959,* 2nd ed. Cambridge: Cambridge University Press.

Denslow, David A., and Mark Rush. 1989. "Supply Shocks and the Interest Rate." *Economic Inquiry* 27 (July): 501–10.

Department of Employment and Productivity. 1971. *British Labour Statistics, Historical Abstract, 1886–1968.* London.

Devine, Theresa, and Nicholas Kiefer. 1991. *Empirical Labor Economics.* Oxford: Oxford University Press.

Dewey, Davis R. 1931. *Financial History of the United States,* 11th ed. New York: Longmans, Green.

Dotsey, Michael. 1985. "The Use of Electronic Funds Transfers to Capture the Effect of Cash Management Practices on the Demand for Demand Deposits." *Journal of Finance* 40 (December): 1493–1503.

DRI/McGraw-Hill. 1996. *DRI Basic Economics.* Lexington, MA: McGraw-Hill.

Easterlin, Richard A. 1968. *Population, Labor Force, and Long Swings in Economic Growth.* New York: Columbia University Press.

Eaton, Jonathan, Mark Gersovitz, and Joseph E. Stiglitz. 1986. "The Pure Theory of Country Risk." *European Economic Review* 30 (June): 481–513.

Economic Report of the President. Washington, DC: U.S. Government Printing Office, various issues.

Economist Intelligence Unit, Ltd. (U.K.). 1987. *Country Profile, Saudi Arabia, 1987–88.* London.

Eisner, Robert. 1986. *How Real Is the Federal Deficit?* New York: Free Press.

Eisner, Robert, and Paul Pieper. 1984. "A New View of the Federal Debt and Budget Deficits." *American Economic Review* 74 (March): 11–29.

Eisner, Robert, and Robert H. Strotz. 1963. "Determinants of Business Investment." In Commission on Money and Credit, *Impacts of Monetary Policy.* Englewood Cliffs, NJ: Prentice-Hall.

Eissa, Nada, and Jeffrey B. Liebman. 1996. "Labor Supply Response to the Earned Income Tax Credit." *Quarterly Journal of Economics* 111 (May): 605–36.

Esposito, Louis. 1978. "Effect of Social Security on Saving: Review of Studies Using U.S. Time Series Data." *Social Security Bulletin* 41 (May): 9–17.

Evans, Paul. 1987a. "Interest Rates and Expected Future Budget Deficits in the United States." *Journal of Political Economy* 95 (February): 34–58.

Evans, Paul. 1987b. "Do Budget Deficits Raise Nominal Interest Rates? Evidence from Six Industrial Countries." *Journal of Monetary Economics* 20 (September): 281–300.

Evans, Paul. 1988. "Do Budget Deficits Affect the Current Account?" Unpublished. Ohio State University, August.

Fair, Ray C. 1979. "An Analysis of the Accuracy of Four Macroeconometric Models." *Journal of Political Economy* 87 (August): 701–18.

Fair, Ray C. 1987. "International Evidence on the Demand for Money." *Review of Economics and Statistics* 69 (August): 473–80.

Fama, Eugene F. 1975. "Short-Term Interest Rates as Predictors of Inflation." *American Economic Review* 65 (June): 269–82.

Fama, Eugene F. 1983. "Financial Intermediation and Price Level Control." *Journal of Monetary Economics* 12 (July): 7–28.

Farber, Henry S. 1995. "Are Lifetime Jobs Disappearing? Job Duration in the United States: 1973–1993." National Bureau of Economic Research, working paper no. 5014, February.

Fay, Jon A., and James L. Medoff. 1985. "Labor and Output over the Business Cycle: Some Direct Evidence." *American Economic Review* 75 (September): 638–55.

Feinstein, C. H. 1972. *National Income, Expenditures and Output of the United Kingdom, 1855–1965.* Cambridge: Cambridge University Press.

Feldstein, Martin S. 1974. "Social Security, Induced Retirement, and Aggregate Capital Accumulation." 1974. *Journal of Political Economy* 82 (September/October): 905–28.

Feldstein, Martin S., and Andrew Samwick. 1992. "Social Security Rules and Marginal Tax Rates." National Bureau of Economic Research, working paper no. 3962, January.

Ferguson, James M., ed. 1964. *Public Debt and Future Generations.* Chapel Hill: University of North Carolina Press.

Fischer, Stanley. 1977. "Long-Term Contracts, Rational Expectations and the Optimal Money Supply Rule." *Journal of Political Economy* 85 (February): 191–206.

Fisher, Irving. 1926. "A Statistical Relation between Unemployment and Price Changes." *International Labor Review* 13 (June): 785–92. Reprinted as "I Discovered the Phillips Curve." *Journal of Political Economy* 81 (March/April): 496–502.

Fisher, Irving. 1930. *The Theory of Interest.* New York: Macmillan.

Fisher, Irving. 1971. *The Purchasing Power of Money,* 2nd ed. (1st ed, 1922). New York: Augustus Kelley.

Fleisher, Belton M., and Thomas J. Kniesner. 1984. *Labor Economics: Theory, Evidence and Policy,* 3rd ed. Englewood Cliffs, NJ: Prentice-Hall.

Flood, Robert P., and Peter M. Garber. 1980. "An Economic Theory of Monetary Reform." *Journal of Political Economy* 88 (February): 24–58.

Friedman, Milton. 1956. "The Quantity of Money—A Restatement." In *Studies in the Quantity Theory of Money.* Chicago: University of Chicago Press.

Friedman, Milton. 1957. *A Theory of the Consumption Function.* Princeton, NJ: Princeton University Press.

Friedman, Milton. 1960. *A Program for Monetary Stability.* New York: Fordham University Press.

Friedman, Milton. 1968a. "Free Exchange Rates." In *Dollars and Deficits.* Englewood Cliffs, NJ: Prentice-Hall.

Friedman, Milton. 1968b. "Inflation: Causes and Consequences." In *Dollars and Deficits.* Englewood Cliffs, NJ: Prentice-Hall.

Friedman, Milton. 1968c. "The Role of Monetary Policy." *American Economic Review* 58 (March): 1–17.

Friedman, Milton. 1969. *The Optimum Quantity of Money and Other Essays.* Chicago: Aldine.

Friedman, Milton, and Anna J. Schwartz. 1963. *A Monetary History of the United States, 1867–1960.* Princeton, NJ: Princeton University Press.

Friedman, Milton, and Anna J. Schwartz. 1970. *Monetary Statistics of the United States.* New York: Columbia University Press.

Fullerton, Don. 1982. "On the Possibility of an Inverse Relationship between Tax Rates and Government Revenues." *Journal of Public Economics* 19 (October): 3–22.

Garber, Peter M. 1982. "Transition from Inflation to Price Stability." *Carnegie-Rochester Conference Series on Public Policy* 16 (Spring): 11–42.

Geweke, John. 1986. "The Superneutrality of Money in the United States: An Interpretation of the Evidence." *Econometrica* 54 (January): 1–22.

Glass, Carter. 1927. *An Adventure in Constructive Finance.* New York: Doubleday, Page & Co.

Goldfeld, Steven M. 1973. "The Demand for Money Revisited." *Brookings Papers on Economic Activity,* no. 3, pp. 577–638.

Goldfeld, Steven M. 1976. "The Case of the Missing Money." *Brookings Papers on Economic Activity,* no. 3, pp. 683–730.

Goldfeld, Steven M., and Daniel E. Sichel. 1990. *The Demand for Money.* In Benjamin M. Friedman and Frank H. Hahn, eds., *Handbook of Monetary Economics,* vol. 1. Amsterdam: North Holland.

Goodfriend, Marvin. 1986. "Monetary Mystique: Secrecy and Central Banking." *Journal of Monetary Economics* 17 (January): 63–92.

Goodfriend, Marvin. 1987. "Interest Rate Smoothing and Price Level Trend Stationarity." *Journal of Monetary Economics* 19 (May): 335–48.

Gordon, Donald F. 1974. "A Neo-Classical Theory of Keynesian Unemployment." *Economic Inquiry* 12 (December): 431–59.

Gorton, Gary. 1986. "Banking Panics and Business Cycles." Unpublished. Federal Reserve Bank of Philadelphia, February.

Gray, Jo Anna. 1976. "Wage Indexation: A Macroeconomic Approach." *Journal of Monetary Economics* 2 (April): 221–36.

Greenwood, Jeremy. 1983. "Expectations, the Exchange Rate and the Current Account." *Journal of Monetary Economics* 12 (November): 543–70.

Grossman, Gene M., and Elhanan Helpman. 1991. *Innovation and Growth in the Global Economy.* Cambridge, MA: MIT Press.

Grossman, Herschel I. 1979. "Risk Shifting, Layoffs and Seniority." *Journal of Monetary Economics* 4 (November): 661–86.

Haberler, Gottfried. 1939. *Prosperity and Depression,* 2nd ed. Geneva: League of Nations.

Hall, Robert E. 1977. "Investment, Interest Rates, and the Effects of Stabilization Policies." *Brookings Papers on Economic Activity,* no. 1, pp. 61–103.

Hall, Robert E. 1979. "A Theory of the Natural Unemployment Rate and the Duration of Unemployment." *Journal of Monetary Economics* 5 (April): 153–70.

Hall, Robert E. 1980a. "Employment Fluctuations and Wage Rigidity." *Brookings Papers on Economic Activity,* no. 1, pp. 91–123.

Hall, Robert E. 1980b. "Labor Supply and Aggregate Fluctuations." *Carnegie-Rochester Conference on Public Policy* 12 (Spring): 7–33.

Hall, Robert E. 1982. "The Importance of Lifetime Jobs in the U.S. Economy." *American Economic Review* 72 (September): 716–24.

Hall, Robert E. 1989. "Consumption." In Robert J. Barro, ed., *Modern Business Cycle Theory.* Cambridge, MA: Harvard University Press.

Hamermesh, Daniel. 1977. *Jobless Pay and the Economy.* Baltimore: Johns Hopkins University Press.

Hamermesh, Daniel. 1995. "Myth and Measurement: The New Economics of the Minimum Wage, Comment." *Industrial and Labor Relations Review* 48 (July): 835–38.

Hamilton, James D. 1983. "Oil and the Macroeconomy since World War II." *Journal of Political Economy* 91 (April): 228–48.

Hamilton, James D. 1985. "Uncovering Financial Market Expectations of Inflation." *Journal of Political Economy* 93 (December): 1224–41.

Hawtrey, Ralph G. 1932. "The Portuguese Bank Notes Case." *Economic Journal* 42 (September): 391–98.

Hayek, Friedrich A. 1945. "The Use of Knowledge in Society." *American Economic Review* 35 (September): 519–30.

Hercowitz, Zvi. 1981. "Money and the Dispersion of Relative Prices." *Journal of Political Economy* 89 (April): 328–56.

Hercowitz, Zvi. 1982. "Money and Price Dispersion in the United States." *Journal of Monetary Economics* 10 (July): 25–38.

Hicks, John. 1937. "Mr. Keynes and the 'Classics.'" *Econometrica* 5 (April): 147–59.

Hicks, John. 1946. *Value and Capital,* 2nd ed. Oxford: Oxford University Press.

Howard, David H. 1976. "The Disequilibrium Model in a Controlled Economy: An Empirical Test of the Barro-Grossman Model." *American Economic Review* 66 (December): 871–79.

Ingram, James C. 1983. *International Economics.* New York: Wiley.

International Monetary Fund. *International Financial Statistics,* various issues.

Jackman, Richard, Richard Layard, and Stephen Nickell. 1996. "Structural Aspects of OECD Unemployment." Unpublished. London School of Economics, February.

Jevons, W. Stanley. 1896. *Money and the Mechanism of Exchange.* New York: D. Appleton.

Jones, Alice H. 1980. *Wealth of a Nation to Be.* New York: Columbia University Press.

Jones, Robert A. 1976. "The Origin and Development of Media of Exchange." *Journal of Political Economy* 84 (August): 757–76.

Judd, John P., and John L. Scadding. 1982. "The Search for a Stable Money Demand Function." *Journal of Economic Literature* 20 (September): 993–1023.

Katz, Lawrence F., and Bruce D. Meyer. 1988. "The Impact of the Potential Duration of Unemployment Benefits on the Duration of Unemployment." Unpublished. Harvard University, May.

Katz, Lawrence F., and Kevin M. Murphy. 1992. "Changes in Relative Wages, 1963–1987: Supply and Demand Factors." *Quarterly Journal of Economics* 107 (February): 35–78.

Kendrick, John W. 1961. *Productivity Trends in the United States.* Princeton, NJ: Princeton University Press.

Kenny, Lawrence W. 1991. "Cross-Country Estimates of the Demand for Money and Its Components." *Economic Inquiry* 29 (October), 696–705.

Keynes, John Maynard. 1935. *The General Theory of Employment, Interest and Money.* New York: Harcourt Brace.

King, Robert G., and Charles I. Plosser. 1984. "Money, Credit and Prices in a Real Business Cycle." *American Economic Review* 74 (June): 363–80.

Klein, Benjamin. 1974. "Competitive Interest Payments on Bank Deposits and the Long-Run Demand for Money." *American Economic Review* 64 (December): 931–49.

Kormendi, Roger C. 1983. "Government Debt, Government Spending, and Private Sector Behavior." *American Economic Review* 73 (December): 994–1010.

Kormendi, Roger C., and Phillip G. Meguire. 1984. "Cross-Regime Evidence of Macroeconomic Rationality." *Journal of Political Economy* 92 (October): 875–908.

Kreinin, Mordechai E. 1961. "Windfall Income and Consumption—Additional Evidence." *American Economic Review* 51 (June): 388–90.

Kroszner, Randall S., and Raghuram G. Rajan. 1994. "Is the Glass-Steagall Act Justified? A Study of the U.S. Experience with Universal Banking Before 1933." *American Economic Review* 84 (September): 810–32.

Kuznets, Simon. 1948. "Discussion of the New Department of Commerce Income Series." *Review of Economics and Statistics* 30 (August): 151–79.

Kydland, Finn E., and Edward C. Prescott. 1977. "Rules Rather than Discretion: The Inconsistency of Optimal Plans." *Journal of Political Economy* 85 (June): 473–91.

Kydland, Finn E., and Edward C. Prescott. 1990. "Business Cycles: Real Facts and a Monetary Myth." Federal Reserve Bank of Minneapolis, *Quarterly Review,* Spring, pp. 3–18.

Lahaye, Laura. 1985. "Inflation and Currency Reform." *Journal of Political Economy* 93 (June): 537–60.

Laidler, David E. 1985. *The Demand for Money: Theories and Evidence,* 3rd ed. New York: Harper and Row.

Landsberger, Michael. 1970. "Restitution Receipts, Household Savings and Consumption Behavior in Israel." Unpublished. Research Department, Bank of Israel.

Law, John. 1966. *Money and Trade Considered* (1705). New York: Augustus Kelley.

Leimer, Dean, and Selig Lesnoy. 1982. "Social Security and Private Saving: New Time Series Evidence." *Journal of Political Economy* 90 (June): 606–29.

Lilien, David M. 1982. "Sectoral Shifts and Cyclical Unemployment." *Journal of Political Economy* 90 (August): 777–93.

Lindsey, Lawrence B. 1987. "Individual Taxpayer Response to Tax Cuts, 1982–1984." *Journal of Public Economics* 33 (July): 173–206.

Lipsey, Richard E. 1960. "The Relation between Unemployment and the Rate of Change of Money Wage Rates in the United Kingdom, 1862–1957: A Further Analysis." *Economica* 27 (February): 1–31.

Long, John B., Jr., and Charles I. Plosser. 1983. "Real Business Cycles." *Journal of Political Economy* 91 (February): 39–69.

Loungani, Prakash. 1986. "Oil Price Shocks and the Dispersion Hypothesis." Rochester Center for Economic Research, working paper no. 33, January.

Loungani, Prakash, and Mark Rush. 1991. "The Effects of Changes in Reserve Requirements on Investment and GNP." Unpublished. Federal Reserve Bank of Chicago, December.

Loungani, Prakash, Mark Rush, and William Tave. 1990. "Stock Market Dispersion and Unemployment." *Journal of Monetary Economics* 25 (June): 367–88.

Lucas, Robert E., Jr. 1967. "Adjustment Costs and the Theory of Supply." *Journal of Political Economy* 75 (August): 321–34.

Lucas, Robert E., Jr. 1977. "Understanding Business Cycles." *Carnegie-Rochester Conference on Public Policy* 5:7–29.

Lucas, Robert E., Jr. 1980. "Two Illustrations of the Quantity Theory of Money." *American Economic Review* 70 (December): 1005–14.

Lucas, Robert E., Jr. 1981. *Studies in Business-Cycle Theory,* Cambridge, MA: MIT Press.

Macaulay, Frederick R. 1938. *The Movement of Interest Rates, Bond Yields and Stock Prices in the United States since 1856.* New York: National Bureau of Economic Research.

MaCurdy, Thomas E. 1981. "An Empirical Model of Labor Supply in a Life-Cycle Setting." *Journal of Political Economy* 89 (December): 1059–85.

Malthus, Thomas R. 1809. *An Essay on the Principle of Population.* Washington, DC: R. C. Weightman.

Mankiw, N. Gregory, and Jeffrey A. Miron. 1986. "The Changing Behavior of the Term Structure of Interest Rates." *Quarterly Journal of Economics* 101 (May): 211–28.

Mankiw, N. Gregory, Jeffrey A. Miron, and David N. Weil. 1987. "The Adjustment of Expectations to a Change in Regime: A Study of the Founding of the Federal Reserve." *American Economic Review* 77 (June): 358–74.

Mansfield, Edwin. 1985. *Microeconomics,* 5th ed. New York: Norton.

Marston, Stephen T. 1976. "Employment Stability and High Unemployment." *Brookings Papers on Economic Activity,* no. 1, pp. 169–203.

McCallum, Ben T. 1979. "The Current State of the Policy-Ineffectiveness Debate." *American Economic Review* 69 (proceedings, May): 240–45.

McCallum, Ben T. 1989. "Real Business Cycle Models." In Robert J. Barro, ed., *Modern Business Cycle Theory.* Cambridge, MA: Harvard University Press.

McClure, Alexander K. 1901. *Abe Lincoln's Yarns and Stories.* New York: W. W. Wilson.

McCulloch, J. Huston. 1980. "The Ban on Indexed Bonds, 1933–77." *American Economic Review* 70 (December): 1018–21.

Miron, Jeffrey A. 1986. "Financial Panics, the Seasonality of the Nominal Interest Rate, and the Founding of the Fed." *American Economic Review* 76 (March): 125–40.

Miron, Jeffrey A. 1988. "A Cross-Country Comparison of Seasonal Cycles and Business Cycles." Unpublished. University of Michigan, October.

Mishkin, Frederic S. 1982. "Does Anticipated Monetary Policy Matter?" *Journal of Political Economy* 90 (February): 22–51.

Mishkin, Frederic S. 1984. "Are Real Interest Rates Equal across Countries? An Empirical Investigation of International Parity Conditions." *Journal of Finance* 39 (December): 1345–57.

Mitchell, B. R. 1980. *European Historical Statistics, 1750–1975,* 2nd ed. London: Macmillan.

Mitchell, B. R., and H. G. Jones. 1971. *Second Abstract of British Historical Statistics.* Cambridge: Cambridge University Press.

Mitchell, B. R., and P. Deane. 1962. *Abstract of British Historical Statistics.* Cambridge: Cambridge University Press.

Modigliani, Franco, and Richard Brumberg. 1954. "Utility Analysis and the Consumption Function: An Interpretation of Cross-Section Data." In Kenneth Kurihara, ed., *Post-Keynesian Economics.* New Brunswick, NJ: Rutgers University Press.

Molle, Willem. 1980. *Regional Disparity and Economic Development in the European Community.* Farnborough, England: Saxon House.

Morgan Guaranty Trust. 1983. *World Financial Markets.* New York, February.

Mulligan, Casey B. 1995a. "Pecuniary and Nonpecuniary Incentives to Work in the U.S. during World War II." Unpublished. University of Chicago, February.

Mulligan, Casey B. 1995b. "The Intertemporal Substitution of Work—What Does the Evidence Say?" Unpublished. University of Chicago, June.

Mulligan, Casey B., and Xavier Sala-i-Martin. 1996. "Financial Technologies: Implications for Money Demand and Monetary Policy." National Bureau of Economic Research, working paper no. 5504, March.

Mundell, Robert A. 1968. *International Economics* New York: Macmillan.

Mundell, Robert A. 1971. *Monetary Theory.* Pacific Palisades, CA: Goodyear.

Musgrave, Richard. 1959. *Theory of Public Finance.* New York: McGraw-Hill.

Mussa, Michael. 1979. "Empirical Regularities in the Behavior of Exchange Rates and Theories of the Foreign Exchange Market." *Carnegie-Rochester Conference Series on Public Policy* 11:9–58.

Muth, John F. 1961. "Rational Expectations and the Theory of Price Movements." *Econometrica* 29 (July): 315 35.

Nelson, Charles R., and G. William Schwert. 1977. "Short-Term Interest Rates as Predictors of Inflation: On Testing the Hypothesis that the Real Rate of Interest Is Constant." *American Economic Review* 67 (June): 478–86.

Neumark, David, and William Wascher. 1992. "Employment Effects of Minimum and Subminimum Wages: Panel Data on State Minimum Wage Laws." *Industrial and Labor Relations Review* 46 (October): 55–81.

Neumark, David, and William Wascher. 1995a. "The Effects of Minimum Wages on Teenage Employment and Enrollment: Evidence from Matched CPS Surveys." Unpublished. Michigan State University, July.

Neumark, David, and William Wascher. 1995b. "The Effect of New Jersey's Minimum Wage Increase on Fast-Food Employment: A Re-Evaluation Using Payroll Records." Unpublished. Michigan State University, November.

Ochs, Jack, and Mark Rush. 1983. "The Persistence of Interest Rate Effects on the Demand for Currency." *Journal of Money, Credit and Banking* 15 (November): 499–505.

O'Driscoll, Gerald P., Jr. 1977. "The Ricardian Nonequivalence Theorem." *Journal of Political Economy* 85 (February): 207–10.

Organization for Economic Cooperation and Development. 1994. *The OECD Jobs Study,* Part 2: *The Adjustment Potential of the Labour Market.* Paris.

Organization of American States. *Statistical Bulletin of the OAS,* various issues.

Patinkin, Don. 1948. "Price Flexibility and Full Employment." *American Economic Review* 38 (September): 543–64.

Patinkin, Don. 1956. *Money, Interest and Prices.* New York: Harper and Row.

Phelps, Edmund S. 1970. "The New Microeconomics in Employment and Inflation Theory." In *Microeconomic Foundations of Employment and Inflation Theory.* New York: Norton.

Phillips, A. W. 1958. "The Relation between Unemployment and the Rate of Change of Money Wage Rates in the United Kingdom, 1861–1959." *Economica* 25 (November): 283–99.

Pigou, Arthur C. 1947. "Economic Progress in a Stable Environment." *Economica* 14 (August): 180–88.

Pinera, Jose. 1996. *Empowering Workers: The Privatization of Social Security in Chile*. Washington, DC: Cato Institute.

Plosser, Charles I. 1982. "The Effects of Government Financing Decisions on Asset Returns." *Journal of Monetary Economics* 9 (May): 325–52.

Plosser, Charles I. 1987. "Fiscal Policy and the Term Structure." *Journal of Monetary Economics* 20 (September): 343–67.

Portes, Richard, and David Winter. 1980. "Disequilibrium Estimates for Consumption Goods Markets in Centrally Planned Economies." *Review of Economic Studies* 47 (January): 137–59.

Protopapadakis, Aris A., and Jeremy J. Siegel. 1987. "Are Money Growth and Inflation Related to Government Deficits? Evidence from Ten Industrialized Economies." *Journal of International Money and Finance* 6:31–48.

Ramaswami, Chitra. 1983. "Equilibrium Unemployment and the Efficient Job-Finding Rate." *Journal of Labor Economics* 1 (April): 171–96.

Rees, Albert E. 1959. "Patterns of Wages, Prices and Productivity." In Charles Myers, ed., *Wages, Prices, Profits and Productivity*. New York: Columbia University Press.

Ricardo, David. 1957. "Funding System." In P. Sraffa, ed., *The Works and Correspondence of David Ricardo*. Cambridge: Cambridge University Press.

Rogoff, Kenneth S. 1989. "Reputation, Coordination, and Monetary Policy." In Robert J. Barro, ed., *Modern Business Cycle Theory*. Cambridge, MA: Harvard University Press.

Romer, Christina D. 1986. "Spurious Volatility in Historical Unemployment Data." *Journal of Political Economy* 94 (February): 1–37.

Romer, Christina D. 1987. "Gross National Product, 1909–1928: Existing Estimates, New Estimates, and New Interpretations of World War I and Its Aftermath." National Bureau of Economic Research, working paper no. 2187, March.

Romer, Christina D. 1988. "The Prewar Business Cycle Reconsidered: New Estimates of Gross National Product, 1869–1908." Unpublished. University of California, Berkeley, June.

Romer, David. 1993. "The New Keynesian Synthesis." *Journal of Economic Perspectives* 7 (Winter): 5–22.

Romer, Paul M. 1990. "Endogenous Technological Change." *Journal of Political Economy* 98 (October): S71–S102.

Rotwein, Eugene, ed. 1970. *David Hume—Writings on Economics*. Madison: University of Wisconsin Press.

Runkle, David E. 1991. "Liquidity Constraints and the Permanent Income Hypothesis: Evidence from Panel Data." *Journal of Monetary Economics* 27:73–98.

Rush, Mark. 1985. "Unexpected Monetary Disturbances during the Gold Standard Era." *Journal of Monetary Economics* 15 (May): 309–22.

Rush, Mark. 1986. "Unexpected Money and Unemployment." Unpublished. University of Florida, September.

Sachs, Jeffrey D. 1981. "The Current Account and Macroeconomic Adjustment in the 1970s." *Brookings Papers on Economic Activity* no. 1, pp. 201–68.

Samuelson, Paul A. 1939. "A Synthesis of the Principle of Acceleration and the Multiplier." *Journal of Political Economy* 47 (December): 786–97.

Sargent, Thomas J. 1982. "The Ends of Four Big Inflations." In Robert E. Hall, ed., *Inflation: Causes and Effects.* Chicago: University of Chicago Press.

Sargent, Thomas J., and Neil Wallace. 1975. "Rational Expectations, the Optimal Monetary Instrument, and the Optimal Money Supply Rule." *Journal of Political Economy* 83 (April): 241–54.

Sargent, Thomas J., and Neil Wallace. 1981. "Some Unpleasant Monetarist Arithmetic." Federal Reserve Bank of Minneapolis, *Quarterly Review,* Fall, pp. 1–17.

Scoggins, John F. 1990. "Supply Shocks and Net Exports." Unpublished. University of Alabama at Birmingham.

Siegel, Jeremy J. 1979. "Inflation-Induced Distortions in Government and Private Saving Statistics." *Review of Economics and Statistics* 61 (April): 83–90.

Simons, Henry C. 1948. "Rules versus Authorities in Monetary Policy." In *Economic Policy for a Free Society.* Chicago: University of Chicago Press.

Sims, Christopher A. 1980. "Comparison of Interwar and Postwar Business Cycles: Monetarism Reconsidered." *American Economic Review* 70 (May): 250–57.

Solon, Gary. 1985. "Work Incentive Effects of Taxing Unemployment Benefits." *Econometrica* 53 (March): 295–306.

Solow, Robert M. 1956. "A Contribution to the Theory of Economic Growth." *Quarterly Journal of Economics* 70 (February): 65–94.

Spindt, Paul A. 1985. "Money Is What Money Does: Monetary Aggregation and the Equation of Exchange." *Journal of Political Economy* 93 (February): 175–204.

Stuart, Charles E. 1981. "Swedish Tax Rates, Labor Supply and Tax Revenues." *Journal of Political Economy* 89 (October): 1020–38.

Summers, Robert, and Alan Heston. 1988. "A New Set of International Comparisons of Real Product and Price Levels, Estimates for 130 Countries, 1950–1985." *The Review of Income and Wealth* 34 (March): 1–25.

Summers, Robert, and Alan Heston. 1996. *Penn-World Tables, Version 5.6*, available on the internet at www.nber.org/pwt56.html.

Taylor, John B. 1980. "Aggregate Dynamics and Staggered Contracts." *Journal of Political Economy* 88 (February): 1–23.

Thornton, Henry. 1978. *An Enquiry into the Nature and Effects of the Paper Credit of Great Britain* (1802). Fairfield, NJ: Augustus Kelly.

Timberlake, Richard H., Jr. 1978. *The Origins of Central Banking in the United States.* Cambridge, MA: Harvard University Press.

Tobin, James. 1956. "The Interest-Elasticity of Transactions Demand for Cash." *Review of Economics and Statistics* 38 (August): 241–47.

Tobin, James. 1971a. "A General Equilibrium Approach to Monetary Theory." In *Essays in Economics,* vol. 1: *Macroeconomics.* Chicago: Markham.

Tobin, James. 1971b. "Deposit Interest Ceilings as a Monetary control." In *Essays in Economics,* vol. 1: *Macroeconomics,* Chicago: Markham.

Topel, Robert, and Finis Welch. 1980. "Unemployment Insurance: Survey and Extensions." *Economica* 47 (August): 351–79.

Ureta, Manuelita. 1992. "The Importance of Lifetime Jobs in the U.S. Economy, Revisited." *American Economic Review* 82 (March): 322–35.

U.S. Department of Commerce. 1993. *Fixed Reproducible Tangible Wealth in the United States, 1925–89.* Washington, DC.

U.S. Department of Commerce. 1975. *Historical Statistics of the U.S., Colonial Times to 1970*. Washington, DC.

U.S. Department of Commerce. 1986. *National Income and Product Accounts of the U.S., 1929–1982*. Washington, DC.

U.S. Department of Commerce. *Statistical Abstract of the United States,* various issues.

U.S. Department of Commerce. *Survey of Current Business,* various issues.

Van Ravestein, A., and H. Vijlbrief. 1988. "Welfare Cost of Higher Tax Rates: An Empirical Laffer Curve for the Netherlands." *De Economist* 136:205–19.

Walre de Bordes, J. van. 1927. *The Austrian Crown.* London: King.

Welch, Finis. 1995. "Myth and Measurement: The New Economics of the Minimum Wage, Comment." *Industrial and Labor Relations Review* 48 (July): 842–49.

Winston, Gordon C. 1966. "An International Comparison of Income and Hours of Work." *Review of Economics and Statistics* 48 (February): 28–39.

World Bank. 1994. *Averting the Old Age Crisis.* Oxford: Oxford University Press.

Glossary

absolute form of PPP The version of purchasing-power parity that involves levels of exchange rates and prices.

acyclical Having no regular relation with the business cycle, that is, with detrended real GDP.

adjusted gross income Gross income less adjustments for tax purposes, such as business and moving expenses and deferred compensation through pension plans.

after-tax marginal product of labor The marginal product of labor less the tax levied on the resulting increase in product.

after-tax rate of return to investment The real rate of return from investment less the tax levied on the resulting increase in net product.

after-tax real interest rate The real interest rate less the tax paid on the interest earnings.

aggregate-consistency conditions Conditions on quantities that must hold when we add up the actions of all participants in a market—for example, the total of goods sold equals the total bought, and the total of funds lent equals the total borrowed. In the basic model, we use market-clearing conditions to ensure that the aggregate-consistency conditions are satisfied.

aggregate supply–aggregate demand model An approach that combines the Keynesian *IS/LM* model with a condition that determines the price level to equate the aggregates of supply and demand.

anticipated money growth The public's forecast of the rate of monetary growth, based on the historical relationship between the quantity of money and economic variables.

AS-AD model See *aggregate supply–aggregate demand model.*

autonomous change in demand An unexplained shift in the aggregate demand for commodities.

average tax rate The ratio of taxes to a measure of income. See *marginal tax rate.*

balance on capital account The net acquisition of interest-bearing assets from abroad.

balance of international payments The summary statement of a country's international trade in commodities, bonds, and international currency.

balanced budget A situation in which there is no change in the real amount of money and bonds issued by government; zero real saving by government.

banking panic Simultaneous runs on many banks and financial institutions, featuring attempts by many depositors to convert their deposits into currency.

barter Direct exchange of one good for another, without the use of money. See *medium of exchange.*

Board of Governors of the Federal Reserve System The seven-member group, appointed by the U.S. president, that makes most decisions of the Federal Reserve System.

bond A contract that gives the holder (lender) a claim to a specified stream of payments from the issuer (borrower).

boom A period in which aggregate economic activity or real gross national product is high and rising.

Bretton Woods System A system of international payments established after World War II in which each country pegged the exchange rate between its currency and the U.S. dollar. The United States exchanged dollars for gold at a fixed price ($35 per ounce), thus pegging the value of each country's currency to gold.

budget constraint The equation relating the sources of funds in a period, such as income from the commodity market and initial assets, to the uses of funds in that period, such as consumption and end-of-period assets.

budget line A graph of the combinations of consumptions over two periods that satisfy the two-period budget constraint.

burden of the public debt The possible negative effect of the public debt on saving and investment and, hence, on the stock of capital available later.

chain-weighted real GDP A method for constructing real GDP in which the relative-price weights continually adjust for the changing composition of production.

closed economy An economy isolated from the rest of the world.

common currency A regime in which all countries use the same currency and quote prices in units of this currency.

complete Keynesian model A version of the Keynesian theory that assumes sticky nominal wage rates but a perfectly flexible general price level.

conditional convergence The idea that poor countries grow faster than rich ones for given values of government policies, propensities to save and have children, and other variables.

constant-growth-rate rule A rule for monetary policy in which a specified monetary aggregate grows at a constant rate.

constant returns to scale The property of some production functions that a proportionate increase in all inputs results in an equiproportionate increase in output.

consumer durables Consumable commodities purchased by households that last for a long time, such as automobiles, furniture, and appliances.

consumer nondurables and services Consumable commodities purchased by households that last for a short time.

consumer price index (CPI) A weighted average of prices of consumer goods relative to a base year.

convergence The tendency of a poor economy to grow at a higher rate per capita than a rich economy and thereby to catch up to the rich economy.

costs of intermediation The total cost of operating a financial intermediary.

countercyclical Moving in the direction opposite to the business cycle, that is, to detrended real GDP.

crowding out (from government deficits) The decline in private investment that may result from a tax cut financed by a government budget deficit.

crowding out (from government consumption) The decrease in private consumption and investment that results from an increase in government consumption.

currency Non-interest-bearing paper money issued by the government.

current-account balance The value of goods produced by domestic residents (including the net factor income from abroad) plus net transfers from abroad, less the expenditure by domestic residents on goods; if the current-account balance is positive (negative), then the current account is in surplus (deficit).

decreasing returns to scale The property of some production functions that a proportionate increase in all inputs results in a less than proportionate increase in output.

deflation A sustained decrease in the general price level over time. See *inflation*.

demand deposits Deposits held at a financial institution that can be withdrawn at face value without restrictions.

demand for money The amount of money that someone desires to hold, expressed as a function of the volume of spending, the interest rate, transaction costs, and other variables.

depreciation The wearing out of capital goods over time; often expressed as a fraction of the stock of capital.

desired stock of capital The stock of capital chosen by a producer, depending on factors such as the marginal product of capital, the real interest rate, and the depreciation rate.

devaluation An action by the central bank of a country that raises the number of units of its currency that exchange for other currencies; a rise in the exchange rate.

diminishing marginal productivity A characteristic of the production function by which successive increments of an input yield progressively smaller increments in output.

direct investment abroad Purchase of capital goods that are located in foreign countries.

discount factor The relative value of a dollar in different periods of time; for example, between one period and the next, the nominal discount factor is one plus the nominal interest rate.

discount rate of Fed The interest rate charged on loans from the Federal Reserve to financial institutions.

discouraged workers Workers who leave the labor force following a period of unemployment.

discretionary policy A setup in which government policy is not restricted by prior commitments.

disintermediation The decline in the use of the services of financial intermediaries that results when the public moves away from holding deposits toward direct holding of bonds and mortgages.

disposable personal income Personal income less taxes.

distributional effects Shifts in the distribution of resources across households, with no change in the aggregate of resources; changes such that some sectors in the economy gain at the expense of others.

domestic credit The total of the central bank's claims on the domestic economy. In the United States, the bulk of domestic credit takes the form of U.S. government securities held by the Federal Reserve. See *Federal Reserve credit*.

double coincidence of wants The situation required for barter to take place, in which the type and quantity of goods offered by one trader match those desired by the other trader.

duration of jobs The average length of time that a job is expected to last; the duration of jobs is inversely related to the job-separation rate.

duration of unemployment The length of time that a spell of unemployment is expected to last. The duration of unemployment is inversely related to the job-finding rate.

economies of scale in the demand for money The property of the demand for money that the desired average real money holding increases less than proportionately with a rise in real income.

employment   The number of persons working at jobs in the market sector.

endogenous growth   Long-run economic growth that is explained by the interactions within a model.

endogenous money   The automatic response of the quantity of money to changes in the economy. Money is endogenous under the gold standard or in regimes in which the monetary authority targets nominal interest rates or the price level.

European Currency Unit (ECU)   A weighted average of all currencies of countries that belong to the European Union. The ECU is used as a currency unit by the European Monetary System.

European Monetary System (EMS)   Arrangement whereby several European countries maintained nearly fixed exchange rates among their currencies. The system began in 1979 and pretty much broke down in 1992.

excess demand   A situation in which, at the prevailing price, the quantity demanded in a market exceeds the quantity supplied.

excess reserves   The difference between the total reserves held by financial institutions and the amount required to be held under the reserve requirement of the Federal Reserve.

excess supply   A situation in which, at the prevailing price, the quantity supplied in a market exceeds the quantity demanded.

exchange rate   The number of units of the currency of a country that trade for one unit of another currency, such as the U.S. dollar.

Exchange Rate Mechanism (ERM)   The setup used by the European Monetary System (EMS) to maintain fixed exchange rates among the members' currencies.

expectation of inflation   The public's forecast of the inflation rate.

expectational Phillips curve   The relation between unexpected inflation and the unemployment rate. According to this curve, an unexpected increase in the inflation rate has a negative effect on the unemployment rate.

expected real interest rate   The real interest rate that is expected to be earned (or paid) after adjusting the nominal interest rate by the expectation of inflation.

experience rating (for unemployment insurance)   The feature of the U.S. program of unemployment insurance that taxes employers more heavily if they have a history of a higher job-separation rate.

exports   Goods that are produced by the residents of a country but are sold to foreigners.

Federal Funds market   The market for very short-term borrowing and lending between financial institutions, primarily commercial banks.

Federal Funds rate   The interest rate on loans made in the Federal Funds market.

Federal Open-Market Committee (FOMC)   A committee of the Federal Reserve that has responsibility for open-market operations.

Federal Reserve credit   The sum of the Fed's holdings of loans to depository institutions, U.S. government securities, and miscellaneous assets. The total of the Fed's claims on the government and the private sector. See *domestic credit*.

financial intermediaries   Institutions that obtain funds from deposits made by individuals and make loans to households and businesses. Examples are banks, savings and loan associations, and money-market funds.

firm An economic organization that employs and supervises various factors of production and then sells its products to consumers or other firms.

fiscal policy The choice of levels of government spending, taxation, and borrowing to influence the level of aggregate economic activity.

fixed exchange rate A system in which countries peg the exchange rate between their currency and other currencies, such as the U.S. dollar. Examples of fixed-exchange rate regimes are the gold standard, the Bretton Woods System, the Exchange Rate Mechanism of the European Monetary System, and a setup with a common currency.

flat-rate tax A kind of income tax in which the amount of tax is a constant fraction of taxable income. See *graduated-rate tax*.

flexible exchange rate The system of international payments, prevalent since the early 1970s, in which countries allow the exchange rates for their currencies to fluctuate so as to clear the exchange market.

full-employment deficit The government deficit after adjusting for the automatic response of government spending and taxes to recession or boom; an estimate of what the deficit would be if the economy were operating at a full-employment level.

fully funded system (for social security) A system in which each individual's payments accumulate in a trust fund, and retirement benefits are paid out of the accumulated funds. See *social security; pay-as-you-go system*.

general market clearing Simultaneous clearing of all markets. See *market-clearing approach; Walras' law of markets*.

general price level The dollar price per unit of an aggregate of commodities.

globalization The increased tendency for production and other economic activities to be carried out on a worldwide basis.

gold standard A system of international payments under which countries agree to buy or sell gold for a fixed amount of their currencies. The high point of this system was from 1890 to 1914.

government budget deficit (or surplus) In real terms, the increase (or decrease) in the real value of the government's obligations to the private sector in the forms of money and bonds.

government consumption expenditure and gross investment Expenditures by government on consumption goods and capital goods. The consumption part includes an estimate of the imputed rental income on the stock of public capital.

governmental budget constraint The equation showing the balance between total expenditures and total revenues of the government.

government's revenue from printing money The real income that government obtains by increasing the quantity of high-powered money. In the United States this revenue accrues to the Federal Reserve and is subsequently transferred to the U.S. Treasury. See *inflation tax*.

graduated-rate tax A kind of income tax in which the marginal tax rate rises with taxable income. See *flat-rate tax*.

Great Depression The decline in aggregate economic activity in the United States that occurred from 1929 to 1933.

gross domestic product (GDP) The market value of an economy's domestically produced goods and services over a specified period of time.

gross investment Purchases of capital goods with no adjustment for the depreciation of the existing capital goods.

gross national product (GNP) The total market value of the goods and services produced by the residents of a country over a specified period of time; GNP equals gross domestic product plus the net factor income from abroad.

gross private domestic investment Total private expenditure on investment goods, including business spending on plant and equipment, the net change in business inventories, and residential construction. This total contains no adjustment for the depreciation of the existing capital goods.

gross saving Saving measured without adjustment for depreciation of capital stocks. The total gross saving of an economy equals GNP less private consumption expenditure and government consumption.

high-powered money The total amount of Federal Reserve Notes (currency) and non-interest-bearing deposits (reserves) held at the Fed by depository institutions; the monetary base.

human capital Skills and training that are embodied in workers and add to productivity.

hyperinflation A period with an extraordinarily high inflation rate, such as that in Germany after World War I.

implicit GDP price deflator The price index that relates the gross national product, measured in nominal terms, to real GDP.

imports Goods that are produced in foreign countries and purchased by the domestic residents of a country.

income effect Another term for a wealth effect.

increasing returns to scale The property of some production functions that a proportionate increase in all inputs results in a more than proportionate increase in output.

indexation A system of contracts in which payments are revised upward or downward according to increases or decreases in the general price level so as to keep the real value of payments independent of inflation; *inflation correction*.

indifference curve A graph showing the combinations of two items, such as consumption and work effort, that yield the same level of utility.

inferior goods Goods for which the wealth effect is negative.

infinite horizon The household's planning horizon when plans extend into the indefinite future; a concept used in models that stress the role of intergenerational transfers.

inflation A sustained increase in the general price level over time.

inflation correction Another term for *indexation*.

inflation rate The percentage change in a price index between two periods of time.

inflation tax The revenue that the government gets by printing money (and thereby causing inflation). See *government's revenue from printing money*.

interest rate The ratio of the interest payment to the amount borrowed; the return to lending or the cost of borrowing.

interest-rate parity The equalization of interest rates across countries, taking account of an adjustment for prospective changes in exchange rates.

interest-rate targeting A setup in which the monetary authority attempts to keep a designated nominal interest rate close to a target value. In this regime, the quantity of money is endogenous.

intermediate goods   Commodities that are purchased for resale or for use in the production and sale of other commodities.

international currency   International media of exchange, such as gold or U.S. currency, held by central banks.

intertemporal-substitution effect   The effect on current consumption (leisure) when the cost of future consumption (leisure) changes relative to that of current consumption (leisure).

inventories   Stores of commodities held by businesses either for sale or for use in production.

investment accelerator   The positive effect of changes in output on investment demand. See *Keynesian investment function.*

investment demand   The quantity of investment that is desired by firms and households, expressed as a function of the real interest rate, the depreciation rate, and the existing stock of capital.

involuntary unemployment   The inability of workers to obtain employment at the prevailing market wage; a feature of Keynesian theory.

irrelevance result for systematic monetary policy   The theoretical finding that a policy of changing the quantity of money in response to the state of economy is predictable and therefore powerless to affect the economy.

irreversible investment   The property that, once output has been used to form new capital goods, the process cannot be reversed by consuming the capital. Because investment is irreversible, uncertainty about the returns to investment can reduce or delay investment spending.

IS curve   A graph used in Keynesian theory to show the combinations of aggregate output and the interest rate that satisfy the condition that aggregate output equals the aggregate demand for commodities.

IS/LM model   The analytical tool used in Keynesian theory to study the simultaneous determination of aggregate output and the interest rate.

job-finding rate   The rate at which workers move from being unemployed or outside of the labor force to being employed.

job-separation rate   The rate at which workers move from being employed to being unemployed or outside of the labor force.

Keynesian consumption function   The dependence of consumption demand on income and the interest rate; a central element of Keynesian theory.

Keynesian cross diagram   The graph in Keynesian theory that depicts the determination of the level of aggregate output for a given interest rate.

Keynesian investment function   The dependence of investment demand on output and the interest rate; an important element of Keynesian theory.

Keynesian model   The theory developed by John Maynard Keynes that sought to explain aggregate business fluctuations. The failure of prices to adjust to clear markets is a central element of this model.

labor force   The total number of employed workers plus the number of unemployed.

labor hoarding   The tendency of firms to retain their workers during a recession in which production and sales decline. Labor hoarding may explain the tendency for measured labor productivity to fall in recessions and rise in booms.

Laffer curve A graph showing that tax revenues initially rise as the marginal tax rate rises but eventually reach a maximum and subsequently decline with further increases in the marginal tax rate.

law of one price The condition that identical goods in different places must sell at the same dollar price.

legal tender A characteristic of money, whereby its use as a medium of exchange is reinforced by government statute.

lender of last resort The role of the central bank as a provider of loans to financial institutions during crises.

life-cycle model The theory of the choices of consumption and leisure that are made when the planning horizon is equal to the individual's expected remaining lifetime; it predicts that an individual will build up savings during working years and exhaust them during retirement years. See *infinite horizon*.

liquidity constraint The negative effect on consumer demand from the inability to borrow at the "going" interest rate.

LM curve A graph used in Keynesian theory to show the combinations of aggregate output and the interest rate that satisfy the condition that the demand for money equals the given quantity of money.

long-term contracts Agreements between buyers and sellers or between firms and workers that specify the terms of exchange over a number of periods.

lump-sum tax A tax paid by an individual to the government in which the amount paid does not depend on any characteristic of the individual, such as income or wealth.

lump-sum transfer A transfer payment from the government to an individual in which the amount paid does not depend on any characteristic of the recipient, such as income or wealth.

M1 The definition of money as the sum of currency plus checkable deposits plus travelers' checks; a measure of the volume of assets that serve regularly as media of exchange.

marginal product of capital (MPK) The increment of output obtained per unit increment in the input of physical capital, while holding fixed any other inputs.

marginal product of labor (MPL) The increment of output obtained per unit increment in labor input while holding fixed any other inputs; the slope of the graph of the production function relating output to labor input.

marginal propensity to consume The effect of a change in income on consumption demand.

marginal propensity to invest The effect of a change in output on investment demand.

marginal propensity to save The effect of a change in income on desired saving.

marginal propensity to spend The effect of a change in income (or output) on the total demand for goods, whether for consumption or investment.

marginal tax rate The fraction of an additional dollar of income that must be paid as tax. In a graduated-rate system, this tax rate varies in accordance with the level of income. See *average tax rate*.

market-clearing approach The viewpoint that prices, such as the interest rate and the general price level, are determined to clear all markets, such as those for credit and commodities; that is, supply equals demand in each market.

medium of exchange The commodity or other item that people use as a means of paying for purchases; *money*.

menu costs Costs of a lump-sum type that must be paid to adjust a nominal price or wage. New Keynesian models rely on these costs to rationalize the sluggish adjustment of prices or wages.

microeconomic foundations The theoretical analysis of individual behavior that underlies the macroeconomic model of the economy.

minimum wage The amount below which the wage rate paid by a firm cannot legally fall.

monetarism A school of thought, based on the quantity theory of money, that changes in the nominal quantity of money primarily account for movements in the price level in the long run and for fluctuations in real economic activity in the short run.

monetary accommodation The response of the nominal quantity of money to a change in the nominal amount demanded. Accommodation tends to occur in regimes in which the monetary authority targets nominal interest rates or in other setups in which money is endogenous.

monetary approach to the balance of payments Analyses of the balance of international payments and exchange rates that stress the quantity of money and the demand for money in each country.

monetary base See *high-powered money*.

monetary reform A fundamental change in the monetary system or in the formulation of monetary policy.

monetize the deficit Raise revenue to meet interest payments on government debt by increasing the quantity of money.

money The usual means of payment or *medium of exchange* in an economy. Money also serves as a store of value. Money may take the form of paper currency, commodities, or deposits at financial institutions.

money multiplier The ratio of M1 to the monetary base.

multiple expansion of deposits The effect of an increase in the monetary base on the volume of deposits held at financial institutions.

multiplier The change in aggregate output per dollar autonomous increase in aggregate demand; assumed in simple Keynesian models to be positive and greater than one.

national income The income earned from aggregate production; gross national product adjusted for depreciation and sales and excise taxes.

national-income accounts The summary statement of gross national product and its components during a year.

national saving The total saving carried out by the residents of a country; the sum of private and public saving.

natural unemployment rate The average unemployment rate that prevails in the economy, depending on the average rates of job separation and job finding.

net domestic product (NDP) Gross domestic product less depreciation.

net exports The difference between the value of exports and the value of imports.

net factor income from abroad Net income earned by the residents of a country from claims on foreign assets and from labor supplied to foreign countries.

net foreign investment The change in a country's net holdings of interest-bearing assets from abroad plus the change in its international currency.

net investment The change in the capital stock; gross investment minus the amount of depreciation.

neutrality of money The theoretical finding that once-and-for-all changes in the nominal quantity of money affect nominal variables, such as the general price level, but do not affect real variables, such as real gross national product.

new Keynesian economics Models that attempt to explain the role of sticky prices and aggregate demand in the Keynesian framework. The new models incorporate elements of imperfect competition and allow for menu costs of changing prices.

nominal Measured in current dollar magnitudes; valued at current dollar prices; unadjusted for changes in the general price level.

nominal deficit The current dollar value of the government's *real deficit*.

nominal exchange rate The exchange rate between one currency and another. The term emphasizes the distinction from the real exchange rate, a measure that adjusts the nominal exchange rate for differences in national price levels.

nominal interest rate The amount paid as interest per dollar borrowed for each period; the rate at which the nominal value of assets that are held as bonds grows over time.

nominal saving The current dollar value of real saving, calculated by multiplying real saving by a price index.

nontraded goods Goods, such as services and real estate, that do not enter readily into international commerce.

open economy An economy that conducts trade with the rest of the world.

open-market operations The purchase or sale of government securities by the Federal Reserve in exchange for newly created high-powered money.

outflow (inflow) of capital The positive (negative) balance on capital account for a country.

outside of the labor force The classification of a person who is neither employed nor currently looking for a job.

pay-as-you-go system (for social security) A system in which benefits to retired persons are financed by taxes on the current working generation.

perceived relative price The ratio of the observed price in a local market to the perceived general price level.

perfect competition The assumption that the individuals who participate in a market view themselves as sufficiently small that they can buy or sell any amount without affecting the established price.

perfect foresight A situation in which expectations of inflation or of other variables are accurate, so that there are no forecast errors.

permanent income The hypothetical amount of real income that, when received constantly throughout the individual's planning horizon, has the same real present value as the actual flow of income; the per-period equivalent of the total present value of income. A temporary change in income entails a less than equivalent change in permanent income.

personal consumption expenditure Purchases of goods and services by households for use in consumption.

personal income Income received directly by persons; national income adjusted for undistributed corporate profits, social security contributions, transfer payments, and some other items.

Phillips curve The relationship between nominal variables, such as the inflation rate, and real variables, such as the unemployment rate or the growth rate of aggregate output.

physical capital Capital inputs into production, such as machinery and buildings.

planning horizon   The number of future periods that enter the household's budget constraint; the length of time for which the household plans consumption and leisure choices.

policy rule   A rule or commitment for governmental actions with regard to money or other variables.

present value   The value of future dollar amounts, after dividing by the discount factor.

principal of bond   The amount borrowed, to be repaid at maturity.

private fixed capital   The sum of producers' durable equipment and structures and residential structures; a measure of the private capital stock that excludes business inventories and consumer durables other than homes.

procyclical   Moving in the same direction as the business cycle, that is, with detrended real GDP.

producer price index (PPI)   A weighted average of prices of raw materials and semifinished goods, relative to base-year prices.

producers' durable equipment and structures   The measure of physical capital that includes machinery and buildings used in production.

production function   The relationship between the quantity of output obtained and the quantities of inputs into production, such as labor and capital.

productivity slowdown   A reduction in the rate of growth of output per worker, thought to have occurred in the United States after the early 1970s.

profit   The difference between revenues and costs for a firm.

public debt   The volume of interest-bearing government obligations to the public.

purchasing-power parity (PPP)   The condition that the ratio of the exchange rates for the currencies of any two countries must equal the ratio of the prices of goods in each country.

quantity theory of money   The theory that changes in the nominal quantity of money account for the majority of long-run movements in the general price level.

rate of monetary growth   The percentage increase in the nominal quantity of money between two periods.

rational expectations   The viewpoint that individuals make forecasts or estimates of unknown variables, such as the general price level, in the best possible manner, utilizing all information currently available.

real-balance effect   The effect of a change in wealth resulting from a change in the general price level; the wealth effect of a rise in the real value of money balances.

real business cycle theory   A theory of business fluctuations that relies on real disturbances rather than monetary shocks. This theory emphasizes shifts to the production function and usually assumes full market clearing and rational behavior of individuals.

real deficit   The change in the real value of the government's obligations to the public in the form of money and bonds.

real exchange rate   The exchange rate between two currencies divided by the ratio of the price levels in the two countries.

real gross national product   The gross national product (GNP) divided by a price index to adjust for changes in the average level of market prices; GNP in constant dollars.

real interest rate   The rate at which the real value of dollar assets that are held as bonds grows over time; the interest rate on an asset after adjusting for inflation.

real rate of return from investment The net real proceeds from investment over one period expressed relative to the real cost of the investment.

real saving The change in the real value of assets of a household or of the economy as a whole.

real terms Measured in units of commodities; valued at base-year prices; dollar magnitudes that are adjusted for inflation by deflating by a price index.

real wage rate The value in real terms of the dollar amount paid for an hour of labor services.

recession A period of decline in the level of aggregate economic activity or real gross domestic product.

Regulation Q The legal limit (applicable in previous years) imposed by the Federal Reserve on the interest rate payable on time deposits and savings deposits held at banks.

relative form of PPP The version of purchasing-power parity that involves changes in exchange rates and prices.

replacement ratio (for unemployment insurance) The ratio of unemployment benefits to the prior wage earnings of a worker.

reservation wage The wage rate that is just high enough to induce someone to accept a job.

reserve requirement The requirement imposed by the Federal Reserve that depository institutions must hold a certain quantity of reserves. For each category of deposits, the requirement is specified as a fraction of the amount of deposits.

reserves (of depository institutions) The total amount of currency and non-interest-bearing deposits at the Fed held by banks and other depository institutions.

revaluation An increase in the value of a country's currency in terms of another currency, such as the U.S. dollar.

Ricardian equivalence theorem The theoretical finding that, given the amounts of government consumption, an increase in current taxes has the same effect on the economy as an equal increase in the government budget deficit.

saving The change in an individual's assets during a period of time.

saving rate The ratio of saving to income. The gross saving rate is the ratio of gross saving (including depreciation of capital) to gross income.

savings deposits Deposits held at banks that usually allow funds to be withdrawn without penalty with a 30-day notice of withdrawal.

seasonally adjusted data Adjustment of quantities for normal seasonal variations. Seasonal adjustments are important for most national-accounts variables, such as real gross domestic product and its components, and also for monetary aggregates.

short-side rule (for determining quantities) The condition that the quantity of output or sales in a situation of excess demand or excess supply is determined by the lesser of the quantity demanded and the quantity supplied.

skill-biased technological progress Technological change, possibly involving the increased use of computers, that tends to raise the demand for skilled labor relative to that for unskilled labor. This type of technological change is thought to underlie the rise in wage inequality during the 1980s.

social security Transfer payments made by government to households through social insurance programs such as old age and survivors' insurance and disability insurance.

speculation (on exchange rates) Sale (or purchase) of a currency in exchange for another currency whenever a devaluation (or revaluation) is expected.

stagflation A situation in which a recession is accompanied by high and rising inflation.

steady state A situation in which the rate of growth of the economy is zero so that the capital stock, output, consumption, gross investment, and work effort are all constant. In a situation of steady-state growth, these variables grow at constant rates, rather than staying constant.

sterilization An action by the central bank of a country that prevents increases (decreases) in the amount of international currency from increasing (decreasing) the quantity of money in the country.

stock market A market in which people trade shares of ownership in firms. The owners of stock receive the dividends paid out by firms.

substitution effect The response of households to changes in the relative costs of obtaining any two goods, such as consumption and leisure.

superior goods (or normal goods) Goods for which the wealth effect is positive.

superneutrality of money The theoretical finding that a change in the pattern over time of monetary growth does not affect real variables, such as aggregate output and the real interest rate. See *neutrality of money*.

supply shock Changes that alter the supply of goods. Important sources of supply shocks are shifts to the production function, changes in marginal tax rates, and variations in the relative price of primary commodities, such as oil.

supply-side economics The study of the causes and effects of changes in the supply and productivity of factors of production. This approach emphasizes the negative effect of income taxes on the incentive to work.

surplus (deficit) on current account A positive (negative) current-account balance.

taxable income Adjusted gross income minus the value of tax exemptions.

tax-exempt income Income from production, interest earnings, or government transfers that is not liable for income taxes.

technological progress Improved knowledge about methods of production that shifts the production function upward.

temporary layoffs Job separations in which the worker is usually rehired within a few months.

terms of trade The price of a country's tradable goods expressed relative to the price of a market basket of the world's tradable goods; often approximated by the ratio of a country's export prices to its import prices.

time deposits Deposits at banks and other depository institutions that have a stated maturity date and carry penalties for early withdrawal.

tradable goods Goods that are actually exchanged or could potentially be exchanged with foreign countries.

trade balance The difference between the value of exports of goods and services and the value of imports of goods and services.

transaction costs Costs incurred in the process of making sales or purchases, such as brokerage fees or the cost of the time involved.

transfer payments Transfers of funds from government to individuals, such as welfare payments, that do not constitute payments for goods and services.

unanticipated money growth   The difference between the actual amount of monetary growth and anticipated money growth.

underground economy   The collection of economic activities from which the income earned is not reported and therefore not taxed.

unemployment   The situation of a worker who has no job and is looking for work.

unemployment insurance   The government program of providing temporary benefits to workers who have lost their jobs and are currently unemployed.

unemployment rate   The ratio of the number of unemployed workers to the total number of employed and unemployed workers; the fraction of the labor force that is unemployed.

unexpected inflation   The difference between the actual rate of inflation and the expectation of inflation; the forecast error made in predicting inflation.

utility   The level of happiness of a household, measured in units called utils. Utility increases with increases in either consumption or leisure. See *utility function*.

utility function   The relationship between the amount of utility obtained and the amounts of consumption and labor chosen by the household.

utilization rate   The percentage of time that capital is used in production; for example, an increase in the number of shifts per day in a factory increases the utilization rate of machinery.

vacancies   The difference between the number of job openings at firms and the level of employment.

value added   The increase in value of product at a particular stage of production.

vault cash   Currency held by a depository institution.

velocity of money   The ratio of the dollar volume of transactions per period to the average money holding; the number of times per period that the average dollar turns over in making transactions.

wage rate   The dollar amount paid to a worker in exchange for an hour of labor services.

Walras' law of markets   The finding that if all but one of the conditions for general market clearing hold, then the final one must hold as well; this result follows because households' budget constraints must be satisfied.

wealth effect   The response of consumption and leisure (or labor) to changes in the household's opportunities for increasing utility. An increase (decrease) in wealth occurs when the household can raise (must reduce) consumption while leisure remains unchanged.

Author Index

SUBJECT INDEX

nominal monetary aggregates
and, 709–10
barter exchange
commodity market and, 92–93
defined, 125, 822
base money
economic growth and, 712–15
financial intermediation and
prices and, 676–77, 684
Baumol-Tobin money model, 140
benchmark values, wartime
government consumption
and, 452
Big Mac example of purchasing-
power parity (PPP),
602–3
bimetallic standard, fixed exchange
rates and, 608
Board of Governors of the Federal
Reserve System, 660, 684,
822
bonds
credit market, 94–96
defined, 125, 822
foreign bonds and open U.S.
economy, 555–63
gold clauses, 253
government bonds and public
debt, 509, 515–16
indexation of, 256–57, 260–61
interest rates and, 195*n*
open-market purchase of,
667–68, 671–73
privately issued bonds, 515–16
boom periods
defined, 51, 822
output per worker, 19–21
real GDP and, 4
unemployment rate and, 4–6
borrowings
balance sheet of financial
intermediaries and, 650–51
from Federal Reserve System
(FRS), 657–59

Brazil, international borrowing and
lending and, 570–71
Bretton Woods System
defined, 633, 823
fixed exchange rates and, 607–8,
632
world prices and, 614–15
budget constraint,
commodity market, 96–104
defined, 51, 823
demand for money and,
154–59
government bonds and, 516–21
government expenditures,
440–44
governmental budget constraint,
271–72
household budget line, 101–3
income tax and, 483–84, 543
infinite horizon, 272–74
investment and, 328–31
microeconomic foundation of
macroeconomics, 23–25
multi-period constraints,
113–17
over two periods, 98–100
present values, 100–101
public debt and household
budget constraints, 521–25
single period, 96–98
Walras' law of markets, 170–72
work effort, 111–12
budget deficits
current account deficits,
557–63, 567, 590
government budget constraints
and, 517–20
budget line
defined, 823
household consumption, 102–4
interest rate and intertemporal
substitution, 109–11
wealth effects of consumption,
107–8

burden of public debt, 535, 543,
823
business cycles. *See also* real
business cycles
aggregate output and, 4–5
characteristics of U.S.
fluctuations, 8–11
economic growth, 29
employment and
unemployment during,
378–79
incomplete information and,
744–45
Keynesian economic model, 31,
786–92, 799
money and, 721–22, 750–51
Phillips curve and, 695–96
private investment and, 311–14
production function and, 72–73
supply shocks, recession and
unemployment during,
379–83
world markets and tax ratios
and, 580–81

calculated GDP, exclusions from,
36–37
calculus, for transaction costs, 141
Canada
exchange rates for, 599
price levels in, 622–23
real exchange rates, 625, 627
capacity utilization, employment
and unemployment, 378
capital
absence of resale market and,
326
changes in stock of, 390–96
constant-returns models of
economic growth, 420–21
as consumable good, limits of,
320–21
deficit-financed tax cuts and,
540

Keynesian model and shifts in, 782–83

macroeconomic models using, 133

microeconomic foundation of macroeconomics, 25–26

nominal wage rate and, 227–28

payments period and, 147

properties of, 143–44

quantity as factor in, 177–78

quantity of money equals quantity demanded, 177–78

real-balance effect, 156–57

supply shock and price levels, 184–86

transition in inflation rates and, 290

deposit insurance liability, government deficit and, 518

depository institutions
loans to, 664–67
open-market operations, 663–64

deposits
bank panics and, 678–81
of financial intermediaries, 654
interest rates and financial intermediation, 655
monetary aggregates and, 668–74
multiple expansion of, 669–74
regulation of interest rates on, 655–57

depreciation
capital goods, 319–20
capital stock changes and, 393–96
current-account balances and exchange rates, 629–31
defined, 51, 824
gross investment and, 392
investment and, 41
investment demand and, 325
purchasing-power parity (PPP) and, 600–604

real exchange rates and, 627–28

deregulation, amount of financial intermediation and, 675–76

desired stock of capital, 323–24, 346, 824

detrended GDP, 9–10
private investment and, 15–16
procyclical behavior of labor input, 223–27

detrended real wage rate, procyclical behavior of labor input, 223–27

detrended unemployment rate, detrended GDP and, 20–21

devaluation
defined, 633, 824
fixed exchange rates and, 615–17
of international currency, 613

diminishing marginal productivity, defined, 84, 824
work effort and, 61

direct investment
defined, 589, 824
world markets and open U.S. economy and, 555

discount factor
defined, 125, 824
present values, 100–101

discount rates
balance sheet of financial intermediaries and, 651
borrowing from Federal Reserve and, 657–59
deficit-financed tax cuts and, 537–40
defined, 824
of Fed, defined, 684
loans to depository institutions, 666–67

discouraged workers
defined, 384, 824
labor force movement and, 364

discrete time, real and nominal interest rate, 251

discretionary policy
defined, 752, 824
inflation in, 746–50

disequilibrium
Keynesian economic theory and, 757–58
market clearing and, 170

disintermediation
defined, 684, 824
deposits and, 656

disposable personal income, defined, 52, 824
measurement of GDP, 45–46

distribution effects
commodity market-clearing, 174–77
defined, 199, 824
minimum wage and unemployment, 375–76
redistribution of wealth, 294

distribution of wealth,
during hyperinflation, 294
tax rate changes and tax revenue and, 495–97

domestic credit
defined, 633, 824
exchange rates and, 596–99

double coincidence of wants
barter exchange and, 93
defined, 126, 824

duration of jobs
defined, 384, 824
job separation demographics and, 367–70

duration of unemployment, 369–70
benefits, 372
defined, 384, 824
in job matching model, 355–56

earned-income tax credit
income taxes and, 482
transfer payments and, 499

experience rating
    defined, 384, 825
    unemployment insurance and,
       371
exports
    current-account balances and
       exchange rates, 629–31
    defined, 52, 825
    GDP measurement, 40
    as ratios to nominal GDP,
       561–63
    during recession, 315
    world markets and open U.S.
       economy and, 557–63
external effects of tax rate, 491
Exxon Valdez oil spill, time
      variations in real wage rates,
      216, 218

favorable shocks
    job matching model and,
       355–56
    marginal product of capital and,
       343–44
    production function shifts and,
       340–44
federal deposit insurance, banking
      panics and, 692
Federal Deposit Insurance
      Corporation (FDIC),
      680–81
Federal Deposit Insurance
      Corporation Improvement
      Act (FDICIA), 681
Federal Funds market
    balance sheet of financial
       intermediaries and, 60
    defined, 685, 825
Federal Funds rate
    balance sheet of financial
       intermediaries and, 60
    defined, 685
federal individual income tax,
      477–79

Federal Open Market Committee
      (FOMC), 660, 662–63, 685,
      825
Federal Reserve Board, 655
Federal Reserve credit, 661–62,
      684, 825
Federal Reserve System (FRS)
    balance sheet of financial
       intermediaries and, 651
    banking panics and, 678–81
    Board of Governors, 660
    borrowing from, 657–59
    changes in reserve requirements,
       681–82
    discount rates and, 711
    establishment of, 659–62
    as financial intermediary,
       659–74
    government revenue from, 472
    indexed bonds, 256–57
    as lender of last resort, 679–80
    loans to depository institutions,
       665–67
    monetary base and monetary
       aggregates, 667–74
    money supply policies, 738–39
    neutrality of open-market
       operations, 674–75
    open-market operations,
       527–28, 662–65
    price levels and, 8, 676–77
    public debt and, 510
    revenue from creation of money,
       440–43
    world prices under fixed
       exchange rates, 614–15
federal revenues. *See also*
      government revenues; state
      and local revenues
    as fraction of total government
       revenue, 475–76
    taxation as source of, 472–76
financial assets
    budget constraints, 97–98

credit market, 96
interest-rate parity and, 604–7
microeconomic foundation of
    macroeconomics, 25
optimal cash management
    model, 137–44
price levels and distribution of,
    693
financial innovations, demand for
    money and, 153
financial instruments, demand for
    money and, 238
financial intermediaries
    amount of, 675–82
    balance sheet of, 649–54
    banking panics and, 677–81
    borrowing from federal reserve,
       657–59
    changes in reserve requirements,
       681–82
    checkable deposits and M1,
       645–48
    control of monetary base,
       662–65
    credit market and, 648–59
    defined, 685, 825
    deposit interest rates and, 655
    deposits and earning assets,
       654, 683
    earning assets, 650
    Federal Reserve System and,
       659–74
    loans to depository institutions,
       665–67
    macroeconomic model, 30
    monetary base and monetary
       aggregates, 667–74
    open-market operations,
       neutrality of, 674–75
    price levels and, 676–77
    regulation of interest rates on
       deposits, 655–57
    reserves, required and excess,
       651–54

government budget deficit, 509
  budget constraints and,
    517–20
  defined, 544, 826
  macroeconomic effects,
    538–39
  wealth effect of tax cuts and,
    535–40
  world markets and tax rates
    and, 578–81, 588–89
government consumption
  government expenditure and,
    436–39
  monetary fluctuations and,
    692
  permanent changes in, 459–62
  real interest rates during
    wartime and, 454–59
  tax rate changes and tax revenue
    and, 493–97, 501
  temporary changes in, 444–46
  wartime experiences in, 450–59
  world markets and, 575–77
government expenditure
  commodity market clearing and,
    446–50
  cross-country comparisons,
    438–39
  data on, 435–39
  defined, 52, 826
  GDP measurement, 39
  Keynesian economic model
    and, 778–79
  macroeconomic model, 30
  real GDP and, 16–17
  during recession, 314–15
  transfer payments, 498–500
  world markets and open U.S.
    economy and, 558–63
government investment, relative to
    GDP, 436–39
government mortgage associations,
    as financial intermediaries,
    649

government revenue. *See also*
    federal revenues; state and
    local revenues
  federal share of, 474–75
  from money printing, 295–97,
    300, 826
  public debt and, 529–32
  state and local government
    share of, 473–74
  tax rate changes and, 493–97
  U.S. sources of, 472–76
Governors' Conference, Federal
    Reserve and, 659–60
graduated-rate tax, 477–79, 502,
    826
Great Depression
  banking panics during, 679–81
  defined, 52, 826
  public debt ratio to GNP and,
    513–15
  real federal deficit and, 520
  real GDP during, 4
  unemployment rate during,
    5–6
gross domestic product (GDP). *See
    also* real GDP
  aggregate economic
    performance, 1
  budget deficit ratios to, 579–81
  components of, 10–17
  currency as percentage of, 134
  current-account deficit ratio to,
    580–81
  current-account surplus ratio to,
    574–75
  cyclical components of, 9–10
  defined, 52, 826
  expenditure measurement,
    37–41
  household output and, 60–61
  income measurement, 43–46
  inventory investment, ratio to,
    313–14
  measure of aggregate output, 2

net factor payments as ratio to,
    562–63
net U.S. transfers abroad,
    563
nominal *vs.* real GDP, 33–37
price levels, 47–50
private investment, ratio to,
    311–14
production measurement,
    41–43
ratio of government revenue to
    GNP/GDP, 475–76
ratio of money to, 135–36
velocity of money and,
    148–51
world markets and open U.S.
    economy and, 559–63
gross investment
  defined, 52, 319, 827
  economic growth and, 403–6
  GDP measurement, 39
gross investment demand, 325
  absence of resale market and,
    326
gross national product (GNP). *See
    also* GDP for all statistics
    after 1959
  defined, 52, 827
  government receipts as ratio of,
    475–76
  income measurement and,
    45–47
  net foreign debt and, 571
  production and, 43
  public debt ratio to, 510–15
  wartime government
    consumption and, 450–59
  world markets and open U.S.
    economy and, 559–63
gross private domestic investment
  defined, 52, 827
  GDP measurement, 39
  real GDP and, 13–15
gross product, defined, 320

wealth effect of tax rate changes and, 491

incomplete information

monetary effects of output, work and investment, 735–37

monetary policy and, 738–39

perceived changes in neutrality of money, 738

real variables and effects of money on, 737–38

significance of, 742–43

stagflation and, 739–40

increasing returns to scale, 394–96

defined, 424, 827

indexation

defined, 252, 263, 827

of money, 647

indexed bonds, 256–57, 260–61

indexes of prices, limitations of, 742–43

indifference curve

defined, 84, 827

now *vs.* later consumption, 103–5

production function and, 70–72

substitution effect, 79–80

two-period consumption, 105–7

work and consumption, 67–72

indirect taxes, national income measurement of GDP, 45

inferior goods

defined, 85, 827

wealth and, 76–77

infinite horizon

budget constraints over, 272–74

defined, 126, 827

multi-period budget constraints, 116–17

inflation

actual *vs.* expected, 248–49

annual growth rates for prices, money and output, 238–42

anticipated changes in monetary growth and, 287–89

anticipated inflation effects, 294–95

consumer price index (CPI), 48–49

correction (indexation), 252, 827

cross-country comparisons of nominal and real variables and, 701–3

cross-country data on, 238–46

currency growth rate and, 243–46

defined, 53, 264, 827

discretionary policy, 746–50

dynamics of, 286–93

flexible exchange rates and, 618–21

government revenue from money printing, 295–97

gradual adjustment of demand for money and, 287–89

historical trends in economic growth and, 403–6

interest rates and, 237–38, 245–46

interest-rate parity and, 606–7

in Keynesian model, 784–86, 799

macroeconomic model, 28–29

market-clearing model, 269–300

monetary growth and nominal inflation, 277–86

as monetary phenomenon, 247–48

money and prices during German hyperinflation, 290–93

nominal and real interest rates and, 253–57

nominal deficit and, 518

nominal *vs.* real deficit and, 518–20

overstatement of measured inflation and real wages, 226–27

Phillips curve and, 693–96

price levels and, 7

public debt and household budget constraints, 524–25

real and nominal interest rate, 249–51

real effects of, 294–97

real exchange rates and, 623–29

time-series data on, 246–49

transition from one rate to another, 290

wartime government consumption and, 456–59

inflation correction, defined, 264, 827

inflation tax, defined, 296, 300, 827

inflow of capital

defined, 590

world markets and open U.S. economy and, 557

infrastructure components of government consumption, 445–46

insurance companies, as financial intermediaries, 649

interest (interest rate). *See also* nominal and real interest rate

aggregate commodity supply and demand, 172–77

aggregate-consistency conditions, 168–72

cash management cost and, 140–44

on checkable deposits, 648

clearing of commodity market, 220, 222n

consumption patterns and, 91, 108–11

credit market, 95

currency and, 93

government consumption and
clearing of commodity
market, 449–50
gradual adjustment of demand,
327
household budget constraints,
328–31
irreversibility of, 325
Keynesian economic model
and, 772–74
macroeconomic model, 29
monetary effects, with
incomplete information,
735–37
public debt and, 530–32
real fixed investment categories,
310–12
social security taxes and,
500
temporary changes in
government consumption
and, 444–46
investment accelerator
defined, 801, 828
Keynesian economic model
and, 773–74
investment banks, separation from
commercial banks, 655
investment companies, as financial
intermediaries, 649
investment demand, 321–28
cyclical behavior of current-
account balances, 573–75
defined, 346, 828
local market stock of goods and,
725–26
marginal product of capital
(MPK) and, 342–44
permanent upward shift in
production and, 341
properties of, 324–25
quantitative effects on, 328
terms of trade in world markets
and, 584–86

world markets and tax rates,
577–78
involuntary unemployment
defined, 801, 828
sales rationing in Keynesian
model and, 761–62
irrelevance result for systematic
monetary policy, 739,
752
irreversible investment, 325–28,
346, 828
IS terminology, 775, 801, 828
IS/LM model
business cycles and, 31
cyclical properties of Keynesian
model and, 786–92
defined, 53, 828
fiscal policy and, 778–79
general market clearing and,
783
Keynesian economic theory
and, 774–86, 798–99
price levels and, 779–81
Italy
exchange rates for, 598–99
price levels in, 621–22
real exchange rates, 624–26

Japan
exchange rates for, 599
price levels in, 622–23
real exchange rates, 623–24
job matching model
components of, 352–57
search by firms, 356–57
job turnover, natural
unemployment rate
and, 361
job-finding rate
defined, 384, 828
in job matching model, 355–56
natural unemployment rate and,
358–65, 383
during recessions, 378–79

job-separation rate, 357–58
defined, 358, 385, 828
labor force movement and, 364
natural unemployment rate and,
358–65, 383
during recessions, 378–79

Keynesian consumption function,
764–65, 801, 828
Keynesian cross-diagram, 766–71,
801, 828
Keynesian investment function,
772, 801
Keynesian model of economic
theory
aggregate supply–aggregate
demand model, 787–89
aggregate-consistency
conditions, 170
business cycles and, 31–32,
757–58
consumption function, 764–65
cyclical properties of, 786–92
defined, 828
demand for money and, 782–83
employment determination, 771
fiscal policy, 778–79
inflation in, 784–86
interest rate in, 774–86
investment accelerator, 773–74
investment demand and, 325
investment function, 772
IS/LM analysis, 774–86
long-term contracts, 794–98
macroeconomics models and,
27–28, 53
market clearing and, 783
multiplier in, 767–71
output determination, 765–74,
777–78
Phillips curve and, 695–96,
715–16
price level changes, 779–81
quantity of money, 782

Keynesian model of economic
theory *(continued)*
    sales rationing and, 760–62
    simple macroeconomic models,
        758–65
    sticky prices and new
        economics, 792–98
    supply side of, 783–84
    variations in output and interest
        rate, 777–78
    work effort choices in, 762–63

labor. *See also* work effort
    cyclical behavior, 18–21
    income measurement of GDP,
        44–46
    macroeconomic model, 28
    real GDP and, 17–21
labor force
    defined, 350, 385, 828
    movements in and out of,
        362–65
    population growth and, 398
    women's participation in,
        365–70
labor hoarding
    defined, 801, 828
    in Keynesian economic model,
        791–92
labor input
    capital productivity and, 344
    in Keynesian model, 762–63
    supply shock and, 183–84
    tax rate changes and, 492
    tax rate changes and tax revenue
        and, 493–97
labor market
    clearing of, 207–8, 217–19,
        229–30
    commodity market clearing and,
        219–22
    demand for labor, 209–12
    equalizing of marginal product
        of labor across firms, 211–12

frictions in, 351
job separations and, 357–58
in macroeconomic model,
    228–29
monetary growth rate and,
    284–85
nominal wage rates, 227–28
production function
    improvement and, 220–22
public services and, 461
real wage rate behavior and,
    223–27
response to time variations in
    real wage rates, 215–16
setup of, 208–9
supply and consumption
    demand, 213–17
unemployment and, 351
wage rate and, 223–27
labor unions, unemployment rate
    and, 376–77
Laffer curve
    defined, 829
    tax rate changes and tax revenue
        and, 494–95, 497, 501–2
Laspeyres indexes of prices, 50*n*.9
law of one price
    defined, 589, 829
    in world markets, 554
legal tender
    currency as, 134
    defined, 160, 829
leisure
    consumption and, 64–70
    credit market and, 98
    household budget constraints
        and demand for money,
        155–59
    interest rate and choices in,
        112–13
    marginal (physical) product of
        labor (MPL) and, 123–24
    marginal product of labor (MPL)
        and, 123–24

supply shock and, 183–84
wealth effects and work effort,
    111–12
lender of last resort
    banking panics and, 679–81
    defined, 685, 829
less-developed countries (LDC),
    convergence hypothesis
    of economic growth and,
    417–18
level of work effort,
    microeconomic foundation
    of macroeconomics,
    23–24
life-cycle model
    defined, 126, 829
    planning horizon, 115–16
liquid assets, bank panics and,
    677–78
liquidity constraint
    defined, 802, 829
    Keynesian consumption
        function, 765
LM curve, 776, 802, 829
loan markets
    deficit-financed tax cuts and,
        536–40
    world markets and government
        consumption, 576–77
loans
    balance sheet of financial
        intermediaries, 650
    to depository institutions,
        665–67
    financial intermediaries and,
        648–49
local markets
    clearing of, 726–28
    disturbances to, 728–30
    goods supply in, 724–26
    imperfect information about
        money and price levels,
        730–45
    imperfect information in, 732

856

capital productivity and, 344
clearing of commodity market,
220
cyclical components, 224–25
defined, 230, 833
demand for labor and, 210,
229–30
equalization of MPL across,
211–12
labor supply and consumption
demand, 213–17
local market stock of goods and,
725–26
time variations in, 214–17
wartime government
consumption and, 457–59
real-balance effect
defined, 160
demand for money and, 156–57
recession
changes in reserve requirement
and, 682
cyclical behavior of money and
price levels and, 705–6
cyclical component of real GDP
and, 9–10
defined, 55, 833
employment and
unemployment during,
377–79
GDP components during,
314–15
job reallocation during, 381–83
nominal monetary aggregates
and, 709–11
output per worker, 19–21
public debt ratio to GNP and,
515
real federal deficit and, 520
real GDP and, 4
supply shocks and, 379–83
unemployment rate and, 4–6
Regulation Q
defined, 686, 833

regulation of interest on
deposits and, 655–57
relative form of purchasing-power
parity (PPP), 601
defined, 634, 833
relative prices, local market
clearing model, 723–30
replacement ratio
defined, 385, 833
unemployment insurance and,
371
reservation wage
defined, 385, 833
job matching model and,
354–55
reserve requirement
amount of financial
intermediation with,
675–76
changes in, 681–82
defined, 686, 833
ratio to checkable deposits,
651–52
reserves
balance sheet of financial
intermediaries, 649
of depository institutions, 686,
833
required and excess reserves,
651–54
retail money-market mutual funds,
135
retirement benefits. See social
security
revaluation
defined, 635, 833
fixed exchange rates and,
615–17
revenue from creation of money,
295–97
government budget constraint
and, 440–43
Ricardian equivalence theorem
defined, 522–25, 545, 833

public debt and household
budget constraints, 522–25
world markets and tax rates,
578–81, 588–89
risk-based insurance premiums,
banking panics and, 681

sales rationing, Keynesian
economic theory and,
760–62
sales taxes, 481
Saudi Arabia, international
borrowing and lending in,
571
saving
after-tax real interest rate and,
484–85, 501
budget constraints, 98
budget deficits and, 538–39
capital stock changes and,
391–92
credit market, 96
deficit-financed tax cut and,
526–27, 534–40
defined, 127, 424, 833
economic growth and, 402
household budget constraints,
523–25
increase in, 393
interest rate and, 112–13
public debt and, 520–21
social security and, 540–42
windfall income and, 121
world markets and tax rates,
578–81, 588
savings and loan associations, as
financial intermediaries,
649
savings deposits
defined, 686, 833
financial intermediaries and,
646
school enrollment, unemployment
patterns and, 375–76

taxable income, 477–79, 503,
834
taxation
on bonds, 253
change in tax rate and, 486–97
commodity market-clearing,
447, 487–88
corporate profits taxes, 480–81
earned-income tax credit, 499
effects of higher rates, 488–90
federal individual income tax,
477–79
government budget constraints
and, 440–43
government consumption
and income taxation, 447,
492–93
government revenue in U.S.
and, 472–76
household budget constraints,
483–84, 522–25
Keynesian economic model
and, 779
long-run effects of, 490–92
property taxes, 481
public debt and, 522–25, 529–32
ratio of government revenue to
GNP/GDP, 475–76
real federal deficit and, 520
sales and excise taxes, 481
social security tax, 480
state and local income tax, 479
substitution effects, 484–86
tax rate and tax revenues,
493–97
theoretical model of income tax,
481–86
timing of, 532–34
transfer payments and, 271,
471, 498–500
types of, 476–81
world markets and tax rates,
577–78, 588
taxes, macroeconomic model, 30

tax-exempt real income, 482, 500,
503, 834
technological progress
capital stock changes and,
393–96
convergence hypothesis and,
415
defined, 424, 834
demand for money and, 146–47,
153–54
economic development and,
399–402, 422
international credit market and,
568–75
saving rate, 402
skill-biased technological
progress, 226–27
theories on economic growth
and, 419–20
velocity of money and,
150–51
teenage unemployment rates,
minimum wage and,
373–76
temporary abode of purchasing
power, money as, 137
temporary layoffs
defined, 385, 834
unemployment insurance and,
371
terms of trade
current-account balances and
exchange rates, 630–31
defined, 590, 834
nontraded goods, 586–87
purchasing-power parity (PPP)
and, 601–4
in world markets, 582–87
time deposits
defined, 686, 834
financial intermediaries and,
646–47
time pattern of money holdings,
138–39

time-series data
economic growth and, 403–6,
422–23
inflation and monetary growth,
246–49
total employment, labor input and
productivity, 17–21
total worker-hours, labor input and
productivity, 17–21
tradable goods
defined, 590, 834
world markets and, 582–86
trade balance
defined, 590, 834
world markets and open U.S.
economy and, 557–63
transaction costs
anticipated inflation and,
294–95
commodity market-clearing,
174
defined, 137, 160, 834
demand for money and, 146–47,
151–54, 197–98
monetary growth rate and,
286
optimal cash management
model, 138–44
real effects of money and,
157–59
transaction interval, variables in,
141–44
transfer payments
defined, 55, 834
GDP measurement, 39–40
government budget constraints
and, 440–43
government spending and,
437–39
international transfers (foreign
aid), 558–63
monetary growth and, 270–72
net U.S. transfers abroad, ratio
to GDP, 563